WESTMAR COLLEGE LIBRARY

W9-AFL-261

THE

ELDER PLINY'S CHAPTERS

ON THE

HISTORY OF ART

batissimam ipsorum astifi
cum quipraesenteserant
iudicio.cum apparuit eam et
se qua omnes secundam asua
quisq; iudicassent. haeceft
polycliti proxima abeaphi
diae. tertia clesilae. quar
ta cydonis. quintaphrae
monis. phidiae. praeter io
uem olympium quemnemo
aemulatur. fecit exaebore
aeque mineruam athenis.
quaeeft inparthenone ftans
ex aere uero. praeter amozo
nem supradictam mineruã
tam eximiae pulchritudi
nis. ut formae cognomen
acceperit. fecit &cliducum.
&aliam mineruam quam
romae paulus aemilius.
adaedem fortunae huiusce
diei dicauit. item duo fig
na quaecatulus ineadem
aede palliata. &alterum co
lossi con nudum. primusq;
aftem fore uticen.. aperu

isse atquedemonstrasse
merito iudicatur. poly
clitus sicyonius hagela
dae discipulus diadume
num fecit molliter iuue
nem centumtalentis no
bilitatum. idem &dory
phorum uiriliter pueru
fecit. &quem canona
artificesuocant. linia
menta artis exeo peten
tes uel uti alege quadam.
solusquehominum ar
temipsam fecisse artis
opere iudicatur. fecit &
deftringentem se. &nu
dum talo incessentem
duosque pueros item
nudos. talis ludentesqui
uocantur aftragalizon
tes &sunt inciti in p.
Atrioduo.hocopere nul
lum apsolutius pleriq;
iudicant. itemmercuri
um. quifuit lysimachaeae.
herculem quiromae

THE
ELDER PLINY'S CHAPTERS

ON THE

HISTORY OF ART

TRANSLATED BY

K. JEX-BLAKE

CLASSICAL LECTURER AT GIRTON COLLEGE, CAMBRIDGE

WITH COMMENTARY AND HISTORICAL INTRODUCTION

BY

E. SELLERS

FORMER STUDENT OF GIRTON COLLEGE, CAMBRIDGE,
AND OF THE BRITISH SCHOOL AT ATHENS

AND

ADDITIONAL NOTES CONTRIBUTED BY DR. HEINRICH LUDWIG URLICHS

Preface to the First American Edition and Select Bibliography
1896–1966
by
RAYMOND V. SCHODER, S.J.
Professor of Classical Archaeology, Loyola
University, Chicago.

ARGONAUT, INC., PUBLISHERS
CHICAGO   MCMLXVIII

709.38
P728

N
5610
.P6
1968

Library of Congress Catalogue Card No. 66–19183

First Printing 1968

Copyright © 1968 by Argonaut Inc., Publishers
737 North Michigan Avenue
Chicago, Illinois 60611

Manufactured in the United States of America
First American Edition
All Rights Reserved

72515

PREFACE TO THE AMERICAN EDITION

The reappearance of this book will be widely welcomed. It is still the best treatment of its subject in any language, and it deserves this availability to a wider audience. It should stimulate further study in the fascinating and complicated area of art history in ancient Greece — which attracted Pliny's attention so extensively when he was writing his technical account of minerals and metallurgy at the close of his great encyclopedia, fortunately providing us these detailed excursuses on Greek artists and their achievements.

Pliny's passages on art history are uniquely useful among our varied sources of information. He fills in many gaps, providing our only clues to the existence or the accomplishments of hundreds of ancient artists in bronze, marble, painting, and mosaics. His stories and anecdotes, salvaged for us from Greek treatises now lamentably lost, give human interest and substance to many famous names. He raises problems as well, leading to more vigorous and precise research and still posing many challenges today. Where Pliny is our only basis of information, art history is deeply in his debt. In the case of the few works still extant about which he writes there is the different facet of his interest: a chance to compare his statements and appraisal with the evidence of the art object itself or its surviving copy. It is now possible to illustrate much of what Pliny is talking about, and study of his text should not be in isolation from this evidence.[1] Pliny himself shows little artistic insight or sensitivity — what interests him is mostly a work's startling realism, or an artist's originality

---

[1] See the starred items in section E of the Supplementary Bibliography below.

(*ingenium*) or distinctive bent (*argumentum*), and always the money value of the masterpiece in the Rome of his day. He was too busy and hurried to give time to esthetic analysis, even if capable of that, which is doubtful in view of his factual and scientific bent of mind. Primarily, he was curious about art history as a human phenomenon and as a huge mass of material needing classification for better understanding. He knew that that was the interest of most of his Roman readers also and he felt that his combination of facts and anecdotes from many scattered sources would appeal. We should not complain that he leaves *us* unsatisfied, though we may regret that he does not include data about architecture, vase painting, gem and ivory carving—which simply fell out-side the scope of his plan. What he does give us is valuable and interesting in many ways, and we owe him appropriate study.

Since this re-issue is a photographic copy of the 1896 edition, it has not been possible to revise and augment the introduction and commentary at those places where later studies could contribute new data or insights. Instead, the book has been brought up to date by way of the Supplementary Biblio-graphy which lists practically anything of importance done in the past seventy years in the area of Pliny's passages on art. This has been compiled by extensive research and with the aid of bibliographical data scattered through the lists by Lambrino, Marouzeau, *L'Année Philologique,* Le Bonniec, and others. I have re-arranged the information into five categories, supplied more complete publication data, and spelled out all periodical titles instead of resorting to the usual maze of esoteric abbreviations. Sections A, B, and C, directly dealing with Pliny, are as complete as I can make them. The items listed in C can serve as new footnotes to the text, indicating where to find whatever has been published since 1896 on any matter in Sellers' selections, in the sequence of Pliny's chapters. I have often given brief indication of what particular articles discuss. Section E lists major books particularly useful as background or development of matters which Pliny treats;

most of these books have extensive bibliographies of their own, which will suffice as guide to further study.

In the following pages, I will try to sketch the main developments in the interpretation of Pliny's chapters on art which have resulted from these writings.

LATER EDITIONS OF PLINY ON ART

A year after Sellers' book appeared, the Teubner text of Pliny N.H. 31-37 was published, edited by Mayhoff (A 1).[2] This has since generally replaced the text of Detlefsen which Sellers basically followed, but it is weakened by over-reliance on the earlier work by Jan, and it too frequently re-writes the Latin without any manuscript evidence, where Mayhoff thinks he knows what Pliny must or should have said. Later scholars have re-established the primacy of the *Codex Bambergensis* (10th century) for the last six books of Pliny, followed in authority by the *Codex Riccardianus,* and it is safer to stay close to their readings.

Only one book comparable to Sellers' has appeared in the past seventy years — further tribute to the lasting merits of her brilliant work. This is the edition by Silvio Ferri (A 2), which includes all the selections in Sellers and several more that are worth adding. Ferri gives a facing translation into Italian and running footnotes of very uneven quality, often adding much that is illuminating but also omitting much that is in Sellers — partly because he assumes that one will be using her notes also, which he admires. Ferri's text is rather eclectic, drawn from Detlefsen, Mayhoff, Sillig, and *Codex Bambergensis,* with a number of new readings of his own, including two of considerable extent and interest (cp. his list of them on p. 40). His Introduction surveys Plinian scholarship from 1850 to 1945 in a succinct but rather rambling way,[3] with bibliographical references that are clumsy and

---

2 These parenthetical references indicate section and entry in the Supplementary Bibliography, 1897-1966, pp. L - Y below.

3 There is a shorter survey by E. Pernice in Otto's *Handbuch der Archäologie,* 1. 314 - 323 (Munich, Beck, 1939).

incomplete. The book was poorly proof-read, and the Latin text too often departs from the manuscripts, though it usefully incorporates many good suggestions by various scholars, and a brief critical apparatus is provided. Other handy features are the list of dates of the Olympiads (p. 37), the table of equivalent measurements in ancient and in metric values (p. 38), the index of names and topics (pp. 297-300), and the list of special technical and art-criticism terminology (pp. 301-302). Altogether a very useful edition, but not really replacing Sellers, though extensively supplementing her notes.

The Bude edition of Pliny 34 (A 3) is an admirable work, and if the subsequent two books are as well edited and annotated this will be an indispensable guide to Pliny's treatise on art. The text is soberly conservative, based primarily on *Codex Bambergensis* but with careful consideration of other MSS and of scholars' conjectures — which are duly reported in the notes but rarely introduced into the text itself; the critical apparatus gives all major MSS variants. The careful French translation is richly annotated, with full use of all relevant scholarship on the various problems and data. Sellers' notes are often quoted and her material incorporated. This commentary is of the greatest value on all levels of study of Pliny's text. The introduction is extensive and most useful. It parallels Sellers' general study of Pliny's sources, but in a different way and in the light of all subsequent literature on that complex topic. Xenocrates, Antigonus, and Varro are shown to be Pliny's chief authorities, but Sellers' position (xxi-xxii) that Xenocrates, via Varro, is the source of both the chronology and the art-critique of the artists treated in 34.49-52 is refuted and the direct influence of Nepos on Pliny is rejected. Pliny's own contributions are shown to be much more extensive and significant than Sellers and some others thought. The whole discussion of Pliny's sources is made more clear by discussing it in several divisions instead of all together, since different sections of Pliny's text draw on different predecessors. Very helpful are two charts (pp. 70-74, 82-84) which show in specific detail which sections of 34.53-71 and of 34.72-83 are ascribable to several distinct sources.

The Loeb edition of Pliny 33-37 (A 4, 5) makes no pretense of scholarly commentary or introduction; it simply presents Mayhoff's text, without some of his arbitrary changes, and a clear English translation, with a minimum of explanatory footnotes. Similarly, the various selections in translation of Pliny on art (A 6, 7, 8) are for reading only, not the needs of scholarship.

THE DEVELOPMENT
OF PLINIAN SCHOLARSHIP SINCE SELLERS

Sellers' Introduction and commentary brilliantly utilized the complex researches of 19th century German scholars on Pliny, presenting the results in a clear and specific analysis of the background to Pliny's treatise on art and in very intelligent notes below the text. Before 1895, the main interest and effort of Plinian scholars had been in recognizing, identifying, and analyzing the multiple influences and sources underlying Pliny's various statements. Jahn, Brieger, Schreiber, Brunn, Furtwängler, Oehmichen, L. Urlichs, H. Urlichs, Robert, Dalstein, Voight, Detlefsen, and Munzer had between 1850 and 1895 ingeniously analyzed every part and aspect of Pliny's statements on art history with a view to ascribing each assertion to its particular source among Pliny's authorities. Much of their work was unquestionably sound, though many details and emphases have been modified since. Sellers' Introduction is still the best synthesis of all this complicated mass of data and theories, along with the good summary of antecedent scholarship in Kalkmann's major book of 1898 (B 2).

As Ferri points out, a whole new era of Plinian research opened with the publication of Münzer's *Quellenkritik* in 1897 (B 1). He boldly studied the whole of the *Natural History* for Pliny's methods, procedures, sources, usefully comparing Pliny with comparable passages in Cato and with the actual content and tenor of extant material from older writers whom Pliny used. Münzer showed that there are four distinct procedures followed by Pliny in his use of sources: (1) collecting into a synthesis his recollections from varied quick reading of earlier treatises; (2) taking careful notes from his study of various authorities, and transcribing these directly into his treatise; (3) taking some established author's material and re-organizing it around a new point of view or emphasis; (4) accepting some authority's list or account, but amplifying it with other data from diverse origins. Thus Pliny is no mere copyist or 'mosaicist', nor is he a simple follower of any one predecessor for a given problem; rather he intelligently chooses what seems to him the best data for each particular matter he is treating and often works up a new synthesis of several sources by fusing them around his own viewpoint, inserting opinions of his own or others into his main authority's treatment — usually after presenting the latter's basic facts as a unit. Münzer felt that Pliny primarily relied on Augustan-era compilations of data, controlling these by checking against older Greek treatises. Among these Roman authorities would be Piso and Valerius Antias, cited by Pliny at 34.14.

Detlefsen's studies (B 4, 5, 6) are sensible and careful researches into the lists of artists which Pliny must have used. He argues that there must have been a catalog of Greek art in Rome, probably of the Vespasian era, and a kind of encyclopedic dictionary of Greek art, in Greek, which Pliny consulted regularly; also that the Acts of the Censors (e.g. 73 A.D.) supplied information on famous works of art in possession of the Roman State. This is doubted by other scholars.

Rabenhorst (B 7, 8) presented vigorous views on the importance of Verrius Flaccus as a source for Pliny, down-graded Varro's influence and the reliability of Pliny's *Indices Auctorum,* and over-emphasized Pliny's primary reliance on compilations of art history made at Rome after 25 A.D. Klotz (B 9) toned down some of these views and defended the basic accuracy of Pliny's indices.

Kalkmann's important book (B 2) had already correctly emphasized Duris of Samos as the main source of the anecdotes on artists related by Pliny, and Mucianus as Pliny's chief authority for details based on a traveller's personal observation of art in Greece. From the discrepancies and duplications occasionally found in Pliny's lists, Kalkmann argued that he drew from several manuals, encyclopedias, lists of artists (including one in Greek independent of Varro's catalog compiled from Xenocrates and Antigonus). He showed that most of the technical ideas on art in Pliny must come from Xenocrates' treatises (he was both practicing artist and writer on art) as expanded and re-organized by Antigonus — who, as Robert had demonstrated in 1888, worked up a canon of artists and schools centered about Peloponnesian masters, whereas Xenocrates had stressed Attic and Pergamene movements. Kalkmann pointed out that Pliny dates artists by their period of eminence rather than their birth, and organizes his dates around Olympiads, probably drawing on a Greek treatise by Apollodorus in iambic trimeters whose fragments Jacoby has published (B 5a).

Schweitzer's book on Xenocrates (B 13) is of major importance. He shows how basic this artist-writer's ideas were for later treatises, and considers Xenocrates the real Father of Art History. He reinforces and supplements the evidence for Xenocrates' influence marshalled at length in Sellers' Introduction, pp. xvi-xxxvi, refuting her objections (p. xx, note 2) to calling Xenocrates an Athenian rather than from Sicyon. Schweitzer claims that Xenocrates invented the evolutionary key to art history — that each style-period has a founder, developers, culminating master. He shows that Xenocrates also established basic technical criteria: symmetry, rhythm, composition, perspective, diligence, distinctive special skills, use of color-contrast and tonalities, He omitted dates, which a generation later Antigonus added to his account, along with anecdotes mostly culled from Duris and more emphasis on Attic and Pergamene sculptors. Ferri in his Introduction, pp. 25-27, handily collects the passages in Pliny which seem to stem ultimately from Xenocrates, adding the passage in Quintilian (12.10.1-12) which is a sort of 'Pergamene canon' of Greek painters and sculptors (pp. 28-29).

Jahn, Dilthey, and Münzer had pointed out significant parallels between various Greek literary epigrams and remarks of Pliny, often on the same art objects referred to in the epigrams, and Sellers gave many interesting examples (pp. lxviii-lxxii). Kalkmann subsequently emphasised this element in the background to Pliny, and Ferri devotes pp. 16-17 of his Introduction to reiterating the relevance of such study, citing many specific examples. This area is one in which Ferri had earlier made a considerable contribution. His 1942 article on the Greek terminology of art criticism (B 16) shows how the ancient Greek mind tended to express art appreciation in terms and categories similar to those used in qualifying literary styles. Epigrams are thus naturally apt for a brief striking appraisal of a work of art, and in Hellenistic times many such were produced and widely known. Pliny clearly drew on them in many passages, borrowing their consciously clever phraseology for succinct characterization of some famous art works.

Even more important, Ferri shows, is the rhetorical usage out of which these Hellenistic epigrams grew. Many Greek terms of art criticism (and their Latin equivalents) can really only be properly understood in the light of their meaning in rhetorical definitions — e.g. *quadratus, multiplicasse, consummasse.* Later Greek writers developed a special genre of descriptions of art works in rhetorical and moralizing vein, known as *ekphrasis.* The clearest examples of this device still extant are the Descriptions (*Ekphraseis*) of Callistratus, from the third century A.D. (D 3); other examples or approximations are found in Philostratus (D 2) and here and there in Lucian (D 4). These somewhat artificial analyses of paintings and sculptures are rooted in a long rhetorical tradition going back to the Sophists and even in a sense to Homer's similes and descriptions, so apt and vivid. Ferri well argues from all this (Introduction, pp. 16-17) that Pliny's frequent echoing of rhetorical-artistic terminology shows that he drew much directly from Greek sources, not just from recent Roman compilations. The Greeks enjoyed evaluating the artistic qualities of a painting or a sculpture analogously to those of a speech or poem, and Pliny followed their example.

In further development of his thesis that Pliny relied much

more directly on Greek sources than has been hitherto appreciated, Ferri analyzes Pliny's subdivisions of his material in Books 33, 34, 35 (Introduction, pp. 18-23), showing that they clearly go back to Greek writers long before his own time. An actual example is extant, in the Greek list of painters and sculptors dating to Hellenistic times and published by Diels in 1904 (reprinted in Ferri, p. 29). Internal qualities of Pliny's lists betray Greek origin: the lists often go in order of descending merit (e.g. 33.154-159: *maxime laudatus . . . proximi ab eo . . . post hos celebratus . . . item laudantur*); within divisions, artists are often named in alphabetical order, frequently in regular groups of three or four or five or ten or twelve. Greeks would tend to presume that such groupings are intended by Nature and that a writer's task is to discover and report them. Confirmation is claimed from the very fact that no such artificial classification is given in Book 36 for marble sculptors — because Pliny's Greek catalog did not fit the vast array of such works then in Rome, or because he had no Greek list available for artists in marble only, and did not have time to make up his own in the Greek fashion.

The latest extensive study of Pliny is that in Pauly-Wissowa by W. Kroll (with some sections by Ziegler, Hanslik, others), a general study of the man and his work and a detailed analysis of the Natural History, with rather full attention to the sections on art history (B 19). It is essentially a survey of earlier scholarship on Pliny, primarily focused on stating the facts.

Just as study of Pliny helps to a grasp of the history of Greek art, continuing progress in the interpretation of Greek art itself, in the light of archeological and critical developments, often throws light on certain passages in Pliny and can be hoped to do so in the future. An example is the discussion by Rhys Carpenter on pp. 232-236 of his recent *Greek Sculpture* (E 17) on the development of anatomic naturalism in third century B.C. sculpture. He analyzes Pliny's passage (35.153) on the innovation by Lysistratus, brother of Lysippus, arguing that Pliny's *hominis imaginem . . . e facie ipsa primus omnium expressit* does not refer to portraits at all, but only to a new technique of comparing casts made from various surface parts of the living body with the traditional canonic rendering, and revising the canon in the light of this new anatomical information. That is, *facies* is to be taken in its more generic meaning of "form, external appearance," not specifically as facial features. The reason for this interpretation of Pliny's statement, which Carpenter considers accurate when thus understood, is that in fact extant examples of portraiture do not show a sudden change to individualized realism in the early third century, as they certainly would if Lysistratus' new technique were primarily concerned with portraiture. Rather it is the whole body which now becomes more precise anatomically and more individualized, though this new movement toward mimetic fidelity and away from an impersonal canon soon showed up in portraiture also, which took on a closer resemblance to individual countenances in their variations from a simplified generic norm. Sellers' note on 35.153 has a point, however, on the other side. She refers to the vividly realistic bronze portrait of a boxer found at Olympia. This is commonly ascribed to the late fourth century B.C., by some authorities thought to be the portrait of the boxer Satyros made by Silanion — who flourished around 330 B.C. (see the illustration and discussion in Lullies and Hirmer, E 39, No. 238-239). Such debates will continue, to the advantage of both Plinian studies and a more accurate understanding of Greek art.

It will be seen from the above survey that Plinian studies have made considerable progress in the past seventy years, and have taken on a new direction. Sellers' book stands as a fruit and summation of the earlier period when the chief interest was in *Quellenforschung,* disentangling the varied sources behind Pliny's statements and appraisals. Studies since her book and Münzer's (B 1) have been more concerned with a broader understanding of Pliny's meaning and ways of expression, with interpretation of his terminology, and with direct reference to actual extant Greek art for mutual illumination of art and text. The key books listed in section E of the Supplementary Bibliography are therefore a real part of Plinian studies today; and his chapers on art should be basic background to their study too.

From the more recent work on Pliny it has become clear that he is a more authentic scholar and more original writer than was formerly realized. He is seen now as a true *vir curiosus,* assiduously studying a vast range of authorities to arrive at an understanding of the truth, and creatively re-organizing past knowledge around his own viewpoints and lines of interest. We should therefore radically modify Sellers' statement (p. xiii) that we should regard Pliny's work "as nothing more than a compilation from other records, in which personal observation plays no part outside the range of contemporary events." Also her conclusion (p. xciii) that "the tendency of modern research is to lessen more and more the importance of Pliny's personal contribution in his account of the artists." And her idea that Pliny got his data from Greek writers only via Varro, who himself got them from some single compilation (p. xv). No one surely would be more pleased than Eugenie Sellers herself to see Pliny now more highly esteemed for his true scholarship and fundamental originality.

RAYMOND V. SCHODER, S.J.
LOYOLA UNIVERSITY, CHICAGO
June, 1966

SUPPLEMENTARY BIBLIOGRAPHY 1897 - 1966

(Sections A, B, D are in chronological order; D, E are selective only)

A. EDITIONS OF PLINY'S TEXT ON ART

1. Carl Mayhoff, *Naturalis Historiae Libri, Vol.* 5: *XXXI - XXXVII* (Leipzig, Teubner, 1897)
2. Silvio Ferri, *Plinio il Vecchio: Storia delle Arti Antiche* (Rome, Palombi, 1946)
3. H. le Bonniec and H. Gallet de Santerre, *Pline l'Ancien: Histoire Naturelle, Livre XXXIV* (Paris, Les Belles Lettres, 1953) — in Budé series
4. H. Rackham, *Pliny: Natural History, Vol. IX: Libri XXXIII-XXXV* (London, Heinemann, 1952)—in Loeb Classical Library
5. D. E. Eichholz, *Pliny: Natural History, Vol. X: Libri XXXVI - XXXVII* (London, Heinemann, 1962) — in Loeb Classical Library
6. Walter Schürmeyer, *Von der Bildhauerei und der Baukunst, aus der 'Historia Naturalis'* (Frankfurt, Kunstgewerbe Bibliotek, 1925)—selections from Books 34-36 in German translation, brief notes
7. Paul Turner, *Selections from the History of the World, Commonly Called the Natural History of C. Plinius Secundus, Translated by Philemon Holland* (Carbondale, Ill., Southern Illinois University Press, 1962)—selections from Books 34-36 on pp. 373-456
8. J. Newsome, *Pliny's Natural History: a Selection from Philemon Holland's Translation* (Oxford, Clarendon Press, 1964) — selections from Books 34-36 on pp. 272-317

B. GENERAL STUDIES OF PLINY'S CHAPTERS ON ART

1. F. Münzer, *Beiträge zur Quellenkritik der Naturgeschichte des Plinius* (Berlin, Weidmann, 1897)
2. A. Kalkmann, *Die Quellen der Kunstgeschichte des Plinius* (Berlin, Weidmann, 1898)

3. L. Traube, "Zu Plinius Kunstgeschichtlichen Büchern," *Hermes* 33 (1898). 345 - 351

4. D. Detlefsen, *Untersuchungen über die Zusammensetzung der Naturgeschichtes des Plinius* (Berlin, Weidman, 1899)

5. D. Detlefsen, "Die Eigenen Leistung des Plinius für die Geschichte der Künstler," *Jahrbuch des Deutschen Archäologischen Instituts* 16 (1901). 75 - 107

5 a. F. Jacoby, *Apollodors Chronik: Eine Sammlung der Fragmente* (Berlin, Weidmann, 1902)

6. D. Detlefsen, "Die Benutzung des Zensorischen Verzeichnisses der Naturalis Historia des Plinius," *Jahrbuch des Deutschen Archäolgischen Instituts* 20 (1905). 113-122

7. M. Rabenhorst, *Die Zeitangaben Varronischer und Capitolinischer Aera in der Naturalis Historia* (Berlin, Ebeling, 1905)

8. M. Rabenhorst, "Die Indices Auctorum und die wirklichen Quellen der Naturalis Historia," *Philologus* 65 (1906). 567 - 603

9. A. Klotz, "Die Arbeitsweise des Plinius und die Indices Auctorum," *Hermes* 42 (1907). 323 - 329

10. Paul Ahlgrimm, *Zur Quellen der Naturalis Historia des Plinius* (Schwerin, Gymnasium Fredericianum, 1911)

11. A. Reinach, "Notes Critiques aux chapitres de Pline relatifs a l'histoire de l'art," *Révue de Philologie* 38 (1914). 245 - 254

12. B. Warnecke, "Pline et sa dépendance des sources grecques," in *Recueil d'Études Dediées á S—A. Gebelev* (Leningrad, Academie des Sciences, 1924), pp. 661 - 662 — in Russian; French summary

13. B. Schweitzer, *Xenocrates von Athen: Beiträge zur Geschichte der Antiken Kunstforschung und Kunstanschauung* (Halle, Niemeyer, 1932) — a source used by Pliny

14. H. N. Wethered, *The Mind of the Ancient World: A Consideration of Pliny's Natural History* (London, Longmans, 1937) — pp. 193 - 233 are on art sections

15. A. C. Moorhouse, "A Roman's View of Art," *Greece and Rome* 10 (1940). 29 - 35

16. S. Ferri, "Note esegetiche ai giudizi d'arte di Plinio il Vecchio," *Annali della Scuola Normale Superiore di Pisa*

1942, pp. 69 - 116 — on Greek terminology of art criticism

17. H. le Bonniec, *Bibliographie de l'Histoire Naturelle de Pline l'Ancien* (Paris, Les Belles Lettres, 1946)

18. J. M. C. Toynbee, *Some Notes on Artists in the Roman World,* 5 fascicles (Bruxelles, Latomus, 1950) — includes Pliny's lists

19. W. Kroll et al., "Plinius der Ältere," article in Pauly-Wissowa-Kroll, *Real-Encyclopädie der Klassischen Altertumswissenschoft* 21 (1951), cols. 271 -439—cols. 392-406 are on Books 33 - 36

C. STUDIES OF PARTICULAR PASSAGES IN PLINY 33-37 ON ART

(for similar studies before 1897, see le Bonniec's Bibliography [B 17], pp. 46 - 55. Numbers in parentheses are those of Pliny's Chapters)

1. (on 34. 9 - 17) B. Schweitzer, "Xenocrates von Athen," *Schrift Königsberger Gelehrter Gesellschafts* 9 (1932). 1 - 52

2. (on 34. 10, 75, 83, 84) A. Daentl, "Textkritische Bemerkungen zu Plinius' Natural Historia," *Philologische Wochenschrift* (1932). 60 - 62

3. (34. 19) G. M. A. Richter, "Pliny's Five Amazons," *Archaeology* 12 (1959). 111 - 115

4. (34. 19) A. W. Lawrence, "Cessavit Ars: Turning Points in Hellenistic Sculpture," in *Mélanges d'Archéologie et d' Histoire Offerts 'a Ch. Picard* (Paris, Presses Universitairs, 1949), 581 - 585

5. (34. 45) Fr. Préchac, *Le Colosse de Néron: son Attitude et ses Vicissitudes d'après les Textes et les Monnaies* (Paris, Rollin et Feuardent, 1920)

6. (34. 50) K. Schefold, "Ante Cuncta Laudabilis," *Mitteilungen des Deutschen Archäologischen Instituts, Römische Abteilung* 57 (1942). 245 - 256 — on Leochares

7. (34. 52) M. Bieber, "Damophon and Pliny," *American Journal of Archaeology* 45 (1941). 94 - 95

8. (34. 52) M. Bieber, "Pliny and Graeco-Roman Art," in *Hommages `a J. Bidez et F. Cumont* (Bruxelles, Latomus, 1949), 39 - 42

9. (34. 55) E. Müller-Graupa, "Der 'Astragalobolos' des Polyklet," *Philologische Wochenschrift* 42 (1922). 208 - 215

10. (34. 56) S. Ferri, "Un Emendamento a Plinio N. H. 34. 56, e l'Herakles di Würzburg," *Rendiconti dell' Accademia dei Lincei* 11 (1935). 770 - 774 — proposes reading "excetram armo sustinentem" instead of "hagetera arma sumentem."

11. (34. 56) S. Ferri, "Una statuetta Romana di Ercole e un Passo di Plinio," *Bolletino d'Arte* 29 (1936). 437 - 441

12. (34. 56) V. Ussani, "Per un Emendamento a Plinio," *Rendiconti dell' Accadèmia dei Lincei* 13 (1937). 251 - 254 — objects to Ferri's argument in No. 10, 11

13. (34. 56, 65) S. Ferri, "Nuovi Contributi esegetici al 'Canone' della scultura Greca," *Rivista dell' Istituto di Archeologia, Roma* 6 (1940). 117 - 152

14. (34. 56, 65) S. Ferri, "Signa Quadrata," *Rivista di Filologia e di Istruzione Classica* 1938, pp. 163 - 166 — on symmetry in Polyclitus and Lysippus

15. (34. 56, 65) E. S. McCartney, "Signa Quadrata," *Classical Weekly* 25 (1931). 80

16. (34. 59) A. S. Arvanitopoulos, "Dia Tinōn Ergōn ho Pythagoras enikēse ton Myrōna," *Polemon* 1 (1929 - 30). 96 — proposes reading "eumden vicit et Leontisco" instead of "eodem vicit et Leontiscum"

17. (34. 61 - 68) Theo. Homolle, "Pline commenté par E. Delacroix," *Comptes Rendus de l'Académie des Inscriptions et Belles-Lettres* (1921). 261 - 269 — on Lysippus and Polyclitus

18. (34. 70, 86) H. Gallet de Santerre, "Un Oubli de Pline l'Ancien: le cas du Sculpteur Antenor," *Révue Archéologique* 24 (1945). 107 - 110

19. (34. 71) S. Ferri, "L'Anabeblēmenē di Kalamis," *La Parola del Passato* 6 (1951). 128 - 129 — refers to Sosandra statue, confused with 'Aspasia'

20. (34. 71) P. Orlandini, "Ancora sulla Sosandra di Calamide," *Archaeologia Classica* 3 (1951). 93—supports Ferri, that Sosandra is same statue as 'Aspasia'

21. (34. 74) A. Raubitschek, "Zu altattischen Weihinschriften," *Oesterreichische Jahreshefte* 31 (1938). 41-42 Beiblätter —a votive inscription signed by Cresilas

22. (34. 78) R. Pichon, "Le Témoinage de Pline sur Hégias," *Revue des Études Grecques* 21 (1908). 119

23. (34. 79) H. le Bonniec and H. Gallet de Santerre, "Lyciscos et Langon," *Revue Archéologique* 24 (1945). 110 - 114 — restore mention of Lykiskos

24. (34. 81) G. Rizza, "Una nuova pelike a figure rosse e lo Splanchnoptes di Styphax," *Annuario della Scuola Archeologica di Atene* 22 (1960). 321 - 345—a vase in Catania illustrating this statue

25. (34. 82) Th. Birt, "Marginalien," *Philologus* 83 (1928). 164 - 169 — critique of the passage

26. (34. 84) B. Schweitzer, "Zur frühpergamenischen Kunst," *Jahrbuch des Deutschen Archäologischen Instituts* 54 (1939). 403 - 413

27. (34. 84) A. Schober, "Zur Geschichte Pergamenischer Künstler," *Jahreshefte des Oesterreichischen Archäologischen Instituts in Wien* 31 (1939). 142 - 149

28. (34. 84) A. Schober, "Zur Zeitbestimmung Pergamenischer Künstler," *ibid.* 32 (1940). 73 - 82

29. (34. 84) A. Schober, "Zu den Weihgeschenke eines Attalos in Athen," *Mitteilungen des Deutschen Archäologischen Instituts, Römische Abteilung* 54 (1939). 82 - 98

30. (34. 87) H. N. Fowler, "Pliny, Pausanias, and the Hermes of Praxiteles," *Transactions of American Philological Association* 31 (1900). 37 - 45

31. (34. 88) A. Mahler, "Niceratos," *Jahrbuch des Deutschen Archäologischen Instituts* 20 (1905). 26 - 31

32. (35. 2) N. W. DeWitt, "Portraits in Bedrooms," *Classical Bulletin* 32 (1956). 68

33. (35. 2) E. Coche de la Ferté, "Imagines Majorum ou Portraits de Momies?", *Revue des Arts* 2 (1953). 54 - 55 —

on 'Fayum style' painted portraits

34. (35. 10) G. Becatti, "Letture Pliniane: Le opere d'arte nei monumenta Asini Pollionis e negli Horti Serviliani," in *Studi in Onore di A. Calderini e R. Paribeni* (Milano, Ceschina, 1956), Vol. 3, pp. 199 - 201

35. (35. 20) A. Stein, *Der Römische Ritterstand* (Munich, 1927) — p. 378 on Turpilius

36. (35. 49) A. Maiuri, "Picturae Ligneis Formis Inclusae," *Rendiconti dell'Accademia d'Italia* 1 (1940). 138 - 160

37. (35. 50) H. Peters, "Zu Plinius N. H. 35. 50," *Geschichtsblätter für Technik* 3 (1916). 341 — on sulphurous yellow color

38. (35. 58) L. B. Lawler, "Lucida Veste," *Transactions of American Philological Association* 69 (1938). 423 - 438 — read "lucida," not "tralucida"

39. (35. 61, 75, 102, 120, 124, 155) A. Daentl, "Textkritische Bemerkungen zu Plinius' Naturalis Historia," *Philologische Wochenschrift* (1932) 60 - 62

40. (35. 62) A. J. B. Wace, "The Cloaks of Zeuxis and Demetrios," *Jahreshefte des Oesterreichischen Archäologischen Instituts* 39 (1952). 111 - 118 — new evidence on material and decoration

41. (35. 67 - 69) R. Bianchi Bandinelli, "Piccoli Problemi da Risolvere: Parrasio, Linea, Spazio, Volume," *La Critica d' Arte* 3 (1938). 4 - 11

42. (35. 70) J. Carcopino, "Critique et Correction d'un Texte de Pline permettant de retrouver et de placer au nombre de ses 'Auctores' Decius Epulo, familier de Tibère," *Bulletin de la Société Nationale des Antiquaires de France* (1922). 157 - 165

43. (35. 70) J. Carcopino, "Attideia II: l'Archigalle de Parrhasios," *Mélanges d'Archéologie et d'Histoire* 40 (1923). 267

44. (35. 87 - 88) A. de Ridder, "Protogène," *Révue des Études Grecques* 28 (1915). 282

45. (35. 99, 110) H. Fuhrmann, *Philoxenos von Eretria* (Göt-

tingen, 1931) — Chap. IV treats No. 99, Chap. II treats No. 110

46. (35. 101) C. Torr, "Protogenes of Kaunos," *Classical Review* 4 (1890). 231 - 232

47. (35. 108) A. Severyns, "Deux Erreurs de Pline l'Ancien," in *Melanges P. Thomas* (Bruges, Imprimerie Saint-Catherine, 1930). 627 - 632

48. (35. 110) G. Bagnani, "Pictura Compendiaria," *American Journal of Archaeology* 66 (1962). 194—discusses its meaning

49. (35. 115) W. Fröhner, "Kleinigkeiten, 5," *Philologus* 71 (1912). 165 — interpretation

50. (35. 115 - 120) C. Cichorius, "Zu Romischen Malern," *Philologus* 76 (1927). 325

51. (35. 120) L. Traube, "Zu Plinius Kunstgeschichtlichen Büchern," *Hermes* 33 (1898). 345 - 351

52. (35. 122, 149) E. Schiavi Gazzola, "Ritrovamento della Tecnica Pittorica dell'Encausto," in *Atti del VII Congresso Internazionale di Archeologia* 1 (1961). 155 - 158

53. (35. 135) G. Becatti, "Metrodoro e Paolo Emilio," *Cahiers Archéologiques* 6 (1941). 70 - 73

54. (35. 140) Charles Picard, "Sur une Peinture perdue de Ctésilochos," *Révue Archéologique* 1958, Vol. 1. 99 - 100 — compares Ionian relief in Istanbul on rebirth of Dionysus

55. (35. 143) K. Schwarz, "Zu Plinius N. H. 35. 143," *Philologische Wochenschrift* 1941, p. 335 — suggests reading "pistoris" instead of "pictoris"

56. (35. 143) E. Diehl, "Zu Plinius N. H. 35. 143," *ibid.* 1941, pp. 575 - 576 — rejects reading proposed by Schwarz (No. 55)

57. (35. 149) O. Donner von Richter, "Ueber die eingesetzten Holztafeln in Pompeji und die Pliniusstelle 35. 149," *Mitteilungen des Kaiserlichen Deutschen Archäologischen Instituts, Römische Abteilung* (1899). 119 - 140

58. (36. 9) F. Brommer, "Beiträge zur Griechischen Bildhauergeschichte," *Mitteilungen des Deutschen Archäologischen In-*

stituts, Berlin 3 (1950). 80 - 98 — on Dipoinos and Skyllis as first marble sculptors in Argolid

59. (36. 9 - 43) C. Brakman, "Plinius: Naturalis Historia 36. 9 - 43," *Opstellen* 3 (1932). 88

60. (36. 12) J. D. Beazley, "The Epigram of Boupalos and Athenis," *Journal of Hellenic Studies* 59 (1939). 282 — reconstructs the distich referred to by Pliny

61. (36. 22) O. Waldhauer, "Myron's Anus Ebria and the Drunken Woman in Munich," *American Journal of Archaeology* 50 (1946). 241 - 246

62. (36. 25) K. Kerenyi, "Das Werk des Skopas für Samothrake," *Symbolae Osloenses* 31 (1951). 141 - 154

63. (36. 29) J. Six, "Zum ersten Satyrpaar bei Plinius 36. 29," *Jahreshefte des Oesterreichischen Archäologischen Instituts* 21 - 22 (1924). 251 - 252

64. (36. 29) H. Sichtermann, "Zur Achill und Chiron-Gruppe," *Mitteilungen des Deutschen Archäologischen Instituts, Römische Abteilung* 64 (1957). 98 - 110 —the IV cent. B.C. Greek basis for the painting found at Herculaneum

65. (36. 30) H. W. Law, "The Mausoleum," *Journal of Hellenic Studies* 59 (1939). 92 - 102

66. (36. 31, 32, 43) A. Daentl, "Textkritische Bemerkungen zu Plinius' Naturalis Historia," *Philologische Wochenschrift* (1932). 60 - 62

67. (36. 31) G. Donnay, "L'Amazonomachie de Mausolée d' Halicarnasse," *L'Antiquité Classique* 26 (1957). 383 - 403 —assigns the extant fragments to the four sculptors mentioned by Pliny, some to each

68. (36. 32) S. Reinach, "L'Hécate de Ménestrate," pp. 307 - 318 of his *Cultes, Mythes, et Religions II* (Paris, Leroux, 1906)

69. (36. 35) Th. Reinach, "Vénus Accroupie," *Comptes Rendus de l'Académie des Inscriptions et Belles-Lettres,* IV Serie 25 (1897). 138 — read "sese Daedalsas"

70. (36. 84, 91) P. J. Enk, "De Labyrinthi Imagine in Foribus Templi Cumani Insculpta," *Eranos* 56 (1958). 322 - 330

71. (36. 184) M. Renard, "L'Asarotos Oikos de Sosos," *Révue*

des Études Latines 33 (1955). 57 - 58

72. (36. 184) M. Renard, "Pline l'Ancien et la Motif de l' Asarōtos Oikos," in *Hommages à M. Niedermann* (Bruxelles, Latomus, 1956). 307 - 314

73. (36. 184 - 189) D. Gioseffi, "La terminologia dei Sistemi di Pavimentazione Marmorea e una Pagina della Naturalis Historia," *Rendiconti della Accademia dei Lincei,* Serie 8, No. 10 (1955). 572 - 595

D. OTHER ANCIENT SOURCES ON THE HISTORY OF CLASSICAL ART

1. Pausanias, *Description of Greece*: Translation and Commentary by J. G. Frazer, 6 vols. (London, Macmillan, 1913)

2. Philostratus, *Images*: Text, Translation, Notes by Arthur Fairbanks in Loeb Classical Library series (London, Heinemann, 1931) — with illustrations

3. Callistratus, *Descriptions*: Text, Translation, Notes by Arthur Fairbanks, in same Loeb volume as Philostratus (No. 2)

4. Lucian, *Essays in Portraiture*: Text, Translations, Notes by A. M. Harmon, in Loeb Classical Library, Vol. IV of Lucian (London, Heinemann, 1925)

5. Laterculi Alexandrini: relevant list of artists is reprinted in Ferri (A2), p. 29

6. H. Stuart Jones, *Select Passages from Ancient Writers Illustrative of the History of Greek Sculpture* (new enlarged reissue of 1895 edition, Chicago, Argonaut, 1966)

7. A. Reinach, *Recueil Millet: Textes Grecs et Latins Relatifs à l'Histoire de la Peinture Ancienne*, I (Paris, Klincksieck, 1921)

8. Phyllis Lehmann, *Statues on Coins of Southern Italy and Sicily in the Classical Period* (New York, Bittner, 1946)

9. Leon Lacroix, *Les Reproductions de Statues sur les Monnaies Grecques* (Liège, Université de Liège, 1949)

10. J. Marcadé, *Recueil des Signatures des Sculpteurs Grecs,* I (Paris, Boccard, 1959)

11. F. Imhoof-Blumer and Percy Gardner, *Ancient Coins Illustrating Lost Masterpieces of Greek Art* (Chicago, Ar-

gonaut, 1965)—expanded new edition of their "Numismatic Commentary on Pausanias," (originally in *Journal of Hellenic Studies* 1885-1887) by Al. N. Oikonomides. New section on the coins of Athens and addenda

12. J. J. Pollitt, *The Art of Greece* 1400 - 31 *B.C.*: *Sources and Documents* (Englewood Cliffs, N.J., Prentice-Hall, 1965) — briefly annotated translation of some of the ancient texts on Classical art in Overbeck's *Schriftquellen* (infra, p. xcviii), with addition of passages on architecture from Vitruvius

E. SOME MAJOR BOOKS ON CLASSICAL ART
(*=important source of illustrations)

1. Ezio Aletti, *La Tecnica della Pittura Greca e Romana, e l'Encausto* (Rome, Airone, 1951)
2. P. E. Arias, *Mirone* (Firenze, Sansoni, 1940)
3. P. E. Arias, *Skopas* (Rome, Bretschneider, 1952)
4. Alberto d'Arzago, *La Grande Pittura Greca dei Secoli V e IV ante Cristo* (Milano, Vita e Pensiero, 1955)
*5. John Barron, *Greek Sculpture* (London, Studio, 1965)
6. J. D. Beazley and B. Ashmole, *Greek Sculpture and Painting* (Cambridge University Press, 1932)
7. H. G. Beyen and W. Volgraff, *Argos et Sicyone*: *Études Relatives `a la Sculpture Grecque de Style Sèvere* (Den Haag, Nijhoff, 1948)
*8. M. Bieber, *The Sculpture of the Hellenistic Age,* Revised Edition (New York, Columbia University Press, 1961)
*8a M. Bieber, *Alexander the Great in Greek and Roman Art* (Chicago, Argonaut 1965)
*9. Raymond Bloch, *Etruscan Art,* Revised Edition (Greenwich, Conn., New York Graphic Society, 1965)
*10. John Boardman, *Greek Art* (London, Thames & Hudson, 1964)
*11. Maurizio Borda, *La Pittura Romana* (Milano, Società Editrice Libraria, 1958)
12. Maurizio Borda, *La Scuola di Pasiteles* (Bari, Adriatica, 1953)

13. Blance Brown, *Ptolemaic Paintings and Mosaics and the Alexandrian Style* (New York, Archaeological Institute of America monograph, 1957)

14. S. Brunnsäker, *The Tyrant Slayers of Kritios and Nesiotes* Lund, Ohlsson, 1955)

15. Ernst Buschor, *Phidias der Mensch* (Munich, Munchener Verlag, 1948)

16. Rhys Carpenter, *Greek Art: A Study of the Formal Evolution of Style* (Philadelphia, University of Pennsylvania Press, 1962)

17. Rhys Carpenter, *Greek Sculpture: A Critical Review* (Chicago, University of Chicago Press, 1960)

18. J. Charbonneaux, *Greek Bronzes* (New York, Viking, 1962)

*19. J. Charbonneaux, *La Sculpture Grecque Archaïque* (Paris, Cluny, 1939)

*20. J. Charbonneaux, *La Sculpture Grecque Classique,* 2 vols. (Paris, Cluny, 1943)

21. L. Curtius, *Die Klassische Kunst Griechenlands* (Potsdam, Athenaion, 1938) — this is Vol. II of his *Die Antike Kunst*

*22. P. Demargne, *Aegean Art* (London, Thames & Hudson, 1964) — on origins of Greek style

23. W. Deonna, *Dédale: La Statue de la Grèce Archaïque,* 2 vols. (Paris, Boccard, 1930)

*24. *Enciclopedia dell'Arte Antica Classica e Orientale,* 8 vols. (Rome, Enciclopedia Italiana, 1958—)—detailed articles on all artists, periods, fields

*25. *Encyclopedia of World Art,* 16 vols. (New York, McGraw-Hill, 1959-   )—good coverage of most aspects of Classical art, excellent illustrations

*26. Adolf Furtwängler, *Masterpieces of Greek Sculpture,* new enlarged edition by Al. N. Oikonomides (Chicago, Argonaut, 1964) — a major work of interpretation

*27. Mabel Gabriel, *Masters of Campanian Painting* (New York, Bittner, 1952)

*28. Percy Gardner, *Archaeology and the Types of Greek Coins* (Chicago, Argonaut, 1965)

*28a. G. Q. Giglioli, *Arte Greca,* 2 vols. (Milano, Vallardi, 1955)

*29. G. M. A. Hanfmann, *Roman Art* (Greenwich, Conn., New York Graphic Society, 1964)

*30 B. V. Head and G. F. Hill, *A Guide to the Principal Coins of the Greeks* (London, British Museum, 1932) — an enlarged edition in 1959

*31. Helga Heintze, *Römische Porträt Plastik* (Stuttgart, Günther, 1961)

32. F. P. Johnson, *Lysippus* (Durham, N.C., Duke University Press, 1927)

* 33. Colin M. Kraay ~ M. Hirmer, *Greek Coins as Art* (London, Thames & Hudson, 1966) — the best collection of photographs, with excellent text

*34. W. Kraiker, *Die Malerei der Griechen* (Stuttgart, Kohlhammer, 1958)

*35. W. Lamb, *Greek and Roman Bronzes* (London, 1929; Enlarged Edition, Chicago, Argonaut, 1966)

36. A. P. Laurie, *Greek and Roman Methods of Painting: Some Comments on the Statements Made by Pliny and Vitruvius about Wall and Panel Painting* (Cambridge University Press, 1910)

37. H. Léchat, *Phidias et la Sculpture Grecque au Ve Siècle* (Paris, Boccard, 1924)

*38. Georg Lippold, *Die Griechische Plastik* (Munich, Beck, 1950)

*39. R. Lullies and Max Hirmer, *Greek Sculpture,* Revised Edition (London, Thames & Hudson, 1960) — the finest photo collection of Greek originals; with notes

40. A. Mahler, *Polyklet und seine Schule* (Leipzig, 1902)

*41. A. Maiuri, *Roman Painting* (Geneva, Skira, 1953)

*42. H. P. L'Orange and P. J. Nordhagen, *Mosaics: From Antiquity to the Early Middle Ages* (London, Paul Hamlyn, 1965) — the best general survey

43. R. Paribeni, *Il Ritratto nell'Arte Antica* (Milano, Treves, 1934)

*44. Charles Picard, *Manuel d'Archéologie Grecque: La Sculpt-ure*, 4 vols. (Paris, Picard, 1935 -   )—the fullest treatment in any language

*45. E. Pfuhl, *Malerei und Zeichnung der Griechen*, 3 vols. (Munich, Bruckmann, 1923)

*46. E. Pfuhl, *Masterpieces of Greek Drawing and Painting*, 2nd edition (London, Chatto & Windus, 1955)

*47. S. Reinach, *Répertoire des Peintures Grecques et Romaines* (Paris, Leroux, 1922)—extensive collection of sketches of ancient paintings

*48. S. Reinach, *Répertoire de là Statuaire Grecque et Ro-maine*, 6 vols. (Paris, Leroux, 1906 - 1930) — sketches of nearly all extant Classical statues

*49. G. M. A. Richter, *Archaic Greek Art* (Oxford University Press, 1949)

50. G. M. A. Richter, *Greek Painting: The Development of Pictorial Representation from Archaic to Greco-Roman Times* (New York, Metropolitan Museum, 1952) — a booklet, illustrated from vase paintings

*51. G. M. A. Richter, *A Handbook of Greek Art*, 4th edition (London, Phaidon, 1965)—handy over-all survey, with 500 illustrations

*52. G. M. A. Richter, *Kouroi: Ancient Greek Youths* (Lon-don, Phaidon, 1960) — best collection of this type of archaic statuary

*53. G. M. A. Richter, *Portraits of the Greeks,* 3 vols. (Green-wich, Conn., New York Graphic Society, 1965) — ful-lest study of all extant important examples

*54. G. M. A. Richter, *The Sculpture and Sculptors of the Greeks,* 3rd edition (New Haven, Conn., Yale University Press, 1950) —excellent survey; 775 illustrations

55. G. S. Rizzo, *Prassitele* (Milano, Treves, 1932)

*56. M. C. Robertson, *Greek Painting* (Geneva, Skira, 1959) — illustrated from vases mostly

57. Georg Rodenwaldt, *Die Kunst der Antike* (Berlin, Pro-pyläen Verlag, 1927) — excellent survey

*58. Karl Schefold, *Meisterwerke Griechischer Kunst* (Basel, Schwabe, 1960)

*59. R. V. Schoder, SJ, *Masterpieces of Greek Art,* revised edition (Greenwich, Conn., New York Graphic Society, 1965) — survey, all in color; extensive text

60. W. H. Schuchhardt, *Die Epochen der Griechischen Plastik* (Baden-Baden, Grimm, 1959)

*61. C. Seltman, *Approach to Greek Art* (London, Studio, 1948)

*62. C. Seltman, *Greek Coins,* 2nd edition (London, Methuen, 1955) — handy survey

*63. C. Seltman, *Masterpieces of Greek Coinage* (Oxford, Cassirer, 1949) — excellent artistic examples in good photos

64. C. Walston, *Alkamenes and the Establishment of the Classical Type in Greek Art* (Cambridge University Press, 1926)

*65. Max Wegner, *Greek Masterpieces of Art* (New York, Braziller, 1960)

66. J. White, *Prespective in Ancient Drawing and Painting* (London, Hellenic Society, 1956) — important technical analysis

PREFACE

THE text printed in the following pages is based upon that of *Detlefsen*, but free use has been made of both earlier and later critical auxiliaries. We differ from Detlefsen mainly in adhering more closely to the *Codex Bambergensis*, whose superiority in respect of those parts of the *Historia* now reproduced must be regarded as incontestable. Our short critical apparatus is limited to notices of our deviations from Detlefsen, or of readings offering special interest or difficulty. For brevity's sake the name of Detlefsen stands in our apparatus not only for his own readings but also for those of the scholars whose views he adopts. In none but a few important cases do we print Detlefsen's sources. I have to thank *Mr. Fischer* of Bamberg for kindly verifying a number of readings in the Bambergensis, and *Dr. Leitschuh*, Chief Librarian at Bamberg, for permission to reproduce in facsimile a page of the famous codex. The present text has been prepared under the guidance of *Dr. Ludwig Traube*, who, moreover, has generously placed at our disposal a number of his own readings or conjectures.

Out of the many problems which even this short selection from the *Historia Naturalis* offers, the Introduction professes to deal only with the question of Pliny's Greek sources for the history of art; it touches upon his Roman authorities only in so far as these were the channel through which the Greek authors reached him. The question is one which, so far from being, as was supposed, either exhausted or incapable of solution, is still in its infancy. Where an earlier school was content to trace back Pliny's debt to his Roman predecessors, a newer method of inquiry enables the student to work backwards not only from the Roman to the Greek authors, but from one Greek author to another. So it is that, returning to the Introduction after an interval, it became clear to me (see footnotes on p. xliii f.) that in matters of anecdote and biography Antigonos of Karystos was seldom, if ever, to be regarded as an ultimate source, and was to a far greater extent than I had at first supposed the debtor of Duris. Nay, I believe that we may in time recover (to some extent) the authorities which Duris himself had at his command. I am profoundly indebted to *Dr. F. Münzer* for reading and criticizing the proofs of the Introduction up to p. lxxiii, and for allowing me to publish as footnotes and *Addenda* the suggestive remarks made to me in the course of a detailed correspondence.

I have endeavoured to make the notes printed below the text a real commentary to the author's meaning, not a bundle of bibliography. Modern commentators might still lay to heart the criticism passed by Scaliger on the Pliny of his friend Dalecampius : *le bon homme est docte, mais il farcit trop ses annotations de je ne sais quelle fatraille d'auteurs* . . . But wherever further revision showed that I had done but scant justice to important though dissentient views I have tried to remedy the omission in the *Addenda*. There too a few notes are printed the necessity for which occurred to me later, and reference given to quite recent literature.

One group of contributions has been made to this book calling for special notice. When my work was already advancing towards completion, I learnt that *Dr. H. L. Urlichs* was himself engaged upon an edition of the same parts of

Pliny. With ready generosity, however, Dr. Urlichs offered me at once for my own book a number of his notes, which we agreed should be printed in square brackets and marked with his initials H. L. U. Subsequently, however, Dr. Urlichs informed me, to my regret and surprise, that the present edition would block the way for his own; accordingly, since he had given us notes, whose value is undeniable, we acceded to his request that his name should be placed as a third on our title-page. In fairness to Dr. Urlichs, I should add that his contributions and his responsibility begin and end with the notes that bear his initials.

Besides those scholars who have given me constant and special help, I have to thank *Mr. A. S. Murray, M. S. Reinach,* and *Professor Wilhelm Klein* for many friendly hints, *Mr. Bernhard Berenson* for helping me to a better understanding of passages concerned with the technique of art, and *Director G. von Laubmann* for the singular privileges accorded to me as a reader in the Royal Library at Munich. Above all am I beholden to my friend *Miss K. Jex-Blake,* not only for undertaking the translation, but for her liberality in allowing certain readings to be printed, of whose soundness she was not fully convinced. She has also found time, amid the arduous tasks imposed by College lecturing, to compile both Indices, and to assist in the revision of the book throughout.

EUGÉNIE SELLERS.

Schwabing, Munich.
July, 1896.

CORRIGENDA.

Page xv, note 3, l. 2, *for* Inaug. *read* Isag.

Page 77, commentary, column 2, n. on Timotheus, *for* xxxvi, 35 *read* xxxvi, 30

Page 171, translation, l. 6, for *Mnasitheus* read *Mnasitheos*

CONTENTS

PLINY THE ELDER

Born A.D. 23, killed in the eruption of Vesuvius A.D. 79.

Preface to Nat. Hist. §§ 17–19.

MY thirty-six volumes contain twenty thousand matters worthy of attention (for, as Domitius Piso says, they ought to be a storehouse, not a book), gathered from some two thousand books, but few of which are known to the learned, owing to the abstruse nature of their contents, and from one hundred chief authorities. I have included a great number of facts which had escaped earlier writers or become known only to a later age, and yet I cannot doubt that I too have omitted much, for I am but a man, and that a busy one, and can devote to these studies only my leisure time, that is, the hours of the night—for I would have none among you believe that I am idle even then. My days belong to you, I give to sleep only the time that may purchase health, and feel fully rewarded in that I add to the hours of my life while dallying, as Marcus Varro has it, with the Muses. For surely we live but in our waking hours.

Plin. Epist. III, 5 (to Baebius Macer), §§ 10–12 ; 14–16.

(My uncle) never read any book without making extracts, and often declared that no book was so bad as not to contain some useful passage. After enjoying the sun he usually took a cold bath, then ate a few morsels and took a short nap, after which, as if it were a new day, he devoted himself to study till dinner-time. While he dined he had a book read aloud and made notes rapidly. I remember that once the reader mispronounced something, and one of the company called him back and made him repeat the passage. 'Surely you understood?' said my uncle. His friend admitted it. 'Then why did you want him to go back?' said he, 'we have lost more than ten lines through your interruption.' . . . He only laid aside his studies when in the bath, and, when I say bath, I mean the actual bathing-chamber, for while he was being scraped and rubbed he used to listen to reading or dictate something. On a journey he threw himself entirely into study, as if he were snatching a holiday from everything else; at his side with book and tablets was a secretary wearing warm cuffs on his hands in winter, so that even the severity of the weather could not steal a moment from his studies; and this too was why he rode in a litter in Rome. I can remember his blaming me for walking; I need not, he said, have lost those hours, for he thought all time lost that was not given to study.

INTRODUCTION

THE *Historia Naturalis* of Pliny was intended not only to embrace the whole of the Natural Sciences, but to consider them in their application to the Arts and Crafts of Civilized Life. Hence it is that in a work, whose title would least suggest it, a short yet complete History of Art finds a logical place within the scheme. To Pliny the arts of chasing in silver and of casting in bronze are simply the indispensable complement of the chapters on metals, while, in the same way, the arts of sculpture, of painting, and of gem-engraving come under the head of kinds of earth and precious stones. Pliny's larger and compacted purpose might thus, on the face of it, seem to condemn this present detachment of the History of Art for separate treatment. But that general commentary on Pliny in the light of modern research, to which the texts of *Sillig* and *L. von Jan* were but to serve as preliminaries [1], seems likely, owing to the multifarious contents of the *Historia*, to remain in the region of unachieved possibilities, if not further away still—in Utopia : *il faut plus d'un homme pour écrire sur le grand Pline* [2]. Meanwhile, from the nature of the subject, the Plinian account of Ancient Art and Artists forms an episode sufficiently complete in itself to be made, without further apology, the subject of a special inquiry.

In the Dedicatory Letter addressed with the *Historia* to the co-Emperor Titus, Pliny has himself announced that the 'twenty thousand matters worthy of attention' contained in the thirty-six volumes of his work were 'gathered from some two thousand books' [3]; we must therefore regard his work as nothing more than a compilation from other records, in which personal observation plays no part outside the range of contemporary events.

---

[1] The gigantic scheme had been conceived by Lorenz Okens (1779–1859) ; see Stark, *Archäologie der Kunst*, p. 264.

[2] *Scaligerana* (ed. 1667), p. 189.

[3] *Praef.* § 17.

An irreparable accident, however—the total loss of the art-
literature which preceded Pliny—has given to the books with
which we are here concerned an unique value. It so happens
that from his pages only can we now obtain something like
a connected impression of the art-literature of the Greeks, as
it lay open, if no longer actually to him, at any rate to some
of his immediate predecessors. For although Pliny in his Preface
makes a great show of acknowledgement to his authorities, and
announces his intention, which he duly carried out, of compiling
Indices of their names [1], a very slight acquaintance with his work
is sufficient to show that for no part of it did he ever read
a Greek author systematically through [2], while for the history of
the artists we are safe in asserting that not one of these authors
was directly consulted. If the names of Apelles, of Melanthios,
of the Sikyonian Xenokrates, of biographers such as Antigonos

---

[1] These lists are suffixed in the
MSS. to the table of contents of each
book, with which they together make
up the first book of the *Historia*, and
are also given singly before each book;
they contain the names of 146 Roman
and 327 foreign authors. For the con-
venience of the reader I print here the
Indices to Bks. xxxiv–xxxvi, italicizing
the names of the writers upon art:

Libro xxxiv continentur (here follow the contents) . . . *Ex auctoribus*: L. Pisone, Antiate, Verrio, *M.
Varrone*, Cornelio Nepote, Messala
Rufo, Marso poeta, Boccho, Iulio
Basso qui de medicina Graece scripsit,
Sextio Nigro qui item, Fabio Vestale.
Externis : Democrito, Metrodoro
Scepsio, *Menaechmo* qui de toreutice
scripsit, *Xenocrate* qui item, *Antigono*
qui item, *Duride* qui item, *Heliodoro*
qui de Atheniensium anathematis
scripsit, *Pasitele* qui de mirabilibus
operibus scripsit, Timaeo qui de medicina metallica scripsit, Nymphodoro, Iolla, Apollodoro, Andrea,
Heraclide, Diagora, Botrye, Archedemo, Dionysio, Aristogene, Democle,
Mneside, Xenocrate Zenonis, Theomnesto.
Lib. xxxv continentur . . . *Ex auc-*

toribus: Messala oratore, Messala
sene, Fenestella, Attico, *M. Varrone*,
Verrio, *Nepote Cornelio*, Deculone,
Muciano, Melisso, Vitruvio, Cassio
Severo, Longulano, *Fabio Vestale* qui
de pictura scripsit. *Externis*: *Pasitele*,
*Apelle, Melanthio, Asclepiodoro, Eu-
phranore, Parrhasio, Heliodoro* qui
de anathematis Atheniensium scripsit,
Metrodoro qui de architectonice scripsit, Democrito, Theophrasto, Apione
grammatico, Timaeo qui de metallica
medicina scripsit, Nymphodoro, Iolla,
Apollodoro, Andrea, Heraclide, Dia-
gora, Botrye, Archedemo, Dionysio,
Aristogene, Democle, Mneside, Xeno-
crate Zenonis, Theomnesto.
Lib. xxxvi continentur . . . *Ex auctoribus*: *M. Varrone*, C. Galba, Cincio,
Muciano, Nepote Cornelio, L. Pisone,
Q. Tuberone, Fabio Vestale, Annio
Fetiale, Fabiano, Seneca, Catone
censorio, Vitruvio. *Externis* : Theo-
phrasto, *Pasitele*, Iuba rege, Nicandro,
Sotaco, Sudine, Alexandro polyhis-
tore, Apione Plistonico, Duride,
Herodoto, Euhemero, Aristagora,
Dionysio, Artemidoro, Butorida,
Antisthene, Demetrio, Demotele,
Lycea.
[2] See Teuffel, p. 761.

of Karystos, or Duris of Samos, figure in the *Indices*, rousing the curiosity and ambition of the modern scholar, they are there simply because Pliny had found them quoted by the Roman authors from whom he habitually drew—in this case by Varro, who, in turn, had presumably taken his own information on the subject from a single writer in whose pages the others were already cited. Thus, although the Plinian *Indices* might mislead us into believing that his work was a mosaic, a piecing together of the several statements of all the authors, Greek or Roman, whose names he quotes, we shall find, on the contrary, that it resembles a stratification of which the superimposed layers can still be distinguished at many points, even though at a number of others they have so run together as to baffle analysis.

The result of such an analysis, if complete, would be nothing less than to isolate and restore to each writer his own contribution; nothing proves so well the difficulty of the task as the great amount of labour already expended in this direction. And this brings me to record the debt which every student of the Plinian art-books owes to the scholars by whose undaunted industry Pliny and his authors have gradually been brought into right relation : to *Otto Jahn,* who by detecting the homogeneous character of a number of scattered art-criticisms, and pointing out their immediate Varronian authorship and ultimate Greek origin, laid a solid basis for all future research in this field [1]; to *A. Brieger,* who made the first attempt to determine the names of the Greek writers whose views Varro had latinized [2]; to *Heinrich Brunn,* who first tried to restore Pliny's system of quotation from his authors [3]; to the scholars—among them *Theodor Schreiber* [4], *Adolf Furtwängler* [5], *Gustav Oehmichen* [6], *Karl Robert* [7],

[1] O. Jahn : *Ueber die Kunsturtheile des Plinius* in *Berichte der Sächs. Gesellschaft d. Wissenschaften,* 1850, pp. 105–142.

[2] A. Brieger : *De Fontibus Librorum, xxxiii–xxxvi, Nat. Hist. Plin. quatenus ad artem plasticam pertinent.* Dissert. Greifswald, 1856.

[3] H. Brunn : *De Auctorum Indicibus Plinianis.* Disp. Inaug. Bonn, 1856.

[4] Th. Schreiber : *Quaestionum de Artificum Aetatibus in Plin. Nat.*

Hist. Lib. relatis Specimen. Dissert. Leipzig, 1872.

[5] A. Furtwängler : *Plinius u. seine Quellen über die Bildenden Künste* in Supplebd. ix der Jahrbb. f. Klass. Phil. Leipzig, 1877.

[6] G. Oehmichen : *Plinianische Studien zur geographischen und kunsthistorischen Literatur.* Erlangen, 1880.

[7] C. Robert : *Archäologische Märchen aus alter u. neuer Zeit,* Berlin, 1886 (ch. i–iv and vi–viii).

L. von Urlichs [1], and his son *H. L. Urlichs* [2],—who, following in the steps of these pioneers, developed or corrected their views; and last, but not least, to *F. Münzer*, who only the other day [3], when the question had begun to show signs of exhaustion, gave it a new stimulus through his vigorous attempt to ascertain the Greek element in Pliny by a minute comparison of those parts suspected to be Greek with the extant fragments of certain authors mentioned in the *Indices*. In what follows, I propose to bring together, in a survey of the gradual growth of the Plinian history of the artists, such results as have been attained, carrying forward by the way the task of identifying and disengaging the Greek writers upon art mentioned by Pliny.

§ 1. *Xenokrates of Sikyon* (*fl. about* 280 B.C.).

In the criticisms or verdicts upon celebrated artists, now disjointedly scattered throughout the Plinian narrative, but recognized by Otto Jahn (*op. cit.*) as vitally interdependent, we touch at once upon the original groundwork. These criticisms have it in common that they all culminate in a broad statement of the special services rendered to art by the artist in question; they are presented for the most part as the effect produced by the artist's works upon the critic; and they are all consistently free from anecdote or epigram, in contrast to the phraseological character of so much of the ancient art-criticism. Their principle is most readily grasped in the judgements passed upon the five most famous statuaries—Pheidias, Myron, Polykleitos, Pythagoras, and Lysippos—in xxxiv, 54–65. It is instructive minutely to analyze these criticisms when freed so far as may be from the additions made to them by later writers [4]. In the following scheme I have indicated, within square brackets, the nature of these additions.

---

[1] L. Urlichs: *Die Quellenregister zu Plinius letzten Büchern.* Progr. Würzburg, 1878.

[2] H. L. Urlichs: *Über Griechische Kunstschriftsteller.* Dissert. Würzburg, 1887.

Besides the works cited as of leading importance, mention may also be made of the two following dissertations: J. Dalstein, *Quibus Fontibus Plinius in Artificum Historia usus sit*, Metz, 1885: and H. Voigt, *De Fontibus earum quae ad artes pertinent partium Nat. Hist. Plin. quaestiones.* Halle, 1887.

[3] F. Münzer: *Zur Kunstgeschichte des Plinius* in Hermes, vol. xxx, 1895.

[4] In doing this I have been guided almost entirely by the analysis of Münzer, *op. cit.* p. 502 ff.

I. Pheidias.

Phidias praeter Iovem Olympium ... fecit ex ebore ... Minervam Athenis, quae est in Parthenone stans, ex aere vero (*follows allusion to 'Amazon' in* § 53) ... Minervam tam eximiae pulchritudinis ut formae cognomen acceperit. fecit et cliduchum [*follows mention of an Athena in Rome, of two draped figures and a nude colossos, all from Rom. Museogr.* p. xci] primusque artem toreuticen aperuisse atque demonstrasse merito iudicatur.

II. Polykleitos.

Polyclitus Sicyonius Hageladae discipulus diadumenum fecit [*follows epigrammatic qualification*, p. lxviii, *and price paid for the Diadumenos*, p. lxxiv], idem et doryphorum [*follows epigrammatic qualification; second mention under the name 'canon' of the doryphoros*, p. xli] fecit et destringentem se et nudum telo incessentem [*follows mention of knucklebone players, at Rome, in Hall of Titus*, p. xcii; *of a Hermes at Lysimacheia, on authority of Mucianus*, p. xc; *of a Herakles at Rome*] hagetera arma sumentem [*follows from an anecdotic source, the mention of Artemon surnamed 'periphoretos'*—Add. p. 235] hic consummasse hanc scientiam iudicatur et toreuticen sic erudisse ut Phidias aperuisse. proprium eius est uno crure ut insisterent signa excogitasse, quadrata tamen esse ea ait Varro et paene ad exemplum.

III. Myron.

Myronem Eleutheris natum Hageladae et ipsum discipulum bucula maxime nobilitavit [*follows allusion to epigrams upon the heifer*], fecit et canem et discobolon et Perseum et pristas et Satyrum admirantem tibias et Minervam, Delphicos pentathlos, pancratiastas [*follows mention* (a) *of a Herakles in Rome*, (b) *of the grave of a grasshopper and locust, see Comm.* p. 46, l. 4, (c) *of an Apollo restored to Ephesos by Augustus*, p. lxxxix]. primus hic multiplicasse veritatem videtur, numerosior in arte quam Polyclitus et in symmetria diligentior, et ipse tamen corporum tenus curiosus animi sensus non expressisse, capillum quoque et pubem non emendatius fecisse quam rudis antiquitas instituisset.

IV. Pythagoras.

Vicit eum Pythagoras Reginus ex Italia pancratiaste Delphis posito ; eodem vicit et Leontiscum ; fecit et stadiodromon Astylon qui Olympiae ostenditur et Libyn puerum tenentem tabellam eodem loco et mala ferentem nudum [*follows mention, from an epigram, of the Philoktetes at Syracuse*, p. lxix], item Apollinem serpentemque eius sagittis configi [*follows mention, from an anecdotic source, of the 'Citharoedus' at Thebes*, Münzer *op. cit.* p. 525], hic primus nervos et venas expressit capillumque diligentius. (πρῶτον δοκοῦντα Πυθαγόραν ῥυθμοῦ καὶ συμμετρίας ἐστοχάσθαι—Diogenes Laertios, viii, 46.)

V. Lysippos.

[*The account of Lysippos opens with an anecdote given on the authority of Duris*, p. xlvi.]

(Lysippus) fecit . . . destringentem se [*follows its dedication at Rome ;*

anecdote of Tiberius's passion for the statue], nobilitatur Lysippus et temulenta tibicina et canibus ac venatione [*mention, on authority of Mucianus* (p. lxxxvii), *of the chariot of the Sun at Rhodes*]. fecit et Alexandrum Magnum multis operibus a pueritia eius orsus [*follows Nero's maltreatment of the statue*]. idem fecit Hephaestionem Alexandri Magni amicum [*its ascription by other authorities to Polykleitos ; Pliny's own comment,* p. xciii], item Alexandri venationem quae Delphis sacrata est, Athenis Satyrum, turmam Alexandri in qua amicorum eius imagines summa omnium similitudine expressit [*mention of removal of the group to Rome*], fecit et quadrigas multorum generum. statuariae arti plurimum traditur contulisse capillum exprimendo, capita minora faciendo quam antiqui, corpora graciliora siccioraque, per quae proceritas signorum maior videretur. *non habet Latinum nomen symmetria* quam diligentissime custodit nova intactaque ratione quadratas veterum staturas permutando [*follows apothegm quoted from Duris,* p. lxii f]. propriae huius videntur esse argutiae operum custoditae in minimis quoque rebus.

To which may be added :

VI. Pupils of Lysippos, and Telephanes of Phokaia.

Filios et discipulos reliquit laudatos artifices Laippum, Boedan, sed ante omnes Euthrycraten, quamquam is constantiam potius imitatus patris quam elegantiam austero maluit genere quam iucundo placere. itaque optume expressit Herculem Delphis et Alexandrum Thespis venatorem et Thespiadas, proelium equestre, simulacrum ipsum Trophonii ad oraculum, quadrigas complures, equum cum fuscinis, canes venantium. huius porro discipulus fuit Tisicrates et ipse Sicyonius, sed Lysippi sectae propior, ut vix discernantur complura signa, ceu senex Thebanus et Demetrius rex, Peucestes Alexandri Magni servator, dignus tanta gloria. artifices qui compositis voluminibus condidere haec miris laudibus celebrant Telephanen Phocaeum ignotum alias, quoniam in Thessalia habitaverit, et ibi opera eius latuerint, alioqui suffragiis ipsorum aequatur Polyclito, Myroni, Pythagorae. laudant eius Larisam et Spintharum pentathlum et Apollinem [*follows, from a different source, a variant explanation of the obscurity of Telephanes*].

It is now a commonplace of archaeology that these closely connected criticisms were designed to establish a comparison of the five principal artists (*insignes*), based upon their gradual conquest of the problems of symmetry and proportion, and of certain minor technical details such as the rendering of the hair, of the sinews, or the veins : Pheidias discovers the possibilities of statuary ; Polykleitos perfects it and makes his statues rest their weight on one leg, yet he fails because his figures are too square and monotonous ; Myron surpasses him by attaining not only to symmetry but to variety, yet he fails in the rendering of the hair ; Pythagoras is more successful with hair and moreover learns how to express the sinews and the muscles ;—at this point we are brought up short by finding that, in Pliny, nothing is said of the relation of Pythagoras to symmetry. This is however an omission for which the Roman author, Pliny or Varro, is responsible; for the record of that artist's contribution to symmetry is preserved in the passage quoted above from Diogenes Laertios [1] (cf. Comm. p. 48). There we learn that Pythagoras was considered the first artist to aim not only at symmetry but also at rhythm—in other words at the correct rendering of proportion, not only in figures at rest, but also in figures in motion. Lysippos, finally, achieves the perfect proportion, by modifying in a manner peculiar to himself the ancient canons, and solves by the way the minor technical difficulties in the rendering of the hair. The guiding thought is analogous to that which prompted Dionysios to classify the orators into inventors of their art— εὑρεταί, and its perfectors—τελειωταί [2].

The mention of Varro in § 56 certainly proves, as Jahn saw, that he was Pliny's immediate authority for the whole series of the criticisms; but it is equally certain that they did not originate with him. So rigid a scheme of artistic development would be a most unlikely product of the varied and miscellaneous literary activity of that compiler. It is moreover strongly coloured by the partisanship of a school and obviously devised to the honour of the Sikyonian Lysippos, the greatest artists falling into place as his precursors. Besides, the words *non habet latinum nomen symmetria* . . . in § 65 show sufficiently that Varro had only been translating from the Greek. He appears here as the intermediary between Pliny and the Greeks precisely as, in the earlier books of the *Historia*, Trogus or Nigidius Figulus are named as authorities for facts or observations drawn by these writers from Aristotle [3].

The Greek author whose views on the gradual development of art passed, through Varro, into the pages of Pliny was not only a warm admirer of the Sikyonians, but, to judge from the exclusive

---

[1] Furtwängler, *Plinius u. seine Quellen*, p. 70.

[2] Dionysios Halik. *De Dinarcho iud.*: Περὶ Δεινάρχου τοῦ ῥήτορος οὐδὲν εἰρηκὼς ἐν τοῖς περὶ τῶν ἀρχαίων γραφεῖσιν, διὰ τὸ μήτε εὑρετὴν ἰδίου γεγονέναι χαρακτῆρος τὸν ἄνδρα, ὥσπερ τὸν Λυσίαν, καὶ τὸν Ἰσοκράτην, καὶ τὸν Ἰσαῖον· μήτε τῶν εὑρημένων ἑτέροις τελειωτήν, ὥσπερ τὸν Δημοσθένην, καὶ

τὸν Αἰσχίνην, καὶ Ὑπερείδην ἡμεῖς κρίνομεν.

[3] Nigidius is quoted for Aristotle in ix, 185, Trogus in xi, 275, 276; see F. Aly, *Zur Quellenkritik des älteren Plinius*, p. 10 f.; Montigny, *Quaestiones in Plin. Nat. Hist de Animalibus Libros*. Bonn,1844; Teuffel, p. 761.

stress which he lays upon certain sides of technical progress, an artist judging from the standpoints which he had himself been trained to esteem most highly. We have not far to go to fix upon his name. He must be, as Robert first definitely pointed out[1], that Xenokrates, himself a pupil of two distinguished Sikyonians, Teisikrates and Euthykrates, who is cited in the Index to Bk. xxxiv and in § 83 as having written on bronze statuary, and in xxxv, 68 upon painting[2]. In the latter passage he is named conjointly with Antigonos, another art-writer, who, as we shall presently see, is in great measure responsible for the additions of epigrammatic or anecdotic character made to the earlier history by Xenokrates.

But the scheme of development propounded in the famous five criticisms involves a curious anachronism: Myron is made posterior to Polykleitos, Pythagoras posterior to both. That this anachronism cannot be due to mere negligence appears from the carefully thought-out nature of the context. I think it is clear from the remark preserved in Diogenes, concerning the *rhythm* contributed to statuary by Pythagoras, that, alongside considerations of symmetry and proportion, the idea of an evolution from figures at rest to figures in motion influenced the chronological order adopted by the author of the criticisms. After the stately seated or standing gods, goddesses, and temple-attendants of Pheidias come first the quiet athletes of Polykleitos, just shifting the weight of the body to one leg as in the act of walking, then

---

[1] *Archäologische Märchen aus alter und neuer Zeit*, pp. 28 ff. A. Brieger, *De Fontibus*, p. 46, had first pointed out that the verdicts on the bronze statuaries could be traced beyond Varro back to Antigonos and Xenokrates; cf. also Th. Schreiber, *Quaestionum de Artif. Aetat.*, p. 27 ff., and Furtwängler, *op. cit.* p. 68; but it was Robert who first disentangled the special contribution of Xenokrates.

[2] His identification with the Athenian Xenokrates, son of Ergophilos, of the inscriptions from Oropos and Elateia (Loewy, *Inschriften der Griechischen Bildhauer*, 135 *a, b, c*) appears to me, on the other hand, doubtful (see Comm.). The strongest argument in its favour is that Loewy, 135 *a, b*, are from Oropos, a region for which both Teisikrates, the master of Xenokrates, and Thoinias, son of Teisikrates, were at one time active (*I. G. B.* 120-122 *a*). But it is strange that an Athenian, who in inscribing his name was careful in at least two cases (*I. G. B.* 135 *a*, and the new inscription—also from Oropos—'Εφημ. ἀρχ. 1892, 51, cf. Diels, *Anzeiger*, 1893, p. 138 f.) to record the country of his birth, should have come so completely to identify himself with the Sikyonians as did the Plinian writer, or have so often entirely passed over, or dismissed with only a passing allusion, the famous artists of his own country.

the works—athletes also for the greater part—of Myron and Pythagoras. Now, if we place the Myronian 'Diskobolos' with its audacious movement next to the Polykleitan 'Diadumenos' or 'Doryphoros,' and adopt the recent conjecture[1], which attributes to Pythagoras the fine boxer in the Louvre[2], and the athlete in violent motion of the Boboli gardens[3]—two statues which surpass even the Diskobolos in movement and animation—we shall at least understand how, at a time when art-criticism in our modern sense was scarcely existent, such statues would give rise to the perverse chronology of §§ 55–59.

The account of the pupils of Lysippos is obviously inseparable from the account of Lysippos himself. To Telephanes we shall return presently. Before we proceed to track out Xenokrates further, we should, however, note the significant fact that wherever, in the passages just discussed, the locality of a work of art is either given or can be recovered from other sources, it lies within a restricted geographical beat, comprised by Olympia (§§ 54, 59), Delphoi (§§ 57, 59, 64, 66), Lebadeia, Thespiai, and Thebes (§§ 66, 67), and finally Athens (§§ 54, 64)[4]. From this we may gather that Xenokrates (who probably had little opportunity for distant travel) confined himself to the mention of monuments of which he had personal knowledge.

A glance at the chronological tables of §§ 49–52 shows them to be by the author of the criticisms; in the one as in the other Pheidias opens the series—Lysippos with the brilliant attendance of sons and pupils closes it. If the Xenokratic authorship of the chronology needed confirmation, we should find it in the fact that Polykleitos, Myron, Pythagoras, are placed in the same curious order as in the verdicts. The activity of Xenokrates cannot have extended much beyond Ol. 121, the date he assigns to the pupils of Lysippos, and it is noteworthy that, although his treatise was extensively enlarged by later writers, yet the period with which it closed was adopted as representing the close of art in Greece. *Cessavit deinde* (after Ol. 121) *ars*, writes Pliny, *ac rursus Olympiade CLVI revixit*, the *revixit* not so much

---

[1] Furtwängler, *Masterpieces of Greek Sculpture*, p. 171 f; cf. E. Reisch, *Weihgeschenke*, p. 44.

[2] Phot. Giraudon, 1207.

[3] Phot. Arndt-Bruckmann (*Einzelverkauf*), 96.

[4] Cf. Münzer, *op. cit.* p. 505. Of the works whose locality is not indicated, the Athena *tam eximiae pulchritudinis* of Pheidias (see Comm. to xxxiv, 54, l. 2), the cow of Myron, ε his Perseus were at Athens.

marking a real revival as affording a convenient formula to introduce the Greek artists who decorated at Rome the famous monuments erected by Q. Metellus Macedonicus [1].

It is evident that the chronological and narrative parts of the Xenokratic treatise had originally formed one consistent whole, which some later writer afterwards subdivided into a chronology and alphabetical lists (cf. p. lxxx). The five most famous artists, however, and the pupils of Lysippos were left, owing to their great reputation, in the original Greek order, though sundered from the chronology. Moreover, Telephanes of Phokaia (§ 68) and Praxiteles (§§ 69-71) were assigned places—in no sort of chronological order—between the pupils of Lysippos and the first alphabetical list. The reasons for the exception made in their favour are sufficiently instructive. The Xenokratic character of the account of Telephanes comes out in the comparison instituted to Polykleitos, Myron, and Pythagoras, whose names are given in the same order as in the verdicts; since, however, Xenokrates had not deemed Telephanes worthy of comparison with the two greatest names—with either Pheidias, the founder, or Lysippos the perfecter of the art—he had also not accredited him with any distinct contribution to the progress of statuary. Now the comparison of Telephanes to Polykleitos, Myron, and Pythagoras on the one hand, and the absence of any precise estimate of his merits on the other, were explained by some later Greek writer in a rationalizing anecdotic manner, alien to Xenokratic practice: Telephanes was excellent, the reasoning seems to be, or he could not be compared to great names, but he must have been obscure or we should hear more about him; and as Xenokrates had given a list of works, some, or all, of which were in Thessaly [2], their remoteness was made the reason for the artist's want of fame: *quoniam in Thessalia habitaverit et ibi opera eius latuerint*. These additions are so nicely welded into the Xenokratic account that they must have been made at a quite early date, as we shall see by Antigonos (p. xxxvi). Puzzled by the mention of this excellent yet unknown artist, the Roman authors next introduced him under cover of their Greek authorities: *artifices qui haec condidere* (i.e. Xenokrates and Antigonos) *miris laudibus celebrant*

---

[1] The *cessavit* and *revixit* first explained by Brunn, *K. G.* i. p. 504 f. Cf H. L. Urlichs, *Griechische Kunstschriftsteller*, p. 31 f.

[2] A region to which Xenokrates might easily have extended his researches northwards from Phokis and Boeotia.

Telephanem Phocaeum, and placed him outside the *insignes*, but yet in a more distinguished place than the alphabetical lists. Practically the same happened in the case of Praxiteles (§§ 69–71). This artist appears to have been only summarily discussed by Xenokrates[1], who, like the rest of his school and Lysippos himself, was exclusively a worker in bronze, and therefore only wrote concerning works in bronze, entirely ignoring the marble sculpture wherein lay the chief strength of Praxiteles and the new Attic school. Yet Praxiteles was much too great a favourite of the Romans for a Roman writer to be content with assigning to him a place among the artists of the alphabetical lists, so he linked him on to Telephanes with a *quoque*, adducing as an apology for not placing Praxiteles among the *insignes* that he was *marmore felicior ideo et clarior*. The argument practically comes to: Praxiteles also, like Telephanes, has an excuse for the place assigned to him—in his case not want of fame, but the fact that he is better known as a worker in marble than as a worker in bronze[2].

An analysis of the first alphabetical list (§§ 74–83) will reveal further traces of Xenokrates. In the subjoined tables I have marked with an X those artists the account of whom seems Xenokratic, and placed within square brackets the names of artists or works manifestly introduced from other sources.

X. *Alcamenes: encrinomenos*[3].
X. *Aristides: quadrigae bigaeque.*
    [*Amphicrates: Leaena*, periegetic, see Comm. and p. lxxxvi.]
X. *Bryaxis: Aesculapius, Seleucus.*
X. *Boedas: adorans.*
    [*Baton: Apollo, Iuno*, Roman museography, cf. p. xci f.]
    [*Cresilas: volneratus, Pericles*, both from epigrams, see Comm. and p. lxix.]
    [*Cephisodotus: ara*, on authority of Heliodoros, p. lxxv.]
X. *Canachus:* [*Apollo*, anecdotic, see Comm. and p. lxxxviii] *celetizontes pueri.*
X. *Chaereas: Alexander, Philippus.*
X. *Ctesilaus: doryphorus, Amazon.*
    [*Demetrius: Lysimache* (inscrip., p. lxxxvi), *Minerva mus.* (periegetic),
        Simon (literary source, p. lxv, note 1).]

---

[1] Münzer, *op. cit.* p. 507, considers the Xenokratic material to be somewhat as follows: *Praxiteles ...fecit ex aere. . . . Proserpinae raptum item catagusam, et Liberum patrem et Ebrietatem nobilemque una Satyrum, quem Graeci periboeton cognominant ... item stephanusam, pseliumenen,* *Oporan* (where M. wrongly retains *canephoram*).

[2] I am indebted to Dr. H. L. Urlichs for giving me what I believe to be the correct explanation of the passage.

[3] The list is based on that of Oehmichen, *Plin. Studien*, p. 163 f.

X. *Daedalus: destringentes se.*
X. *Dinomenes: Protesilaus, Pythodemus.*
X. *Euphranor:* [*Alexander Paris* (epigr. p. lxix), *Minerva, Latona* (Roman museogr.)], *quadrigae bigaeque, cliduchus. Virtus et Graecia; mulier adm. et ador.; Alex. et Philippus.* [*Eutychides: Eurotas* (epigr. p. lxix f.).]
X. *Hegias: Minerva, Pyrrhus, celetizontes.* [*Hagesias: Hercules in Pario colonia* (Mucianus, p. xc).]
X. *Isidotus: buthytes.* [*Lycius: puer sufflans* (epigr. p. lxx)], *Argonautae.* [*Leochares: Ganymedes* (epigr. p. lxx), *Autolycus* (literary source, p. xlv, note 1), *Jupiter, Apollo* (Rom. museogr.), *Lyciscus* (epigr. p. lxxiii, note 2).]
X. *Lycius: puer suffitor.* [*Menaechmus: vitulus* (epigr. p. lxxiii, note 2).]
X. *Naucydes: Mercurius, discobolus, immolans arietem.*
X. *Naucerus: luctator anhelans.* [*Niceratus: Aesculapius et Hygia* (Roman museogr.).]
X. *Pyromachus: quadriga cum Alcibiade.*
X. *Polycles: Hermaphroditus.*
X. *Pyrrhus: Hygia et Minerva.*
X. *Phanis: epithyusa.* [*Styppax: splanchnoptes* (periegetic and epigr. p. lxx).] [*Silanion: Apollodorus, Achilles, epistates* (epigr. p. lxx).] [*Strongylion: Amazon* (Roman anecdote, cf. p. xcii).] [*Theodorus: se ipse fudit* (anecdotic).] [*Xenocrates: copia signorum* (Antigonos).]

Reference to the text of Pliny will show that the works of the nineteen artists marked X are enumerated with a simple directness which contrasts as forcibly as possible with the literary allusions, anecdotic tags, and epigrammatic descriptions attaching to the notices of the names placed in brackets. This same directness characterized the lists of works of the *insignes*, and is a clear mark of Xenokratic authorship. Ten of these names, moreover, still retain their place in the Xenokratic chronology (*Alcamenes, Aristides, Canachus, Daedalus, Dinomenes, Euphranor, Hegias, Naucydes, Pyromachus, Polycles*).

An attentive study shows how a second, a third, and perhaps even a fourth hand worked over or added to the Xenokratic material, sometimes to its suppression. *Cephisodotus, Eutychides, Leochares*, all appear in the Xenokratic chronology, but, if any of their works were mentioned, these have been omitted to make way for others which brought the added interest of anecdote or epigram ; in the case of Euphranor (§ 77) the mention of the ' Paris,' derived from an epigram, was prefixed to the arid Xenokratic lists. This method of introducing new material from other sources has led to the double mention of *Lycius* (§ 79) and of *Hegias* (§ 78), the latter of whom appears the second time, under the alternative form of his name, *Hagesias*. As to the mention of Xenokrates himself (§ 83), it is probable that if it had come from him its wording would be at once more modest and less vague. I therefore adopt Münzer's suggestion (*op. cit.* p. 509) that it is due to the reverence ('Pietät') of the later writer, who worked the Xenokratic treatise into his own, namely Antigonos. A number of other additions, made from evident Roman sources, or concerning works to be seen at Rome, in Varro's or Pliny's day, need no comment here. In the same way certain additions came to be made also to the chronology. The most obvious is the notice of Seilanion (see p. xlix, note 2, and Add. to Comm. on xxxiv, 51), who is tacked on to the artists of Ol. 113.

The Plinian account of the bronze-workers from § 49 to § 83 represents roughly, then, the original compass of that portion of the treatise of Xenokrates which treated of the period from the great revival after the Persian wars down to the sons and pupils of Lysippos, in Olympiads CXIII and CXXI. But it would be an error to suppose that this history of statuary took no notice of the earlier phases of the art. Through some accident which we are now no longer in a position to determine, the whole earlier part seems however to have been suppressed, with the exception of one unmistakable fragment, which oddly enough has found its way to the beginning of Pliny's account of the sculptors in marble (xxxvi, 9–10). The passage, as it now stands, is a little mosaic of most diverse materials, but the original Xenokratic conception is still evident from the stress laid upon the early fame of the Sikyonian workshops, from the fact that Dipoinos and Skyllis, the scene of whose labours lay chiefly in Sikyon and adjacent or dependent regions, are chosen among all archaic craftsmen to represent the beginnings of their art [1]. Their works had been of wood (note on xxxvi, 10) and could thus fall within the range of a writer upon bronze statuary, describing the gradual evolution from wood or wood gilt to metal. To the Xenokratic

---

[1] The Xenokratic kernel of the passage has been rightly detected by Münzer (*op. cit.* p. 523), whom it is therefore surprising to find support-ing the view that Xenokrates left the whole of the archaic period unnoticed (*ib.* p. 505).

contention that the art of sculpture in bronze was elaborated by
Daidalid artists on the mainland of Greece, a later writer—
presumably Antigonos (p. xliii f)—adjusted the account of the rise
of sculpture in marble in the islands of the Aegean, under the
auspices of Chian sculptors. Thus it was that the Xenokratic
account of Dipoinos and Skyllis came in time to be placed at the
opening of a history of sculpture in marble, where it has long
proved a crux to archaeologists [1]. We have learnt, then, that
Xenokrates, in treating of the bronze-workers, began with
the earliest beginnings. The current notion that he took no
account of archaic bronze statuary is as false as it is arbitrary [2].
It is not improbable that, if the Xenokratic account of the
statuaries, as we have it in Pliny's thirty-fourth book, opens with
Pheidias, this is somehow due to a very ancient misunderstanding
of the statement that ' Pheidias first revealed the capabilities of
sculpture and indicated its methods.' We shall immediately see
how a similar expression, in the case of the painter Apollodoros,
misled both ancient and modern critics into the erroneous supposition that the Greek writers—Xenokrates *in primis*—had
ignored the early painters.

The Xenokratic history of the painters, preserved in Pliny's
thirty-fifth book, can be recovered far more completely than that
of the bronze-workers. Since in xxxv the alphabetical principle
does not make its appearance till § 138, where it is employed to
group together artists of comparatively minor importance, the
original scheme is, in parts at least, still sufficiently clear.

Xenokrates is quoted by name, along with Antigonos, as the
authority for the verdict upon Parrhasios (§ 68). The judgement
in its essence is so indubitably his, as a comparison with the
judgement passed upon Lysippos and his son Euthykrates (xxxiv,
66) proves, that if the later writer's name appears it can only

---

[1] Münzer, *loc. cit.*

[2] Cf. among others Robert, *Arch.
Märchen*, pp. 36, 41, where the
post-dating of Kritios and Nesiotes
(§ 49) is explained by supposing that
the fame of their ' Tyrant-Slayers '
would attract the attention of the
compiler of the chronology, who,
since he ignored the archaic period,
made them into contemporaries of
Pheidias, the earliest bronze-worker

known to him. I take it rather that
Xenokrates, having but very few dates
at his command (see Comm. on xxxiv,
49), grouped about Pheidias, as their
representative, a number of other
artists who had been engaged upon the
restoration of Athenian monuments
after the Persian sack. The anachronism at any rate affords no proof
that Xenokrates had neglected the
archaic period.

be in his character of compiler, or 'editor,' of the Xenokratic history.

(Lysippus) statuariae arti plurimum traditur *contulisse* capillum exprimendo, capita minora faciendo quam antiqui, corpora graciliora siccioraque, per quae proceritas signorum maior videretur. non habet Latinum nomen *symmetria quam diligentissime custodit* nova intactaque ratione quadratas veterum staturas permutando, vulgoque dicebat ab illis factos quales essent homines, a se quales viderentur esse. propriae huius videntur esse *argutiae* operum custoditae in minimis quoque rebus. filios et discipulos reliquit laudatos artifices Laippum, Boedan, sed ante omnes Euthrycraten, quamquam is constantiam potius imitatus patris quam *elegantiam* austero maluit genere quam iucundo placere.

Parrhasius Ephesi natus et ipse multa *contulit. primus symmetrian picturae dedit,* primus *argutias* voltus, *elegantiam* capilli, venustatem oris, confessione artificum in lineis extremis palmam adeptus. haec est picturae summa suptilitas. corpora enim pingere et media rerum est quidem magni operis sed in quo multi gloriam tulerint, extrema corporum facere et desinentis picturae modum includere rarum in successu artis invenitur. ambire enim se ipsa debet extremitas et sic desinere ut promittat alias pone se ostendatque etiam quae occultat. hanc ei gloriam concessere Antigonus et Xenocrates qui de pictura scripsere, praedicantes quoque, non solum confitentes [1].

But the criticism of Parrhasios is closely linked with a row of similar criticisms, not only interconnected, but dictated by the same spirit as the judgements passed upon the statuaries [2]. Robert has pointed out that identical standards were set up in each case, while the final appreciations were similarly formulated; as Pheidias (xxxiv, 54) discloses the possibilities of statuary, so Apollodoros (xxxv, 60) discloses those of painting. The initiative of either master was carried further in the one art by Polykleitos (xxxiv, 56), by Zeuxis (xxxv, 64) in the other. Both these artists, however, fail in the rendering of proportion, a point in which Myron (xxxiv, 57) and Parrhasios (xxxv, 68) surpass them. The former is *symmetria diligentior* than Polykleitos; of the other it is said that *primus symmetrian picturae dedit.* Pythagoras (xxxiv, 59) and Euphranor (xxxv, 128) each progress towards the attainment of symmetry; of the one the critics said πρῶτον . . . συμμετρίας δοκοῦντα ἐστοχάσθαι, of the other *primus videtur . . . usur-*

---

[1] I have chosen these two passages for comparison, because of the marked verbal similarities, but of course the real counterpart, among the painters, of Lysippos, among the statuaries, was Apelles.

[2] Robert, *Arch. März.* p. 67 ff., conveniently prints the passages side by side. After the detailed analysis of the verdicts upon the bronze-workers, it seems sufficient to refer to the text.

passe symmetrian. The highest mastery, finally, is embodied in Lysippos (xxxiv, 65) and in Apelles (xxxv, 79).

We may now proceed to recover traces of Xenokrates in the earlier sections of xxxv. It has been noted above that the contribution to symmetry, made respectively by Pythagoras and Euphranor, was couched in almost identical terms. But the statement that Pythagoras was the first to mark the sinews and the muscles, *primus nervos et venas expressit,* recalls the improvements attributed in an early part of the History of the Painters to Kimon of Kleonai : *articulis membra distinxit, venas protulit* (§ 56)[1]. That both are from the same hand is indubitable.

Again, the criticism of Kimon is inseparable from a whole series of similar passages, in which the earlier stages of painting were discussed. These began at § 16, and, after sundry excursus on paintings in Rome and on colours (§ 18 ff.), were resumed again at § 56. When exhibited together, the original coherence of the passages is self-evident[2].

§ 16. Inventam liniarem a Philocle Aegyptio vel Cleanthe Corinthio primi exercuere Aridices Corinthius et Telephanes Sicyonius, sine ullo etiamnum hi colore, iam tamen spargentes linias intus. ideo et quos pingerent adscribere institutum. primus invenit eas colore testae, ut ferunt, tritae, Ecphantus Corinthius.

§ 56. . . . eosque qui monochromatis pinxerint, quorum aetas non traditur, . . . fuisse, Hygiaenontem, Dinian, Charmadan et qui primus in pictura marem a femina discreverit Eumarum Atheniensem figuras omnis imitari ausum, quique inventa eius excoluerit Cimonem Cleonaeum. hic catagrapha invenit, hoc est obliquas imagines, et varie formare voltus, respicientes suspicientesve vel despicientes. articulis membra distinxit, venas protulit, praeterque in vestibus rugas et sinus invenit.

§ 57. Panaenus quidem frater Phidiae etiam proelium Atheniensium adversus Persas apud Marathona factum pinxit. adeo iam colorum usus increbruerat, adeoque ars perfecta erat ut in eo proelio iconicos duces pinxisse tradatur, Atheniensium Miltiaden, Callimachum, Cynaegirum, barbarorum Datim, Artaphernen.

§ 58. . . . Polygnotus Thasius qui primus mulieres tralucida veste pinxit, capita earum mitris versicoloribus operuit plurimumque picturae primus contulit, siquidem instituit os adaperire, dentes ostendere, voltum ab antiquo rigore variare. [*follows mention of a picture in Rome*] hic Delphis aedem pinxit, hic et Athenis porticum quae Poecile vocatur . . . cum partem eius Micon . . . pingeret.

These primitives are represented as not yet sufficiently ad-

---

[1] The parallelism of the two passages is noted—but in a different context—by Hartwig, *Meisterschalen,* p. 165.

[2] I here follow Münzer entirely (*op. cit.* p. 514), who gives the passages freed, so far as possible, from later additions.

vanced to grapple with problems of harmony and symmetry; it
is sufficient for them to attempt to conquer step by step, first
a knowledge of their materials, then by slow degrees the correct
presentment of objects. Philokles, Kleanthes, and the earliest
painters, are scarcely painters at all; they practise mere outline.
Then Ekphantos fills up this outline with red colour. Hygiainon
and his fellows (§ 56) continue to use only one colour till it
occurs to Eumaros to distinguish in painting between the sexes;
this he doubtless does by introducing white for the flesh of
the women [1] *and thus marks the first stage in the progress from
monochrome to polychrome painting.* So far, however, figures
have only been drawn in full face or in profile (though Pliny
nowhere states this, it can be supplied from what follows); but now
Kimon of Kleonai *invents* foreshortening, κατάγραφα [2]. He further
correctly marks the articulations and the muscles, and 'discovers
the wrinkles and the windings of drapery.' Artists, having now
learnt to distinguish between the sexes, to articulate their figures,
and to present them in various attitudes, are able to turn their
attention to distinguishing between individuals. Panainos, accordingly, in his Battle of Marathon, introduces *portraiture.* But
mere draughtsmanship—outline simply filled in with colour—was
susceptible of still further improvements. Thus Polygnotos of
Thasos first permits the draperies to reveal the bodies beneath
them, and shows at the same time how to give movement not
only to the body, as Kimon had done, but also to the face. Then,
the capacities of this limited technique being exhausted, there
appeared on the scenes the great painter Apollodoros (§ 90 above,
p. xxvii), who by discovering 'the fusion and management of
shade [3] '—we should rather say of light—first gave to objects their
real semblance (*primus species instituit*): thus he contributed to
painting its most important factor, and thereby, as an epigrammatist
pointedly said, he 'opened the gates of art' to the great masters
of Greek painting—to Zeuxis and Parrhasios and their illustrious
contemporaries. The coherence of the whole history of the
development and perfection of painting—the consistent logic
which underlies it, of an evolution from the simpler to the more
complex—is so patent that it is incomprehensible how so many

---

[1] Eumaros's innovation is generally
so explained, but I am not aware
that the significance of the introduction of this white colour has ever been
accurately grasped.

[2] See note on xxxv, 56.

[3] ἐξευρὼν φθορὰν καὶ ἀπόχρωσιν
σκιᾶς, Plutarch, *De Glor. Athen.* 2.

scholars—at least in the period between Jahn's Essay and Münzer's—entirely failed to apprehend it.

It remains, however, to ask how in face of this consecutive Treatise by a Greek writer there could ever arise the complaint in xxxv, 54 : *non constat sibi in hac parte* (sc. *historia pictorum*) *Graecorum diligentia multas post olympiadas celebrando pictores quam statuarios ac toreutas, primumque olympiade LXXXX.* The question involves a difficult problem. One can only imagine that the complaint, in its present form, is the result of a misunderstanding; it is not impossible that some later writer, intermediate between the earlier Greek art-writers and the Roman, had found fault with the Greeks for failing to appreciate the naïve charm and simple methods of the painters who lived previous to the innovations of Apollodoros. Such a criticism, combined with the words used by Xenokrates of Apollodoros, *hic primus species instituit*, might lead in time to the supposition that the Greek art-writers had completely failed even to mention pre-Apollodorian painters. The Roman compilers, drawing from books (Pasiteles? p. lxxix) where the names of Xenokrates and Antigonos as authorities for the history of the early painters had long dropped out, piled up as proofs of the supposed inaccuracy of these writers[1] a number of facts[2] for which their Treatises were in reality the chief sources. Theophrastos, also, had been misrepresented in precisely the same manner. According to Pliny (vii, 205) he had attributed the invention of painting to Polygnotos, whereas Theophrastos can have intended nothing more than that Polygnotos was the first painter who could be properly so called ; writing doubtless under the influence of Aristotle's admiration for the ethical qualities of this artist (*Poet.* 1450*a*). Theophrastos had assigned to him the place which the Plinian authors, intent rather upon technical progress, gave to Apollodoros. In truth Pliny's statement as regards Theophrastos, and his or Varro's complaint of the Greek inaccuracy, are, I believe, but the distorted reflection of the old controversy whether draughtsmanship or colouring was the more powerful means of expression. The opinion of Aristotle may be

---

[1] It is universally acknowledged that the Greeks alluded to in the words *Graecorum diligentia* are the main authorities, i.e. Xenokrates and Antigonos (perhaps also Duris); cf. Robert, *Arch. Märchen*, p. 25.

[2] E.g. the activity of Pheidias and Panainos as painters (cf. p. li); the whole list of painters and their works from the early monochromatics down to Polygnotos. The account of Boularchos (§ 55) may have been derived by Varro (cf. p. lxxxiv and Comm. on xxxv, 55) from some independent source.

guessed from his predilection for the pre-Apollodorian Polygnotos [1]. The testimony of Dionysios to the value which a school of criticism, practically unrepresented in Pliny, attached to the pre-Apollodorian paintings is of importance :

'In ancient paintings the scheme of colouring was simple and presented no variety in the tones ; but the line was rendered with exquisite perfection, thus lending to these early works a singular grace. This purity of draughtsmanship was gradually lost; its place was taken by a learned technique, by the differentiation of light and shade, by the full resources of the rich colouring to which the works of the later artists owe their strength [2].'

We learn from this passage that the methods of the later painters were practically looked upon as hostile to those of the earlier, and Xenokrates, a hot partisan of the post-Apollodorians, may well have expressed himself in language which would eventually lead to the erroneous supposition that he had ignored all earlier paintings, from Polygnotos and Panainos up to the early monochromatics.

As we have it in Pliny, the argument against the Greeks is presented with skill and vigour (Comm. on xxxv, 54); the theme was evidently congenial to the Roman authors, who doubtless felt for the archaic the enthusiasm—common to all decadent periods—which was to rouse the subtle satire of Quinctilian [3].

After § 70 it becomes more difficult to follow Xenokrates (cf. Münzer, *op. cit.* p. 516), and scarcely any sentence can be picked out as bearing the indubitable signs of his method. Later writers, as shown by the Plinian *indices*, had, when it came to the artists

---

[1] Bertrand, *Études sur la Peinture*, p. 17, singularly misapprehends Aristotle when he assumes that A. definitely stated his preference for drawing over painting, and translates *Poet.* 1450 b, 'en étalant les plus belles couleurs on ne fera pas le même plaisir que par le simple trait d'une figure.' What A. says is that colours laid on *confusedly* or *indiscriminately* will not produce as much pleasure as simple outline : εἰ γάρ τις ἐναλείψειε τοῖς καλλίστοις φαρμάκοις χύδην, οὐκ ἂν ὁμοίως εὐφράνειεν καὶ λευκογραφήσας εἰκόνα.

[2] Dionys. Halik. *de Isaeo iudic.* 4 εἰσὶ δή τινες ἀρχαῖαι γραφαί, χρώμασι μὲν εἰργασμέναι ἁπλῶς, καὶ οὐδεμίαν ἐν

τοῖς μίγμασιν ἔχουσαι ποικιλίαν, ἀκριβεῖς δὲ ταῖς γραμμαῖς, καὶ πολὺ τὸ χαρίεν ἐν ταύταις ἔχουσαι· αἱ δὲ μετ' ἐκείνας, εὔγραμμοι μὲν ἧττον, ἐξειργασμέναι δὲ μᾶλλον, σκιᾷ τε καὶ φωτὶ ποικιλλόμεναι, καὶ ἐν τῷ πλήθει τῶν μιγμάτων τὴν ἰσχὺν ἔχουσαι.

[3] *Primi, quorum quidem opera non vetustatis modo gratia visenda sunt, clari pictores fuisse dicuntur Polygnotus atque Aglaophon, quorum simplex color tam sui studiosos adhuc habet, ut illa prope rudia ac velut futurae mox artis primordia maximis, qui post eos exstiterunt, auctoribus praeferant, proprio quodam intelligendi, ut mea opinio fert, ambitu.* Quinct. xii, 10.

of the fourth century, a large mass of literature to draw from.
Moreover popular anecdotes concerning the painters now take in
great measure the place of more serious criticism.

The next clear trace of Xenokrates is in the special emphasis
laid (§ 76) upon the fame of the Sikyonian painters. Sikyon,
the cradle of art-painting (§ 16), is now shown to be the home
also of its splendid maturity; as she had produced Lysippos, the
greatest master of statuary, so she produces Apelles, the greatest
master of the rival art of painting, whose contributions to his art
are appraised (§ 79) according to the canons applied to Lysippos
in xxxiv, 65. Though Apelles was probably already an artist of
established renown when he left his native Ephesos to study in
the schools of Sikyon, the claims of his obscurer early masters
must fade entirely before the glorious reputation of Eupompos
and Pamphilos.

The Theban-Attic school, which branched off from the
Sikyonian, with Aristeides I—brother-pupil of Eupompos—also
claimed the attention of Xenokrates. We must recognize with
Robert [1] that the account of Aristeides II in § 98 originates with
him; we note the Xenokratic intent to connect the name of
a great artist with some definite progress or contribution. In
this case the progress accomplished is of ethical rather than of
technical import; Aristeides discovers how to render not only
character but transient emotions [2], and in this there is a vague
reminiscence of the criticism passed upon Myron, that he had
failed to express 'the sensations of the mind.'

Between the two Aristeides must naturally have intervened the
account of Nikomachos, son of Aristeides I, and his pupils,
which in Pliny appears in §§ 108–110, away from its original
context.

After a long digression in §§ 112–121, due, as we shall see, in
part to Varro (p. lxxxiv), in part to Pliny himself (cf. p. xcii), we again
come upon clear traces of Xenokrates in the History of the Painters
in Encaustic [3]. In § 122 we find it stated first that, according to
certain authorities, Aristeides was the *inventor* of encaustic;

---

[1] *Archäologische Märchen*, p. 69;
cf. Münzer, p. 516.

[2] i.e. *perturbationes*: Furtwängler,
Plinius u. s. Quellen, p. 65 f., points
out that this Ciceronian translation of
the Greek πάθη (see Comm.) is presum-

ably due to Varro. It affords one of
the many proofs of the passage of the
Greek Treatises upon Art through
Varro's hands.

[3] Münzer, *op. cit.* p. 517 ff.

immediately after it is asserted that there existed pictures in this technique older than the time of Aristeides, namely those by Polygnotos, by the Parians Nikanor and Mnasilaos, and by Elasippos. In a word, the claims of the island-schools to priority of invention are opposed to the claims of the artists of the mainland, precisely as in xxxvi, 9–12 the Xenokratic contention that statuary was invented by the Daidalids Dipoinos and Skyllis was confronted by Antigonos with the assertion that long before their time sculpture in marble had flourished in the islands of the Aegean (p. xxvi) [1]. Thus it seems safe to conclude that the tradition attaching the invention of Encaustic to the name of Aristeides goes back to Xenokrates, and that Antigonos, faithful to his programme of exhibiting the various sources at his command, appended to it the account now represented in Pliny by the words *aliquanto vetustiores encaustae picturae extitere . . . nisi encaustica inventa*.

The school partisanship of Xenokrates at once betrays itself in § 123 in the preeminence assigned to the Sikyonian Pausias, pupil of the Sikyonian Pamphilos (§ 75), and accordingly brother-pupil of Apelles. Pausias is not only praised as the *first* to achieve fame in the wax technique, but is also credited in true Xenokratic fashion with two distinct contributions : he is the *first* to paint the panels of ceilings, the *first* also to decorate the vaults of roofs. It may be noted at this point that the Plinian division into painters in the ordinary tempera and painters in encaustic was probably no part of the original Greek treatise. Pausias must have been discussed in connexion with Pamphilos and the artists of § 75, while the discussion of Euphranor must have followed upon that of his master Aristeides I. That the pupils of Pausias, Aristolaos (§ 137) and Nikophanes, had also originally been discussed by Xenokrates is almost certain [2]; but the criticism passed upon Euphranor in § 130 is to my mind the last passage in the Plinian narrative of the painters where Xenokratic authorship can be pointed to with certainty. Students, however, will read with interest Münzer's attempts (*op. cit.* p. 518) to disengage further Xenokratic threads.

---

[1] The parallelism has been kindly pointed out to me by Münzer in a private letter; see note 3 on p. xliv.

[2] The epithet *elegans* applied to Nikophanes in xxxv, 111, recalls the *elegantia* attributed to Lysippos, xxxiv, 66, the *elegantia* in rendering of hair attributed to Parrhasios, xxxv, 67.

Before dismissing the history of the painters we still have to note a few scattered passages which afford proof that Xenokrates had not only summed up but analyzed the problems which the great artists in turn had set themselves to solve. The appreciation of Parrhasios (xxxv, 67), with the appended analysis of his special artistic achievement, contained in the words *haec est picturae summa suptilitas . . . occultat*, is a striking instance. That highest and hardest aim of the painter to produce about his figures the illusion of ambient space, of enveloping light and air, could not be more vigorously or happily expressed than in the phrase : *corpora enim pingere et media rerum est quidem magni operis sed in quo multi gloriam tulerint, extrema corporum facere et desinentis picturae modum includere rarum in successu artis invenitur. Ambire enim se ipsa debet extremitas, et sic desinere ut promittat alia post se ostendatque etiam quae occultat* (see Comm.). Again we can, I think, trace the hand of Xenokrates in xxxv, 29, in the analysis of the various effects attempted by painting ; with subtle understanding of artistic procedure it is told how painting after shaking off its early monotony discovered first light and shade, then the effects attainable by the juxtaposition of colours ; finally, how it discovered glow and the passage from the more lit-up to the less lit-up parts of a picture, in a word what the moderns call 'values' (see Comm.) Such observations had doubtless formed part of the history of the development of painting from the early monochromatics to the successors of Apollodoros, and became detached from their original context, perhaps at the time when the Xenokratic Treatise was schematized as noted on p. xxii. Furthermore it is possible that the Treatise had originally included, besides statements of the personal contribution made to the progress of art by the principal artists, and aesthetic analysis of special problems, a discussion of the materials employed. Perhaps therefore we should follow Münzer (*op. cit.* p. 512 ; p. 499 ff.) in crediting Xenokrates with the chapters on colours (xxxv, 29 ff.)[1] and consequently also with the notice of the various kinds of bronze (xxxiv, 9 ff.) employed by the statuaries.

The short account of modelling[2] in clay in xxxv, 151–153, con-

---

[1] After considerable hesitation, we decided on omitting these chapters from the present edition, which is concerned only with those portions of the *Historia* that treat of artists and actual works of art.

[2] Münzer, *op. cit.* p. 509 f. ; cf. Furtwängler, *Plinius u. s. Quellen*, p. 59 f.

tains the last marked traces of Xenokrates that we come across
in Pliny. Boutades, a potter (*figulus*), and of course a Sikyonian,
invents the fashioning of portraits in clay (*fingere ex argilla
similitudines*). To this statement is now attached from another
source an anecdote which represented this Sikyonian workman
as active in Corinth (p. xxxvii). In § 152 a variant version of
the discovery of modelling is given. Then with the words
Butadis inventum we get back to our Sikyonian potter, who,
having learnt to fashion a face in clay, is now the first (*primus*)
to adapt faces to tile ends, whence arose in time the whole
decoration of the eaves of temples. Further, he invents (*invenit*)
how to take moulds off the clay models for statues (*de signis
effigies exprimere*), and is thus the discoverer of the preliminary
indispensable process of casting statues in bronze. Hundreds
of years later another Sikyonian, Lysistratos, the brother of Xenokrates's special hero Lysippos, first discovers (*primus . . . instituit*)
how to take a mould off the living face. Hence the last and
crowning progress of art, the advent of realistic portraiture.
Münzer is certainly right in his conjecture that the account of
modelling was originally prefixed to the history of bronze-statuary,
since bronze-casting presupposed the clay model (see Comm. on
xxxiv, 35, and xxxv, 153), and therefore modelling passed as the
older art : *etenim prior quam statuaria fuit* (xxxiv, 35). The place
which Pliny assigns to modelling in his *History* is an obvious
necessity of his scheme ; clay being the material of modelling,
he is forced to bring the discussion of this art under 'kinds of
earth.'

This closes the list of passages that can be traced back with
any certainty to Xenokrates. It is a proof of the vigour of his
conceptions that they could so impose themselves upon subsequent
writers as never entirely to lose their original character, which
still asserts itself throughout the whole of the Plinian account
of the bronze statuaries and the painters. Nowhere do we grasp
so readily what Pliny's history of art owed to Xenokrates as in the
account of sculpture, given in Bk. xxxvi, where, failing the strong
thread which bound together—at least in considerable parts—
the narrative of the preceding books, we get little more than
a loose patch-work of facts brought together without guiding
thought or dominating interest. Meagre as are the fragments
that we have disengaged, they point back to a critic of other
calibre than the mere maker of anecdote and epigram—to

a critic who, conscientiously endeavouring to judge of works of art on their own merits, fails, not from garrulous digression or the desire to make a witty point, but rather from preconceived theory and love of schematizing. Xenokrates allows nothing for the fantastic freaks of artistic growth; in his rigidly constructed system monochrome is made to precede colour, artists may not attack the problems of drapery till they have solved the rendering of muscle, and the gracious advent of perfect harmony and proportion is presented as the inevitable sum to which each of five artists had contributed his measured share. Besides, in common with most artists who have also been art-critics, he insists upon fixing the measure of artistic achievement in the successful solution of the problems which chiefly interested the school of which he showed himself the jealous partisan. Yet, crude as the scheme must appear to our modern world with its deeper sense of the complexity of things, it should win respect and sympathy as a first genuine attempt to tell the still unfinished tale of the rise and growth of art. And there is even to be traced, at a distance great enough from the modern method of comparison, that same purpose which distinguishes the modern critic—to let the actual monuments tell the tale.

§ 2. *Antigonos of Karystos* (*born about* 295 B. C.).

When a writer aims, like Xenokrates, at formulating his criticism of an artist as the unbiassed impression received from a series of that artist's works, he will be anxious not to impair the strength of this impression by digressive criticism of single works; above all, he will jealously guard the integrity of his judgement against anything that might look like borrowed appreciation. A writer who appraises an artist in the words applied by Xenokrates to Polykleitos will be the last to introduce material so foreign to the final judgement as that which describes how the boy binding a fillet about his head was 'a boy yet a man,' or his companion athlete 'a man yet a boy'—words written, moreover, with a view to rhetorical antithesis rather than to criticism of artistic qualities.

Yet little epigrammatic or anecdotic tags are plentiful even in those parts of the Plinian account which have been shown to be essentially Xenokratic. Such, for instance, are the legends inter-

woven in xxxv, 9 with the account of the early Sikyonian artists
Dipoinos and Skyllis (see Comm.); the rationalizing statements in
xxxv, 16 and 151, intended to reconcile the conflicting claims to
greater antiquity of the art centres of Sikyon and Corinth; the
additions made in xxxv, 59 to the Xenokratic account of Polygnotos and Mikon, to the effect that the former took no payment
for his paintings in the *Stoa Poikile*, while the latter did; the
anecdotic flavour given to the account of Telephanes of Phokaia
(xxxiv, 68), the epigrammatic touch added in xxxv, 61 to express
the connexion between Apollodoros and Zeuxis. These additions
are generally so closely compacted with the original fabric that
it is only recent criticism, the growing recognition of the whole
tendency of the Xenokratic methods, which has detected them as
extraneous. They differ totally, in this respect, from the loose
and not unfrequently awkward additions to the Greek Treatises
made at a later date by Varro or Pliny himself in order to
introduce the mention of works in Rome or allusions to contemporary events.

It becomes evident that the Xenokratic treatise was minutely
worked over by a writer, who used it not simply to quote from,
but as a solid framework into which to fit new material of his
own. This writer, who appears almost as close collaborator of
Xenokrates, must be one of the writers included in xxxiv, 68 in
the words *Artifices qui compositis voluminibus condidere haec*, where
the *haec* refers (see p. xxii) to the previous account of the *insignes*,
which, as we have seen, is Xenokratic in the main. Now in xxxv,
67, in the discussion of Parrhasios, writers upon art are referred
to in similar manner: *confessione artificum in liniis extremis
palmam adeptus (Parrhasius)*. Immediately below, the names of
these *artifices* are given; the one is, as we expected, *Xenocrates*,
the other is *Antigonus*.

Antigonos is no longer a mere name. The brilliant essay in
which Wilamowitz proved his identity with the Antigonos of
Karystos [1], author of a book of Marvels or Ἱστοριῶν παραδόξων

---

[1] v. Wilamowitz-Moellendorff, *Antigonos von Karystos*, in *Philologische
Untersuchungen*, iv, Berlin, 1881;
see Susemihl, *Geschichte der Griechischen Literatur in der Alexandriner
Zeit*, i. p. 519 ff. I consider it superfluous to discuss the question of identity. It was questioned by Diels in
his review of Wilamowitz's book,
Deutsche Lit.-Zeitung, 1882, p. 604
(cf. also Voigt, *De Fontibus Plinianis*
p. 24), and disputed by H. L. Urlichs,
Griechische Kunstschriftsteller, p. 34.
Since then it has been accepted without reserve by Susemihl, and quite
lately by Münzer, *op. cit.* p. 521 ff.

συναγωγή, and of certain Biographies of the Philosophers, from which Diogenes Laertios drew extensively [1], has made almost familiar the artist who was likewise pupil of the philosopher Menedemos of Eretria, who contributed to the revival of Attic sculpture under Attalos and Eumenes of Pergamon, and was at the same time a versatile *littérateur*, equally at home in the poems of Euripides or Philoxenos and in the technical treatises of the painters. Scarcely a strong individuality, perhaps, but a highly finished type of his age in its wide culture and many-sided curiosities. In addition to the passages already referred to (xxxiv, 68 ; xxxv, 66–68), Antigonos is quoted by Pliny in the *Indices* of Books xxxiii and xxxiv as a writer *de toreutice*, and in xxxiv, 84 as one of the sculptors in the service of the Court of Pergamon. Diogenes mentions the sculptors Anaxagoras (ii, 45) and Demokritos (ix, 49) on his authority, and recounts (vii, 7, 187) of a namesake of the philosopher Chrysippos, the physician Chrysippos of Knidos, that he had invented concerning Zeus and Hera certain intolerable obscenities not described by the writers upon painting : ' they are found neither in Polemon, nor in Xenokrates, nor yet in Antigonos [2].'

It further appears from the two following passages that, in his Lives of the Philosophers, Antigonos had allusions to the history and literature of art :

Diogenes ix, 11, 62 : Antigonos of Karystos says in his account of Pyrrhon that he began life in obscurity and poverty, and was at first a painter, and that a picture by him—of very moderate execution—representing torch-bearers, is in the Gymnasium of Elis [3].

Diogenes iv, 3, 4 : On the whole he (Polemon) was the sort of man described by Melanthios in his Book upon Painting, who says that a certain self-reliance and austerity should make itself felt in portraiture, precisely as in character [4].

[1] The fragments of Diogenes referable to Antigonos will be found conveniently put together by Wilamowitz, *op. cit.*

[2] Diog. vii, 7, 187 : οὐδὲ παρὰ τοῖς περὶ πινάκων γράψασι κατακεχωρισμένην (sc. *historiam*)· μήτε γὰρ παρὰ Πολέμωνι μήτε παρὰ Ξενοκράτει (Wilam. *op. cit.* p. 8 ; Köpke, *De Antigono Carystio*, p. 25 note ; the MSS. have παρ' Ὑψικράτει), ἀλλὰ μηδὲ παρ' Ἀντιγόνῳ εἶναι.

[3] Ἀντίγονος δέ φησιν ὁ Καρύστιος ἐν τῷ περὶ Πύρρωνος τάδε περὶ αὐτοῦ,

ὅτι τὴν ἀρχὴν ἄδοξύς τ' ἦν καὶ πένης καὶ ζωγράφος· σώζεσθαί τ' αὐτοῦ ἐν Ἤλιδι ἐν τῷ γυμνασίῳ λαμπαδιστὰς μετρίως ἔχοντας.

[4] Καὶ ὅλως ἦν τοιοῦτος οἷόν φησι Μελάνθιος ὁ ζωγράφος ἐν τοῖς περὶ ζωγραφικῆς· φησὶ γὰρ δεῖν αὐθάδειάν τινα καὶ σκληρότητα τοῖς ἔργοις ἐπιτρέχειν, ὁμοίως δὲ καὶ (so Wilam. p. 64; the MSS. have δὲ κἄν) τοῖς ἤθεσιν. I am not able to apprehend the precise meaning which the words ὁμοίως . . . ἤθεσιν are intended to convey. The sense of the rest of the

Lastly, the learned traveller and antiquary, Polemon of Ilion (contemporary of Ptolemaios V. Epiphanes, 202–131 B.C.), who wrote against Antigonos a controversial work in at least six books[1], gives, in order to combat it, a verbatim quotation from Antigonos. The Polemonic fragment, which is of incomparable interest as affording an insight into the methods of these ancient controversialists, has found its way into the collection of Proverbs of the sophist Zenobios (age of Hadrian); it runs as follows :—

Zen. v. 82 : At Rhamnous is an image of Nemesis ten cubits high, made wholly of marble, the work of Pheidias, holding an apple branch in her hand. From this branch, *according to Antigonos of Karystos*, hangs a little tablet bearing the inscription ' Agorakritos the Parian made me.' But this is no proof (οὐ θαυμαστὸν δέ), for many also have inscribed another's name upon their own works, a complacency which Pheidias probably showed to Agorakritos, whom he loved . . .[2]

These accredited fragments prove the varied experience of Antigonos in the province of art-history : we find him appealing to the testimony of inscriptions as carefully as his rival Polemon, whose industry in this respect won for him the nickname of ὁ στηλοκόπας[3] ; he is ready to apply a phrase in a Treatise upon Portraiture to his characterization of a philosopher ; he had himself written a statistical book upon pictures, containing minute descriptions of their subjects[4] ; nor had he neglected to note the apocryphal tale which connected a certain mediocre picture at Elis with the name of the philosopher Pyrrhon.

The miscellaneous character of his information, and the

passage is finely indicated by Wilamowitz, p. 147 ; cf. also H. L. Urlichs, *Griech. Kunstschrift.* p. 18 ff.

[1] The work bore the title πρὸς 'Αδαῖον καὶ 'Αντίγονον ; of Adaios of Mitylene, who appears to have written upon sculptors, περὶ ἀγαλματοποιῶν (Athenaios, xiii, 606 a), very little is known, cf. Susemihl, *op. cit.* i, p. 518 ; for Polemon, see Susemihl, i, p. 665 ff. ; for the fragments of his treatise against Antigonos, Preller, *Polemonis periegetae fragmenta,* Leipzig, 1838, p. 97 ff. ; Müller, *F. H. G.* iii, p. 132, fr. 56–69 ; for the nature of the controversy, see especially H. L. Urlichs, *op. cit.* p. 33 ff.

[2] 'Ραμνουσία Νέμεσις : ἐν 'Ραμνοῦντι

Νεμέσεως ἵδρυται ἄγαλμα δεκάπηχυ, ὁλόλιθον, ἔργον Φειδίου, ἔχει δὲ ἐν τῇ χειρὶ μηλέας κλάδον. ἐξ οὗ φησιν 'Αντίγονος ὁ Καρύστιος πτύχιόν τι μικρὸν ἐξηρτῆσθαι τὴν ἐπιγραφὴν ἔχον "'Αγοράκριτος Πάριος ἐποίησεν." οὐ θαυμαστὸν δέ· καὶ ἄλλοι γὰρ πολλοὶ ἐπὶ τῶν οἰκείων ἔργων ἕτερον ἐπιγεγράφασιν ὄνομα· εἰκὸς οὖν καὶ τὸν Φειδίαν τῷ 'Αγορακρίτῳ συγκεχωρηκέναι, ἦν γὰρ αὐτοῦ ἐρώμενος, καὶ ἄλλως ἐπτόητο περὶ τὰ παιδικά. It was first conjectured by Wilamowitz, *op. cit.* p. 13 f., that the whole passage goes back to Polemon ; the view has been accepted without reserve by H. L. Urlichs *loc. cit.*

[3] Herodikos, *ap.* Athen. vi, 234 d.

[4] Cf. Wilamowitz, *op. cit.* p. 8.

varying trustworthiness of the quarters whence he obtained it, prove at once that Antigonos, unlike Xenokrates, belonged to the class of people who are curious of facts rather than critical of their significance.

Xenokrates had been guided in his selection of material by a strongly marked principle, whence the comparative ease in recovering and closing up the dissevered members of his treatise. The treatise of Antigonos on the other hand, with its looser method of synthesis, is more difficult to retrace. We cannot point to this or that fragment of the Plinian history as bearing his individual stamp. But we can distinguish certain elements in Pliny which go back to those general sources — art-historical, epigrammatic, anecdotic, &c.—whence we know Antigonos to have drawn, and, on examining these, we shall find the majority of cases to afford such strong proof of his handling that, failing contrary evidence, it will not be unfair to assume the remainder also to have come into Pliny through his medium.

From the fact that Antigonos incorporated the Treatise of Xenokrates into his own work, and from his allusion in his life of Polemon (above, p. xxxviii) to a Treatise upon Portraiture by the painter Melanthios, we may infer that it was he who introduced references to a number of artists as having also written upon their art. These are the bronze-worker Menaichmos (xxxiv, Index and § 80)[1], the painter Apelles (xxxv, Ind. and § 79, § 111), Melanthios, Asklepiodoros and Parrhasios (*ib*. Ind.), and Euphranor (*ib*. Ind. and § 128). Apelles as a writer upon art is fortunately more than a mere name. One trace of the work or works in which he expounded—presumably for the use of his pupils (cf. xxxv, § 111)—the theories of his art has survived, as Robert justly points out[2], in § 107 in the words *Asclepiodorus, quem in symmetria mirabatur Apelles*, which at the close of § 80 had been rendered by *Asclepiodoro de mensuris* (*cedebat Ap*.). If the conjecture be correct for Asklepiodoros it follows that Apelles's appreciation of Melanthios in the grouping of figures was also expressed in the same work. There, likewise, it must have been that he discussed the art of Protogenes (§ 80) and criticized his laborious finish. In fact, from the words *quorum opera cum admiraretur omnibus conlaudatis*, it is fair to assume that besides original theories the Apellian treatise contained criticisms—for the

---

[1] He is otherwise unknown either as artist or writer; see Münzer, *op. cit.*   p. 520, note 1; cf. Susemihl, i, p. 113, note 2.   [2] *Arch. Märchen*, p. 70.

most part favourable—of contemporary artists [1]. The statement as to his own *venustas*, like the *quod manum de tabula sciret tollere*, is the later concrete expression, practically thrown into proverbial formula, of the aims and theories expounded by Apelles as being those of himself and his school.

Antigonos, too, may be responsible for a few more Plinian passages which are faintly coloured by reminiscences of other technical treatises by artists, though these are not definitely alluded to. I have already indicated in the notes that in the words *solusque hominum artem ipsam fecisse artis opere* (*Polyclitus*) *iudicatur* in xxxiv, 55, there appears to lurk an allusion to the book, the Κάνων [2], in which, as we learn more fully from Galenos, Polykleitos had laid down his theories on the proportions of the human body [3]; we have accordingly translated the passage 'he is the only man who is held to have embodied his theory of art in a work of art,' the work being the famous Spear-Bearer, which is here introduced, quite irrespectively of its first mention in § 55, as a separate work under its alternative name of the *Canon* [4].

---

[1] Schubert, *Fleckeisen's Jahrbb.*, Supplementband ix, p. 716, detects a reference to the work of Apelles in Plut. *Dem.* 22 καί φησιν ὁ 'Απέλλης οὕτως ἐκπλαγῆναι θεασάμενος τὸ ἔργον ὥστε καὶ φωνὴν ἐκλιπεῖν αὐτόν. ὀψὲ δὲ εἰπεῖν, μέγας ὁ πόνος καὶ θαυμαστὸν τὸ ἔργον, οὐ μὴν ἔχειν χάριτας, δι' ἃς οὐρανοῦ ψαύειν τὰ ὑπ' αὐτοῦ γραφόμενα.

[2] The passage was first so explained by Otto Jahn, *Rhein. Mus.* ix, 1854, p. 315 f. ('Das Kunstwerk war ein Inbegriff der Regeln der Symmetrie, ein Compendium derselben'), who argued that here *ars* = the theories of art, a compendium of the rules of art, by extension of the meaning common in the rhetors and grammarians ; Cic. *Brut.* 12, 46 *Aristoteles ait . . . artem et praecepta Siculos Coracem et Tisiam conscripsisse.* 12, 48, *similiter Isocratem . . . orationes aliis destitisse scribere, totumque se ad artis componendas transtulisse.* Cf. Quinct. x. 1, 15 (where see Spalding's note); Servius on *Aen.* vii, 787, *legitur in arte.* The Greek τέχνη was commonly used in the same manner, *Life of*

Ten Orators, Isokrates, ii, p. 838 (= Bernardakis, v, p. 164), εἰσὶ δ' οἱ καὶ τέχνας αὐτὸν (sc. *Isocr.*) λέγουσι συγγεγραφέναι. At a later period Jahn abandoned his earlier opinion and saw a latent epigram in the words *solus hominum . . . iudicatur* (*Kunsturtheile*, p. 120); he is followed by Münzer, *op. cit.* 530, note 1.

[3] The few extant fragments of this incomparably interesting work, in which Polykleitos reveals himself as an ancient Leonardo or Albrecht Dürer, have been carefully collected and commented on by H. L. Urlichs, *Griechische Kunstschriftsteller*, p. 1 ff. See also Diels, in *Arch. Anz.*, 1889, p. 10.

[4] It is quite possible that Antigonos, who had added to the Xenokratic mention of Doryphoros and Diadumenos the epigrammatic description which placed the two statues in pointed relation to one another (above, p. xxxvi), now introduced from his acquaintance with the literature of art a second account of the statue in its relation, not to the other works

If the proposed interpretation of the words *artem ipsam fecisse artis opere iudicatur* be correct, it follows that we have traces in xxxv, 74 of another such compendium of art by the painter Timanthes: *pinxit et heroa absolutissimi operis artem ipsam complexus viros pingendi*; i. e., like the Doryphoros of Polykleitos, the ' hero' of Timanthes was to serve as a 'Canon,' as the embodiment of theories which had been expounded in an *ars* or τέχνη.

Finally in § 76 it is said of Pamphilos that he was especially learned in arithmetic and geometry, without which sciences, he used to declare, art could make no progress. H. L. Urlichs[1] has pointed out that these words are distinguished from the ordinary floating apothegm by a precise character such as we should expect from an opinion recorded in a written Treatise ; and indeed an opinion emanating doubtless from the whole artistic personality of Pamphilos could nowhere have been preserved intact so well as in a technical treatise, written, like the work of Apelles, for the guidance of his pupils.

The Zenobian gloss showed that Antigonos had maintained the Agorakritan authorship of the Nemesis at Rhamnous on the ground of the inscription,—an argument against which Polemon, supporting the current attribution to Pheidias, retorts that Pheidias had doubtless permitted his own work to be inscribed with the name of the pupil he loved. Now, since Pliny ascribed the Nemesis quite simply to Agorakritos, without any reference to its attribution to Pheidias by other authorities, or to the Polemonic compromise, there can be little doubt that his ultimate source was Antigonos. Pliny gives the statement, however, in close connexion with the story of a competition between Agora-

---

of the master, but to his theories. This second mention, made with no precise reference to the first, was afterwards understood by the Roman authors to concern a distinct work. In the commentary I have given Furtwängler's explanation that the *Canon* appears in Pliny as a separate work to the *doryphorus*, owing to the introduction of a fresh authority at the words *fecit et quem*. I would differ only in so far that, while F. supposes Pliny to have been the first to combine the two notices, my own opinion is that the combination was already

effected by the Greek authors. It is possible, of course, though scarcely probable, that a Greek writer had already been guilty of assuming the *canon* and *doryphorus* to be separate works.

[1] *Op. cit.* p. 14 ff., where it is shown that the Pamphilos who wrote a work περὶ γραφικῆς καὶ ζωγράφων ἐνδόξων is a distinct person to the painter, and is presumably identical with the Alexandrian grammarian, first century B. C. ; see Urlichs, *Rhein. Mus.* xvi, 1861, pp. 247–258, and Susemihl, i, p. 903 f.

kritos and Alkamenes, and this again follows in natural sequence
upon the mention of these artists in their common relation,
as pupils, to Pheidias. The various episodes are so indis-
solubly linked[1] that the passage as a whole must be referred
to Antigonos. Indeed, that he is Pliny's ultimate authority for
the information concerning Agorakritos is confirmed by the
closing attribution (§ 18, *s. f.*) to Agorakritos of the 'Mother of
the Gods' at Athens : another vindication for that artist—doubtless, this time also, on the evidence of the inscription—of a work
popularly ascribed to Pheidias (*Schriftqu.* 831–833), of which popular
ascription Polemon, whose version is represented in Pausanias,
would not be slow to avail himself. It is noteworthy that by
retailing, though quite generally and in no relation to any one
work, the scandal about Pheidias and Agorakritos (*eiusdem*—sc.
*Phidiae—discipulus fuit Ag. Parius et aetate gratus, itaque e suis
operibus pleraque nomini eius donasse fertur*) Antigonos may have
supplied to Polemon, as Münzer acutely suggests (*op. cit.* p. 522),
the weapon wherewith to combat the Agorakritan authorship of
the Nemesis[2].

We have seen how the Xenokratic accounts of the beginning
of painting in encaustic (xxxv, 121 ; see above, p. xxxii) and of the
beginning of statuary (xxxvi, 9 ; above, p. xxv f.) were combined
by a later writer, surmised to be Antigonos, with variant traditions that proclaimed the priority of invention of the island-schools
over the schools of the mainland. The theory that these combinations or contrasts of traditions were effected at an early date
by Antigonos is now confirmed by the fact that in both cases
appeal is made to the testimony of inscriptions in xxxv, 121 ;
the ἐνέκαεν in an artist's signature is quoted in proof of the
antiquity of encaustic, while in xxxvi, 11–13, the genealogy of
the Chian sculptors 'Melas,' Mikkiades, and Archermos, and the

---

[1] See on this point Furtwängler,
Plinius u. s. Quellen, p. 72, who however does not trace the passage further
back than Varro. That Varro was
the intermediary source is obvious
from the words *quod M. Varro omnibus signis praetulit* ; to the account of
the Nemesis which he found in his
handbook he appended, according to
the wont of travellers, remarks of his
own.

[2] The impression has grown upon
me, since I wrote the above, that
Antigonos drew from Duris the main
part, if not the whole, of his account of
Alkamenes and Agorakritos : the stress
laid upon relations of pupilship,
the supposed competition (p. lxiv),
the hint thrown out of a scandalous
story (see below, p. lx)—above all,
the imaginative element in the tale
of how the discomfited Agorakritos
turned his Aphrodite into a Nemesis—
are so many Duridian traits. Addenda.

mention of works by Boupalos and Athenis, sons of Archermos [1], at Delos, and of works by Archermos at both Delos and Lesbos, are all based upon inscriptional evidence [2] (Münzer, *op. cit.* p. 524 f.). Further, as Münzer indicates (*loc. cit.*), Antigonos went so far in the latter instance as to quarrel with his sources; he corrected the legend according to which Hipponax had driven Boupalos and Athenis to hang themselves in despair [3] by adducing proofs

[1] The genealogy of Boupalos and Athenis is mentioned only once again in literature—in the Scholia to Ar. *Birds*, 574 : Ἀρχερμον (MSS. Ἀρχεννον) γάρ φασι, τὸν Βουπάλου καὶ Ἀθήνιδος πατέρα, οἱ δὲ Ἀγλαοφῶντα τὸν Θάσιον ζωγράφον, πτηνὴν ἐργάσασθαι τὴν Νίκην, ὡς οἱ περὶ Καρύστιον τὸν Περγαμηνόν φασι. There is much to commend Münzer's suggestion (*loc. cit.*) that Karystios of Pergamon (end of second century, Müller, *Fragm. Hist. Graec.* iv, p. 356) appears here by confusion for our Karystian Antigonos, sometime resident in Pergamon. (The words οἱ δὲ ... ζωγράφον are in any case introduced from a source other than that cited for B. and A.) We should thus obtain important confirmation of Antigonos's authorship of the Plinian passage.

[2] The Zenobian gloss alone shows that Susemihl (i, p. 672) does Antigonos an injustice when he credits Polemon with the 'epoch-making' idea of basing researches in the province of art-history and periegesis upon a study of inscriptions. In this connexion we may recall as illustrative of the method employed by Antigonos, without on that account proposing to refer them definitely to him, the notices, derived from the inscriptions on their bases, of the group of Alkibiades and 'Demarate' of Nikeratos (xxxiv, 89), and of the trainer of athletes by Apollodoros (*ib.* 89); for the portrait statue of Lysimache by Demetrius (*ib.* 76), see below, p. lxxvi.

[3] Repeated study of the passage xxxvi, 11–13, convinces me that Anti-

gonos borrowed from Duris of Samos the genealogy of the Chian sculptors and the whole story of Hipponax; especially Duridian is the adjustment to a new set of personages of the story of Archilochos and Lycambes (see Comm.). I am glad to receive on this point confirmation from Münzer, who (in a private letter) explains Antigonos as having corrected Duris somewhat as follows : ' It is true that the Chians were already practising the art of sculpture (i. e. at the time when, according to the Xenokratic theory, the Daidalids were inventing statuary), but it is not true that the verses of Hipponax (as probably maintained by Duris) drove Boupalos and Athenis to death, for works by these artists exist which were created after the portrait of the poet, as, for example, the Delian statue bearing the inscription *non vitibus tantum*, &c.' Moreover, in another note, the gist of which he also allows me to publish, Münzer observes that Antigonos seems likewise to have borrowed from Duris that notice of the existence of paintings in encaustic older than Aristeides which he confronted with the Xenocratic account : ' The appeal to the signature of the otherwise totally unknown Elasippos would be characteristic of Duris (cf. below, p. liii). Equally unknown are Nikanor and Mnasilaos, and it is not clear whether the ethnic *Pariorum* applies also to Polygnotos, and whether this Polygnotos should accordingly be distinguished from the celebrated Thasian artist.' In the to the contrary, again borrowed from inscriptions : *quod falsum est, complura enim in finitimis insulis simulacra postea fecere sicut in Delo quibus subiecerunt carmen non vitibus tantum censeri Chion sed et operibus Archermi filiorum.*

It is reasonable to suppose that Antigonos, who diligently studied the inscriptions carved on the actual monuments, did not neglect so fruitful a source as the literary epigram. He is almost certainly to be credited, as we have seen (p. xxxvi), with the epigrammatic qualification attached to the Xenokratic mention of the Diadumenos and the Doryphoros of Polykleitos, while the ascertained fragments of his writings display a wide-ranging familiarity, not only with the greater poets, but also with the poetasters and epigrammatists of his day[1]. Since, however, the actual extent of his responsibility for the epigrammatic element in Pliny cannot be precisely determined, it will be best to reserve for separate consideration (p. lxviii) material which plays a considerable part in the Plinian descriptions of works of art.

The Lives of the Philosophers reveal Antigonos as a lover of personal anecdote and characteristic *bons mots*[2]. Hence we are naturally disposed to credit him with the anecdotic material which forms so large a bulk of the Plinian narrative, and, as a fact, there are frequent proofs of its passage through his hands. The preservation, however, in the case of one highly distinctive anecdote, of the name of Duris of Samos (xxxiv, 61) enables us to penetrate further—to the very source whence Antigonos drew the larger part of his anecdotes[3].

text I have adopted the reading *Mnasilai* as beyond dispute, but Münzer provides me with a satisfactory proof that the *Arcesilai* of the inferior codices is impossible ; were this reading correct, we should expect to find that Antigonos in his biography of the Akademic Arkesilaos had mentioned this namesake of the philosopher (Antig. Kar. *ap.* Diog. Laert. iv, 45 ; cf. Wilamowitz, p. 70 ff.) ; but he only notes the sculptor Arkesilaos of Paros on the evidence of an epigram of Semonides.

[1] Münzer, *op. cit.* p. 529. Münzer, I may note here, lays considerable stress on the learning of Antigonos, in searching for traces of his art-treatise in Pliny ; he accordingly inclines to trace back to him certain passages which evince literary interest: e. g. the allusions to the ' Banquet ' of Xenophon (xxxiv, 79) and to his Treatise on Horsemanship (*ib.* 76).

[2] See on this point Wilamowitz, *Antigonos*, p. 33.

[3] That Antigonos drew from Duris for his Treatise upon art, and was thus the ' first intermediary ' through which Duridian material found its way into Pliny, was first suggested by Susemihl, i, note 325, p. 588.

3. *Duris of Samos* (*born about* 340 B. C.) ; *the anecdotic element in Pliny.*

Duris, historian and tyrant of Samos, is one of the most striking figures among those older Greek writers whom German scholarship—the researches of Roesiger[1] and Schubert[2], the brilliant sketch by Wachsmuth[3], call for grateful mention—has succeeded in calling back to a new life. The facts we know about his career are few, but the scanty fragments[4] of his writings suffice to prove the strength of his literary personality. Together with his brother Lynkeus he had been a pupil of Theophrastos[5], and, like the later Peripatetics, he became a curious inquirer into personal anecdote, which he freely used for purposes of history. His imagination was stimulated by his studies of the tragedians[6] till he developed into an accomplished master of dramatic anecdote, where heroes and heroines, dressed in appropriate costume, play on a stage whose properties seem inexhaustible. It is to Duris that Plutarch owes some of his most picturesque descriptions—such as the gorgeous pageantry of the return of Alkibiades, and the picture of the admiral's galley entering the harbour with purple sails 'as if some maske had come into a man's house after some great banquet made[7].' Yet Plutarch more than once casts severe doubts on the historical trustworthiness of Duris[8], and the censure has been confirmed by Grote[9].

From Diogenes, who mentions a painter Thales on the authority of Duris (Diog. i, 1, 39 = Duris fragm. 78), we learn that he wrote Lives of the Painters (περὶ ζωγράφων), and, as we shall

---

[1] A. F. Roesiger: (1) *De Duride Samio Diodori Siculi et Plutarchi auctore Diss.*, Göttingen, 1874; (2) *Die Bedeutung der Tyche bei den späteren Griechischen Historikern*, Konstanz, 1880. For Duris, see especially p. 20 f.

[2] Rudolf Schubert: (1) *Die Quellen Plutarchs in d. Lebensbeschreibungen des Eumenes, Demetrios und Pyrrhos*, in Supplementband ix of the *Jahrbücher für Philologie*, pp. 648–833 ; (2) *Geschichte des Agathokles*, Breslau, 1887, p. 13 ff. ; and (3) *Geschichte des Pyrrhus*, Königsberg, 1894, pp. 11–24, give a full and vivid account of Duris.

[3] Curt Wachsmuth, *Einleitung in das Studium der alten Geschichte*, Leipzig, 1895, pp. 543–546; see also Susemihl, i, p. 585 ff.

[4] To the collected fragments in Müller, *F. H. G.* ii, pp. 466–468, must be added the new fragments noted by Schubert, *Pyrrhus*, p. 12.

[5] Athen. iv, 128 a.

[6] Fr. 69, Fr. 70, and the remarks of Schubert, *Pyrrhus*, p. 15.

[7] *Alcib.* xxxii, tr. North, ed. Wyndham, ii, p. 133.

[8] Plut. *loc. cit.* ; *Perikl.* 28, &c.

[9] In reference to the story of Alkibiades' return, *Hist.* vi, p. 368.

presently see (cf. p. xlix), that he also wrote Lives of the Sculptors. Pliny mentions him in the Index to Book XXXIV as having written *de toreutice*. In the same book (§ 61) he appears as the authority for the statement that Lysippos of Sikyon had no master, but that he was originally a coppersmith and ventured upon a higher profession at a word of the painter Eupompos, who in presence of the young craftsman had enounced the dictum that 'nature and not any artist should be imitated.' The story will repay careful analysis. The meeting between the young Lysippos and Eupompos, though not chronologically impossible, belongs to a class of anecdote devised in order to bring the celebrity of one generation into pointed contact with the rising genius of the next. The story of Lysippos and Eupompos reminds one of nothing so much as of those legends invented by the Italian art-historians, on a hint afforded by two famous lines in Dante[1], in order to bring the young Giotto into connexion with Cimabue—legends which represent Giotto neglecting his clothmaker's trade to watch Cimabue at his work, or Cimabue opportunely passing along the road 'da Fiorenza a Vespignano[2]' precisely at the moment that the boy Giotto, while tending his flock, had drawn a sheep with such surprising fidelity that the delighted Cimabue begged Giotto's father to let him have the boy as pupil. But antiquity was rich in similar examples; the young Thukydides was said to have burst into tears of emotion on hearing Herodotos recite his History at Olympia, so that the elder historian was moved to congratulate the father of so gifted a son[3]. The undoubted pupilship of Xenophon to Sokrates was invested, by the later biographers of the philosophers, with the additional interest of that first meeting 'in a narrow lane' where Sokrates, barring the way with his stick, had refused to let the young man pass till he should have answered the question 'where men were made good and virtuous[4].' So, too, an exquisite legend had been spun to connect

---

[1] *Purgat.* xi, 94–96 :
'Credette Cimabue nella pittura
  Tener lo campo, ed ora ha Giotto
    il grido
  Si che la fama di colui oscura.'
The entirely apocryphal character of the Cimabue-Giotto legend has been thoroughly exhibited by Franz Wick- hoff, *Ueber die Zeit des Guido von Siena* (Mitth. des Inst. f. Oesterr.

Geschichtsforschung, Bd. x. pp. 244 ff.).
[2] Vasari ed. Milanesi, p. 370.
[3] Souidas, s. v. *Thuc.*
[4] Diog. Laert. ii, 6, 2 ; the analogy to the Lysippos-Eupompos story is pointed out by H. L. Urlichs, *Griech- ische Kunstschriftsteller*, p. 27. For further instances of such relation- ships cf. Diels, *Rhein. Mus.* xxxi, p. 13 ff.

the greatest of the Sokratic disciples with the master already
from the hour of birth : not only was Plato born the day after
one of Sokrates' birthdays, but on the eve Sokrates had dreamed
of a swan flying from the altar of Eros in the Academy, to take
refuge in his bosom, and lo! as the philosopher was recounting
the vision Ariston brought in the new-born babe, in whom
Sokrates at once divined the swan of his dream[1]. In the case
of Eupompos and Lysippos there was no pupilship to emphasize,
nor could pupilship be invented, since they practised different
arts; yet there remained the temptation to link the most brilliant
of the Sikyonian statuaries, the chosen portraitist of Alexander,
to the celebrity of the passing generation, that greatest of
Sikyonian painters, whose fame had occasioned, in order to
comprise him, a redivision of the schools (xxxv, 75).

The statement that Lysippos had no master arose in great
measure, I take it, out of the good advice put into the mouth of
Eupompos 'to imitate nature and not any artist'—advice which
amounted to an aphorism expressing the naturalistic tendencies
of the Lysippian school. But from saying that Lysippos followed
nature and no special master it was but a step to concluding that
he never had a master at all. Then, once the master's name
suppressed or forgotten, legend and the art-historians might fill
up the gap as they pleased, and the theory of self-taught genius
was the readiest to hand. But here was an opportunity for further
elaboration: the self-taught boy, the poor coppersmith, is destined
to become the leading artist of Sikyon, at that time the
acknowledged head of the Greek schools. Not only so, but he
achieves great wealth, as we learn from another Duridian fragment
preserved in Pliny (xxxiv, 37), but now separated from its original
context[2]. So that the information as to the early career of
Lysippos, which has been accepted with the utmost gravity by
archaeologists and historians of art, is found to resolve itself into
three apocryphal stories : (1) the *autodidaktia* assumed to account
for the artist's master being unknown; (2) the meeting with
Eupompos, intended to bring into presence Sikyon's greatest
painter and her greatest sculptor; (3) the rise from obscurity to
fame and riches. Armed with these observations, we shall have

---

[1] Apuleius, *de Platone* I.

[2] The authorship of Duris for this
passage had been pointed out by
Brieger, *De Fontibus*, p. 61 ; I cannot

understand on what grounds it is
doubted by Susemihl, i, p. 587, note
325. (See also Münzer, *op. cit.*
p. 542.)

no difficulty in detecting the Duridian authorship of a number of other anecdotes preserved in Pliny. We can at once follow Münzer[1] in attributing to him the story which tells how Protogenes, whose master, like that of Lysippos, was unknown (*quis eum docuerit non putant constare*, § 101), began his career in abject poverty (*summa paupertas*) as a ship-painter, yet lived to decorate the most celebrated spot in the world, even the Gateway of the Athenian Akropolis; the story of Erigonos (xxxv, 145), the slave who rubbed in the colours for the painter Nealkes, who yet lived to be a great master himself, and to leave in Pasias a pupil of distinction; further, the kindred story of how the sculptor Seilanion (xxxiv, 51)[2] became famous *nullo doctore*, and yet, like Erigonos, formed a pupil of his own, Zeuxiades. The kinship of the whole group is self-evident, and even if the name of Duris in xxxiv, 61 were not there to reveal the author we should be led to fix upon him, because of the precise parallelism of these stories to that recounted by Plutarch, on the authority of Duris, of how, through the unexpected favour of Philip, Eumenes of Kardia rose from being the son of a poor carrier, who earned a scanty living in the Chersonese, to wealth and position[3]. Such anecdotes seem in measure prompted by the desire to illustrate the changes of Fortune, of that Τύχη whose caprices were so favourite a theme of the Peripatetics[4].

Duris was the author of yet one more anecdote of an artist's rise from obscurity to fame, which has been preserved in two scattered fragments in Pliny and in Diogenes. In Plin. xxxvi, 22 we read : *non postferuntur et Charites in propylo Atheniensium*

---

[1] *Op. cit.* p. 534.

[2] The Duridian authorship is detected by H. L. Urlichs, *op. cit.* p. 28. The notice of Seilanion appears in the chronological table, awkwardly tacked on to the artists of the 113th Olympiad, where it is evidently out of place; Add. to Comm. on xxxiv, 51, 1.

[3] Plut. *Eum.* 1 Εὐμένη δὲ τὸν Καρδιανὸν ἱστορεῖ Δοῦρις πατρὸς μὲν ἀμαξεύοντος ἐν Χερρονήσῳ διὰ πενίαν γενέσθαι, τραφῆναι δὲ ἐλευθερίως ἐν γράμμασι καὶ περὶ παλαίστραν· ἔτι δὲ παιδὸς ὄντος αὐτοῦ Φίλιππον παρεπιδημοῦντα καὶ σχολὴν ἄγοντα τὰ τῶν Καρδιανῶν θεάσασθαι παγκράτια μειρα-

κίων καὶ παλαίσματα παίδων, ἐν οἷς εὐημερήσαντα τὸν Εὐμένη καὶ φανέντα συνετὸν καὶ ἀνδρεῖον ἀρέσαι τῷ Φιλίππῳ καὶ ἀναληφθῆναι. The analogy is pointed out by Münzer, *op. cit.* p. 534, who also refers to Duris all the stories discussed above of artists rising to fame from humble beginnings. The Duridian authorship had become evident to me since analysing the anecdotic material in Pliny in the light of the hints thrown out by H. L. Urlichs, *op. cit.* p. 21 ff. Addenda.

[4] See especially Roesiger, *Bedeutung der Tyche*, passim. Susemihl, i, p. 592.

quas Socrates fecit, alius ille quam pictor, idem ut aliqui putant. In his Life of Sokrates, Diogenes (ii, 5, 4) has the story on the authority of Duris that a Sokrates had begun life in slavery, and as a stone mason[1]. Now, although Diogenes applies this story to the philosopher, there is nothing in the fragment as it stands to show that Duris had this Sokrates in his mind. Indeed, since nothing is known of the slavery of the philosopher[2], there is every reason to suppose that Duris was speaking of the sculptor, and was recounting of him the same tale of modest beginnings as in the cases of Lysippos, of Protogenes, and of Erigonos. Like Erigonos he had been a slave, and in this capacity had practised an inferior branch of the art in which he was afterwards to excel. Like Protogenes, moreover, this man rose from the humblest circumstances to see his works—the famous Charites—*in propylo Atheniensium!* Further, the peculiar use in both passages of *propylon* for the gateway of the Akropolis, instead of the invariable *propylaion* or *propylaia*, affords satisfactory corroborative evidence of their common origin[3]. We get an interesting trace of the story's passage through the hands of Antigonos in the words *alius ille quam pictor, idem ut aliqui putant.* The identity of

---

[1] Diog. Laert. ii, 5, 4 Δοῦρις καὶ δουλεῦσαι αὐτὸν (Σωκράτη) καὶ ἐργάσασθαι λίθους. The statement which immediately follows, concerning the Charites on the Akropolis, which some said (ἔνιοί φασιν) to be by Sokrates, does not concern us ; H. L. Urlichs (*Griechische Kunstschriftst.* p. 43) is certainly right in referring it to another source than Duris.

[2] Duris was quite capable of inventing the story had it suited him ; but in the first place there is nothing to show that he wrote concerning the philosophic Sokrates or any philosophers ; in the second, it is odd that so striking a circumstance as that of the philosopher's slavery, once invented, should not have found its way to any authors besides Diogenes.—As to the legend that the philosopher had been the sculptor of the Charites (Paus. i, 22, 8 ; ix, 35, 3 ; Schol. Aristoph. νεφελαί, 773 ; Souidas, s. v. *Sokrates* : Pliny, it should be noted, knows

nothing about it), it was inevitable that it should arise in face of the said Charites by a namesake, combined with the fact that the father of Sokrates, Sophroniskos, was a sculptor. That the *contaminatio* of philosopher and sculptor occurred at an early period is proved by some Attic coins of Hellenic date bearing the name of an official Sokrates who, in evident allusion to his famous namesake, had the group of the Charites from the Akropolis stamped on the Reverse. (See Furtwängler, *ap.* Roscher, i, p. 881.) The celebrity of the relief, owing to the supposed authorship of Sokrates, accounts for its numerous copies. See note on xxxvi, 32, and Furtwängler, *Statuenkopien im Alterthum*, p. 532 f. (where the writer modifies his earlier view as to the date of the extant Charites reliefs).

[3] Wachsmuth, *Stadt Athen,* i, p. 36, note 2 ; cf. also B. Keil in *Hermes*, xxx, 1895, p. 227.

Sokrates the sculptor with the painter of the same name was maintained against a previous writer who had disputed it. The nature of the controversy recalls at once Antigonos and his hostile critic Polemon[1]. (See Addenda.)

We have seen that one factor in these stories is the desire to account for the absence of any record concerning the masters of certain celebrated artists. We may therefore suspect that a second little group of Plinian anecdotes of sculptors who were *initio pictores* and who exchanged painting for sculpture may be traced back to the same workings[2]. The case of Pheidias (xxxv, 52) is specially deserving of analysis. The ambiguous character of the information concerning the painted shield, upon which his reputation as a painter rests, has been detected by H. L. Urlichs (see Commentary). We may now carry the argument further and recognize in the statement that Pheidias was *initio pictor* an attempt to solve a problem which greatly exercised the ancient art-historian, namely the problem who was the real master of Pheidias.

Three answers to this question may be distinguished in ancient criticism. According to one tradition, Pheidias had, like Myron and Polykleitos, been the pupil of Hagelaidas of Argos[3], a view which has long been shown—by Klein[4], Robert, and others—to be improbable, if not as impossible as it apparently is in the case of Polykleitos[5]. The tradition has all the apocryphal air of those stories, common to all times and countries, which group great names together without regard to temporal probabilities[6]. In certain circles, however, the real fact, as recent morphological study reveals it[7], that Pheidias was the pupil of Hegias, had

---

[1] So H. L. Urlichs, *Gr. Kunstschriftsteller*, p. 43.

[2] Cf. Münzer, *op. cit.* p. 533.

[3] Schol. to Aristoph., *Frogs*, 504, whence the information was copied by Tzetzes and Souidas.

[4] Klein, *Arch.-Ep. Mitth. aus Oesterreich*, vii, p. 64; cf. Robert, *Arch. Märchen*, p. 93 f. ; Furtwängler, *Masterpieces*, p. 53.

[5] Robert, *l. c.*

[6] Lately Ernest Gardner, *Handbook of Greek Sculpt.* i, p. 193, has attempted, by straining the dates to the utmost, to defend the tradition for all three sculptors. Failing, however, sufficient evidence for its truth, a

sound criticism requires us rather to lay it aside, if not absolutely to reject it. The chronological difficulties have been hinted at above. Moreover, by exhibiting Hagelaidas as the master of the three most representative artists of the fifth century, the tradition betrays that tendency which is, to quote a modern writer, ' so easily explained pyschologically, but so fatal to criticism, of making one great name stand for a whole epoch or style.' (Bernhard Berenson, *Lorenzo Lotto, an Essay in Constructive Criticism*, p. 26.) Add.

[7] Furtwängler, *loc. cit.* The Hegias tradition is preserved by Dio Chrysostom, *Or.* lv, περὶ 'Ομ. καὶ Σωκρ. 1.

either remained unforgotten or, as is more probable, had been recovered from the monuments. Neither tradition, however, can have been widely current, for had it been generally reported that Pheidias was the pupil of either artist some mention of the fact, or at least some argument disputing it, would surely have filtered into Pliny, who mentions Hegias twice (xxxiv, 49, 78) and Hagelaidas three times (*ib.* 49, 55, 57), noting, moreover, that the latter artist was the master of Myron and of Polykleitos. The Plinian authors were on a totally different track, and their solution of the problem reveals the existence of a third class of critics, who, ignorant of the Hagelaidas and Hegias theories, filled up the gap in tradition by declaring that the early training of Pheidias was that of a painter. To this theory some writer of the stamp of Duris would give more point by the opportune discovery of a shield reputed to be painted by Pheidias, though, strange to say, unable to fix the whereabouts of so weighty a piece of evidence more precisely than by saying it *had* been at Athens.

But if Duris of Samos is to be held responsible for the story that Pheidias had begun life as a painter it follows that we must likewise trace back to him the similar story concerning Pythagoras of Samos, and hence the whole ridiculous splitting into two of an artist who happened to sign sometimes Σάμιος from the home of his birth, sometimes Ῥηγῖνος from that of his adoption (see Comm.). Πυθάγορας Σάμιος would have a triple interest for Duris: as a native of Samos; as a namesake of the philosopher Pythagoras, also a Samian celebrity, whom Duris had mentioned in his second Book of the History of Samos (fr. 56); and as a famous portraitist of athletes, for Duris, who had himself as a boy won a victory at Olympia (Paus. vi, 13, 5 [1]), appears in later life to have written a book on athletic games, περὶ ἀγώνων [2], the material for which he would doubtless derive in great measure from the inscriptions on the bases of the athlete statues. It was perhaps thus that, coming upon the alternative ethnic of Pythagoras, he jumped at the conclusion that there were two artists of the name. Then, having discovered a Πυθάγορας Σάμιος, it became necessary to find out his master. Klearchos—himself a Rhegine—must be left for Pythagoras of Rhegion (Paus. vi, 4, 3), and so Duris, instead of involving

---

[1] See the reading proposed by Susemihl, i, p. 586, note 323. Schubart's emendation of the corrupt passage seems entirely erroneous.

[2] Susemihl, i, p. 587 f.

himself in false school genealogies, simply filled up the gap by declaring the Samian Pythagoras to have, like Pheidias, begun life as a painter. Finally, since a sentimental harping upon family relationships has been acutely detected by Münzer (*op. cit.* p. 533) as a characteristic of Duridian anecdotes, we may trace back to Duris the mention of Sostratos, the pupil and nephew— *filius sororis*—of Pythagoras of Rhegion. I have noted in the Commentary that there is nothing to lead us to identify this Sostratos with any of the other sculptors of the name, and Duris was nothing loth to provide his heroes with pupils, with children or other near relations, of whom history has otherwise no record. So the Arimnestos (Duris, fr. 56), son of the philosopher Pythagoras, and himself master of the philosopher Demokritos, appears a pure creation of Duris, as, for the rest, do the pupils of Seilanion and of Erigonos.

The whole group of stories we have been considering were precisely of the kind to attract Antigonos of Karystos, who in his Life of Pyrrhon (above, p. xxxviii) had especially noted the poverty and obscurity of the philosopher's early days, adding that he had begun as a painter [1]. In the case of Pythagoras there is a further interesting little proof that the story was handled by Antigonos. The words in § 61, *hic* (*Pyth. Samius*) *supra dicto* (*Pyth. Rhegino*) *facie quoque indiscreta similis fuisse traditur*, contain a sharp criticism, which has amusingly escaped Pliny and before him Varro, upon the statement that the Rhegine and Samian Pythagoras were different persons. The fact of the criticism turning upon a question of identity of artists, no less than the manner in which the criticism is passed, at once betray Polemon of Ilion, the indefatigable assailant of Antigonos, whose error, as regards Pythagoras, Polemon now corrects. 'Your second Pythagoras, my friend Antigonos,' wrote the amused Polemon, 'looks to me suspiciously like your first [2].' 'Polemon's whole book was merely the comprehensive criticism, the improvement and enlargement of that of Antigonos' (Münzer, *op. cit.* p. 526), and it was characteristic of its controversial parts, as H. L. Urlichs was

[1] The analogy between the anecdotes is pointed out by Münzer, *op. cit.* p. 533.

[2] Polemon's authorship of the criticism was rightly detected by H. L. Urlichs, *Griechische Kunstschrift-steller*, p. 39 ff., but I owe it to Prof. W. Klein to have explained to me, as I believe correctly, the whole satirical force of the words *hic supra dicto*, &c. . . .

the first correctly to apprehend, that, while Antigonos had inclined to multiply names and attributions, Polemon on the contrary wished to reduce them[1]. He was wrong in the case of the Agorakritan Nemesis; in that of Pythagoras of Samos and Rhegion he was—as it happens—quite right.

Having thus detected in Pliny a number of anecdotes betraying the Peripatetic, and more especially Duridian, delight in dwelling upon unexpected turns of fortune or upon paradoxical changes of profession, we now turn to another class of story, intended primarily to give point to striking traits of character. In xxxiv, 71 it is recounted of the painter Parrhasios that he made an insolent use of his success, taking to himself the surname of the 'Lover of Luxury' (ἁβροδίαιτος), boasting moreover of his descent from Apollo, and that he had painted Herakles even as the hero had appeared to him in a dream. Finally the artist's intolerable pride finds its highest expression in the insult flung at his rival Timanthes. The story recurs in an amplified form, though with the Apolline descent omitted, in Athenaios, who has the first part of it on the authority of the Peripatetic Klearchos of Soloi.

Athen. xii, p. 543 c [2]: 'Among the ancients ostentation and extravagance were so great that the painter Parrhasios was clothed in purple and wore a golden wreath upon his head, as Klearchos says in his Lives. Parrhasios,

[1] Zenobios, v, 82 (above, p. xxxix); with Athenagoras, Πρεσβεία, 17 (=our App. XI), cf. Paus. ii. 27, 2; see also Paus. i, 24, 8 and the remarks of Furtwängler, *Masterpieces*, p. 412, on the artist of the *Apollo Parnopios*. With the statement preserved in Pliny xxxv, 54, to the effect that the gold-ivory Athena at Elis was the work of Kolotes, it is interesting to compare Paus. vi, 26, 3, where the words εἶναι μὲν δὴ Φειδίου φασὶν αὐτήν (i. e. the Eleian Athena) seem to imply, as Münzer kindly points out to me in an unpublished note, that the authorship of the statue was a controverted point—in other words, the phrase of Pausanias is the echo of a Polemonic criticism such as that surviving in the Zenobian gloss, and that which doubtless attached to the question of the authorship of

the 'Mother of the Gods.'

[2] The alternative account in Athenaios (xv, 687 b) should be compared (lack of space compels omission of the Greek):—
'Though Parrhasios the painter was vain beyond the measure of his art, and had, as the saying goes, drunk deep of the cup of liberty that his pencil gave, yet he had pretensions to virtue, writing on all his paintings at Lindos,
"One who lived in luxury... (ἁβροδίαιτος)."
But a wit, who was, I imagine, angry with him for defiling the delicacy and beauty of virtue by diverting to vulgar luxury the fortune given to him by chance, wrote at the side,
"One worthy of the stick... (ῥαβδοδίαιτος)."
In spite of all, however, he must be

while arrogant beyond what his art warranted, yet laid claim to virtue, and would write on his paintings

One who lived in luxury (ἀβροδίαιτος) and honoured virtue painted this.

' And some person who was stung by the words wrote at the side :—

One worthy of the stick (ῥαβδοδίαιτος), &c.

' He further wrote these lines on many of his works :—

A man who lived in luxury and honoured virtue painted this, Parrhasios born in famous Ephesos. Nor have I forgotten my father Evenor, who begat me as his lawful son, first in my art among all Greeks [1].

' And he spoke a vaunt with no offence in the lines :—

Though they that hear believe not, I say this. For I aver that now have the clear limits of this art been discovered by my hand, and a bound is set that none may overpass. Yet is nothing faultless among mortals [2].

'Once at Samos, when competing with his Aias against an inferior picture, he was defeated; and when his friends condoled with him he said that, for himself, he cared little, but he was grieved for Aias, who was worsted a second time.

' As signs of his luxurious living he wore a purple cloak and had a white fillet upon his head, and leaned upon a staff with golden coils about it, and fastened the strings of his shoes with golden latchets.

' Nor was the practice of his art toilsome to him, but light, so that he would sing at his work, as Theophrastos in his treatise on Happiness tells us. And he uttered marvels when he was painting the Herakles at Lindos, saying that the god appeared to him in a dream and posed himself (rd. αὐτόν) as was fitting for the picture. Hence he wrote upon the painting :—

As many a time in nightly visits he appeared unto Parrhasios, such is he here to look upon [3].'

Jahn has pointed out, in his discussion of the passage [4], that Klearchos had only the story of the artist's effeminacy. That Athenaios derived the rest of his information concerning Parrhasios from another source is manifest from the clumsy repetition of the

pardoned, because he said that he loved virtue. This is the story of Klearchos.

[1] ἀβροδίαιτος ἀνὴρ ἀρετήν τε σέβων
τόδ᾽ ἔγραψα
Παρράσιος, κλεινῆς πατρίδος ἐξ
Ἐφέσου.
οὐδὲ πατρὸς λαθόμην Εὐήνορος, ὅς
ῥά μ᾽ ἔφυσε
γνήσιον, Ἑλλήνων πρῶτα φέροντα τέχνης.

[2] εἰ καὶ ἄπιστα κλύουσι, λέγω τάδε·
φημὶ γὰρ ἤδη

τέχνης εὑρῆσθαι τέρματα τῆσδε
σαφῆ
χειρὸς ὑφ᾽ ἡμετέρης· ἀνυπέρβλητος
δὲ πέπηγεν
οὖρος· ἀμώμητον δ᾽ οὐδὲν ἔγεντο
βροτοῖς.

[3] Οἷος δ᾽ ἐννύχιος φαντάζετο πολλάκι
φοιτῶν
Παρρασίῳ δι᾽ ὕπνου, τοῖος ὅδ᾽
ἐστὶν ὁρᾶν.

[4] Kleine Beiträge z. Geschichte d. alten Literatur (in Sächsische Berichte for 1857), p. 285, note 1.

epigram ἀβροδίαιτος ἀνήρ, as also from the variant details respecting
the artist's headgear—a gold crown in the first passage, a white
fillet in the second. If we analyze the stories in Pliny and in
Athenaios we obtain the following elements :

(1) The story of the artist's effeminacy and luxury, given in
Athenaios, first on the authority of Klearchos, and repeated from
an unnamed author ; in Pliny it occurs combined with that of
the artist's arrogance : *fecundus artifex, sed quo nemo insolentius
usus sit gloria artis habrodiaetum se appellando.*

(2) The boast recorded both in Athenaios and Pliny that
Herakles often appeared to the artist in dreams while he was
engaged upon the hero's picture.

(3) The story, given also by both writers, of the competition
at Samos, and the insult to Timanthes.

(4) The story, preserved *only in Pliny*, of the artist's boasted
descent from Apollo.

It is evident that these *membra disiecta* must all have been
found united in some older writer, from whom they found their
way through different channels into Pliny and Athenaios respectively. Now Klearchos of Soloi was himself a pupil of
Aristotle[1] ; and, although Athenaios does not name his authority
for the rest of the story, it is evident from its character, and from
the mention moreover of Theophrastos for the parenthetical
anecdote that Parrhasios was in the habit of singing at his
work, that we are full among the Peripatetics. Therefore, as
H. L. Urlichs has pointed out, the original authority must be
a Peripatetic who had written upon the painters ; in a word, it
must be Duris of Samos[2]. This conjecture finds confirmation
in the comments respectively made by Schubert[3] and Münzer[4]
on the especial delight which Duris takes in describing details of
dress (above, p. xlvi). It is significant that out of eighty-four
fragments in Müller no less than ten[5] are concerned with elaborate descriptions of costume. Parrhasios the effeminate, with
his purple robe and his golden crown, is reminiscent of the
effeminate Demetrios, with his yellow hair and painted face, of
frag. 27; of the regal Demetrios, with the gold-embroidered robes
and the hair-band shot with gold (μίτρα χρυσόπαστος), of frag. 31.

---

[1] Athen. xv, p. 701 c.
[2] *Griechische Kunstschriftsteller*, p. 25.
[3] *Pyrrhus*, p. 15.
[4] *Op. cit.* p. 536.
[5] Fr. 14, 20, 22, 24, 27, 29, 31, 47, 50, and 64.

But Parrhasios was not the only painter who delighted in gorgeous apparel. According to Pliny (xxxv, 62), his rival Zeuxis carried the same taste so far as to make his appearance at Olympia displaying his own name woven in letters of gold into the embroideries of his garments—*aureis litteris in palliorum tesseris intextum nomen*—a detail which recalls the description of the chlamys of Demetrios, into which was inwoven the vault of heaven with its golden stars and twelve signs of the zodiac[1].

Robert[2] had already pointed out that the similarity of the stories narrated by Athenaios of the costume of Parrhasios, and by Pliny of that of Zeuxis, showed them to be derived from the same author. Since in the case of Parrhasios this author was Duris of Samos, it follows that it is to him also we must refer the Plinian anecdote of the luxury of Zeuxis[3].

A word remains to be said about the epigrams out of which the stories concerning Parrhasios are in great measure elaborated. It was the opinion of Jahn that all the epigrams purporting to have been written by Parrhasios upon himself, and inscribed upon his pictures—with the exception perhaps of the one celebrating the nocturnal apparitions of Herakles—were apocryphal[4]. Jahn included in the same category the self-laudatory epigrams placed in the mouth of the painter Apollodoros by one Nikomachos[5], and the epigram which, according to the orator Aristeides (Or. xlix, vol. ii, p. 521 Dindorf), had been elicited from Zeuxis in answer to the boasts of Parrhasios.

'Listen now,' writes Aristeides, 'to another swaggering painter,' and quotes the following epigram of Zeuxis:

'Herakleia my Fatherland, Zeuxis my name; if any among men pretend to have attained the limits of my art, let him come forward and be proclaimed conqueror. . . . Yet methinks that mine is not the second place[6].'

---

[1] Duris *ap.* Athen. xii, 535 f (= fr. 31): αἱ δὲ χλαμύδες αὐτοῦ ἦσαν ὄρφνινον ἔχουσαι τὸ φέγγος τῆς χρόας, τὸ δὲ πᾶν ⌊*verba suspecta*, Keil] ὁ πόλος ἐνύφαντο χρυσοῦς ἀστέρας ἔχων καὶ τὰ δώδεκα ζῴδια. Cf. Plut. *Demetrios*, 41.

[2] *Arch. Märchen*, p. 80.

[3] The remarks made above will show sufficiently why I have thought it unnecessary to refer either here or in the Comm. to the witty explanation of the *pallia* of Zeuxis as the curtains

hung in front of pictures which he exhibited at Olympia (see *Arch. Ep. Mitth. aus Oesterreich*, xii, 1888, p. 106 f., and the article *Pictura* in Smith's *Dict. of Ant.* vol. ii, p. 410).

[4] *Kleine Beiträge*, p. 286 ff.

[5] *Apud* Hephaistion περὶ μέτρων καὶ ποιημ. iv, 7:
Οὗτος δή σοι ὁ κλεινὸς ἀν' Ἑλλάδα πᾶσαν Ἀπολλό-
δωρος· γιγνώσκεις τοὔνομα τοῦτο κλύων.

[6] Ἡράκλεια πατρίς, Ζεῦξις δ' ὄνομ'·

These poetical criticisms, passed in similar vocabulary by three great contemporary painters upon their own or one another's achievements, seemed suspicious to Jahn.

Bergk, however, saw no reason to dispute their authenticity[1], and in the case of Zeuxis at least it has lately been pointed out that his epigram has a parallel in the acrostic inscribed upon the grave of the rhetor and sophist Thrasymachos of Chalkedon, a younger contemporary of Sokrates : Τοὔνομα Θῆτα Ῥῶ ῎Αλφα Σὰν ῎Υ Μῦ ῎Αλφα Χεῖ Οὖ Σάν, | πατρὶς Χαλκηδών· ἡ δὲ τέχνη σοφίη (Athen. x, 454 f= Anth. App. 359)[2]. We may gather from the observation that Zeuxis stood, as probably also Polykleitos, in close relation to the Sophists[3]. And the same is possibly true also of Parrhasios.

But to return to Duris. We have seen that those episodes of the Zeuxis-Parrhasios legends, designed to point the ethical qualities of the artists, might with certainty be referred to him. Now it has been finely discerned by Robert that the amiable Apelles and Protogenes are conceived as a pendant, so to speak, to the haughty and arrogant Zeuxis and Parrhasios, ' the faults of the older couple serving as a foil to the virtues of the younger. As a contrast to the productive and luxurious Parrhasios, we get Protogenes, struggling with the bitterest poverty, working with the most painstaking care, and accordingly producing but little : *summa paupertas initio artisque summa intentio et ideo minor fertilitas.* The portrait of Apelles is drawn with an even more loving hand ; his *simplicitas*, which manifests itself in his ungrudging recognition of the superiority of masters who surpassed him in special points ; his *comitas*, to which he owed the intimacy of Alexander ; his *benignitas* displayed towards Protogenes—are dwelt upon with admiration, and instances are adduced in their support[4].'

The intercoherence of the two sets of anecdotes is so patent

εἰ δέ τις ἀνδρῶν ἡμετέρης τέχνης πείρατά φησιν ἔχειν δείξας νικάτω· δοκῶ δέ, φησίν, ἡμᾶς οὐχὶ τὰ δεύτερ' ἔχειν.

The resemblance to the second epigram of Parrhasios, quoted by Athenaios, is striking.

duces himself to the reader as : ἐμοὶ ᾿Αγαθίας μὲν ὄνομα, Μύρινα δὲ πατρὶς (Μεμνόνιος δὲ πατήρ), τέχνη δὲ τὰ ῾Ρωμαίων νόμιμα καὶ οἱ τῶν δικαστηρίων ἀγῶνες. See Reitzenstein, *Hermes*, xxiv, 1894, p. 238.

[1] *Lyrici Graeci*, ed. 4, vol. ii, p. 316 f.

[2] Imitated as late as the second half of the sixth cent. A. D. by Agathias (pp. 8, 18, ed. Niebuhr), who intro-

[3] Robert, *Votivgemälde eines Apobaten*, p. 20 ; Diels, *Deutsche Liter.-Ztg.* May 29, 1886, p. 784, and *Arch. Anz.* 1889, p. 10.

[4] *Arch. Märchen*, p. 81.

as of itself to justify us in assuming Duris, to whom we owe the one set, to be the author also of the other. This assumption is confirmed when we look more clearly into the details.

Most of the anecdotes recounted of Apelles and Protogenes are intended, as Robert has already remarked, to give concrete expression, above all, to the moral qualities of the artists, and at times also to their technical excellencies. The famous story of the 'splitting of the line' (xxxv, 80–82), like that of the circle traced by Giotto in presence of the Pope's envoy[1], is merely a comment on the delicate draughtsmanship of Apelles. Protogenes is made to split the line which Apelles divides once more, that the latter's superiority may be only the more triumphantly established by a great rival's acknowledged discomfiture. The setting of this particular anecdote moreover—the description of the studio with the solitary old woman (see Comm.) guarding in the master's absence the large easel with the panel ready to be worked upon—is specially Duridian in its picturesque detail.

The two proverbs attributed to Apelles, 'No day without a stroke' (§ 84), and 'Cobbler, stick to thy last' (§ 85), were intended to bring out his industry, and his respect for the opinion of others, though naturally only in so far as they speak of what they understand. The moralizing tone of the Peripatetic is heard in both the anecdotes elaborated out of the proverbs; nor is it superfluous to note that Duris seems to have had a strong leaning to proverbial sayings, possibly actually to have collected them[2].

The anecdote recounted in §§ 85, 86 of Alexander the Great's visit to Apelles illustrates another of the artist's qualities, his *comitas* or amiability. The kindly snub administered by Apelles to the king is evidently apocryphal, belonging to that class of anecdotes which, as Freeman would say, 'go about the world with blanks for the names[3],' for Ailianos (see Comm.) has it of Zeuxis and a *Megabyzos* or Priest of Kybele. The story of Pankaspe, which, on the other hand, is a comment on the monarch's generosity and self-control, is not only practically inseparable from the first, but Alexander's detection of his artist friend's trouble, and the magnanimous self-denial with which he gives up

---

[1] Vasari, ed. Milanesi, vol. i, p. 383.

[2] See fr. 49 = Zenob. v, 64; fr. 68 = id. ii, 28; fr. 65 = Plut. *Lysander*, 18.

[3] Freeman, *Methods of Historical Study*, p. 134.

to him the most beloved of his mistresses, bear an extraordinary resemblance to the tale recounted by Plutarch (*Demetr.* xxxviii) of how King Seleukos gave up his wife Stratonike to his sick son Antiochos, whose love to his step-mother had been discovered by the physician Erasistratos as the cause of the young man's disease. The Plutarchian story has been traced back to Duris [1], whose partiality for erotic subjects, moreover, is abundantly proved by the extant fragments [2].

The story told in § 87 emphasizes the *benignitas* of Apelles towards all rivals, by singling out for our admiration his conduct in the case of Protogenes. The episode was evidently originally of a piece with the visit recounted in §§ 81, 82. To the story of the horses in § 95 we shall return later (p. lxiv); it may, however, be noted here that it shows the amiable and good-tempered artist losing patience, as in the case of the cobbler, with people pretending to know more about art than himself.

The Duridian character of the story of the rise of Protogenes from poverty to fame (§ 101) has already been noted in another connexion. His homely fare of soaked lupins gives point to his poverty and sobriety. The story in § 103, telling how the froth at the dog's mouth in the picture of 'Ialysos' was rendered by a lucky accident, when all the artist's efforts had failed, is eminently Peripatetic and Duridian in its delighted insistence upon the miracle of chance (*canis* . . . *quem pariter et casus pinxerit; fecitque in pictura fortuna naturam*) [3]. It is almost the anecdotic

---

[1] Schubert, *Pyrrhus*, p. 21.

[2] Cf. fragm. 2, 3, 19, 27, 35, 37, 42, 43, 58, 63. Thus he might possibly be responsible for the story of Pausias and Glykera (xxxv, 125), and for the anecdote recounted in xxxv, 140, of a Queen Stratonike, who may be identical with the Stratonike mentioned above. Perhaps too he had the stories of the lovers of the Knidian Aphrodite (xxxvi, 21) and of the Eros at Parion (*ib.* § 22); the stories, it is true, were derived by Pliny from Mucianus (p. xc), but the latter may quite well have had access to Duris (cf. p. xci) or to art-literature based upon Duris; at any rate we find a similar anecdote recounted by Klearchos of Soloi (fragm. 46 *ap.* Athen.

xiii, p. 605 E), who not impossibly had himself got it from Duris, the statue in question having been at Samos. We learn, moreover, from Athenaios (xiii, p. 606 A), on the authority of Adaios of Mitylene, that it was the work of one Ktesikles (cf. Brunn, *K. G.* i, p. 424): he is otherwise unknown, and the name happens to be identical with that of the painter of 'Stratonike and the Fisherman.'

[3] The similar story recounted of Nealkes (xxxv, 104) is probably a mere *doublette* of that of Protogenes; but there is nothing in the date of Nealkes, as now established by Münzer (see Comm.), to prevent its having originated with Duris.

illustration of a line of Agathon quoted by Aristotle : τέχνη τύχην
ἔστερξε, καὶ τύχη τέχνην [1].' (Addenda.)

The story of the protection accorded by Demetrios (who by
the way is a favourite hero of Duris) to Protogenes [2], and of the
friendly intercourse between the warrior and the artist (§§ 104,
105), recalls the intercourse of Alexander and Apelles. Moreover,
the scenic setting, the description of the artist living *in hortulo
suo* (see Comm.), must be by the hand which had described the
anus una keeping watch in the empty studio. Of the Satyr
upon which Protogenes was at work when Demetrios besieged
Rhodes, Strabo (xiv, p. 652) tells an anecdote characteristic of
Duris. The Satyr was represented leaning against a column
upon which perched a partridge ; now so greatly was the painting
of the bird admired that it detracted from the attention due to
the central figure ; the painter, accordingly, vexed because his
main theme had become subsidiary (τὸ ἔργον πάρεργον γεγονός),
erased the bird. The story is identical in spirit and intention
with that of the boy and grapes painted by Zeuxis, and recounted
by Pliny (xxxv, 66) and Seneca Rhetor (see Comm.). I incline
to credit the Samian historian with the authorship of both. Lastly,
the story of Aristotle's advice to Protogenes to paint the feats of
Alexander is obviously more likely to proceed from the Peripatetic
Duris than from any other of the Plinian authors.

We have thus recovered considerable fragments of as many as
four of Duris's Lives of the Painters. There still remain scattered up and down the Plinian narrative a number of Duridian
passages, which I propose to examine in conclusion.

Closely connected with the anecdotes illustrative of character
comes another series, designed to give concrete form to certain
art-problems which had at different times exercised different
schools. A striking instance is the story told in xxxv, 64, of how
Zeuxis combined the beauty of his Helen painted for Kroton
(the Agrigentum of Pliny is a mistake, see Comm.) from the best
features of the five fairest maidens of that city. The anecdote
embodies the axiom that since 'there is no excellent *Beauty*, that
hath not some strangenesse in the proportions,' the artist, striving
for the ideal perfection, must needs 'take the best Parts out of
Divers Faces to make one Excellent [3].' Both the problem and

---

[1] *Ethics*, vi, 4. See *Addenda.*
[2] The story is also told with only
slight discrepancies by Plutarch in the

Demetrios, for which Duris is one of
the main sources.
[3] Bacon, *Essays*, xliii.

its solution had been discussed by Sokrates in the studio of Parrhasios[1]. Cicero, recounting the story of Zeuxis and the maidens as an illustration of the method he had himself followed in his study of rhetoric, had naturally combined it with the axiom it was originally intended to illustrate. The long passage (*de Invent. Rhet.* ii, 1, 1) is too well known to need full quotation, but the closing words are significant for our purpose, as showing how the anecdote had its rise in philosophic speculations :—

'. . . he (Zeuxis) did not believe that all the excellencies he needed for his beauteous image could be found in one body, for this reason, that nature never puts the perfect finishing touch to all the parts of any one object. Therefore, precisely as though by bestowing everything on the one she would have nothing left for the rest, she confers some benefit, now here now there, which is always inseparable from some defect[2].'

Dionysios (τῶν ἀρχ. κρίσις I), by using the anecdote to prove that we may, out of a varied erudition (πολυμάθεια), combine and inform the indestructible image of Art, shows his thorough appreciation of the philosophic lesson it was intended to convey. To a genial inventor like Duris, trained moreover in philosophic doctrine, may well be attributed the shaping of a story so much more apt to clothe an aesthetic problem than to convey an actual artistic practice. The fable of the five maidens of Kroton is of perennial interest; it haunted the imagination of Raphael, who, writing of his Galatea to Baldassare Castiglione, says that 'per dipingere una bella, mi bisognerei veder più belle,' and at a later date we find it astutely criticized by Bernini[3] (see Add.).

Duris may also be credited, I think, with the expression of another problem of kindred nature, conveyed this time, however, not as an anecdote but as an apothegm. The judgement which Lysippos had passed upon his predecessors (xxxiv, 61), saying that, while *they* represented men as they are, *he* strove to represent them as they appeared to be, expresses, as I have pointed out in the notes, a dominant problem of art, the

---

[1] Xenophon, *Memorab.* iii, 10, 1 : . . . ἐπειδὴ οὐ ῥᾴδιον ἑνὶ ἀνθρώπῳ περιτυχεῖν ἄμεμπτα πάντα ἔχοντι, ἐκ πολλῶν συνάγοντες τὰ ἐξ ἑκάστου κάλλιστα οὕτως ὅλα τὰ σώματα καλὰ ποιεῖτε φαίνεσθαι ; ποιοῦμεν γάρ, ἔφη, οὕτως.

[2] *Neque enim putavit omnia, quae quaereret ad venustatem, uno se in corpore reperire posse ideo, quod nihil*

simplici in genere omnibus ex partibus perfectum natura expolivit. Itaque, tanquam ceteris non sit habitura quod largiatur, si uni cuncta concesserit, aliud alii commodi, aliquo adiuncto incommodo muneratur.

[3] See Baldinucci, *Notizie dei Professori del Disegno da Cimabue in qua* (Firenze, ed. 1847), p. 661.

problem of impressionism *versus* realism. Münzer[1] has lately referred the passage to Antigonos, who records a somewhat similar judgement passed by the philosopher Menedemos upon his predecessors[2]. This, however, only proves the later hand of Antigonos. So illuminating an aphorism could only have arisen in the brain of a far more powerful writer. The Lysippian judgement recalls, as has often been noticed[3], that which Aristotle makes Sophokles pass on himself and Euripides (Arist. *Poetics*, 1460 b[4])—is, in fact, but the application to a new problem of a phrase traditional in Aristotelian circles[5]. It is evident that Duris, who moreover is expressly named by Pliny as the authority for the early career of Lysippos, is far the likeliest of the Plinian authors to be responsible for the Lysippian apothegm[6]. The attribution is corroborated, moreover, by his partiality for such sayings, which he possibly collected systematically in emulation of the ἀποφθέγματα or ἀπομνημονεύματα of his brother Lynkeus[7].

He was an adept at deducing apothegms out of well-known lines of the poets and dramatists, even at the cost of occasional misapplication (Plutarch, *Demetr.* 14, 35, 45, 46; with Athen. vi, 249 c, cf. Odyss. xi, 122; Schubert, *Pyrrhus*, p. 20 f.); and I would therefore likewise refer to him the apothegm of Euphranor to the effect that 'his Theseus was fed on meat, but that of Parrhasios on roses' (xxxv, 128). Münzer has detected in the words the latent reminiscence of an Aristophanic line preserved in Diogenes on the authority of Antigonos[8] (see Comm.), but this

---

[1] *Op. cit.* p. 527.

[2] Antig. Kar. *ap* Diog. ii, 134 (= Wilam. p. 98): τῶν δὲ διδασκάλων τῶν περὶ Πλάτωνα καὶ Ξενοκράτην ἔτι δὲ Παραιβάτην τὸν Κυρηναῖον κατεφρόνει, Στίλπωνα δ' ἐτεθαυμάκει· καί ποτε ἐρωτηθεὶς περὶ αὐτοῦ ἄλλο μὲν οὐδὲν εἶπε πλὴν ὅτι ἐλευθέριος. The resemblance to the Lysippian phrase is little more than formal and verbal.

[3] Among others by Vahlen in the notes to his ed. of the *Poetics* (Leipzig, 1885), p. 265.

[4] 'Further, if it be objected that the description is not true to fact, the poet may perhaps reply,—" But the objects are as they ought to be ": just as Sophokles said that he drew men as they ought to be drawn ; Euripides as they are.' Tr. S. H. Butcher,

p. 95 (for Greek. see Comm.).

[5] To say this, however, is far from admitting the theory of Ottfried Müller (*Kunst-Archäol. Werke*, II. p. 165 ff.), lately revived by Kékulé (*Arch. Jahrb.* viii, 1893, p. 39 ff.), that the original Greek of the Lysippian saying was a slavish imitation of the Sophoklean (Kékulé, p. 45)—and the *quales viderentur esse* of Pliny a clumsy misunderstanding of something like οἵους ἔοικεν εἶναι. On the contrary, the *viderentur* is the very pith of the apothegm, which conveys a problem totally different to the Sophoklean.

[6] Duridian authorship seems hinted at by Diels, *Arch. Anz.* 1893, p. 11.

[7] Ath. vi, 245 ; viii, 337.

[8] I trust I am not misapprehending

is no proof that Antigonos is also responsible for the new turn given to the phrase in the mouth of Euphranor.

There remains to note, with H. L. Urlichs[1] and Münzer[2], that Duris was presumably the source for sundry stories of art-competitions preserved in Pliny. Their authenticity is suspicious, as Jahn long ago maintained[3], because in all of them the competition itself offered no interest whatsoever to the writer, but was merely used—we may at once say invented—in order to bring great artists of the same or adjoining epochs into presence, and often to point some saying supposed to have been uttered on the occasion. The animating idea is the same as in the story which represented the young Lysippos venturing upon the higher paths of art at the bidding of Eupompos. Such is the contest between Parrhasios and Timanthes, already discussed in another connexion (above, p. liv), where we are not even told the subject of the picture by the latter artist; the competition between Zeuxis and Parrhasios with the curtain and the grapes (*ib.* 65); and the kindred anecdote of Apelles' appeal from the verdict of human judges to that of beasts (*ib.* 95).

The story of the four statues of Amazons made in competition by four great artists for the Temple of Ephesos belongs to the same series. The garb it borrows from the legend of the award of the prize of valour after Salamis (see Comm.) sufficiently betrays its apocryphal character, even though it have a groundwork of truth. There is the undoubted existence of four distinct types of Amazons, similar in size and pose; and Furtwängler has lately made the acute suggestion that the anecdote of the evaluation grew out of the order in which four statues of Amazons by the said four masters were exhibited in the Ephesian Artemision (see Comm.). Certainly such an order of exhibition[4], could it be proved, would

---

the *rapprochements* attempted on p. 527 f. of Münzer's article.

[1] *Griechische Kunstschriftsteller*, p. 28 f.

[2] *Op. cit.* p. 534.

[3] *Kleine Beiträge*, p. 289 f.

[4] It may be worth pointing out here that the story of the Four Amazons has a curious parallel, not, I believe, observed before, in Augustine's explanation of the origin of the number of the Muses; it is quoted on the authority of Varro, who of course had

it from Greek art-writers: Aug., *De Doctrina Christiana*, ii, 8: *Non enim audiendi sunt errores gentilium superstitionum qui novem Musas Iovis et Memoriae filias esse finxerunt. Refellit eos Varro, quo nescio utrum apud eos quisquam talium rerum doctior vel curiosior esse possit. Dicit enim civitatem nescio quam, non enim nomen recolo, locasse apud tres artifices terna simulachra musarum, quae in templo Apollinis dono poneret, et quisquis artificum pulchriora for-*

be a fine opportunity for imagining the rivalry of the four artists, precisely as a joint inscription of (the Elder) Praxiteles and Kalamis had given rise to some popular explanation, afterwards elaborated by Duris or a writer of his stamp into the anecdote recorded in xxxiv, 71, of the kind consideration of Praxiteles for the artistic reputation of Kalamis—an anecdote, by the way, that recalls the kindness of Apelles to Protogenes. Finally, the competition between Panainos and a totally unknown Timagoras (xxxv, 58), on the testimony of a *carmen vetustum*, of whose content, however, no hint is given, looks suspiciously like fiction.

There is still one passage in conclusion where Münzer (p. 535) detects, I believe rightly, the influence or authorship of Duris. This is the account of the women painters in xxxv, 147, 'woman' being one of the most favourite Duridian themes [1]. Münzer further remarks that the painter Olympias is a namesake of the mother of Alexander the Great, for whom Duris evinced a lively interest,[2] as for every one connected with Alexander; that Aristarete is the daughter of Nearchos, who, as the namesake of one of Alexander's generals [3], would likewise interest Duris; and that the three women Timarete (xxxv, 59), Irene, and Aristarete, at once daughters and pupils of their respective fathers, Mikon, Kratinos, and Nearchos, are conceived too manifestly on the same pattern to be above suspicion. Finally, the dancer Alkisthenes and the juggler Theodoros, painted by Kalypso, are evident Duridian personages; they recall the θαυματοποιοί, Xenophon and Nymphodoros, of fragm. 44 (=Ath. i, p. 19, f.), where the clever tricks of Xenophon's pupil Kratisthenes of Phlious are described. The analogous formation of the names Alkisthenes—Kratisthenes, Theodoros—Nymphodoros, is certainly significant.

This closes the list of passages that may be attributed with any certainty to Duris. It is most improbable that either Varro or Pliny had direct access to his writings; he seems so certainly the authority of Antigonos for the statement concerning Pythagoras of Samos (above, p. liii), and so many of the passages traced back to

---

masset ab illo potissimum electa emeret. Itaque contigisse ut opera sua quoque illi artifices aeque pulchra explicarent, et placuisse civitati omnes novem atque omnes emptas esse, ut in Apollinis templo dedicarentur. Quibus postea dicit Hesiodum poetam im-

posuisse vocabula. Non ergo Iupiter novem Musas genuit, sed tres fabri ternas creaverunt.

[1] Cf. fragm. 2, 3, 19, 24, 35, 42, 58, 63.

[2] Fr. 24.

[3] Plut. *Alex.* 66, 73 and often.

Duris were likely to interest Antigonos from their purely anecdotic character, that it is not unreasonable to assume that all the Duridian stories we meet with in Pliny were brought in by Antigonos, who had drawn largely from Duris for his Book of Marvels (Münzer, *op. cit.* p. 531). Antigonos presumably did not always give the name of his authority; like Pliny and most ancient writers, he would be willing enough to assume the credit of the greater part of his information, and would only mention his authorities by name in cases where the statements seemed to him to outpass belief. So, too, Varro quoted the *artifices qui condidere haec*, in xxxiv, 68, and again in xxxv, 68 (giving them here a second mention by name), in cases where he felt he needed an excuse for a weak explanation, or a warrant for an over-bold criticism. Thus it was that, after passing through many different hands, the name of Duris of Samos, preserved in xxxiv, 61 in testimony of the incredible story that the great Lysippos of Sikyon had been wholly a self-taught artist, has given us a clue leading us to assign, as I believe, to their right author no inconsiderable portion of the Plinian anecdotes.

At the same time the vindication of these tales for the Samian historian throws considerable light on the nature of his art-writings. They reveal him as above all a biographer in spirit and not only in form. He seeks to bring before his readers the individuality of the man rather than the technical or aesthetic quality of his work. For this purpose he employs popular traditions, giving to these *voces populi* the literary form which was to secure them from oblivion. In the attention he bestowed upon character-drawing, real and fictitious, he was a true product of his age in its newly awakened desire to ascertain the features of great men present or past. The words of Pliny were as true of the third century as of his own : *pariunt ... desideria non traditos vultus, sicut in Homero evenit :* sculptors were not content to portray contemporaries— a Menander or a Poseidippos—but must needs discover and fix for a late posterity the likeness of Aisop, Archilochos, Epimenides, nay of Homer himself [1]. In many cases the monuments are still there to show how nearly a deep intuition of the genius peculiar to each personage portrayed might help to restore the image which no contemporary hand had traced. The same occurred in literature : the Peripatetics, Chamaileon of Herakleia,

---

[1] See the remarks of Wilamowitz, *Antigonos von Karystos*, p. 149 ff.

or Dikaiarchos of Messana—to quote two out of a host—had attempted to reconstruct the lives of Alkman, of Alkaios, or of Semonides. Duris himself had written a biography of Euripides [1], of which recent criticism has recovered at least one characteristic fragment, which tells how Sophokles on receiving the news of the death of Euripides clad himself in robes of mourning. When Duris wrote his biographies of the artists he determined they should be 'Lives' in the most realistic sense of the word, refusing to discuss the works divorced from the artists' personalities. It is little wonder if in essaying to breathe back life into the persons of Lysippos, of Apelles, or Protogenes, his vivid imagination and strong powers of presentment led him, when historic facts failed, to offer telling anecdote in their place.

We may feel impelled from the side of historical verity to echo the complaint of Plutarch that Duris shows, even where not misled by interest, an habitual disregard of truth [2], but we are none the less indebted to him for what is perhaps the most enduring charm in the history of the ancient artists. The stories we have been studying, like those countless others which enliven the pages of Greek history, have their rise in a profoundly popular instinct, in the desire to find expression, at once simple and striking, for distinguishing qualities of temperament or of workmanship. And in their graphic force, that 'power,' if we may borrow from the words which Dionysios applies to the oratory of Lysias, of 'driving home to the senses the subject of discourse [3],' they have entered into the very substance of our thought. While every schoolboy is familiar with the tale of Zeuxis and the grapes, a scholar such as August Boeckh could express his ideal of the learned life in the words *dies diem docet ut perdideris quam sine linea transmiseris*, or the orator Burke sum up the qualities of that masterly state-paper, 'whose every stroke had been justified by historic fact,' in the telling phrase *Thus painters sign their names at Co*.[4]

---

[1] Printed at the commencement of Kirchhoff's ed. Berlin, 1867, vol. i, p. viii. Cf. Schubert, *Pyrrhus*, p. 16.

[2] *Pericl.* xxviii: Δοῦρις μὲν οὖν οὐδ' ὅπου μηδὲν αὐτῷ πρόσεστιν ἴδιον πάθος εἰωθὼς κρατεῖν τὴν διήγησιν ἐπὶ τῆς ἀληθείας. . . . Cicero, however, in his

one allusion to Duris (*Att.* vi, 1, 18) judges him more leniently.

[3] Dion. Hal. *de Lys.* vii δύναμίς τις ὑπὸ τὰς αἰσθήσεις ἄγουσα τὰ λεγόμενα.

[4] Burke, *Works* (ed. 1823), vol. viii, p. 129 (Letters on a Regicide Peace).

IV. Literary Epigrams.

The literary epigram, at once descriptive of a work of art and embodying its criticism or eulogy, was among the most fruitful sources of information at the disposal of ancient writers upon art[1]. It plays accordingly, as Otto Jahn first perceived[2], a considerable part in Pliny's descriptions of pictures or statues, where it becomes of the highest importance to the critic to detect it : for, as it strongly coloured the Plinian narrative, so it has gone on to this day, colouring our appreciation of ancient works of art, nay, predisposing us in many cases to read into them intentions, which are within the expressive range of poetry rather than of the plastic arts. Pliny's own phrase describing what the Apellian Aphrodite owed to the verses written in her praise remains true in greater or less degree of all works extolled in epigrams : *versibus Graecis tali opere, dum laudatur, victo sed illustrato.*

A first list of the Plinian passages based upon epigrams was drawn up by Otto Jahn (*loc. cit.*), and afterwards supplemented by Benndorf[3]. The subjoined list is compiled from theirs, but with some few additions indicated by an asterisk.

1.—xxxiii, 156 Antipater (sc. Diodoros, see note)—qui *Satyrum in phiala gravatum somno conlocavisse verius quam caelasse dictus est.*

   Cf. *Anth. Plan.* 248 :

   τὸν Σάτυρον Διόδωρος ἐκοίμισεν, οὐκ ἐτόρευσεν·
   ἦν νύξῃς, ἐγερεῖς· ἄργυρος ὕπνον ἔχει[4].

2.—xxxiv, 55 Polyclitus . . . diadumenum fecit *molliter iuvenem* . . . et doryphorum *viriliter puerum.*

(The epigrammatic qualification is so finely knitted to the mention of the works that it must have been brought in at a very early date[5].)

3.—xxxiv, 59 Pythagoras—fecit—*claudicantem, cuius ulceris dolorem sentire etiam spectantes* VIDENTUR.

---

[1] See in connexion with the epigrams of the *Anthology* which deal with works of art the admirable essay of J. W. Mackail, *Select Epigrams from the Greek Anthology*, p. 47 ff. ; cf. P. Vitry, *Étude sur les Épigr. de l'Anthol. Pal. qui contiennent la description d'une œuvre d'Art*, in *Rev. Arch.* xxiv. 1894, p. 315 ff.

[2] *Kunsturtheile des Plinius*, p. 118 ff.

[3] *De Anthologiae Graecae Epigrammatis quae ad artes spectant;* diss. Leipzig, 1862.

[4] 'This Satyr Diodorus engraved not, but laid to rest; your touch will wake him; the silver is asleep.' Tr. J. W. Mackail, *op. cit.* p. 179.

[5] Münzer, *op. cit.* p. 529. Dilthey, *Rhein. Mus.* xxvi, 290, first pointed out the epigrammatic juxtaposition of the two works.

Cf. *Anth. Plan.* iv, 113; ll. 1–2:

οἶδα Φιλοκτήτην ὁρόων, ὅτι πᾶσι φαείνει
ἄλγος ἐὸν καὶ τοῖς τηλόθι δερκομένοις[1].

*4.—xxxiv, 70 (Praxiteles) fecit et *puberem Apollinem subrepenti lacertae com-
minus sagitta insidiantem* quem sauroctonon vocant.

Cf. the same or perhaps identical epigram as adopted by
Martial, xiv, 172:

> *Ad te reptanti, puer insidiose, lacertae*
> *Parce; cupit digitis illa perire tuis*[2].

5.—xxxiv, 70 (Praxitelis) spectantur et *duo signa eius diversos adfectus exprimentia, flentis matronae et meretricis gaudentis.* hanc putant
Phrynen fuisse *deprehenduntque in ea amorem artificis et mercedem in voltu meretricis.*

The juxtaposition of the statues is purely epigrammatic; in the
description of Phryne's portrait lurks perhaps a reminiscence of
Anth. Plan. iv, 204 (see Comm.).

*6.—xxxiv, 71 Ipse Calamis et alias *quadrigas bigasque fecit se impari, equis
sine aemulo expressis.*

The rhetorical point betrays the underlying epigram; the
Propertian *Exactis Calamis se mihi iactat equis* (Prop. iii, 9, 10)
is doubtless from the same source, for where should Kalamis
boast of his horses so well as in some epigram purporting to be
written by the artist himself?

7.—xxxiv, 74 Cresilas *volneratum deficientem, in quo possit intellegi quantum
restet animae,*
et *Olympium Periclen dignum cognomine, mirumque in hac arte est
quod nobiles viros nobiliores fecit.*

8.—*ib.* 77 Euphranoris *Alexander Paris est, in quo laudatur quod omnia
simul intellegantur, iudex dearum, amator Helenae et tamen
Achillis interfector.*

9.—*ib.* 78 Eutychides *Eurotam, in quo artem ipso amne liquidiorem plurimi
dixere.*

---

[1] 'I behold Philoktetes. His agony
is made manifest, even to those who
look on from afar.' The analogy to the
Plinian description is pointed out by
Münzer, *l. c.* In the notes I have followed Brunn in quoting *Anth. Plan.*
112 (where the omission of the name
of Philoktetes is perhaps the cause of
its unusual omission in Pliny): 'More
hateful than the Greeks was my maker,
a second Odysseus, who brought back
to me my woeful dire disease. The
rock, my rags and blood and wound
and grief, were not enough, but he has
even wrought my pain in bronze.'

[2] Pointed out by Münzer *op. cit.*
p. 527, note 1.

Cf. *Anth. Pal.* ix, 709 :

> Εὐρώταν ὡς ἄρτι διάβροχον, ἔν τε ῥεέθροις
> εἵλκυσ' ὁ τεχνίτης ἐν πυρὶ λουσάμενον·
> πᾶσι γὰρ ἐν κώλοις ὑδατούμενος ἀμφινένευκεν
> ἐκ κορυφῆς ἐς ἄκρους ὑγρο͜ατῶν ὄνυχας
> ἁ δὲ τέχνα ποταμῷ συνεπήρικεν· ἆ τίς ὁ πείσας
> χαλκὸν κωμάζειν ὕδατος ὑγρότερον [1];

*10.—xxxiv, 79 Lycius . . . fecit *dignum praeceptore puerum sufflantem languidos ignes.*

The description of the 'dying fire,' which was of course not represented in bronze, betrays the epigram.

11.—xxxiv, 79 Leochares *aquilam sentientem quid rapiat in Ganymede et cui ferat parcentemque unguibus etiam per vestem puero.*

Cf. *Anth. Pal.* xii, 221 :

> Στεῖχε πρὸς αἰθέρα δῖον, ἀπέρχεο παῖδα κομίζων
> αἰετέ, τὰς διφυεῖς ἐκπετάσας πτέρυγας·
> στεῖχε τὸν ἁβρὸν ἔχων Γανυμήδεα, μηδὲ μεθείης
> τὸν Διὸς ἥδιστον οἰνοχόον κυλίκων·
> φείδεο δ' αἱμάξαι κοῦρον γαμψώνυχι ταρσῷ,
> μὴ Ζεὺς ἀλγήσῃ, τοῦτο βαρυνόμενος [2].

12.—xxxiv, 80 Naucerus (censetur) *luctatore anhelante.*

The analogy to xxxv, 71, makes it probable that the *anhelante* is from an epigram ; cf. Benndorf, *op. cit.*

xxxiv, 81 Styppax uno celebratur signo, splanchnopte—*Periclis Olympi vernula hic fuit exta torrens ignemque oris pleni spiritu accendens.*

The last words, the insistence on the swelling cheeks of the boy as he blows the fire, clearly point to an epigram. How far removed the real 'Entrail Roaster' would be from the Plinian description may be seen at a glance by studying the boy's statue from the Olympieion at Athens, which has lately been brought, with much probability, into relation with the statue by Styppax (see Comm. on passage).

13.—xxxiv, 81 Silanion Apollodorum fudit . . . *nec hominem ex aere fecit, sed iracundiam.*

(See Add. to the Comm. on the passage.)

---

[1] 'Dragged by the artist through a bath of fire, the Eurotas seems fresh from the water and amidst his streams. He bends to either side while water pours from all his limbs, and the drops fall from his head even to his feet. Art too hath joined in contest with the river; ah, who hath taught the bronze to burst into waves more flowing than the floods ? '

[2] 'Speed on to the heaven divine, go thy way, eagle, with the boy, spreading either pinion wide. Speed on with beauteous Ganymedes, nor suffer the boy to fall who poureth sweetest cups for Zeus. Yet spare to wound the boy with thy crooked talon, lest Zeus sorrow in grief thereat.'

14. —xxxiv, 88 Epigonus ... praecessit in ... *matri interfectae infante miserabiliter blandiente.*

(From an epigram similar to the one on the 'dying mother' by Aristeides in xxxv, 98.)

15.—xxxiv, 141 *Ferreus Hercules*, quem fecit Alcon *laborum dei patientia inductus.*

16.—xxxv, 59 (Zeuxis) fecit et *Penelopen, in qua pinxisse mores videtur.*

17.—*ib.* 69 (Parrhasius) pinxit demon Atheniensium argumento quoque ingenioso. ostendebat namque *varium, iracundum iniustum inconstantem, eundem exorabilem clementem misericordem, gloriosum, excelsum humilem, ferocem fugacemque et omnia pariter.*

18.—*ib.* 70 (Parrhasius) *pueros duos, in quibus spectatur securitas et aetatis simplicitas.*

19.—*ib.* 71 (Parrhasi) duae picturae nobilissimae, *hoplites in certamine ita decurrens ut sudare videatur, alter arma deponens ut anhelare sentiatur.*

20.—*ib.* 94 (Apelles) pinxit et heroa nudum, *eaque pictura naturam ipsam provocavit.*

21.—*ib.* 98 (Aristidis) *oppido capto ad matris morientis ex volnere mammam adrepens infans, intelligiturque sentire mater et timere ne emortuo lacte sanguinem lambat.*

Cf. *Anth. Pal.* vii, 623 :

"Ελκε, τάλαν, παρὰ μητρὸς ὃν οὐκέτι μαστὸν ἀμέλξεις,
ἕλκυσον ὑστάτιον νᾶμα καταφθιμένης·
ἤδη γὰρ ξιφέεσσι λιπόπνοος· ἀλλὰ τὰ μητρὸς
φίλτρα καὶ εἰν Ἀΐδῃ παιδοκομεῖν ἔμαθεν [1].

22.—xxxv, 99 (Aristides pinxit) *supplicantem paene cum voce.*

*23.—*ib.* 99 (Aristides pinxit) *anapauomenen propter fratris amorem.*

(Cf. *Anth. Pal.* vii, 183, 184, and see H. L. Urlichs' note in the Comm. on the passage.)

24.—xxxv, 106 (Protogenis) Satyrus—est, quem anapauomenon vocant, *ne quid desit temporis eius securitati, tenentem tibias.*

(Cf. *Anth. Plan.* 244.)

*25.—xxxv, 138 Antiphilus *puero ignem conflante laudatur ac pulchra alias domo splendescente ipsiusque pueri ore.*

I suspect an epigram from the forced point made in the description of the room 'which is in itself beautiful.'

26.—xxxvi, 21 (Praxitelis Veneris) effigies *dea favente ipsa, ut creditur, facta.*

(Cf. *Anth. Plan.* 159–170.)

27.—xxxvi, 24 Cephisodotus ... *cuius laudatum est Pergami symplegma nobile digitis corpori verius quam marmori inpressis.*

---

[1] 'Drink, poor babe, from thy mother, whose breast thou shalt suck no more ; drink thy last draught from her in death. Now has the sword taken her life, yet a mother's love knows, even in Hades, how to care for her child.'

Cf. Herondas iv, 59 f. [1], quoted in the Comm. on the passage.

Besides the epigrams descriptive of works of art, we may note, for the sake of completeness, the allusion to the epigrams on Myron's cow (xxxiv, 57) and on the *Anadyomene* of Apelles (xxxv, 92); the epigram upon Zeuxis which lurks in the words *ab hoc* (*Apollodoro*) *artis fores apertas, Zeuxis . . . intravit* in xxxv, 61 (see Comm.); the epigram in which Apollodoros reproached Zeuxis with having not learnt—but stolen the art of his masters (*ib.* § 62); finally the reference to the laudatory verses composed by Parrhasios upon himself, discussed above (p. liv f.). In all these descriptive passages it is evident that the writer has been concerned to outstrip rather than to explain the artistic aim. We are confronted by a series of pointed sayings, inspired indeed, or they would miss their effect, by some quality actually existent in the work of art, but using this quality as a theme to be expanded freely into the fluidity of language, whereas the artist had been forced to compress his conceptions within the limits imposed by visible form. Whatever Euphranor's ethical conception of the separate or conflicting traits in the character of Paris, he must perforce combine and fuse them in the portrayal of one single personage. The versifier, on the other hand, remains within the limits of his art if he picks out the qualities suggested rather than definitely indicated by the Paris of Euphranor, and embodies these in a series of consecutive images: thus the Paris of the sculptor will be converted by the epigrammatist from a unit into a triad; the compacted whole is resolved into the judge of the goddesses, the lover of Helen, the murderer of Achilles—each trait calling up in the mind of the reader a distinct sensuous image, whereas the statue, however complex, called up only one. Or, again, the epigram may catch at a purely accidental detail — accidental so far as regards any ethical import—such as the drapery which Leochares gave as a background to his Ganymede, and interpret it to mean what it lay entirely outside the power of the formative arts to express,—the eagle's care to avoid wounding the boy. The achievement of artist and of epigrammatist is bound to be different, because of the dissimilarity of the material with which each clothes his thought. The question touches one of the

---

[1] 'Pray look at this naked child; if I pinch him can you not fancy I shall really hurt him Kynno? For the flesh palpitates in the picture like a warm spring'—(*ut fontes calidi*, v. Crusius, *ad loc.*).

most difficult of all the problems suggested by the study of art, the problem how far the language of form can be translated into that of words, and *vice versa*. It could only be adequately treated in context with the written Greek epigrams of the same class as those we have been considering, and with the various descriptions in ancient literature, outside Pliny, based upon such epigrams; and this, after all, would be only one chapter of a vast discussion that should embrace the literature, whether ancient or modern, that aims at the analysis of works of art. But I have touched upon it here only as a passing protest against the practice, still too common, of searching in what were often but plays of fancy for definite evidence concerning the intention to be conveyed by a work of art. The modern scholar shows himself scarcely less credulous in this respect than Pliny himself, who introduced most of his epigrammatic descriptions by the *intelligere*, which, as we learn from Cicero, was the special term used of the insight and criticism of the man who knows [1].

These descriptive epigrams were doubtless interwoven with the original Xenokratic fabric that underlies the Plinian account at different times. We have seen that some—perhaps even a large number—were certainly due to Antigonos of Karystos. Others may be due to the Greek artist and writer upon art, Pasiteles of Naples (p. lxxvii ff.) ; Varro or Mucianus may have brought in others ; nor need we decide whether Varro, or Pliny, or another Roman, was first guilty of the comic blunder arising from the attribution in xxxiv, 57 to the sculptor Myron of the little monument, sung by two poets of the Anthology, which the girl Myro had raised to her pets, a cricket and a grasshopper [2].

---

[1] *Brutus*, 184 etenim necesse est, qui ita dicat, ut a multitudine probetur, eundem doctis probari ; nam quid in dicendo rectum sit aut pravum, ego iudicabo, si modo is sum, qui id possim aut sciam iudicare : *qualis vero sit orator ex eo, quod is dicendo efficiet poterit intelligi.* See O. Jahn, *loc. cit.* p. 120.

[2] The list of works whose description is based upon literary epigrams should further include the notice in xxxiv, 79 of the group by Leochares of the slave-dealer Lykiskos and a boy 'on whose face may be read the wily craft of the servile character.' Possibly the notice in xxxiv, 88 of Nikeratos' group of Alkibiades and his mother ' Demarate sacrificing by torchlight' belongs to the same class (cf. note 2 on p. xliv). The description in xxxiv, 93 of the Hercules 'wearing the tunic,' considered by Benndorf (p. 55) as epigrammatic, seems inseparable from the notice of the three *tituli* on the statue, and is presumably an observation of Pliny's own, not borrowed from any special source.

V. *Heliodoros of Athens* (*fl.* 150 B.C.).

Heliodorus qui de Atheniensium anathematis scripsit is cited in
the Indices of authors to Books xxxiv and xxxv ; the mention of
his name in the Index to Book xxxiii, which contains no material
that could be derived from him, must be looked upon as an
interpolation.   Till recently the literary personality of Heliodoros
remained so shadowy [1] that all attempts to recover traces of him
in Pliny had proved ineffectual [2].   Now, however, that Bruno Keil [3]
has succeeded in proving Heliodoros to be the source for the
periegetic portions in the Pseudo-Plutarchian *Lives of the Ten
Orators*, it has become possible to ascertain also the extent of
Pliny's debt—and it remains very small—to the Athenian
periegete.

The interest of the results attained by Keil lies almost entirely
outside Pliny ; it will suffice to indicate them briefly.   The passage
in the Life of Hypereides (849 c) concerning the burial-place of
the orator πρὸ τῶν Ἱππάδων πυλῶν, ὥς φησιν Ἡλιόδωρος ἐν τῷ τρίτῳ
περὶ Μνημάτων forms the basis of the inquiry.   The reading of the
MSS. Ἡλιόδωρος, which Ruhnken had unnecessarily altered to
Διόδωρος, has been rightly retained in this place by both Keil (*l.c.*)
and by Bernadakis in the new edition of the *Moralia* (vol. v,
p. 193).   For not only does the date of Heliodoros [4] accord
precisely with the date required by certain other statements of
periegetic nature contained in the *Lives* (cf. in particular
Lyk. 842e=fr. 5[a] Keil [5]), but the information conveyed in these
dateable fragments and in the remaining periegetic passages
scattered through the *Lives* is of a strictly homogeneous
character, which Keil defines as follows (*op. cit.* p. 237, cf. p. 201) :
' The first interest of Heliodoros is for extant monuments ; he gives
details concerning the nature of the monument, its material, its
locality and present condition ; then follow in natural sequence
statements of an historical character, such as the original condition, change of locality, occasional details concerning cost,

---

[1] Seven fragments are collected by
Müller, *F. H. G.* iv, p. 425.   See
also Susemihl, *Geschichte d. Al. Lit.*
i, p. 692 f.

[2] E. g. the attempts of Wachsmuth,
Stadt Athen, i, p. 36, note 2 ; on the
difficulty of the Heliodoran question
see Brieger, *De Fontibus*, p. 33.

[3] *Hermes*, xxx, 1895, pp. 199–240.

[4] After Antiochos Epiphanes (B. C.
175–164), cf. Athen. II, p. 45 c.

[5] Καὶ ἔστιν αὐτῶν (Lykurg. and his
children) τὰ μνήματα ἀντικρὺ τῆς
Παιωνίας Ἀθηνᾶς ἐν τῷ Μελανθίου τοῦ
φιλοσόφου κήπῳ (date of Melanthios
circ. B.C. 150, Keil, *l. c.*).

artists, or donors. These statements are corroborated by the epigrams and inscriptions . . . relative to the monument described [1].'

Now if we turn to Pliny we shall find some four passages which bear this peculiar Heliodoran stamp. Three occur in Book xxxiv, in the first alphabetical list of the bronze-workers; one in Book xxxv, towards the close of the main account of the painters. In xxxiv, § 74, the passage *Cephisodorus Minervam mirabilem in portu Atheniensium et aram ad templum Iovis Servatoris in eodem portu, cui pauca comparantur* (sc. *fecit*) has long been admitted by a number of authorities [2], though on different grounds, to be from a source other than that of the main account. It will repay careful analysis. We know from Pausanias (i, 1, 3) that the 'Minerva' and the 'Jupiter' belonged to the same temple, namely to the Διϲωτήριον, where Zeus and Athena were worshipped respectively as Ϲωτήρ and Ϲώτειρα [3]. Now, if we examine the Plinian passage we note at once a certain looseness of construction, a certain hesitancy in the wording; it is as if Pliny, or the author from whom he quotes, were not fully conscious—or at least fully persuaded—that the 'wondrous Athena' which was to be seen 'in the harbour of Athens' were really in the same place as the altar, which was in the same city, 'in the temple of Zeus the Saviour.' I accordingly believe that we have here the juxtaposition of two statements derived from separate sources. The words *Cephisodorus Minervam mirabilem in portu Atheniensium* would belong to the main account—the mention of the Athena, which was bronze (χαλκοῦ μὲν ἀμφότερα τὰ ἀγάλματα), being in place in a history of bronze-sculpture—while a later hand introduced from another source the mention of the *ara*, another work by Kephisodoros. Now this altar, which would naturally be marble and be decorated with reliefs, is obviously out of place in a history which was only concerned with works in the round and in bronze; this discrepancy, however, was unnoticed by the art-writer (Pasiteles (?), p. lxxx) who made the addition.

---

[1] Cf., in particular, Isokr. 838ᵈ (= Keil, fr. 4ᵇ), the inscription from the statue of Isokrates by Leochares, which Timotheos put up at Eleusis.

[2] Wachsmuth, *Stadt Athen*, i, p. 36, note 2; Furtwängler, *Master-pieces*, p. 145; Oehmichen, *Plin. Studien*, p. 151.

[3] See Comm. p. 60; cf. Liv. xxxi, 30, 9. The whole literature on the passage, both ancient and modern, given by Hitzig and Blümner, *Pausanias*, p. 120 f.

The connecting link was afforded by the name of Kephisodoros. Nor was any special attention bestowed upon the fact that the *ara* which was now mentioned stood not only *in eodem portu*, but actually in the same temple as the Athena. That the addition itself is Heliodoran seems probable from the precision with which the locality of the altar is noted (*ad templum Iovis Servatoris*), whereas the Minerva was simply cited as being *in portu Atheniensium*. The altar moreover—doubtless itself an ἀνάθημα—was a likely object to be included in a work *de anathematis*.

Close by the notice of Kephisodoros occurs the second passage detected as Heliodoran by Keil. The statement in xxxiv, 76 that 'Demetrios made a statue of Lysimache, who was priestess of Athena for sixty-four years,' has a precision of detail, due to the fact that the years of Lysimache's priesthood were taken from the inscription on her statue (see Comm.), unlike anything that meets us in the main account, where such detail is alien to the nature of the inquiry.

With these two passages recognized as Heliodoran by both Keil and Münzer [1] I incline to associate a third, claimed for Heliodoros by Wachsmuth [2], but rejected by Keil (*l. c.*). The passage (xxxiv, 72) concerning the 'Lioness' of Amphikrates, whose name was doubtless taken from the inscribed basis, belongs essentially to a book *de anathematis*, and accordingly to Heliodoros, one of whose works specially described the monuments of the Athenian Akropolis (περὶ τῆς Ἀθήνησιν ἀκροπόλεως, fr. 1–3 Müller). At the same time, it must be admitted that the story related in connexion with the monument has, in its Plinian form, a more imaginative flavour than we find in any of the accredited Heliodoran fragments or in those more recently recovered by Keil. It is possible, therefore, that only the kernel of the passage is Heliodoran, and that the anecdote itself was expanded under the influence of other sources [3].

---

[1] *op. cit.* p. 541.

[2] *loc. cit.* The Heliodoran authorship seems admitted by Gurlitt, *Pausanias*, p. 96.

[3] It is noteworthy that the name of Amphikrates is preserved only in Pliny. As regards the mention of the statue and the anecdote attached thereto, Plut., *Garrul.* 8, and Polyainos, *Stratagem.* viii, 45, appear to draw from the same source as Pliny, while the words of Pausanias (i, 23, 2), λέγω δὲ οὐκ ἐς συγγραφὴν πρότερον ἥκοντα, seem to indicate that Pausanias had the story merely from hearsay; moreover, he has no allusion to the animal's tonguelessness. The story, without mention of the statue, recurs once again in Pliny (vii, 87), and is told by Athen., xiii, 596 f.

We return to safer ground in the passage in Book xxxv, claimed for Heliodoros by Keil. He argues that the sentence (§ 134) *pinxit* (i. e. *Athenion*) *in templo Eleusine Phylarchum et Athenis frequentiam quam vocavere syngenicon* is marked off from the rest of the account of Athenion's pictures by the careful notice of locality, a special Heliodoran characteristic, while the rest of the enumeration, being resumed with *item*, points to the juxtaposition of different sources. Both the 'Phylarchos' and the 'syngenicon,' moreover, being votive offerings, fall within the range of the *de anathematis*.

As already hinted, it seems probable that these additions from Heliodoros to the older text-books of Xenokrates and Antigonos were made by Pasiteles, the Plinian author whom we pass to consider next.

VI. *Pasiteles of Naples.*

This curiously many-sided man [1], at once worker in marble, in ivory, and in bronze, who was a careful student of animal life, who modelled and chiselled, who could raise a chryselephantine statue or make the design for a silver mirror, and who was the master of a considerable school, is known to us only from Pliny and from one mention in Cicero (*de Div.* i, 36, 79). His date is given by the former (xxxiii, 156) as *circa Pompei Magni* (b. 108 B.C., murd. 48 B.C.) *aetatem*. He received the right of Roman citizenship in 88 B.C. (xxxvi, 40, where see Comm.), at a time when he had presumably attained to manhood [2], if not yet to fame. Of his five volumes concerning famous works of art (*quinque volumina scripsit nobilium operum in toto orbe*, xxxvi, 40) we may expect to find traces in Pliny's work, where a distinguished place is assigned to him in the Indices of authors: in the Indices to xxxiii and xxxv he heads the list of Greek writers, in the Index to xxxiv he closes it; for xxxvi he appears as sole Greek authority. Brunn's researches have proved that a writer appearing in so prominent a position must be a main

See Jacobi, *Fleckeisen's Jahrb.* 1873, p. 367 f.; Gurlitt, *loc. cit.*; Kalkmann, *Pausanias der Perieget*, p. 52, note 1; Reisch, *Weihgeschenke*, p. 13, note 1. Grote (*Hist.* iii, p. 332) inclined to accept the story of Leaina, but took no notice of the monument.

[1] The fullest account of Pasiteles is still that of Kékulé, *Die Gruppe des Künstlers Menelaos*, 1870, p. 11 ff.; see also Helbig, *Untersuchungen über die campanische Wandmalerei*, p. 10 f.; Wickhoff, *Wiener Genesis*, p. 26 f.

[2] Kékulé, *op. cit.*, p. 11 f.

authority—yet there is no writer so difficult to lay a definite hold on as Pasiteles, when we come to analyze the Plinian text. The only passage (xxxvi, 40) where he was thought to be cited by name for an expression of opinion has fallen away before Furtwängler's criticism : the reading *admirator et Pasitelis* must be restored in place of the unsatisfactory *admiratur et Pasiteles* of the editions[1]. The attempt of Brieger[2] to detect Pasitelean authorship in passages betraying periegetic interests or points of view, and that of Otto Jahn[3] to detect it wherever a work of art was qualified by the epithet *nobilis,* have likewise been disposed of by Furtwängler, whose own association of Pasiteles, however, with all the more properly artistic criticism in Pliny is in- adequately based upon the fact that Pasiteles was an artist, since, as we have seen, he only shared that qualification with Xenokrates, Antigonos, and others. Nor are there any accredited fragments of his writings which could serve as clues. We are left, in order to account for his singular position in the Indices, with the sole alternative, already indicated by Brunn[4], of accrediting him with a final and wholesale working up of the old Greek Treatises upon art into his own five volumes. That Pasiteles should thus have elected to return to the Treatises of Xenokrates and Antigonos, rather than apply himself to formulate fresh theories and judge- ments, accords admirably with his artistic leanings : he created no style of his own, but turned back to Greek models—at times simply copying them, at others adapting or combining them for the presentment of a new subject[5]. Even as we doubtless owe to him and his school[6] not a few of those copies which have rescued Greek statues from complete oblivion, so we may owe it to his reverence for the art-literature of the Greeks that some part of it has filtered down to us through the subsequent medium of the Roman authors. Thus Varro, and Pliny after him, would quote, as their manner was, the names of Xenokrates,

[1] Furtwängler, *Plinius und seine Quellen,* p. 40 f.

[2] *De Fontibus,* p. 36.

[3] *Kunsturtheile,* p. 124.

[4] *Sitzungsberichte der Münchener Akademie* (phil.-hist. Classe), 1875, p. 313.

[5] On this point see especially Furtwängler, *Eine argivische Bronze* (50, Winckelmannsprogramm, Berlin, 1890), p. 134 f. ; Hauser, *Die neu- attischen Reliefs,* p. 182 ; cf. the interesting summary of Wolters, *Jahrb.* xi, 1896, p. 3 f, and now Furtwängler, *Statuenkopien im Alter- thum,* p. 544 f.

[6] For Stephanos, pupil of Pasi- teles, and Menelaos, pupil of Stephanos, see Commentary on xxxvi, 33.

of Antigonos, and other Greek writers, at second or third hand[1]. And that Pasiteles himself should chance not to be quoted in the actual text, for any of the additions which he made, is natural enough if we suppose that he gave merely an uncoloured enumeration of new material, unaccompanied by striking or disputable comment. For it is clear, if we inspect the cases in which authorities are cited in the Plinian text (xxxiv, 61, 68, &c.), that the mention is in no wise determined by the modern conscientiousness in such matters—not even by a sentiment of honour among thieves—but by the occasional wish to disclaim responsibility (cf. p. lxvi). Pliny, at any rate, thought it sufficient to acknowledge the debt which he owed indirectly to Pasiteles, whom he found cited as main Greek authority in Varro, by assigning him the leading place in the Indices, a place corresponding to that which he doubtless occupied in the Varronian lists of Greek authors[2]. Varro seems to have marked his debt to Pasiteles by a general complimentary allusion to his productiveness both as writer and artist (xxxvi, 40). The *quae fecisse nominatim non refertur* is an addition by Pliny, who, not seizing the precise intention of the passage, expected to find the works of Pasiteles enumerated singly in this particular connexion. He forgets that just above he has mentioned on Varro's authority the gold-ivory Jupiter in the temple of Metellus; Varro himself, who was a contemporary and possibly a friend of Pasiteles[3], must have known his works well.

To Pasiteles, moreover, may be traced almost certainly one important extension of the original Greek treatises. These terminated, as we have seen (p. xxi), with Ol. 121, a date which, though purely accidental, was accepted by subsequent writers

---

[1] That the name of Antigonos reached Pliny only through Pasiteles has been suggested by Wilamowitz, *Antigonos von Karystos*, p. 7.

[2] For Pliny's method of compiling long lists of authors from Varro see in especial the Index to Book viii; it contains the names of twenty-nine Greek authors, not one of which is cited in the text of the work; they appear to have been taken bodily over from Varro, *Re Rust.* i. 1, 8, Pliny even adopting for a long stretch the same order of enumeration; cp. *Amphilocho Athe-*naeo—*Menandris Prienaeo et Heracleote* with the Varronian *item Amphilochus Atheniensis . . . Menandri duo unus Prienaeus alter Heracleotes.* Brunn (*de Indicibus,* p. 48) conjectures that the nine Greek writers περὶ μελιτουργικά, Index to Book xi, were taken straight over by Pliny from the lost work of Hyginus; cf. also Brunn, p. 50, and F. Aly, *Zur Quellenkritik des älteren Plinius,* 1885, p. 7 ff.

[3] Kékulé, p. 17.

as the close of a period of art. It was probably Pasiteles who, while preserving this date as the lower chronological limit for Greek art, brought in the mention of the revival in Ol. 156 (xxxiv, 52)[1]. This revival seems connected with the works of art and decorations executed for the buildings of Metellus, for which at a later date Pasiteles himself had made a Jupiter in ivory and gold. But if Pasiteles be the author of the additions to the chronology of the statuaries he must also be credited with the similar extension of the history of the painters, to include those who flourished from Ol. 156 onwards (xxxv, 135)[2].

To the actual contents of the five volumes *nobilium operum* we have no clue, but from their number a certain width of range may reasonably be argued. The design of Pasiteles was, we may conjecture, to give a general survey of all the arts of antiquity, rather than, like Xenokrates, to develop a definite scheme in relation to the department of art in which he was himself engaged, or which came within the sphere of his personal interest. We may therefore tentatively attribute to him—at any rate without violating any ascertained principle upon which he worked—the otherwise unallotted information in the early parts of xxxiv concerning bronze as used (*a*) for furniture, (*b*) for temple ornaments, (*c*) for statues of the gods, (*d*) for statues of mortals; each category is linked to the following by the purely artificial conception of progress from the less to the more noble. Under these headings the Roman authors afterwards fitted in, as best they could, fresh material concerning Roman art, committing themselves in the process to singular contradictions[3]. Statuary proper, moreover, was further divided into colossal images and lesser images (§ 49). These artificial categories seem likely enough to have been adopted by Pasiteles as a convenient mode of tabulating his vast material. Thus he would further break up the old Greek Treatises into a chronological table and an alphabetical list (above, p. xxii), into which new names or works of special merit were introduced from Heliodoros[4] or other sources, only the *insignes* being reserved for separate treatment. New lists were appended; of these it is significant that the first comprises almost solely the names of artists who were also distinguished for their silver-chasing, a branch of

[1] Münzer, *op. cit.*, p. 538; cf.   *März h.* p. 135, note 1.
Comm. on xxxiv, 52, l. 4.   [3] Cf. Münzer, p. 501.
[2] Münzer, *l. c.*; Robert, *Arch.*   [4] Cf. B. Keil, *Hermes* xxx, 1895, p. 226.

art in which Pasiteles himself specially excelled. Indeed, with regard to the account of the silver-chasers themselves in xxxiii, 154–157, failing information concerning the unknown writers Menaichmos[1] and Menander[2], who appear as authorities in the Index to Bk. xxxiii, or any clue to guide us here to Antigonos, Pasiteles must, for the present, be accepted as authority for the whole passage, with the sole exception of the subsequent interpolations and additions commented upon in the notes.

In Bk. xxxv, again, it may be Pasiteles who divided the painters into two classes, according as they painted in tempera (53–111) or in wax by the process called encaustic (122–149), and who elaborated the curiously artificial theories (§ 149) as to its development. The latter recall the conventional notions of artistic progress unfolded at the commencement of Bk. xxxiv; they are equally devoid of that apprehension of a living growth within a living organism which, in spite of all blunderings, never seems to have deserted Xenokrates. In his written works, as in many of the copies of Greek statuary attributed to him, Pasiteles had caught the sense but not the spirit of the masters he so zealously emulated. Lastly, he arranged the painters of second rank (§§ 138–145), those of third rank (§ 146), and the women painters (§ 148) in three closing alphabetical lists.

That the account of modelling (xxxv, § 151 f.) went through his hands is clear from the exceeding stress he laid upon the indispensable function of modelling in every branch of the plastic arts; his opinion on this subject, quoted by Varro, was probably the main addition Pasiteles made to the original Greek Treatise. That Pasiteles would leave the account of the modellers prefixed to that of the statuaries in bronze is evident from the connexion he established between the two, *plasticen matrem caelaturae et statuariae sculpturaeque dixit.* It has already been noted (p. xxxv) that the exigencies of his plan compelled Pliny to transfer the account to its present awkward position.

Pasiteles is the last writer upon art, properly so called, whose name meets us in the pages of Pliny. His comprehensive work proved not only a rich but a convenient store for the Roman encyclopaedists. Above all does he seem to have been excerpted

---

[1] Above, p. xl, note 1.
[2] Only known through Pliny; cf. Susemihl, i, p. 524, note 47.

by Varro, whose extracts from Pasiteles, altered and re-adapted to
his own purposes by Pliny, have thus survived down to our own
day.

VII. *Varro* (116–28 B. C.)—*Cornelius Nepos* (*circ.* 99–24 B. C.)— *Fabius Vestalis.*

The first step in Plinian criticism went from Pliny back to
Varro as authority for the bulk of the history upon art. In the
light of a clearer analysis, Varro has fallen again into a subordinate place, overshadowed no longer indeed by his debtor
Pliny, but by those earlier authorities to whom he was in his turn
indebted. By the emergence now into a certain definiteness of
the Greek authorities : of Xenokrates and Duris, with their very
distinctive histories, the one of art, the other of the artists ; of
Antigonos in whom this uncongenial and even antagonistic
material was worked up into a singular union ; and of Pasiteles,
who yet further manipulated, rearranged, and amplified it, the
Roman Varro is reduced from his position as authority to the
humbler office of final intermediary. Though he is undoubtedly
the author whom Pliny quotes most frequently in his account of
the Artists [1], as generally throughout the *Historia Naturalis*,
yet any discussion of his literary or scientific personality would
be foreign to the present enquiry [2]. It is perhaps fortunate for
his great reputation that so few of his voluminous writings have
survived : the criticism of their comparatively meagre fragments
will, for the world at large, always be outmatched by that
picture of his learning which we owe to the genius of Cicero
(*Acad. Post.* i, 3, 9), who as a fact neither loved nor admired him,
but who, in order to secure by a counter-compliment the
gratification of his own vanity, was ready to flatter the πολυ-
γραφώτατος *homo* [3]. Neither in the great list of his works preserved
by Jerome, nor outside it, do we come upon traces of any work
exclusively devoted to the history of art. The probability is that
in the case of Varro, as in that of Pliny, this history formed but

---

[1] xxxiv, 56 ; xxxv, 113, 136, 154, 155 ff. ; xxxvi, 14, 17, 39, 41 ; cf. Furtwängler, *Plinius*, p. 56 ff.

[2] For Varro, see especially Teuffel, *Geschichte der Römischen Literatur*, §§ 164-169, and the sketch in Momm-sen, vol. III, p. 602 ff. On Varro's compilatory methods see the just estimate of G. Boissier, *Étude sur la vie et les ouvrages de Varron*, p. 27 ff.

[3] Cic. *Ep. ad Att.* xiii, 18.

an episode of a larger work, such for instance as the section on 'Human Affairs' in the 'Antiquities.' Further, we know from extant fragments[1] that various notices of artists were scattered up and down a number of Varro's lesser works.

It only remains to indicate the few and comparatively insignificant passages which we know, in most cases from Pliny's express mention of him, to be in a more special sense Varronian, for which Varro is, so far as we know, the final and sole authority. Even these I shall be content to summarize very briefly, apologizing for a brevity that may seem disproportioned by reminding the reader that till lately the disproportion has been all to the score of Varro, and that as a fact the value of the Plinian sources increases in the order, not of their nearness to Pliny, but of their approach to the distant fountain-head.

Varro seems occasionally, as in the passage (xxxiv, 69) on Praxiteles, to have modified and doctored the Greek account (above, p. xxii) so as to suit the Roman taste. Occasionally also he brought in parenthetical scraps of interesting or curious information; for instance, to the statement in xxxvi, § 14, that the archaic sculptors worked in marble he tacked on the truly Varronian etymology of the word *lychnites* (see Comm.). For the rest, his additions mostly express his personal opinion, or retail his personal knowledge, in many cases, of contemporaries. Thus from Pliny's paraphrase we learn that to the account he borrowed from his Greek authors of the Nemesis at Rhamnous (xxxvi, 17) he added a sentence expressive of his own admiration of the statue, which he had doubtless seen during his stay at Athens. Thus too his mention of the lady artist Iaia of Kyzikos, a friend of his youth, is adjoined to the lists of women painters (xxxv, 147). In like manner he praises the marvellously naturalistic modelling of fruits by another acquaintance, Possis (*ib.* 155); this is followed (*ib.* 155) by the laudatory notice of the friend of Lucullus, the Athenian Arkesilaos—who may well have been known to Varro— and of Pasiteles (above, p. lxxix). Further, it appears from § 154 that he had combined the Greek account of modelling, as he took it from Pasiteles, with some account of the art in Rome, and in this same connexion of modelling, though scarcely in its present context, he had given yet another reminiscence of his Athenian

---

[1] When the whole of the Varronian fragments dealing with art-questions are collected and analyzed, considerable traces of lost Greek writings are certain to be revealed; see e.g. *Ling. Lat.* ix, 6, 12; *ib.* ix, 18.

visit in his explanation of the term *Ceramicus*. Two statements are still more closely personal: he mentioned that he had once possessed (*habuisse*) a bronze figure by the silver-chaser Mentor (xxxiii, 154), and a marble group of a Lioness and Cupids by Arkesilaos (xxxvi, 41). From his use of the past tense it has been justly surmised that Varro had lost these treasures at the time of the proscriptions of B.C. 43.

It is evident that Varro is the authority for both the genre pictures by Peiraikos and the huge pictures by Serapion, as well as for the portraits by Dionysios (xxxv, 113, 114). All three artists are placed antithetically to one another, and moreover, as we learn from § 148, they were evidently all three contemporaries of Varro. Upon these follows the mention of Kalates, a painter only once again mentioned in literature, namely in Varro's Life of the Roman People (fr. 1 Keil). Lastly, it is at least a significant coincidence that, while the pictures of Antiphilos mentioned by Pliny (*ib.* § 114) were either inside or in the neighbourhood of the Gallery of Pompeius, the same painter is mentioned in Varro's Treatise on Rustic Affairs (iii, 2, 5), in that part of the dialogue which is supposed to take place B.C. 54, a few months after the dedication of the theatre and the Gallery of Pompeius in the Field of Mars [1]. It shows, at any rate, that Varro, writing after his eightieth year, was still interested in the pictures of the Egyptian painter, whom he may have discussed in a previous work.

To Varro likewise Pliny owes, as appears from xxxv, 136, a number of notices of the high prices paid for works of art—mostly pictures. Varro had apparently collected together from his Greek authors a number of these instances, and had at the same time given, for the benefit of Roman readers, the Roman equivalent of the Greek talent: hence the *talentum Atticum $\overline{XVI}$ taxat M. Varro* (*loc. cit.*) of Pliny. Three of the works of art which obtained specially high prices ·are mentioned together in vii, 126 (where, however, there is no reference to Varro's evaluation of the talent), and again separately at different parts of the account of the painters: thus the price paid by Attalos for the 'Dionysos' of Aristeides of Thebes is given again twice in xxxv, 24 and 100; the price, 'its weight in gold,' of the picture by Boularchos, *ib.* 55; lastly, the price paid by Caesar for the 'Aias' and the 'Medeia' of Timomachos, *ib.* 136 [2]. To these

[1] Münzer, p. 541. [2] Münzer, *l. c.*

undoubted instances of Varronian authorship I incline to add as
a fourth the notice of the price paid for the 'Diadumenos' of
Polykleitos (xxxiv, 55).

Cornelius Nepos, who at one time (e. g. Furtwängler, *Plinius*,
p. 25) was credited with the anecdotic portions in Pliny, which
recent criticism has gradually but surely traced back to Duris,
is mentioned in xxxv, 16 as Pliny's authority for the existence
of an early Greek painter Ekphantos, who accompanied the
Corinthian Damaratos in his flight to Italy. Presumably, therefore,
Pliny also obtained from him the mention of the Corinthian
potters, also companions of Damaratos (*ib.* 152). These extracts
may be from the same work of Nepos, dealing apparently with
Roman customs, from which Pliny has citations in other parts of
the *Historia* (ix, 61, 136; x, 60, &c.) [1].

For Fabius Vestalis, *qui de pictura scripsit* (Index, xxxv),
and who possibly had also written on statuary and sculpture,
since he figures in the Indices to xxxiv and xxxvi, not even the
acuteness of Münzer has been able to recover one single fragment
out of the Plinian history. He is entirely unknown [2], save for
the references in Pliny [3] (see Addenda).

VIII. *G. Licinius Mucianus* (date of birth unknown; died before
B. C. 77, cf. Plin. xxxii, 62).

To the History of the Artists which he borrowed from Varro,
Pliny made one notable group of additions from the work in
which his contemporary G. Licinius Mucianus, *ter consul* [4], had
published the more or less trustworthy observations compiled
during a prolonged sojourn in the East. These additions concern
the works of art of the coast cities of Asia-Minor and the adjacent
islands, a region that had practically lain outside the ken of
the Greek art-writers Xenokrates (cf. p. xxi) and Antigonos [5], and
after them of Pasiteles [6].

---

[1] Münzer, p. 542 f.

[2] Teuffel, § 267, 11.

[3] Indices, vii, xxxiv–xxxvi; cf. vii, 213.

[4] Cited Indices to xxxi, xxxiii, xxxv, xxxvi, and repeatedly in the body of the *Historia* (see Detlefsen's Index).

[5] We must except, of course, the traditions derived by Antigonos from Duris concerning the island-schools of the Aegean.

[6] Pasiteles, so far as we can tell, seems not to have enlarged the geographical range of his predecessor, except for the notice of the Greek artists in

Mucianus, coming from the South[1], would first encounter the civilization of the Aegean in Rhodes (v, 132; xix, 12; xxxiv, 36); of the islands which he visited, Delos (iv, 66), Syros (*ib.* 67), and Andros (ii, 231) lay furthest to the West, Samothrake (xi, 167) to the North; along the coast proper he came at least as far as Kyzikos (xxxi, 19). Pliny not unfrequently introduces the notices of works of art extant within this geographical district by such words as *hodie* or *nunc*, showing that he is quoting from a contemporary or recent authority. Finally, we have also to guide us, in our search for the information borrowed by Pliny from Mucianus, our knowledge of the man's superstitious credulousness, of his keen interest for everything marvellous or miraculous[2]. The greater number of the additions to be traced back to Mucianus have been detected by Leopold Brunn in an exhaustive dissertation[3], and accepted as Mucianian by the later commentators of Pliny[4]. The following list of the passages derived from Mucianus in the art-books follows a geographical order from south to north.

I. *Rhodes.*

LINDOS. That Mucianus visited its temple of Athena and noted its treasures and curiosities in detail, appears from xix, 12, where Pliny, specially using the word *nuperrime*, describes on the authority of Mucianus the cuirass of the Egyptian king Amasis, there preserved; each thread in this cuirass was composed of three hundred and sixty-five strands; Pliny adds that Mucianus, who had *verified* the fact, had remarked that 'almost nothing was left of the cuirass owing to these frequent verifications[5].' Hence the following descriptions of works of art in the same temple of Lindos have been justly referred to him[6].

1. xxxiii, 81: a cup, with the strange story attached to it that

---

Rome employed on the buildings of Metellus.

[1] Münzer, *op. cit.*, p. 544.

[2] E. g. he was in the habit of wearing round his neck a fly tied up in a linen rag as a remedy against ophthalmia, Plin. xxviii, 5. I am not concerned here to reconcile such statements with the glowing tributes paid to Mucianus by Tacitus (*Hist.* i, 10; ii, 5, &c.). For an estimate of Mucianus see especially Teuffel, § 314.

[3] *De C. Licinio Muciano*, Diss., Leipzig, 1870.

[4] Cf. Furtwängler, *Plinius und seine Quellen*, pp. 52–56; Oehmichen, *Plinianische Studien*, pp. 141–149.

[5] . . . *Quod se expertum nuperrime prodidit Mucianus ter cos., parvasque iam reliquias eius superesse hac experientium iniuria.*

[6] First by Brieger, *de Fontibus*, p. 59 ff.

it was dedicated by Helena, who had moulded it on her breasts. (L. Brunn, 43.)

2. xxxiii, 155: silver cups chased by Boëthos, the *hodie* showing that Pliny was quoting from a contemporary authority. (L. Brunn, 44.)

RHODES (city): 3. xxxiii, 155: silver cups chased by Akragas and Mys. (L. Brunn, 44.)

4. xxxiv, 36: *Rhodi etiamnum LXXIII signorum esse Mucianus ter cos. prodidit.* (L. Brunn, 12.)

5. *Ib.* 41, 42: the description of the colossus of Rhodes (L. Brunn, 45); it evidently rests on the testimony of an eye-witness, and the delighted insistence on the marvellous appearance (*miraculo est*) of the fallen colossus, and its size and its cost, betrays the special bent of Mucianus [1].

6. *Ib.* § 42: *Sunt alii centum numero in eadem urbe colossi minores* (L. Brunn, 45); the words are inseparable from the notices of the large colossus, and moreover recall xxxvi, 37.

7. xxxv, 69: the picture by Parrhasios of Meleager, Herakles, and Perseus, thrice struck by lightning and yet not effaced— *hoc ipso miraculum auget*—(L. Brunn, 46), the insistence upon the miracle being thoroughly after the manner of Mucianus.

8. To the seven passages on Rhodian works of art, which critics agree in tracing back to Mucianus, should be added the mention in xxxiv, 63, of the chariot of the Sun by Lysippos, *in primis vero quadriga cum Sole Rhodiorum* [2].

ii. *Knidos.*

9. xxxvi, 20, 21 : description of the Aphrodite of Knidos; it is that of an eye-witness, who is interested neither in the motive nor technique of the statue, but whose tourist's curiosity was roused by the story of King Nikomedes, by the tradition that the artist had made two rival statues, the one draped, the other not, and finally by the anecdote of the statue's lover [3].

10. *Ib.* : *Sunt in Cnido et alia signa marmorea inlustrium artificum*—inseparable from the preceding notice of the Aphrodite ; cf. above, 6 and 5 [4].

---

[1] Brieger, *l. c.*

[2] Münzer (p. 504) correctly omits it from the original Xenokratic list of Lysippian works, but makes no further suggestion as to its authorship.

[3] The passage first referred to Mucianus by Furtwängler, *op. cit.*, p. 53 f.; cf. Oehmichen, *op. cit.*, p. 148.

[4] Furtwängler, *l. c.*

III. *Halikarnassos.*

11. xxxvi, 30, 31 : description of the Mausoleion ; it resembles in character that of the Knidian Aphrodite ; the size, the beauty, and the labour expended upon the monument are described, but nothing is said of the subject presented ; the words *hodieque certant manus* point to a contemporary authority [1].

IV. *Miletos.*

12. xxxiv, 75 : Apollo of Kanachos, with the wonderful stag. That this is an addition to the original Greek account of the artist has already been pointed out (above, p. xxii) ; the periegetic character of the description, and the insistence upon trivial pecu-liarities which were perhaps only the result of accident [2], are characteristic of Mucianus [3].

V. *Samos.*

13. xxxv, 93 : portrait of Habron by Apelles [4].

VI. *Ephesos.*

14. xxxvi, 95 : description of Temple of Artemis ; it is evidently from the same hand as xvi, 213 (= App. IV), where Mucianus is quoted by name. Besides, the description bears the same character as that of the Mausoleion (No. 11) : the interest of the describer centred in the wonder of the foundations, in the size and number of the columns, and in the apparition of the goddess to the tired artist.

15. *Ib.* 32 : the Hekate, against whose radiance the guardians of the temple advised visitors to shade their eyes. (L. Brunn, 51.)

16. xxxv, 92 : the portrait of Alexander by Apelles ; the descrip-tion seems by Mucianus ; the price of the work is dwelt upon, and the motive of the thunderbolt mentioned only because *digiti eminere videntur et fulmen extra tabulam esse.* (L. Brunn, 53.)

17. xxxv, 93 : picture of the procession of a Megabyzos by Apelles. (L. Brunn, 53.)

---

[1] First attributed to Mucianus by Furtwängler, *l. c.*

[2] See note on passage. Ernest Gardner, *Handbook of Greek Sculp-ture*, p. 194, note 1, hints at the same possibility. If my memory serves me right, it was Mr. A. S. Murray who, some years ago, in the course of conversation, first suggested to me that the puzzling Plinian description of the stag was a periegetic fable in-vented out of some trivial failure in the casting.

[3] Oehmichen, *Plin. Studien*, p. 142 f.

[4] Oehmichen, p. 146.

18. *Ib.* 129 : picture of the Madness of Odysseus by Euphranor ; Mucianus interpreted the action of Palamedes differently to other authorities [1] (see Comm.).

19. *Ib.* 131 : grave picture of a priest of Artemis by Nikias. (L. Brunn, 54.)

20. xxxiv, 58 : Apollo by Myron, taken away by Antonius and restored to the Ephesians by Augustus, in obedience to a dream. Münzer (p. 544) has astutely detected the apocryphal character of a story invented by a jealous priesthood in emulation of their Samian neighbours. (See Comm. on pass.)

VII. *Smyrna.*

21. xxxvi, 32 : the drunken old woman by Myron (for the epithet *ebria*, see Comm.) [2].

VIII. *Iasos.*

22. xxxvi, 12 : Artemis, by the sons of Archermos [3] ; evidently from the same writer as following fragment [4].

IX. *Chios.*

23. *Ib.* 13 : mask of Artemis by the same artists ; the Mucianian character patent in the description of the face, which appears sad to those who enter the temple, gay to those who leave it.

X. *Pergamon.*

From xxxvi, 131 we learn that Mucianus was in that region ; accordingly we should perhaps refer to him the notices concerning Pergamene art. These are foreign to the original treatises (above, p. xxi) : Xenokrates lived too early to take Pergamon into account ; Antigonos, although himself one of the artists employed by the Pergamene kings (xxxiv, 84), accepted the chronological limit of the Xenokratic Treatises. Pasiteles did the same, marking his only addition to the chronology as a 'Revival' (above, p. lxxix f.). It only remains to conjecture that Pliny took from Mucianus his descriptions of Pergamene works [5].

---

[1] Rightly attributed to Mucianus by Oehmichen, *l.c.*, as against Furtwängler (p. 44), who gave the passage to Pasiteles.

[2] Cf. Furtwängler, *op. cit.*, p. 54.

[3] Oehmichen, p. 147 ; cf. Münzer, *op. cit.*, p. 525, note 1.

[4] That Mucianus visited Iasos appears from ix, 33.

[5] Cf. Münzer, *op. cit.*, p. 544.

24. xxxiv, 84: *Plures artifices . . . Antigonus*; the words *qui volumina condidit de sua arte* may be an addition of Pliny's own.

25. xxxv, 60: *Aiax fulmine incensus* by Apollodoros, the *hodie* pointing clearly to a contemporary authority[1]. (Oehmichen, 71.)

26. xxxvi, 24: the 'symplegma' by Kephisodotos, with the epigram attached thereto. (Oehmichen, 81.)

XI. *Samothrake.*

From xi, 167 it appears that Mucianus visited this island; hence we may refer to him:

27. xxxvi, 25: an Aphrodite and Pothos by Skopas; the words *sanctissimis caerimoniis coluntur* are characteristic of the pious and superstitious Mucianus. (Oehmichen, 78.)

XII. *Parion.*

28. xxxiv, 78: Herakles by Hagesias (Oehmichen, 67). That this is an addition to the early Greek account was pointed out above, p. xxiv. Parion, moreover, only became a *colonia* under Augustus (see Comm.). It was not known as such to Varro, who only refers to it as Parion (cf. vii, 13, in *Hellesponto circa Parium*, on the authority of Varro); thus Mucianus remains the only one of the Plinian authors known to have visited this region at a time when it would be generally described as *P. colonia*.

29. xxxvi, 22: nude Eros by Praxiteles *in Pario colonia*, with the story of its lover Alketas of Rhodes, closely resembling the story of the lover of the Knidian Aphrodite. (Oehmichen, 68.)

XIII. *Lysimacheia.*

30. xxxiv, 56: a Hermes by Polykleitos, no longer extant when Mucianus visited the city[2].

This bald list serves to indicate the immediate indebtedness of Pliny to Mucianus, but there arises the further question whence Mucianus derived his own information. That he relied in great measure, perhaps mainly, on the tales of ciceroni, is evident from the nature of what he relates. Yet in some cases, e. g. in the description of the Mausoleion, or of the colossus of Rhodes, he

---

[1] Furtwängler, *Plinius*, p. 53.

[2] First attributed to Mucianus by Münzer, *op. cit.*, p. 525. In a private note Münzer further points out to me that the description of the temple of Erythreia (xi, 111, and xxxv, 161)—a city which lay in the route of Mucianus —must be referred to this author: ' it has all the characteristic signs: personal observation and interest in the miraculous.'

doubtless had handbooks which informed him of such details as price and size, or gave the names of the artists employed. To ascertain what these handbooks may have been, and whether fragments of Greek writings other than those of the Xenokrates-Antigonos-Pasiteles group reached Pliny through Mucianus, is a task which lies outside the compass of the present essay.

IX. *Pliny's own additions.—Roman Museography. Retrospect.*

Besides the Varronian additions to the material derived from the Greek art-treatises, and besides the material which he derived independently from Varro, Pliny enriched his account of the artists by notices concerning the locality in Rome of a number of Greek works. It is well known that in the days of Pliny, and already long before his time, Rome displayed within her galleries, her temples, and her public places an unrivalled collection of works of art, gathered together from every part of the Hellenic world. From the day when Marcellus had first induced the Romans to admiration of Greek art by displaying the spoils of Syracuse [1], down to that crowning day of a triple triumph when Caesar Augustus celebrated his victory over the last of the Hellenic powers [2], statues and other works of art had come to be as much a part of the pageantry of triumphs as captives or military booty [3]. The solemn dedication of these objects in some public building was the natural sequel of the triumphal procession. The great generals of the Republic [4], and after them the Emperors [5], had shown themselves zealous for the preservation and arrangement of these collections. Only a short while before Pliny compiled

[1] Liv. xxv, 40; see Comm. on xxxv, 24, l. 16.

[2] In 23 B. C.; for the works of art brought to Rome from Alexandria, see Wunderer, *Manibiae Alexandrinae.*

[3] So much so that works of art were even displayed in triumphs over barbaric and Western nations; the art booty acquired from Macedonia by Aemilius Paullus, for instance, seems to have formed an inexhaustible mine whence other conquerors could draw;

cf. Comm. on xxxiv, 54, the statues dedicated by Catulus in the temple of the Fortune of the Day, and on xxxiv, 77, the Minerva dedicated by Q. Lutatius Catulus below the Capitol.

[4] E. g. Gallery of Octavius, xxxiv, 13; Gallery of Pompeius, xxxv, 114, 126, 132.

[5] E. g. Gallery of Octavia, xxxiv, 31; xxxv, 139; xxxvi, 24, 35, &c.; and consult the Museographic Index (ii).

his history of the artists, his patron Vespasian had opened the great Temple of Peace, destined with its surrounding Forum [1] to receive, alongside the treasures of the Temple of Jerusalem, those Greek masterpieces which the greed of Nero had gathered within the Golden House [2]. The pages of Pliny are certainly the richest mine of information concerning the art treasures of Rome. Owing, moreover, to his preference for books over personal observation of actual fact, Pliny not unfrequently records the locality of works of art which had disappeared in his day [3]. Yet a discussion of the sources whence Pliny obtained his museographic information, though of matchless interest for the study of Roman history and topography, lies entirely outside an inquiry concerned with the Greek element in Pliny. It suffices to point out that Pliny doubtless had straight from Varro (p. lxxxiii f.) most of the Roman notices relating to events up to the close of the Republic ; that for the Early Empire, up to the reign of Nero, he may have borrowed from authors such as Deculo [4] or Fenestella [5] ; while his allusions to Nero [6], and his eulogies of the Flavian Emperors, and of the works of art in their possession [7], were probably part of the material he had himself compiled for his own *History of Rome*, a work embracing the period from the accession of Nero to the Judaic triumph of Vespasian and Titus [8].

It is little or nothing, then, of intrinsic importance from our point of view, that Pliny added to the Greek Treatises as he found them excerpted in Varro. At most does he bring the information thus derived from the Greeks into consonance with the taste of his day by occasional flashes of rhetoric, such as the repeated lament over the decay of art [9] ; his outburst of admiration at the power of art, which ' could turn the eyes of the Senate of the Roman people for so many years upon Glaukion and his

---

[1] xxxiv, 84.

[2] *ib.*

[3] This remark applies to a great portion of the Roman statues mentioned in the earlier part of xxxiv. Cf. also xxxiv, 69 (statues by Praxiteles which had stood in front of the Temple of Felicity) ; xxxv, 99, the Dionysos and Ariadne of Aristeides.

[4] From whom he had the anecdote of Tiberius' passion for the *Apoxyomenos* of Lysippos, xxxiv, 62 ; it is

evidently from the same source as the mention of the ' Archigallus' loved by Tiberius, in xxxv, 70 ; see Oehmichen, *Plin. Studien*, p. 123.

[5] Cf. Oehmichen, *op. cit.* p. 125.

[6] xxxiv, 45, 48, 63, 84 ; xxxv, 51, 91, 120, &c.

[7] See especially xxxiv, 84 ; the appreciation of the *astragalizontes* belonging to Titus in xxxiv, 55, and of the *Laocoon* in xxxvi, 37.

[8] *Praef. Hist. Nat.* 20.

[9] Cf. xxxiv, 5 ff. ; xxxv, 4, 29.

son Aristippos, persons otherwise quite obscure[1];' his simulated indignation at the cruelty of Phalaris[2]; and his allusion to the present merited dishonour of that Carthaginian Hercules to whom human victims had once been offered up[3].

In estimating Pliny's account of the artists we must never forget that it was inserted into the *Historia Naturalis* as a digression, which was artificially linked to the history of mineralogy on the pretext of the materials employed. In doing this Pliny was responding rather to the curiosity of his time in artistic matters[4] than following any special inclination of his own. If Pliny cared for art at all, it was only for its most realistic and imitative aspects. He admires the brutal realism of the dog licking her wounds[5], and in the workshop of Zenodoros his enthusiasm is roused by the colossal model which, even when covered with its wax tubings, betrayed an extraordinary likeness to Nero[6]. Occasionally too—and we may pay this tribute to our author as we take our leave of him—we seem to detect that, if he appears too often as an indiscriminating compiler, this is not so much through total lack of the critical faculty as through lack of time. At least he does not omit to rail at those critics who ascribed to Polykleitos (the elder namesake being the only Polykleitos known to him) the statue of Hephaistion, the friend of Alexander, although Hephaistion had lived nearly one hundred years after the artist[7], while in xxxiv, 79 he expresses by a vigorous turn of phrase his astonishment at finding Daidalos, whom in his hurry he confuses with the old Homeric craftsman, figuring among the artists of the historic age[8]. Yet the critical note is rare, and, in the larger inquiry concerning the sources whence Pliny drew, his own estimate of these sources appears but as a trivial accident.

Thus the tendency of modern research is to lessen more and more the importance of Pliny's personal contribution in his account of the artists, as indeed in the whole of his great work. Yet, by a singular irony, the fundamental faults of his work have bestowed upon it a permanent value. He has given us what is better than any original criticism which his century could have produced—a short compilation which is, to borrow the word he

[1] xxxv, 28.
[2] xxxiv, 89. [3] xxxvi, 39.
[4] Cf. Bertrand, *Études*, p. 329 ff., and his remarks, *ib*., on the passages
in Plutarch treating of art.
[5] xxxiv, 38. [6] *ib*. 45–46.
[7] *ib*. 64.
[8] *ib*. 76.

applies to the whole *Historia*, the 'storehouse' or *thesaurus* wherein are consigned fragments from the lost text-books of Xenokrates, from the Biographies of Duris and Antigonos, nay, priceless sayings that had filtered through the ages from the very writings of Apelles and Pamphilos [1].

---

[1] A short but admirably just estimate of the precise value of Pliny's work is given by J. W. Mackail, *Latin Literature*, 1895, p. 197.

BIBLIOGRAPHY [1].

Editions. BARBARUS, Rome, 1492; DALECAMPIUS, Lyons, 1586; GRO-
NOVIUS, Leiden, 1669; HARDUINUS, Paris, 1685; SILLIG, Gotha, 1853–55;
LUDWIG VON JAN, Leipzig, 1854–65; DETLEFSEN, Berlin, 1866–1873;
URLICHS, *Chrestomathia Pliniana*, Berlin, 1857; LITTRÉ (Text and Trans-
lation), Paris, 1883.

AMELUNG, WALTHER: *Die Basis des Praxiteles aus Mantinea*
(Munich, 1895).

ARNDT-BRUCKMANN: *Photographische Einzelaufnahmen antiker
Sculpturen* (Munich, 1893, &c.).

BABELON: *Monnaies de la République Romaine* (Paris, 1885, 1886);
Cabinet des Antiques à la Bibliothèque Nationale (Paris, 1887).

BAUMEISTER: *Denkmäler des Klassischen Alterthums* (Munich
and Leipzig, 1885–1888).

BECKER, W. A.: *Römische Topographie* (being the first vol. of
Handbuch der röm. Alterthümer, Leipzig, 1843).

BERGER, ERNST: *Beiträge zur Entwickelungsgeschichte der Malertechnik* (I and II, Munich, 1893 and 1895).

BERGK: *Poetae Lyrici Graeci* (ed. 4, Leipzig, 1878–82).

BERNOULLI, J. J.: *Römische Ikonographie* (Stuttgart, 1882–1894).

BERTRAND, ÉDOUARD: *Études sur la Peinture et la Critique d'Art
dans l'Antiquité* (Paris, 1893).

BLÜMNER: *Technologie und Terminologie der Gewerbe und Künste
bei den Griechen und Römern* (Leipzig, 1875–1887).

BRUNN, HEINRICH: *Geschichte der Griechischen Künstler* (Brunswick,
1853 and 1859; the second edition, Stuttgart, 1889, is merely a
reprint of the first) = *K. G.*

---

[1] Only the most important works and those most constantly cited in the
notes are given. The bibliography of the Plinian sources will be found on
p. xv f. of the Introduction.

BRUNN–BRUCKMANN: *Denkmäler Griechischer und Römischer Sculptur* (Munich, 1888–1895).

COLLIGNON, M.: *Histoire de la Sculpture Grecque* (vol. I, Paris, 1892) = *Sculpt. Grecque.*

CURTIUS, ERNST: *Stadtgeschichte von Athen* (Berlin, 1891).

DETLEFSEN: *De Arte Romanorum antiquissima* (I, II, III, Glückstadt, 1867, 1868, 1880).

DITTENBERGER AND PURGOLD: *Die Inschriften von Olympia* (Berlin, 1896).

FICK, A.: *Die Griechischen Personennamen* (second edition, Göttingen, 1894).

FÖRSTER, G. H.: *Die Sieger in den Olympischen Spielen* (I, II, Zwickau, 1891, 1892).

FRÄNKEL, MAX: *Die Inschriften von Pergamon* (Berlin, 1890).

FREEMAN, E.: *History of Sicily* (Oxford, 1891–1894).

FRIEDERICHS–WOLTERS: *Die Gipsabgüsse antiker Bildwerke* (Berlin, 1885).

FURTWÄNGLER, A.: *Der Dornauszieher und der Knabe mit der Gans* (Berlin, 1876).

—— *Die Sammlung Sabouroff* (Berlin, 1883, 1887).

—— *Meisterwerke der Griechischen Plastik* (Leipzig—Berlin, 1893).

—— *Masterpieces of Greek Sculpture*, ed. by E. Sellers London, 1895).

—— *Statuenkopien im Alterthum* (Munich, 1896).

GARDNER, E. A.: *A Handbook of Greek Sculpture* (London, 1896).

GARDNER, P.: *The Types of Greek Coins* (Cambridge, 1883).

GARDNER, P., and IMHOOF–BLUMER: *A Numismatic Commentary on Pausanias* (London, 1887, reprinted from *Journal of Hellenic Studies*).

GARDTHAUSEN, V.: *Augustus und seine Zeit* (Leipzig, 1891, 1896).

GILBERT, OTTO: *Geschichte und Topographie der Stadt Rom* (Leipzig, 1883–1890).

GURLITT, W.: *Ueber Pausanias* (Graz, 1890).

HARTWIG, PAUL: *Die Griechischen Meisterschalen* (Stuttgart and Berlin, 1893).

HEAD, B. V.: *Guide to the Coins of the Ancients* (second edition, London, 1881).

HELBIG: *Wandgemälde der vom Vesuv verschütteten Städte Campaniens* (Leipzig, 1868) = *Wandgem.*

—— *Untersuchungen über die Campanische Wandmalerei* (Leipzig, 1873) = *Untersuch.*

HELBIG : *Guide to the Public Collections of Classical Antiquities in Rome*, English ed. by James, F., and Findlay Muirhead (Leipzig, 1895)=*Class. Ant.*

HILLER VON GAERTRINGEN : *Inscriptiones Graecae Insularum Rhodi, Chalces, Carpathi cum Saro Casi* (Berlin, 1895).

HITZIG AND BLÜMNER : *Pausaniae Graeciae descriptio* (I, 1 Attica, Berlin, 1896).

HOLLAND, PHILEMON : *The Historie of the World, commonly called the Natural Historie of C. Plinius Secundus* (London, 1635).

JACOBI, FRANZ : *Grundzüge einer Museographie der Stadt Rom zur Zeit des Kaisers Augustus* (Part I, Spires, 1884).

JAHN, OTTO : *Kleine Beiträge zur Geschichte der Alten Literatur* (in Sächsische Berichte, Leipzig, 1857, p. 284).

JORDAN, H.: *Topographie der Stadt Rom im Alterthum* (1871–1885).

KIEPERT, H., ET HUELSEN, CH.: *Formae Urbis Romae Antiquae* (Berlin, 1896).

KROKER, E.: *Gleichnamige Griechische Künstler* (Leipzig, 1883).

KUHNERT, E.: *Statue und Ort in ihrem Verhältniss bei den Griechen* (in the Jahrbücher f. Classische Philologie, Supplementband xiv, Leipzig, 1884).

KÜLB, H.: *C. Plin. Secundus Naturgeschichte übersetzt und erläutert von* . . . (Stuttgart).

LANGE, JULIUS : *Fremstilling af Menneskeskikkelsen i dens aeldeste Periode indtil Hoj depunktet af den graeske Kunst* (Kopenhagen, 1892).

LOEWY, E.: *Untersuchungen zur Griechischen Künstlergeschichte* (Vienna, 1883)=*Untersuch.*

—— *Inschriften Griechischer Bildhauer* (Leipzig, 1885)=*I. G. B.*

MARQUARDT : *Privatleben der Römer* (Leipzig, 1886).

—— *Römische Staatsverwaltung* (Leipzig, 1894).

MAYHOFF : *Lucubrationes Plinianae* (1865).

—— *Novae Lucubrationes Plinianae* (1874).

MOMMSEN, TH.: *Römische Geschichte* (7th edition, Berlin, 1882).

—— *Res Gestae divi Augusti* (Berlin, 1883).

—— *Römisches Staatsrecht* (Leipzig, 1887, 1888).

—— *Römische Forschungen* (Berlin, 1864).

—— *Geschichte des Römischen Münzwesens* (Berlin, 1860).

MÜLLER, J.: *Der Stil des älteren Plinius* (Innsbruck, 1883).

MÜLLER, OTTFRIED : *Handbuch der Archaeologie der Kunst* (third edition, by Welcker; Stuttgart, 1878).

MURRAY, A. S. : *A Handbook of Greek Archaeology* (London, 1892).

OTTO : *Sprichwörter der Römer* (Leipzig, 1890).

OVERBECK : *Schriftquellen zur Geschichte der Bildenden Künste bei den Griechen* (Leipzig, 1868) = *S. Q.*

PAULY : *Real-Encyclopädie* (new edition, by G. Wissowa, Stuttgart, 1893–).

PREGER : *Inscriptiones Graecae Metricae ex scriptoribus praeter Anthologiam collectae* (Leipzig, 1891).

PRELLER : *Römische Mythologie* (third edition, by H. Jordan, Berlin, 1881).

—— *Griechische Mythologie* (fourth edition, by C. Robert, Berlin, 1894).

RAOUL-ROCHETTE : *Peintures antiques inédites* (Paris, 1836).

REINACH, S. : *Chroniques d'Orient* (1883–1895, reprinted from Revue Archéologique).

—— *Antiquités du Bosphore Cimmérien* (Paris, 1892).

—— *Bronzes figurés de la Gaule Romaine* (Paris, 1894).

REISCH, EMIL : *Griechische Weihgeschenke* (Leipzig, 1890).

ROBERT, C. : *Bild und Lied* (Berlin, 1881).

—— *Die Iliupersis des Polygnot*, Halle'sches Winckelmannsprogramm xvii (Halle, 1893).

—— *Die Marathonschlacht in der Poikile, und weiteres über Polygnot*, Halle'sches Winckelmannsprogramm xviii, 1895.

—— *Votivgemälde eines Apobaten nebst einem Excurs über den sog. Ares Borghese*, Halle'sches Winckelmannsprogramm xix, 1895.

ROSCHER, W. H. : *Lexikon der Griechischen und Römischen Mythologie* (Leipzig, 1884–).

v. SCHNEIDER, ROBERT : *Album auserlesener Gegenstände der antiken Sammlungen des allerh. Kaiserhauses* (Vienna, 1895).

SCHREIBER, THEODOR : *Die Alexandrinische Toreutik* (Leipzig, 1894).

—— *Hellenistische Reliefbilder* (Leipzig, 1894).

SILLIG, JULIUS : *Dictionary of the Artists of Antiquity* (trans. by H. W. Williams, London, 1837).

SUSEMIHL : *Geschichte der Griechischen Literatur in der Alexandrinerzeit* (I, II, Leipzig, 1891, 1892).

TEUFFEL : *Geschichte der Römischen Literatur* (fifth edition, by L. Schwabe, Leipzig, 1890).

TURNEBUS : *Adversariorum libri* xxx (Paris, 1580).

URLICHS, LUDWIG V. : *Anfänge der Griechischen Künstlergeschichte* (Würzburg, 1871, 1872).

—— *Die Malerei in Rom vor Caesar's Dictatur* (Würzburg, 1876).

URLICHS, LUDWIG V. : *Griechische Statuen im Republikanischen Rom* (Würzburg, 1880).

—— *Das hölzerne Pferd* (Würzburg, 1881).

—— *Pergamenische Inschriften* (Würzburg, 1883).

—— *Arkesilaos* (Würzburg, 1887).

WACHSMUTH, C.: *Die Stadt Athen im Alterthum* (I, II, Leipzig, 1874, 1890).

WEISSHÄUPL : *Grabgedichte der Griechischen Anthologie* (Vienna, 1889).

WICKHOFF, FRANZ : *Die Wiener Genesis* (Vienna, 1895).

WINCKELMANN : *Geschichte der Kunst des Alterthums* (first edition, 1763 ; I quote from the Vienna edition of 1776).

—— *History of Ancient Art*, tr. by G. Henry Lodge (London, 1881).

WUNDERER : *Manibiae Alexandrinae, eine Studie zur Geschichte des römischen Kunstraubes* (Würzburg, 1894).

Ann. Inst. = *Annali dell' Istituto di Corrispondenza Archeologica* (Rome, 1829–1885).

Ant. Denkm. = *Antike Denkmäler, herausgegeben vom K. Deutschen Archäologischen Institut* (Berlin, 1887).

Arch. Anz. = *Archäologischer Anzeiger* (a supplement printed at the end of the *Archäologisches Jahrbuch*).

Arch. Ep. Mitth. = *Archäologische Epigraphische Mittheilungen aus Oesterreich-Ungarn.*

A. Z. = *Archäologische Zeitung* (Berlin, 1843–1885).

Ath. Mitth. = *Mittheilungen des K. deutschen Archäologischen Instituts, Athenische Abtheil.* (Athens, 1876–).

Berl. Phil. Woch. = *Berliner Philologische Wochenschrift.*

B. C. H. = *Bulletin de Correspondance Hellénique* (Athens, 1877).

Bull. Inst. = *Bullettino dell' Istituto di Corrispondenza Archeologica* (Rome, 1829–1885).

Class. Rev. = *Classical Review* (London, 1887–).

Δελτ. = Δελτίον Ἀρχαιολογικόν (Athens, 1888–).

'Εφ. 'Αρχ. = 'Εφημερὶς 'Αρχαιολογική (Athens, 1883–).

Fleckeisen's Jahrb. = *Neue Jahrbücher für Philologie u. Pädagogik* (ed. Fleckeisen u. Masius).

Hermes = *Hermes, Zeitschrift für Classische Philologie* (Berlin, 1866–).

Jahrb. = *Jahrbuch des K. deutschen Archäologischen Instituts* (Berlin, 1886–).

J. H. S. = *Journal of Hellenic Studies* (London, 1880–).

Mon. Inst.=Monumenti inediti dell' Istituto di Corrispondenza Archeologica (Rome, 1829–1885).

Rev. Arch.=Revue Archéologique (Paris, 1844–).

Rhein. Mus.=Rheinisches Museum für Philologie.

Röm. Mitth.=Mittheilungen des K. deutschen Archäologischen Instituts, Röm. Abtheil. (Rome, 1886–).

T. J. B.=Topographischer Jahresbericht (contributed to the Römische Mittheilungen).

Woch. f. Klass. Phil.=Wochenschrift für Klassische Philologie (Berlin).

C. I. A.=Corpus Inscriptionum Atticarum (Berlin, 1873–).

C. I. G.=Corpus Inscriptionum Graecarum (Berlin, 1828–1870).

C. I. G. S.=Corpus Inscriptionum Graeciae Septentrionalis (vol. I, Berlin, 1892).

C. I. L.=Corpus Inscriptionum Latinarum (Berlin, 1863–).

C. I. Rhen.=Corpus Inscriptionum Rhenarum (Elberfeld, 1867–).

MANUSCRIPTS REFERRED TO.

Bamb.=the *Codex Bambergensis* M. V. 10, of the ninth to tenth century (see our plate); in the Royal Library at Bamberg (it contains only the last six books of the *Hist. Nat.*).

Ricc.=the *Codex Riccardianus* M. II. ii. 488, written about the year 1100 according to Detlefsen, but probably older; in the *Bibliotheca Riccardiana* at Florence.

Voss.=the *Codex Vossianus Latinus* 61 in folio, of the ninth century (cf. Chatelain, *Paléographie des Classiques Latins*, pl. cxli); in the University Library at Leiden.

Lips.=the *Codex Lipsii* 7 (see Geel, *Cat.* n. 465), copied from the *Vossianus* when this codex was more complete than it is now, and before it had been corrected (cf. Chatelain, pl. cxlii); in the University Library at Leiden.

e corr.=*e correctione* and refers to the corrections introduced into a MS. by a later hand.

reliqui=the remaining codices save the particular codex or codices anywhere quoted.

* * =a corrupt reading which has not yet been satisfactorily restored.

† printed before an artist's name in the English translation signifies that the artist is so far known only from Pliny.

C. PLINII SECUNDI

NATURALIS HISTORIAE

LIBER XXXIII §§ 154–157
LIBER XXXIV §§ 5–93 ; 140–141

(CAELATURA ET STATUARIA)

I. CAELATURA.

154 MIRUM auro caelando neminem inclaruisse, argento
multos. maxime tamen laudatus est Mentor de quo supra
diximus. quattuor paria ab eo omnino facta sunt, ac iam
nullum extare dicitur Ephesiae Dianae templi aut Capitolini
incendiis. Varro se et aereum signum eius habuisse scribit. 5
155 proximi ab eo in admiratione Acragas et Boethus et Mys

§ 154. 2. maxime . . . laudatus:
the silver chasers are arranged in
order of merit in four groups (a) *max.
laudatus*, (b) *proximi ab eo*, (c) *post hos
celebrati*, (d) *item laudantur*. Within
each of these groups the names are
arranged alphabetically, Benndorf, *de
Anthol. Graec. Epigramm. quae ad
artes spectant*, p. 52, note 1. The
main account, derived, through a
Roman source, from some Greek
writer, is interrupted (1) by the
mention of Varro's statue; (2) by a
description (*extant . . . habuit*) of
chased works in Rhodes, drawn presumably from Mucianus (Brieger, *de
Fontibus Plin.* p. 60), Introd. p. lxxxvi;
(3) by the quotation of an epigram.

de quo supra diximus: the reference is to vii, 127, where the cups
of Mentor are again alluded to as
being in the Ephesian and Capitoline
temples. The reader, however, would
naturally think of (xxxiii. 147) *Lucius
uero Crassus orator duos scyphos Men-
toris artificis manu caelatos* HS. c̄ (sc.
emptos habuit); but this statement
being at variance with the present one,
they must have been made indepen-

dently and at different times; the
present passage seems a later addition,
taken straight from vii, 127 (Furtwängler, *Plinius u. s. Quellen*, p. 57,
note 1).

3. quattuor paria: cups are mentioned in pairs, xxxiii, 147 (quoted
above); xxxiv, 47 (*duo pocula Calamidis manu*); below § 156 (*in duobus
scyphis*). It was apparently customary
to decorate the pair with one continuous subject, as is expressly stated
in the case of the cups by Zopyros (cf.
Furtwängler, *Dornauszieher*, p. 96,
note 63) and known from extant instances, e. g. the superb pairs of cups
from Bernay, Schreiber, *Alex. Toreutik*, 54*, 55* (= Babelon, *Cab. des
Antiques*, pl. 51 and 14, with Kentaurs and Kentauresses); *ib.* 67*, 68*;
ib. 63*, 64* (at Naples) = *Mus. Borb.*
xiii, pl. 49.

4. Ephesiae . . . incendiis: vii,
127. The fire, which occurred in B.C.
356, gives us a lower limit for the
date of Mentor. For the numerous
passages in ancient authors referring
to this, the most celebrated silver
chaser of antiquity, see Overbeck's

I. SILVER CHASING.

CURIOUSLY enough, none have become famous as gold chasers, 154 many as chasers of silver. Of these the most esteemed is that *Mentor*, whom I have already mentioned. He made four pairs of cups in all, none of which, it is said, are extant; they perished when the temples of Artemis at Ephesos and of Jupiter on the Capitol were burnt down. Varro speaks of a bronze statue in his possession also from the hand of Mentor. Next to him †*Akragas*, 155 *Boethos*, and *Mys* were had in great admiration. Works by these

---

Schriftquellen, 2169–2181. The Capitoline fire occurred B. C. 83, during the Civil War, Appian, Ἐμφ. i, 83.

§ 5. **Varro**: cf. xxxvi, 41, where Varro is likewise cited both as author and owner.—Like a number of other *caelatores* (so Kalamis, Ariston, Eunikos) Mentor was also a sculptor in bronze.

§ 155. 6. **Acragas**: the name, which is that of the eponymous river-god of Agrigentum (Ailian, Ποικ. Ἱστ. ii, 33), shows him to have been a native of that city, whose early connexion with Rhodes (cf. T. Reinach, *Rev. Arch.* xxiv, 1894, p. 178), would account for the artist seeking a field for his activity in the brilliant and art-loving city of Rhodes (cf. Museogr. Index) founded B.C. 408; at present, however, we have no nearer clue to his date. Against the theory of Th. Reinach, *op. cit.* pp. 170–180, that a chaser Akragas never existed, but was merely assumed owing to a misunderstanding of the legend ΑΚΡΑΓΑΣ on coins inserted as the *umbilici* of silver cups, Hans Dragendorff in *Terra*

Sigillata, p. 58, maintains that when a coin impression decorates the interior of a cup, it is always the only ornament and therefore inadmissible for cups decorated in relief, like those of Akragas. For names derived from river-gods cf. Αἴσηπος, as early as the sixth century (see Fick, *Gr. Personennamen*, p. 347, where a further list of such names is given). That the chaser Akragas appears only in Pliny need not astonish us: to mention only Epigonos (xxxiv, 88), this apparently very famous artist was up to the date of the Pergamene finds known from Pliny alone.

Boethus: xxxiv, 84. Cic. *Verr.* II, iv, 14, § 32 . . . *hydriam Boëthi manu factam.* A gem representing the wounded Philoktetes, signed ΒΟΗΘΟΥ is probably to be referred to him (Furtwängler, *Gemmen m. Künstlerinschriften*, Jahrb. iii, pl. VIII, 21 and p. 216).

Mys: he was a contemporary of Parrhasios (xxxv, 65, 68–73), from

fuere. exstant omnium opera hodie in insula Rhodiorum,
Boethi apud Lindiam Minervam, Acragantis in templo
Liberi patris in ipsa Rhodo Centauros Bacchasque caelati
scyphi, Myos in eadem aede Silenos et Cupidines. Acragantis et venatio in scyphis magnam famam habuit. post 5
156 hos celebratus est Calamis. et Antipater quoque Satyrum
in phiala gravatum somno conlocavisse verius quam caelasse
dictus est. Stratonicus mox Cyzicenus, Tauriscus, item
Ariston et Eunicus Mitylenaei laudantur et Hecataeus et
circa Pompei Magni aetatem Pasiteles, Posidonius Ephesius, 10
Hedys,Thrakides qui proelia armatosque caelavit, Zopyrus
qui Areopagitas et iudicium Orestis in duobus scyphis
HS [XII] aestimatis. fuit et Pytheas cuius duae unciae
✶ X̄ venierunt. Ulixes et Diomedes erant in phialae
157 emblemate Palladium subripientes. fecit idem et cocos 15
magiriscia appellatos parvolis potoriis, e quibus ne exem-

---

11. Hedys, Thrakides] *Furtwängler, Fleckeisen's Jahrb.* v, xxii, 1876,
p. 507 ; hedystrachides *Bamb.* ; iedis thracides *reliqui* ; Hedystrachides *Sillig,
Detlefsen* ; Telesarchides *coni. Dilthey ap. Benndorf, de Epigr.* p. 53.

whose designs he executed the Ken-
tauromachia on the shield of the
Athena Promachos (Paus. i, 28, 2).
The epigram, from a cup at Herakleia
(Athen. xi, p. 782 B), beginning Γραμ-
μαὶ Παρρασίοιο, τέχνα Μυός . . . must
however, owing to the expression
τέχνα τινός, which does not occur in
pre-Imperial times, be a later forgery ;
Preger, *Inscript. Graec. Metr.* p. 142,
note 185.

1. exstant . . . Cupidines: while
the introduction of the word *hodie*
points to a recent authority, the repetition of the artists' names in a different
order, marks the sentence as an interpolation (Introd. p. lxxxvii).

3. Centauros : for the subject cf.
the cups in the Biblioth. Nationale
and in Naples mentioned above.

5. venatio : Dragendorff (*loc. cit.*)
suggests that the hunting scene on the
silvered terra-cotta cups, *Ann. d. Inst.*
1871 Pl. Q, and kindred compositions
may be derived from the *venatio* of

Akragas. in scyphis—the plural as
usual because two cups or perhaps a
set were decorated with one continuous
subject.

6. Calamis : xxxiv, 47, 71.

§ 156. 6. Antipater : the name of
the writer of an epigram has been
substituted for Diodoros, the real
name of the artist, and moreover that
required by the alphabetical arrangement ; cf. *Anth. Plan.* 248

Τὸν Σάτυρον Διόδωρος ἐκοίμισεν, οὐκ
    ἐτόρευσεν.
ἢν νύξῃς, ἐγερεῖς· ἄργυρος ὕπνον ἔχει.
an epigram similar to the one quoted
in the words *gravatum ... caelasse.*
Introd. p. lxviii.

8. Stratonicus : xxxiv, 85 ; he is
mentioned Athen. xi, p. 782 B, among
the ἔνδοξοι τορευταί.

Tauriscus : in xxxvi, 33 Pliny
expressly distinguishes him from the
sculptor of the same name.

9. Ariston, Eunicus . . . Hecataeus : xxxiv, 85.

three are still to be seen in the island of Rhodes: by Boethos in the temple of Athena at Lindos, by Akragas cups with figures of Kentaurs and Bacchantes in the temple of Dionysos in the city of Rhodes, and in the same temple cups by Mys, with figures of Seilenoi and Erotes. Cups decorated round the interior with hunting scenes by Akragas were also well known. Next in merit to these chasers came *Kalamis*, †*Antipater*—whose sleeping Satyr **156** was said to have been not chased but laid to rest within the cup—, *Stratonikos* of Kyzikos, and †*Tauriskos*. Other famous chasers are †*Ariston* and †*Eunikos* of Mitylene, †*Hekataios*, *Pasiteles*, a contemporary of the Great Pompeius, †*Poseidonios* of Ephesos, *Hedys*, †*Thrakides*, whose favourite subjects were battles and warriors, and †*Zopyros*, who represented the court of the Areiopagos and the trial of Orestes on a pair of cups valued at 1,200,000 sesterces [£10,500 circ.]. †*Pytheas* too made a cup weighing two ounces which sold for 10,000 denarii [£350 circ.]; the design on the interior represented Odysseus and Diomedes stealing the Palladion. He further made small drinking cups in the shape of **157** cooks, called μαγειρισκία, the delicate chasing of which was so liable

---

10. **Pasiteles**: xxxv, 156; xxxvi, 39 f. and above § 130. Cic. *de Div.* i. 36, 79 mentions a toreutic work by him representing the infant Roscius wrapped in the coils of a serpent. Possibly Pasiteles was influenced in the presentation of the subject by the 'infant Herakles strangling the snakes' of Zeuxis (xxxv, 63).

Posidonius: xxxiv, 91.

11. **Thrakides**: for the name cf. Fick, *op. cit.* p. 141. The corrupt *Hedys* conceals a name whose initial letter lies between P—T.

12. **Areopagitas . . . Orestis**: i. e. Orestes undergoing his trial before the Areiopagos, the subject being spread over both cups. Cf. Winckelmann, *Mon. Ined.* pl. 151 for a silver cup in the Corsini coll. representing this subject; better reproduced by Michaelis, *Das Corsinische Silbergefäss*, Leipzig, 1859.

13. **fuit et**: like the *habuit et* below, introduces a new artist who had no place in the canonical lists quoted in

Pliny's main authority. Pytheas and Teuker, therefore, lived presumably in the period subsequent to Pasiteles. The continuance of silver chasing at least as late as the reign of Nero is proved by the case of Zenodoros (xxxiv, 47). The decay of which Pliny complains only applies to his own time; nor need we attach too precise a meaning to this, or the similar complaint on the decay of painting in xxxv, 4, both being evidently rhetorical, cf. Oehmichen, *Plinianische Studien*, p. 161 f.; Furtwängler in *Berl. Phil. Wochenschr.*, 1895, p. 814.

14. **Ulixes et Diomedes**: for the subject cf. the celebrated Spada relief, Schreiber, *Hell. Reliefbilder*, pl. VII, the gem, signed Calpurnius Felix, *Jahrbuch* iii, 1888, Pl. x, 7; cf. Furtwängler, *ib.* p. 312; and the relief on the neck of one of the Bernay oinochoai, Babelon, *Cab. des Ant.* pl. 41.

§ 157. 15. **cocos**: [i.e. silver cups in the shape of figurines.—H. L. U.]

16. **magiriscia**: from μάγειρος, a

plaria quidem liceret exprimere, tam opportuna iniuriae
subtilitas erat.   habuit et Teucer crustarius famam, subito-
que ars haec ita exolevit ut sola iam vetustate censeatur,
usuque attritis caelaturis, si nec figura discerni possit, auctoritas constet.   5

II. STATUARIA.

5   QUONDAM aes confusum auro argentoque miscebatur, et
tamen ars pretiosior erat, nunc incertum est peior haec sit
an materia, mirumque, cum ad infinitum operum pretia
creverint, auctoritas artis extincta est.   quaestus enim causa
ut omnia exerceri coepta est quae gloriae solebat—ideo 10
autem etiam deorum adscripta operi, cum proceres gentium
claritatem et hac via quaererent—adeoque exolevit fundendi
aeris pretiosi ratio ut iamdiu ne fortuna quidem in ea re ius
6 artis habeat.   ex illa autem antiqua gloria Corinthium
maxime laudatur.   hoc casus miscuit Corintho, cum cape- 15
retur, incensa, mireque circa id multorum adfectatio furit,
quippe cum tradatur non alia de causa Verrem quem
A.U.C. 711. M. Cicero damnaverat proscriptum cum eo ab Antonio,
quoniam Corinthiis cessurum se ei negavisset.   ac mihi
maior pars eorum simulare eam scientiam videtur ad segre- 20
gandos sese a ceteris magis quam intellegere aliquid ibi
7 suptilius, et hoc paucis docebo.   Corinthus capta est olym-

---

4. si nec] *Urlichs in Chrestom.* p. 301 ; sine *Bamb.*; ne *reliqui, Detlefsen.*
11. autem] *om. omnes praeter Bamb., Detlefsen.*

---

cook. [The subject influenced perhaps
by the Middle or New Comedy.—
H. L. U.]

   2. Teucer: possibly identical with
the gem engraver Τεῦκρος (cf. *Jahrb.*
iii, p. 323).

   crustarius: this shows him to
have been especially a worker of
ἐμβλήματα or *crustae*, i.e. of figures
in relief, wrought separately and
attached to the object to be decorated;
cf. Cic. *Verr.* II, iv, 22, § 49 *duo
pocula non magna, verum tamen cum
emblemate*: also Juv. i, 76.   Add.

   § 5. 6. auro argentoque: up to

now the amount of precious metals
yielded by the analysis of ancient
bronzes is so small as scarcely to warrant Pliny's statement that gold and
silver were regularly employed in
the most ancient Greek alloys; cf.
Blümner, *Technol. u. Terminol.* vol.
iv, p. 178 ff.; O. Müller, *Handbuch*
306, Daremberg and Saglio, s. v. *aes.*

   § 6. 15. hoc casus miscuit: cf.
Florus, ii, 16; this and several other
anecdotes (see in especial Paus. ii, 3, 3,
and Plut. *De Pyth. Or.* 2, p. 395 B)
were invented to account for the origin
of Corinthian bronze when the secret

to injury that it was impossible to take a cast of them. *Teuker* also enjoyed some reputation for his embossed work. The whole art then suddenly disappeared so completely that nowadays we only value wrought silver for its age, and reckon its merit established when the chasing is so worn that the very design can no longer be made out.

II. BRONZE STATUARY.

BRONZE was formerly alloyed with both gold and silver, and yet 5 the workmanship used to be more valuable than the metal; now *Decay of bronze work.* it is hard to say which is worse. It is extraordinary that when the price given for works of art has risen so enormously, art itself should have lost its claim to our respect. The truth is that the aim of the artist, as of every one else in our times, is to gain money, not fame as in the old days, when the noblest of their nation thought art one of the paths to glory, and ascribed it even to the gods. The process of founding valuable bronze is so completely lost that for generations even fortune has not been able to secure the results formerly ensured by skill.

Of the bronzes renowned in antiquity, the Corinthian is the 6 most esteemed. An accident first produced this alloy in the fire *Corinthian bronze.* which followed on the sack of Corinth and the rage for it is marvellously widespread. For instance, there is a story that when Antony proscribed Cicero he also proscribed Verres (whose 43 B.C. condemnation Cicero had once procured), simply because Verres had refused to give up to him his Corinthian bronzes. In my own opinion, however, most people affect a knowledge of the subject solely to exalt themselves above the common herd, without having any real insight into it; this I can prove in a few words. Corinth was taken in the third year of the hundred and 7

of its mixture had been lost. Pliny sees the impossibility of reconciling the story of the Corinthian alloy and the dates of famous statues, but instead of questioning the truth of the story, he proceeds to deny *in toto* the existence of Corinthian bronzes, though it is excellently and repeatedly attested: e.g. Martial, xiv, 172, 177, and often. The reader will feel reminded of the witty satire in Petronius, *Sat.* 50, on Corinthian bronze and its wonderful alloy.

18. **proscriptum ab Antonio:** cf. Seneca Rhetor, *Suas.* vi, vii, *passim.* For the use to which Augustus put the proscriptions, in order to obtain Cor. bronzes, see Suet. *Aug.* 70; cf. Plin. xxxvii, 81, where Nonius is proscribed by Antonius for the sake of a fine opal.

piadis CLVIII anno tertio, nostrae urbis DCVIII, cum ante
saecula fictores nobiles esse desissent, quorum isti omnia
signa hodie Corinthia appellant.   quapropter ad coar-
guendos eos ponemus artificum aetates.   nam urbis nostrae
annos ex supra dicta comparatione olympiadum colligere 5
facile erit.   sunt ergo vasa tantum Corinthia quae isti
elegantiores modo ad esculenta transferunt, modo in lu-
8 cernas aut trulleos nullo munditiarum dispectu.   eius tria
genera : candidum argento nitore quam proxime accedens
in quo illa mixtura praevaluit, alterum in quo auri fulva 10
natura, tertium in quo aequalis omnium temperies fuit.
praeter haec est cuius ratio non potest reddi, quamquam
hominis manu sed ad fortunam temperatur in simulacris
signisque, illud suo colore pretiosum ad iocineris imaginem
vergens, quod ideo hepatizon appellant, procul a Corinthio, 15
longe tamen ante Aegineticum atque Deliacum, quae diu
optinuere principatum.

9   Antiquissima aeris gloria Deliaco fuit mercatus in Delo
celebrante toto orbe, et ideo cura officinis.   tricliniorum
pedibus fulcrisque ibi prima aeris nobilitas, pervenit deinde 20
et ad deum simulacra effigiemque hominum et aliorum
animalium.

10   Proxima laus Aeginetico fuit.   insula et ipsa est, nec
quod ibi gigneretur, sed officinarum temperatura nobilitata.
bos aereus inde captus in foro boario est Romae.   hoc erit 25
exemplar Aeginetici aeris, Deliaci autem Iuppiter in
Capitolio in Iovis Tonantis aede.   illo aere Myron usus

§ 7. 2. fictores : from meaning literally a modeller in clay, the word *fictor*
is extended to workers in bronze ; see
note on xxxv, 153.

4. ponemus . . . aetates : in §§
49–52.

nam : elliptical 'for of course, as
I shall draw from a Greek source,
I shall give them only in Olympiads,'
Furtwängler, *Plinius*, p. 19 ; for the
ellipse cf. xxxv, 137 (*nam Socrates*);
xxxvi, 32 (*nam Myronis illius*), where
see note.

7. lucernas : the familiar oval oil
lamp with flat top.

8. trulleos : apparently identical
with the *pelvis*, a basin to wash hands
or feet.   For a pelvis of bronze cf.
Juv. x, 64 ; for one of Corinthian
bronze, Orelli, 3838.

§ 8. 9. candidum argento : for
some bronze objects found at Suessula,
really containing small quantities of
gold and silver, see Blümner *op. cit.*
p. 184, note 5.

§ 9. 18. Deliaco : mentioned three
times, along with Corinthian bronze by
Cicero, *pro Sext. Rosc. Am.* 46, 133 ;
Verr. II, ii, 34, § 83 ; *ib.* 72, § 176.

mercatus in Delo : i.e. the fair

fifty-eighth Olympiad, that is, the year of Rome 608 [146 B.C.], centuries later than the celebrated workers, whose statues our amateurs still assume to be all of Corinthian bronze. I shall prove that they are wrong by giving the dates of the artists, for it will be easy to turn the Olympiads into years of Rome by referring to the two corresponding dates given above. It follows that the only vessels of Corinthian bronze are those which these connoisseurs use as dishes or lamps or basins, with no regard for their workmanship.

There were three varieties of Corinthian bronze—a white 8 bronze, that shone almost like silver, and contained a very large proportion of that metal; a second, in which a reddish tinge of gold prevailed; and a third, in which the three metals were blended in equal proportions. There is also a fourth alloy, of which no scientific account can be given; it is employed for images and statues, and though it is produced by the hand of man, yet fortune partly determines the result. It is known as ἡπάτιζον from the peculiar tint, verging on liver colour, which is its chief merit. It is inferior to the bronze of Corinth, but superior to those of Aigina and Delos, though these were long thought the best.

The bronze most celebrated in early times was that of Delos, 9 for as all nations resorted to the market of the island, great care *Delian bronze.* was bestowed on the manufacture of bronze. It was first employed there for the feet and framework (Add.) of couches, and afterwards its use was extended to images of the gods, and figures of men and animals.

Aiginetan bronze was the next to become celebrated. Aigina 10 also is an island; it had no mines, but owed its reputation to *Aiginetan bronze.* the admirable alloys produced in its foundries. A bronze bull, *Bull in* taken from Aigina, and now in the Cattle Market at Rome, may *Cattle* stand for an example of Aiginetan bronze, and the Jupiter in the *Market.* temple of Jupiter the Thunderer on the Capitol for an example of *Statue of Jupiter the Thunderer.*

held in connexion with the quinquennial festival of Apollo and Artemis.

21. ad deum simulacra: cf. § 15 *transit deinde ars vulgo ubique ad effigies deorum*: the imagined progress of art from furniture to images of gods and hence to images of men and animals is purely conventional; see Münzer, *Hermes* xxx, 1895, p. 501.

§10. 23. Aeginetico: the alloy was renowned because of the famous artists who employed it. For a vivid picture of the Aiginetan School, see Collignon, *Sculpt. Grecque*, i, 280–307.

25. in foro boario: Tac. *Ann.* xii, 24.

27. Iovis Tonantis aede. Cf. xxxvi, 50. A small temple built (B.C.

est, hoc Polycletus, aequales atque condiscipuli, sed aemu-
latio et in materia fuit.

11   Privatim Aegina candelabrorum superficiem dumtaxat
elaboravit, sicut Tarentum scapos. in his ergo iuncta com-
mendatio officinarum est. nec pudet tribunorum militarium 5
salariis emere, cum ipsum nomen a candelarum lumine
inpositum appareat. accessio candelabri talis fuit Theonis
iussu praeconis Clesippus fullo gibber et praeterea et alio
12 foedus aspectu, emente id Gegania HS L̄. eadem osten-
tante in convivio empta ludibrii causa nudatus atque 10
inpudentia libidinis receptus in torum, mox in testamentum,
praedives numinum vice illud candelabrum coluit et hanc
Corinthiis fabulam adiecit, vindicatis tamen moribus nobili
sepulchro per quod aeterna supra terras Geganiae dedecoris
memoria duraret. sed cum esse nulla Corinthia candelabra 15
constet, nomen id praecipue in his celebratur, quoniam
Mummi victoria Corinthum quidem diruit, sed e compluri-
bus Achaiae oppidis simul aera dispersit.

13   Prisci limina etiam ac valvas in templis ex aere facti-
A.U.C. 587. tavere. invenio et a Cn. Octavio qui de Perseo rege nava- 20
lem triumphum egit factam porticum duplicem ad circum
Flaminium quae Corinthia sit appellata a capitulis aereis
columnarum, Vestae quoque aedem ipsam Syracusana super-
ficie tegi placuisse. Syracusana sunt in Pantheo capita

22) by Augustus near the great temple
of Jupiter Capitolinus to commemorate
his miraculous escape from death by
lightning (Suet *Aug*. 29); *Mon. Ancyr.*
xix, 4, 5; Mommsen, *Res Gestae*,
p. 81. The temple appears on coins
of Augustus, Cohen, *Aug.* 178-180;
184-186. For the bronze statue by
Leochares, see below § 79.

Myron . . . Polycletus, §§ 55-
58.

§ 11. 5. tribunorum . . . salariis:
cf. Juv. iii, 132.

6. a candelarum lumine: the
etymology is Varronian; cf. Varro,
ap. Servius on *Aen.* ii, 225 . . . *ut in
quo figunt candelam candelabrum
appellant, sic in quo deum ponunt*

delubrum   dicunt; and Macrob.
Satur. iii, 4, 2; cf. Martial, xiv, 43.

8. Clesippus: the slave was of
course a Greek (Κλήσιππος). The
story is attested by an inscription (close
of Republic) *C. I. L.* i, 805, *Clesippus-
Gegánius mag. Capit̲ol̲]-mag. luperc.
viat. tr.* apparently belonging to the
sepulchre mentioned in § 12.

§ 13. 19. limina etiam ac valvas:
either of massive bronze or plated,
Marquardt, *Privatleben der Römer*,
p. 223 ff.

20. Cn. Octavio: the portico (built
B.C. 167) stood in the Campus
Martius near the Circus Flaminius
and the theatre of Pompeius. It was
burnt down and rebuilt by Augustus

Delian bronze. Aiginetan bronze was employed by Myron, and *Bronzes used by Myron and Polykleitos.* Delian by Polykleitos. These two artists were contemporaries and fellow-pupils, who carried their rivalry even into their choice of a material.

At Aigina it was the trays, at Tarentum the stems of cande-11 labra which were specially elaborated, so that the efforts of several *Cande-labra.* workshops combine to recommend these utensils. They are things without even a name except the one which they borrow from the light of their own candles, and yet we are not ashamed to give as much for them as the year's pay of a military tribune. Theon, the auctioneer, once included in the same lot as *Story of Clesippus and Gegania.* one of these candelabra a slave, a fuller named Clesippus, who was humpbacked and altogether hideous. The lot was bought for 50,000 sesterces (£440 circ.) by Gegania, who displayed her 12 purchase at a banquet, and exposed Clesippus naked to the ridicule of the company, yet afterwards, through sheer wantonness, made him her lover, and at last her heir. Thus enriched, he worshipped the candelabrum as a deity, providing yet another story about Corinthian bronzes. Morality, however, was avenged in the magnificent tomb that he built only to keep the remembrance of Gegania's infamy alive upon the earth. Although none of these candelabra are really Corinthian, yet they are called so because Mummius destroyed Corinth ; people forget that his victory also scattered the bronzes of various other Greek cities.

In early times the thresholds and folding-doors in temples 13 were commonly made of bronze. I find, too, that Gnaeus *Thresh-olds.* Octavius, who was granted a triumph for his naval victory over 167 B.C. King Perseus, built a gallery with double colonnade by the Circus of Flaminius, called the Corinthian Gallery, from the small bronze capitals of its columns. A decree was also passed that the temple of Vesta should be roofed with plates of Syracusan bronze.

(Festus, p. 178 ; *Mon. Anc.* xix, 4, 2–4. Mommsen, *Res Gestae*, p. 80), after the Dalmatian Triumph, B. C. 33. It must be distinguished from the *porticus Octaviae*, § 31. *Invenio* shows that Pliny is quoting from an ancient authority; either the building no longer existed in his day, or the outer colonnade had not been restored after the fire, so that the remarks as to the columns apply to the pre-Augustan building. (See O. Gilbert, *Gesch. u.*

Top. der Stadt Rom iii, p. 250, n. 2.)

23. **Vestae** . . . tegi : cf. xxxiii, 57.

24. **placuisse** : probably after the great fire of B.C. 241, cf. vii, 141.

in **Pantheo** : built (B. C. 27) by Agrippa in his third consulate. This earlier building was altered to its present shape in the reign of Hadrian. For recent discoveries and literature, cf. C. Hülsen in *T. J. B.* iv, p. 305 (*Röm. Mitth.* viii, 1893) and Gardthausen *Augustus* ii, p. 430 f.

columnarum a M. Agrippa posita. quin etiam privata opu-
lentia eo modo usurpata est. Camillo inter crimina obiecit
A.U.C. 363. Spurius Carvilius quaestor ostia quod aerata haberet in
domo.

14   Nam triclinia aerata abacosque et monopodia Cn. 5
Manlium Asia devicta primum invexisse triumpho suo quem
duxit anno urbis DLXVII L. Piso auctor est, Antias quidem
heredes L. Crassi oratoris multa etiam triclinia aerata vendidisse. ex aere factitavere et cortinas tripodum nomine
Delphicas, quoniam donis maxime Apollini Delphico dica- 10
bantur. placuere et lychnuchi pensiles in delubris aut
arborum mala ferentium modo lucentes, quale est in templo
Apollinis Palatini quod Alexander Magnus Thebarum ex-
A.U.C. 419. pugnatione captum in Cyme dicaverat eidem deo.

15   Transiit deinde ars vulgo ubique ad effigies deorum. 15
Romae simulacrum ex aere factum Cereri primum reperio
A.U.C. 270. ex peculio Spuri Cassi quem regnum adfectantem pater
ipsius interemerit. transit et a diis ad hominum statuas

9. nomine] nomine ac *Bamb.*; nomine a *Voss.*

3. **Spurius Carvilius**: his part in
the trial is mentioned only by Pliny.

ostia quod aerata: καὶ δῆτα καὶ
θύραι τινὲς ἐλέγοντο χαλκαῖ παρ'
αὐτῷ φανῆναι τῶν αἰχμαλώτων. Plut.
Camill. xii.

§ 14. 5. **abacosque**: the use of
abaci as sideboards appears really to
date from the conquest of Asia, Marquardt, *Privatleben*, p. 319.

Cn. Manlium: Liv. xxxix, 6, 7
*ii primum lectos aeratos . . . et quae
tum magnificae supellectilis habe-
bantur monopodia et abacos Romam
advexerunt.*

6. **Asia devicta**: cf. xxxiii, 148.

7. **L. Piso**: Lucius Calpurnius
Piso, surnamed Frugi; cos. B.C. 133;
frequently quoted by Pliny, Teuffel,
G. R. L. § 132, 4.

Antias, Valerius, fl. ab. 45 B.C.;
frequently quoted by Pliny; Teuffel,
§ 155, 2.

9. **nomine**: cf. Diodoros, xvi, 26.
The corrupt *ac* of the MSS. must

arise from a copyist's misunderstanding
of *Delphicas* as a separate object.

11. **lychnuchi**: originally lamp-
stands (λυχνοῦχοι), whence the name
was transferred to the whole candelabrum, Marquardt, *op. cit.* p. 711;
Daremberg et Saglio, s.v. *candelabrum.*

pensiles: Verg. *Aen* i, 726; Petron.
Sat. 30 *et lucerna bilychnis de camera
pendebat.*

12. **quale**: sc. *candelabrum*, to be
supplied from § 12.

templo Apollinis: dedicated by
Augustus B.C. 27, cf. xxxvi, 32.

§ 15. 15. **Transiit . . . ars**: note
on § 9.

16. **simulacrum**: restricted as
usual to images of the gods, while
statua is more particularly used for
mortals. The notion that the Cassian
simulacrum was the first of its kind
at Rome is in flagrant contradiction to the mention in § 33 of a
Hercules, consecrated by Evander and
of Numa's Janus; moreover since in

Syracusan bronze was also employed by Marcus Agrippa for the capitals of the columns in his Pantheon. Wealthy individuals even adopted this fashion for their private houses. The quaestor Spurius Carvilius accused Camillus among other things of having had bronze plated doors to his house. 391 B.C. *Plated doors.*

The practice of using bronze for couches, side-boards and tables supported on a single foot, was first introduced, according to Lucius Piso, by Gnaeus Manlius, after the conquest of Asia, when he triumphed in the year of Rome 567 [187 B.C.]. Antias adds that the heirs of Lucius Crassus, the orator, sold a number of bronze couches. The cauldrons of tripods were also made of bronze; they were called *Delphicae*, because they were the gift most frequently dedicated to the Delphic Apollo. Hanging lamps in shrines were also made of bronze, and lamps with the lights fixed like apples on trees, as for instance, the lamp now in the temple of Apollo of the Palatine, which Alexander the Great carried off when he took Thebes, and dedicated, also to Apollo, at Kyme. 14 *Household furniture.* *Delphic tripods.* *Hanging lamps.* 335 B.C.

Later on bronze was universally employed for statues of the gods. I find that at Rome the first bronze image was made in honour of Ceres out of the confiscated property of Spurius Cassius, who was put to death by his father because he aimed at becoming king. From figures of the gods, bronze came to be used in various ways for statues and images of men. The 15 *Statues of gods and of mortals.* 484 B.C.

§§ 21, 29, a whole series of portraits from the period of the Kings and early Republic are mentioned, it is irreconcilable with the theory that art progressed from the statues of gods to those of men. Pliny is quoting from a variety of sources, without even attempting to harmonize them.

Cereri: in her temple near the Great Circus, vowed by Aulus Postumius the victor at Regillus, B.C. 493; for its paintings and plastic decorations see xxxv, 154.

17. pater ipsius: cf. Liv. ii, 41, 10 *sunt, qui patrem auctorem eius supplicii ferant : eum cognita domi causa verberasse ac necasse, peculiumque filii Cereri consecravisse ; signum inde factum esse et inscriptum 'ex Cassia familia datum.'* Dionysios (viii, 79),

on the other hand, speaks of several statues. The story involves a complicated problem. There is much to commend the view of Gilbert, *Rom* ii, p. 243, note 2 *s. f.* that the consecration to Ceres, the special patroness of the plebeians, of the private property of Cassius was an extension—more accurately an ironic application (*Verhöhnung*) of the *lex sacrata* for the protection of the Trib. Pl. (cf. Liv. iii, 55) *ut qui trib. pl. nocuisset eius caput Ioui sacrum esset, familia ad aedem Cereris Liberi Liberaeque venum iret ;* Dionys. x, 42 where the Patricians who offend against the assembly of the people convened under the Tribunes are punished by confiscation of their property to Ceres (τὰς οὐσίας αὐτῶν ἱερὰς εἶναι Δήμητρος).

atque imagines multis modis. bitumine antiqui tinguebant
eas, quo magis mirum est placuisse auro integere. hoc
nescio an Romanum fuerit inventum, certe etiam Romae
16 non habet vetustatem. effigies hominum non solebant ex-
primi nisi aliqua inlustri causa perpetuitatem merentium, 5
primo sacrorum certaminum victoria maximeque Olympiae,
ubi omnium qui vicissent statuas dicari mos erat, eorum
vero qui ter ibi superavissent ex membris ipsorum simili-
17 tudine expressa, quas iconicas vocant. Athenienses nescio
an primis omnium Harmodio et Aristogitoni tyrannicidis 10
publice posuerint statuas. hoc actum est eodem anno quo
A.U.C. 245. et Romae reges pulsi. excepta deinde res est a toto orbe
terrarum humanissima ambitione, et in omnium municipiorum
foris statuae ornamentum esse coepere prorogarique memoria
hominum et honores legendi aevo basibus inscribi, ne in 15
sepulcris tantum legerentur. mox forum et in domibus
privatis factum atque in atris honos clientium instituit sic
colere patronos.

18   Togatae effigies antiquitus ita dicabantur. placuere et
nudae tenentes hastam ab epheborum e gymnasiis exem- 20
plaribus, quas Achilleas vocant. Graeca res nihil velare,

19. ita] ista *Riccard., Voss.* (*e corr.*); sta *Voss.*

1. **bitumine**: in order to give a
patina to the new bronze.

2. **auro**: xxxiii, 61, 82; xxxiv, 63.
The custom of gilding statues was
known in Greece, cf. the gilt statue
of Gorgias of Leontinoi, Paus. x, 18,
7 (Plin. xxxiii, 83, where, however,
it is stated that the Gorgias was of
solid gold), and the gilt Phryne by
Praxiteles, Paus. x, 15, 1; cf. Blümner,
Technol. iv, p. 308 ff.

4. **non habet vetustatem**: the
oldest recorded Roman instance of a
statua aurata is to M'. Acilius Glabrio
(B.C. 131), Liv. xl, 34, 5 *quae prima
omnium in Italia est statua aurata.*

§ 16. 6. **Olympiae**: the long
list of athlete statues began with the
ancient cypress wood statue of Praxi-
damas of Aigina, who won the prize

for boxing, Ol. 59 (= B.C. 544). Paus.
vi, 18, 7.

7. **ubi omnium . . . iconicas
vocant**: Lessing has made these
words the text for a famous passage
in the *Laokoon* (ii, § 13). Visconti
(*Iconographie Grecque*, Discours pré-
lim. p. viii, n. 4) arguing from Lucian,
ὑπὲρ τῶν εἰκόνων xi, takes *iconicas* to
mean ' grand comme nature '; Prof.
Klein, however, in a note which he
kindly allows me to publish, points
out that Pliny's statement bears an
apocryphal character, which has escaped every one save perhaps Blümner
in his Comm. on Lessing's *Laokoon*,
p. 503. It is evident that the discrepancies between ideal and iconic
statues were explained by Pliny,
or his author, as the result of an

ancients tinted the figures with bitumen, which makes the later practice of gilding them the more curious. This may very well be a Roman invention, and certainly even at Rome it is not of great antiquity. The ancients did not make any statues of **16** individuals unless they deserved immortality by some distinction, *Victors at Olympia.* originally by a victory at some sacred games, especially those of Olympia, where it was the custom to dedicate statues of all those who had conquered, and portrait statues if they had conquered three times. These are called *iconic.* (See Addenda.)

The Athenians were, I believe, introducing a new custom **17** when they set up statues at the public expense in honour of *Public benefactors.* Harmodios and Aristogeiton, who killed the tyrants. This occurred in the very year in which the kings were expelled from **509** B.C. Rome. A refined ambition led to the universal adoption of the custom, and statues began to adorn the public places of every town ; the memories of men were immortalized, and their honours were no longer merely graven on their tombstones, but handed down for posterity to read on the pedestals of statues. Later on the rooms and halls of private houses became so many public places, and clients began to honour their patrons in this way.

Formerly statues were dedicated wearing the toga. Nude **18** statues holding a spear were also in favour, modelled after young *Draped and nude* men in the gymnasia ; these were called Achillean. The Greek *statues.*

improbable rule, simply because the ancients had no habit of applying historical criticism to art, and consequently of discriminating between the works of a time when only the type was aimed at, from those of periods when art had advanced to individual portraiture. It is instructive to compare with Pliny's words a passage in Dio Chrysostom, *Or.* xxi, 1 περὶ κάλλους, where he attempts to explain the difference between the statues of an earlier and a later date by alleging physical degeneration. The difference observable in the Olympic statues generally, distinguished *pre-* from *post-* Lysippian portraiture; as it is very well said in xxxv, 153 *hic* (Lysistratos) *et similitudines reddere instituit, ante eum quam pulcherrimas facere studebatur.*

§ 17. 10. **Harmodio et Aristogi-**

toni: below § 70.

§ 18. 19. **togatae effigies**: such as the statues of the kings, § 23.

20. **tenentes hastam**: statues of athletes in the scheme of the Polykleitan Doryphoros, or leaning on their spear. *Achilleas* (from Achilles, the typical hero of the ephebes) a convenient generic term under which to group such portraits, Furtwängler, *Plinius,* p. 47, note 11. The custom of portraying mortals other than athletes in heroic nudity *during their lifetime,* seems to have been introduced by Alexander and his successors ; cf. the bronze portrait of a Hellenistic ruler in the Museo delle Terme (Helbig, *Class. Ant.* 1052).

21. **Graeca . . . addere**: no precise historical information can be drawn from these words, which merely contain a broad comparison between

at contra Romana ac militaris thoraces addere. Caesar quidem dictator loricatam sibi dicari in foro suo passus est. nam Lupercorum habitu tam noviciae sunt quam quae A.U.C. 617. nuper prodiere paenulis indutae. Mancinus eo habitu sibi 19 statuit quo deditus fuerat. notatum ab auctoribus et 5 L. Accium poetam in Camenarum aede maxima forma statuam sibi posuisse, cum brevis admodum fuisset. equestres utique statuae Romanam celebrationem habent orto sine dubio a Graecis exemplo, sed illi celetas tantum dicabant in sacris victores, postea vero et qui bigis vel quadrigis 10 vicissent. unde et nostri currus nati in iis qui triumphavissent. serum hoc, et in his non nisi a divo Augusto seiuges, aut elephanti.

20 Non vetus et bigarum celebratio in iis qui praetura functi curru vecti essent per circum, antiquior columnarum, 15 sicuti C. Maenio qui devicerat priscos Latinos, quibus ex

13. aut] *E. Sellers*; sicut *codd.*, *Detlefsen.*

the typical Greek athlete statues and the numerous Roman portraits of late Republican and Imperial times.

1. **thoraces**: the statue of Augustus in the Vatican, Helbig, *Class. Ant.* 4, well illustrates the combination of the military element with the nude athletic type. As a reminiscence of the athlete statues the legs are left bare, but the Emperor wears the cuirass, with the mantle rolled round below the waist.

2. **loricatam**, sc. **effigiem**: belonging to the class of statues just mentioned, of which there are numerous examples, see Rohden in *Bonner Studien*, pp. 1–80. Very little is known about this particular statue of Caesar or the spot in his Forum where it stood. Pliny the Younger (*Ep.* viii, 6, 14) says that a decree of the Senate in favour of Pallas, the freedman of Claudius, was put up *ad statuam loricatam divi Iulii.*

3. **Lupercorum**, i. e. with only a goatskin about the loins, like the priests of Lupercus at the festival of the Lupercalia (Ov. *Fast.* v. 101).

5. **quo deditus fuerat**: *nudus ac*

post tergum religatis manibus Vell. Paterc. II, i, 5.

not. ab auctoribus: probably the statue was no longer extant when Pliny wrote.

§ **19. 6. L. Accium**: the tragic poet, B. C. 170–103. There is no reliable copy of the statue, Bernoulli, *Röm. Iconographie*, i, p. 289.

Camenarum = Musarum, in the first region, *Porta Capena.*

10. **postea vero**: the notion that art progressed from the representations of statues of horsemen to chariot-groups, is in harmony with the formalizing theories of the growth of art, hinted in § 9 and § 15, but it is the inverse of fact (cf. Münzer, *op. cit.* p. 502): the race with four-horsed chariots was introduced at Olympia, Ol. 25 (B. C. 680), the race on horseback (ἵππος κέλης), Ol. 33 (B. C. 648), and the race with two-horsed chariots, Ol. 93 (B. C. 408). The earliest monument of a victor on his four-horsed chariot was that of Kleosthenes of Epidamnos by Hagelaidas, Ol. 66 (B. C. 516), Paus. vi, 10, 2.

custom was to leave the body quite nude; but the Roman and military custom was to add a breastplate, while Caesar, when Dictator, allowed a statue of himself wearing a cuirass to be set up in his forum. Statues in the dress of the Lupercals are as recent an innovation as those lately introduced wearing short cloaks. Mancinus set up a statue in his own honour, wearing the dress in which he had been given up to the enemy. I find it mentioned by some authors that Lucius Accius the poet set up in his own honour in the temple of the Camenae a statue, which was of great size, although he was a very small man. *Lupercals. C. Hostillius Mancinus; 137 B.C. 19 Lucius Accius.*

Equestrian statues, which are so common at Rome, were undoubtedly first borrowed from Greece. The Greeks, however, only dedicated equestrian statues of those who had been victors on horseback at the sacred games; later on we find statues of the victors in the two and four-horse chariot races. From this arose our custom of setting up chariots in honour of those who had triumphed. Until recent times this was unknown, and chariots drawn by six horses or by elephants were only introduced by the god Augustus. *Equestrian statues. Chariots.*

The erection of two-horse chariots in honour of those who as praetors have led the procession round the Circus is also of late date. The custom of erecting statues on columns is more ancient, witness the column in honour of Gaius Maenius, conqueror of the Ancient Latins, a people to whom the Romans were *20 Statues on columns. G. Maenius.*

---

11. **currus**: Juv. viii, 3, mentions the statue of a *triumphator* standing erect in his triumphal car in the *vestibulum*.

13. **seiuges**: a gilt chariot, drawn by six horses, had already been dedicated to Jupiter Capitolinus in B.C. 169, by the Consul P. Cornelius (*seiuges in Capitolio aurati* Liv. xxxviii, 35, 4). Pliny's meaning must be that under Augustus the team of six horses was first used for other than religious purposes. Mommsen, *Staatsrecht*, i, 3rd ed. p. 395, n. 1, points out that, according to Dio Cassius, lix, 7, Caligula was the first to drive in the circus with six horses: τὸ ἅρμα τὸ πομπικόν . . . ἐξ ἵπποι εἴλκυσαν· ὃ μήπώποτε ἐγεγόνει.

elephanti: from Pliny's words

it might be inferred that *triumphal* chariots were drawn by elephants as early as Augustus, whereas this occurred for the first time in the reign of Alexander Severus, cf. Aelius Lampridius, *Vita Al. Sev.* 57, 4. The chariots drawn by elephants on early imperial coins refer to the *Pompa circensis*, Marquardt, *Staatsverw.* ii, p. 586, note 7. Addenda.

§ 20. 15. per circum, sc. *Maximum*, on the occasion of the *Ludi Apollinares*, instituted B.C. 212. For the praetorial *biga*, cf. Mommsen, *Staatsrecht*, i, 3rd ed., p. 394, note 4; pp. 412, 447.

columnarum: from § 26 it is evident that the *columnae* were statues placed on high pedestals.

16. **C. Maenio**: cf. vii, 212. He

foedere tertias praedae populus R. praestabat, eodemque
in consulatu in suggestu rostra devictis Antiatibus fixerat
anno urbis CCCCXVI, item C. Duillio qui primus navalem
A.U.C. 494. triumphum egit de Poenis, quae est etiam nunc in foro,
21 item L. Minucio praefecto annonae extra portam Trige- 5
A.U.C. 315. minam unciaria stipe conlata—nescio an primo honore tali
a populo, antea enim a senatu erat—praeclara res, nisi
frivolis coepisset initiis. namque et Atti Navi statua fuit
A.U.C. 702. ante curiam—basis eius conflagravit curia incensa P. Clodii
A.U.C. 304. funere—fuit et Hermodori Ephesii in comitio, legum quas 10
22 decemviri scribebant interpretis, publice dicata. alia causa,
alia auctoritas M. Horati Coclitis statuae, quae durat hodie-
A.U.C. 246. que, cum hostes a ponte sublicio solus arcuisset. equidem
et Sibyllae iuxta rostra esse non miror, tres sint licet: una
quam Sextus Pacuius Taurus aed. pl. restituit, duae quas 15
M. Messalla. primas putarem has et Atti Navi, positas

had conquered the Latins with Furius
Camillus ; *additus triumpho honos,
ut statuae equestres eis, rara illa
aetate res, in foro ponerentur* Liv.
viii, 13, 9. The statue of Camillus had
stood on the old Rostra (§ 23), and
was apparently still extant in the days
of Pliny the Younger (see *Paneg.* 55,
6). The exact site of the statue of
Maenius is unknown, cf. Jacobi,
Museographie, p. 60.

1. ex foedere, i. e. the treaty concluded by Sp. Cassius in B.C. 493,
cf. *Röm. Forsch.* ii, p. 163, note 22.

2. Antiatibus : the orator's platform was from that time called the
rostra (Liv. viii, 14, 12). For its
statues, see Gilbert, *Rom*, p. 153, note 3.

3. C. Duillio : a portion of the inscribed basis, restored in antiquity,
belonging to the *columna Duilia*, was
found in 1565 (Helbig, *Class. Ant.* 543;
C. I. L. i, 195).

4. de Poenis. After the battle
of Mylae, B.C. 260.

§ 21. 5. L. Minucio : his column,
surmounted by the statue, is shown on
the reverse of a denarius of B.C. 129
of C. Minucius Augurinus (Babelon,

Monn. de la Rép. Rom., ii, p. 228;
Mommsen, *Röm. Münzw.* p. 550, no.
265). Livy, iv, 16, 2, mentions only
a gilt ox erected in honour of Minucius.

praefecto annonae : Liv. iv, 12, 8,
cf. Hirschfeld, *Verwaltungsgeschichte*,
p. 134.

6. unciaria stipe collata: according to Mommsen, *Staatsrecht*, iii,
p. 1185, note 3, this possibly means
that the expenses were met by volun-
tary contributions, whereas they otherwise fell to the *Aerarium*.

8. frivolis, because the statue was
set up in honour of the supposed
miracles of the whet-stone (Liv. i, 36)
and of the *Ficus ruminalis.* For
Pliny's scepticism in these matters see
xv, 77.

Atti Navi : he was represented
as under average height, and wearing
the priestly fillet (Dionysios iii, 71,
5). The statue stood on the left of
the steps leading up to the curia
(Livy, *loc. cit.*). The mention of
this statue, in confirmation of the
statement *antea enim a senatu*, brings
with it a long digression, thoroughly

bound by treaty to give one third of the spoils taken in war. In the same consulship, in the year of Rome 416 [338 B.C.], he defeated the people of Antium, and fixed the beaks of their ships upon the platform in the forum. Another column, in honour of Gaius Duillius, who enjoyed the first naval triumph for his victory over the Carthaginians, is still standing in the forum. Another was set up outside the Porta Trigemina, in honour of Lucius Minucius, chief commissioner of the corn supply, and for it a rate of one twelfth of an *as* was levied. This was, I believe, the first time this honour was conferred by the people, for previously it had been left in the hands of the Senate. Certainly the distinction were an honourable one save for the slight grounds for which it was first conferred. For instance, there was in front of the Senate House a statue of Attus Navius, the base of which was destroyed when the Senate House was burnt down at the funeral of Publius Clodius, and in the comitium there was another, dedicated at the public expense, of Hermodoros, the Ephesian, who expounded the laws drawn up by the Decemvirs. Very different were the reasons which entitled Horatius Cocles to the statue which is still standing: single-handed he had held the Sublician bridge against the foe. Nor am I astonished that a statue, or even three statues, of the Sibyl should stand near the Rostra. One of these was replaced by Sextus Pacuvius Taurus, when plebeian aedile, and the two others by Marcus Messala. I should consider these statues and that of Attus Navius, which date from the reign of Tarquin the Ancient, to be the earliest we have, were it not that on the Capitol

The 'Rostra.'

C. Duillius; 260 B.C.

21

Lucius Minucius. 439 B.C.

Statue of Attus Navius. 52 B.C.

Hermodoros; 450 B.C.

22

Horatius Cocles. 508 B.C.

The three Sibyls.

---

in Pliny's manner, on ancient statues in Rome; the subject of the statues raised on columns is not resumed till § 27.

fuit, i.e. the statue had disappeared when Pliny wrote.

10. **Hermodori**: cf. Strabo xiv, p. 642; Cic. *Tusc. Disp.* v, 36, 105. The statue presumably stood in front of the old rostra, by the Twelve Tables upon which the laws were inscribed. It had been removed in Pliny's day, cf. Jacobi, *Museographie*, p. 50.

§ 22. **12. Horati Coclitis**: below § 29. The statue stood *in comitio* Liv. ii, 10, 12; afterwards removed to

the *area Volcani* Aul. Gell. iv, 5, 1. Cocles was represented full-armed, with perhaps an indication of his lameness, Dionysios v, 25; Plut. *Publ.* xvi.

14. **iuxta rostra**, i.e. the old rostra. These new Sibyls are probably identical with the τρία φᾶτα mentioned by Procop. *De Bell. Goth.* i, 25, p. 122, as standing between the curia and the temple of Janus (O. Gilbert, *Rom*, iii, p. 228, note 2).

15. **Sextus Pacuius Taurus**, probably identical with the trib. pl., B.C. 27.

aetate Tarquinii Prisci, ni regum antecedentium essent in
23 Capitolio. ex his Romuli et Tatii sine tunica, sicut et
Camilli in rostris. et ante aedem Castorum fuit Q. Marci
Tremuli equestris togata, qui Samnites bis devicerat capta-
A.U.C. 448. que Anagnia populum stipendio liberaverat.   inter anti- 5
quissimas sunt et Tulli Cloeli, L. Rosci, Spuri Nauti,
A.U.C. 316. C. Fulcini in rostris, a Fidenatibus in legatione interfectorum.
24 hoc a re p. tribui solebat iniuria caesis, sicut aliis et P. Iunio,
A.U.C. 524. Ti. Coruncanio, qui ab Teuta Illyriorum regina interfecti
erant.   non omittendum videtur quod annales adnotavere 10
tripedaneas iis statuas in foro statutas.   haec videlicet mensura honorata tunc erat.   non praeteribo et Cn. Octavium
ob unum SC. verbum.   hic regem Antiochum daturum se
responsum dicentem virga quam tenebat forte circum-
scripsit priusque quam egrederetur circulo illo responsum 15
A.U.C. 592. dare coegit.   in qua legatione interfecto senatus statuam
poni iussit quam oculatissimo loco, eaque est in rostris.
25 invenitur statua decreta et Taraciae Gaiae sive Fufetiae
virgini Vestali, ut poneretur ubi vellet, quod adiectum
non minus honoris habet quam feminae esse decretam. 20
meritum eius ipsis ponam annalium verbis : quod campum
Tiberinum gratificata esset ea populo.

1. regum. Cf. xxxiii, 9, 10, 24.

in Capitolio: cf. Appian, 'Εμφ.
i, 16, where Tib. Gracchus is killed
by the doors of the temple of Capitoline
Jupiter near the statues of the kings.

§ 23. 2. sine tunica, i. e. wrapped
in the toga alone, cf. Aul. Gell. vi,
12; Asconius (on Cic. pro Scaur. 30)
says that the younger Cato as praetor
used to lay aside the tunic *ex vetere
consuetudine, secundum quam et
Romuli et Tatii statuae in Capitolio
et in rostris Camilli fuerunt togatae
sine tunicis.* The difference of costume
shows that the statues of the kings were
put up at different dates. Pliny's information seems derived from Verrius,
cf. xxxiii, 63 *tunica aurea triumphasse
Tarquinium Priscum Verrius docet.*

et Camilli : see the passage from
Asconius quoted above.

3. Q. Marci Tremuli: Liv. ix, 43,
22 *statua equestris in foro decreta
est quae ante templum Castoris posita
est*; cf. Cic. *Phil.* vi, 5, 13. For a possible echo of the statue see Mommsen,
Röm. Münzw. p. 549, n. 263.

qui . . . liberaverat : these words
appear to come from an inscription
in Saturnine verse, qui bís devícit
Sámni | -teís Anágniámque ‖ cepít
populúm stipéndi | ó líberavit (Urlichs
in *Chrestom.* p. 307).

5. stipendio : according to the
treaty concluded by Sp. Cassius in
B. C. 486, the Hernicans had been entitled to a third of the war booty;
on this clause see Mommsen, *Röm.
Forsch.* ii, p. 163, n. 22.

inter antiquissimas sunt : the
use of the present shows that
Pliny is transcribing direct from his

we have the statues of Tarquin's predecessors. Among these the figures of Romulus and Tatius are without the tunic, and so is that of Camillus on the Rostra. In front of the temple of Castor there also stood an equestrian statue of Quintus Marcius Tremulus wearing the toga. He had conquered the Samnites in two battles, and by taking Anagnia had freed Rome from payment of the war tax. The statues on the Rostra to Tullus Cloelius, Lucius Roscius, Spurius Nautius, and Gaius Fulcinus, ambassadors killed by the people of Fidenae, are also among the earliest. This honour was usually paid by the state to those who had been killed in violation of the law of nations; it was done in many cases, notably that of Publius Junius and Tiberius Coruncanius, who were put to death by Teuta, queen of Illyricum. It is worth noticing that according to the annals the statues set up in the forum on these occasions were three feet high; apparently this was the height in vogue in those days. I shall mention the statue of Gnaeus Octavius, on account of one clause in the decree of the Senate. King Antiochos had wished to delay an answer, whereupon Octavius drew a circle round him with a rod which he chanced to have in his hand, and compelled the king to give an answer before he stepped outside the circle. Octavius was killed while on this embassy, and the Senate ordered a statue to be set up in his honour 'in as visible a place as possible': the statue accordingly stands on the Rostra. I find a decree giving a statue to Taracia Gaia or Fufetia, a Vestal virgin, 'to be placed where she pleased,' a clause no less to her honour than the actual dedication of a statue to a woman. According to the words of the annals, which I will quote, she received these honours *'because she had presented to the people the field by the Tiber.'*

23 Ancient kings.

Q. M. Tremulus.

306 B.C.

Roman ambassadors killed by the Fidenates.

438 B.C.

24

230 B.C. Publius Junius and Tiberius Coruncanius.

Cn. Octavius.

162 B.C.

25 Taracia Gaia.

author; the statues had already disappeared in Cicero's time: *Lars Tolumnius rex Veientium quattuor legatos populi Romani Fidenis interemit, quorum statuae steterunt usque ad meam memoriam in rostris. Phil.* ix, 2, 4.

§ 24. 8. P. Iunio, Ti. Coruncanio. Polybios, ii, p. 131 (ed. Büttner-Wobst), calls them Γάϊος and Λεύκιος (Κορογκάνιοι). They had been sent to put down piracy on the Illyrian coast.

11. **tripedaneas** refers not only to the last-mentioned statues, but also to those of the ambassadors to the Fidenates.

12. **Cn. Octavium,** § 13, murdered at Laodicea in B.C. 162; cf. Cic. *Phil.* ix, 2, 4 *statuam videmus in rostris.* By a confusion Pliny attributes to Octavius an act performed by C. Popilius Laenas, on the occasion of his embassy to Antiochus IV Epiphanes in B.C. 168, Cic. *Phil.* viii, 8, 23; Liv. xlv, 12.

§ 25. 18. **Taraciae Gaiae sive Fufetiae ... populo:** this curious

26   Invenio et Pythagorae et Alcibiadi in cornibus comitii
A.U.C. 411. positas, cum bello Samniti Apollo Pythius iussisset
fortissimo Graiae gentis et alteri sapientissimo simulacra
A.U.C. 666. celebri loco dicari. eae stetere donec Sulla dictator ibi
curiam faceret. mirumque est illos patres Socrati cunctis 5
ab eodem deo sapientia praelato Pythagoran praetulisse
aut tot aliis virtute Alcibiaden et quemquam utroque
27 Themistocli. columnarum ratio erat attolli super ceteros
mortales, quod et arcus significant novicio invento. primus
tamen honos coepit a Graecis, nullique arbitror plures 10
statuas dicatas quam Phalereo Demetrio Athenis, siquidem
CCCLX statuere nondum anno hunc numerum dierum
A.U.C. 670. excedente, quas mox laceravere. statuerunt et Romae in

8. tolli *omnes praeter Bamb.*, *Detlefsen.*

statement is best examined in the light of a passage from Aulus Gellius, vii, 7, 1–4 *Accae Larentiae et Gaiae Taraciae, sive illa Fufetia est, nomina in* antiquis annalibus *celebria sunt. earum alterae post mortem, Taraciae autem vivae amplissimi honores a populo Romano habiti. et Taraciam quidem virginem Vestalem fuisse lex Horatia testis est, quae super ea ad populum lata. qua lege ei plurimi honores fiunt, inter quos ius quoque testimonii dicendi tribuitur* 'testabilis'*que una omnium feminarum ut sit datur. id verbum est legis ipsius* Horatiae ; con*trarium est in* duodecim tabulis *scriptum :* improbus intestabilisque esto. *praeterea si quadraginta annos nata sacerdotio abire ac nubere voluisset, ius ei potestasque exaugurandi atque nubendi facta est munificentiae et beneficii gratia, quod campum Tiberinum sive Martium populo condonasset.* Though the personality of Taracia is clearly defined in this passage, it cannot be supposed that the region of the Campus Martius had been so late as republican times in the possession of a single person, and that a Vestal virgin ; close examination shows the aitiological nature of the whole story.

The privileges granted to Taracia are simply the common privileges of all the Vestals ; in order to account for these the story of the gift of the land was adapted from the myth of Acca Larentia. Taracia is in fact a mere double of Larentia ; her name betrays an evident connexion with Tarutius, the Tuscan husband of Acca Larentia, to whom he leaves the Ager Turax, i. e. the Campus Tiberinus (Plut. *Rom.* v.), which Larentia in turn bequeaths to the Roman people ; a genuine myth which has for kernel the fact that the region of the Campus Martius had once been Etruscan (see Plut. *Publ.* viii, where the story of the gift and the privileges is substantially the same, but the name of the heroine is Ταρκυνία ; cf. Liv. ii, 5, 2 *ager Tarquiniorum*). A statue was possibly put up to the mythical Vestal, benefactress of the Romans, but as no statue is mentioned either by Gellius or Plutarch (see Detlefsen, *De Art. Rom. Ant.* ii, p. 13), and as Pliny does not say he saw the statue, but merely that the annals stated that one was decreed, it is probable that the statue only existed in the anecdote, and that its mention represented what was

I find that statues of Pythagoras and Alkibiades were erected **26** *Pythagoras and Alkibiades.* at the corners of the comitium, after an oracle of the Pythian Apollo, delivered in the course of the Samnite war, had ordered that a statue in honour of the bravest man of Hellenic birth, **343 B.C.** and another in honour of the wisest should be dedicated in a much frequented place.   These statues remained until the dictator Sulla built the Council Chamber there.   It is strange **88 B.C.** that the Senate of the day chose Pythagoras in preference to Sokrates, whom Apollo had declared to be wiser than all men, or that they chose Alkibiades before many other brave men, and in fact that they selected any one for either quality in preference to Themistokles.

The use of the columns was to raise the statues above **27** *Origin of statues raised on columns and on arches.* ordinary men, and this is also the purpose of the arches which have been recently introduced.   The Greeks, however, were the first who conferred statues as a mark of honour, and I imagine that no man has had so many statues dedicated to him as Demetrios of Phaleron at Athens, inasmuch as three hundred *Demetrios of Phaleron;* and sixty were set up at a time when the year only contained that number of days.   All these statues were afterwards broken *Gaius Marius Gratidianus.* up.   At Rome too the tribes put up statues in every street in

84 B.C.

most likely another clause of the *lex Horatia*, namely, the right of the Vestals to have their portrait-statues erected. O. Gilbert, *Rom*, ii, p. 112, note 3.

The praenomen *Gaia* was given to *Taracia* in order to latinize her; cf. Tanaquil, who also bore the Latin names of *Gaia Cecilia*.   The alternative name *Fufetia* is according to Gilbert *loc. cit.* probably Etruscan. For the masculine *Fufetius* cf. the famous Alban dictator Metius Fufetius, Liv. i, 23, 4 &c.

§ 26. 1. **Pythagorae et Alcib. in cornibus,** ἐπὶ τῆς ἀγορᾶς Plut. *Num.* viii.

5. **curiam:** altered and enlarged by Sulla (B. C. 88), who caused many of the statues in or in front of the curia to be removed. This new curia was burnt in B.C. 52, on the occasion of the riots at the funeral of Clodius

(§ 21), and rebuilt by Faustus Sulla, son of the dictator.

§ 27. 8. **columnarum:** resumes the subject of § 21.

9. **arcus:** on which stood statues and chariots.   The oldest known instance is the arch or *fornix* of Q. Fabius Maximus Allobrogicus (B.C. 120) of which remains are to be seen close to the temple of Faustina.   The simpler *fornix* developed into the elaborate triumphal arches of the Emperors.

12. **nondum,** i. e. before the reform of the calendar by Julius Caesar. Add.

13. **laceravere:** on the entrance of Demetrios Poliorketes into the city, Strabo ix, p. 398; Diogenes Laertios v, 5, 75 f.   Pliny evidently has this statement as to the number of statues put up to Demetrios from Varro (see *Imagines*, *ap.* Nonius, p. 528 M.); cf. Wachsmuth, *Stadt Athen*, p. 611, note 1. Addenda.

omnibus vicis tribus Mario Gratidiano, ut diximus, easdem-
que subvertere Sullae introitu.

28 Pedestres sine dubio Romae fuere in auctoritate longo
tempore, et equestrium tamen origo perquam vetus est
cum feminis etiam honore communicato Cloeliae statua 5
equestri, ceu parum esset toga eam cingi, cum Lucretiae
ac Bruto, qui expulerant reges propter quos Cloelia inter
29 obsides fuerat, non decernerentur.   hanc primam cum
Coclitis publice dicatam crediderim—Atto enim ac Sibyllae
Tarquinium ac reges sibi ipsos posuisse verisimile est—nisi 10
Cloeliae quoque Piso traderet ab iis positam qui una opsides
fuissent, redditis a Porsina in honorem eius, e diverso Annius
Fetialis equestrem, quae fuerit contra Iovis Statoris aedem
in vestibulo Superbi domus, Valeriae fuisse Publicolae con-
sulis filiae, eamque solam refugisse Tiberimque transnata- 15
visse ceteris opsidibus qui Porsinae mittebantur interemptis
Tarquinii insidiis.

30 L. Piso prodidit M. Aemilio C. Popilio iterum cos.
a censoribus P. Cornelio Scipione M. Popilio statuas circa
forum eorum qui magistratum gesserant sublatas omnis 20
praeter eas quae populi aut senatus sententia statutae essent,
eam vero quam apud aedem Telluris statuisset sibi Sp.
Cassius qui regnum adfectaverat etiam conflatam a censori-

1. **Mario Gratidiano, ut diximus**: xxxiii, 132; he introduced
a method of testing the *denarii* issued
by the mint (cf. Cic. *de Off.* iii, 20,
80). According to Mommsen (*Röm.
Münzw.* p. 388) this would be insufficient to account for the almost divine
honours paid to him; it seems more
than probable that he also withdrew
the plated coins from circulation.

§ 28. 6. **Lucretiae ac Bruto**:
of the statue of Lucretia nothing
more is known. The statue of Brutus
stood near those of the kings (§ 23)
on the Capitol; see Plut. *Brutus*, i,
where the statue is described as holding a drawn sword.

§ 29. 11. **ab iis qui . . . fuissent**:
Livy (*loc. cit.*) says simply that the

Romans awarded the statue ; see
Nitzch, *Röm. Annalistik*, p. 52.

12. **e diverso ... Valeriae**: cf.
Plutarch, *Publ.* xix. The doubt as
to the name shows that the statue
bore no inscription.   Neither Pliny
nor Livy could probably have seen
it, since Dionysios (v, 35) speaks of
it as having disappeared in his day.
From Seneca (*Consol. ad Marciam*,
16) and Plutarch *loc. cit.*, it appears
that it was restored at a later date
(cf. Urlichs, *Quellen-Register*, p. 5).

Annius Fetialis: only known
from Pliny (*Indices* to xvi, xxxiii,
xxxvi).

13. **Iovis Statoris**, ii, 140. The
temple stood on the Sacred Way,
at the commencement of the *Clivus*

honour of Gaius Marius Gratidianus, as I have said, and overthrew them again when Sulla entered the city.   83 B.C.

It is certain that standing statues were customary in Rome at 28
a very early date.   Still the first equestrian statues are extremely *Compara-*
old, and women shared the honour of them with men when *antiquity*
Cloelia, as if it were not enough that she should be re- *of standing*
presented wearing the toga, was granted such a statue, though *equestrian*
none were given to Lucretia and Brutus, and yet they had *statues.*
expelled that royal family for whose interests Cloelia was a *Cloelia.*
hostage.   I should readily believe this statue and that of Cocles 29
to be the first dedicated by the state (for it is probable that Tar- 508 B.C.
quinius set up those to Attus and the Sibyl, and that the kings
each set up their own), were it not for Piso's statement that the
statue to Cloelia was raised by her fellow-hostages, who were sent
back by Porsenna in honour of her.   Annius Fetialis on the other
hand says that the equestrian statue which stood opposite the
temple of Jupiter the Upholder in the vestibule of the house of
Tarquin the Proud was that of Valeria, the daughter of the consul *Valeria.*
Publicola.   She alone, he says, escaped and swam across the
Tiber, while the other hostages sent to Porsenna were treacherously
killed by Tarquinius.   Lucius Piso states that in the second con- 30
sulship of Marcus Aemilius and Gaius Popilius all the statues of 158 B.C.
magistrates standing round the forum, except those which had been *Removal of*
set up in accordance with a decree of the people or of the Senate, *statues of*
were removed by the censors Publius Cornelius Scipio and Marcus *magistrates*
Popilius.   The one near the temple of Earth, set up in his own *not erected*
honour by Spurius Cassius, who aimed at the kingship, was further *people or*
melted down by the censors; thus even in the matter of a statue *the Senate.*

Palatinus, near the arch of Titus; the
house of Tarquin was close to it (Liv.
i, 41, 4), cf. Liv. ii, 13, 11 *in summa
sacra via fuit posita virgo insidens
equo,* without any closer definition of
the spot.

§ 30. 21. **praeter eas** : the measure
would be intended to prevent the
crowding of public places by statues
put up by private individuals (*loca
tueri*) ; Mommsen, *Staatsrecht,* ii,
p. 437, cf. Liv. xl, 51, 3.

23. **conflatam a censoribus** : not
of course by the censors mentioned
above, or the sentence would have

ended at *conflatam.*   For the duties
of censors as regards the removing of
statues, cf. Mommsen, *op. cit.,* p. 443.
As there were, however, no censors
in the days of Spurius Cassius
(office created B. C. 445), we must conclude that Pliny's account is incorrect.
According to Mommsen (*Röm. Forschungen,* ii, p. 167, note 28) Piso,
in recounting the events of A. U. C. 596,
may have stated that Sp. Cassius had
set up a statue in his own honour on
the spot where at a later date stood
the temple of Tellus (vowed B. C. 268
and ded. B. C. 252 by P. Sempronius

bus. nimirum in ea quoque re ambitionem providebant
31 illi viri. exstant Catonis in censura vociferationes mulieribus
A.U.C. 570. statuas Romanis in provinciis poni. nec tamen potuit in-
hibere quo minus Romae quoque ponerentur, sicuti Corneliae
Gracchorum matri, quae fuit Africani prioris filia. sedens 5
huic posita soleisque sine ammento insignis in Metelli publica
porticu, quae statua nunc est in Octaviae operibus.

32   Publice autem ab exteris posita est Romae C. Aelio
A.U.C. 469. tr. pl. lege perlata in Sthennium Stallium Lucanum qui
Thurinos bis infestaverat. ob id Aelium Thurini statua et 10
corona aurea donarunt. idem postea Fabricium donavere
A.U.C. 472. statua liberati obsidione, passimque gentes in clientelas ita
receptae, et adeo discrimen omne sublatum ut Hannibalis
etiam statuae tribus locis visantur in ea urbe cuius intra
A.U.C. 543. muros solus hostium emisit hastam.   15

33   Fuisse autem statuariam artem familiarem Italiae quoque et vetustam indicant Hercules ab Evandro sacratus,
ut produnt, in foro boario, qui triumphalis vocatur atque
per triumphos vestitur habitu triumphali, praeterea Ianus
geminus a Numa rege dicatus, qui pacis bellique argumento 20
colitur digitis ita figuratis ut CCCLXV dierum nota per

---

3. Romanis statuas *omnes praeter Bamb.*, *Detlefsen.*

Sophus), and that this statue was
melted down when he was con-
demned—some such statement mis-
leading Pliny into the double error of
supposing (1) that the statue stood in
the temple of Tellus, (2) that the
second measure recounted above was,
like the first, carried out by censors,
whom he was naturally at a loss to
name.

2. **illi viri** ; used by Pliny to cover
his ignorance of the censor's names.

§ **31. mulieribus**: cf. Cato's speech
on the *Lex Oppia*, as narrated by
Livy, xxxiv, 2–4 ; for his dislike of
statues in general cf. the anecdote
told by Plutarch, *Praec. Gerend. Reip.*
xxvii, B (Bernardakis, v, p. 115).

4. **Corneliae**: vii, 57 ; Plutarch
C. Gracchus, iv. The rectangular
basis of this statue was found in 1878

on the site of the porticus Octaviae ;
it is inscribed (*a*) *Opus Tisicratis*,
(*b*) *Cornelia Africani f*(ilia) *Graccho-*
rum (sc. *mater*). (*b*) is the earlier
inscription ; it is probable that the
statue of Cornelia was destroyed in
the great fire of A.D. 80, after which
the basis was used a second time for
some copy of a work of Teisikrates
(§ 67), Löwy, *I. G. B.* 493. Cf.
Bernoulli, *Röm. Iconogr.* i, p. 72 ff.
From the shape of the basis, Cornelia
appears to have been represented
seated, in the scheme familiar from
the so-called statues of Agrippina.

6. **Metelli ... porticu** : erected
by Q. Metellus Macedonicus after his
triumph B.C. 146. On its site Augustus
built in honour of his sister the famous
porticus Octaviae.

§ **32. 9. lege perlata** : this measure

they provided against possible ambition.   We know the protests 31
of Cato, in his censorship, against the statues set up to Roman 184 B.C. *Protests of Cato the Censor against statues of women.*
women in the provinces, and yet he could not prevent their being
set up in Rome itself, for example to Cornelia the mother of
the Gracchi and daughter of the elder Africanus.   It is a seated
figure, remarkable as having shoes without thongs, which was
formerly in the public colonnade of Metellus and is now in
the galleries of Octavia.

The first statue set up at Rome at the cost of a foreign 32
nation was to Gaius Aelius, tribune of the people.   He had *Statues erected by foreign cities.*
carried a law against Sthennius Stallius Lucanus, who had on two
occasions molested the people of Thurii.   They in return pre- 285 B.C.
sented Aelius with a statue and a golden crown, and later on
also gave a statue to Fabricius, who had delivered them from 282 B.C.
a siege.   This method of receiving a people into clientship
became very general, and all distinction was so completely lost
that statues of Hannibal can be seen in three places in a city *Statues of Hannibal in Rome.*
within whose walls he, alone among its enemies, has hurled his
spear. 211 B.C.

That there was an ancient art of statuary, native to Italy, 33
is proved by the tradition which assigns to Evander the con- *Native Italian statuary.*
secration of the Hercules in the Cattle Market, which is known
as the triumphal Hercules and draped at every triumph in *Hercules.*
a triumphal robe.   There is moreover the two-headed Janus *Two-headed Janus.*
dedicated by King Numa, which is honoured as marking peace
or war; his fingers are bent to form 365, which is the number of

---

is mentioned only in this passage;
nothing further is known of this statue
or that of Fabricius.

13. **Hannibalis:** brought either
from Carthage or from Asia Minor.

§ 33. 16. **statuariam:** see on *toreuticen* in § 54.

17. **Hercules:** in the ancient shrine
(Tac. *Ann.* xv, 41: *magna ara fanum-
que, quae praesenti Herculi Arcas
Evander sacraverat*) near to which,
at a later date, was built the round
temple of Hercules, which contained
the paintings of Pacuvius; Peter *ap.*
Roscher, i, 2911 ff.; cf. note on xxxv,
19), and below on § 33.

19. **Ianus geminus:** in his temple

near the curia at the N.E. end of the
Forum. The head of the statue appears
on the oldest Roman libral asses
(Roscher s. v. *Janus*, Mommsen, *Röm.
Münzw.* p. 175). One of the faces
looked towards the West and the
Great Forum, the other towards the
East and the Forum Julium (cf. Pro-
cop. *Bell. Goth.* i, 25).

20. **pacis bellique arg.:** *indicem
pacis bellique fecit* Liv. i, 19, 2.

21. **digitis ita figuratis:** this
curious statement is confirmed by
Macrobius, *Sat.* i, 9, 10, and John
Lydos, περὶ μηνῶν, i, 4. A number of
ingenious explanations are quoted in
Hardouin's note on the passage.

significationem anni temporis et aevi esse deum indicent.
34 signa quoque Tuscanica per terras dispersa quin in Etruria
factitata sint non est dubium.   deorum tantum putarem ea
fuisse, ni Metrodorus Scepsius cui cognomen a Romani
A.U.C. 489. nominis odio inditum est propter M M statuarum Volsinios 5
expugnatos obiceret.   mirumque mihi videtur, cum statuarum origo tam vetus Italiae sit, lignea potius aut fictilia
deorum simulacra in delubris dicata usque ad devictam
35 Asiam, unde luxuria.   similitudines exprimendi quae prima
fuerit origo, in ea quam plasticen Graeci vocant dici con- 10
venientius erit, etenim prior quam statuaria fuit.   sed haec
ad infinitum effloruit multorum voluminum operi, si quis
plura persequi velit, omnia enim quis possit ?

36   M. Scauri aedilitate signorum M M M in scaena tan-
A.U.C. 695. tum fuere temporario theatro.   Mummius Achaia devicta 15
A.U.C. 608. replevit urbem non relicturus filiae dotem.   cur enim non
cum excusatione ponatur ?   multa et Luculli invexere.
Rhodi etiamnum LXXIII signorum esse Mucianus ter
cos. prodidit, nec pauciora Athenis, Olympiae, Delphis
37 superesse creduntur.   quis ista mortalium persequi possit 20
aut quis usus noscendi intellegatur ?   insignia maxime et
aliqua de causa notata voluptarium sit attigisse artificesque
celebratos nominavisse, singulorum quoque inexplicabili
multitudine, cum Lysippus MD opera fecisse prodatur,
tantae omnia artis ut claritatem possent dare vel singula, 25
numerum apparuisse defuncto eo, cum thensaurum effre-
gisset heres, solitum enim ex manipretio cuiusque signi

12. operi *Bamb.*; opere *reliqui, Detlefsen.*   18. LXXIII] *Bamb. Ricc.*;
LXXIII *Voss.* (*teste Detlefsen*); *numerus aperte corruptus.*

1. aevi esse deum : ὡσεὶ τοῦ αἰῶνος
πατέρα, John Lydos, *loc. cit.*
§ 34. 4. Metrodorus Scepsius :
born about B.C. 145 ; Müller, *F. H. G.*
iii, pp. 202–205 ; Susemihl, *Griech.*
Lit. in der Alexandr. Zeit, ii, p.
352 ff.
7. lignea : in Italy, as in Greece,
statuary began with the wooden idols
which not unfrequently remained
objects of worship even in the greatest
periods of art, e. g. the Athene Polias

of olive wood in the Erechtheion at
Athens, Paus. i, 26, 6 ; 27, 1 ; ii,
25, 1, &c.
fictilia : xxxv, 157.
§ 35. 11. prior quam statuaria :
since a bronze statue presupposed
a clay model, note on xxxv, 153.
§ 36. 14. M. Scauri aedilitate :
viii, 64, xxxv, 127. For the theatre
see xxxvi, 5, 50, 113–115, 189; it
was erected in the Campus Martius,
but the exact spot is unknown.

days in the year, and by thus indicating the year they mark him
as the god of time and the age. We also find, scattered in 34
different countries, statues in the Tuscan style, which must
certainly have been made in Etruria. I should incline to think
that these were only figures of the gods, did not Metrodoros of
Skepsis, whose other name of μισορωμαῖος or Roman-Hater was
given him from his hatred of Rome, accuse us of having taken
Volsinii for the sake of its two thousand statues. To me it seems 265 B.C.
strange that, though statuary in Italy has so ancient an origin, *Images of*
wood or
the images of the gods dedicated in the shrines were by preference *terra-cotta*
made of wood or of terra-cotta until the conquest of Asia intro- *preferred*
in the
duced luxury. It will be better to speak of the origin of the model- *temples.*
ling of portraits when we treat of the art which the Greeks call 35
πλαστική, as it is earlier than statuary. The latter art has been
infinitely developed; a fuller discussion would require many
volumes, an exhaustive treatise is scarcely possible.

Marcus Scaurus in his aedileship adorned the stage of a mere 36
temporary theatre with three thousand statues. Mummius filled 58 B.C.
Statues in
all Rome with sculpture after his conquest of Achaia, and yet *Theatre of*
I must add in his favour that he eventually died too poor to *Marcus*
Scaurus.
leave his daughter a dowry. The Luculli too brought over a 146 B.C.
number of statues; seventy-three thousand are still to be seen at A.D. 67, 70,
Rhodes, according to Mucianus, who was three times consul, 72.
and it is supposed that at least as many still remain at Athens,
Olympia and Delphoi. A detailed knowledge of all these is 37
unattainable and would moreover serve no purpose; still I should
like to touch on the most famous, and those which any particular circumstance has made noteworthy, and to name the
illustrious artists. Even the works of individual sculptors are
too numerous to be catalogued; Lysippos, for example, is said to 1500
have made fifteen hundred pieces of statuary, all of such merit *statues by*
Lysippos.
that any one alone would bring him fame. Their number was

15. **Achaia devicta**: xxxiii, 149.

16. **dotem**: cf. Frontinus, *Strateg.*
iv, 3, 15.

17. **et Luculli**: i.e. L. Licinius,
the conqueror of Mithridates, cos. B.C.
74 (xxxv, 125, 155), and his brother
Marcus, below § 39; cos. B.C. 73;
triumphed B.C. 71.

18. **Rhodi etiamnum**: Jerome
(see Addenda) *Chron.* Ol. 184, 4,

ed. Schoene, p. 139: *templa Rho-*
diorum depopulatus est Cassius, but
from Pliny it appears that the
plundering cannot have been so
thorough as set forth either by Appian
ἐμφυλ. iv, 81, Val. Max. i, 5, 8, or
Orosius, vi, 18, 3.

Mucianus: see Introd. p. lxxxv.

§ 37. 24. **Lysippus**: the anecdote
of the money-box may be traced

38 denarios seponere aureos singulos. evecta supra humanam
fidem ars est successu, mox et audacia. in argumentum
successus unum exemplum adferam, nec deorum hominumve
similitudinis expressae. aetas nostra vidit in Capitolio,

A.U.C. 822. priusquam id novissime conflagraret a Vitellianis incensum, 5
in cella Iunonis canem ex aere volnus suum lambentem,
cuius eximium miraculum et indiscreta veri similitudo non
eo solum intellegitur quod ibi dicata fuerat, verum et satisdatione, nam quoniam summa nulla par videbatur, capite
tutelarios cavere pro ea institutum publice fuit.   10

39   Audaciae innumera sunt exempla. moles quippe
excogitatas videmus statuarum, quas colossaeas vocant,
turribus pares. talis est in Capitolio Apollo tralatus a

A.U.C. 681. M. Lucullo ex Apollonia Ponti urbe, XXX cubitorum,
40 D talentis factus, talis in campo Martio Iuppiter a Claudio 15
Caesare dicatus, qui devoratur Pompeiani theatri vicinitate,
talis et Tarenti factus a Lysippo XL cubitorum. mirum in
eo quod manu, ut ferunt, mobilis—ea ratio libramenti est—
nullis convellatur procellis. id quidem providisse et artifex
dicitur modico intervallo, unde maxime flatum opus erat 20
frangi, opposita columna. itaque magnitudinem propter
difficultatemque moliendi non attigit eum Fabius Verru-

A.U.C. 545. cosus, cum Herculem qui est in Capitolio inde transferret.
41 ante omnis autem in admiratione fuit Solis colossus Rhodi,

---

back to Duris, below § 51 ; Introd.
p. xlviii.

1. denarios : the Roman golden
denarius was worth about £1, but the
reference here must be to the στατήρ =
16s. nearly. Introd. p. lxxxiv.

§ 38. 4. in Capitolio : after the
temple had been burnt down in B.C. 83,
Sulla undertook its reconstruction,
which was eventually carried out by Q.
Lutatius Catulus, who dedicated the
new temple in B. C. 69. It was burnt
again *a Vitellianis*, Tac. *Hist.* iii, 71.

6. in cella Iunonis ; on the
right of the central cella of Jupiter ;
the cella on the left was dedicated to
Minerva.

9. capite: cf. xxxvi, 29 . . . *capi-*
tali satisdatione fama iudicet dignos
(i. e. two statuary groups).

§ 39. 13. Apollo: Καλάμιδος ἔργον.
Strab. vii, p. 319.

§ 40. 15. a Cl. Caesare. Claudius
restored the theatre of Pompeius
after a fire, and probably dedicated
the Jupiter on the same occasion. Tac.
Ann. iii, 72.

16. Pompeiani theatri ; near the
Great Circus.

17. factus a Lysippo : it represented Zeus, and according to Strabo,
p. 278, was the tallest colossus after
that of Rhodes.

discovered when his heir broke open his money-box after his death, for it was his custom to lay by a piece of gold out of the price he received for each statue.

Art has made extraordinary progress, in technique first and afterwards in audacity.   As an example of successful technique I shall mention a figure representing neither god nor man.   Before the last fire on the Capitol, caused by the soldiers of Vitellius, our own generation could see in the temple of Juno a bronze dog licking its wound: the wonderful workmanship and absolutely life-like treatment are sufficiently proved not only by the sacred spot where the work was dedicated, but also by the unusual guarantee demanded for it.   No sum of money was considered equivalent: it was a public ordinance that the curators should pledge their lives for its safety. *38 Technical progress. A.D. 69. Bronze dog.*

Of audacity countless instances can be given.   For example artists have conceived the idea of gigantic statues called *colossi*, as tall as towers.   Of this class is the Apollo in the Capitol, brought from Apollonia in Pontos by Marcus Lucullus; it is forty-five feet high, and cost five hundred talents [£120,000].   Another is the Jupiter dedicated in the Field of Mars by Claudius Caesar, which, however, is dwarfed by its proximity to the theatre of Pompeius.   Yet another is the Zeus at Tarentum by Lysippos, which is 40 cubits [58 ft.] in height and is noteworthy because the weight is so nicely balanced that the colossus can, they say, be turned round by a touch of the hand, and yet cannot be overthrown by the wind.   The artist is said to have provided against this by placing a column a little way off, on the side where it was most necessary to break the violence of the wind.   The size of the statue and the difficulty of transporting it prevented Fabius Verrucosus from touching it, although he brought the Herakles in the Capitol from Tarentum.   The most marvellous of all, however, is the statue *39 Colossi. (a) Apollo in the Capitol. B.C. 73. (b) Jupiter in the Field of Mars. 40 (c) Zeus by Lysippos, at Tarentum. B.C. 209. (d) Herakles in the Capitol. 41*

mirum . . . procellis : periegetic explanation.

22. non attigit Fabius : cf. Liv. xxvii, 16, 8.

23. Herculem : Λυσίππου ἔργον, Strabo, *loc. cit.* The hero was represented without weapons and seated, resting his head on his left hand ; cf. Niketas Akominatos *de signis Constantinop.*, p. 859. Near the Hercules stood a bronze equestrian statue of

Fabius himself (Plut. *Fab. Max.* xxii), which he doubtless set up in imitation of Carvilius.

§ 41. 24. ante omnis . . . in admiratione : cf. Luc. *Jup. Trag.* 11. It was even reckoned among the Seven Wonders of the world. The notion that it stood with one foot on each of the moles which formed the entrance to the harbour while ships passed full sail between its legs was unknown to

A.U.C. 527. quem fecerat Chares Lindius, Lysippi supra dicti discipulus.
LXX cubitorum altitudinis fuit. hoc simulacrum post LVI
annum terrae motu prostratum, sed iacens quoque miraculo
est. pauci pollicem eius amplectuntur, maiores sunt digiti
quam pleraeque statuae. vasti specus hiant defractis mem- 5
bris, spectantur intus magnae molis saxa quorum pondere
stabiliverat eum constituens. duodecim annis tradunt effectum CCC talentis quae contigerant ex apparatu regis
42 Demetrii relicto morae' taedio opsessa Rhodo. sunt alii
centum numero in eadem urbe colossi minores hoc, sed 10
ubicumque singuli fuissent, nobilitaturi locum, praeterque
43 hos deorum quinque quos fecit Bryaxis. factitavit colossos
et Italia. videmus certe Tuscanicum Apollinem in bibliotheca templi Augusti quinquaginta pedum a pollice, dubium
aere mirabiliorem an pulchritudine. fecit et Sp. Carvilius 15
A.U.C. 461. Iovem qui est in Capitolio victis Samnitibus sacrata lege
pugnantibus e pectoralibus eorum ocreisque et galeis. amplitudo tanta est ut conspiciatur a Latiari Iove. e reliquiis
limae suam statuam fecit quae est ante pedes simulacri eius.
44 habent in eodem Capitolio admirationem et capita duo quae 20
A.U.C. 697. P. Lentulus cos. dicavit, alterum a Charete supra dicto
factum, alterum fecit ... dicus conparatione in tantum victus
45 ut artificum minime probabilis videatur. verum omnem
amplitudinem statuarum eius generis vicit aetate nostra
Zenodorus Mercurio facto in civitate Galliae Arvernis per 25

the ancients, and arose in the Middle
Ages. See Cecil Torr, *Rhodes in
Ancient Times*, p. 96 f.

2. **LXX** cub. altitudinis: presumably from Varro, the measurement
being practically identical with that
given by Vibius Sequester (*Colossus
Rhodi altus pedes CV*), who is known
to have drawn from Varro, Urlichs,
Quellen-Reg. p. 11.

hoc simulacrum . . . Bryaxis:
the picturesque description of the
prostrate colossus, and the mention of
the hundred other colossal statues in
Rhodes, have been rightly referred to
Mucianus by Brieger, *de Font. Plin.*

p. 60. Introd. p. lxxxvii.

8. ex apparatu: Plut. *Demetr.* 20.

9. opsessa Rhodo: vii, 126;
xxxv, 104, 105.

§ 42. 12. Bryaxis: below, § 73.

§ 43. 13. Tuscanicum Apollinem:
from what we know of Etruscan workmanship, Pliny's admiration must be
prompted by patriotism.

in bibliotheca: belonging to
the temple of Augustus (xii, 94),
built by Tiberius and Livia in B.C.
14, Dio Cassius, lvi, 46; cf. Suet.
Tib. 74 *in bibliotheca templi novi.*
Gilbert, *Rom,* iii, p. 121, n. 3; it also
contained, besides the customary busts

of the Sun at Rhodes, made by Chares of Lindos, a pupil of the *(e) Colossus* Lysippos already mentioned.   It was seventy cubits [102 feet] in *of Rhodes by Chares* height, and after standing for fifty-six years was overthrown by an *of Lindos.* earthquake, but even as it lies on the ground it arouses wonder. B.C. 227. Few men can clasp their arms about its thumb, its fingers are taller than most statues and wide caverns gape within its broken limbs, while inside can be seen huge fragments of rock, originally used as weights to steady it.   According to tradition, its construction lasted twelve years, and cost 300 talents [£72,000], contributed by the Rhodians out of the siege-train left with them by King 42 Demetrios when he wearied of the siege of Rhodes.   There are *Other* a hundred smaller colossal statues in this city, any one of which *colossal statues at* would have made famous the place it adorned, besides five *Rhodes.* representing gods, made by Bryaxis.   In Italy too colossal *Five by Bryaxis.* statues have been made; we have before our eyes the Tuscan 43 Apollo, in the library of the temple of Augustus, which mea- *Tuscan Apollo.* sures 50 feet from its toe.   It is not easy to say whether the *Colossal* beauty of the statue or of the bronze is the more worthy of *statues in* wonder.   After the victory over the Samnites, who fought *Italy.* bound by a solemn vow, Spurius Carvilius made from their B.C. 293. breastplates, greaves, and helmets the Jupiter in the Capitol, *Jupiter.* a·statue large enough to be visible from the temple of Jupiter Latiaris.   From the filings he made a statue of himself, to 44 stand at the feet of the other.   Two heads, also placed on the *Colossal* Capitol, deserve to be admired.   They were dedicated by *heads.* Publius Lentulus : one is the work of the Chares mentioned above, the other is by . . . dikos, who however suffers by the comparison so as to seem a most unattractive artist.   In 45 our own times however Zenodoros exceeded the proportions *Zenodoros.* of all other statues of this class.   His Mercury was made in *His* Gaul, in the state of the Arverni; he spent ten years upon *Mercury.*

---

of illustrious men, a statue of Minerva, Plin. vii, 210.

16. **victis Samnitibus** : cf. Liv. x, 38-46. It is at least curious that Livy in his elaborate account of the triumph of B.C. 293 should only mention the temple of *Fors Fortuna* (x, 46, 14) as erected out of the booty. A. Schaeffer (*Comm. phil. in hon. Momms.* p. 7) accordingly supposes the statue to have been set up at a

later date, and that Pliny, or his author, confused the first and second consulship of Carvilius.

18. **Latiari Iove** : on the Mons Albanus (Monte Cavo).

§ 44. 21. **Charete supra dicto** : in § 41. Pliny is the only author who mentions any work of Chares besides the *Colossus.*

§ 45. 25. **Zenodorus** : perhaps an Alexandrian established in Gaul, see S.

annos decem, HS [$\overline{CCCC}$] manipreti, postquam satis artem
ibi adprobaverat, Romam accitus a Nerone, ubi destinatum
illius principis simulacro colossum fecit CXIXS pedum
longitudine, qui dicatus Soli venerationi est damnatis sceleri-
46 bus illius principis. mirabamur in officina non modo ex 5
argilla similitudinem insignem, verum et de parvis admodum
surculis quod primum operis instaurati fuit. ea statua
indicavit interisse fundendi aeris scientiam, cum et Nero
largiri aurum argentumque paratus esset et Zenodorus
scientia fingendi caelandique nulli veterum postponeretur. 10
47 statuam Arvernorum cum faceret provinciae Dubio Avito
praesidente, duo pocula Calamidis manu caelata, quae Cassio
Salano avonculo eius praeceptori suo Germanicus Caesar
adamata donaverat, aemulatus est ut vix ulla differentia
esset artis. quanto maior Zenodoro praestantia fuit, tanto 15
magis deprehenditur aeris obliteratio.

48   Signis quae vocant Corinthia plerique in tantum capiuntur
ut secum circumferant, sicut Hortensius orator sphingem
Verri reo ablatam, propter quam Cicero illo iudicio in
altercatione neganti ei aenigmata se intellegere respondit 20
debere, quoniam sphingem domi haberet. circumtulit et
Nero princeps Amazonem, de qua dicemus, et paulo ante

3. CXIXS] *Urlichs in Chrestom. Plin.*; CVIS *Detlefsen*; qui nonaginta
Bamb.

Reinach, *Bronzes Figurés de la Gaule
Romaine*, p. 12, who shows that the
name is met with principally in Syria
and Egypt.

Arvernis : where Mercury had a
celebrated ritual in his temple on the
Puy de Dôme; see Addenda.

3. **colossum** : in the vestibule of
the Golden House, Suet. *Nero*, 31.

4. **dicatus Soli venerationi** : i. e.
by Vespasian, Suet. *Vesp.* 18, who set
up the colossus on the Sacred Way,
Dio Cassius, 66, 15; Martial, *Spect.* 2,
i, 71, 6. The basis may still be seen *in
situ* between the temple of Venus and
Rome and the Colosseum. Com-
modus replaced the head by a portrait
head of himself (Herodian, i, 5, 9),
and gave to the statue attributes of

Hercules, which were afterwards removed (Aelian Lamprid. *Commod.* 17,
10). The size of the Neronian colossus
became proverbial, *C. I. L.* viii, 1,
212, p. 36, l. 82. Cf. in xxxv, 51,
the colossal painted portrait of Nero.

§ **46. 5. mirabamur** : practically
the only instance where Pliny speaks
from personal observation.

in **officina** : sc. *aeraria*, cf. below,
§ 134; xvi, 23; xviii, 89; *C. I. L.* vi,
8455, &c. Addenda.

6. **argilla** : i. e. the πρόπλασμα,
cf. xxxv, 155.

7. **surculis** : the *surculi* must, I
think, be the τρυπήματα or wax tubes
with which the wax model was
covered previous to its being cased
in loam ; these tubes were intended

it and received in payment forty million sesterces [£350,000 circ.]. After he had won his reputation in Gaul, Nero summoned him to Rome, where he made a colossal statue 119½ feet in height. It was originally intended to represent the Emperor, but after Nero's crimes had met with their punishment, it was dedicated to the worship of the Sun. In his workshop **46** our wonder was excited not only by the extraordinary likeness in the clay model, but by the slender tubing which was the first stage towards the completion of the work. This statue proved that the secret of the composition of bronze was lost, since Nero had been ready to provide the gold and silver, and in modelling and chasing Zenodoros was the equal of any ancient artist. When he made the statue for the Arverni, during **47** the governorship of Dubius Avitus, he imitated two cups, chased by the hand of Kalamis, which Germanicus Caesar had prized very highly, and had given to Cassius Silanus his tutor, the uncle of Dubius, with such nicety that scarcely any difference can be detected between the original and the copy. Thus the artistic cunning of Zenodoros only strengthens the proof that the art of alloying bronze was forgotten.

His colossal Nero.

He copies two cups by Kalamis.

The figures known as Corinthian are often so much prized that **48** the owners carry them about with them, as the orator Hortensius did the figure of a sphinx which he had taken from his client Verres. The image was mentioned in the course of the trial, for when Hortensius declared that he could not guess riddles, Cicero replied that he should be able to do so since he kept a sphinx in his house. Nero when Emperor also took about with him an Amazon

Great value of Corinthian bronzes. Sphinx of Hortensius.

Nero's Amazon.

to produce in the loam-coating holes for the pouring in of the bronze, and the letting out of the air. The colossal wax cast of a horse covered with tubings, Clarac, *Musée de Sc.* i, pl. v, figs. 5, 6, p. 101 ff., exactly illustrates what I imagine would be the appearance which the Neronian colossus presented when Pliny saw it. Oddly enough neither Clarac nor Blümner (cf. *Technol.* iv, p. 325) comment, so far as I am aware, on this interesting passage.

8. **indicavit interisse:** cf. § 5.

§ **47.** 11. **Dubio Avito.** Tac. *Ann.* xiii, 54.

12. **Calamidis:** xxxiii, 156; xxxvi, 36.

13. **praeceptori:** in oratory. Ovid addressed the *Pontic Ep.* ii, 5, to Salanus.

§ **48.** 18. **Hortensius:** the celebrated orator and art amateur, repeatedly mentioned by Pliny, viii, 211; ix, 170; xxxv, 130, &c.

21. **sphingem:** according to Plut. *Apophthegm. Rom. Cic.* ii. it was silver, but according to the same author, *Cic.* vii, 2, it was of ivory. See Addenda.

22. **de qua dicemus:** below, § 82.

C. Cestius consularis signum, quod secum etiam in proelio
habuit.   Alexandri quoque Magni tabernaculum sustinere
traduntur solitae statuae, ex quibus duae ante Martis Ultoris
aedem dicatae sunt, totidem ante regiam.

49   Minoribus simulacris signisque innumera prope artificum 5
multitudo nobilitata est, ante omnis tamen Phidias Atheniensis Iove Olympio facto ex ebore quidem et auro, sed et
ex aere signa fecit. floruit autem olympiade LXXXIII, circiter CCC urbis nostrae annum, quo eodem tempore aemuli
eius fuere Alcamenes, Critias, Nesiotes, Hegias, et deinde 10
olympiade LXXXVII Hagelades, Callon, Gorgias Lacon,
rursus LXXXX Polyclitus, Phradmon, Myron, Pythagoras,
50 Scopas, Perellus. ex his Polyclitus discipulos habuit

7. Olympiae *omnes praeter Bamb., Detlefsen.*

1. **C. Cestius.** Tac. *Hist.* v, 10.

consularis signum : where Fröhner (*Rhein. Mus.,* 1892, p. 292)
proposes *consularis ⟨laris⟩ signum.*
But Pliny is concerned merely with
proving what store was laid by Corinthian bronzes, and not with their
subjects.   If he specifies Nero's
Amazon, it is only because it had
become a familiar object.

2. **tabernaculum :** Pliny has here
misunderstood the Greek word σκηνή
= tent *or* canopy.   The description
in the original can only have been of
the golden Nikai, which according to
Diodoros (xviii, 26) supported at
each of its corners the canopy of the
chariot upon which Alexander's corpse
was borne to Alexandria ; Urlichs,
Chrest. p. 314.

3. **Martis Ultoris :** in the forum
of Augustus, dedicated B.C. 2. *Mon.
Anc.* (iv) xxi, 21-22 ; Mommsen, *Res
Gestae,* p. 88.

4. **regiam :** close to the temple
of Vesta.

§ **49.** 5. **Minoribus,** i. e. *colossis
supradictis.*

7. **Iove Olympio,** § 54; xxxvi,
18.

8. **floruit** = ἤκμαζε.

olymp.   LXXXIII :   probably
date of commencement of Parthenon.
Then about Pheidias as representative
are grouped—failing more precise historical information—other artists connected with the restoration of Athens
after the Persian wars and its subsequent embellishment.   The group of
the Tyrant-slayers, made by Kritios and
Nesiotes (archonship of Adeimantos
B.C. 477, *Marm. Par.*), replaced the
older group by Antenor, which had
been carried away by Xerxes (§ 70).
Hegias appears as contemporary of
K. and N. (cf. Lucian, *Rhet. Praec.* 9) ;
Alkamenes worked chiefly for Athens
(*Schriftquell.* 812-822).   The following groups likewise, when they can be
determined at all, seem the result of
similar uncritical combinations.   As
a rule the given Olympiad strictly
refers only to the first artist in each
group.

circiter : i. e. more accurately, 306.

9. **aemuli :** the epithet is applied
quite loosely, and means little more
than ' of rival merit ': so in xxxvi, 30,
the fellow-workers of Skopas on the
Mausoleion are called his *aemuli;* in

which will be mentioned later on, and a little earlier Gaius Sestius, a consular, had a statue which he even took into battle. It is said too that the tent of Alexander the Great was *Tent of* always supported by statues, of which two have been dedicated *Alexander.* in front of the temple of Mars the Avenger, and two in front of the Regia.

The number of artists whose reputation rests on images and 49 statues of smaller size can hardly be counted. *Pheidias* of *Chronology of the* Athens, however, stands first of all with his Olympian Zeus. *principal* This was of ivory and gold, but he also worked in bronze. He *artists.* flourished in the eighty-third Olympiad [448–445 B.C.], about three hundred years after the foundation of Rome. Of the same date were his rivals, *Alkamenes, Kritios, Nesiotes,* and *Hegias.* In the eighty-seventh Olympiad [432–429 B.C.] came *Hagelaidas, Kallon* and the Laconian *Gorgias,* and in the ninetieth [420–417 B.C.] *Polykleitos, Phradmon, Myron, Pythagoras, Skopas,* †*Perellos.*

xxxv, 64, illustrious contemporaries of Zeuxis figure as his *aequales et aemuli;* cf. also xxxv, 124.

11. **Hagelades** : a contemporary of the Elder Kanachos; flourished circ. B. C. 515–485, Robert, *Arch. März*h. pp. 39, 93. He is placed in Ol. 87, because his Herakles, Ἀλεξίκακος (in Melite, Schol. Aristoph. Βάτραχοι, 504), like the Apollo Alexikakos of Kalamis, Paus. i, 3, 4 (cf. Brunn, *K. G.* i, p. 126), was connected in the popular imagination with the staying of the great Plague in the third year of the Peloponnesian war—the association arising of course from the epithet (Brunn, i, p. 68). The real occasion for the dedication of the Herakles remains obscure ; cf. Robert, *loc. cit.;* Studniczka, *Röm. Mitth.* ii, 1887, p. 99, note 27 ; Wolters, *Ath. Mitth.* xvi, 1891, p. 160. The mention of Hagelaidas brings with it that of his contemporaries, Gorgias and Kallon. See Addenda.

Callon : it is uncertain whether the Eleian Kallon (Paus. v, 25, 4; 27, 8 = *I. G. B.* 33), or his more celebrated Aiginetan namesake (*I. G. B.* 27 ; Paus. ii, 32, 5 ; iii, 18, 8).

Gorgias: *I. G. B.* 36 = *C. I. A.* iv, 373 (214).

12. **Polyclitus:** § 55, possibly dated by the gold and ivory Hera, which he made for the new Heraion at Argos, after the fire of B.C. 424. Together with Polykleitos are grouped, besides Phradmon (probably a real contemporary, Paus. vi, 8, 1, below, § 53), Myron and Pythagoras, for no other reason, I imagine, than that, all three masters being celebrated for their statues of athletes, they fitted in better with him than with any other fifth-century artist for whom a date could be found. As a fact the best activity of Myron falls within the first half of the century (Furtwängler, *Masterpieces,* p. 182), while Pythagoras, as we know from his statues of athletes whose victories ranged from B.C. 488–480, was considerably the older artist.

13. **Scopas** : he appears here by a singular anachronism : in xxxvi, 30, he is correctly dated from the Mausoleion at Halikarnassos. The error is however insufficient reason for assuming (with Klein and Robert cf. *Arch. Märchen,* p. 46) an elder Skopas.

Argium, Asopodorum, Alexim, Aristidem, Phrynonem, Dinonem, Athenodorum, Demean Clitorium, Myron Lycium.
LXXXXV olympiade floruere Naucydes, Dinomenes,
Canachus, Patroclus, centesima secunda Polycles, Cephisodotus, Leuchares, Hypatodorus, CIIII Praxiteles, Eu- 5
51 phranor, centesima septima Aetion, Therimachus. CXIII
Lysippus fuit, cum et Alexander Magnus, item Lysistratus
frater eius, Sthenis, Euphron, Sofocles, Sostratus, Ion,

1. Argium Asopodorum *Detlefsen.* Phrynonem Dinonem *omnes praeter*
Bamb., [Dinonem] *Detlefsen.*   8. Sofocles] *coni. Loewy in Inschr. Gr.*
Bildh. 103ᵃ *p.* 384; fucles *Bamb.*; icles *Ricc., Voss.*; Eucles *Jan, Detlefsen.*

§ 50. 1. **Asopodorum**: a later
artist than the Asopodoros who worked
on the bathron of Praxiteles of Kama-
rina at Olympia (*I.G.B.* 30). See Add.

Alexim: if identical with the
father of Kantharos of Sikyon in § 85
(the pupil of Eutychides; Paus. vi,
3, 6), he must have been a pupil of
Polykleitos II. His insertion here
would be due to an error of Pliny.

2. **Athenodorum, Demean**: mentioned together, Paus. x, 9, 7, as employed on the Lakedaimonian votive
offering set up at Delphoi in comme-
moration of Aigospotamoi (B. C. 405).

Lycium: as his father appears in
the same Olympiad with Polykleitos,
he is placed in the Ol. of the sons of
Polykleitos; but he was already a
flourishing artist in B.C. 446, if Lolling
(Δελτίον, 1889, p. 181 ff.) is right in
referring the statues of horsemen (Paus.
i, 22, 4), on whose basis his signature
occurs, to the expedition of Perikles
to Euboia.

3. **Naucydes**: § 80, son of Patrokles (*I. G. B.* 86), and brother of
Daidalos of Sikyon, Paus. vi, 34;
I. G. B. 88–89. On his relation
to the older Polykleitos, next to
whose statue of Hera at Argos had
stood a Hebe by Naukydes, Paus.
ii. 17, 4 (the two statues on coins of
Argos, P. Gardner, *Num. Comm.* I, xv),
see Furtwängler, *Masterpieces*, p. 226,
and cf. Robert, *Arch. Märch.* p. 104 ff.

Dinomenes: below, § 76.

4. **Canachus**, i.e. the younger:
a Sikyonian and a pupil of Polykleitos
(Paus. vi, 13, 7). His chronology,
like that of Patrokles, is determined
by the fact that he worked on the
votive offering of Aigospotamoi (Paus.
x, 9, 7).

Polycles: § 80.

Cephisodotus: father of Praxiteles? (Brunn, *K. G.* i. p. 269) or elder
brother? (Furtwängler, *Masterpieces*,
p. 295). His chronology seems determined by his Eirene holding the
infant Ploutos, which should probably
be dated shortly after B.C. 375 'to
correspond with the institution of the
annual offering to Eirene consequent
on the victories of Timotheus' (Furtwängler, *loc. cit.*).

5. **Leuchares** = Leochares. Cf.
Leutychides = Leotychides in Herodotos. For his works, see below, 79
and xxxvi, 30. The extant dates for
his activity are comprised between
(*a*) a period previous to the banish-
ment of Timotheus in B.C. 355, for
whom he made a statue of Isokrates
(Heliodoros *ap.* Ps. Plut. *Vita X
Orat. Isocr.* 27), and (*b*) the year in the
reign of Alexander, when, in conjunc-
tion with Lysippos, he made Alexander's Lion Hunt (below on § 64).

Hypatodorus: he is possibly
identical with the H. who, in con-
junction with another artist Sostratos,

The following were pupils of Polykleitos, *Argeios, Asopodoros,* 50 *Alexis, Aristeides,* †*Phrynon,* †*Deinon, Athenodoros,* and *Demeas* of Kleitor. Myron was the master of *Lykios.* In the ninety-fifth Olympiad [400–397 B.C.] *Naukydes* flourished, with *Deinomenes,* *Kanachos,* and *Patroklos ;* in the hundred and second [372–369 B.C.], *Polykles, Kephisodotos, Leuchares, Hypatodoros ;* in the hundred and fourth [364–361 B.C.], *Praxiteles* and *Euphranor ;* in the hundred and seventh [352–349 B.C.], *Aetion* and †*Therimachos.* *Lysippos* lived in the hundred and thirteenth [328–325 B.C.], in 51 the days of Alexander the Great ; so also did his brother *Lysistratos,* as well as *Sthennis,* †*Euphron, Sophokles, Sostratos,* †*Ion,*

made for the Arkadian Aliphera (previous to B.C. 372, see Brunn, *K. G.* ii, p. 295) a bronze Athena, Paus. viii, 26, 5; Polyb. iv, 78. He must however be a distinct personality from the Hypatodoros who, with his colleague Aristogeiton, made for a certain Orchomenian the monument of which the inscribed basis is still extant (*I. G. B.* 101). The archaic style of the epigraphy (Kirchhoff, *Studien*, 4th ed., p. 142, note 1) compels us to follow Robert (*Hermes*, xxv, 1890, p. 412 ff., and *Hall. Winckelmannspr.* xviii, 1895, p. 4 ff.) in referring the artists to the early part of the fifth century. To this date accordingly we must also refer their group set up at Delphoi by the Argives, whatever view we may take of the date of the Attico-Argive victory at Oinoë which the group commemorated, or was supposed to commemorate Paus. x, 10, 3 (see especially Robert, *ll. cc.*, and Furtwängler, *Masterpieces*, p. 41).

Praxiteles : dated with reference to his activity in Mantineia (Paus. viii, 9, 1), the third year of Ol. 104 (B. C. 462) being the date of the great battle (Furtwängler, *Plinius*, p. 21).

Euphranor : although he appears here as a sculptor (§ 77), the clue to his date is afforded by his painting, in the Stoa of Zeus Eleutherios at Athens (Paus. i. 3, 4), of the cavalry engagement that preceded the battle of Mantineia (*equestre proelium*, xxxv, 129).

6. **Aetion, Ther. :** Aetion being only known as a painter (xxxv, 78), and Therimachos being unknown except for this passage and xxxv, 78, it is reasonable to suppose with Furtwängler (*loc. cit.*) that the whole passage, *centesima . . . Therimachus,* has been interpolated from xxxv, 78.

§ 51. 7. **Lysippus :** his ἀκμή is determined by the central Olympiad of the reign of Alexander. (Loewy, *Untersuch.* p. 64.)

Lysistratus, xxxv, 153.

8. **Sthenis** of Olynthos, *inf.* § 90. From *I. G. B.* 83 we learn that he was a fellow-worker of Leochares; and from *I. G. B.* 103[a] (cf. on *I. G. B.* 541, p. 370) that he was still active in the reign of Lysimachos (B. C. 306–281).

Sofocles : Loewy's reading is made practically certain by Bulle's observation (*Olympia*, Bd. ii, p. 156) that the bases from the statues of riders by Sophokles at Olympia (*I. G. B.* 123–125) closely resemble, in form and profile, the basis (*I. G. B.* 103[a]) of Sthennis from the Amphiareion at Oropos. This near connexion of the two artists explains the place assigned to them in the Plinian chronology.

Sostratus : probably identical with the Sostratos, son of Euphranor, *I. G. B.* 105.

Silanion—in hoc mirabile quod nullo doctore nobilis fuit,
ipse discipulum habuit Zeuxiaden—CXXI Eutychides,
Euthycrates, Laippus, Cephisodotus, Timarchus, Pyromachus.
52 cessavit deinde ars, ac rursus olympiade CLVI revixit, cum
fuere longe quidem infra praedictos, probati tamen, Antaeus, 5
Callistratus, Polycles Athenaeus, Callixenus, Pythocles,
53 Pythias, Timocles.   ita distinctis celeberrimorum aetatibus
insignes raptim transcurram reliqua multitudine passim
dispersa.   venere autem et in certamen laudatissimi, quamquam diversis aetatibus geniti, quoniam fecerant Amazonas, 10
quae cum in templo Dianae Ephesiae dicarentur, placuit
eligi probatissimam ipsorum artificum qui praesentes erant
iudicio, cum apparuit eam esse quam omnes secundam a sua
quisque iudicassent. haec est Polycliti, proxima ab ea Phidiae,
54 tertia Cresilae, quarta Cydonis, quinta Phradmonis.   Phidias 15

1. **Silanion**: from Paus. vi, 4, 5
we learn that he made a statue of
Satyros of Elis, who appears as winner
of a double victory in a catalogue of
the Amphiaraia (*C. I. G. S.* 414).
According to a conjecture of J. Dela-
marre (*Rev. de Phil.* xviii, p. 162 *sqq.*)
this catalogue belongs to the same
period as *C. I. G. S.* 4253 (under archonship of Niketas B.C. 332–1), and
C. I. G. S. 4254 (archonship of Kephi-
sophon B.C. 329–8).   It would thus
appear that the date assigned by Pliny
to Seilanion is correct. For his works,
cf. below, § 81. See Addenda.

nullo doctore, i. e. his school dia-
dochy had been lost ; cf. the similar
case of Lysippos. Introd. p. xlvii ff.

2. **Zeuxiaden**: known from one
of the Mattei inscriptions (*I. G. B.* 483–
485) as sculptor of a statue of Hypereides (d. B.C. 322). See Addenda.

Eutychides: below, § 78 ; xxxv,
141. The date assigned to him by
Pliny coincides approximately with
the restoration of Antiocheia by Seleukos, Ol. 119, 3 = B.C. 302. For the
new city E. made an allegorical figure
of Tyche supported on the river-god
Orontes—a work of which a copy has

survived in the exquisite statue in the
Vatican, Helbig, *Class. Ant.* 376.

3. **Euthycrates**: § 66. *Laippus*
(*ibid.*) = the Daippos of Paus. vi, 12,
6 ; 16, 5. The name is correctly
given below, § 87. Either Pliny in
transcribing from the Greek mistook
Δ for Λ, or he is quoting from a Latin
author who had already been guilty
of the blunder.

Cephisodotus, Timarchus: sons
of Praxiteles, *Vit. X Orat. Lykurg.*
38. The fact that they made a statue
of Menander (Paus. i, 21, 1, *I. G. B.*
108 = *C. I. A.* ii. 1370), who died
B.C. 291, shows that they were
older than the sons of Lysippos.
After the great masters, their pupils
are lumped together without any strict
chronological order (cf. Furtwängler,
Masterpieces, p. 309).

Pyromachus: there appear to
have been several artists of that name,
see below on § 80, § 84 ; xxxv, 146.

§ 52. 4. **cessavit deinde ars**:
marks the end, not of a period of art,
but of Pliny's main Greek authority
(cf. the similar break in the account
of the Painters, xxxv, 135), Brunn,
K. G. i, p. 504 f. Between B.C. 296

and *Seilanion*. It is remarkable that *Seilanion* owed nothing to the instruction of any master; his own pupil was *Zeuxiades*. In the hundred and twenty-first Olympiad [B.C. 296–293] came *Eutychides, Euthykrates, Laippos, Kephisodotos, Timarchos*, and *Pyromachos*. A period of stagnation followed, and again a revival 52 in the hundred and fifty-sixth Olympiad [B.C. 156–153], the age of †*Antaios, Kallistratos, Polykles* of Athens, †*Kallixenos*, †*Pythokles*, †*Pythias* and *Timokles*, artists of merit, but still far below those already mentioned.

Having given the dates of the most celebrated artists, I shall 53 touch briefly on the great names, and group the others under various heads. The most famous artists, although born at some distance of time from each other, still came into competition, since each had made a statue of an Amazon, to be dedicated in the temple of Artemis at Ephesos, when it was decided that the prize should be awarded to the one which the artists themselves, who were on the spot, declared to be the best. This proved to be the statue which each artist placed second to his own, namely that of Polykleitos; the statue of Pheidias was second, that of Kresilas third, Kydon's fourth, and Phradmon's fifth. *The five most famous make Amazons for a competition.*

Besides his Olympian Zeus, a work which has no rival, Pheidias 54

and the 'revival' in B.C. 156 came the great school of Pergamon, which Pliny omits in his chronological table, but which he mentions below, § 84. The *revixit* in B.C. 156 appears connected with the family of Polykles, father of Timokles and Timarchides (below, § 92; xxxvi, 35), and grandfather of Polykles II and of Dionysios, who made the statues for the temples of Juno and Jupiter erected by Q. Metellus Macedonicus, B.C. 149, cf. Gurlitt, *Pausanias*, p. 361 ff.; Loewy, *I. G. B.* p. 177.

6. **Callistratus**: perhaps identical with the artist mentioned, Tatian p. 36, 14, ed. Schwartz (Brunn, *K. G.* i, p. 535).

§ 53. 9. quamquam . . . geniti: by which Pliny attempts to reconcile his chronology (where Polykleitos is placed twenty-eight years after Pheidias) with the story of the competition.

10. **Amazonas**: since four Amazon

types, distinct in conception, but with external resemblances of type and dress have been identified (Furtwängler, *Masterpieces*, p. 128 ff.), the story of the competition contains a kernel of truth. Two of the extant statuary types can be traced back to Kresilas and Polykleitos respectively.

11. **placuit** . . . **iudicassent**: we have here in another garb the identical anecdote told by Herodotos, viii, 123, Plut. *Themist.* xvii, of the allotting of the prize of valour after Salamis.

15. **Cresilae** . . . **Cydonis**. In three out of the four extant inscriptions of his name, Kresilas calls himself Κυδωνιάτης (*I. G. B.* 45–47; for the inscription recently found at Delphoi cf. Furtwängler, *Masterpieces*, p. 116); it is evident that Pliny's Latin author in transcribing from the Greek forged out of a form Κύδων, the name of a fifth artist (cf. O. Jahn, *Sächs. Ber.* 1850, p. 37).

praeter Iovem Olympium quem nemo aemulatur fecit ex
ebore aeque Minervam Athenis, quae est in Parthenone stans,
ex aere vero praeter Amazonem supra dictam Minervam
tam eximiae pulchritudinis ut formae cognomen acceperit.
fecit et cliduchum et aliam Minervam quam Romae Paulus 5
Aemilius ad aedem Fortunae Huiusce Diei dicavit, item duo
signa quae Catulus in eadem aede palliata et alterum
colossicon nudum, primusque artem toreuticen aperuisse
55 atque demonstrasse merito iudicatur.   Polyclitus Sicyonius Hageladae discipulus diadumenum fecit molliter 10
iuvenem centum talentis nobilitatum, idem et doryphorum
viriliter puerum.   fecit et quem canona artifices vocant liniamenta artis ex eo petentes veluti a lege quadam, solusque
hominum artem ipsam fecisse artis opere iudicatur.   fecit

§ 54. 1. Iovem Olympium:
xxxvi, 18, where the gold-ivory
Minerva is also described.

3. Minervam . . . pulchr. : i. e.
the bronze Athena surnamed the
'Lemnia,' Paus. i, 28, 2 ; Lucian,
εἰκόνες 4 ; for extant copies of the
statue, Furtwängler, *Masterpieces*, pp.
4 ff. ; see Add.

5. cliduchum : votive portrait
statue of a priestess, same subject by
Euphranor, below § 78. See Add.

P. Aemilius : probably on the
occasion of his triumph after Pydna
(B.C. 168). For the magnificent
statues and works of art which he
brought from Makedonia see Liv.
xlv, 33; they filled 250 chariots
which graced his triumph. Plut. *Aem.
Paull.* 32; cf. Vell. Pater. i, 9.

6. Fortunae Huiusce Diei: on
the Palatine where was a *Vicus
huiusce diei* (Gilbert, iii, p. 422);
there was another temple of *Fortuna
H. D.* in *campo* (see R. Peter *ap.*
Roscher, i, 1514. *C. I. L.* i, p. 298 f.).

7. Catulus: i. e. the Elder, who
on the day of the battle against the
Cimbri εὔξατο . . . ἀνασχὼν τὰς χεῖρας
καθιερώσειν τὴν τύχην ἡμέρας ἐκείνης.
Plut. *Marius*, 26: Plin. xvii, 2. Whence
Catulus obtained these Pheidian works

remains uncertain. Cf. Urlichs, *Gr.
Statuen in Rep. Rom*, p. 9 f.

palliata: i. e. portraits (cf. the *palliati*, xxxv, 136), while the *colossus
nudus* presumably represented a hero
or local god; cf. H. L. Urlichs in
Woch. f. Klass. Philol. 1894, 488.

alterum: the *duo palliata* are
to be considered as one group, in
apposition to *alterum*, by an extension
of the construction of xix, 34; xxi,
128; xx, 9; xxxv, 71. H. L. Urlichs
loc. cit. See Addenda to p. 38, 5.

8. primusque aperuisse : this
criticism forms, together with the
similar criticisms attached to Myron,
Polykleitos, Pythagoras and Lysippos,
a consecutive *canon* or series of axioms
intended to link with definite great
names the successive steps in the
development of bronze-casting. After
Pheidias, the reputed discoverer of the
possibilites of the art, each artist is
appraised in his relation to symmetry,
the highest award falling to Lysippos,
Otto Jahn, *Kunsturtheile des Pl.* p.
128 ff.; C. Robert, *Arch. Märch.*
p. 28 ff. For the author of the verdicts
cf. below on § 56. Introd. p. xvi ff.

toreuticen; a term applied by
Pliny to the whole of statuary as
opposed to *pictura* (cf. xxxv, 77),

made in ivory the Athena at Athens, which stands erect in the *Artists of first rank. Pheidias.* Parthenon. In bronze, besides the Amazon already mentioned, he made an Athena of such passing beauty that she was sur- named the Fair. He also made a Key-Bearer, or κλειδοῦχος, another Athena which Aemilius Paullus dedicated at Rome in front of the temple of the Fortune of the Day, two draped statues dedicated by Catulus in the same temple, and a nude colossal statue. He is rightly held to have first revealed the capabilities of sculpture and indicated its methods.

Polykleitos of Sikyon was a pupil of Hagelaidas. He made **55** an athlete binding the diadem about his head, which was famous *Polykleitos of Sikyon.* for the sum of one hundred talents [£21,000 circ.] which it realized. This διαδούμενος has been described as 'a man, yet a boy': the δορυφόρος or spear-bearer as 'a boy, yet a man.' He also made the statue which sculptors call the 'canon,' referring to it as to a standard from which they can learn the first rules of their art. He is the only man who is held to have embodied the principles of his art in a single work. He also made

while *Statuaria ars* is, according to Latin usage, reserved for bronze statu- ary; cf. § 35; § 65; xxxv, 156; xxxvi, 15, 37.

§ **55. 9. Sicyonius**: by Plato (*Protag.* p. 311 C) Pol. is called ᾽Αργεῖος; cf. also *I. G. B.* 91; Furt- wängler, *Masterpieces*, p. 255 ff. It is natural that a confusion as to the exact place of his birth should have arisen, as his family appear to have migrated from Argos to Sikyon (*I. G. B.* 89).

10. **Hag. discipulus**: this is chro- nologically impossible—the activity of Hagelaidas reaching back as far as Ol. 65 = B. C. 520, that of Polykleitos as low down as Ol. 90 = B. C. 420 (above, § 49), Robert, *Arch. Märchen*, p. 92 ff. By a loose juxtaposition the greatest Argive master in the fifth century is made into the pupil of the greatest Argive master in the sixth.

diadumenum . . . puerum: the neat antithesis points to an epi- gram as the source of this statement, Dilthey, *Rhein. Mus.* xxvi, p. 290.

The Doryphoros represented an athlete carrying his palaistric javelin. The most complete copy of the Diadou- menos is the Vaison statue (*Br. Mus. Cat.* i, 500); of the Doryphoros the statue in Naples (Collignon, *Sculpture Grecque*, i, pl. xii). See Addenda.

11. **centum talentis**; cf. vii, 126, where the same price is paid by Attalos for a picture by Aristeides of Thebes. Introd. p. lxxxiv.

12. **et quem canona**: the 'canon' was, however, identical with the Doryphoros (see the passages *Schrift- quell.* 953 ff.). It erroneously appears here as a separate statue, the comment on the Doryphoros *qua* canon being, as Furtwängler, *Masterpieces*, p. 229, note 4, detected, taken from a different source to what precedes; cf. Münzer, *Hermes*, xxx, 1895, p. 530, note 1.

14. **artem ipsam fecisse**: ap- parently an allusion to the treatise on art by Polykleitos, called the *Canon*. What Pliny states in epigrammatic form is told more plainly by Galenos περὶ τῶν ῾Ιπποκρ.

et destringentem se et nudum telo incessentem duosque
pueros item nudos talis ludentes qui vocantur astragalizontes et sunt in Titi imperatoris atrio—hoc opere nullum
56 absolutius plerique iudicant—item Mercurium qui fuit Lysimacheae, Herculem qui Romae, hagetera arma sumentem, 5
Artemona qui periphoretos appellatus est. hic consummasse
hanc scientiam iudicatur et toreuticen sic erudisse ut Phidias
aperuisse. proprium eius est uno crure ut insisterent signa
excogitasse, quadrata tamen esse ea ait Varro et paene ad
57 unum exemplum. Myronem Eleutheris natum Hageladae et 10
ipsum discipulum bucula maxime nobilitavit celebratis versibus laudata, quando alieno plerique ingenio magis quam
suo commendantur. fecit et canem et discobolon et Perseum

---

1. telo] *Benndorf in Gesammelte Stud. zur Kunstgesch. Festschr. für A.
Springer*, 1885, *pag.* 260; talo *codd. Detlefsen.* 3. *vide* Addenda.

καὶ Πλατ. δογμ. 5: ἔργῳ τὸν λόγον
ἐκβεβαίωσε, δημιουργήσας ἀνδριάντα
κατὰ τὰ τοῦ λόγου προστάγματα καὶ
καλέσας δὴ καὶ αὐτὸν τὸν ἀνδριάντα
καθάπερ καὶ τὸ σύγγραμμα, κανόνα ;
cf. xxxv, 74 (Timanthes) *pinxit et
heroa . . . artem ipsam complexus
viros pingendi.* Introd. p. xli.

1. destringentem se: i.e. an
ἀποξυόμενος.

telo incessentem : Furtwängler
(*Masterpieces*, p. 249) compares Ovid,
Metam. 14, 402 *saevisque parant
incessere telis.* See also Woelfflin,
in *Archiv für Lat. Lexicogr.* ix, 1894,
p. 119 ff. Addenda.

2. astragalizontes: [possibly for
a votive or grave monument, *Woch.
f. Klass. Phil.* 1895, 548. For a
kindred subject on a Roman sarkophagos, see Helbig, *Class. Ant.* 97.
—H. L. U.] See Add. to p. 42, 5.

3. et sunt . . . atrio : this addition
concerning the Roman locality of the
astragalizontes is loosely co-ordinated
to the main account ; cf. Oehmichen,
Plin. Studien, p. 119. Introd. p. xxxvii.

§ 56. 4. fuit: before the destruction of Lysimachea by the Thracians in
Ol. 145, 4 = B.C. 197 (Liv. xxxiii, 38, 11).

Lysimacheae: built B.C. 309 by

Lysimachos in the Thracian Cher-
sonnese. Where the statue had previously stood is not known.

5. **hagetera** : the Doric form
points to a metrical epigram which
was doubtless inscribed on the basis
of the statue ; cf. H. L. Urlichs in
Woch. f. Klass. Phil. 1894, p. 1299 ff.

6. **Artemona** : according to
Ephoros (*ap.* Plut. *Per.* 27), A. was an
engineer who directed the blockading
works during the siege of Samos by
Perikles. Owing to his lameness, he
was carried about in a litter, whence
he received the surname Periphoretos.
Plutarch adds, however, that the story
was confuted by Herakleides of Pontos,
who showed from Anakreon (cf.
Bergk, *Poetae Lyr.* iii, p. 261, Fr.
21-46, where see note), that Art.
Periphoretos lived long before the
Samian war. It is evident that there
was *contaminatio* between the two
namesakes, the engineer becoming
credited with the surname of the
notorious voluptuary, while the story
of the lameness was invented to account for it. Addenda.

7. **hanc scientiam** : harks back
to § 54 *Phidias . . . primus artem
toreuticem aperuisse.*

an athlete scraping himself, a nude figure advancing with a weapon, and two boys, also nude, playing with knucklebones, who are known as the ἀστραγαλίζοντες [dice-players], and are now in the Hall of the Emperor Titus. Many people think that the faultless execution of this work has never been surpassed. Other works of his are 56 a Hermes, which was at Lysimacheia; a Herakles at Rome; a captain or ἀγητήρ putting on his armour; and finally a portrait of Artemon, known by the name of περιφόρητος or 'Man in the litter.' He is considered to have brought the scientific knowledge of statuary to perfection, and to have systematized the art of which Pheidias had revealed the possibilities. It was his peculiar characteristic to represent his figures resting their weight on one leg; Varro however says that they are square and almost exactly after the same type.

Myron was born at Eleutherai, and was also a pupil of 57 Hagelaidas. He is best known by his heifer, thanks to the well- *Myron of Eleutherai.* known verses written upon it, for people very generally owe their reputation to the talent of others, rather than their own. He also made a dog, and a δισκοβόλος, or athlete hurling the disk, a Perseus, sawyers, a Satyr gazing with wonder at the

8. **uno crure ut insisterent**: implies a shifting of the weight from one leg to the other in the act of walking, and therefore accurately describes the favourite Polykleitan attitude of 'arrested motion.' Had the figure been represented at rest with its whole weight on one leg, the expression used must have been *uni cruri insist.*, Michaelis, *Ann. d. Inst.* 1878, p. 29 (cf. J. Lange, *Fremstilling*, p. 466).

9. **quadrata . . . ait Varro**: the mention of Varro shows that the criticism of Polykleitos and consequently the kindred criticisms of the remaining four artists were derived from him, though Varro himself was of course drawing directly or indirectly from a Greek author, whom we now know to have been Xenokrates of Sikyon (§ 83), Introd. p. xvi ff.

quadrata = τετράγωνα, cf. Plato, *Protag.* 344 a.

§ 57. 10. **Myronem . . . Hage-**

ladae: the pupilship can neither be proved nor disproved; possibly, however, the tradition only arose from a general likeness between the early works of Myron and those of Hagelaidas. Furtwängler, *Masterpieces*, p. 196. Introd. p. li, note 6.

Eleutheris: on the frontier between Boeotia and Attica (cf. *I. G. B.* 417).

11. **bucula**: the heifer (doubtless a votive offering) had originally stood in Athens, Cic. *Verr.* II, iv, 60, § 135. Later it was transferred to Rome, where Prokopios (*Bell. Goth.* iv, 21) saw it in the *Forum Pacis.*—No less than thirty-eight of the epigrams alluded to are extant (collected in Overbeck, *Schriftquell.* 550–588).

13. **canem**: votive-offering, cf. *Anth. Pal.* vi, 175; 176. The list of works down to *Delph. pentathlon* is alphabetic (Petersen, *A. Z.* xxxviii, 1880, p. 25).

discobolon: the best copy is

et pristas et Satyrum admirantem tibias et Minervam,
Delphicos pentathlos, pancratiastas, Herculem qui est apud
circum maximum in aede Pompei Magni. fecisse et cicadae
monumentum ac locustae carminibus suis Erinna significat.
58 fecit et Apollinem quem ab triumviro Antonio sublatum 5
restituit Ephesiis divus Augustus admonitus in quiete.
primus hic multiplicasse veritatem videtur, numerosior in
arte quam Polyclitus et in symmetria diligentior, et ipse
tamen corporum tenus curiosus animi sensus non expressisse,
capillum quoque et pubem non emendatius fecisse quam 10
59 rudis antiquitas instituisset.   vicit eum Pythagoras Reginus ex Italia pancratiaste Delphis posito ; eodem vicit
et Leontiscum ; fecit et stadiodromon Astylon qui Olympiae
ostenditur et Libyn, puerum tenentem tabellam eodem loco
et mala ferentem nudum, Syracusis autem claudicantem, 15

14. loco, et *Detlefsen.*

in Palazzo Lancellotti (Collignon,
Sculpture Grecque, i, pl. xi).

Perseum: presumably identical
with the Perseus by Myron on the
Akropolis (Paus. i, 23, 7).

1. **pristas :** Dalecampius was the
first to give the true meaning of the
word ; Furtwängler, *Dornauszieher*,
p. 89, note 30, correctly explained
the curious subject as a votive offering;
cf. H. L. Urlichs in *Woch. f. Klass.
Phil.* 1893, p. 220 f.   See Addenda.

Satyrum . . . et Minervam =
Paus. i, 24, 1 ; Collignon, *Sculpture
Grecque*, i, p. 465 f. Petersen, *loc.
cit.*, showed that the two must be
considered as one group owing to the
alphabetical enumeration noted above.

3. **in aede Pompei Magni :**
this new temple of H. was presumably near to the *ara maxima* in the
foro boario, the chief centre of the
hero's worship (Gilbert iii, p. 434 ;
cf. H. Peter *ap.* Roscher i, 2918 ; cf.
above on § 33 ; xxxv, 19). Pompeius
had probably dedicated it on the
occasion of his last triumph in B.C. 61,
and brought the Herakles from Asia
Minor (cf. Urlichs, *Chrest.* p. 139).

Vitr. 3, 2, 5 : *aedes . . . Herculis
Pompeiani.*

4. **Erinna :** Hardouin (1685) had
already detected that this ridiculous
statement arose from a confusion between Μυρών and the maiden Μυρώ, for
whom the poetess Erinna must have
written an elegy similar to the extant one by Anyte (*Anth.* vii, 190).

Ἀκρίδι τᾷ κατ' ἄρουραν ἀηδόνι καὶ
δρυοκοίτᾳ
τέττιγι ξυνὸν τύμβον ἔτευξα Μυρώ.

§ 58. 5. **sublatum restituit :** cf.
Mon. Anc. (xxiv) iv, 49–51 : *In
templis omnium civitatium provinciae
Asiae victor ornamenta reposui, quae
spoliatis templis is cum quo bellum
gesseram privatim possederat.* Mommsen, *Res Gestae*, p. 95 f.   Münzer,
op. cit. p. 545, suspects the Ephesian
story of being a *doublette* of Augustus'
restoration of Myronian works to
Samos, recounted Strabo xiv, 1, 14.

7. **multiplicasse veritatem :** explained by Brunn (*K. G.* i, p. 151) to
mean that Myron ' widened the range
of representation in art, inasmuch as
he laid hold on moments disclosed by
attentive observation of nature, but not

pipes and Athena, winners in the five contests at Delphoi, pankratiasts, and the Herakles which is near the great Circus in the temple of the great Pompeius. A poem by Erinna also tells us that he made the monument of a cicada and a locust; he also **58** made the Apollo which was taken from the Ephesians by the triumvir Antonius, and restored to them by the god Augustus, in obedience to a dream. He was apparently the first to multiply truth; he was more productive than Polykleitos, and a more diligent observer of symmetry. Still he too only cared for the physical form, and did not express the sensations of 'he mind, and his treatment of the hair of the head and of the pubes continued to betray an archaic want of skill.

Pythagoras of Rhegion in Italy surpassed Myron with the **59** pankratiast placed at Delphoi; with the same statue he also sur- *Pythagoras* passed Leontiskos. He further made the statues of the runner *of Rhegion.* Astylos and of a Libyan, which are to be seen at Olympia; for the same place he made the boy holding a tablet, and a nude male figure bearing apples. At Syracuse is a statue by him of a man

utilized before.' A striking example of course is the Diskobolos, represented in the act of hurling the disk.

numerosior : cf. xxxv, 130, *diligentior quam numerosior* ; ibid. § 138 *numerosaque tabula* [*numerosus* in Pliny always of number; cf. vii, 101, 143; x, 176 *numerosiora in fetu*; xv, 8, and often.—H. L. U.].

9. animi sensus : the translation given above is from Pater, *Greek Studies*, p. 301.

§ 59. 12. eodem . . . Leontiscum : Leontiskos was a winner both in the Pythian and Olympic games, whose portrait was made by Pythagoras (Paus. vi, 4, 3). He figures here as an artist, doubtless through misunderstanding of some Greek sentence such as ἐνίκα καὶ τοῦτον ποιῶν καὶ Λεοντίσκον, i. e. 'he conquered, both when he made the pankratiast and when he made the Leontiskos' (Urlichs, *Rhein. Mus.* 1889, p. 261).

13. Astylon : Paus. vi, 13, 1.

qui Olympiae ostenditur : belongs to *Libyn* as well as to

Astylon. In the following sentence, likewise, *eodem loco* belongs to both *puerum* and *mala ferentem nudum;* cf. the analogous construction in xxxiii, 5 *murrina ex eadem tellure et crystalina effodimus.* (H. L. Urlichs in *Görlitz. Verhandl.* p. 330.)

14. Libyn, i. e. Mnaseas of Kyrene. Paus. vi, 13, 7 ; 18, 1.

puerum . . . tabellam : probably an iconic πινάκιον, Reisch, *Weihgeschenke*, p. 44. The statue may be identical with that of the boy victor Protolaos, Paus. vi, 6, 1 ; cf. H. L. Urlichs, *loc. cit.* See Addenda.

15. mala ferentem : cf. the statue of Theognetos, who carried πίτυος τῆς γ' ἡμέρου καὶ ῥοιᾶς καρπόν, Paus. vi, 9, 1. Pythagoras's statue of Euthymos (*I. G. B.* 29, Paus. vi, 6, 4–6) is mentioned in Bk. vii, 152.

claudicantem : the identification of this statue with a wounded Philoktetes is due to Gronovius (Blümner, *Comm. to Lessing's Laokoon*, p. 508 f.). The following words *cuius . . . videntur* are evidently epi-

cuius ulceris dolorem sentire etiam spectantes videntur, item
Apollinem serpentemque eius sagittis configi, citharoedum,
qui Dicaeus appellatus est, quod, cum Thebae ab Alexandro
caperentur, aurum a fugiente conditum sinu eius celatum
esset. hic primus nervos et venas expressit capillumque 5
60 diligentius. fuit et alius Pythagoras Samius, initio pictor,
cuius signa ad aedem Fortunae Huiusce Diei septem
nuda et senis unum laudata sunt. hic supra dicto facie
quoque indiscreta similis fuisse traditur, Regini autem
61 discipulus et filius sororis fuisse Sostratus. Lysippum 10
Sicyonium Duris negat ullius fuisse discipulum, sed primo
aerarium fabrum audendi rationem cepisse pictoris Eupompi
responso. eum enim interrogatum, quem sequeretur antecedentium, dixisse monstrata hominum multitudine naturam
62 ipsam imitandam esse, non artificem. plurima ex omnibus 15
signa fecit, ut diximus, fecundissimae artis, inter quae destringentem se quem M. Agrippa ante Thermas suas dicavit
mire gratum Tiberio principi. non quivit temperare sibi in
eo, quamquam imperiosus sui inter initia principatus, trans-

grammatic ; *Anth. Plan.* iv, 112, of
a bronze Philoktetes, seems to refer
to the work of Pythagoras, the unusual omission of the name of the
hero portrayed accounting for its
omission by Pliny (cf. Brunn, *K. G.* i,
p. 134).

2. configi : for the construction
cf. xxxv, 144 (*pinxit*) *ab Oreste matrem et Aegisthum interfici.*

citharoedum : a Theban poet
named Kleon. The inscription on his
statue is quoted by Athenaios, i,
p. 19 b, who adds the story of the
gold on the authority of Polemon ; cf.
Preger, *Inscriptiones*, 140.

5. hic primus nervos : his relation to *symmetry* is not given by
Pliny. It is preserved however,
by Diogenes Laërtios viii, 46 : οἱ δὲ
καὶ . . . ἀνδριαντοποιὸν 'Ρηγῖνον γεγονέναι φασὶ Πυθ. πρῶτον δοκοῦντα
ῥυθμοῦ καὶ συμμετρίας ἐστοχάσθαι.
καὶ ἄλλον ἀνδριαντοποιὸν Σάμιον
(Furtwängler, *Plinius*, p. 70).

§ 60. 6. fuit et alius : in Paus.
vi, 4, 3, Pythagoras is called 'Ρηγῖνος,
and immediately after (vi, 6, 4) he is
named as the artist of the statue of
Euthymos. Now on the basis of the
Euthymos (*I. G. B.* 23), Pythagoras
signs himself Σάμιος ; it is clear
therefore that the *Samius* and the
Rheginus were one and the same person. He was probably among the
Samians who migrated to Italy in Ol.
71 (Herod. vi, 23) and became subjects
of Anaxilas of Rhegion (Loewy on
I. G. B. 23). He evidently signed
sometimes with the one sometimes
with the other ethnic, a fact which
misled some art historian into dividing
him into two persons. A critic corrected this blunder and stated his belief
that the two were identical, a remark
which would afford the clue to Pliny's
ridiculous statement about the likeness. It is noteworthy that Diogenes
(*loc. cit.*) is likewise guilty of dividing
the sculptor into two.

limping, the pain of whose ulcer even the spectators seem to feel. He also made an Apollo piercing a serpent with his arrows, and a man with a cithara, which bears the name of δίκαιος [the Just], because when Thebes was taken by Alexander, a fugitive concealed B.C. 335. some money in its bosom, where it remained safely hidden. He was the first to make the sinews and veins duly prominent, and to bestow greater pains on the hair. A second Pythagoras, 60 a Samian, was a painter in early life. Near the temple of the Fortune of the Day are seven nude figures by him, and an old man, which are praised. According to tradition his personal resemblance to the other Pythagoras was so strong that the two could be mistaken; it was the Rhegine Pythagoras, however, of whom Sostratos was the pupil and nephew.

Duris declares that Lysippos of Sikyon was no man's pupil; 61 that he was originally a coppersmith, and was encouraged to ven- *Lysippos* ture on a higher path by the words of Eupompos. That painter *of Sikyon.* when asked which of the earlier artists he followed, pointed to a crowd of people, and replied that nature should be imitated and not any artist. Lysippos produced more works than any 62 other artist, possessing, as I have said, a most prolific genius. Among them is the man scraping himself, which Marcus Agrippa dedicated in front of his baths. In this statue the Emperor Tiberius took a marvellous delight, and though capable of self-

6. initio pictor: so of Pheidias xxxv, 54.

7. ad aedem Fortunae H. D.: above § 54; it seems to have contained a real Museum; the *septem signa* need not have formed a group, but were seven athlete statues, collected together into one place for the first time at Rome. To these was added the portrait of an old man by the same artist (cf. H. L. Urlichs in *Woch. f. Klass. Phil.* 1894, p. 488, and Sauer, *Anfänge d. Stat. Gruppe,* p. 20, note 73).

8. facie quoque indiscreta: cf. the similar expressions above § 38; vii, 53; xxxv, 88 *similitudinis indiscretae, &c.*

10. Sostratus: his identity with Sostratos, sixth in artistic descent from Aristokles of Sikyon (Paus. vi, 9, 3), is quite doubtful. On this

Sostratus see Münzer, *Hermes,* 1895, p. 533.

§ 61. 11. negat ullius fuisse discipulum: in other words the name of his master was lost, cf. Seilanion above § 51, Protogenes in xxxv, 101.

12. pictoris Eupompi: xxxv, 75, among the *aequales et aemuli* of Zeuxis. On chronological grounds there is nothing to prevent Eupompos as an old man from having known the young Lysippos. The anecdote, however, was probably concocted in order to bring into connexion the greatest painter and the greatest sculptor of Sikyon; cf. Introd. p. xlvii f.

14. naturam... non artificem: a hit at the schools which worked according to a fixed *canon.* Introd. p. xlviii.

§ 62. 16. ut diximus: above, § 37.

17. thermas: at the back of the Pantheon. See Addenda.

tulitque in cubiculum alio signo substituto, cum quidem tanta
populi Romani contumacia fuit ut theatri clamoribus reponi
apoxyomenon flagitaverit princepsque quamquam adamatum
63 reposuerit.   nobilitatur Lysippus et temulenta tibicina et
canibus ac venatione, in primis vero quadriga cum Sole 5
Rhodiorum.   fecit et Alexandrum Magnum multis operibus
a pueritia eius orsus.   quam statuam inaurari iussit Nero
princeps delectatus admodum illa, dein, cum pretio perisset
gratia artis, detractum est aurum, pretiosiorque talis existimabatur etiam cicatricibus operis atque concisuris in quibus 10
64 aurum haeserat remanentibus.   idem fecit Hephaestionem
Alexandri Magni amicum, quem quidam Polyclito ad-
scribunt, cum is centum prope annis ante fuerit, item
Alexandri venationem quae Delphis sacrata est, Athenis
Satyrum, turmam Alexandri in qua amicorum eius imagines 15
A.U.C. 608. summa omnium similitudine expressit—hanc Metellus Macedonia subacta transtulit Romam—fecit et quadrigas multo-
65 rum generum.   statuariae arti plurimum traditur contulisse

§ 63. 4. temulenta tibicina : a
votive or grave statue, cf. the *anus
ebria* of Myron, xxxvi, 32 ; the *psaltria* by the painter Leontiskos, xxxv,
141, &c.

5. canibus ac venatione : cf. the
Alexandri ven. below, § 64. Large
hunting groups came largely into
vogue from Alexander onwards ; cf.
Kuhnert, *Statue und Ort*, p. 331. Urlichs (*Skopas*, p. 196) believes that the
fine fragment of a rider from the
Mausoleion (Brit. Mus.) had formed
part of such a group.

Sole Rhodiorum : for a head of
Helios with Lysippian characteristics,
found in Rhodes, cf Hartwig, 'Testa di
Helios,' *Röm. Mitth.* ii, pp. 159–166.

6. Alexandr. Magnum : the most
famous was the Alexander with the
spear (Plut. περὶ τῆς ᾽Αλ. τύχης ii,
2) ; the motive seems reproduced in
the nude bronze portrait in the Terme
Mus. (Helbig, *Class. Ant.* 1052 ;
Ant. Denkm. i, 5 ; Furtwängler,
Masterpieces, p. 364, n. 2).   For

portraits of Alexander see Koepp,
Winckelmannsprogramm, 1892. The
story told in Bk. vii, 125 (cf. Plut.
Alex. iv), that Lysippos alone was
privileged to make bronze statues of
Alexander, must like the similar stories
of Apelles (xxxv, 85) and Pyrgoteles
(xxxvii, 8) be accepted *cum grano*.

§ 64. 13. cum is centum prope
annis : Pliny's difficulty arises from his
only knowing of the Elder and more
famous Polykleitos, whereas a younger
P. is known from Paus. vi, 6, 2 (also
I. G. B. 92).   Since the greater artists
often become credited with the works
of their less illustrious *confrères*, it is
probable that, as Loeschcke (*A. Z.*
1878, p. 10 ff.) has already pointed
out, the Hephaistion really was by the
younger Polykleitos. So too a number
of the works by the pupils of Pheidias
came to be reckoned as by the master
himself. Introd. p. xciii.

14. venationem . . . Delphis :
dedicated by Krateros on the occasion
narrated by Plutarch (*Alex.* 40), who

control in the first years of his reign, he could not refrain from
having the statue removed into his private chamber, substituting
another in its place. The populace of Rome resented this so
deeply that they raised an outcry in the theatre, demanding the
restitution of the ἀποξυόμενος, to which the emperor was fain to
yield, in spite of the passion he had conceived for the statue.
Lysippos has also won fame by his drunken flute-player, his dogs 63
and huntsmen, and above all by the four-horse chariot and the
figure of the Sun made for the Rhodians. He also made a number
of portraits of Alexander the Great, beginning with one of him as
a boy, which the Emperor Nero, who was greatly charmed with the
statue, ordered to be gilded. Then, as this costly addition spoiled
the beauty of the work, the gold was removed, and the statue was
considered more valuable without it, in spite of the scars upon it
and the incisions for fixing the gold. Further he made a statue 64
of Hephaistion, the friend of Alexander the Great, which some
ascribe to Polykleitos, although that artist lived almost a hundred
years earlier. We have also from his hand an Alexander in
a hunting group, which is consecrated at Delphoi, a Satyr at
Athens and a troop of Alexander's bodyguard, in which all his
friends' portraits are rendered with great fidelity. This group
was transported to Rome by Metellus after the conquest of 146 B.C.
Makedonia. By Lysippos also are various four-horse chariots. His 65
chief contributions to the art of sculpture are said to consist

states that the work was executed
conjointly with Leochares. According
to Loeschcke (*Jahrb.* iii, 1888, p.
139 f.) an echo of this work has survived on a relief from Messene in the
Louvre (*loc. cit.* pl. vii), cf. also Hans
Dragendorff, *Terra Sigillata*, p. 57.

15. **turmam Alexandri**: i. e. the
twenty-five officers who had fallen in
the first attack at the Granikos. A
statue of Alexander formed the centre
of the group, Vell. Paterc. i, 11, 3.

amicorum . . . imagines: this
assertion has been supposed to clash
with the statement that the dead were
buried on the battle-field (Arrian i,
16, 5). But seeing how extensively
portraiture was encouraged in the
circle of Alexander, there doubtless
were extant portraits of the officers,

which would serve Lysippos as guide;
cf. the undoubted portraits on the
'Alexander' sarkophagos from Sidon,
where, however, we can hardly suppose
the persons represented to have given
the artist sittings.

16. **Macedonia subacta**: the group
had stood in Dion, probably in the
temenos of Zeus, where were the statues
of the Makedonian kings (Heuzey,
Mont Olympe, p.118). Arrian, writing
A.D. 124, mentions it as still at
Dion, probably because he is quoting
from some life of Alexander written
previous to the Roman conquest.

17. **Romam**: first in the *porticus
Metelli*, which was afterwards ab-
sorbed into the *porticus Octaviae* (Vell.
Paterc. *loc. cit.*). The statues were on
the *area* (cf. Varro *ap.* Macrob. iii,

capillum exprimendo, capita minora faciendo quam antiqui,
corpora graciliora siccioraque, per quae proceritas signorum
maior videretur. non habet Latinum nomen symmetria
quam diligentissime custodit nova intactaque ratione quadratas veterum staturas permutando, vulgoque dicebat ab 5
illis factos quales essent homines, a se quales viderentur esse.
propriae huius videntur esse argutiae operum custoditae in
66 minimis quoque rebus. filios et discipulos reliquit laudatos
artifices Laippum, Boedan, sed ante omnes Euthycraten,
quamquam is constantiam potius imitatus patris quam 10
elegantiam austero maluit genere quam iucundo placere.
itaque optime expressit Herculem Delphis et Alexandrum
Thespis venatorem et Thespiadas, proelium equestre, simulacrum ipsum Trophonii ad oraculum, quadrigas complures,
67 equum cum fuscinis, canes venantium. huius porro 15
discipulus fuit Tisicrates et ipse Sicyonius, sed Lysippi
sectae propior, ut vix discernantur complura signa, ceu
senex Thebanus et Demetrius rex, Peucestes Alexandri

---

13. Thespiadas] *om. Bamb., Detlefsen.*   15. fiscinis *Bamb., Detlefsen.*

4, 2) in front of the temples—Jupiter
and Juno (*frontem aedium spectant*
Velleius *loc. cit.*), cf. xxxvi, 35, 40.

§ 65. 3. symmetria: so in xxxv,
67, 128 Pliny retains the Greek word,
although, as Otto Jahn has pointed
out (*Kunsturtheile*, p. 131) *proportio*
or *commensus* afforded an adequate
Latin equivalent. For a like reluc-
tance to translate a Greek word which
had come to have a precise meaning
cf. xxxv, 98 *quae vocant Graeci ethe.*

6. quales viderentur esse: Pliny,
or his authority, is here finding a
formula for the conflict between the
desire to represent things *as they are
known to be*, and that of presenting
them *as they appear to be*. The *form*
of the aphorism seems influenced by the
words Aristotle puts into the mouth of
Sophokles, *Poet.* 1460 b: Σοφοκλῆς ἔφη
αὐτὸς μὲν οἴους δεῖ ποιεῖν, Εὐριπίδην δὲ
οἵοι εἰσίν (cf. also in *Poet.* 1448, ff. the
judgement passed on Polygnotos, Pau-
son and Dionysios), Introd. p. lxii f.

7. argutiae operum: cf. xxxv,
67 *Parrhasius . . . dedit primus argutias voltus;* Cic. *Brutus,* 45, 167
and O. Jahn's note.

§ 66. 8. filios et discipulos: the
notice of the sons of Lysippos is from
the same author as the preceding five
appreciations. Introd. p. xxi.

9. Laippum: above § 51; cf.
§ 87.— Boedan: below § 73.—
Euthykraten: § 83.

10. quamquam . . . maluit: points
to a reaction within the Lysippian
school to the older and severer Argive
manner.

constantiam: cf. Petron. 88 *Lysippum, statuae unius lineamentis
inhaerentem, inopia extinxit.*

12. itaque optime: explanatory,
not of the preceding *quamquam,* but
of the general excellence of E. (Blümner, *Rhein. Mus.* xxxii, p. 610).

13. Thespiadas: a Praxitelean
subject, xxxvi, 39; so his father made
for the same Thespiai an Eros, as

in his vivid rendering of the hair, in making the heads smaller
than older artists had done, and the bodies slimmer and with
less flesh, thus increasing the apparent height of his figures.
There is no word in Latin for the canon of symmetry [συμμετρία]
which he was so careful to preserve, bringing innovations which
had never been thought of before into the square canon of the
older artists, and he often said that the difference between himself and them was that they represented men as they were, and
he as they appeared to be.   His chief characteristic is extreme
delicacy of execution even in the smallest details.

He left artists of high reputation in his sons and pupils, Laippos, **66**
✝ Boedas, and above all Euthykrates ; the latter however imitated *Pupils of*
not so much the refinement as the perseverance of his father, *Lysippos.*
choosing to win approval by an austere rather than a lighter style
of execution.   In this manner he made for Delphoi an admirable
statue of Herakles, for Thespiai an Alexander hunting, a group of
the Thespiades and a combat between horsemen, a statue of
Trophonios within his oracular cave, several chariots with four
horses, a horse carrying hunting prongs, and hunting dogs.

His pupil was Teisikrates, also a native of Sikyon, who **67**
followed more closely the school of Lysippos, so that many of his *Teisikrates*
works can hardly be distinguished from those of the master : *pupil of*
witness his portrait of an old man at Thebes, of king Demetrios *Euthy-*
and of Peukestes, who saved Alexander's life and well deserves *krates.*
the honour of a statue.

Praxiteles before him. It may be
that the Thespians owed to the bounty
of Alexander (whose allies they had
become in B. C. 335) these Lysippian
bronzes, rivals of the celebrated Praxitelean marbles. (So Klein, *Jahrb.* ix,
1894, p. 166.)

   proelium equestre : a votive offering like the *turmam Alexandri*, § 64,
cf. Kuhnert, *Statue u. Ort*, p. 331.
[From *simulacrum* to *canes* we have
an inverted alphabetical list.—H.L.U.]

   14. **ad oraculum** : the actual cave
as distinct from the temple, which
contained a statue of the god by
Daidalos (Paus. ix, 39, 8), and another
by Praxiteles (*ib.* § 4).

   15. **fuscinis** : two-pronged spears,
such as are used by Meleager and

Mopsos on the cylix by Glaukytes and
Archikles in Munich (Klein, *Meister-
sign.* p. 77 = Gerhard, *Auserlesene
Vasenbilder*, iv, 235). Further, on an
archaic cylix from Kameiros (mentioned, *A. Z.* xxiv, 1866, p. 296),
Bellerophon, riding Pegasos, is represented with a similar pronged fork ;
also in hands of one of the huntsman
on two amphoras in Berlin (Furtwängler, *Cat.* 1705, 1706), otherwise
the pronged fork is known only as
a fishing implement. The horse, the
quadrigae just mentioned, and the
following *canes* (cf. note on *canem*
in § 57) all belong to the usual class
of votive offerings.

   § 67. 16. **Tisicrates** : § 83.

   18. **senex Thebanus** : not Pindar

68 Magni servator, dignus tanta gloria. artifices qui compositis voluminibus condidere haec miris laudibus celebrant Telephanen Phocaeum ignotum alias, quoniam in Thessalia habitaverit, et ibi opera eius latuerint, alioqui suffragiis ipsorum aequatur Polyclito, Myroni, Pythagorae. 5 laudant eius Larisam et Spintharum pentathlum et Apollinem. alii non hanc ignobilitatis fuisse causam, sed quod se regum Xerxis atque Darei officinis dediderit, existimant. 69 Praxiteles quoque marmore felicior, ideo et clarior fuit. fecit tamen et ex aere pulcherrima opera : Proserpinae 10 raptum, item catagusam, et Liberum patrem, et Ebrietatem nobilemque una Satyrum quem Graeci periboeton cognominant, et signa quae ante Felicitatis aedem fuere, Veneremque quae ipsa aedis incendio cremata est Claudii principatu, 70 marmoreae illi suae per terras inclutae parem, item stepha- 15

as some have supposed—or the name would almost certainly have been preserved, but merely a portrait. Furtwängler, *Dornauszieher*, p. 92.

Demetrius : i. e. Poliorketes, became king B.C. 307, died B.C. 283.

Peucestes : *tribus iaculis confossus, non se tamen scuto, sed regem tuebatur* Q. Curtius ix, ch. 5, 21 ; the episode occurred during a siege in the territory of the Oxydrakai, or according to Arrian vi, 10, and Plutarch, *Alex.* lxiii, in that of the Malloi.

§ **68.** 1. **artifices qui** : i. e. Xenokrates and Antigonos, see Introd. p. xxii. **haec**, i. e. everything mentioned §§ 49-68.

3. **Phocaeum** : from the Ionian Phokaia, Φωκαῖος ; cf. Furtwängler, *Masterpieces*, p. 57. It is unnecessary to look upon the word as a variant for *Phocensis*.

6. **Larisam** : it is worth noting in this connexion the beautiful head of the nymph Larissa on the coin, P. Gardner, *Types*, pl. vii, 17 ; *Rev.* horse and horseman treated in a style reminiscent of Parthenon frieze.

7. **alii non** : see Introd. *loc. cit.* The names of Xerxes (B.C. 485-465)

and of Dareios (the First B.C. 521-485, the Second B.C. 425-405) are apparently only introduced to attach the statement to well-known names. The dates are plainly irreconcilable.

§ **69.** 10. **Proserpinae raptum** : the extant representations of the Rape of Persephone have been carefully collected by Förster, *Raub u. Rückkehr d. Perseph.* in *Philologus*, Supplementband iv. A number are reproduced by Overbeck, *Atlas d. Kunst Myth.* Taf. 17, 18 ; none however can be referred with any certainty, or even probability, to the group by Praxiteles. Förster hesitatingly suggests that the coin of Kasa (Overb. *K. M. Münztafel*, ix, 12) reproduces the group of Praxiteles. The subject of the Rape was treated by the painter Nikomachos, xxxv, 108.

11. **item** : introduces a new subject, **catagusa** : the true meaning was given as early as by Dalecampius, τὴν κατάγουσαν *quae pensa nendo ducet unde et* κάταγμα ; so independently Loeschcke, *A. Z.* 38 (1880), p. 102 f. The meaning of κατάγειν is further discussed by Förster, *loc. cit.* p. 719 ; H. L. Urlichs (*Woch. f. Klass. Phil.*

Those sculptors who have written treatises on the subject give **68**
high praise to Telephanes of Phokaia, who is otherwise unknown, *Telephanes of Phokaia.*
since, they say, he lived in Thessaly, where his works remained
unnoticed.   These writers however adjudge him a place beside
Polykleitos, Myron and Pythagoras, praising his statues of Larissa,
of Spintharos, a winner in the five contests, and of Apollo.
Others give a different reason for his comparative obscurity,
saying that he passed into the service of king Xerxes and of
Dareios.

Praxiteles also, though more successful and consequently **69**
better known as a worker in marble, created admirable works *Praxiteles.*
in bronze : a rape of Persephone, the κατάγουσα or Girl Spinning,
a Dionysos, a figure of Intoxication grouped with an admirable
Satyr known among the Greeks as the περιβόητος or Renowned,
and also the statues which stood in front of the temple of
Felicity, and an Aphrodite which was also destroyed when the
temple was burned down in the reign of Claudius, the worthy
peer of his famous marble Aphrodite.   Other works of his are **70**
the στεφανοῦσα, or woman presenting a wreath, the ψελιουμένη, or

1894, p. 227 f.) compares for the
motive the spinning maiden, Furtwängler, *Samml. Sabouroff,* Pl. xix ;
and the bronze statue, Munich, *Glypth.*
314. I take the κατάγουσα to have
been a grave statue ; for spinning and
similar motives on graves, see Weisshäupl, *Grabgedichte der Gr. Anthol.*
p. 77, note 3.

Liberum patrem : [it is usual to
understand the Dionysos as forming
a group with the two following statues,
but the fact that up to *Veneremque*
the enumeration of single works is
given by *et,* shows that Pliny, at any
rate, understood the Dionysos as a
separate statue, and the figure of Intoxication and the Satyr only (their
close connexion being indicated by
the use of -*que*) as forming a group
together ; the second *et* is omitted in
Cod. Bamb., but in cases of omission
of syllables or even words, little faith
can be put in this otherwise excellent
MS.—H. L. U.]. This observation
disposes of a recent conjecture *Liberum*

ebriolatum (*Mus. Ital. d. Antich.
Class,* iii, p. 787) ; not only is it irreconcilable with the evidence of the
MSS., but the use of the word *ebrio-
lare,* only known from a fragment
of the *Hetaera* of Laberius (*ap.* Nonius,
108, 6), is quite unproved for prose
writers.

13. Felicitatis aedem : on the
Triumphal Street (Dio Cassius 43,
21) built by L. Lucullus, B.C. 151 ;
see note on xxxvi, 39. The *signa*
being bronze are of course distinct
from the marble *Thespiades* of xxxvi,
39 ; a number of Praxitelean works had
been gathered together in the precinct
of Felicitas, just as the temple of the
Fortune of The Day contained works
by Pheidias and Pythagoras (above,
§§ 54, 60).

15. marmoreae illi : xxxvi, 20.

§ 70. stephanusam : probably in
a group with an athlete, in which
case the στεφανοῦσα would be the
personification of the festal city where
the athletic victory had been won ;

nusam, pseliumenen, oporan, Harmodium et Aristogitonem
tyrannicidas, quos a Xerxe Persarum rege captos victa
Perside Atheniensibus remisit Magnus Alexander. fecit
et puberem Apollinem subrepenti lacertae comminus sagitta
insidiantem quem sauroctonon vocant. spectantur et duo 5
signa eius diversos adfectus exprimentia, flentis matronae
et meretricis gaudentis. hanc putant Phrynen fuisse deprehenduntque in ea amorem artificis et mercedem in vultu
71 meretricis. habet simulacrum et benignitas eius, Calamidis enim quadrigae aurigam suum inposuit, ne melior in 10
equorum effigie defecisse in homine crederetur. ipse Calamis
et alias quadrigas bigasque fecit se impari, equis sine aemulo
expressis. sed, ne videatur in hominum effigie inferior,

1. oporan] *Ricc.*; operan *Voss.*; ephoram *Bamb.*; canephoram *Urlichs in
Chrest.*, *Detlefsen.*   12. sem̃ pari equis *Bamb.*, *corr. Traube*; equis semper
reliqui, Detlefsen.

cf. Athen. xii, 534 D : ὁ μὲν (sc.
πίναξ) εἶχεν Ὀλυμπιάδα καὶ Πυθιάδα
στεφανούσας αὐτόν ('Ἀλκιβιάδην). For
the artistic motive cf. the relief in the
Akrop. Mus., *A. Z.* 1869, 24 = Friederichs-Wolters, 1188. [From *Stephan.*
to *Harmod. et Arist.* we have an
inverted alphabetical list (cf. § 66);
this confirms the MS. reading *oporan*.
—H. L. U.]

1. pseliumenen : for an analogous
motive see the little bronze, *Jahrb.* ix
1894, pl. xi; its connexion with Praxiteles cannot however be pressed
further.

oporan : [for a personification of
autumn cf. Ar. Εἰρήνη 523 ff., where
ὀπώρα is brought in to wed Trygaios;
thus the subject, which fits excellently
into the Praxitelean series, is also
proved to have been a conception
familiar in the fifth and fourth centuries, H. L. U.].

2. quos a Xerxe ... Alexander:
since this statement is true only of the
group by Antenor, Paus. i, 8, 5, it
seems probable that the mention of
Praxitelean Tyrant-Slayers is due
to a confusion. Urlichs, *A. Z.* 1861,

p. 144, supposes the displacement of a
heading *Antenor*, belonging probably
to the alphabetical list which begins
in § 72.

3. Magnus Alexander: so also
Arrian, *Anab.* iii, 7, 8 ; Antiochos
according to Paus. *loc. cit.*; Seleukos
according to Val. Max. ii, 10, *ext.* 1.

4. subrepenti lacertae : from
a descriptive epigram ; cf. Martial,
xiv, 172.

5. sauroctonon : finest replica in
Louvre, phot. Giraudon 1200.

6. flentis . . . gaudentis : epigrammatic antithesis, cf. the *molliter
iuvenis* and *viriliter puer* of § 55.
The statues were certainly only jux-
taposed in the epigram. The *flens
matrona*, like the similar figures by
Sthennis (below § 90) was a portrait
statue for a grave ; Praxiteles is known
to have made at least two grave
monuments ; (*a*) the warrior and his
horse, Paus. i, 2, 3 ; (*b*) the monument to which *C. I. G.* 1604 belonged;
cf. Furtwängler, *Dornauszieher*, p. 91,
note 43; above note on *catagusa*. For
the artistic motive see the fine statue
in the Louvre, phot. Giraudon 1174.

woman clasping a bracelet on her arm, ὀπώρα or Autumn, and statues of Harmodios and Aristogeiton, the Slayers of the Tyrant. These were carried off by Xerxes, king of the Persians, and restored to Athens by Alexander the Great after his conquest of Persia. He also made a young Apollo with an arrow watching a lizard as it creeps up with intent to slay it close at hand; this is known as the σαυροκτόνος or Lizard-slayer. There are two statues by him expressing contrary emotions, a mourning matron and a rejoicing courtesan. The latter is believed to be Phryne. The sculptor's love may be read in the whole statue, and Phryne's satisfaction is depicted on her face.

There is also a statue which testifies to the kindness of Praxiteles, for he made a charioteer for a four-horse chariot by Kalamis, not wishing it to be thought that Kalamis failed in the man after succeeding in the horses. Kalamis made other four and two-horse chariot-groups with varying success, though unrivalled in his horses. And yet, for it must not be thought that

71

Kindness of Praxiteles towards Kalamis.

---

7. **putant Phrynen**: doubtless correctly; it should be noted, however, that Pliny mentions neither of the celebrated statues of Phryne at Thespiai and at Delphoi, Furtwängler, *loc. cit.*

8. **mercedem**: the meaning is not altogether clear; the words may contain an allusion to the μισθός given by Praxiteles to Phryne, in the shape of the Eros which she dedicated at Thespiai, *Anth. Plan.* 204 (cf. Benndorf, *Epigr.* p. 53). Again the *merces* may refer to Phryne's reward in the artist's love; or—in the lower sense of payment—it may contain an allusion to her venality as *meretrix*.

§ 71. 10. **aurigam suum imposuit**: since Kalamis (above § 47; xxxiii, 156; xxxvi, 36) flourished in the early part of the fifth century, the *auriga* must have been by the Elder Praxiteles (Klein, *Arch. Ep. Mitth.* 1879, p. 8; Benndorf, *Cultusbild der Athena Nike*, p. 47; Furtwängler, *Masterpieces*, p. 102 ff., &c.). A division of labour in the case of important monuments was quite common, e. g. for Hieron,

Onatas makes the chariot, while Kalamis makes the κέλητες ἵπποι at either side, Paus. vi, 12, 1. [In the case of the Younger (?) Praxiteles it is expressly mentioned as noteworthy, that for a grave monument he made *both* the horse and the horseman: καὶ τὸν ἵππον καὶ τὸν στρατιώτην Paus. i, 2, 3.—H. L. U.] The inscription on the *bathron* of the chariot gave the names of both artists, and the juxtaposition was sufficient to give rise to the story of the *benignitas*. The chariot was of course a votive offering, a ὑπόμνημα τῆς νίκης (cf. in this book §§ 64, 86, 88; xxxv, 27, 99, 108, 141, &c.). Introd. p. lxv.

12. **se impari, equis sine aemulo expressis**: the reading, while derived straight from Cod. Bamb., further brings out an epigrammatic antithesis; the full meaning is as follows: 'This same K. failed through his inability to do the human figure, in other chariot-groups as a whole, albeit the horses taken alone were unrivalled'; cf. Prop. iii, 9, 10 *exactis Calamis se mihi iactat equis.* Introd. p. lxix.

72 Alcman poeta nullius est nobilior. Alcamenes Phidiae discipulus et marmorea fecit et aereum pentathlum qui vocatur encrinomenos, at Polycliti discipulus Aristides quadrigas bigasque. Amphicrates Leaena laudatur. scortum haec lyrae cantu familiaris Harmodio et Aristogitoni con- 5 silia eorum de tyrannicidio usque in mortem excruciata a tyrannis non prodidit, quamobrem Athenienses, et honorem habere ei volentes nec tamen scortum celebrasse, animal nominis eius fecere atque, ut intellegeretur causa honoris, 73 in opere linguam addi ab artifice vetuerunt.   Bryaxis 10 Aesculapium et Seleucum fecit, Boedas adorantem, Baton Apollinem et Iunonem qui sunt Romae in Concordiae 74 templo, Cresilas volneratum deficientem in quo possit

1. Alcman poeta] *E. Sellers*; alcamen et *Bamb.* (alcame et *e corr.*); alchimena *reliqui*; Alcmena *Detlefsen*.

1. **Alcman poeta**: it was pointed out by Benndorf (*op. cit.* p. 47) that the original reading had been corrupted by the neighbouring *Alcamenes*. The readings *Alcmena* or *Alcumena* are unsatisfactory, since the subject could hardly be reckoned among *hominum effigies*. The reading *Alcman poeta* now proposed meets this difficulty, while the subject falls within the range of Kalamis. He is known to have worked for Sparta from Paus. x, 16, 4 (cf. Klein, *Arch. Ep. Mitth.* 1881, p. 84), and might well be called upon to execute a statue of its greatest poet. For a statue of Alkman cf. *Anth. Pal.* vii, 709, an epigram which Weisshäupl (*Grabgedichte der Gr. Anth.* p. 45) suggests may have belonged to a statue of the poet at Sparta, cf. also *Anth. Pal.* vii, 18, 19. *Nobilior*—cf. *nobilis* applied below to the portrait of Perikles by Kresilas.

§ 72. **Alcamenes**: above § 49, xxxvi, 16.

3. **encrinomenos**: *encrinomenos vocatur, qui athletis adnumeratur, id est qui in eorum numero recipitur*, so Turnebus (*Advers.* p. 486, cf. the note of Dalecampius) explains the

term with reference to the ἔγκρισις ἀθλητῶν. Modern commentators, however, generally refer the epithet to the statue, and explain it as *approved, chosen, classical* or *canonical* ('classisch' 'mustergiltig,' Urlichs in *Chrest.* p. 325; cf. O. Jahn, *Kunsturtheile,* p. 125; H. L. Urlichs, *Blätter f. d. bayr. Gymnasialsch.* 1894, pp. 609–613). But the ἔγκρισις ἀθλ. (Lucian, ὑπὲρ τῶν εἰκόν. 11; cf. Xen. *Hell.* iv, 1, 10), lit. the 'examination' of the athletes (*probatio* Cic. *Off.* i, 144) was too well known as an athletic term for the epithet ἐγκρινόμενος as applied to the portrait of an athlete to be understood in any other sense than the one given to it above. The present participle, instead of the more usual ἐγκριθείς (cf. the inscr. Ross. *Griech. Königsreisen,* i, p. 96) shows that the athlete was represented in the act of submitting to the ἔγκρισις. The occurrence of the epithet *Encrinomenus* as a Roman proper name (*C. I. L.* v, 1, 4429), by proving its familiarity, suffices to discredit the old emendation of Barbarus *encriomenos*, which had lately come again into favour. The proposed identification of the *encrinomenos* with the statue of an athlete holding he was inferior to others in representing the human figure, no artist has better portrayed the poet Alkman.

Alkamenes, a pupil of Pheidias, produced works in marble as 72 well as a winner in the five contests in bronze, called the ἐγκρινόμενος [undergoing the test]. A pupil of Polykleitos, *Aristeides*, made chariots with four horses and with two. †*Amphikrates* is famous for his λέαινα or Lioness: this Leaina was a courtesan, intimate through her playing on the lyre with Harmodios and Aristogeiton, whose plot of assassination she refused to betray, although tortured to death by the tyrants. The Athenians were anxious to pay her honour, and yet unwilling to commemorate a courtesan by a statue; they accordingly made a figure of the animal whose name she bore, and to indicate their reason for honouring her, they forbade the artist to give it a tongue. *Bryaxis* made an Asklepios and a Seleukos; †*Boedas* a praying 73 figure, *Baton* the Apollo and Hera which are in the temple of Concord at Rome, *Kresilas*, a wounded man at the point 74

Monument of Leaina.

---

the disc preparatory to the throw (Brit. Mus. and Vatican; Helbig, *Class. Ant.* 331, where see literature) is, to say the least, open to doubt.

Aristides : possibly identical with the painter, master of Euphranor, xxxv, 75 ; Kroker, *Gleichnamige Künstler*, p. 25.

4. **Leaena** : vii, 87 ; the story, told also Plut. *de Garrul.* 8 ; Paus. i, 23, 1 ; Polyainos, Στρατηγήμ. viii, 45 ; cf. Cicero, *Glor.* i, fr. 12 (all without mention of artist's name), is an obvious invention. Had the 'Lioness' been originally connected with the Tyrant-Slayers her monument must have stood by theirs ἐν Κεραμεικῷ (Arrian, *Anab.* iii, 16, 8), instead of at the entrance to the Akropolis (Paus. *loc. cit.*). Further, since the oldest authorities, Herodotos and Thukydides, in their account of the murder of the Tyrants, know nothing of this Leaina, it is probable that she was an ordinary votive-offering; the fact that the artist had failed to give the animal a tongue, or that in the course of time the tongue had got broken away, having given rise to the anecdote

(cf. also Athen. xiii, 596 f.) Introd. p. lxxvi, note 3.

§ 73. 10. Bryaxis : above § 42 ; xxxvi, 30.

11. **Aesculapium** : for Megara he made an Asklepios grouped with Hygieia, Paus. i, 40, 6.

Seleucum : i.e. Nikator, reigned B.C. 312–280 ; cf. below § 86; for his portraits see Wolters, *Röm. Mitth.* iv, 1889, pp. 32–40.

Boedas : above § 66.

adorantem : in the scheme doubtless of the 'Praying Boy' (Berlin, *Cat.* 2), cf. *Jahrb.* i, 1886, p. 1 ff. (Conze); for the type of the *adorans* on coins *Jahrb.* iii, 1886, p. 286 ff. (Imhoof-Blumer), on a gem *ib.* I. p. 217 (Furtwängler).

Baton : below § 91 ; known from *I. G. B.* 61, as a native of Herakleia.

12. **Concordiae templo** : at the base of the Capitol, vowed B.C. 367 by Camillus, and built after his death by the State; restored by Tiberius (ded. A.D. 9). It was the most usual meeting place of the Senate.

§ 74. 13. Cresilas : above § 53.

vulneratum : apparently identical

intellegi quantum restet animae et Olympium Periclen
dignum cognomine, mirumque in hac arte est quod nobiles
viros nobiliores fecit. Cephisodorus Minervam mirabilem
in portu Atheniensium et aram ad templum Iovis Servatoris
75 in eodem portu, cui pauca comparantur, Canachus Apollinem 5
nudum qui Philesius cognominatur in Didymaeo Aeginetica
aeris temperatura, cervumque una ita vestigiis suspendit ut
linum subter pedes trahatur alterno morsu calce digitisque
retinentibus solum, ita vertebrato dente utrisque in partibus
ut a repulsu per vices resiliat. idem et celetizontas pueros, 10
Chaereas Alexandrum Magnum et Philippum patrem eius

3. Cephisodorus] *Bamb.*; Cephissidorus *reliqui.*　　　8. inlitum *Bamb.*
　　　　　　　　　　trahantur *Bamb.*

with the statue of Dieitrephes
pierced by arrows, Paus. i, 23, 3
(where the artist is not named); the
extant inscription ('Ερμόλυκος Διειτρέ-
φος άπαρχεν· Κρεσίλας έπόεσεν *I. G. B.*
46) should place this beyond a doubt,
were it not that the epigraphy is too
early for the date of Dieitrephes, who
according to Pausanias was identical
with the Athenian general mentioned
Thuc. vii, 29 (B. C. 414); cf. Kirchhoff
on *C. I. A.* i, 402. Furtwängler
(*Masterpieces*, p. 122) accordingly
proposes to identify the Dieitrephes
of the statue with an older namesake, father of the Nikostratos, who
was a general at the commencement
of the Peloponnesian war (Thuc. iii,
75; iv, 119, 129). For possible reproductions of the statue see Furtwängler, *op. cit.* figs. 48, 49, 50
(against his views cf. C. Robert, *Hall.
Winckelmannspr.* 1895, p. 21 f.).

1. **Periclen**: for the portrait
(without name of artist), cf. Paus. i,
25, 1. Its inscribed basis was discovered in 1888, see Δελτίον, 1889,
p. 36 ff. (Lolling). A terminal portrait of Perikles, extant in several
replicas (*Br. Mus. Cat.* i, 549; Helbig,
Class. Ant. 281, where see literature)
has been identified as a copy of the
Kresilaian portrait. Addenda.

3. **Minervam mirabilem . . . et
aram**: cf. Paus. i, 1, 3: θέας δὲ ἄξιον
τῶν ἐν Πειραιεῖ μάλιστα 'Αθηνᾶς ἐστι
καὶ Διὸς τέμενος· χαλκοῦ μὲν ἀμφότερα
τὰ ἀγάλματα, ἔχει δὲ ὁ μὲν σκῆπτρον
καὶ νίκην, ἡ δὲ 'Αθηνᾶς δόρυ. The
τέμενος has been shown to be probably
contemporary with the restoration of
the Peiraios by the architect Hippo-
damos of Miletos (Arist. *Pol.* ii, 8, 1),
under Perikles (so Wachsmuth, *Stadt
Athen,* ii, p. 141 f.). Thus, if the
monuments mentioned by Pliny and
Pausanias are, as seems reasonable to
suppose, identical, Kephisodoros would
be an artist of the Periklean age.—
I see no reason for following Furtwängler (*Masterpieces*, p. 145 f.) in
assuming a displacement of Pliny's
notes, and giving the works mentioned
to Kresilas (cf. B. Keil in *Hermes*, xxxi,
1895, p. 225). Introd. p. lxxv; Add.

§ 75. 5. **Apollinem**: it was the
exact replica of the same artist's Apollo
at Thebes, except that the latter was
of wood, cf. Paus. ix, 10, 2; ii, 10, 4;
the type is reproduced both on the
autonomous and Imperial coinage of
Miletos, *A. Z.* 18, ix, pl. vii, and page
90 (= Collignon, *Sculpt. Grecque*,
fig. 153) and in the 'Payne-Knight
bronze' (Br. Mus.); cf. Furtwängler,
ap. Roscher i, 451: the god, nude,

of death, whose face betrays how fast his life is ebbing, and also an Olympian Perikles, worthy of the epithet. The marvel *Perikles.* of his art is that it made famous men yet more famous. †*Kephisodoros* made a wondrous Athena in the harbour of Athens, and in the same city, in the temple of Zeus the Saviour, an altar to which few are comparable. *Kanachos* made the nude Apollo, 75 which is named the Lover and is in the temple at Didyma, of Aeginetan bronze, and with it a stag so poised upon its feet, *Apollo and* that a thread can be drawn beneath them while the heel and toe *Stag.* alternately catch the ground, both parts working with a jointed mechanism in such a way that the impact suffices to make them spring backwards and forwards. He also made boys on race-horses. †*Chaireas* made an Alexander the Great and his father

stands erect, holding a small stag on the palm of his R. hand, and the bow in his L. The work was executed previous to Ol. 71, 3 (= B. C. 494), in which year Dareios (Herod. vi, 19; Paus. viii, 46, 3, erroneously says Xerxes) sacked Miletos and took away the statue. The Apollo was restored by Seleukos Nikator, Paus. *loc. cit.* and i, 16, 3.

6. **Philesius**: aitiology sought to explain the epithet by allusion to Apollo's love for Branchos (Strabo, xiv, p. 634), so Varro, *p.* schol. to Statius, *Thebais*, viii, 198 (ed. Lindenbrog, p. 282 f.); Macrobius (*Sat.* i, 17, 2) gives a symbolic explanation.

Aeginetica temp.: above § 8.

7. **suspendit**: for the meaning given above cf. xxxvi, 117 *theatra iuxta duo fecit amblissima ligno, cardinum singulorum versatili suspensa libramento.* From the word *solum* it is evident that Pliny conceived the stag to have its feet on the ground, an arrangement however which is in irreconcilable contradiction to the testimony of the coins, which show the stag resting on the god's hand. We must suppose, therefore, that the exact place of the stag was not described in the original account, and that Pliny, unacquainted with the statue, assumed, naturally enough,

either that the animal was on the ground, or, according to a scheme familiar from statues of Artemis (also for Apollo in the gem *Cades, Impronte,* iv, 19, 20) that its hind feet were on the ground while its front feet were held in the hand of the god. It is evident that in the *inlitum* of cod. *Bamb.* we have a corruption, while the *linum* of the later codices is a mere interpolation intended to get an ordinary Latin word out of the corrupt reading; the original word must have given the instrument provided with the *dens vertebratus.* Whether the stag was in reality provided with some curious mechanism, or whether the fact that it had been cast separate and did not accurately fit on to the god's palm had given rise to an explanation which has a flavour of concoction, it is now impossible to tell (cf. however the ingenious article of Petersen, *A. Z.* xxxviii, 1880, pp. 22, 192).

10. **repulsu**: cf. xi, 164 *pare eodem praegnas veneno impresso dentium repulsu virus fundit in morsus* (Petersen).

celetizontas pueros: cf. on the Akropolis the bronze statue of Isokrates as παῖς κελητίζων. Lives of Ten Orators, *Isokr.* 42; at Olympia Aisypos, son of Timon, Paus. vi, 2, 8 ; cf. *id.* vi, 12, 1. A κελητίζων on the

76 fecit, Ctesilaus doryphoron et Amazonem volneratam,
Demetrius Lysimachen quae sacerdos Minervae fuit LXIIII
annis, idem et Minervam quae *musica* appellatur, quoniam
dracones in Gorgone eius ad ictus citharae tinnitu resonant,
idem equitem Simonem qui primus de equitatu scripsit. 5
Daedalus et ipse inter fictores laudatus pueros duos destringentes se fecit, Dinomenes Protesilaum et Pythodemum
77 luctatorem.   Euphranoris Alexander Paris est, in quo
laudatur quod omnia simul intellegantur, iudex dearum,
amator Helenae et tamen Achillis interfector.   huius est 10
Minerva Romae quae dicitur Catuliana, infra Capitolium
A.U.C. 676. a Q. Lutatio dicata, et simulacrum Boni Eventus, dextra
pateram, sinistra spicam ac papavera tenens, item Latona

---

1. Ctesilaus] *Sillig, Detlefsen*; G. tesilaus *Bamb.*; desilaus *reliqui.*
3. myetica *Bamb.*

coin of Tarentum, Head, *Guide*, pl.
24, 7. Addenda.

§ 76. 1. Ctesilaus : the name,
though uncommon, is a good Greek
formation (cf. the formations ending
-λεως, -λαος in Fick, *Gr. Personennamen*, pp. 186 ff.), so that I see no
grounds for altering the reading to
Kresilas as proposed by Bergk
(*Zeitschr. d. Alterth. Wissensch.* 1845,
p. 962), who is followed by most
archaeologists. The argument derived
from the Amazon (§ 53), though
strong, is scarcely sufficient.

2. Demetrius : the famous ἀν-
θρωποποιός, Lucian, *The Liars*, 18.

Lysimachen = Paus. i, 27, 4 : πρὸς
δὲ ναῷ τῷ τῆς Ἀθηνᾶς, the following information is derived from the
inscription on the basis of the statue,
Töpffer, *Att. Geneal.* 128 ; for a
similar inscr. from the Akropolis (but
belonging to a larger statue) of a
priestess who had served (?) [ἐξή]κοντα
δ' ἔτη [κ]αὶ τέσσαρ[α], see *I. G. B.* 64 ;
Hitzig and Blümner, *Paus.* p. 295.

3. musica : the reading is an
obvious interpolation, to make sense
out of the corrupt *myetica ;* the epithet
is not found of Athena or any other

god. Fröhner in *Rhein. Mus.* 1892,
p. 292, proposes to read *mystica* for
myetica, adding that 'the mysterious
resonance of the aegis recalled the
music of the Eleusinian mysteries
when the Hierophant struck the
ἠχεῖον.' Dr. Traube suggests that the
reading might possibly be *mycetica*, i.e.
' the Roarer '—μυκητικός as an epithet
of Poseidon occurs *ap.* Cornutos, *Nat.
Deor.* ch. 22, p. 42, Lang—it is quite
possible that an aitiological explanation, derived from the resonance of the
bronze aegis, had been found for an
epithet of which the original meaning
had been forgotten.

5. de equitatu: περὶ ἱππικῆς Xen.
de Re Eq. i, 3.

6. Daedalus : son of Patrokles
(*I. G. B.* 88, 89 ; Paus. vi, 3, 9, cf.
above § 50). D. signs Σικυώνιος
(*I. G. B.* 89) and seems to be the first
member of the family who migrated
to Sikyon ; cf. Furtwängler, *Masterpieces*, p. 225.

et ipse : marks Pliny's astonishment at the appearance of Daidalos
among the bronze-workers (rightly explained by Oehmichen, *Plin. Studien*,
p. 192), perhaps because the only

Philip. † *Ktesilaos* made a δορυφόρος, or Spear-bearer, and 76
a wounded Amazon ; *Demetrios* a statue of Lysimache, who was
priestess of Athena for sixty-four years. He also made the
Athena called the Musical because the snakes of her Gorgon
resound to the notes of the cithara, and an equestrian statue of
Simon, the first writer on horsemanship. *Daidalos*, who appears
here among the famous statuaries, made two boys scraping themselves, *Deinomenes* a Protesilaos and a portrait of Pythodemos
the wrestler. A statue of Alexander Paris by *Euphranor* is 77
said to display every phase of the Trojan's character : he is *Statue of Paris in*
at once the judge of the goddesses, the lover of Helen, and yet *his triple*
the slayer of Achilles. The Athena at Rome known as the *aspect.*
Minerva of Catulus, which was dedicated below the Capitol by
Quintus Lutatius, is by Euphranor ; so is the statue of Good B.C. 78.
Luck holding in the right hand a bowl, and in the left an ear
of corn and a poppy. He also made a Leto with the new-

personage of the name with whom he
is familiar is the mythical Daidalos
(vii, 198, 209 ; xxxvi, 85, cf. vii, 205).

destringentes se : for the motive
cf. §§ 55, 62.

7. Dinomenes : above § 50 ;
distinct from the artist of the first
century who made the statues of Io
and Kallisto (Paus. i. 25, 1 ; *I. G. B.*
233), cf. Gurlitt, *Pausanias*, p. 267 ff.

§ 77. 8. Euphranoris : above
§ 50; xxxv, 128. His activity ranges
from B.C. 375–330.

Alexander Paris : the second name
is added to distinguish him from the
king. The statue has not yet been
identified among our copies, Furtwängler, *Masterpieces*, p. 357 ff. and
Robert, *Hall. Winckelmannsprogr.*
xix, 1895, p. 20 ff. arrive at sur-
prisingly different results. Addenda.

11. infra Capitolium : Urlichs
(*Griechische Statuen im Rep. Rom*,
p. 11) suggests on the open space
afterwards occupied by the temple of
Vespasian.

12. Q. Lutatio, i. e. *Catulo* : after
the fire of B.C. 85, the restoration of
the Capitoline temple and adjacent
buildings was entrusted to him ; cf.

Tacit. *Hist.* iii, 72 ; Plutarch, *Popl.*
15 ; above xxxiii, 57, &c. It is not
known whence he obtained Greek
works of art ; possibly from the inexhaustible booty of Aemilius Paulus ;
cf. Urlichs, *loc. cit.*

Boni Eventus : from the description it is evident that the statue
originally represented the Greek Triptolemos (Urlichs, *Chrestom.* p. 326),
and was re-christened as a Roman
agrarian divinity. Fröhner (*Méd. de
l'Empire Romain*, p. 35) was the
first to recognize the type on the
obverse of a bronze medal of Hadrian :
youth, holding in one hand two ears
of corn and two poppies, and in the
other a libation cup, is sacrificing at
an altar. For a still better reproduc-
tion on a gem (*Br. Mus. Cat.* 929) cf.
Furtwängler, *op. cit.* p. 350, where
the gem is made the starting-point for
a suggestive reconstruction of the
works of Euphranor.

13. Latona . . . sustinens : the
work is still unknown ; cf. E. Reisch,
' Ein vermeintliches Werk des Euphranor' in *Festgruss aus Innsbruck
an die Phil. Versamml. in Wien*,
1893.

puerpera Apollinem et Dianam infantis sustinens in aede
78 Concordiae. fecit et quadrigas bigasque et cliduchon eximia
forma, et Virtutem et Graeciam, utrasque colossaeas, mulierem admirantem et adorantem, item Alexandrum et
Philippum in quadrigis, Eutychides Eurotam, in quo artem 5
ipso amne liquidiorem plurimi dixere. Hegiae Minerva
Pyrrhusque rex laudatur, et celetizontes pueri, et Castor ac
Pollux ante aedem Iovis tonantis, Hagesiae in Pario colonia
79 Hercules, Isodoti buthytes. Lycius Myronis discipulus fuit,
qui fecit dignum praeceptore puerum sufflantem languidos 10
ignes et Argonautas, Leochares aquilam sentientem quid
rapiat in Ganymede et cui ferat parcentemque unguibus
etiam per vestem puero, Autolycum pancrati victorem propter
quem Xenophon symposium scripsit, Iovemque illum tonantem in Capitolio ante cuncta laudabilem, item Apollinem 15
diadematum, Lyciscum mangonem, puerum subdolae ac

2. cliduchon] *Barbarus*; cliticon *Bamb.*, *Detlefsen*; cliticum *reliqui*.
16. luciscus langonem *reliqui*.

1. aede Concordiae: above § 73.
§ 78. 2. cliduchon: a subject also
treated by Pheidias, § 54.

4. admirantem et adorantem =
ἀποβλέπουσαν 'looking up with awe
at the image of the divinity,' Furtwängler, *Plinius*, p. 46, cf. *Dornauszieher*, p. 87, note 19.

Alexandrum et Philippum: a
suitable occasion for these statues
would be the battle of Chaironeia,
where Al. had distinguished himself
by the side of Philip.

5. Eutychides: above § 51; distinct from his two later namesakes
(*a*) *I.G.B.* 143; (*b*) *I.G.B.* 244-249,
and recently Homolle in *Bull. Corr.
Hell.* 1894, p. 336 f. To the pupil
of Lysippos, Studniczka (*Jahrb.* ix,
1894, p. 211) inclines to attribute the
superb sarkophagos ' of Alexander '
from Sidon.

Eurotam: cf. the Orontes that
supports the city of Antioch by the
same artist; above note on § 51.

6. plurimi: i.e. the writers of
epigrams, Benndorf, *Epigr.* p. 54; cf.

Anth. Pal. ix, 709 (Introd. p. lxx).

Hegiae: for an older namesake,
master of Pheidias, see § 49; for a
Hegias in the reign of Claudius see
I.G.B. 332.

7. Pyrrhusque rex: for portraits
of this king (born B.C. 319, died
272), see Six, *Röm. Mitth.* vi, p. 279;
Helbig in *Mélanges d'Arch. et d'Hist.*
xiii, 1893, pl. i, ii, pp. 377 ff.
The addition of *rex* gives such precision to Pliny's statement that it is
unnecessary to suppose that we have
in the words *Hegiae . . . laudatur* a
confused repetition of the *Pyrrhus
Hygiam et Minervam* of § 80 (cf.
Wolters, *Ath. Mitth.* xvi, 1891, p.
155, note 2).

8. Iovis tonantis: above § 10;
below § 79.

Hagesiae: 'Ηγησίας instead of
the more familiar diminutive 'Ηγίας,
so Ζεύξιππος for Ζεῦξις Plat. *Prot.*
318 B (cf. Fick, *Gr. Personennamen*,
p. 35).

Pario colonia: v, 141, founded
by the Parians, Milesians, and Ery-

born Apollo and Artemis in her arms, now in the temple of
Concord, and chariots with four and two horses, a κλειδοῦχος or 78
Key-bearer, of great beauty, a statue of Valour, and one of
Hellas, both of colossal size, a woman in wonder praying, and
Alexander and Philip in four-horse chariots. *Eutychides* made
an image of the Eurotas of which many have said that the
artist's skill is clearer than the stream itself.

The Athena and the king Pyrrhos by *Hegias* are praised, so
are his boys riding on racehorses, the Kastor and Polydeukes which
stand in front of the temple of Jupiter the Thunderer, and also
the Herakles of *Hegesias* in the colony of Parion, and the βουθύτης,
or Slayer of the Ox, by *Isodotos*. *Lykios* was a pupil of Myron ; in 79
the boy blowing a dying fire he created a work worthy of his
master ; he also made statues of the Argonauts. The eagle of *Eagle*
Leochares appears to know how precious a burden it is ravishing *ravishing*
Ganymede.
in Ganymede and to what master it bears him, and its talons
hold the boy tenderly though his dress protects him. He
also made a statue of Autolykos, who was victorious in the pankration and in whose honour Xenophon wrote the Banquet ; the
celebrated Zeus with the thunderbolt in the Capitol, a work of
supreme excellence ; an Apollo wearing the diadem ; the slave-
dealer Lykiskos and a boy, on whose face may be read the wily

thraians, Strabo, xiii, p. 588, 14 ; it
was made into a Roman colony by
Augustus (*Colonia Pariana Julia
Augusta*).

§ 79. 9. Lycius Myronis : § 50.

10. puerum sufflantem: same subject treated by the painter Antiphilos
xxxv, 138. The work is of course distinct from the *puer suffitor* below, and
from the boy, also by Lykios, holding
the holy water basin on the Akropolis,
Paus. i, 23, 7, but the kinship of the subjects shows where the artistic strength
of Lykios lay (cf. Wolters, *Ath.
Mitth.* xvi, 1891, p. 153 ff. and Mayer,
Arch. Jahrb. viii, 1893, p. 218 f.).

11. Leochares : § 50. [His works
are enumerated in two alphabetical
groups : from *aquilam* to *Iovem*, and
after *item* from *Apollinem* to *puerum*.
—H. L. U.]

aquilam . . . Ganymede : a copy

of this work has been recognized in
the statuette, Helbig, *Class. Ant.* 400.

13. Autolycum : winner in the
Pankration at the greater Panathenaia
Ol. 89, 3 = B.C. 422 (the fictitious date
of the 'Banquet,' Athen. v, p. 216 d),
murdered B.C. 404 by the Thirty
Tyrants. Since Leochares lived into
the reign of Alexander, there can be
no question of his having made a portrait of Autolykos, but the latter was
sufficiently celebrated to have—like
Miltiades and other heroes of Athenian
history—statues raised to him after
death (cf. Klein, *Arch. Ep. Mittheil.*
vii, 1883, p. 72).

14. Iovemque illum tonantem :
the motive of the statue may be recovered from coins ; Cohen, *Médailles
Impériales*, 2nd ed. i, p. 88; Roscher,
ii, 748. Above § 10.

16. Lyciscum mangonem : Ur-

80 fucatae vernilitatis, Lycius et ipse puerum suffitorem. Me-
naechmi vitulus genu premitur replicata cervice. ipse
Menaechmus scripsit de sua arte. Naucydes Mercurio et
discobolo et immolante arietem censetur, Naucerus luctatore anhelante, Niceratus Aesculapium et Hygiam . . . qui 5
sunt in Concordiae templo Romae. Pyromachi quadriga
ab Alcibiade regitur. Polycles Hermaphroditum nobilem
fecit, Pyrrhus Hygiam et Minervam, Phanis Lysippi
81 discipulus epithyusan. Styppax Cyprius uno celebratur
signo, splanchnopte—Periclis Olympii vernula hic fuit exta 10
torrens ignemque oris pleni spiritu accendens—Silanion
Apollodorum fudit, fictorem et ipsum, sed inter cunctos
diligentissimum artis et iniquom sui iudicem, crebro perfecta

5. Hygiam] Hygiam fecit *Detlefsen.*

lichs (*Chrestom.* p. 328) refers the
subject to the influence of the Middle
Comedy. Λυκίσκος, as title of a play
by Alexis, is preserved by Athen. xiii,
p. 595 d; the *puer* must have formed
a group with the *mango;* but Pliny,
who is here giving an asyndetic
enumeration of single works, seems
to have understood them to be separate statues, cf. Furtwängler, *Dornauszieher,* p. 91, note 44 (against
the reading *Lyciscus langonem,* which
has lately again come into favour, see
Friedländer's note to Martial, ix, 50).

1. suffitorem: presumably holding
a censer suspended by chains; cf.
Mayer, *op. cit.* p. 222.

§ 80. 2. replicata cervice: i. e.
in the scheme known from the Nike
sacrificing an ox on the balustrade of
the Temple of Athena Nike, cf. Cecil
Smith in *J. H. S.* vii, 1886, pp. 275 ff.

3. scripsit de sua arte : Introd.
p. xl.

Naucydes: above § 50. His *immolans arietem* has been identified,
but on purely fanciful reasons, with
the Phrixos burning the thigh of a ram
on the Akropolis, Paus. i, 24, 2 (cf.
Furtwängler, *Masterpieces,* p. 231).

4. luctatore anhelante: epigram-

matic, cf. xxxv, 71, *ut anhelare sentiatur ;* Reisch, *Weihgeschenke,* p. 45.

5. Niceratus : Νικήρατος Εὐκτή-
μονος Ἀθηναῖος, Fränkel, *Inschr. aus
Perg.* 132; also *I. G. B.* 147, 496;
works conjointly with Phyromachos,
ib. 118 (from Delos).

Aesculapium et H.: Fränkel (*loc.
cit.*) suggests that the group was originally made for the *Asklepieion* at
Pergamon, in which case it was presumably transferred to Rome when
the Romans inherited the Pergamene
treasures by the will of Attalos II, 133
B. C.

6. Pyromachi : note on *Niceratus*
above; for an older namesake cf.
§ 51.

quadriga: possibly as a pendant to
the group by Nikeratos of Alkibiades
and his mother sacrificing, § 88
(Fränkel, *loc. cit.*).

7. Polycles : not identical with
the artist of § 50, while his identity
with the Polykles of § 52 (= xxxvi, 35)
is uncertain. Nothing is known of his
Hermaphrodite; it cannot of course
have been the marble recumbent figure,
extant in so many replicas ; it should
perhaps be sought for among the
standing types of the Hermaphrodite

craft of the servile character. *Lykios* too made a boy burning perfumes.

By *Menaichmos* we have a calf on which a man is setting 80 his knee as he bends its neck back; Menaichmos also wrote a book on his art. The fame of *Naukydes* rests on his Hermes, his δισκοβόλοs or Disk-thrower, and his man sacrificing a ram; that of †*Naukeros* on his panting wrestler. *Nikeratos* ⟨made⟩ the Asklepios and Hygieia now in the temple of Concord at Rome. By *Pyromachos* we have a four-horse chariot driven by Alkibiades. *Polykles* made a famous Hermaphrodite, *Pyrrhos* a Hygieia and an Athena, †*Phanis*, the pupil of Lysippos, an ἐπιθύουσα, or woman sacrificing.

†*Styppax* of Cyprus is known by one statue only, the σπλαγχνόπ- 81 της, or Roaster of Entrails. This was a slave of Perikles the *The 'Roaster of* Olympian; he is roasting entrails and blowing hard on the fire to *Entrails.'* kindle it till his cheeks swell. *Seilanion* cast a portrait of Apollo-doros, who was also a statuary, and among the most painstaking, a severe critic of his own work, who often broke up a finished

(e. g. *Berlin Cat.* 193; see Herrmann *ap.* Roscher, i, pp. 2324 ff.). Addenda.

8. **Hygiam et Minervam**: from the extant inscription ('Αθηναῖοι τῇ 'Αθηναίᾳ τῇ 'Υγιείᾳ || Πύρρος ἐποίησεν 'Αθηναῖος *I. G. B.* 53) it appears that Pliny made one work into two. The statue is mentioned Paus. i, 23, 4 (without name of artist), Plutarch, *Per.* 13, who says it was dedicated by Perikles to commemorate the miraculous cure of a favourite work-man employed on the Propylaia (see note on *vernula* below). Wolters, however, has shown on technical evidence (*Ath. Mitth.* xvi, 1891, p. 153 ff.) that the statue must have been dedicated at a period subsequent to the commencement of the Peloponnesian war, and that Plutarch's narrative must consequently be a mere invention.

§ 81. 9. **Styppax Cyprius**: I see no reason for the doubts with regard to this name expressed by Loewy *Untersuch.* p. 30, against which see also Wolters, *Ath. Mitth.* xvi, 1891, p. 156, note 1.

10. **splanchnopte**: the motive of the statue and a probable copy are fully discussed by M. Mayer, *Jahrb.* viii, 1893, p. 224 and pl. iv.

Periclis Ol. vernula: the story is told fully, xxii, 44; in spite of dis-crepancies it is apparently identical with the one narrated by Plutarch of the Athena Hygieia. The cause for the dedication of a statue by so im-portant a personage as Perikles would naturally be eagerly sought for; the vicinity of the *splanchnoptes* to that of Athena in her character of 'Healer' suggested a connexion between the two, and accounts for the legends told by Pliny and Plutarch. Cf. Wol-ters, *loc. cit.*; Kuhnerdt, *Stat. u. Ort*, p. 274.

12. **Apollodorum**: the date proved for Seilanion (§ 51) makes it impossible to identify the Apollodoros either with the Sokratic philosopher (fl. B. C. 430–360) or with the artist of *I. G. B.* 55 (in Pre-Eukleidan characters). *I.G.B.* 218 records a third of the name. For the painter A. see xxxv, 60.

signa frangentem, dum satiari cupiditate artis non quit,
82 ideoque insanum cognominatum ; hoc in eo expressit, nec
hominem ex aere fecit, sed iracundiam, et Achillem nobilem,
item epistaten exercentem athletas, Strongylion Amazonem
quam ab excellentia crurum eucnemon appellant, ob id in 5
comitatu Neronis principis circumlatam. idem fecit puerum
quem amando Brutus Philippensis cognomine suo inlustravit.
83 Theodorus, qui labyrinthum fecit Sami, ipse se ex aere
fudit, praeter similitudinis mirabilem famam magna sup-
tilitate celebratus. dextra limam tenet, laeva tribus digitis 10
quadrigulam tenuit translatam Praeneste, tantae parvitatis
ut—mirum dictu—eam currumque et aurigam integeret alis
simul facta musca. Xenocrates Tisicratis discipulus, ut alii
Euthycratis, vicit utrosque copia signorum. et de sua

8. fecit Sami, ipse] *editores ante Sillig* ; fecit, Sami ipse *Detlefsen*.   12.
mirum dictu] *coni. Traube* ; miraculo pictam *Bamb.* ; totam *reliqui, Detlefsen.*

§ 82. 2. nec hominem . . . sed irac. : O. Jahn (*Kunsturtheile*, p. 112) detected in these words a latent epigram ; the phraseology, however, which was originally confined to colloquial language and used as a rule in a disparaging sense, had become universal in Pliny's day ; cf. Quinct. x, 1, 112 *non iam hominis nomen sed eloquentiae habeatur ;* H. S. Jones, *Class. Rev.* 1893, p. 224, cf. Baehrens, *Catullus*, p. 608. See Addenda.

4. epistaten . . . athletas : votive statue, put up presumably by the athletes of a gymnasium ; thus the gymnasiarchs Menas and Metodoros at Sestos and Pergamon receive statues for honourable discharge of their duties, likewise the Κοσμητής Nymphodotos at Athens receives a statue in the palaistra *C. I. A.* iii, 1104, see Kuhnerdt, *Statue u. Ort*, p. 308 [the words *exercentem athletas* were probably taken from the descriptive epigram on the statue.—H. L. U.]

Strongylion : *I. G. B.* 52 gives the inscr. belonging to his δούριος ἵππος (Paus. i, 23, 8), which from the allusion in Aristoph. Ὄρνιθες, 1128, must

have been erected shortly before that play was produced in B. C. 414.

Amazonem : we possibly have its copy in the charming equestrian statuette in Naples (Friederichs-Wolters, 1781 ; the opinion first expressed by Hoffman in Overbeck's *Plastik*, ed. 4, i, p. 506, note 14). By representing the Amazon on horseback, S. could not only display her legs, but likewise find scope for his talent as a sculptor of animals (Paus. ix, 30, 1).

6. circumlatam : above § 48 ; we may conclude from this fact that the Amazon was a statuette.

7. cognomine suo : *Bruti puer*, Martial, ii, 77 ; ix, 50 ; xiv, 171.

§ 83. 8. Theodorus : his date may be approximately determined by the fact that he worked for Kroisos (B. C. 560–546), Herod. i, 51, and for Polykrates, Herod. iii, 41 (B. C. 532 ?–521), cf. xxxvii, 3. That there was only one artist of the name has now been admitted even by Overbeck (*Plastik*, 4th ed. 1893, p. 78).

labyrinthum . . . Sami : i. e. the Heraion, of which his father Rhoikos (Herod. iii, 60) was the first archi-

statue, being unable to reach the ideal he aimed at; from this
he was called 'the madman.' This characteristic Seilanion ren- 82
dered, and made his bronze not a portrait of an individual, but
a figure of Vexation itself. He also made a famous Achilles,
and a trainer exercising his athletes. *Strongylion* made the Amazon surnamed the εὔκνημος from the beauty of her legs; it was
because of this special feature that the Emperor Nero carried
the statue about in his train. He also made the boy which
Brutus of Philippi loved, and made illustrious by his name.
Theodoros, the maker of the labyrinth at Samos, also cast a portrait 83
of himself in bronze, famed as a wondrous likeness, and also
celebrated for the extreme delicacy of the workmanship. The
right hand holds a file, while three fingers of the left hand
support a tiny team of four horses, which is now at Praeneste, *Tiny*
so small that the team, marvellous to relate, with chariot and *chariot and*
team by
charioteer could be covered by the wings of a fly which the artist *Theodoros.*
made to accompany it. *Xenokrates* was a pupil of Teisikrates, or,
according to some authorities, of Euthykrates; he outdid both in

tect; cf. xxxvi, 90, where the purely
mythical *labyrinthus Lemnius* is a
mistake of Pliny for *lab. Samius*
(Urlichs, *Anfänge*, 1871, p. 3, cf.
Klein in *Arch. Ep. Mitth.* ix, 1885,
p. 184); of Rhoikos and Theodoros
at least we know that they were *indigenae* not of Lemnos but of Samos
(Σάμιοι, Paus. viii, 14, 8; Ῥοῖκος
ἐπιχώριος, sc. of Samos, Herod. *loc. cit.*

ipse se : cf. the portrait of the
Kretan Cheirisophos, presumably by
himself, next to his gilt statue of
Apollo at Tegea, Paus. viii, 53, 7.

10. **laeva . . . quadrigulam** : it
is generally supposed that the little
chariot was engraved on the base of
a scarab (see e. g. the scarab, *Brit.
Mus. Cat. of Gems*, pl. D, 254);
Benndorf, *Zts. für Oesterr. Gymnasien*,
1873, p. 406. Theodoros was a
famous gem-graver; yet the extant
marvels of μικροτεχνία accomplished
in the goldsmith's art show that the execution in the round of a microscopic
chariot was no technical impossibility;
see note on *Mymercides*, xxxvi, 43.

11. **Praeneste** : where the celebrated temple of *Fortuna Primigenia*,
like so many of the temples in Rome
(cf. Friedländer, *Darstellungen*, ii,
pp. 154 ff.), must have contained all
sorts of curiosities (see R. Peter *ap.*
Roscher, i, 1545).

12. **mirum dictu**: xviii, 160, so
facile dictu, xxviii, 20; *rarum
dictu*, xiv, 132; *incredibile dictu*,
xxxv, 88.

eam : i. e. the team proper as distinct from the *currus* and the *auriga*,
likewise in xxxvi, 36 *quadriga currusque*.

13. **Xenocrates**: his identity with
the Xenocrates of Athens, son of
Ergophilos of *I. G. B.* 135 a and b
(from Oropos), of *I. G. B.* 135 c (from
Elateia), and of Ἐφημ. ἀρχαιολ. 1892,
52 (from Oropos), though usually
accepted, is nothing less than proven.
See Introd. p. xx, note 2.

Tisicratis : *I. G. B.* 120, from
Oropos.

14. **Euthycratis** : above § 67
[from the fact that this and the two

84 arte composuit volumina. plures artifices fecere Attali et
Eumenis adversus Gallos proelia, Isigonus, Pyromachus,
Stratonicus, Antigonus qui volumina condidit de sua arte.
Boethi, quamquam argento melioris, infans amplexando
anserem strangulat. atque ex omnibus quae rettuli clarissima 5
quaeque iam sunt dicata a Vespasiano principe in templo
Pacis aliisque eius operibus, violentia Neronis in urbem con-
85 vecta et in sellariis domus aureae disposita. praeterea sunt
aequalitate celebrati artifices, sed nullis operum suorum
praecipui, Ariston qui et argentum caelare solitus est, Cal- 10
lides, Ctesias, Cantharus Sicyonius, Dionysodorus Critiae
discipulus, Deliades, Euphorion, Eunicus et Hecataeus
argenti caelatores, Lesbocles, Prodorus, Pythodicus, Polygnotus idem pictor e nobilissimis, item e caelatoribus
86 Stratonicus, Scymnus Critiae discipulus. nunc percensebo 15

4. amplexando] *Traube*; sex anno *Bamb.* (sex annis *e corr.*) ; eximiae *Voss.* ;
eximie *Ricc.*, *Detlefsen* ; annosum *coni. Buecheler in Herondas*, p. 25 ;
vi annosum *coni. R. Meister in Mimiamben des Herondas*, p. 708. 11. Dionysius, Diodorus *Detlefsen* ; Diodorus *Bamb.*; dionysiodorus *Ricc.*, *Voss.*

preceding names contain the common
element -κρατης it would appear that
the bearers all belonged to the same
family, cf. Fick, *Griech. Personennamen*, p. xi.—H. L. U.].

1. **volumina** : Introd. p. xvi.

§ 84. **Attali** : i.e. Attalos I, B.C.
241–197.

2. **Eumenis** : i.e. II, B.C. 197–159.

Gallos : *Attalus eos rex saepe fudit
fugavitque*, Liv. xxxviii, 17, 15, the
dates however are obscure (see Loewy
on *I. G. B.* 154, pp. 117 f.); the
other victories commemorated in the
Pergamene inscriptions are those of
Attalos I over Antiochos Hierax in
228 B.C.

Isigonus : neither his name nor
those of Stratonikos (below § 90) or
Antigonos, have turned up among
the Pergamene inscriptions; Michaelis
(*Jahrb.* viii, 1893, p. 131) accordingly
proposes to alter the *Isigonus* of Pliny
to *Epigonus*, but on grounds which
are insufficient.

Pyromachus : above § 80.

3. **volumina** : Introd. p. xxxvi.

4. **Boethi** : of Chalkedon (Paus.
v, 17, 4, where Schubart, however,
reads Καρχηδόνιος) ; identical with the
silver-chaser of xxxiii, 155. In the
Heraion of Olympia Pausanias saw
the gilt statue of a boy by him.
quamquam elliptical, i.e. 'although
more renowned as a silver chaser, yet
I may mention . . .' The artist of
the portrait of Antiochos Epiphanes
(*I. G. B.* 210) belongs to a later
period, while a third Boëthos, belonging to the first quarter of the first
century B.C., is known from *Bull. d.
Corr. Hell.* xi, p. 263.

infans : preserved in a number of
replicas, Munich, *Glypt.* 140; Capitol, Helbig, *Class. Ant.* 518. The
same subject (without the artist's
name) is mentioned Herond. iv, 31
τὴν χηναλώπεκα ὡς τὸ παιδίον πνίγει |
πρὸ τῶν ποδῶν γοῦν εἴ τι μὴ λίθος
τοὔργον | ἐρεῖς λαλήσει· (ed. O. Cru-

the number of statues that he produced, and he also wrote books on his art.

The battles of Attalos and Eumenes against the Gauls were represented by several artists, †*Isigonos*, *Pyromachos*, *Stratonikos* and *Antigonos* who also wrote books on his art.

Boëthos, though greater as a worker in silver, made a child hugging a goose till he throttles it.

The best of all the works I have mentioned have now been dedicated at Rome by the emperor Vespasian in the temple of Peace and in his other galleries, Nero having first brought them by the strong hand to Rome, and placed them in the apartments of the Golden House.

I add a list of artists whose works are of equal excellence, though no single one is of supreme merit. Such are *Ariston*, who also worked in silver, †*Kallides*, †*Ktesias*, *Kantharos* of Sikyon, *Dionysodoros* the pupil of Kritios, †*Deliades*, †*Euphorion*, *Eunikos* and *Hekataios*, the silver chasers; †*Lesbokles*, †*Prodoros*, †*Pythodikos*, and *Polygnotos*, who was also among the most famous painters. Others who were also silver chasers were *Stratonikos* and †*Skymnos* the pupil of Kritios.

84
Works commemorating the victories of Attalos and Eumenes.
Boëthos.

85
Artists of second rank.

sius, who suggests the basis alone to have been of marble—cf. *Anth. Pal.* ix, 719—and accordingly assumes identity with the Plinian group, cf. *Untersuchungen zur Mimiamben des Herondas* 1892, p. 82). Identity likewise assumed by Buecheler and Meister (above text notes). The action of the child, who is really squeezing the goose in his embrace, is exactly described by the word *amplexando*, as now restored from the reading of Cod. Bamb. Addenda.

5. ex omnibus . . . clarissima: rhetorical flattery intended to please Pliny's patron Vespasian, cf. xxxvi, 102; so too Josephus, *Bell. Jud.* vii, 5, 7 (Niese, vol. vi, p. 591) says: πάντα . . . εἰς ἐκεῖνον τὸν νεὼ (sc. *Templ. Pac.*) συνήχθη καὶ κατετέθη, δι᾽ ὧν τὴν θέαν ἄνθρωποι πρότερον περὶ πᾶσαν ἐπλανῶντο τὴν οἰκουμένην. The *templum Pacis* was ded. A. D. 75, after the conquest of Judaea; full literature Gilbert, *Rom* iii, p. 135, note 3.

7. violentia Neronis: for hatred of Nero, cf. above § 45, xxxv, 51, 120. Introd. p. xcii.

§ 85. 9. aequalitate: i.e. of merit, Furtwängler, *Plinius*, p. 11.

10. Ariston: xxxiii, 156; a painter of the name, xxxv, 110-111; cf. on *I. G. B.* 275 a.

Callides: a painter of the name in Lucian, *Dial. Meretr.* viii, 3, cf. Brunn, *K. G.* ii, p. 311.

11. Cantharus: son of Alexis, pupil of Eutychides (above § 78), Paus. vi, 3, 6; 17, 7.

Dionysodoros: an artist of the name, *I. G. B.* 243 (from Delos, B. C. 110); a painter, xxxv, 146.

Critiae: perhaps identical with the Kritios in § 49.

12. Eunicus et Hec.: xxxiii, 156.

13. Polygnotus: xxxv, 58; known as a sculptor only from Pliny.

15. Stratonicus: presumably identical with the Str. of § 84 and of § 90.

eos qui eiusdem generis opera fecerunt, ut Apollodorus,
Androbulus, Asclepiodorus, Aleuas philosophos, Apellas
et adornantes se feminas, Antignotus et luctatores, perixyo-
menum tyrannicidasque supra dictos, Antimachus, Athenodorus feminas nobiles, Aristodemus et luctatores bigasque 5
cum auriga, philosophos, anus, Seleucum regem.   habet
87 gratiam suam huius quoque doryphorus.   Cephisodoti
duo fuere: prioris est Mercurius Liberum patrem in infantia
nutriens, fecit et contionantem manu elata, persona in
incerto est.   sequens philosophos fecit.   Colotes qui cum 10
Phidia Iovem Olympium fecerat philosophos, item Cleon et
Cenchramis et Callicles et Cepis, Chalcosthenes et comoedos
et athletas, Daippus perixyomenon, Daiphron et Damo-

§ 86. 1. qui eiusdem generis :
for the practice of classifying works
of art according to the artistic motive cf. Furtwängler, *Dornauszieher*,
pp. 20 f.

    Apollodorus: above § 81.

    2. Asclepiodorus : a painter of the
name, xxxv, 107.

    philosophos : Furtwängler, *Dorn-
auszieher*, pp. 24 f., has pointed out
that under this rubric must be understood not only philosophers in a restricted sense, but in general portraits
of distinguished personages.

    Apellas : son of Kallikles, makes
for Olympia the chariot of Kyniska
(*I. G. B.* 99 = Paus. vi, 1, 6), sister of
Agesilaos (died B.C. 360) of Sparta.
Cf. note on Callicles in § 87. Add.

    3. adornantes se : cf. the *pseli-
umene* in § 70.

    Antignotus : an artist of the name,
I. G. B. 314–316 (Augustan).

    4. supra dictos : descriptive of
the actual personages portrayed ; unnecessary difficulty has been caused
(cf. Loewy on *I. G. B.* 314) by assuming that they referred to the group
mentioned in § 70.

    Athenodorus : xxxvi, 37.

    5. Aristodemus : according to Ta-
tian, p. 36, 9 (ed. Schwartz), makes a
statue of Aisop, i.e. a work which

would fall under the heading of
philosophi.

    6. anus : votive portraits of priest-
esses, such as that of Lysimache, above
§ 76. Furtwängler, *Dornauszieher*, p. 26.

    Seleucum regem : above § 73.

    7. quoque : [i.e. as well as the
more celebrated Doryphoros of Polykleitos in § 55.—H. L. U.].

    § 87. Cephisodoti duo : (*a*) the
artist of the Eirene, Paus. ix, 16,
1, possibly father or brother of the
great Praxiteles (cf. note on § 50) ; (*b*)
a son of Praxiteles, xxxvi, 24.

    8. Mercurius . . . nutriens : the
motive is identical with that of the
Praxitelean Hermes. Addenda.

    9. manu elata : the raised hand
not being an action of Greek oratory
(where even to allow the hand to
protrude much from the cloak was
thought unseemly, Aischines *c. Tim.*
25), it is probable that the statue belonged to the class *adorantes*, and
that its gesture was misinterpreted by
a Roman writer as being the familiar
manus elata of the Roman orators
(Milchhöffer, *Arch. Studien H. Brunn
dargeb.* 1892, p. 39). A recent conjecture *manu velata* as the equivalent
of the ἐντὸς τὴν χεῖρα ἔχων of Aisch.
loc. cit. has met with little favour, cf.
S. Reinach in *Chron. d'Orient*, 1893,

I will now enumerate those who made statues of the same class, as *Apollodoros,* †*Androboulos, Asklepiodoros* and †*Aleuas,* who made philosophers; *Apellas,* who also made women adorning themselves, *Antignotos,* who also made wrestlers, a περιξυόμενος or athlete scraping himself, and statues of the tyrant-slayers whom I have mentioned, and †*Antimachos* and *Athenodoros,* who made statues of renowned women. *Aristodemos* also made wrestlers, two-horse chariots with charioteer, and figures of philosophers, of old women, and of king Seleukos; his Spear-bearer too has a charm of its own. There were two artists of the name of *Kephisodotos ;* by the first we have a Hermes nursing the infant Dionysos. He also made a statue of a man haranguing with uplifted hand; the person represented is not known. The younger *Kephisodotos* made statues of philosophers, and so did *Kolotes,* who had worked with Pheidias on his Olympian Zeus, *Kleon, Kenchramos, Kallikles,* and †*Kepis ; Chalkosthenes* also made statues of comic actors and athletes. *Daippos* made a περιξυόμενος or athlete scraping himself, † *Daiphron, Damokritos,* and †*Daimon* philosophers

p. 9; W. Gurlitt in *Berl. Phil. Woch.* 1895, p. 1230.

persona in incerto : [i. e. the inscription was effaced, or no longer extant.—H. L. U.] So Pausanias, vi, 15, 7, speaks of the statue of an unknown individual as ἀνὴρ ὅστις δή.

10. **Colotes:** xxxv, 54.

11. **Cleon :** of Sikyon, pupil of Antiphanes, himself pupil of Polykleitos, Paus. v, 17, 4, where a bronze Aphrodite by him is mentioned; *ib.* 21, 3 (two bronze Zanes, *I. G. B.* 95, 96); the remaining four statues by him (vi, 1, 5 ; 3, 10 ; 8, 5 ; 9, 2 ; 10, 9) all belong to the class *athletae.* For his school cf. Furtwängler, *Masterpieces,* p. 278.

12. **Cenchramis:** *I. G. B.* 70, 71 (both from Athens), where he is named with Polymnestos (*I. G. B.* 72). Add.

Callicles : son of Theokosmos of Megara, Paus. vi, 7, 1 (where his statue of the illustrious περιοδονίκης Diagoras of Rhodes is mentioned); father of Apellas (above § 86). F. Hauser (*Röm. Mittheil.* x, 1895, pp. 97–119) would see in him the artist

of the lovely bronze head of the boy-pugilist, Munich, *Glypt.* 302, and of the original of the basalt statue of another pugilist in the Terme Mus. (*ib.* pl. I).

Chalcosthenes : apparently an error for *Chaecosthenes* (Καϊκοσθένης), brother of Dies and son of Apollonides, *I. G. B.* 113-117, 220, see note on xxxv, 155. In connexion with the votive-statues of *comoedi* mentioned here, it is interesting to note that *I. G. B.* 220 is from the theatre of Dionysos at Athens ; cf. Δελτίον, 1891, p. 84, 1. Like Epigonos (§ 88) he is known only from Pliny and the inscriptions.

13. **Daippus :** above § 51; for athlete statues by him cf. Paus. vi, 12, 6 ; 16, 5.

Damocritus : From Paus. vi, 3, 5 we learn that he was a Sikyonian, a pupil of Pison of Kalaureia (Paus. x, 9, 8), and fifth in school descent from the Attic artist Kritios. His identity with the Δημόκριτος of *I. G. B.* 484 and Diogenes Laertios, ix, 49 is doubtful.

88 critus et Daemon philosophos. Epigonus omnia fere prae-
dicta imitatus praecessit in tubicine et matri interfectae
infante miserabiliter blandiente. Eubuli mulier admirans
laudatur, Eubulidis digitis computans. Micon athletis spectatur, Menogenes quadrigis. nec minus Niceratus omnia quae 5
ceteri adgressus repraesentavit Alcibiaden lampadumque
89 accensu matrem eius Demaraten sacrificantem. Tisicratis
bigae Piston mulierem inposuit, idem fecit Martem et Mercurium qui sunt in Concordiae templo Romae. Perillum
nemo laudet saeviorem Phalaride tyranno, cui taurum fecit 10
mugitus hominis pollicitus igni subdito, et primus expertus
cruciatum eum iustiore saevitia. huc a simulacris deorum

11. et] *Bamb.* ; ex *reliqui* ; exprimere *Detlefsen.*

§ 88. 1. **Epigonus** : known from
a series of Pergamene inscriptions.
Fränkel, *Inschriften aus Pergamon*,
12 ; 21–28 ; 29 ; 31 (= *I. G. B.* 157) ;
32 (= *I. G. B.* 157 a). The great
bathron to which 21–28 belongs commemorates the close of the war in B. C.
228, against Antiochos and the Galatai.

omnia fere : rhetorical ; cf. *clarissima quaeque* in § 84 ; *omnibus fere
quae fecit*, xxxvi, 13.

2. **tubicine** : since Epigonos
worked for the Pergamene kings, it
has been suggested that his *tubicen*
represented a Gaul with his war
trumpet such as the famous 'dying
Gaul' of the Capitol (Helbig, *Class.
Ant.* p. 398, where see literature).
[The statue, however, may, as Winckelmann suggested, have been simply the
votive-portrait of the winner in the
contest of heralds, such as that of
Archias of Hybla at Delphoi, cf. Pollux, iv, 92, Preger, *Inscr.* 143, or that
of Phorystas at Olympia, *I. G. B.*
119. For a *tubicen* by the painter
Antidotos see xxxv, 130.—H. L. U.]
Add.

matri interfectae : for the motive cf. xxxv, 98; S. Reinach (*Rev.
des Études Grecques,* 1894, p. 41 ff.)
suggests that the group was of a

Gaulish mother and her child, and
belonged to the same series as the
'Dying Gaul' and the so-called
'Arrius and Paeta' of the Villa Ludovisi, Helbig, *Class. Ant.* 884.   Add.

3. **Eubuli** : his name has been
suggested in *I. G. B.* 235. For his
mulier admirans cf. above § 78.

4. **Eubulidis** : his name alter-
nates with that of Eucheiros (below
§ 91) on a series of inscriptions
(*I. G. B.* 223–229, 544) belonging
apparently to one family of artists ;
dates uncertain.

digitis computans : [the gesture
which is expressive of pondering or
meditation might be given to any
number of portraits of *philosophi ;* cf.
Lucian, *Timon,* 122, συνεσπακὼς τοὺς
δακτύλους πρὸ τὸ ἔθος τῶν λογισμῶν ;
Plin. *Ep.* ii, 20, 3 : *composuit vultum,
intendit oculos, movet labra, agitat
digitos, computat.* This observation,
coupled with the fact that, had the
digitis computans been the portrait of
a celebrated man, the name would
not have been forgotten, disposes of
Milchhöffer's theory (*Arch. Studien
H. Brunn dargebr.* pp. 37 ff.) that
the personage represented was Chrysippos.—H. L. U.]

Micon : identical with the painter,

Epigonos produced examples of almost all the subjects I have 88
mentioned, and surpassed them in his trumpeter and his infant *Dead mother and child by Epigonos.*
piteously caressing its dead mother.   †*Euboulos* is praised for
his woman in amazement, and *Euboulides* for his man reckoning
on his fingers.   *Mikon's* athletes are admired, and the four-horse
chariots of *Menogenes*.   *Nikeratos* too attempted the same subjects as these artists, and also made statues of Alkibiades and
his mother Demarate sacrificing by torchlight.   *Piston* made a 89
woman, to be placed in a two-horse chariot by *Teisikrates*, also
the statues of Ares and of Hermes which stand in the temple of
Concord at Rome.   *Perillos* it is impossible to praise: he showed *Bull of Phalaris.*
a cruelty greater than that of the tyrant Phalaris, for whom he
made a bull, promising that if a fire were lighted under it the
cries of the man inside would sound like the animal's bellowing,
a torture which cruelty for once righteous made him the first to
suffer.   From representations of gods and men he had dragged

xxxv, 59. The fact that he made
statues of athletes has been confirmed
by *I. G. B.* 41, from the statue of
the περιοδονίκης Kallias (Ol. 77 =
B. C. 472); and *I. G. B.* 42.

5. **Niceratus**: above § 80, where
see note on his Alkibiades.

6. **lampadum accensu**: i.e. she
held a torch, possibly in each hand;
the word *accensu*, however, makes
me suspect a latent epigram, Introd.
p. xliv, note 2.

7. **Demaraten**: her name was
however Δεινομάχη, Plat. *Alc.* 105,
d, &c. [The name Demarate may
have crept into Pliny's authority
through an error in transcribing the
inscription on the group.—H. L. U.]

§ 89. **Tisicratis**: above § 83;
mulierem inposuit, cf. § 71 on
Kalamis and the Elder Praxiteles;
the *mulier* was possibly a Nike.

9. **Perillum**: the Latin form. He
also appears as Perilaos in Lucian,
according to whom (*Phal.* i, 11) he
was a native of Akragas; for the late
notion that he was an Athenian, see
Freeman, *Hist. of Sicily*, ii, p. 75,
note 2.

10. **Phalaride**: vii, 200; B.C. 570-

564 is now generally accepted as the
date of his τύραννις, Bentley, *Diss. on
the Epistles of Phalaris* (ed. 1699),
pp. 27 ff.; Freeman, *Sicily*, ii, pp.
458 f.

taurum fecit: the earliest mention of the brazen bull is by Pindar,
Pyth. i, 184; its mechanism is fully
described by Polybios, xii, 25. The
bull was reputed to have been taken
to Carthage on the sack of Akragas by the Carthaginians, B. C. 403;
it was brought back and restored
to the Carthaginians by the Younger
Scipio, Cic. *Verr.* II, iv, 34, § 73.
See Freeman, *op. cit.* Appendix,
vii, where the story of the bull is
fully discussed. It early became
a *locus communis* of rhetoric (cf.
Kalkmann in *Rhein. Mus.* xlii,
1887, pp. 513 ff.), which accounts
for the high colouring of Pliny's
language. Introd. p. xciii.

11. **mugitus hominis**: *Mugiet,
et veri vox erit illa bovis*, Ovid, *Trist.*
iii, 11, 48.

primus expertus: cf. Diodoros,
ix, 19; Ovid, *loc. cit.*; and *Ars Amat.*
1, 653; Lucian, *Phalaris*, i, 12.

hominumque devocaverat humanissimam artem.   ideo tot
conditores eius laboraverant ut ex ea tormenta fierent!
itaque una de causa servantur opera eius, ut quisquis illa
90 videat oderit manus.   Sthennis Cererem, Iovem, Minervam
fecit, qui sunt Romae in Concordiae templo, idem flentes 5
matronas et adorantes sacrificantesque.   Simon canem et
sagittarium fecit, Stratonicus caelator ille philosophos,
91 Scopas *uterque*, athletas autem et armatos et venatores
sacrificantesque Baton, Euchir, Glaucides, Heliodorus,
Hicanus, *Iophon*, Lyson, Leon, Menodorus, Myagrus, Poly- 10
crates, Polyidus, Pythocritus, Protogenes idem pictor e
clarissimis, ut dicemus, Patrocles, Pollis, Posidonius qui
et argentum caelavit nobiliter, natione Ephesius, Periclymenus, Philon, Symenus, Timotheus, Theomnestus, Timarchides, Timon, Tisias, Thrason.   ex omnibus autem 15

8. scopas] *codd.*; copas *Gerhard, Detlefsen.*   10. Iophon] *Urlichs in*
Chrest. p. 91; olophon *Bamb.*; lophon *reliqui.*

§ 90. 4. Sthennis: above § 51.

5. flentes matronas: grave portrait statues, cf. above on § 70.

6. adorantes sacrificantesque:
cf. §§ 73, 78. On these rubrics see
the remarks of Furtwängler, *Dorn-*
auszieher, pp. 22 ff.

Simon: his identity with the Aiginetan artist of the name (Paus. v,
27, 2), employed with Dionysios of
Argos on the Olympic votive-offer-
ings of Phormis of Mainalos, is
uncertain.

canem et sagittarium: i. e. a
votive-portrait of a Kretan or Scythian
bowman with his dog; cf. Furtwängler,
op. cit., p. 93.

7. Stratonicus: xxxiii, 156; above
§§ 84, 85.

8. Scopas uterque: although the
MSS. are unanimous, no satisfactory
sense can be got out of the reading.
Skopas, as the name of the artist, is
quite in place in the alphabetical
enumeration, but we cannot follow
Klein (*Arch. Ep. Mitth.* iv, p. 22 ff.)
in assuming a lacuna after *uterque,* or
in seeing in the *uterque* a confirma-

tion of his double Skopas (above note
on § 49, l. 13). My own view is that the
uterque is a very ancient corruption,
and conceals the name of the work of
art made by Skopas. It has also been
suggested that *scopas* is the acc. pl.
either of σκώψ (Satyric dancers, see
Urlichs's note in *Chrest.* p. 331) or
σκόπας (Satyr on the look-out), in
which case the *uterque* would refer
back to Simon and Stratonikos.
ΣΚΟΓΑ< is inscribed above a Satyr
on a vase with the Apotheosis of
Herakles (Munich, Jahn *Cat.* 384=
Mon. d. Inst. iv, pl. 41, *Ann.* xi, *Tav.*
d'Agg. O); but the fact that the
next Satyr is inscribed ΥΒΡΙΣ shows
that we have here no generic term,
but merely an epithet applied to one
particular Satyr (cf. the ἀποσκοπεύων
of Antiphilos in xxxv, 138). Finally
besides the *copas* (= castanet dancers),
of Gerhard, Urlichs in *Pergamen.*
Inschriften, p. 23, has suggested
scyphos. See Addenda.

§ 91. athletas: for this and the
following rubrics cf. *adorantes sacri-*
ficantesque above.

down the most humanizing of arts to this level, and the early masters had only laboured to the end that instruments of torture should be created by its means. The works of Perillos, in consequence, are preserved only that whoever sees them may loathe the hand that made them. *Sthennis* made statues of Demeter, **90** Zeus and Athena, which are at Rome in the temple of Concord; also matrons weeping, praying, or sacrificing. *Simon* made a dog and an archer, *Stratonikos*, known also as a silver chaser, made statues of philosophers, and Skopas . . .

We have statues of athletes, armed men, hunters, and men **91** sacrificing, by *Baton, Eucheir,* †*Glaukides, Heliodoros,* †*Hikanos,* *Artists* †*Iophon, Lyson, Leon, Menodoros, Myagros, Polykrates,* †*Polyeidos,* *who made statues of* *Pythokritos, Protogenes,* who was also, as will be said later on, *athletes.* a painter of the highest renown, *Patrokles,* †*Pollis, Poseidonios,* an Ephesian by nationality, who is also famous for his silver chasing, *Periklymenos, Philon, Symenos, Timotheos, Theomnestos, Timar-chides, Timon,* †*Teisias,* and *Thrason.*

Baton: above § 73.

Euchir: note on *Eubulidis* above § 88.

Heliodorus: xxxvi, 35.

10. Iophon: the *olophon* of *Bamb.* points to a longer name. Loewy, *Untersuch.* p. 39, note 31 suggests Herophon (*I. G. B.* 280, from a basis found at Olympia).

Lyson: he made a statue of *Demos* which stood in the Bouleuterion at Athens, Paus. i, 3, 5.

Leon: perhaps = *I. G. B.* 148.

Menodoros: an artist of the name made a copy of the Eros of Praxiteles at Thespiai, Paus. ix, 27, 4.

Myagrus: of Phokaia, Vitruv. iii, *Praef.* 2.

Polycrates: for a doubtful inscription with this name cf. *I. G. B.* 482.

11. Pythocritus: son of Timocharis of Rhodes, *I. G. B.* 174–176, *Ath. Mitth.* xvi, 1891, pp. 120 f. = *Jahrb.* ix, 1894, p. 41. It is interesting to note that *I. G. B.* 174 belonged to the statue of a priest, i. e. to the class *sacrificantes* (Brunn, *K. G.* i, p. 461);

while *I. G. B.* 176, from the statue of an Olympic winner, belongs to the class *athletae.*

12. Patrocles: above § 50.

Posidonius: xxxiii, 156.

13. Periclymenus: Tatian, p. 35, 28 (ed. Schwartz), τί μοι διὰ τὸν Περικλύμενον γύναιον (Eutychis Plin. vii, 34), ὅπερ ἐκύησε τριάκοντα παῖδας, ὡς θαυμαστὸν ἡγεῖσθε τὸ κατανοεῖν ποίημα; Brunn, *K. G.* i, p. 473.

14. Philon: Tatian, p. 36, 17 (ed. Schwartz), mentions a statue of Hephaistion (cf. above § 64) by him; he would thus belong to the age of Alexander.

Symenus: *I. G. B.* 84 (latter half of sixth century).

Timotheus: xxxvi, 35.

Theomnestus: a painter of the name, xxxv, 107.

Timarchides: xxxvi, 35.

15. Timon: probably = *I. G. B.* 234 (from Athens).

Thrason: a figure of Hekate and a fountain, a Penelope and Eurykleia (in a group?) are mentioned, Strabo, xiv, p. 641; cf. Brunn, *K. G.* i, p. 421.

92 maxime cognomine insignis est Callimachus semper calumniator sui. nec finem habentis diligentiae, ob id catatexitechnus
appellatus, memorabili exemplo adhibendi et curae modum.
huius sunt saltantes Lacaenae, emendatum opus sed in quo
gratiam omnem diligentia abstulerit.   hunc quidem et 5
pictorem fuisse tradunt.   non aere captus, nec arte, unam
A.U.C. 698. tantum Zenonis statuam Cypria expeditione non vendidit
Cato, sed quia philosophi erat, ut obiter hoc quoque noscatur
93 tam inane exemplum.   in mentione statuarum est et
una non praetereunda, quamquam auctoris incerti, iuxta 10
rostra, Herculis tunicati, sola eo habitu Romae, torva facie,
sentiensque suprema tunicae.   in hac tres sunt tituli: L.
A.U.C. 691. Luculli imperatoris de manubiis, alter: pupillum Luculli
filium ex S. C. dedicasse, tertius: T. Septimium Sabinum
aed. cur. ex privato in publicum restituisse.   tot certaminum 15
tantaeque dignationis simulacrum id fuit.

12. sentientique *reliqui.*   tunica *reliqui.*

§ 92. 1. **Callimachus**: his date
can be approximately fixed at the
close of the fifth century, from the fact
that he is credited (Vitr. iv, 1, 10)
with the 'invention,' i. e. introduction
into Greece, of the Corinthian capital,
which Skopas (Paus. viii, 45, 5) employed in the temple at Tegea (Ol.
96 = B. C. 396).   Addenda.

calumniator sui: cf. Quint. x,
1, 115: *inveni qui Calvum prae-
ferrent omnibus, inveni qui Ciceroni
crederent, eum nimia contra se ca-
lumnia verum sanguinem perdidisse.*

2. **catatexitechnus**: Paus. i, 26,
7; Vitruv. *loc. cit.*: *Call. qui propter
elegantiam ac subtilitatem artis
marmoreae ab Atheniensibus catatexitechnus fuerat nominatus;* Brunn,
K. G. i, p. 254 aptly compares the
use of κατατήκειν in Dionys. *H. de vi
Dem.* 51: Οὐ γὰρ δή τοι, πλάσται μὲν
καὶ γραφεῖς ἐν ὕλῃ φθαρτῇ χειρῶν εὐ-
στοχίας ἐνδεικνύμενοι τοσούτους εἰσ-
φέρονται πόνους, ὥστε καὶ φλέβια καὶ
πτίλα καὶ χνοῦς καὶ τὰ τούτοις ὅμοια
εἰς ἄκρον ἐξεργάζεσθαι καὶ κατατήκειν
εἰς ταῦτα τὰς τέχνας.

4. **saltantes Lacaenae**: Furtwängler (*Masterpieces*, p. 438; *ib.* fig.
179) inclines to recognize the type in
the dancing girls wearing the Kala-
thiskos so common on later reliefs
and gems.

5. **gratiam . . . abstulerit**: this
judgement flatly contradicts the words
of Vitruvius quoted above (cf. also Paus.
loc. cit.); an interesting evidence of diver-
gence of opinion among ancient critics.

et pictorem fuisse: cf. of Pythagoras, § 60; of Pheidias, xxxv, 54.

7. **Zenonis**: he was born at Kition.
His features are known from the bust
at Naples, Schuster, *Ueber die erhal-
tenen Porträts der Gr. Philosophen,*
pl. iv, 1, 1 a.

Cypria expeditione: vii, 113,
when Cato went to Cyprus as *Quaestor
cum iure practorio* to confiscate the
property of Ptolemy, which was put
up to auction.

§ 93. 10. **auctoris incerti**: this
suffices to discredit the proposed
identification of this statue with the
Herakles of Polykles, mentioned Cic.
ad Att. vi, 1, 17.

Of all artists, however, *Kallimachos* has received the most dis- 92
tinctive name. He was always too severe a critic of himself, and *Kallimachos, ' the
incessantly laborious; from this he received the surname of *Niggler.'*
κατατηξίτεχνος, or the Niggler—a noteworthy warning that even
diligence has its limits. By him we have a group of Spartan
girls dancing, a work of faultless technique, which has, however,
lost all charm through over elaboration. Some authorities say
that Kallimachos was also a painter.

The statue of Zeno was the only one which Cato did not sell 56 B.C.
when commissioner in Cyprus; this, however, was not because
he valued the bronze or the workmanship, but because the statue
was that of a philosopher, a trivial incident, yet not unworthy of
passing notice.

In speaking of statues there is one which ought not to be 93
omitted, although the artist is unknown. It stands close to the *Herakles
wearing
Rostra, and represents Herakles wearing the tunic; it is the only *the tunic.*
one of him in Rome in that dress: the wild expression of the
face shows that he is feeling the last agonies of the tunic. There
are three inscriptions upon it: one states that it is part of the
plunder taken by Lucius Lucullus, the second that the son of 63 B.C.
Lucullus, while still a minor, dedicated it in pursuance of a decree of the Senate, the third that Titus Septimius Sabinus when
curule aedile made it once more a public monument. These
inscriptions show the rivalry occasioned by the statue, and the
value set on it.

11. **torva facie**: the description
shows clearly to what school the
Herakles belonged; the hero trying
to extricate himself from the burning
robe irresistibly recalls the Laokoon
tearing away the snakes. That the
tunica was the fatal robe sent by
Deianeira is a suggestion first made
by Turnebus, *Advers.* lib. xvi, 487.
Though the reading *sentiensque
suprema tunicae* is not absolutely
beyond suspicion, I see no reason for
following Peter (*ap.* Roscher, i, 2941)
in denying (cf. Urlichs in *Chrest.*
p. 333) the allusion to the poisoned
tunic. The subject seems to have been
represented in painting by Aristeides
(Polybios, *ap.* Strabo, viii, p. 381).

12. **tres sunt tituli**: showing that
the statue had changed place three
times; where it stood on its first
dedication is unknown. The son of
Lucullus re-dedicated it near the (old)
Rostra. Then, owing to the numerous
changes which took place in the Forum
it was removed and fell into private
hands; the restoration by T. Septimius Sab. was in virtue of his office
as aedile, by which he had charge of
public buildings and statues.

13. **de manubiis**: on the occasion
of his triumph B.C. 63.

pupillum: he was the ward of
Cato (Cic. *de Fin.* iii, 2) and Cicero
(*Att.* xiii, 6).

140   Aristonidas artifex cum exprimere vellet Athamantis
furorem Learcho filio praecipitato residentem paenitentia,
aes ferrumque miscuit ut robigine eius per nitorem aeris
relucente exprimeretur verecundiae rubor.   hoc signum
141 exstat hodie Rhodi.   est in eadem urbe et ferreus Hercules, 5
quem fecit Alcon laborum dei patientia inductus.   videmus et Romae scyphos e ferro dicatos in templo Martis
Ultoris.

1. **Aristonidas :** xxxv, 146, where
his son Mnasitimos is mentioned
among the painters *non ignobiles ;* cf.
I. G. B. 197 (inscr. more completely
given by Hiller von Gaertringen,
I. G. Ins. i, 855),which shows that M.
was also a sculptor like his father.

Athamantis furorem : recalls such
subjects as Herakles grieving for his
madness, xxxv, 141.   The Athamas
was perhaps inspired by the *Ino* of
Euripides, where the murder of Lear-
chos occurred.

4. **verecundiae rubor :** cf. Plu-

The artist *Aristonidas* in a statue representing Athamas after **140** the murder of his son sought to depict fury giving place to *Use of iron in* repentance, and mixed copper and iron, that the rust might show *statues.* through the metallic lustre of the copper and express the blush of shame; this statue exists to this day at Rhodes, where also is **141** a Herakles which *Alkon* bethought himself to cast in iron, in allusion to the fortitude of the god under his labours. We can also see cups of iron at Rome, dedicated in the temple of Mars the Avenger.

tarch's description of the Iokasta of Seilanion, Σνμπ. v, 1, 2, cf. πῶς δεῖ τὸν νέονποιημ. ἀκ. iii, 30.

6. **Alcon** : according to Brunn, *K. G.* ii, p. 402 (cf. i, p. 466) he is

perhaps identical with the chaser Alkon, Athen. xi, p. 469 A, the Pseudo - Virgil, *Culex*, 66 ; Ovid, *Metam.* xiii, 683 ff.

7. **Martis ultoris** : above § 48.

C. PLINII SECUNDI

NATURALIS HISTORIAE

(PICTURA ET PLASTICE)

I. PICTURA.

15 DE picturae initiis incerta nec instituti operis quaestio est. Aegyptii sex milibus annorum apud ipsos inventam priusquam in Graeciam transiret adfirmant vana praedicatione, ut palam est, Graeci autem alii Sicyone alii apud Corinthios repertam, omnes umbra hominis lineis circumducta, itaque 5 primam talem, secundam singulis coloribus et monochromaton dictam postquam operosior inventa erat, duratque 16 talis etiam nunc. inventam liniarem a Philocle Aegyptio vel Cleanthe Corinthio primi exercuere Aridices Corinthius et Telephanes Sicyonius, sine ullo etiamnum hi colore, iam 10 tamen spargentes linias intus. ideo et quos pingerent ad-

§ 15. 1. incerta: in vii, 205 Pliny had already given two different versions.

2. Aegyptii: their contention was obviously a true one; the *vana praedicatione* is drawn from a Greek writer anxious to claim the invention of painting for Greece.

4. Sicyone: for its claims to artistic preeminence cf. below, § 75, xxxvi, 9, and note on xxxiv, 55; it is probable that Corinth was the earlier artistic centre, and that priority was claimed for Sikyon, when, in the latter half of the fifth century, it began to assume the leadership of the Peloponnesian schools. The allusion to Sikyon, and the theoretical character of the following genesis of painting

(Introd. p. xxviii f.) point to Xenokrates as authority.

5. umbra . . . circumducta: this theory is purely arbitrary; it rests on the conventional supposition that the simpler method necessarily precedes the more complex—that pictures in outline precede pictures where the contours are filled in, and monochrome painting polychrome. The historical study of the monuments, i. e. of early painted fictile wares, has shown, however, that the operation was reversed in both cases; cf. Robert, *Arch. Märchen*, p. 121 ff. Studniczka (*Jahrb.* ii, 1887, p. 148 ff.) has made a vigorous attempt to reconcile fact with the Plinian tra-

I. PAINTING.

THE origin of painting is obscure, and hardly falls within the scope of this work.   The claim of the Egyptians to have discovered the art six thousand years before it reached Greece is obviously an idle boast, while among the Greeks some say that it was first discovered at Sikyon, others at Corinth.   All, however, agree that painting began with the outlining of a man's shadow; this was the first stage, in the second a single colour was employed, and after the discovery of more elaborate methods this style, which is still in vogue, received the name of monochrome.

The invention of linear drawing is attributed to † *Philokles* of Egypt, or to *Kleanthes* of Corinth.   The first to practise it were † *Arideikes* of Corinth, and † *Telephanes* of Sikyon, who still used no colour, though they had begun to give the inner markings, and from this went on to add the names of the personages they

15
Obscurity of its origin.

16
Philokles of Egypt.
Kleanthes of Corinth.
Arideikes of Corinth.
Telephanes of Sikyon.

dition; see also Hollwerda in *Jahrb.* v, 1890, p. 256 f. and C. Smith, art. PICTURA in Smith's *Dict. Ant.* p. 400 f., who gives a lucid analysis of the question.

§ 16. 8. **inventam liniarem**: the use of *invenio* like that of *primus* (cf. note on xxxiv, 54) must not be pressed; it arises from the determination, already noted in the case of the bronze statuaries, to connect each stage of a progress with one definite name.

Philocle Aegyptio: harks back to the Egyptian tradition; Münzer, *Hermes*, xxx, 1895, p. 512, note 1.

9. **Cleanthe**: known from Strabo, viii, p. 343, as the painter of (*a*) an Ilioupersis, (*b*) a Birth of Athena (cf. Athen. viii, 346 C); for the probable style of these paintings cf. Studniczka, *op. cit.* p. 153.

11. **adscribere institutum**: the names of the personages portrayed were used ornamentally to fill up space, as often on black-figured vases.

scribere institutum. primus invenit eas colore testae, ut
ferunt, tritae, Ecphantus Corinthius. hunc eodem nomine
alium fuisse quam quem tradit Cornelius Nepos secutum
in Italiam Damaratum Tarquinii Prisci regis Romani patrem
fugientem a Corintho tyranni iniurias Cypseli mox docebi- 5
mus.

17   Iam enim absoluta erat pictura etiam in Italia. exstant
certe hodieque antiquiores urbe picturae Ardeae in aedibus
sacris, quibus ego quidem nullas aeque miror, tam longo
aevo durantis in orbitate tecti veluti recentis. similiter 10
Lanivi, ubi Atalante et Helena comminus pictae sunt nudae
ab eodem artifice, utraque excellentissima forma, sed altera
18 ut virgo, ne ruinis quidem templi concussae. Gaius princeps
tollere eas conatus est libidine accensus, si tectori natura
permisisset. durant et Caere antiquiores et ipsae. fate- 15
biturque quisquis eas diligenter aestimaverit nullam artium
celerius consummatam, cum Iliacis temporibus non fuisse
eam appareat.

1. invenit]_codd.; inlevit *Haupt, Detlefsen*.

1. **invenit**: the manuscript reading is defended by Holwerda (*op. cit.*
p. 259, note 54) who points out that
invenire eam colore testae tritae corresponds to *picturam invenire singulis
coloribus* above. For *primus invenit*
cf. below, §§ 151, 152.

testae tritae : the process, which
is known only from this passage,
probably died out early, Blümner,
Technol. iv, p. 478 f.

2. **Ecphantus** : the name is that
of a painter inscribed on the *columna
Naniana* (*I. G. B.* 5); the identity
suggested by Studniczka (*op. cit.* p.
151) is quite uncertain.

3. **alium fuisse quam** : attempts
to reconcile two variant traditions—
namely the attribution of the invention
of painting proper to Ekphantos, and
the Italian tradition that painting was
perfect in Italy long before the arrival
of the Greeks. Cf. § 152, where the
fictores who followed Damaratos into
Italy are mentioned.

4. **Damaratus**: below § 152; Tac.
Ann. xi, 14; Dionysios H. iii, 46 ff.,
Strabo v, p. 219, viii, p. 378, &c.

5. **mox docebimus** : Furtwängler
(*Plinius*, p. 25 f.; cf. Robert, *Arch.
Märchen*, p. 123) has shown that the
proof follows immediately: *iam
enim . . .*

§ 17. 8. **Ardeae** : iii, 56; for the
paintings by M. Plautius in its temple
of Juno, below, § 115; for paintings
in temple of Castor and Pollux see
Servius on *Aen.* i, 44 (Thilo i, p. 31) :
*nam Ardeae in templo Castoris et
Pollucis in laeva intrantibus* (cf.
below, § 154) *post forem Capaneos
pictus est fulmen per utraque tempora
traiectus.*

11. **Lanivi** : iii, 64; viii, 221.

12. **altera ut virgo** : for the
ellipse of the first *altera* cf. below,
§ 71 *hoplites in certamine ita
decurrens ut sudare videatur,* alter
arma deponens ut . . . and see note on
xxxiv, 54, l. 7.

painted. The invention of painting with colour made, it is said, from powdered potsherds, is due to †*Ekphantos* of Corinth. *Ekphantos of Corinth.* I shall show presently that this Ekphantos is distinct from that namesake of his who, according to Cornelius Nepos, followed Damaratos, the father of Tarquin the Ancient, in his flight to Italy from Corinth to escape the insults of the tyrant Kypselos, for by that time painting in Italy also had already reached high perfection. To this day we may see in the temples of Ardea paintings older than the city of Rome, which I admire beyond any others, for though unprotected by a roof they remain fresh after all these years. At Lanuvium again are two nude figures by the same artist, of Atalanta and Helen, painted side by side. Both are of great beauty, and the one is painted as a virgin; they have sustained no injury though the temple is in ruins. The Emperor Caligula, who was fired by a passion for these figures, would undoubtedly have removed them if the composition of the stucco had allowed of it. Caere possesses some still more ancient paintings. No one can examine these carefully without confessing that painting reached its full development more rapidly than any other art, since it seems clear that it was not yet in existence in Trojan times.

17

Antiquity of painting in Italy.

Paintings at Ardea.

Atalanta and Helen at Lanuvium.

18

Paintings at Caere.

Rapid development of the art.

13. **ne ruinis quidem concussae** : one may conjecture that the Atalanta and Helena had once formed part of a larger composition which was partially destroyed in Pliny's time. Engelmann (*ap.* Roscher, i, p. 1964) conjectures that the painting had originally represented a mortal counterpart of the 'Judgement of Paris'— on the analogy of a bronze Etruscan cista at Berlin (Friederichs, *Bronzen*, 542, cf. *Arch. Anz.* 1889, p. 42),where Paris appears in conversation with three nude women Felena (Helen), Ateleta (Atalanta) and Alsir (?). Helen was a favourite subject of the Etruscan artists ; cf. Gerhard, *Etr. Spiegel*, iv, 373-382.

§ 18. 14. **libidine accensus** : for similar stories cf. below, § 70 ; xxxiv, 62.

tectori natura : below, § 173. For the elliptical construction of *si permisisset* cf. Tac. *Ann.* ii, 46 ; *spera-*

baturque rursum pugna, ni *Maraboduus castra* subduxisset.

15. **Caere**, iii, 51 ; an interesting series of paintings from Caere (Cervetri) now in the Brit. Mus. has been published by A. S. Murray, *J. H. S.* x, 1889, pl. vii, pp. 243-252, who justly points out their dependence on Greek models. In asserting the independent development of painting in Italy, Pliny has evidently been misled by his patriotism. A similar, but somewhat later, series of paintings from Caere in the Louvre, *Mon. Inst.* vi, vii, pl. 30.

17. **Iliacis temporibus** : the statement is based on the Homeric poems, where, with the exception of the νῆες μιλτοπάρῃοι, and the ἵππου παρήιον (*Il.* iv, 141) which 'a woman of Paionia or Maionia dyes with purple,' there are no allusions to painting ; see O. Müller, *Handbuch*, p. 51.

19   Apud Romanos quoque honos mature huic arti contigit,
siquidem cognomina ex ea Pictorum traxerunt Fabii claris-
simae gentis, princepsque eius cognominis ipse aedem Salutis
pinxit anno urbis conditae CCCCL, quae pictura duravit
ad nostram memoriam aede ea Claudi principatu exusta. 5
proxime celebrata est in foro boario aede Herculis Pacuvi
poetae pictura.   Enni sorore genitus hic fuit, clarioremque
20 artem eam Romae fecit gloria scaenae.   postea non est
spectata honestis manibus, nisi forte quis Turpilium equitem
Romanum e Venetia nostrae aetatis velit referre pulchris 10
eius operibus hodieque Veronae exstantibus.   laeva is manu
pinxit, quod de nullo ante memoratur.   parvis gloriabatur
tabellis extinctus nuper in longa senecta Titedius Labeo
praetorius, etiam proconsulatu provinciae Narbonensis functus,
21 sed ea re in risu etiam contumeliae erat.   fuit et principum 15
virorum non omittendum de pictura celebre consilium.
A.U.C. 709. cum Q. Pedius nepos Q. Pedii consularis triumphalisque et
a Caesare dictatore coheredis Augusto dati natura mutus
esset, in eo Messala orator, ex cuius familia pueri avia
fuerat, picturam docendum censuit, idque etiam divus 20
Augustus comprobavit, puer magni profectus in ea arte
22 obiit.   dignatio autem praecipua Romae increvit, ut existimo,

§ 19. 2. **Fabii clariss. gentis** : *An
censemus, si Fabio, nobilissimo homini,
laudi datum esset quod pingeret, non
multos apud nos futuros Polyclitos et
Parrhasios fuisse ?* Cic. *Tusc. Disput.*
i, 2, 4.   The first *Pictor* is of course
distinct from the historian (b. about
B.C. 254; Teuffel, 116).

3. **aedem Salutis** : since the
temple was dedicated by C. Junius
Bubulcus, a hero of the second
Samnite war, B.C. 311, and consecrated by him as Dictator, B.C. 302
(Liv. ix, 43, 25), the pictures probably
related to his exploits in Apulia
(Urlichs, *Malerei in Rom*, p. 7). From
Valerius Max. viii, 14, 6 it appears
that they were extensive compositions,
covering perhaps the two long walls of
the cella. Dionysios, xvi, 6, praises the
fine drawing, and sharp clean contours

of these wall-paintings.   (Against the
proposed identification of a wall painting from the Esquiline, *Bull. Comm.*
1889, pl. xi, xii, as 'riproduzione in
piccolò' of the pictures in the temple
of Salus, see Hülsen, *Röm. Mitth.*
1891, p. 111.)

6. **foro boario aede Herculis** :
this temple, which was called *aedes
Aemiliana* (according to Scaliger's
emendation of Festus, p. 242) was
either founded or restored with great
splendour by Aemilius Paullus the
conqueror of Pydna ; cf. H. Peter, *ap.*
Roscher, i, p. 2909 f. It was natural,
as Urlichs (*Malerei*, p. 17) points out,
that he should employ to decorate it
Pacuvius, who had written in his
honour the *Praetexta Paulus* (Ribbeck,
Röm. Trag. 326), and whose intimacy with Laelius, the bosom friend

Among the Romans too this art was early had in honour, see- 19
ing indeed that so distinguished a family as the Fabii drew from *Painting in Rome.*
it the name of Pictor [Painter]; and the first of the name actually *Fabius Pictor.*
painted the temple of Safety, in the year of Rome 450 [304 B.C.].
These paintings lasted until my day, when the temple was burned
down in the reign of Claudius.   Soon afterwards the poet *Pacu-* *Pacuvius.*
vius won great renown through his paintings in the temple of
Hercules in the Cattle Market.   The mother of Pacuvius was
a sister of Ennius, whence it came about that the drama lent
a new lustre to the art of painting at Rome.   Since that time. 20
however, the profession of painter has received no honour at the
hands of men of good birth, unless we except in our own time
Turpilius, a Roman knight from Venetia, whose excellent pictures *Turpilius.*
are still to be seen at Verona.   He painted with his left hand,
a peculiarity noted of no artist before him.   *Titedius Labeo*, who *Titedius Labeo.*
died not long ago in extreme old age, was proud of the little
pictures that he painted: he was of praetorian rank and had even
been governor of Narbonensis, yet his art only brought upon him
ridicule and even scorn.   Nor must I omit the famous decision 21
with regard to painting arrived at by eminent statesmen. *Quintus* *Quintus Pedius.*
Pedius (grandson of that Quintus Pedius who had been consul,
had enjoyed a triumph and was named by the dictator Caesar as 45 B.C.
co-heir with Augustus) having been dumb from his birth, it so
befell that Messala, the orator, to whose family the boy's grand-
mother belonged, advised that he should be taught to paint.   The
god Augustus approved of the idea, and the boy had made great
progress in the art when he died.   The esteem which the Romans 22

of Aemilius' son Scipio, is known to
us from Cicero (*Laelius*, 7, 24).

§ 20. 9. honestis manibus : cf.
Cic. *Tusc. Disp. loc. cit.*, and the
ironical words applied to Fabius
Pictor by Val. Max. viii, 14, 6.

Turpilium : possibly a descen-
dant of the Turpilius who wrote comedies, and was a contemporary of
Terence (Ribbeck, *Com.* 2nd ed. 85).

11. Veronae : probably Pliny's
birthplace, since in Praef. 1 he speaks
of Catullus as his *conterraneus*.

13. Titedius Labeo : Tac. *Ann.*
ii, 85.

§ 21. 17. Q. Pedii consularis : he

was the grandson of Caesar's elder
sister ; he triumphed Dec. 13, B.C. 45,
after his Spanish campaign (Appian,
Bell. Civ. iii, 22, 23, 94–96), was
consul with Augustus in B.C. 43, in
which year he died.

18. coheredis dati : Suet. *Julius*,
83.

19. Messala orator : B.C. 64–A.D.
8 (Teuffel, 222), quoted in the indices
to Bks. ix, xxxiii, xxxv ; restores the
ancient Sibyls, xxxiv, 22.   Cf. also
vii, 90, and above, § 8.

avia : i.e. the wife of Q. Pedius,
the legatee of Caesar.

§ 22. 22. dignatio ... increvit :

a M'. Valerio Maximo Messala, qui princeps tabulam pictam proelii quo Carthaginienses et Hieronem in Sicilia vicerat, proposuit in latere curiae Hostiliae anno ab urbe condita CCCCLXXXX. fecit hoc idem et L. Scipio, tabulamque

A.U.C. 565. victoriae suae Asiaticae in Capitolio posuit, idque aegre 5 tulisse fratrem Africanum tradunt haut inmerito, quando

23 filius eius illo proelio captus fuerat. non dissimilem offensionem et Aemiliani subiit L. Hostilius Mancinus qui primus Carthaginem inruperat situm eius oppugnationesque depictas proponendo in foro et ipse adsistens populo spectanti 10 singula enarrando, qua comitate proximis comitiis con-

A.U.C. 609. sulatum adeptus est. habuit et scaena ludis Claudii Pulchri
A.U.C. 655. magnam admirationem picturae, cum ad tegularum simili-tudinem corvi decepti imaginem advolarent.

24   Tabulis autem externis auctoritatem Romae publice fecit 15 primus omnium L. Mummius cui cognomen Achaici victoria

A.U.C. 608. dedit.   namque cum in praeda vendenda rex Attalus ✕⌈VI⌉ emisset tabulam Aristidis, Liberum patrem, pretium miratus suspicatusque aliquid in ea virtutis quod ipse

on Roman triumphal pictures generally see the excellent remarks of Raoul-Rochette, *Peint. Ant.* p. 303 f., and recently Wickhoff, *Wiener Genesis,* p. 30 f.

1. **M'. Valerio Maximo Messala:** cos. B.C. 263 ; cf. vii, 214.

3. **in latere curiae Host.** : see-ing the numerous changes undergone by the Curia between the date of Messala and that of Cicero, the iden-tity of the picture with the *tabula Valeria* (Cicero *in Vat.* 9, 21 ; *ad Fam.* xiv, 2, 2) is improbable (it seems ac-cepted by Becker, *Röm. Top.* p. 326, note 99, and recently by Gilbert, *Ge-schichte u. Top.* iii, p. 165, note 2 ; Urlichs, *Malerei,* p. 9, suggests that the exhibition was only temporary). The date usually assigned to Messala's victory is A. U. C. 491 = B.C. 263.

4. **L. Scipio** : he triumphed on the last day of the intercalary month of B.C. 188, but his splendid games were not celebrated till B.C. 186 (cf. xxxiii, 138). It is not known on

which of the two occasions he exhi-bited the picture of his exploits (cf. Urlichs, *op. cit.* p. 14).

5. **aegre tulisse** : the injury felt was far-fetched ; from Val. Max. ii, 10 2, we learn that Antiochos treated the son with marked courtesy, and sent him back *celeriter.*

§ 23. 8. **Aemiliani** : the offence presumably consisted in the omission from the picture of any allusion to the timely help of Scipio, Appian, Λιβ. 113 ff.; cf. *ibid.* 134, where a graphic account is given of the en-thusiasm with which the Romans received the news of the fall of Carthage.

12. **scaena** : i. e. the *scaenae frons* or wall of the stage-buildings, upon which the scenic decorations were hung, cf. § 65.

Claudii Pulchri : aedile B.C. 99 ; on his games see viii, 19 ; Val. Max. ii, 4, 6 *C. Pulcher scenam va-rietate colorum adumbravit vacuis ante pictura tabulis extentam.*

gave to painting was greatly increased (so it seems to me) by the action of Manius Valerius Maximus Messala. He first caused his victory over the Carthaginians and Hiero in Sicily to be painted on wood, and exhibited the picture at the side of the Curia Hostilia in the year of Rome 490 [264 B.C.]. Following his example Lucius Scipio exhibited in the Capitol a picture representing his Asiatic victory, a step which not unnaturally displeased his brother 'the African,' whose son had been taken prisoner in the battle. In the same way Lucius Hostilius Mancinus, who had been the first to enter Carthage, incurred the anger of Scipio Aemilianus by exhibiting in the forum pictures of the site of Carthage and the various attempts to storm it, while he himself stood by, telling the whole story to the crowd of spectators with a geniality which at the next elections won him the consulship. At the games given by Claudius Pulcher, the painting of the scenery excited great wonder, the very crows being deceived by the painted tiles and flying down to settle on them. *M'. Val. Max. Messala commemorates his victory by a picture.* *L. Scipio Asiaticus.* 189 B.C. **23** *L. Hostilius Mancinus.* 145 B.C. 99 B.C.

Foreign pictures, however, were first publicly brought into vogue at Rome by Lucius Mummius, surnamed the Achaean from his victories. At the auction of the spoils, King Attalos had bid for a picture of Dionysos by Aristeides the sum of 600,000 denarii [£21,000 circ.], whereupon Mummius, surprised at the price offered, and suspecting some merit in the picture which escaped **24** *Mummius introduces foreign pictures.* 146 B.C.

14. **corvi decepti**: cf. below, §§ 65, 66, and 155.

§ 24. 16. **L. Mummius**: in xxxiii, 149, however, the introduction of foreign pictures into Rome is attributed to Scipio's Asiatic victories; while Liv. xxv, 40, states that the first enthusiasm for Greek pictures at Rome was a result of the capture of Syracuse by Marcellus: *ceterum inde primum initium mirandi Graecarum artium;* cf. also Cato's speech as given Liv. xxxiv, 4 (below note on § 157), and Plut. *Marcell.* xxi.

17. **in praeda vendenda**: the notion of an auction is inaccurate: according to Paus. vii, 16, 8, Mummius had taken to Rome the most valuable works of art, and handed over to Philopoimen (see next note) the less important objects.

rex Attalus: see vii, 126. As a fact Attalos himself was not present at Corinth (Paus. vii, 16, 1); he had only sent an auxiliary force to the Romans, under the command of Philopoimen. There is a further inaccuracy in the account of the purchase: according to Polybios (*apud* Strabo, viii, p. 381), who was an eye-witness, the Roman soldiers were already using the pictures as dice-boards, when Philopoimen offered a hundred talents to Mummius in case he should feel disposed to assign the picture to Attalos' share of the booty. For the paintings collected by Attalos, see Fränkel, *Jahrb.* vi (1891), pp. 49-60, 'Gemälde-Sammlungen u. Gemälde-Forschung in Pergamon.'

18. **Aristidis**: below, §§ 98-100.

Liberum patrem: below, § 99.

nèsciret, revocavit tabulam Attalo multum querente et in
Cereris delubro posuit, quam primam arbitror picturam
25 externam Romae publicatam. deinde video et in foro
positas volgo. hinc enim ille Crassi oratoris lepos agentis
sub Veteribus, cum testis compellatus instaret : dic ergo, 5
Crasse, qualem me noris? talem, inquit, ostendens in tabula
pictum inficetissime Gallum exerentem linguam. in foro
fuit et illa pastoris senis cum baculo, de qua Teutonorum
legatus respondit interrogatus, quantine eum aestimaret,
donari sibi nolle talem vivom verumque.   10

26 Sed praecipuam auctoritatem publice tabulis fecit Caesar
dictator Aiace et Media ante Veneris Genetricis aedem
dicatis, post eum M. Agrippa vir rusticitati propior quam
deliciis. exstat certe eius oratio magnifica et maximo
civium digna de tabulis omnibus signisque publicandis, 15
quod fieri satius fuisset quam in villarum exilia pelli. verum
eadem illa torvitas tabulas duas Aiacis et Veneris mercata
est a Cyzicenis HS. [XII]. in thermarum quoque calidissima parte marmoribus incluserat parvas tabellas paulo
ante, cum reficerentur, sublatas.   20

---

1. in **Cereris delubro**: xxxiv,
15; below, §§ 99, 154. Strabo, *loc.
cit.* τὸν δὲ Διόνυσον [sc. 'Αριστείδου]
ἀνακείμενον ἐν τῷ Δημητρείῳ τῷ ἐν
'Ρώμῃ κάλλιστον ἔργον ἑωρῶμεν· ἐμ-
πρησθέντος δὲ τοῦ νεὼ συνηφανίσθη καὶ
ἡ γραφὴ νεωστί.

§ 25. 4. **Crassi oratoris** : Cicero
(*de Orat.* ii, 66, 266 ; cf. Quinct. vi, 3,
38, where see Spalding's note) attributes the witticism to the orator, C.
Julius Caesar Strabo (Teuffel, 153, 3).

5. **sub veteribus** : sc. *tabernis*,
cf. § 113; these shops, with a colonnade in front of them, stood facing the
Sacra Via, on the site afterwards occupied by the *Basilica Julia*. The
tribunal, where the scene is imagined,
may have stood close to the *Regia* ;
cf. Jordan, *Top.* i, 2, p. 382, note 92.
Cicero, *loc. cit.*, has *sub novis*, i. e. on
N. side of the Forum.

6. in **tabula** : Cic. *loc. cit. in*

Mariano scuto Cimbrico. The pro-
truding tongue was probably apotro-
paic (cf. Urlichs in *Chrestom.*, p. 343) ;
being misunderstood it gave occasion
to the witticisms recorded by Pliny,
Cicero and others with Quinctilian,
perhaps also to the remark in Liv.
vii, 10, 5 : (*Gallum*) *linguam etiam
ab irrisu exserentem.*

§ 26. 12. **Aiace et Media** : vii,
126 = App. I ; below, §§ 136, 145.

ante V. G. aedem : whereas
in § 136 the same pictures are said to
be *in V. G. aede ;* the latter seems
the likeliest ; the first variant is probably due to Pliny's carelessness ; cf.
Münzer, *op. cit.* p. 542. The temple
was vowed by Caesar at Pharsalos
(B.C. 48), ded. with the Forum, Sept.
24 or 25, B.C. 46 (but see *Mon. Ancyr.*
iv, 12 ; Mommsen, *Res Gestae*, p. 84 f.).

13. **M. Agrippa** : B.C. 63–A.D. 12 ;
Teuffel, 220, 10–14.

his own eyes, withdrew it, in spite of the protests of Attalos, and afterwards dedicated it in the temple of Ceres. This was, I believe, the first foreign picture publicly dedicated at Rome. Later on I see that they were constantly put up even in the 25 Forum, a custom which gave the orator Crassus an opening for a witticism. He was pleading a case close to the Old Shops, when a witness under examination said to him, 'Pray what do you take me for, Crassus?' 'Just such a man as that,' answered Crassus, pointing to a coarse picture of a Gaul with his tongue out. In the Forum too was the picture of an old shepherd with his staff, of which the envoy of the Teutons said, when asked what he thought it was worth, that he would not take such a man at a gift, even if he were alive and real.

But the highest public tribute to painting was paid by the 26 dictator Caesar when he dedicated the Aias and the Medeia in front of the temple of Venus the Mother, and after him by Marcus Agrippa, whose natural tastes inclined to rustic simplicity rather than to the refinements of luxury; a magnificent speech of his at least is extant, fully worthy of the first citizen in the state, urging that all pictures and statues should be made public property—certainly a wiser plan than to consign them to exile in our country houses. Yet the rude Agrippa bought two pictures—an Aias and an Aphrodite—from the people of Kyzikos for 1,200,000 sesterces [£10,500 circ.], and further, in the hottest chamber of his baths were some small pictures, let into the marble, which were removed not long ago in the course of a restoration.

Caesar's patronage. Aias and Medeia. Agrippa.

Aias and Aphrodite from Ky-zikos.

17. **Aiacis et Veneris**: nothing further is known of either picture; the grounds for identifying either or both with the Ajax and Medea purchased by Caesar (Welcker, Helbig, Urlichs, &c.) are purely fanciful. From the *post eum* we may assume that Agrippa's purchases were later than Caesar's, and the price paid for the pictures was not the same (cf. § 136 where the price paid by Caesar is given). The question is fully discussed by F. Brandstätter, *Timomachos*, p. 16 ff. The occasion for Agrippa's purchases, and the spot where he exhibited them, are unknown. He may have bought the pictures as aedile

in B.C. 33, or to adorn the buildings which several years later were carried out under his direction (the *Septa Julia* in B.C. 26; the *Thermae* and the *Porticus Neptunia* in the following year; cf. Brandstätter, *loc. cit.*).

18. **thermarum**: immediately behind the Pantheon: the *calidissima pars* must be identical with the *caldarium*.

19. **incluserat**: according to a custom general in Roman times; cf. below the pictures in the Curia Julia (§ 27). The six celebrated monochrome pictures in red on white marble slabs (Naples) had been let into the wall in a similar manner; cf.

27   Super omnis divus Augustus in foro suo celeberrima in
parte posuit tabulas duas quae Belli faciem pictam habent
et Triumphum, item Castores ac Victoriam. posuit et quas
dicemus sub artificum mentione in templo Caesaris patris.
A.U.C. 725. idem in curia quoque quam in comitio consecrabat duas 5
tabulas inpressit parieti. Nemean sedentem supra leonem
palmigeram ipsam adstante cum baculo sene cuius supra
caput tabella bigae dependet, Nicias scripsit se inussisse,
28 tali enim usus est verbo. alterius tabulae admiratio est
puberem filium seni patri similem esse aetatis salva differentia 10
supervolante aquila draconem complexa. Philochares hoc
suum opus esse testatus est. inmensam, vel unam si tantum
hanc tabulam aliquis aestimet, potentiam artis, cum propter
Philocharen ignobilissimos alioqui Glaucionem filiumque
eius Aristippum senatus populi Romani tot saeculis spectet. 15
posuit et Tiberius Caesar minime comis imperator in templo
ipsius Augusti quas mox indicabimus.

29   Hactenus dictum sit de dignitate artis morientis. quibus
coloribus singulis primi pinxissent diximus, cum de his pig-
mentis traderemus in metallis: monochromata ea genera 20
picturae vocantur. qui deinde et quae invenerint et quibus
temporibus, dicemus in mentione artificum, quoniam indicare
naturas colorum prior causa operis instituti est. tandem

6. impressit parieti, Nemean *usque ad* bigae (bige *Voss.*, bigere *Bamb.*,
palmigere *Bamb. e corr.*) dependet. Nicias *Detlefsen; interpunctionem corr.*
Traube. 20. metallis: monochromata . . . vocantur] *Littré*; metallis. qui
monochromata—ea genera picturae vocantur—*Detlefsen, vid. errata, vol.* v
pag. 250.

Robert, *Hall. Winckelm. progr.* xix,
1895, p. 5 f.; Raoul-Rochette, *Pein-*
tures, p. 162 ; Wickhoff, *Wiener Gene-*
sis, p. 70.

§ 27. 1. in foro . . . parte : below,
§ 93, in *fori sui celeberrimis partibus.*

2. Belli faciem . . . et Triumphum
= below, § 93 *Belli imaginem re-*
strictis ad terga manibus, Alexandro
in curru triumphante ; ib. *Castorem*
et Pollucem cum Victoria.

3. quas dicemus : i. e. the Anadyomene of Apelles in § 91.

5. in curia : sc. *Julia,* ded. by

Augustus B.C. 29: it had been begun by Caesar to replace the *Curia*
of Sulla.

6. inpressit parieti : cf. note on
incluserat in § 26.

Nemean . . . Nicias : §§ 130,
131. The *Nemea* was the personification of the festal city; the *senex*
with the staff one of the judges in the
games; the tablet with the chariot
indicated the particular contest of
which the picture was the memorial
(Brunn, *K. G.* ii, p. 194) ; cf. in Paus.
i, 22, 7 the picture commemorating

Above all the god Augustus placed in the most frequented part 27
of the Forum which bears his name, two pictures, the one containing *Augustus. Pictures in*
figures of War and of Triumph, the other Kastor and his twin, *his forum.*
with Victory. He also dedicated in the temple of his father Caesar *In temple*
certain pictures which I shall mention when I enumerate the artists. *of Caesar.*
Furthermore he let into the wall of the Council Chamber which *In Curia.*
he consecrated in the Comitium two pictures. On the one, which 29 B.C.
represents the nymph Nemea holding a palm and seated on a *by Nikias.*
lion, while an old man with a staff stands by, above whose head
is suspended a tablet with a two-horse chariot, Nikias has written
that he burned in the painting, using that very word [ἐνέκαεν]. In 28
the other picture we admire the marked resemblance between *2. Picture by Philo-*
a young man and his aged father, although the difference of age *chares of*
is not lost; an eagle with a snake in its talons is flying over their *Glaukion and Aris-*
heads. Philochares lays claim to the painting as his work. *tippos.*
Marvellous is the power of art, judged by this work alone, since
Philochares could turn the eyes of the Senate of the Roman
people for so many years upon Glaukion and his son Aristippos,
persons otherwise quite obscure. Tiberius Caesar too, rude *Tiberius.*
prince though he was, dedicated in the temple of Augustus
pictures which I shall name later on.

I have said enough concerning the dignity of a decaying art. 29
When treating of pigments in my account of metals I named the
colours used singly by the early painters; paintings in that style
are called monochromes. Subsequent innovators, together with
the character and date of their inventions, I shall treat of in my
account of the artists, since the scheme of my work obliges me
first to describe the composition of the pigments employed.

the victory of Alkibiades in the Nemean games: ἵππων δέ οἱ νίκης τῆς ἐν
Νεμέᾳ ἐστὶ σημεῖα ἐν τῇ γραφῇ; also
the *pinax* wtih *biga* on the 'Ikaorios'
relief (Br. Mus. = Friederichs-Wolters,
1844).

8. inussisse i. e. ἐνέκαεν: cf. 122.

§ 28. 9. alterius tabulae: since
placed in the open air, presumably
likewise in encaustic. The eagle and
snake, like the *tabella bigae*, must
have referred to the event commemorated by the picture. How the
work of Nikias came into the hands
of Augustus is unknown (§ 131); as

to the picture of Philochares, Wunderer (*Manubiae Alexandrinae*, p. 23)
suggests that it belonged to Augustus's Egyptian spoils.

11. Philochares: perhaps identical with the vase-painter, brother of
the orator Aischines, mentioned
derisively (ἀλαβαστοθήκας γράφων) by
Demosthenes, *Fals. Leg.* p. 415, 237
(Ol. 109, 2 = B. C. 343).

17. mox indicabimus: in § 131.

§ 29. 19. diximus: in xxxiii,
117.

20. monochromata: *ibid.*; cf.
above, § 15; below, § 56.

se ars ipsa distinxit et invenit lumen atque umbras, differentia
colorum alterna vice sese excitante. postea deinde adiectus
est splendor, alius hic quam lumen. quod inter haec et
umbras esset appellarunt tonon, commissuras vero colorum
et transitus harmogen.

5

50   Quattuor coloribus solis immortalia illa opera fecere—ex
albis Melino, e silaciis Attico, ex rubris Sinopide Pontica,
ex nigris atramento—Apelles, Aetion, Melanthius, Nicomachus, clarissimi pictores, cum tabulae eorum singulae
oppidorum venirent opibus. nunc et purpuris in parietes 10
migrantibus et India conferente fluminum suorum limum,
draconum elephantorumque saniem nulla nobilis pictura est.
omnia ergo meliora tunc fuere, cum minor copia. ita est,
quoniam, ut supra diximus, rerum, non animi pretiis ex-
cubatur.

15

51   Et nostrae aetatis insaniam in pictura non omittam. Nero
princeps iusserat colosseum se pingi CXX pedum linteo,
incognitum ad hoc tempus. ea pictura cum peracta esset

1. **lumen atque umbras:** cf.
xxxiii, 160; below, § 131.

2. **alterna vice sese excitante:**
this passage should be studied in
connexion with Aristotle's doctrine, in
the third book of the *Meteorologica*,
of the juxtaposition of colours;
cf. with relation to the Plinian
words: μέλαν παρὰ μέλαν ποιεῖ τὸ
ἠρέμα λευκὸν παντελῶς φαίνεσθαι
λευκόν *Meteor.* p. 375 a, 20. See on
the whole subject, Bertrand, *Études*,
pp. 150–160.

3. **splendor:** the meaning suggested for this word by Blümner,
Technol. iv, p. 428 is '*reflexion*' (for
reflected lights cf. § 138). But reflexion comes simply under the same
heading as treatment of light, whereas
the words of Pliny, *alius hic quam
lumen*, expressly show that *splendor*
was a totally different factor to light.
In truth it was neither more nor less
than the 'glow' which—as distinct
from any treatment of light and shade

—is so marked a quality of certain
Renascence and modern artists (e. g.
Titian, Turner). Külb rightly trans-
lates 'Glanz.' Introd. p. xxxiv.

4. **tonon:** what the modern French
would call 'values,' i. e. the passages
from the more lit up parts in a picture
to the less, the 'value' being the
quantity of light in a given colour.

commissuras . . . colorum:
the arrangement of colours, resulting
in ἁρμογή, or what the moderns
would call the general 'tone' of a
picture.

§ **50. 6. Quattuor coloribus:**
cf. Cic. *Brutus* 18, 70 *similis in
pictura ratio est, in qua Zeuxin et
Polygnotum et Timanthem et eorum
qui non sunt usi plus quam quattuor
coloribus, formas et lineamenta lau-
damus ; at in Aetione, Nicomacho,
Protogene, Apelle iam perfecta sunt
omnia.* These words do not necessarily
contradict the statement of Pliny or
prove that the later painters used more

Art at last differentiated itself and discovered light and shade, the several hues being so employed as to enhance one another by contrast. Later on glow—a different thing to light—was introduced. The transition between light and shade they called τόνος, but the arrangement of hues and the transition from one colour to another harmonization or ἁρμογή.

Four colours only—white from Melos, Attic yellow, red from **50** Sinope on the Black Sea, and the black called 'atramentum'— *Four colours* were used by Apelles, Aetion, Melanthios and Nikomachos in *used by early* their immortal works; illustrious artists, a single one of whose *artists.* pictures the wealth of a city could hardly suffice to buy, while now that even purple clothes our walls, and India contributes the ooze of her rivers and the blood of dragons and of elephants, no famous picture is painted. We must believe that when the painter's equipment was less complete, the results were in every respect better, for as I have already said, we are alive only to the worth of the material and not to the genius of the artist.

In our own days too painting has known an extravagance which **51** must not be forgotten: the Emperor Nero ordered a colossal por- *Colossal portrait* trait of himself, 120 feet in length, to be painted on canvas, a thing *of Nero on canvas.*

than four colours. The *perfecta omnia* need mean no more than that they had learnt endless combinations of the four colours, whereas the older painters used them pure or knew but of few combinations. The colour effects produced by Apelles and his contemporaries being far more elaborate than anything attempted in the period of Polygnotos, it is natural that the employment of only four colours should, in their case, be dwelt upon with special admiration. As an example of what can be accomplished with only four colours, the student will remember the 'Christ crowned with thorns' by Titian in the Munich Pinakothek (1114); cf. Morelli, *Galleries of Munich and Dresden*, p. 58 (Transl. C. J. Ffoulkes). The 'four colours' are elaborately discussed by Bertrand, *Études*, pp. 132–144. [The names Apelles — Nicomachus are in alphabetical order. H. L. U.]

8. **Apelles:** below, § 92 *legentes meminerint omnia ea* (sc. *opera*) *quattuor coloribus facta.*

11. **India...limum:** i. e. *indigo*, cf. xxxiii, 163; above, §§ 46, 49.

12. **draconum elephantorumque saniem:** also called *cinnabaris*, 'dragon's blood'; in viii, 34, Pliny gives a wonderful account of its production; cf. xxxiii, 116.

14. **ut supra diximus:** xxxv, 4: *honorem non nisi in pretio ducentes;* cf. the similar rhetorical complaint in xxxiv, 5.

§ 51. 17. **colosseum:** a counterpart to the colossal statue by Zenodoros in xxxiv, 45.

18. **incognitum:** if still unknown in Pliny's day, the practice of painting on canvas soon became general, as is witnessed by the portraits from the Fayoum; cf. Cecil Smith, *Pictura*, p. 329; Berger, *Beiträge*, ii, p. 52 f.

H

in Maianis hortis, accensa fulmine cum optima hortorum
52 parte conflagravit. libertus eius cum daret Anti munus
gladiatorum, publicas porticus occupavit pictura, ut constat,
gladiatorum ministrorumque omnium veris imaginibus redditis. hic multis iam saeculis summus animus in pictura, 5
pingi autem gladiatoria munera atque in publico exponi
coepta a C. Terentio Lucano. is avo suo a quo adoptatus
fuerat triginta paria in foro per triduum dedit tabulamque
pictam in nemore Dianae posuit.

53   Nunc celebres in ea arte quam maxima brevitate per- 10
curram, neque enim instituti operis est talis executio, itaque
quosdam vel in transcursu et in aliorum mentione obiter
nominasse satis erit, exceptis operum claritatibus quae et
54 ipsa conveniet attingi sive exstant sive intercidere. non
constat sibi in hac parte Graecorum diligentia multas post 15
olympiadas celebrando pictores quam statuarios ac toreutas,
primumque olympiade LXXXX, cum et Phidian ipsum
initio pictorem fuisse tradatur clipeumque Athenis ab eo
pictum, praeterea in confesso sit LXXX tertia fuisse fratrem
eius Panaenum, qui clipeum intus pinxit Elide Minervae 20

1. **Maianis hortis**: *C. I. L.* vi,
6152, 8668, where they are mentioned
along with the *horti Lamiani*,
which as we learn from Phil. Jud.
περὶ ἀρετ. καὶ πρεσβ. 2, p. 597, ed.
Mangey (cf. Becker, *Röm. Top.* p. 542,
note 1142), were close to the gardens
of Maecenas on the Esquiline.

§ **52.** 2. **Anti**: iii, 57 ; it was the
birthplace of Nero (Suet. *Nero* 6).

4. **gladiatorum . . . imaginibus**:
numberless representations of gladiators have come down to us in
mosaics ; such as the mosaic from
Trêves (Baumeister, *Denkm.* pl. xci) ;
cf. the great mosaic with portraits of
athletes in the Lateran (Helbig,
Class. Ant. 704).

7. **C. Terentio Lucano**: possibly
identical, according to Mommsen,
with the *Terentius Lucanus* on the
coin *Röm. Münzw.* p. 554, 164 (and
note 278).

9. **in nemore Dianae**: i. e. the

grove of Nemi ; cf. xvi, 242 and
Strabo, v, p. 239.

§ **53.** 10. **Nunc celebres . . . per-
curram** : cf. xxxiv, 53.

13. **claritatibus** : [xxviii, 87 *in
ceteris claritates animalium aut
operum sequemur* = for the rest, I
shall note remarkable animals . . .
H. L. U.]

§ **54.** 14. **non constat sibi . . .
adiutor** : the supposed proofs of
Greek inaccuracy are skilfully cumu-
lated, (*a*) *non constat sibi* . . . (*b*) § 56
quid quod in confesso . . . (*b*) § 57
quod si recipi necesse est . . . , the
argument culminating in § 58 in the
words *chronicorum errore non dubio*,
after which the case of Polygnotos is
thrown in as a kind of postscript.
The complaint was, however, unjust
and originally based on a misunderstanding, see Introd. p. xxx.

17. **olympiade LXXXX** : below,
§ 60.

previously unheard of. When the picture was finished, it was struck by lightning in the gardens of Maius, and burned together with the greater part of the gardens. A freedman of this emperor 52 gave a gladiatorial show at Antium, at which the public colonnades were adorned by a picture of all the gladiators and attendants, *Portraits of* portrayed from the life. Realistic portraiture indeed has for *gladiators.* many generations been the highest ambition of art; Gaius Terentius Lucanus, however, was the first to have a picture of a gladiatorial show painted and to exhibit it in public. He showed thirty pairs of gladiators in the Forum for three days, in honour of his grandfather, who had adopted him: moreover he dedicated a picture of them in the grove of Diana.

I now propose to mention the most famous painters as briefly 53 as may be, for a detailed account would be inconsistent with the *History of painters.* scheme of my work. It will therefore be enough if I give some artists only a passing notice, or name them in connexion with others; though I must still make a separate mention of the most renowned paintings, whether they be still in existence or whether they have perished. On this point the Greeks have 54 made a mistake in placing the painters many years later than the *Erroneous chronology* bronze workers and metal chasers, and in giving the ninetieth *of the* Olympiad [420–417 B.C.] as the date of the earliest painter, over-*Greeks.* looking the tradition that *Pheidias* himself was originally a painter, *Pheidias.* and painted a shield at Athens. It is further acknowledged that *Panainos* brother of Pheidias, who lived in the eighty-third *Panainos.*

18. initio pictorem : cf. xxxiv, 60 *Pythagoras Samius initio pictor* and Introd. p. li.

clipeum: the shield introduced without any further definition has an apocryphal air (cf. Münzer, *op. cit.* p. 553, and Introd. *loc. cit.*). It cannot of course be that of the Athena Parthenos as Urlichs (*Chrest.* p. 346), Robert (*Arch. Märch.* p. 24), and Furtwängler (*Masterpieces*, p. 45), would have it, for so important a fact would have been noted; besides, we have the express statement in xxxvi, 18 that the inner side of the shield of the Parthenos was carved in relief, H. L. Urlichs, *Woch. f. klass. Phil.* 1895, p. 548.

tradatur : H. L. Urlichs (*loc. cit.*) points out that the expression is

opposed to *in confesso sit*, i. e. hearsay to ascertained fact.

19. LXXX tertia : the date is loosely assumed for Panainos, as being that of his brother Pheidias, xxxiv, 49; Robert, *op. cit.* p. 25; Furtwängler, *op. cit.* p. 40 f.

20. Panaenum : Panainos is again mentioned below, in his proper order in the history of the development of painting, without any reference to this first notice, which is from a different source, cf. Introd. p. xxviii f. and p. li f. *Fratrem*, so also Paus. v, 11, 6: ἀδελφιδοῦς Strabo viii, p. 354.

intus pinxit : with the device of a cock (Paus. vi, 26, 3, where the Athena is simply attributed to Pheidias). Introd. p. liv, note 1.

Elide: from xxxvi, 177 (=App.

H 2

72515

quam fecerat Colotes discipulus Phidiae et ei in faciendo
55 Iove Olympio adiutor.   quid quod in confesso perinde est
Bularchi pictoris tabulam, in qua erat Magnetum proelium,
a Candaule rege Lydiae Heraclidarum novissimo, qui et
Myrsilus vocitatus est, repensam auro? tanta iam dignatio 5
picturae erat.   circa Romuli id aetatem acciderit necesse
est, etenim duodevicensima olympiade interiit Candaules
A.U.C. 37. aut, ut quidam tradunt, eodem anno quo Romulus, nisi
fallor, manifesta iam tunc claritate artis, adeo absolutione.
56 quod si recipi necesse est, simul apparet multo vetustiora 10
principia eosque qui monochromatis pinxerint, quorum
aetas non traditur, aliquanto ante fuisse, Hygiaenontem,
Dinian, Charmadan et qui primus in pictura marem
a femina discreverit Eumarum Atheniensem figuras omnis
imitari ausum, quique inventa eius excoluerit Cimonem 15
Cleonaeum.   hic catagrapha invenit, hoc est obliquas
imagines, et varie formare voltus, respicientes suspicientesve
vel despicientes.   articulis membra distinxit, venas protulit,

VIII) it appears that Panainos also
decorated with paintings the walls of
the temple of Athena.

1. **Colotes**: xxxiv, 87. *Iove Olympio*: xxxiv, 54; xxxvi, 18.

§ 55. 3. **Magnetum proelium**:
according to vii, 126, a defeat
(*excidium*), but the precise event is
unknown. S. Reinach (*Rev. des Ét.
Grecques*, 1895, p. 175 ff.), justly
comments on the strangeness of the
tradition that a Greek painter immortalized a Greek defeat, and tries to
prove the *excidium* to have crept into
Pliny's account by confusion with the
celebrated defeat—or rather exter-
mination—of the Magnetes by the
Treres in B. C. 651 (Strabo xiv, p.
647), which gave rise to the proverbial τὰ Μαγνητῶν κακά. R. wishes
to refer the picture to some one of
the Magnete victories alluded to by
Strabo (*loc. cit.*) on the testimony of
Kallinos (cf. also Wilamowitz in
Hermes, xxx (1895), p. 177 ff.).   But
where so much is uncertain, we shall

hesitate before throwing overboard our
only piece of positive information—the
excidium of vii, 126 (= App. I).

6. **circa Romuli aetatem**: the
synchronism is based on Herod. i, 12,
who gives the death year of Kandaules = accession of Gyges = *floruit*
of Archilochos, and must be connected with Cicero (*Tusc. Disp.* i,
13), who places Archilochos *regnante
Romulo;* cf. Münzer, *op. cit.* p. 542:
cf. Introd. p. lxxxiv.

§ 56. 11. **monochromatis**: above,
§§ 15, 29.

14. **discreverit**: as in black-figured
vases, by painting the flesh parts of
the women white (Introd. p. xxix).
Indeed a conventional difference between the colouring of the sexes seems
to have been observed down to the
latest time. Thus albeit Alexander was
remarkable for his fair skin, Apelles
in his portrait of the king οὐκ ἐμι-
μήσατο τὴν χρόαν, ἀλλὰ φαιότερον καὶ
πεπινωμένον ἐποίησεν Plut. *Al.* iv, 120.

Eumarum: the name is still known

Olympiad [448–445 B.C.], painted at Elis the inner surface of the shield belonging to an Athena by Kolotes, a pupil of Pheidias and his assistant in executing the Olympian Zeus. Again, is it not an undisputed fact that a picture of the defeat of the Magnetes by the painter *Boularchos* was bought by Kandaules, also called *Boular-* Myrsilos, the last Lydian king of the line of the Heraklids, for its *chos.* weight in gold, a proof of the honour already paid to painting? This must have taken place in the days of Romulus, for Kandaules died in the eighteenth Olympiad [708–705 B.C.], or, according to some authorities, in the same year as Romulus, and already then, B.C. 717. unless I am mistaken, the art had attained to greatness, even to perfection. And if we must accept this, it follows that its first origin 58 is much older, and that the early painters in monochrome, whose *Painters* dates have not been handed down to us, lived some time before. *in mono-* Such, for example, were †*Hygiainon*, †*Deinias*, † *Charmadas*, *chrome.* †*Eumaros* of Athens, who was the first to mark the difference *Eumaros* between man and woman in painting, and who ventured to *of Athens.* imitate every sort of figure, and *Kimon* of Kleonai, who developed *Kimon of* the inventions of Eumaros. He devised κατάγραφα, or profile *Kleonai.* drawings, and represented the features in different postures, looking backwards or upwards or downwards. He marked the attachments of the limbs, gave prominence to the veins, and also

only from Pliny, for the reading Εὔμαρος on the basis from the Akropolis, bearing the signature of Antenor (*Jahrb.* ii, 1887, p. 135 f.) is quite uncertain (cf. Hartwig, *Meisterschalen*, p. 154). Further, the conjecture of Urlichs, *Eumari* (*Hölz. Pferd*, p. 14 n. 12), for the corrupt *Arimnae* in Varro, *Ling. Lat.* ix, 6, 12, is impossible; see Spengel's critical apparatus, p. 198.

figuras = ' position' by a slight extension of one meaning given to the word by Cicero, *Verres* II, i, 21, 57, *non solum numerum signorum, sed etiam uniuscuiusque magnitudinem, figuram, statum litteris definiri vides*, upon which see Pseudo-Asconius, p. 174, 7 (ed. Orelli) *figura est circa gestum situmque membrorum* (Blümner, *Rhein. Mus.* 26, p. 353).

15. **Cimon**: cf. the improvements attributed to him by Ailian, ποικ. ἱστ. viii, 8.

16. **catagrapha**: the word is susceptible of meaning ' foreshortening' (Holwerda, *Jahrb.* v, 1890, p. 258; Hartwig, *Meisterschalen*, p. 156 f., Lange, *Fremstilling*, pp. 429, 464), and this was possibly the meaning intended by the Greek author, for profile figures, which had existed from the earliest times, could on no theory, however conventional, be interpreted as audacious inventions. It is clear however that Pliny or his Latin author understood *catagrapha* as simply = profile, since this is the meaning he gives to the Greek equivalent *obliqua imago* in § 90, where see note.

17. [**respicientes suspicientesve vel despicientes**: sudden change from asyndeton to disjunctive particle, cf. xxviii, 63 *contra renum aut lumborum, vesicae cruciatus*, J. Müller, *Stil*, p. 69. H. L. U.]

18. **membra . . . protulit**: cf. on

57 praeterque in vestibus rugas et sinus invenit. Panaenus
quidem frater Phidiae etiam proelium Atheniensium ad-
A.U.C. 264. versus Persas apud Marathona factum pinxit. adeo iam
colorum usus increbruerat, adeoque ars perfecta erat ut in
eo proelio iconicos duces pinxisse tradatur, Atheniensium 5
Miltiaden, Callimachum, Cynaegirum, barbarorum Datim,
Artaphernen.

58   Quin immo certamen etiam picturae florente eo in-
A.U.C. 306. stitutum est Corinthi ac Delphis, primusque omnium certavit
cum Timagora Chalcidense, superatus ab eo Pythiis, quod 10
et ipsius Timagorae carmine vetusto apparet chronicorum
errore non dubio. alii quoque post hos clari fuere ante
LXXXX olympiadem, sicut Polygnotus Thasius qui primus
mulieres tralucida veste pinxit, capita earum mitris versicoloribus operuit plurimumque picturae primus contulit, 15
siquidem instituit os adaperire, dentes ostendere, voltum

59 ab antiquo rigore variare. huius est tabula in porticu
Pompei, quae ante curiam eius fuerat, in qua dubitatur an
ascendentem cum clupeo pinxerit an descendentem. hic

---

1. vestibus rugas] *Traube*; veste brugas *Bamb.*; verrugas *reliqui*; veste
rugas *Detlefsen*.

xxxiv, 59, the improvements attributed
to Pythagoras of Rhegion. Introd.
p. xxvii.

57. 3. apud **Marathona**: on a wall
of the στοὰ ποικίλη (§ 59). The picture
was ascribed by other writers to Mikon
(Arrian, *Anab.* vii, 13, 5 ; Ailian, περὶ
ζώων vii, 38 ; Sopatros, διαιρ. ζητημ. i,
8), and may have been the work of both
painters, Wachsmuth, *Stadt Athen* ii,
p. 503. Others again (see Ailian, *loc.
cit.*) gave it to Polygnotos. Pausanias
in his description of the paintings of
the Poikile, i, 15, names no artists.
For the latest reconstruction of the
picture see Robert, *Hall. Winckelmannspr.* xviii, 1895. Addenda.

5. iconicos duces: the year of
the battle being B. C. 490, and the
Stoa dating presumably from Kimon's
recall in B.C. 457 (Furtwängler,
Masterpieces, p. 41), there can be no
question of real portraiture ; but the

tradition of the names attaching to
each figure would be carefully preserved ; perhaps too there was an
attempt at characterization, so that
in a history of the development of
painting Panainos might pass as the
first to have essayed portraiture (Introd. p. xxviii f.).

6. **Miltiaden** : his name was not
inscribed, but he was characterized
by his gesture of exhortation, Aischines *c. Ktesiph.* 186, &c., see Wachsmuth's fine criticism of the passage,
op. cit. p. 506, note 2. For the
motive see the warrior on the gold
sheath in the Hermitage, Benndorf,
Gjölbaschi p. 157 fig. 143 = *Compte
Rendu* 1864, pl. v, 1.

Callimachum, Cynaegirum : Ail.
loc. cit. τοὺς ἀμφὶ τὸν Κυνέγειρον
καὶ Ἐπίζηλόν τε καὶ Καλλίμαχον,
cf. Wachsmuth, *op. cit.* p. 510 f. The
omission of Epizelos in Pliny is

discovered the wrinkles and the windings of drapery.   Furthermore Panainos the brother of Pheidias painted the battle between
the Athenians and Persians at Marathon.   So extensively were
colours now used, so perfect had technique now become, that he
is actually said to have given the real portraits of the commander
on both sides, of Miltiades, Kallimachos and Kynaigeiros among
the Athenians, of Datis and Artaphernes among the barbarians.

Panainos. Picture of battle of Marathon. — 57

Nay more, competitions for painters were instituted at Corinth
and Delphoi in the time of Panainos, when in the first contest he
tried for the prize against *Timagoras* of Chalkis, who conquered
him, as we know from an old epigram by Timagoras himself, at
the Pythian games; an evident proof that the chroniclers are
wrong in their dates.   Yet other painters became famous before
the ninetieth Olympiad [420–417 B.C.], as for example *Polygnotos*
of Thasos, who first painted women with transparent garments
and gave them headdresses of various colours.   This artist made
a first serious contribution to the development of painting by
opening the mouth, showing the teeth, and varying the stiff
archaic set of the features.   He painted the picture now in the
gallery of Pompeius and formerly in front of his Council Chamber,
representing a warrior armed with a shield, about whom people
argue as to whether he is ascending or descending.   He also

Painting competi- tions. — 58
448 B.C. Timagoras of Chalkis.
Polygnotos of Thasos.
His 'warrior.' — 59

---

curious. The heroes are mentioned
as an indivisible triad by Plutarch,
Glor. Ath. 3, Diogenes Laert. i, 56.

§ 58. 9. **Corinthi ac Delphis**: i.e.
at the Isthmian and Pythian festivals
(*Pythiis* below); for contests between painters cf. §§ 65, 72 and
Introd. p. lxiv.

13. **Polygnotus**: son of the first
Aglaophon, and brother of Aristophon
(§§ 60, 138).

qui primus: introduces as usual,
the artist's special contribution to the
progress of his art, Introd. p. xxviii f.

14. **tralucida veste**: Ailian, ποικ.
ἱστ. iv, 3 ἱματίων λεπτότητας; Lucian,
εἰκόνες 7 ἐς τὸ λεπτότατον ἐξειργασ-
μένην (of the drapery of Kassandra in
the Nekuia).

§ 59. 17. **porticu Pompei**: in
the immediate vicinity of Pompeius's
theatre.

18. **curiam**: Gilbert, *Rom.* iii,
p. 325; numerous works of art
were collected by Pompeius in the
complex of buildings about his
Theatre.

in qua dubitatur: the warrior
(perhaps Kapaneus, cf. Benndorf, *op.
cit.* p. 190; pl. xxiv, A. 4: *Anth. Plan.*
iv, 106) was presumably on a ladder,
and it was difficult to tell whether he
was climbing up or coming down again.
Robert, *Hall. Winckelmannsprogr.*
xviii, 1895, p. 67, suggests that
the *tabula* was the votive picture of
an *apobates*, of whom it was uncertain
whether he was stepping up to, or
down from, his chariot; for the subject
see the beautiful monochrome picture
on white marble slab (Naples, Helbig,
Wandgemälde 1405[b]), published by
Robert, *Hall. Winckelmannsprogr.*
xix, 1895.

Delphis aedem pinxit, hic et Athenis porticum quae Poecile
vocatur gratuito, cum partem eius Micon mercede pingeret.
vel maior huic auctoritas, siquidem Amphictyones, quod
est publicum Graeciae concilium, hospitia ei gratuita de-
crevere.   fuit et alius Micon qui minoris cognomine distin- 5
guitur, cuius filia Timarete et ipsa pinxit.

60   LXXXX autem olympiade fuere Aglaophon, Cephisodorus, Erillus, Evenor pater Parrhasi et praeceptor maximi
pictoris de quo suis annis dicemus, omnes iam inlustres, non
tamen in quibus haerere expositio debeat festinans ad lumina 10
artis in quibus primus refulsit Apollodorus Atheniensis
LXXXXIII olympiade.   hic primus species exprimere
instituit primusque gloriam penicillo iure contulit.   eius est
sacerdos adorans et Aiax fulmine incensus, quae Pergami

---

1. **Delphis aedem**: i. e. the
Λέσχη or covered portico where
people met to converse. The pictures,
which included an Ilioupersis and a
Nekuia are described in Paus. x, 25–
31. For modern reconstructions see
Robert, *Hall. Winckelmannspr.* xvi,
1892 and xvii, 1893.

Poecile: where next to Mikon's
Amazonomachia (below) Polygnotos
painted an *Ilioupersis*. Next to
this again came the *Marathon* by
Mikon and Panainos (above). For
the distribution of the pictures see
Benndorf, *op. cit.* p. 156, and the new
arrangement proposed by Robert in
Hall. Winckelmannspr. xviii, 1895,
p. 44.   The pictures, as appears
from Synnesios, *Ep.* 135 (= Overb.
Schriftquell. 1057), were not mural
paintings in the ordinary sense, but
were painted on wooden boards or
panels; cf. Wachsmuth, *Stadt Athen*,
ii, p. 504.

2. **gratuito**: cf. Melanthios (cf.
Wilamowitz, *Arist. u. Athen.* p. 287,
n. 37) *ap.* Plutarch, *Kimon*, iv, p. 431 :
αὐτοῦ γὰρ δαπάναισι θεῶν ναοὺς
ἀγοράν τε
Κεκροπίαν κόσμησ' ἡμιθέων
ἀρεταῖς.

(The *ναοί* here referred to are those of
Theseus and the *Anakes*, Harpokration *s. v.* Πολύγνωτος.)

partem eius Micon: he painted
the battle of Theseus and the Amazons, Paus. i, 15, 2 ; Arrian vii, 13, 5,
where few will agree with Graef (*ap.*
Pauly *s. v.* AMAZONEN p. 1778) in
defending the old reading Κίμων ; cf.
Robert, *loc. cit.* p. 47, note 2. Mikon
was also a sculptor, xxxiv, 88, where
see note.

3. **Amphictyones**: the reward
they gave was more probably for the
decoration of the Λέσχη ; while for
his work at Athens he received the
Attic citizenship, Harpokration, *l. c.*

6. **Timarete**: below, § 147.

§ 60. 7. **LXXXX** autem Olymp.:
as in the case of the sculptors (xxxiv,
49), the first painter in each Olympiad is dated from a work brought
into connexion with an important
historical event ; about this central
date his contemporaries, whether
older or younger, are roughly grouped,
cf. Robert, *Arch. März.* p. 66 f.

Aglaophon: son of Aristophon
(below, § 138), and accordingly nephew
of Polygnotos (Plato, *Gorg.* p. 448 B)
and grandson of the first Aglaophon.

decorated the temple at Delphoi and at Athens the Painted Portico *He paints*
[στοὰ ποικίλη], as it is called. For this he took no money, while *the Lesche at Delphoi,*
Mikon, to whom part of the work was entrusted, accepted pay- *and at*
ment. The position he thus won for himself was all the greater, *Athens the Stoa*
so much so that the Amphyktionic council, or national assembly *Poikile.*
of Hellas, decreed that he should be a public guest. There was *Mikon.*
Mikon the
another *Mikon*, distinguished as 'the younger,' whose daughter *Younger.*
Timarete was also an artist.

In the ninetieth Olympiad [420–417 B.C.] lived *Aglaophon*, 60
†*Kephisodoros*, †*Erillos* and *Evenor*, the father and master of *Great masters*
the great artist Parrhasios, whom I shall mention in due time. *of the*
They were all painters of note, yet they need not prevent my *ninetieth Olympiad.*
hastening on to the true luminaries of art, among whom the
first to shine was *Apollodoros* of Athens in the ninety-third *Apollo-*
Olympiad [408–405 B.C.]. He was the first to give his figures *doros of Athens.*
the appearance of reality, and he first bestowed true glory on
the brush. He painted a priest in prayer, and an Aias struck *His works*
by lightning, which is still to be seen at Pergamon. No picture *1. Priest,*
2. Aias.

His date (Robert, *loc. cit.*) seems
determined by his picture of Olympias
and Pythias crowning Alkibiades
(Satyros *ap.* Athen. xii, p. 534 D),
painted to commemorate the chariot
victories of Ol. 90 (Grote, *Greece*, v,
p. 456 f.) or Ol. 91 (Rutgers) ; see
G. H. Förster, *Die Olympischen
Sieger*, i, p. 20 f. The companion
picture of Alkibiades in the lap of
Nemea was by Aristophon, Plut.
Alkib. xvi, Paus. i, 22, 6 (artist
unnamed). Satyros, *loc. cit.*, attributes
it however to the son.

8. **Evenor, pater Parrhasi** : Paus.
i, 28, 2. *suis annis* below, § 67.

11. **Apollodorus** : Overb. *Schriftquell.* 1641–1646.

12. **primus species** ... primusque **gloriam** : belongs to the series
of Xenokratic art judgements begun in
§§ 15–16 ; 56–58 : cf. Introd. p. xxix.

species : evidently the vague translation of some Greek technical term ;
cf. Jahn, *Kunsturtheile*, p. 138.
The discovery attributed to Apollodoros by Plutarch (*Glor. Ath.* ii) was

the φθορὰ καὶ ἀπόχρωσις σκιᾶς—(an
advance also attributed to Zeuxis,
Quinct. xii, 10, 4 *prior luminum
umbrarumque invenit rationem*) i. e.
he showed how to render—not the
shadow cast, but the graduated
passage from light to shadow on
curved surfaces (Lange, *Fremstilling*,
p. 465 ; cf. above, *tonon* and *harmogen*
in § 29). In this connexion may be
noted the attempt at expressing by
shadow the curving of surfaces, on
two interesting polychrome lekythoi
of the Berlin Museum (*Cat.* 2684,
2685—the latter published in facsimile
by Winter, *Winckelmannsprogr.* 1895,
cf. *id.* p. 9).

14. **sacerdos adorans** : votive
portrait ; cf. the *sacerdos adstante
puero* of Parrhasius (§ 70) the *sup-
plicans paene cum voce* of Aristeides
(§ 99).

Aiax fulmine incensus : Verg.
Aen. i, 43 ff. *ipsa* (sc. *Minerva*)
*Iovis rapidum iaculata e nubibus
ignem | disiecitque rates, evertitque
aequora ventis | illum expirantem*

spectatur hodie. neque ante eum tabula ullius ostenditur
61 quae teneat oculos. ab hoc artis fores apertas Zeuxis
Heracleotes intravit olympiadis LXXXXV anno quarto,
audentemque iam aliquid penicillum—de hoc enim adhuc
loquamur—ad magnam gloriam perduxit, a quibusdam falso 5
in LXXXVIIII olympiade positus. confuisse necesse est
Demophilum Himeraeum et Nesea Thasium, quoniam
62 utrius eorum discipulus fuerit ambigitur. in eum Apollodorus supra scriptus versum fecit, artem ipsis ablatam
Zeuxim ferre secum. opes quoque tantas adquisivit ut in 10
ostentationem earum Olympiae aureis litteris in palliorum
tesseris intextum nomen suum ostentaret. postea donare

6. positus. confuisse] *Traube*; positus cum fuisse (fuisset *omnes praeter
Bamb.*) *codd.*; positus, cum quo fuisse *Ritschl, Detlefsen.*

transfixo pectore flammas | turbine
corripuit scopuloque infixit acuto; cf.
Odyss. iv, 499 ff. [The *fulmine incensus* of the subject not (as Furtwängler, *Plinius*, p. 53 suggests) of
the picture, in which case Pliny would
use *tabula*, cf. below, § 69.—H. L. U.]

Pergami : Introd. p. xc.

§ 61. 2. fores apertas : [ii, 31
*rerum fores aperuisse Anaximander
... traditur*; the metaphor is common
to Silver Latin, cf. Plin. *Epist.* i, 18, 4
*illa (actio) ianuam famae (mihi)
patefecit.* Because a similar expression
occurs, Babrios, Proem. l. 29, there is
no need to follow Schneidewin, *Rhein.
Mus.* vii (1850), p. 479, in thinking
that Pliny's words go back to a Greek
metrical epigram, cf. also Müller,
Stil, p. 126 ff. H. L. U.] At the
same time, the words exactly express
the position which the Greek writers
(Introd. p. xxix) assigned to Apollodoros at the opening of a series of
painters who, masters of their art,
each brought towards the final perfection to be attained by Apelles (§ 79)
a definite contribution : Apollodoros
among the painters is the counterpart
of Pheidias among the statuaries,
Robert, *Arch. März.* p. 67 f. (Introd.

p. xxvii).   Therefore the words must
represent some closely similar Greek
expression; for an analogous paraphrase cf. Add. to note on xxxiv, 81.

3. Heracleotes : Plato, *Protag.*
318 B ὁ νεανίσκος ὁ νῦν νεωστὶ ἐπιδημῶν
Ζεύξιππος ὁ Ἡρακλεώτης (on the identity
of Zeuxis and Zeuxippos see Fick,
Griech. Personennamen, pp. 35, 132).
The dialogue being imagined as taking
place in B. C. 424, it is impossible to
reconcile this mention of Zeuxis with
the tradition that he was born at
Herakleia (founded B.C. 432), except
by either holding Plato guilty of an
anachronism (and likewise Xenophon,
who alludes to Z. in the 'Banquet,'
of which the scene is laid in B. C. 422),
or supposing with Robert (*Hall.
Winckelmannsprogr.* xix, 1895, p. 18),
that the parents of Zeuxis removed as
colonists to Herakleia when he was
already a boy of nine or ten. The artist
was evidently at home in Lower Italy
(he paints for Agrigentum, Kroton,
&c.); it is out of the question to
assume that he was born at the older
Pontic Herakleia. Addenda.

Ol. 95, anno quarto : the occasion for the date assigned to him here
is unknown. Since the 'Alkmena,'

by any of his predecessors really rivets the gaze. It was he who 61
opened the gates of art through which *Zeuxis* of Herakleia *Zeuxis of*
passed in the fourth year of the ninety-fifth Olympiad [397 B.C.], *Herakleia,*
giving to the painter's brush (for of the brush alone I speak as
yet) the full glory to which it already aspired. Zeuxis is erroneously placed by some in the eighty-ninth Olympiad [424–
421 B.C.]; it is evident that † *Demophilos* of Himera and † *Neseus taught by*
of Thasos were among his contemporaries, seeing that there is a *Demophilos*
controversy as to which of the two was his master. In an epigram 62 *or Neseus.*
written against him by the Apollodoros whom I mentioned above,
it is said that 'Zeuxis bore away with him the art he had stolen
from his masters.' He amassed great wealth, and in order to *His wealth,*
make a parade of it at Olympia he showed his name woven in *luxury,*
golden letters into the embroideries of his garments. Later on *and pride.*

which belongs to his later period (see
below Urlichs' note on *postea*), was
yet painted previous to B.C. 406, in
which year Agrigentum was destroyed
by the Carthaginians, Zeuxis must
have been an artist of note long
before B.C. 398; cf. also the
passage from Plato quoted above.
On the other hand the ascription to
Z. of the Ἔρως . . . ὁ γεγραμμένος
ἔχων στέφανον ἀνθέμων, Ar. *Acharn.*
991 (play produced B.C. 425), rests
only on the doubtful authority of the
scholia.

4. **adhuc**: i. e. in opposition to
encaustic painting in § 149.

5. **falso**: Quinct. xii, 10, 4, dates
Zeuxis, and Parrhasios *circa Pelopon-
nesia ambo tempora*, from the fact
that Xenophon (*Memorab.* iii, 10, 1)
records a conversation between Parrhasios and Sokrates. The earlier
date was the correct one.

7. **Demophilum**: distinct from
the Damophilos (below, § 154, where
see note) who decorated the temple of
Ceres.

Himeraeum: Ἱμέρα on the N.
coast of Sicily.

Thasium: the ethnic suggests that
Neseus belonged to the circle of
Polygnotos (§ 58) of Thasos. Robert,
loc. cit., points out that the young

Zeuxis very possibly placed himself
under this master, on his arrival in
Athens.

§ 62. 9. **ipsis**: sc. *Demophilo et
Nesea* (Traube). Benndorf, *Epigr.* p.
30, and Jahn, *Kleine Beiträge*, p. 284,
explain it as *sibi sociisque*, which is
impossible.

10. **in ostentationem**: the story
of the gorgeous robes worn by Zeuxis
has its counterpart in the gorgeous
robes of his rival Parrhasios (Athen.
xii, 543 C—D), Introd. p. lvii.

12. **tesseris intextum**: the best
explanation seems that of Urlichs,
Chrest. p. 345; he takes the *tesserae*
to have been small squares (of stuff)
upon which the name was embroidered,
and quotes Vopiscus, *Carinus* 20
*inscriptum est adhuc in choraulae
pallio Tyrianthino Messalae nomen
uxoris* (ed. H. Peter); see in Casau-
bon's edition, vol. ii, p. 851 ᵃ, Sau-
maise's note, who in reference to the
Plinian passage explains *tesserae =*
κύβοι, and quotes Hesychius (*s. v.*
κύβος) οἱ Σαλαμίνιοι λέγουσι κύβον
τὸ τοῦ ἱματίου σημεῖον.

postea: [i. e. in his latter period;
the Alkmena and the Pan must therefore be reckoned among the artist's
later works.—H. L. U.]

opera sua instituit, quod nullo pretio satis digno permutari
posse diceret, sicuti Alcmenam Agragentinis, Pana Archelao.
63 fecit et Penelopen in qua pinxisse mores videtur, et athletam,
adeoque in illo sibi placuit ut versum subscriberet celebrem
ex eo, invisurum aliquem facilius quam imitaturum.   magni- 5
ficus est et Iuppiter eius in throno adstantibus diis et
Hercules infans dracones strangulans Alcmena matre coram
64 pavente et Amphitryone.   reprehenditur tamen ceu grandior
in capitibus articulisque, alioqui tantus diligentia ut Agragentinis facturus tabulam quam in templo Iunonis Laciniae 10
publice dicarent inspexerit virgines eorum nudas et quinque
elegerit, ut quod in quaque laudatissimum esset pictura
redderet.   pinxit et monochromata ex albo.   aequales eius
et aemuli fuere Timanthes, Androcydes, Eupompus, Parrha-
65 sius.   descendisse hic in certamen cum Zeuxide traditur, et 15
cum ille detulisset uvas pictas tanto successu ut in scaenam

2. **Alcmenam**: probably identical with the picture in § 63.

Archelao: for whom Zeuxis decorated the palace at Pella, Ailian ποικ. ἱστ. xiv, 17.

3. **mores**: in the sense given to it by Horace, *Ep.* i, 1, 57 *est animus tibi, sunt mores.* Some commentators however (chief among them Winckelmann), have understood *mores* to be a translation of the Greek ἦθος, whereby endless difficulties have arisen, seeing that ἦθος was precisely the quality in which, according to Aristotle, *Poet.* 6, 11, Zeuxis was deficient. But ἦθος in its strictly philosophical sense had no precise Latin equivalent, as we learn from Quinct. vi, 2, 8, and from Pliny himself (below, § 98, where see note); cf. Brunn, *K. G.* ii, p. 86 f.; Jahn, *Kunsturtheile,* p. 105 f.

5. **invisurum**: μωμήσεταί τις μᾶλλον ἢ μιμήσεται; the proverb is attributed by Plutarch (*Glor. Ath.* 2), and Hesychios to Apollodoros. The saying recurs from early times in a variety of forms; Bergk, *Lyr. Graec.* ii, p. 318, Benndorf, *Epigr.* p. 27, n. 3;

cf. Preger, *Inscript. Gr. Metr.* 193. Introd. p. lvii.

6. **Iuppiter . . . Amphitryone**: the whole subject is preserved on a vase-painting in the Brit. Mus.; A. S. Murray, *Class. Rev.* 1888, p. 327; id. *Handb. of Greek Arch.* p. 376. Add.

§ 64. 8. **reprehenditur tamen**: the *tamen* presupposes a sentence of praise, which has fallen out. Quinctilian (xii, 10, 5) says of Zeuxis *plus membris corporis dedit . . .* but praises him on the same grounds that Pliny blames him, another instance of conflicting criticisms in antiquity; cf. note on Kallimachos in xxxiv, 92.

9. **articulisque**: literally the joints (knuckles, wrists, ankles, &c.) and so by extension the extremities; see Robert, *Arch. Märch.* p. 76, *Hall. Winckelmannsprogr.* xix, 1895, p. 25. An almost identical criticism is passed upon Euphranor in § 128. Zeuxis is represented in the same relation to Apollodoros as Polykleitos xxxiv, 56 to Pheidias (*ib.* 54). On the Xenokratic authorship see Introd. p. xxvii.

Agragentinis: from Cic. (*Invent.* ii, 1, 1) it appears that this picture he began to make presents of his pictures, saying that they were beyond all price. In this way he gave his Alkmena to the city of Agrigentum and his Pan to Archelaos. He also painted a Penelope, in whom he embodied virtue's self, and an athlete with whom he was so well pleased that he wrote beneath it the line thenceforward famous : 'Another may carp more easily than he may copy.' He also painted a superb Zeus enthroned amid the assembled gods, with the infant Herakles strangling the snakes in presence of his trembling mother Alkmena and of Amphitryon. Zeuxis is criticized however as having exaggerated the heads and extremities of his figures ; for the rest he bestowed such minute pains upon his work that before painting for the people of Agrigentum a picture to be dedicated in the temple of Hera on the Lakinian promontory, he inspected the maidens of the city naked, and chose out five, whose peculiar beauties he proposed to reproduce in his picture. He also painted monochromes in white. *Timanthes, Androkydes, †Eupompos* and *Parrhasios* were contemporaries and rivals of Zeuxis. The story runs that Parrhasios and Zeuxis

His gifts of the 'Alkmena,' and the 'Pan.' 63

64 *For the temple of Hera Lakinia he paints a picture taken from the five most beauteous maidens of the city.*

65 *His contemporaries.*

is identical with the famous Helena (below, § 66).

10. Iunonis Laciniae : Cicero, *loc. cit.*, says the Helena was painted for the Krotoniates ; so too Dionysios H. (*de veter. script. cens.* 1), and this is doubtless correct, for as Freeman remarks (*Sicily*, vol. ii, p. 402, note 3) 'the Lakinian Hera, at home at Kroton, would have no place at Akragas' (cf. Roscher, i, p. 2086).

11. inspexerit virgines : Lange (*Fremstilling*, p. 354 n.) points out that the anecdote gives concrete expression to the saying that the best parts must be taken 'out of divers Faces, to make one Excellent,' cf. Xenoph. *Mem.* iii, 10, 2 ; Cicero and Dionysios (*ll. cc.*) incorporate the axiom with the anecdote which illustrates it. See Introd. p. lxi f.

13. ex albo : i. e. on a dark ground, perhaps in imitation of marble reliefs (cf. Blümner, *Technol.* iv, p. 420, note 4), whereas monochrome paintings were usually carried out in red (*cinnabar, minium, rubrica, sinopis*, Plin. xxxiii, 117), presumably on a white

ground. Of the latter technique we have imitations in the pictures painted in red colour on the white marble slabs in Naples. Semper's theory (*Stil*, i, p. 470, ed. 1) that these had once been polychrome pictures in encaustic, whose colours were destroyed by the heat of the lava, has been disproved by Helbig, *Wandgemälde*, 170[b]; cf. Robert, *Hall. Winckelmannsprogr.* xix, 1895, p. 9 ; on the contrary, the slabs admirably prove the practice of painting in monochrome.

14. Timanthes : below, § 73.

Androcydes : of Kyzikos ; according to Plutarch (*Pel.* xxv) he painted at the time of the liberation of the Kadmeia (B.C. 379) the picture of a battle in which both Epameinondas and Pelopidas had been engaged ; i. e. probably the battle mentioned *Pel.* iv (Brunn, *K. G.* ii, p. 124). From Athen. viii, p. 341 A, we learn that he was celebrated for his accurate painting of fish.

Eupompus : below, § 75.

§ 65. 16. uvas pictas : cf. below, §§ 66, 155 ; above, § 23.

ut in scaenam : i. e. the pictures

aves advolarent, ipse detulisse linteum pictum ita veritate repraesentata ut Zeuxis alitum iudicio tumens flagitaret tandem remoto linteo ostendi picturam atque intellecto errore concederet palmam ingenuo pudore, quoniam ipse 66 volucres fefellisset, Parrhasius autem se artificem. fertur et 5 postea Zeuxis pinxisse puerum uvas ferentem, ad quas cum advolassent aves, eadem ingenuitate processit iratus operi et dixit : uvas melius pinxi quam puerum, nam si et hoc consummassem, aves timere debuerant. fecit et figlina opera, quae sola in Ambracia relicta sunt, cum inde Musas Fulvius 10 Nobilior Romam transferret. Zeuxidis manu Romae Helena est in Philippi porticibus, et in Concordiae delubro Marsyas 67 religatus. Parrhasius Ephesi natus et ipse multa contulit. primus symmetrian picturae dedit, primus argutias voltus, elegantiam capilli, venustatem oris, confessione artificum in 15 lineis extremis palmam adeptus. haec est picturae summa

were exhibited in the theatre, and hung on the *scaenae frons*, or front wall of the stage-buildings.

§ 66. 7. pinxisse puerum: a mere *doublette* of the preceding anecdote; the story is also told Senec. Rhet. *Controv.* x, 5 (34), 27.

9. figlina opera: Pyrrhus had probably inherited these works as king of Macedonia. Zeuxis, it will be remembered, had worked for King Archelaos, above, § 62.

10. sola . . . relicta sunt : doubtless because these painted terra-cottas were architectural decorations, and could not be removed without injury to the buildings; Liv. xxxviii, 9, 13 *signa aenea marmoreaque et tabulae pictae, quibus ornatior Ambracia quia regia ibi Pyrrhi fuerat . . . sublata omnia avectaque ; nihil praeterea tactum violatumve,* cf. Raoul-Rochette, *Peintures,* p. 51.

Ambracia: the capital of King Pyrrhus : for its art treasures cf. Polyb. xxii, 13, 9; Liv. *loc. cit.*

Musas : these statues, which probably dated from the reign of Pyrrhus,

were dedicated by Fulvius in the Temple of *Hercules Musarum,* with a statue of Herakles as Μουσα-γέτης (see in this connexion Eumenius of Autun *pro restaurandis scholis,* vii, in *Paneg. Lat.* ed. Baehrens, p. 121 ; cf. also Ovid, *Fasti,* vi, 804). The Muses are figured on the reverse of the coins of Q. Pomponius Musa (reproduced and fully discussed by O. Bie, *Die Musen in d. antiken Kunst,* pp. 24–44). The tragic Muse is preserved in a statuette of the Vatican (Clarac, 507, 1013), while a head from Frascati in the Brit. Mus.(Friederichs-Wolters,1445) seems to reproduce the head of another; cf. Amelung, *Basis des Praxiteles,* p. 44. For the one extant basis, see *Bull. d. Inst.* 1869, p. 3 ff.—The temple was surrounded by the *porticus Philippi,* and was close to the *porticus Octaviae* on the W. side of the *Circus Flaminius.*

11. Helena : the mention of the Muses which Fulvius brought to Rome, suggests to Pliny two more works by Zeuxis, noted by him as

entered into competition, Zeuxis exhibiting a picture of some *Competi-*
grapes, so true to nature that the birds flew up to the wall of the *tion be-*
tween
stage. Parrhasios then displayed a picture of a linen curtain, *Zeuxis and*
realistic to such a degree that Zeuxis, elated by the verdict of the *Parrha-*
sios.
birds, cried out that now at last his rival must draw the curtain *The cur-*
and show his picture. On discovering his mistake he surrendered *tain and*
the grapes.
the prize to Parrhasios, admitting candidly that he had deceived
the birds, while Parrhasios had deluded himself, a painter. After **66**
this we learn that Zeuxis painted a boy carrying grapes, and when *Boy with*
the birds flew down to settle on them, he was vexed with his own *grapes.*
work, and came forward saying, with like frankness, ' I have
painted the grapes better than the boy, for had I been perfectly
successful with the latter, the birds must have been afraid.' He
also modelled certain terra-cottas which were the only works of art
left in Ambrakia when Fulvius Nobilior brought the statues of the
Muses to Rome. The paintings in Rome by the hand of Zeuxis *Helen.*
are : the Helen in the gallery of Philip and the bound Marsyas *Marsyas*
bound.
in the temple of Concord. *Parrhasios*, a native of Ephesos, also **67**
made great contributions to the progress of art. He first gave *Parrha-*
sios.
painting symmetry, and added vivacity to the features, daintiness
to the hair and comeliness to the mouth, while by the verdict of
artists he is unrivalled in the rendering of outline. This is the

being also in Rome. In making
this addition he forgets that he
had already mentioned the Helena,
when quoting from his main authority.
His oversight is, however, the easier
to explain as in the previous passage
the name of the picture had not been
given.

12. **Philippi porticibus:** built by
L. Marcius Philippus, the step-father
of Augustus, round the *T. Hercules
Musarum* (above); Suet. *Aug.* 29 ;
Ovid, *Fasti*, vi, 801 ; cf. Gilbert, *Rom.*
iii, p. 248.

Concordiae delubro: note on
xxxvi, 73.

Marsyas religatus: the representations of Marsyas bound are
all cited by Jessen *ap.* Roscher, ii,
2450 ff. None, however, can be traced
back with any certainty to Zeuxis's
picture. A reminiscence of the whole
composition perchance survives in the

relief of a marble vase at Naples,
A. Z. 1869, taf. 18.

§ 67. 13. **Ephesi natus:** Strabo
xiv, p. 642 ; *Anth. App.* lix, 2.

14. **primus symmetrian pict.
dedit:** his achievement as a painter
marks a similar advance upon that of
Zeuxis (§ 64) to Myron's (xxxiv, 57)
upon that of Polykleitos among the
statuaries, Introd. p. xxvii.

argutias: note on xxxiv, 65.

15. **confessione artificum:** refers
to the artists and art-historians Antigonos and Xenokrates (below, § 68) ;
cf. *artifices qui condidere haec* in
xxxiv, 68, where the same two writers
are meant, Introd. p. xxxvii.

in lineis: cf. Quinct. xii, 10, 4
*examinasse (Parrh.) subtilius lineas
traditur.*

16. **haec est picturae . . . occultat:** the passage is of unique aesthetic
interest (Introd. p. xxxiv), it expresses

suptilitas. corpora enim pingere et media rerum est quidem
magni operis sed in quo multi gloriam tulerint, extrema corporum facere et desinentis picturae modum includere rarum
68 in successu artis invenitur. ambire enim se ipsa debet extremitas et sic desinere ut promittat alia post se ostendatque 5
etiam quae occultat.   hanc ei gloriam concessere Antigonus
et Xenocrates qui de pictura scripsere, praedicantes quoque,
non solum confitentes.   et alia multa graphidis vestigia
exstant in tabulis ac membranis eius, ex quibus proficere
dicuntur artifices.   minor tamen videtur sibi comparatus in 10
69 mediis corporibus exprimendis. pinxit demon Atheniensium
argumento quoque ingenioso. ostendebat namque varium,
iracundum iniustum inconstantem, eundem exorabilem
clementem misericordem, gloriosum, excelsum humilem,
ferocem fugacemque et omnia pariter. idem pinxit et 15
Thesea, quae Romae in Capitolio fuit, et navarchum thoracatum, et in una tabula, quae est Rhodi, Meleagrum, Herculem, Persea, haec ibi ter fulmine ambusta neque obliterata
70 hoc ipso miraculum auget. pinxit et archigallum, quam

---

5. alia sponse (sponte *e correctione*) *Bamb.* (*scriptum erat* alias pos se ; *an*
alias post se ? *Traube*).

the dominant effort of painting to
represent objects not only as relieved
from the flat, but *as occupying space.*
It is suggestively discussed by Bertrand, *Études*, p. 65 ff.

1. media rerum : i. e. the modelling of the particular face chosen for
presentation, as it lies between its
bounding lines, without any necessary
suggestion of the parts which are
concealed from view.

2. extrema . . . modum includere : the subtle meaning conveyed
by these words is more easily felt
than translated.   The idea is that the
supreme difficulty and consequently
the supreme achievement of painting
consists in bringing the painted outline (*modus desinentis picturae*) into
agreement with the contour of the
figure.

4. ambire . . . extremitas : Ber-

trand (*loc. cit.*) translates ' il faut en
effet que les *contours s'enveloppent
eux-mêmes.*'   In other words, the contours must be so drawn *as to appear
to clasp what is behind them.*

§ 68. 5. ut promittat alia post
se : the meaning is so clear, the
aesthetic lesson so true, that I have
decided on keeping Detlefsen's reading, but not without hesitation, for the
MSS. are in favour of *alias* (sc. *extremitates*) *post se*—a reading recommended
by Dr. Traube.   The meaning of
this alternative reading would be : in
any object, the face which the artist
chooses for presentation forms, where
it leaves off, a line against the background.   But another view of the
same object would have afforded a
different system of bounding lines, of
extremitates, and as any object may
be viewed from an endless number

highest subtlety attainable in painting. Merely to paint a figure in relief is no doubt a great achievement, yet many have succeeded thus far. But where an artist is rarely successful is in finding an outline which shall express the contours of the figure. For the 68 contour should appear to fold back, and so enclose the object as to give assurance of the parts behind, thus clearly suggesting even what it conceals. Preeminence in this respect is conceded to Parrhasios by Antigonos and Xenokrates, writers on *Judgement* painting, who indeed not only concede but insist upon it. Many *of Antigonos and* other traces of his draughtmanship remain, both in pictures and *Xeno-* on parchments, which are said to be instructive to artists. Still, *krates.* if tried by his own standard, he fails in modelling. He painted 69 an ingenious personification of the Athenian 'Demos,' discovering *His works.* it as fickle, passionate, unjust, changeable, yet exorable, compassionate and pitiful, boastful, proud and humble, bold and cowardly, in a word, everything at once. He also painted the Theseus formerly in the Capitol at Rome, an admiral in armour, and Meleager, Herakles and Perseus in a picture at Rhodes, where it has thrice been set on fire by lightning without being destroyed, a miracle which increases our wonder.

---

of points, there is no limit to its bounding lines. It therefore becomes the business of the great artist, to give assurance, although working on the flat, of these hidden lines. This notion of fugitive, pursuant outlines, though somewhat rhetorical and over-subtilized, would also convey its peculiar truth.

9. **tabulis** : either small tablets, containing the artist's sketches for his large pictures, or, if in the usual sense of easel pictures, we must understand these *tabulae* to have been left unfinished, with the design merely sketched in.

§ 69. 11. **demon Atheniensium**: cf. the same subject by Euphranor, Paus. i, 3, 3 ; below note on § 129.

16. **Thesea**: the picture was originally in Athens (Plut. *Thes.* iv), whence it may have been brought by Sulla.

fuit: i.e. it was destroyed by the fire of B.C. 70 ; cf. xxxiii, 154 ; xxxiv, 38.

17. **quae est Rhodi** : Mucianus is therefore presumably the authority here followed by Pliny, Introd. p. lxxxvi f.

Meleagrum, Herculem, Persea ; grouped in a 'Santa conversazione,' such as were becoming popular in the period of Parrhasios ; they had little mythological significance, save as presenting, pleasantly grouped together, two or more of the popular national gods or heroes ; cf. the 'Aineias, Kastor and Polydeukes' in § 71. (Robert, *Bild u. Lied*, p. 45.)

18. **ter fulmine ambusta** : the stress laid on the miraculous circumstance confirms the authorship of Mucianus, Introd. *loc. cit.*

§ 70. 19. **archigallum** : literally the word would apply to the chief of the priests of Kybele. But the following anecdote shows that the picture more probably represented the figure of a nude boy, surnamed the *archi-*

picturam amavit Tiberius princeps atque, ut auctor est
Deculo, HS. [LX] aestimatam cubiculo suo inclusit. pinxit
et Thressam nutricem infantemque in manibus eius et Philiscum et Liberum patrem adstante Virtute, et pueros duos in
quibus spectatur securitas et aetatis simplicitas, item sacer- 5
71 dotem adstante puero cum acerra et corona. sunt et duae
picturae eius nobilissimae, hoplites in certamine ita decurrens
ut sudare videatur, alter arma deponens ut anhelare sentiatur. laudantur et Aeneas Castorque ac Pollux in eadem
tabula, item Telephus, Achilles, Agamemnon, Ulixes. fecun- 10
dus artifex, sed quo nemo insolentius usus sit gloria artis,
namque et cognomina usurpavit habrodiaetum se appellando
aliisque versibus principem artis et eam ab se consummatam,
super omnia Apollinis se radice ortum et Herculem, qui est
Lindi, talem a se pictum qualem saepe in quiete vidisset. 15
72 ergo magnis suffragiis superatus a Timanthe Sami in Aiace
armorumque iudicio herois nomine se moleste ferre dicebat
quod iterum ab indigno victus esset. pinxit et minoribus
tabellis libidines, eo genere petulantis ioci se reficiens.

gallus, owing to some physical peculiarity (cf. Klein, *Arch. Ep. Mitth.*
xii, 1888, p. 123); perhaps therefore
the picture should be reckoned among
the *libidines* mentioned below in § 72.

1. amavit Tiberius: cf. the
similar story told of the *Apoxyomenos*
of Lysippos, xxxiv, § 62.

3. Thressam nutricem: a votive
portrait put up in gratitude for the
services of a favourite nurse; cf. Furtwängler, *Dornauszieher*, p. 95, or a
grave picture; cf. *Anth. Pal.* vii,
663 :

'Ο μικκὸς τόδ' ἔτευξε τᾷ Θρείσσᾳ
Μήδειος τὸ μνᾶμ' ἐπὶ τᾷ ὁδῷ, κἠπέ-
γραψε Κλείτας.
ἐξεῖ τὰν χάριν ἁ γυνὰ ἀντ' ἐκείνων
ὧν τὸν κῶρον ἔθρεψ'. ἔτυμ' ὧν ἔτι
ΧΡΗΣΙΜΑ τελευτᾷ.

From *pinxit et Thr. nutr.* down to *et
corona* we seem to have part of the
old account of Parrhasios by Xenokrates; Münzer, *op. cit.* p. 515; cf.
Introd. p. xxvii.

Philiscum: a poet of the Middle
Comedy; Kock, *Fragm. Com. Graec.*
vol. ii, p. 443.

5. sacerdotem adstante puero:
cf. above, note on § 60.

§ 71. 6. duae picturae: apparently
composed as pendants; the description is epigrammatic, Benndorf, *Epigramm.* p. 55, Introd. p. lxxi.

9. Aeneas Castorque ac Pollux:
for this group of heroes, who have
no mythological connexion with one
another, cf. above, note on § 69.

10. Telephus, Achilles, Agamemnon, Ulixes: i.e. a picture representing the healing of Telephos by
the rust from the sword of Achilles
(xxxiv, 152), in presence of Agamemnon and of Odysseus. Robert (*Bild.
u. Lied.* p. 35) conjectures the picture
to have been inspired by the lost play
of Euripides; but Vogel (*Scenen
Euripid. Trag. in gr. Vasengemälden*,
p. 18) rightly points out that Euripides had assigned too marked a part

He also painted a priest of Kybele : a picture of which the 70
Emperor Tiberius was enamoured, and which, according to
Deculo, although valued at 6,000,000 sesterces (£52,500 circ.), he
placed in his private apartments. Furthermore he painted a
Thrakian nurse with an infant in her arms ; a portrait of Philiskos,
Dionysos by the side of Virtue, two boys whose features express
the confidence and the simplicity of their age, and a priest with
a boy at his side holding a censer and a wreath. Two other 71
pictures by him are most famous, a hoplite in a race who seems to
sweat as he runs, and a hoplite laying aside his arms, whose
labouring breath we seem to hear. His picture of Aineias, Kastor
and Polydeukes is praised, so is his Telephos with Achilles, Agamemnon and Odysseus. He was a prolific artist, but carried his *His luxury
and arrog-*
success with an arrogance that none have equalled ; he called *ance.*
himself ἀβροδίαιτος [the luxurious] and said in another epigram
that he was the prince of painting, that he had brought it to the
highest point of perfection, and more than all that he was of the
seed of Apollo, and had painted the Herakles at Lindos precisely *Herakles at
Lindos.*
as he had often seen him in sleep. Hence it was that when he 72
was defeated by a large majority of votes in a competition with *Competition with*
Timanthes at Samos, the subject of his picture being Aias and *Timanthes.*
the award of the arms, he said in the name of the hero that he
was grieved at being worsted a second time by an unworthy rival.
He also painted small pictures of licentious subjects, seeking

in the action to Klytaimnestra, for
her to have been left out in a picture
taken straight from his drama. Vogel
therefore points to the Telephos of
Aischylos as the source of Parrhasios'
inspiration.

12. **habrodiaetum**: from the epigram preserved Ath. xii, p. 543 D,
= *Anthol. App.* 59 = Bergk. *L. G.* ii,
pp. 320, 635, 1 ; cf. O. Jahn, *Kleine
Beiträge*, p. 286 ff. ; Introd. p. lv.

13. **consummatam**: from the epigram Athen. xii, p. 543 E = *Anthol.
App.* 60 = Bergk, ii, p. 321, 636, 2 ; cf.
the epigram composed by Zeuxis upon
himself, Aristeides, *Or.* 49, ii, p. 521
= Bergk, ii, pp. 318, 634.

14. **super omnia . . . ortum**: according to Jahn (*loc. cit.*) these words
are from a lost epigram of similar
character to those preserved in Athe-

naios.

15. **talem . . . pictum**: Athen. xii,
543 F = *Anth. App.* 61 = Bergk, p. 321,
636, 3 ; these verses were probably inscribed on the picture ; cf. the epigram
which Parrhasios composed for his
picture of Hermes, Themistios *Orat.*
ii, p. 34 (Dindorf).

§ 72. 16. **a Timanthe** : the name of
Parrhasios' rival is given only by Pliny ;
the story of the competition also
Athen. xii, 543 E, Ailian, ποικίλη ἰστ.
ix, 11. Introd. p. liv f.

in Aiace armorumque iudicio :
it is unnecessary to suppose from
these words that ' The award of the
Arms ' was also the subject of the
picture by Timanthes.

19. **libidines**: one instance on record is his 'Meleager and Atalanta,'
Suet. *Tib.* 44 ; Polemon (*ap.* Athen.

73 nam Timanthi vel plurimum adfuit ingenii. eius enim est
Iphigenia oratorum laudibus celebrata, qua stante ad aras
peritura cum maestos pinxisset omnes praecipueque patru-
um, et tristitiae omnem imaginem consumpsisset, patris
ipsius voltum velavit quem digne non poterat ostendere. 5
74 sunt et alia ingenii eius exempla, veluti Cyclops dormiens
in parvola tabella, cuius et sic magnitudinem exprimere
cupiens pinxit iuxta Satyros thyrso pollicem eius metientes.
atque in unius huius operibus intellegitur plus semper quam
pingitur et, cum sit ars summa, ingenium tamen ultra artem 10
est. pinxit et heroa absolutissimi operis artem ipsam complexus viros pingendi, quod opus nunc Romae in templo
75 Pacis est.   Euxinidas hac aetate docuit Aristiden praeclarum artificem, Eupompus Pamphilum Apellis praeceptorem.
est Eupompi victor certamine gymnico palmam tenens. 15

xiii, p. 567 B) makes the same charge
of πορνογραφία against Aristeides,
Pausias and Nikophanes; cf. also
Euripides, *Hippol.* 1005.

§ 73. 1. **Nam**: resumes the subject
from *victus esset.*

Timanthi: a native of Kythnos,
Quinct. ii, 13, 13. Eustathios (on
Il. p. 1343, 60), whose authorities
are rarely trustworthy, calls him
Σικυώνιος. It must be by confusion
with a later Timanthes, who painted
the battle of Aratos against the
Aitolians at Pellene in Arkadia, in
B. C. 240 (Plut. *Arat.* 32), and who
was therefore presumably a Sikyonian.

2. **oratorum**: cf. Cic. *Orator*, 22,
74 *pictor* (name not mentioned) *ille
vidit, cum immolanda Iphigenia tristis
Calchas esset, tristior Ulixes, mae-
reret Menelaus, obvolvendum caput
Agamemnonis esse, quoniam sum-
mum illum luctum penicillo non posset
imitari.*   That the Iphigeneia was a
stock rhetorical subject is proved by
Quinct. (*loc. cit.*) and Val. Max. viii,
11, ext. 6. A famous Pompeian wall-
painting, representing the sacrifice
(Helbig, *Wandgemälde*, 1304 = phot.
Alinari 12027), shows Agamemnon

with head completely veiled, but since
Iph. is being carried, and not standing, we must see in it only a later
adaptation of the picture by Timanthes (cf. also Helbig, *op. cit.* 1305, and
the mosaic in *A. Z.* 1869, taf. xiv).
The ancients entertained two distinct
views as to the veiling of Agamemnon; Pliny and Quinctilian arguing
that the painter did not show the
features of the father, in order to save
dignitas, while Cicero and Valerius
Maximus argued that he had recourse
to this means because the highest
pain cannot be expressed in art.
Both ancient and modern criticisms
are discussed by Blümner, *Comm.* to
Lessing's *Laokoon,* p. 506 f. As
Blümner points out, the veiling motive
in sorrow is common both in painting
and poetry; *e. g.* Euripides veils the
head of Agamemnon in the description
of the identical scene, *Iph. Aul.* 1550;
cf. also Brunn, *K. G.* ii, p. 124.
According to Quinctilian, this picture
gained for Timanthes the prize over
Kolotes of Teos.

4. **consumpsisset**: cf. the similar story of Euphranor, Val. Max.
viii, 11, ext. 5.   According to Eusta-

relaxation in this wanton humour. To return—*Timanthes* was a painter above all curious in invention, for by him is that Iphigeneia praised by the orators, whom he depicted standing by the altar ready for death. Having represented all the onlookers and especially her father's brother as plunged in sorrow and having thus exhausted every presentment of grief, he has veiled the face of her father for which he had reserved no adequate expression. There are other examples of his inventiveness; for instance, being desirous to emphasize, even in a small picture, the huge size of a sleeping Cyclops, he painted some Satyrs at his side, measuring his thumb with a thyrsos. He is the only artist whose works always suggest more than is in the picture, and great as is his dexterity, his power of invention yet exceeds it. He also painted a hero, a picture in which he touched perfection, having comprehended in it the whole art of painting the male figure. The picture is now at Rome in the temple of Peace.

In this period †*Euxeinidas* was the master of *Aristeides*, a famous artist, and †*Eupompos* of *Pamphilos*, who in turn was the master of Apelles. We have by Eupompos a victor in an athletic contest holding a palm. So great was this artist's reputation that

73 Iphigeneia of Timanthes.

74 Sleeping Cyclops.

Hero in temple of Peace at Rome.

75 New division of the schools into the Attic, Ionic and Sikyonian.

thios (*l. c.*), whose statement, however, savours of concoction, Timanthes was inspired to veil the head of Agamemnon, by the similar device employed by Homer in describing the grief of Priam, *Il.* xxiv, 162.

§ 74. 6. Cyclops dormiens: the presentation of this subject in painting was doubtless influenced by the *Kyklops* of Euripides, in which the Satyrs were brought on the stage with Polyphemos; Robert, *Bild u. Lied*, p. 35; Winter, *Jahrb.* vi, 1891, p. 272, who rightly refuses to refer the picture (with Klein) to the younger Timanthes.

11. artem ipsam complexus: the similarity of expression with xxxiv, 55, *solusque hominum autem ipsam fecisse artis opere iudicatur*, suggests that the *heros* of Timanthes, like the Doryphoros of Polykleitos, was a canonical figure intended to illustrate the artist's theories of proportion; cf. Kalkmann, *Jahrb.* x, 1895, p. 84, note 147; Introd. p. xli.

12. in templo Pacis: note on xxxiv, 84.

§ 75. 13. Aristiden: identical with the Aristeides of § 111, the master of Euphranor, where Pliny however confuses him with his grandson Aristeides the Theban. According to Kroker (*Gleichnamige Gr. Künstler*, p. 33) and Furtwängler (*Masterpieces*, p. 349) he is further probably identical with the sculptor of xxxiv, 72, pupil of Polykleitos; the dates favour the supposition.

14. Eupompus: xxxiv, § 61; above, § 64.

15. palmam tenens: a number of examples of a youth with palm in the left hand, and raising the crown to his head with the right, are collected by Milchhöfer, *Arch. Stud. Brunn dargebracht*, 1892, p. 62, ff.; they probably go back to the type created by Eupompos, Furtwängler, *Masterpieces*, p. 256; cf. also Reisch, *Griech. Weihgeschenke*, p. 41.

ipsius auctoritas tanta fuit ut diviserit picturam in genera.
quae ante eum duo fuere—Helladicum et Asiaticum appella-
bant—propter hunc, qui erat Sicyonius, diviso Helladico
76 tria facta sunt, Ionicum, Sicyonium, Atticum.   Pamphili
cognatio et proelium ad Phliuntem ac victoria Atheniensium, 5
item Ulixes in rate.   ipse Macedo natione, sed primus in
pictura omnibus litteris eruditus, praecipue arithmetica et
geometria, sine quibus negabat artem perfici posse, docuit
neminem talento minoris—annuis X D—quam mercedem et
77 Apelles et Melanthius dedere ei.   huius auctoritate effectum 10
est Sicyone primum, deinde et in tota Graecia, ut pueri ingenui omnia ante graphicen, hoc est picturam in buxo,
docerentur recipereturque ars ea in primum gradum libera-
lium.   semper quidem honos ei fuit ut ingenui eam exerce-
rent, mox ut honesti, perpetuo interdicto ne servitia doce- 15
rentur.   ideo neque in hac neque in toreutice ullius qui
78 servierit opera celebrantur.   clari et centesima septima
olympiade exstitere Aetion   ac Therimachus.   Aetionis

4. **tria facta sunt** : above note on
§ 72. 'It is difficult to say wherein
this great local superiority consisted,
which tempted, moreover, wealthy
amateurs, like Ptolemy II and Attalos, to purchase at enormous prices
galleries of old Sikyonian masters.
Plutarch uses a special term for it,
χρηστογραφία, which is usually explained as indicating the reaction in
art against the methods of Zeuxis
and his contemporaries.' (C. Smith,
art. PICTURA, Smith's *Dict. Ant.* p.
413.)

§ 76. 5. **cognatio**: it may have
been a grave picture placed upon a
family grave, cf. in sculpture a similar
family gathering on the Eastern pediment of the tomb known as the
'Nereid monument' (Brit. Mus.),
Michaelis, *A. Z.* 1845, pl. xxxiv, p.
145. Or it may have been merely a
votive commemorative picture.   For
similar subjects cf. the *cognatio
nobilium* of Timomachos (136), the
frequentia of Athenion (134), the

syngenicon of Oinias (143), finally
the *stemmata* of Koinos (139).

**proelium ad Phliuntem ac vic-
toria** : = **victoria Atheniensium in
proelio ad Phliuntem** : hendiadys,
cf. Müller, *Stil*, pp. 109, 15. The
picture is generally supposed to have
represented the episode narrated by
Xenophon, *Hellenika*, vii, 2, 18–23,
when the Phliasians and Athenians
under the command of Chares surprised and put to flight the Sikyonian
troops (B.C. 367); Brunn, *K. G.* ii, p.
132 f.; Schaefer, *Demosthenes*, i, p.
103 ff.; cf. Grote, *Greece*, viii, p. 258.

6. **Macedo**: from Amphipolis
(Souidas).   His birthplace is of importance as giving the probable clue
to the subsequent connexion of his
pupil Apelles—and possibly to that
of Lysippos—with the Makedonian
court. (Against his identification, on
the insufficient testimony of the scholia,
with the Pamphilos of Aristoph. *Plut.*
385, see Judeich, *Fleckeisen's Jahrb.*
1890, p. 758.)

A. THE THEBANO-ATTIC SCHOOL.

Euxeinidas, *fl. circ.* 400 B.C.; § 75.

Aristeides I (§§ 75; 108; 111; xxxiv. 72?)

Nikomachos, son §§ 108-109.

Aristeides II, *Thebanus*, son §§ 98-100; 110.

Nikeros, son § 111.

Philoxenos of Eretria, § 110.

Ariston, son §§ 110; 111.

Antorides, § 111.

Euphranor, §§ 111; 128.

Antidotos, § 130.

Nikias (II), §§ 130-132.

B. THE SIKYONIAN SCHOOL.

Eupompos, *fl. circ.* 400 B.C.; § 75.

Pamphilos, §§ 75-76; 123.

Apelles, §§ 79-97.

Perseus, § 111.

Melanthios, §§ 76; 80.

Aristolaos, son § 137.

Pausias, §§ 123-127.

Nikophanes, § 137.

Sokrates, § 137.

it occasioned a new division of the schools of painting. Before
his time there had been two schools, known as the Helladic
proper and the Asiatic; but now the Helladic was subdivided
in his honour, and thus the schools became three, the Ionic, the
Sikyonian and the Attic, Eupompos himself being a Sikyonian.

By Pamphilos we have a family group, the victorious engage- **76**
ment of the Athenians at Phlious, and a picture of Odysseus on *Pamphilos, master*
his raft. A Makedonian by birth, Pamphilos was the first painter *of Apelles.*
who was thoroughly trained in every branch of learning, more *367* B.C.
particularly in arithmetic and geometry; without which, so he
held, art could not be perfect. He taught no one for less than
a talent [£210 circ.]—that is, five hundred denarii [£17 10s.
circ.] a year—the fee paid him both by Apelles and by Melanthios.
It was owing to his influence that first at Sikyon, and after- **77**
wards throughout Greece drawing, or rather painting, on tablets *Drawing taught to*
of boxwood, was the earliest subject taught to freeborn boys, and *freeborn*
that this art was accepted as the preliminary step towards a liberal *boys.*
education. It was at any rate had in such honour that at all
times the freeborn, and later on persons of distinction practised
it, while by a standing prohibition no slaves might ever acquire
it, and this is why neither in painting nor in statuary are there
any celebrated works by artists who had been slaves.

In the hundred and seventh Olympiad [352–349 B.C.] lived **78**
Aetion and †Therimachos, both painters of note. By Aetion are *Aetion and Therimachos.*

7. **praecipue arithmetica . . .
posse**: these words are probably
derived from a Treatise on Painting
by Pamphilos; see Introd. p. xliii.

9. **quam mercedem . . . Apelles**:
Ἤνθει γὰρ ἔτι δόξα τῆς Σικυωνίας
μούσης καὶ χρηστογραφίας, ὡς μόνης
ἀδιάφθορον ἐχούσης τὸ καλόν, ὥστε
καὶ Ἀπελλῆν ἐκεῖνον ἤδη θαυμαζό-
μενον ἀφικέσθαι καὶ συγγενέσθαι τοῖς
ἀνδράσιν ἐπὶ ταλάντῳ, τῆς δόξης μᾶλλον ἢ τῆς τέχνης δεόμενον μεταλαβεῖν.
Plut. *Arat.* xiii.

10. **Melanthius**: §§ 50, 80; and
Index to this book. From Antigonos
of Karystos, *ap.* Diogenes L. iv, 3, 18
(Introd. p. xxxviii), we learn that he
wrote περὶ ζωγραφικῆς; Melanthios
was also a master of Apelles (perhaps
after the death of Pamphilos), who,

with other pupils, assisted him in the
votive picture for Aristratos of Sikyon
(Plut. *loc. cit.*).

§ **77. 11. pueri ingenui** = ἐλευ-
θέριοι: cf. Aristotle, *Polit.* v (viii), 3,
p. 1338 δοκεῖ δὲ καὶ γραφικὴ χρήσι-
μος εἶναι πρὸς τὸ κρίνειν τὰ τῶν τεχ-
νιτῶν ἔργα κάλλιον· οὐδ' αὖ καθάπερ ἡ
γυμναστικὴ πρὸς ὑγίειαν καὶ ἀλκήν·
οὐδέτερον γὰρ τούτων ὁρῶμεν γινό-
μενον ἐκ τῆς μουσικῆς. λείπεται τοίνυν
πρὸς τὴν ἐν τῇ σχολῇ διαγωγήν, ἐς
ὅπερ καὶ φαίνονται παράγοντες αὐτήν·
ἣν γὰρ οἴονται διαγωγὴν εἶναι τῶν
ἐλευθέρων, ἐν ταύτῃ τάττουσιν.

§ **78. 18. Aetion et Therimachus**:
cf. note on xxxiv, 50. Therimachos is
otherwise unknown, Aetion is a favourite artist of Lucian, who has given
a famous description of his Alexander

sunt nobiles picturae Liber pater, item Tragoedia et
Comoedia, Semiramis ex ancilla regnum apiscens, anus
lampadas praeferens et nova nupta verecundia notabilis.
79 verum et omnes prius genitos futurosque postea superavit
Apelles Cous olympiade centesima duodecima. picturae 5
plura solus prope quam ceteri omnes contulit, voluminibus
etiam editis quae doctrinam eam continent. praecipua eius
in arte venustas fuit, cum eadem aetate maximi pictores
essent. quorum opera cum admiraretur omnibus conlaudatis,
deesse illam suam Venerem dicebat, quam Graeci Charita 10
vocant, cetera omnia contigisse, sed hac sola sibi neminem
80 parem. et aliam gloriam usurpavit, cum Protogenis opus
inmensi laboris ac curae supra modum anxiae miraretur,
dixit enim omnia sibi cum illo paria esse aut illi meliora,
sed uno se praestare, quod manum de tabula sciret tollere, 15
memorabili praecepto nocere saepe nimiam diligentiam. fuit
autem non minoris simplicitatis quam artis. Melanthio
dispositione cedebat, Asclepiodoro de mensuris, hoc est
81 quanto quid a quoque distare deberet. scitum est inter
Protogenen et eum quod accidit. ille Rhodi vivebat, quo 20
cum Apelles adnavigasset avidus cognoscendi opera eius

and Roxana ('Hρόδ. ἡ 'Aετίων, 4);
cf. εἰκόνες, 7, περὶ τῶν ἐπὶ μισθ. συν.
42 ; cf. Cicero, Brutus, xviii, 70
(quoted above, note on § 50).

2. Semiramis: Brunn (K. G. ii,
p. 245) points out that the nuptials
of S. and Ninos may have been conceived as a sort of mythical counterpart to those of Alexander and Roxana.

anus . . . nova nupta : of course
in one picture. The anus is doubtless
the mother of the bride, to whom the
δᾳδουχεῖν, the carrying of the δᾳδες
νυμφικαί, usually fell (Hermann-Blüm-
ner, Lehrbuch, p. 275; Furtwängler,
S. Sabouroff, i. 58, 59; cf. the attendant (?) holding torches on the
marriage vases or λουτροφόροι). The
torch was doubtless made the occasion for effects of light; cf. the
marriage of Alexander and Roxana,

where Hephaistion holds a torch, the
marriage feast of Peirithoos by Hippys
(Athen. xi, p. 474), which was lit up
by a hanging candelabrum. The
enumeration from Tragoedia to anus
is asyndetical—et being reserved to
link Comoedia to Trag. (both in one
picture) and nova nupta to anus
—so that I cannot follow Brunn
(K. G. ii, p. 245) and Furtwängler
(Dornauszieher, p. 96, n. 57), in
understanding the words anus . . .
notabilis to be descriptive of the
picture of the Nuptials of Semiramis.

§ 79. 5. Apelles Cous : Ovid,
ArsAmat. iii, 401, Pont. Epist. iv, 1,
29 ; but Strabo (xiv, p. 642), Lucian,
διαβολ. 2, and after him Tzetzes (Chil.
viii, 392) call him an Ephesian; that
this is correct is proved by Herondas,
iv, 72 ('Eφεσίου 'Aπελλέω) who certainly would not have made Apelles

the well-known pictures of Dionysos, of Tragedy and Comedy, of Semiramis rising from slavery to royal power, and of an old woman carrying lamps and a bride, whose shamefacedness is very apparent.

Apelles of Kos, however, in the hundred and twelfth Olympiad **79** [332–329 B.C.] excelled all painters who came before or after him. *Apelles of Kos.* He of himself perhaps contributed more to painting than all the *His written Treatises.* others together; he also wrote treatises on his theory of art. The grace of his genius remained quite unrivalled, although the very greatest painters were living at the time. He would admire their *His estimate of the works of his contemporaries and of his own.* works, praising every beauty and yet observing that they failed in the grace, called χάρις in Greek, which was distinctively his own; everything else they had attained, but in this alone none equalled him. He laid claim to another merit: when admiring **80** a work of Protogenes that betrayed immense industry and the most anxious elaboration, he said that, though Protogenes was his equal or even his superior in everything, he yet surpassed that painter in one point—namely in knowing when to take his hand from a picture; a memorable saying, showing that too much care may often be hurtful. His candour was equal to his genius: he acknowledged the superiority of Melanthios in the distribution of figures, and that of Asklepiodoros in perspective arrangement, that is in giving the accurate distances between different objects.

A neat story is told of him in connexion with Protogenes, who **81** was living in Rhodes. Thither Apelles sailed, eager to see the *His visit to Protogenes.*

into an Ephesian, if he could have claimed him for his native Kos. The tradition that the artist was a Koan arose because at Kos were some of his most celebrated works, among them the *Anadyomene.*

6. voluminibus editis: cf. § 111; it must be from these writings of Apelles that the judgements he passed upon his contemporaries were originally derived (Introd. p. xl).

7. praecipua venustas: Quinct. xii, 10, 6 *ingenio et gratia, quam in se ipso maxime iactat, Ap. est praestantissimus.* According to Plutarch (*Demetr.* xxii), and Ailian (ποικ. ἱστ. xii, 41) this judgement on himself was passed when he saw the Ialysos of Protogenes (§ 102).

9. quorum opera cum adm.: i. e. in his writings.

§ 80. 12. Protogenis: below, §§ 81, 101–106.

opus miraretur: presumably the Ialysos.

15. manum de tabula: = χεῖρ’ ἀπὸ τραπέζης; Petron. 76 *postquam coepi plus habere, quam tota mea patria habet, manum de tabula;* also used of school-boys trifling in their master's absence, cf. Cic. *ad Fam.* vii, 25 *sed heus tu, manu de tabula!* (Otto, *Sprichwörter*, p. 210).

17. Melanthio: above, § 76.

18. Asclepiodoro: below, § 107.

§ 81. 19. scitum est: the following anecdote appears to be elaborated out of the admiration which Apelles

fama tantum sibi cogniti, continuo officinam petiit. aberat
ipse, sed tabulam amplae magnitudinis in machina aptatam
una custodiebat anus. haec foris esse Protogenen respondit
interrogavitque a quo quaesitum diceret. ab hoc, inquit
Apelles, adreptoque penicillo lineam ex colore duxit sum- 5
82 mae tenuitatis per tabulam, et reverso Protogeni quae gesta
erant anus indicavit. ferunt artificem protinus contempla-
tum subtilitatem dixisse Apellen venisse, non cadere in
alium tam absolutum opus, ipsumque alio colore tenuiorem
lineam in ipsa illa duxisse abeuntemque praecepisse, si 10
redisset ille, ostenderet adiceretque hunc esse quem quaereret, atque ita evenit. revertit enim Apelles et vinci
erubescens tertio colore lineas secuit nullum relinquens
83 amplius subtilitati locum. at Protogenes victum se confessus
in portum devolavit hospitem quaerens, placuitque sic eam 15
tabulam posteris tradi omnium quidem, sed artificum prae-
A.U.C. 757. cipuo miraculo. consumptam eam priore incendio Caesaris
domus in Palatio audio, spectatam nobis ante spatiose nihil
aliud continentem quam lineas visum effugientes inter egregia
multorum opera inani similem et eo ipso allicientem omnique 20
84 opere nobiliorem. Apelli fuit alioqui perpetua consuetudo
numquam tam occupatum diem agendi ut non lineam du-
cendo exerceret artem, quod ab eo in proverbium venit.
idem perfecta opera proponebat in pergula transeuntibus,
atque ipse post tabulam latens vitia quae notarentur aus- 25
cultabat vulgum diligentiorem iudicem quam se praeferens,
85 feruntque reprehensum a sutore, quod in crepidis una pauci-
ores intus fecisset ansas, eodem postero die superbo emenda-

---

2. aptatam una] *Bamb.* ; aptatam picturae una *reliqui, Detlefsen.*

---

had professed for Protogenes in his
writings, see Introd. p. xl.

3. una ... anus : Leo, *Plautinische
Forschungen* (1895), p. 65, calls attention to the part played in classical
literature by the single *ancilla* or the
anus. Like the *pistrinum* she is, so
to speak, one of the requisites of the
contented life. We get the *ancilla*
in the amusing anecdote, Cic. *de Orat.*
ii, 276, while Chrysippos ἤρκεῖτο
γραιδίῳ, μόνῳ, Demetrios *ap.* Diog.

Laert. vii, 7, 185. The motive is
Homeric ὥσπερ ὁ Λαέρτης ... γρηὶ σὺν
ἀμφιπόλῳ, Teles, p. 25 (ed. Hense).

5. lineam ... duxit : the anecdote
belongs to the same category as
Giotto's O, Vasaried. Milanesi I, p.383.

§ 83. 17. consumptam ... audio :
oral tradition.

§ 84. 23. in proverbium : i. e.
nullus dies sine linea; cf. Otto, *Sprichwörter*, p. 194.

24. pergula : cf. Ulpian, *Digest.*

works of a man only known to him by reputation, and on his arrival immediately repaired to the studio.   Protogenes was not at home, but a solitary old woman was keeping watch over a large panel placed on the easel.   In answer to the questions of Apelles, she said that Protogenes was out, and asked the name of the visitor: 'Here it is,' said Apelles, and snatching up a brush he drew a line of extreme delicacy across the board.   On the return **82** of Protogenes the old woman told him what had happened. *They split a line, in* When he had considered the delicate precision of the line he at *friendly* once declared that his visitor had been Apelles, for no one else *emulation.* could have drawn anything so perfect.   Then in another colour he drew a second still finer line upon the first, and went away, bidding her show it to Apelles if he came again, and add that this was the man he was seeking.   It fell out as he expected; Apelles did return, and, ashamed to be beaten, drew a third line of another colour cutting the two first down their length and leaving no room for any further refinement.   Protogenes owned himself **83** beaten and hurried down to the harbour to find his visitor; they agreed to hand down the painting just as it was to posterity, a marvel to all, but especially to artists.   It perished, I am told, A.D. 4. in the first fire of the house of the Caesars on the Palatine. Formerly we might look upon it; its wide surface disclosed nothing save lines which eluded the sight, and among the numerous works by excellent painters it was like a blank, and it was precisely this that lent it surpassing attraction and renown.

Apelles further made it an unvarying rule never to spend a day, **84** however busy, without drawing a line by way of practice; hence *His in-* the proverb.   It was also his habit to exhibit his finished works *dustry.* to the passers-by in a balcony, and he would lie concealed behind the picture and listen to the faults that were found with it, regarding the public as more accurate critics than himself.   There is **85** a story that when found fault with by a cobbler for putting one *The critical* loop too few on the inner side of a sandal, he corrected the *cobbler.* mistake.   Elated by this the cobbler next day proceeded to find fault with the leg, whereupon Apelles thrust out his head in

---

ix, 3, 5, § 12 *cum pictor in pergula clipeum vel tabulam expositam habuisset eaque excidisset, et transeunti damni quid dedisset.* (It has been shown by F. Marx in *Studia Luciliana*, 1882, p. 16 f. that in Lucilius xv,

6, the old reading *pergula pictorum* should be altered to *pergula fictorum*, which is adopted by Buecheler.) For *pergulae* at Pompei, see Mau, *Röm. Mitth.* ii, 1887, p. 214 ff.

tione pristinae admonitionis cavillante circa crus, indignatum
prospexisse denuntiantem ne supra crepidam sutor iudicaret,
quod et ipsum in proverbium abiit. fuit enim et comitas
illi, propter quam gratior Alexandro Magno frequenter in
officinam ventitanti—nam, ut diximus, ab alio se pingi 5
vetuerat edicto—sed in officina imperite multa disserenti
silentium comiter suadebat rideri eum dicens a pueris qui
86 colores tererent. tantum erat auctoritati iuris in regem
alioqui iracundum. quamquam Alexander honorem ei
clarissimo perhibuit exemplo, namque cum dilectam sibi 10
ex pallacis suis praecipue, nomine Pancaspen, nudam pingi
ob admirationem formae ab Apelle iussisset eumque, dum
paret, captum amore sensisset, dono dedit ei magnus animo,
maior imperio sui, nec minor hoc facto quam victoria aliqua.
87 quippe se vicit, nec torum tantum suum sed etiam adfectum 15
donavit artifici, ne dilectae quidem respectu motus, cum
modo regis ea fuisset, modo pictoris esset. sunt qui Venerem
anadyomenen ab illo pictam exemplari putent. Apelles et
in aemulis benignus Protogeni dignationem primus Rhodi
88 constituit. sordebat suis ut plerumque domestica, percon- 20
tantique quanti liceret opera effecta parvum nescio quid
dixerat, at ille quinquagenis talentis poposcit famamque
dispersit se emere ut pro suis venderet. ea res concitavit
Rhodios ad intellegendum artificem, nec nisi augentibus
pretium cessit. imagines adeo similitudinis indiscretae 25
pinxit ut—incredibile dictu—Apio grammaticus scriptum
reliquerit quendam ex facie hominum divinantem, quos
metoposcopos vocant, ex iis dixisse aut futurae mortis annos

§ 85. 2. ne supra crepidam sutor:
cf. Valer. Max. viii, 12, ext. 3; Otto,
Sprichwörter, p. 97. Introd. p. lix.

3. enim: corroborates *idem praeferens*, ignoring the intervening anecdote.

5. ut diximus: in vii, 125 = App. I;
cf. note on xxxiv, 63.

6. in officina: the following anecdote is told by Plutarch (*de Tranquill.
Anim.* 12), concerning the megabyzos
(§ 93), while Ailian, Ποικ. Ἱστ. ii, 2,
tells it of Zeuxis and a megabyzos.

7. qui colores tererent: τὰ παι-
δάρια τὰ τοῦ Ζεύξιδος τὴν μηλίδα τρί-
βοντα κατεγέλα, Ailian, *loc. cit.*

§ 86. 11. Pancaspen: ὄνομα ἦν
Παγκάσπη, τὸ δὲ γένος Λαρισσαία,
Ailian, Ποικ. Ἱστ. xii, 34. Lucian
(εἰκόνες, 7) calls her Πακάτη.

§ 87. 18. anadyomenen: = *exeuntem e mari*, below, § 91.

exemplari: according to Athen.
xiii, p. 590 F, the model was Phryne,
while according to *Anth. Plan.* 179
Apelles, like Praxiteles (xxxvi, 21),

a passion and bade the cobbler 'stick to his last,' a saying which has also passed into a proverb.

The charm of his manner had won him the regard of Alexander *Friendship* the Great, who was a frequent visitor to the studio, for, as we have *of Alexan-* *der and* said, he had issued an edict forbidding any one else to paint his *Apelles.* portrait. But when the king happened to discourse at length in *Story of* *Pankaspe.* the studio upon things he knew nothing about, Apelles would pleasantly advise him to be silent, hinting that the assistants who ground the colours were laughing at him; such power did his **86** personality give him over a king habitually so passionate. Yet Alexander gave him a signal mark of his regard: he commissioned Apelles to paint a nude figure of his favourite mistress Pankaspe, so much did he admire her wondrous form, but perceiving that Apelles had fallen in love with her, with great magnanimity and still greater self-control he gave her to him as a present, winning by the action as great a glory as by any of his victories. He **87** conquered himself and sacrificed to the artist not only his mistress but his love, and was not even restrained by consideration for the woman he loved, who, once a king's mistress, was now a painter's. Some believe that she was the model for the Aphrodite rising from the sea.

Friendly even to his rivals, Apelles was the first to establish in **88** Rhodes the reputation of Protogenes, who, as so many in their *Kindness* *of Apelles* own homes, was neglected by his countrymen. When asked by *to Proto-* Apelles the prices of his finished works, he mentioned some *genes.* trifling sum, upon which Apelles offered fifty talents [£10,500 circ.] for each, and spread a report that he was buying the pictures to sell as his own. This stirred up the Rhodians to a better appreciation of the artist, but not until they offered a still higher price would Apelles give up the pictures.

His portraits were such perfect likenesses that, incredible as it *His aston-* may sound, Apio the grammarian has left it on record that *ishing* *merits as* a physiognomist, or μετωποσκόπος as they are called, was able to *portrait* *painter.*

---

was privileged to see the goddess herself: αὐτὰν ἐκ πόντοιο τιθηνητῆρος Ἀπελλῆς | τὰν Κύπριν γυμνὰν εἶδε λοχευομέναν.

§ 88. 25. similit. indiscretae: xxxiv, 60 *facie quoque indiscreta similis*, and note.

26. incredibile dictu: hence Pliny

waives the responsibility and immediately names his authority.

Apio grammaticus: *Praef.* 25, xxx, 18, and often in Pliny; flor. reign of Caligula. Müller, *F. H. G.* iii, 506–516.

28. metoposcopos: cf. Suet. *Titus* 2.

89 aut praeteritae vitae.   non fuerat ei gratia in comitatu
Alexandri cum Ptolemaeo, quo regnante Alexandriam vi
tempestatis expulsus subornato fraude aemulorum plano
regio invitatus ad cenam venit, indignantique Ptolemaeo et
vocatores suos ostendenti, ut diceret a quo eorum invitatus 5
esset, arrepto carbone extincto e foculo imaginem in pariete
deliniavit, adgnoscente voltum plani rege inchoatum proti-
90 nus.   pinxit et Antigoni regis imaginem altero lumine
orbam primus excogitata ratione vitia condendi, obliquam
namque fecit, ut quod deerat corpori picturae deesse potius 10
videretur, tantumque eam partem e facie ostendit quam
totam poterat ostendere.   sunt inter opera eius et exspirantium imagines.   quae autem nobilissima sint non est
91 facile dictu.   Venerem exeuntem e mari divus Augustus
dicavit in delubro patris Caesaris, quae anadyomene vocatur, 15
versibus Graecis tali opere, dum laudatur, victo sed inlus-

§ 89. 1. non fuerat ei gratia :
the following is a mutilated and somewhat different account of the events
narrated at length by Lucian (διαβολ.
4), for which, according to Lucian,
Apelles took vengeance by painting
his famous 'Calumny.'   Both the
versions have an aitiological flavour, and probably arose in great
measure out of the picture itself (for
the historical inaccuracies in Lucian's
story see Brunn, *K. G.* ii, p. 208).   For
the latest discussion of the Calumny,
and especially of the influence of
Lucian's description on artists of the
Renascence, see R. Förster in *Jahrb.
d. Preuss. Samml.* 1887, p. 29 ff.

3. aemulorum : from Lucian, *loc.
cit.*, we learn that the Egyptian painter
Antiphilos (§§ 114, 138) was among
them.

5. vocatores : i. e. the slaves in
charge of the invitations or *vocationes*,
Seneca, *Ira* iii, 37, 4 ; Suet. *Calig.*
39, &c.

§ 90. 8. altero lumine orbam :
Ant. was accordingly surnamed μονό-
φθαλμος and Κύκλωψ, Polyb. v, 67, 6 ;
Ailian, Ποικ. Ἰστ. xii, 43.

9. obliquam : Brunn, *K. G.* ii,
p. 10 ; Quinct. ii, 13, 12 *habet in pictura speciem tota facies ; Apelles tamen
imaginem Antigoni latere tantum
altero ostendit, ut amissi oculi deformi-
tas lateret.*   These words prove beyond
the possibility of doubt that the *obliqua imago* of Antigonos was a simple
portrait in profile.   Hartwig, however,
(*Meisterschalen,* p. 157) argues that
to disguise a defect a simple profile
would be unworthy of the inventiveness
of so great an artist as Apelles, and,
starting from the meaning which he
claims for *catagrapha* (above, § 56,
where see note), tries to show that the
portrait was in ¾ and foreshortened.
The portrait of the squinting Tommaso
Inghirami by Raphael (original in
Pal. Inghirami at Volterra ; the picture
in the Pitti is only a copy), which
Hartwig quotes in support of his
theory, seems as a fact to emphasize
rather than conceal the physical defect.

12. exspirantium imagines :
acutely explained by Brückner (*Sitz-
ungsber. d. Wiener Akademie*, vol.
116, p. 519, note 4) as grave pictures

tell from the portraits alone how long the sitter had to live or had already lived. When in Alexander's train he had been on un- 89 friendly terms with Ptolemy, during whose reign he was once driven into Alexandria by a violent storm. On Apelles appearing at a banquet, to which his rivals had maliciously induced the king's fool to invite him, Ptolemy flew into a passion, and pointing to his chamberlains bade him say from which of them he had received the invitation, whereupon the painter snatching up a charred stick from the hearth traced on the wall a likeness, in whose first strokes the king at once recognized the face of the fool.

He also painted a portrait of king Antigonos, who was blind of 90 one eye, being the first to devise a means of concealing the *He paints king* infirmity by presenting his profile, so that the absence of the eye *Antigonos.* would be attributed merely to the position of the sitter, not to a natural defect, for he gave only the part of the face which could be shown uninjured. There are among his works some pictures of dying people, though it were difficult to say which are the best. His Aphrodite rising from the sea was dedicated by the god 91 Augustus in the temple of his father Caesar: she is known as the *'Aphrodite rising from* ἀναδυομένη, being, like other works of the kind, at once eclipsed *the sea.'* yet rendered famous by the Greek epigrams written in her praise.

representing death-scenes; cf. the γραπτὸς τύπος, described *Anth.* vii, 730; cf. also *ib.* vii, 170; Weisshäupl, *Die Grabgedichte der Gr. Anthologie*, 97 ff.; further, Paus. ii, 7, 3 praises the excellent painting of a grave picture at Sikyon, of Xenodyke, who died in childbirth; cf. in sculpture the grave relief of Malthake from the Peiraieus, see Friederichs-Wolters, 1042. Praxiteles (xxxiv, 70), Nikias (below, § 132), Nikomachos (mon. of Telestes, § 109), likewise decorate graves; cf. the *iuvenis requiescens* of Simos, § 143.

13. quae autem nobilissima sint: [refers not to *opera* but to *imagines;* rapid changes of gender or number are common in Pliny, Mayhoff, *Lucubr. Plin.* (1865) p. 83; cf. J. Müller, *Stil,* p. 56.—H. L. U.].

§ 91. 14. exeuntem e mari = *anadyomenen*, above, § 87. From numerous descriptions (Overb. *Schrift-*

quellen, 1847–1866) we learn that the goddess was represented wringing her hair, in a type which was likewise adapted to statuary (Helbig, *Class. Ant.* 254). For the picture itself see Benndorf, *Athen. Mitth.* 1876, p. 50.

15. in delubro patris Caesaris: the picture was previously in the Koan Asklepieion, whence Augustus obtained it by remitting 100 talents of the Koan tribute; Strabo xiv, p. 657. Since Ovid (exiled A.D. 8) mentions the Anadyomene in *Trist.* ii, 527 f., the picture must have been in Rome previous to the year of his exile. For further discussion of the dates see Wunderer, *Manibiae Alexandrinae,* p. 8.

16. victo sed inlustrato : 'surpassed' inasmuch as the poet can give expression to more things than the painter who is limited to one moment;

trato, cuius inferiorem partem corruptam qui reficeret non
potuit reperiri, verum ipsa iniuria cessit in gloriam artificis.
consenuit haec tabula carie, aliamque pro ea substituit Nero
92 principatu suo Dorothei manu.   Apelles inchoaverat et
aliam Venerem Coi superaturus famam illam suam priorem. 5
invidit mors peracta parte, nec qui succederet operi ad prae-
scripta liniamenta inventus est.   pinxit et Alexandrum
Magnum fulmen tenentem in templo Ephesiae Dianae viginti
talentis auri.   digiti eminere videntur et fulmen extra
tabulam esse—legentes meminerint omnia ea quattuor colo- 10
ribus facta—manipretium eius tabulae in nummo aureo
93 mensura accepit, non numero.   pinxit et megabyzi sacerdotis Dianae Ephesiae pompam, Clitum cum equo ad
bellum festinantem, galeam poscenti armigerum porrigentem.
Alexandrum et Philippum quotiens pinxerit enumerare 15
supervacuum est.   mirantur eius Habronem Sami, Menan-

<hr>

5. famam] etiam *omnes praeter Bamb., Detlefsen.*

for the idea conveyed by *inlustrato*
cf. xxxiv, 57, of the heifer of Myron,
*celebratis versibus laudata, quando
alieno plerique ingenio magis quam
suo commendantur.*

3. substituit : this may be an
exaggeration, as the picture of Apelles
seems still to have been in existence under Vespasian, when Suetonius
(*Vesp.* 18) speaks of its being again
restored : *Coae Veneris . . . refectorem
insigni congiario magnaque mercede
donavit.*

§ 92. 4. inchoaverat : Cic. *Fam.*
i, 9, 15, and *Off.* iii, 2, 10.

8. fulmen tenentem = κεραυνο-
φόρον, i. e. deified.   Plutarch (περὶ
τῆς 'Αλ. τύχης, ii, 2) relates that it was
said of this picture that there were
two Alexanders, the son of Philip
who was invincible, and the Alexander of Apelles who was inimitable.
It is a fascinating conjecture of King
(*Anc. Gems* i, p. xii), followed by
Furtwängler, *Jahrb.* iv (1889), p. 69,
that an ancient copy of this famous
picture is extant in the carnelian in
St. Petersburg (*Jahrb.* iii, pl. xi, 26).

The position of the right arm holding
the thunderbolt in the gem is specially
significant.

9. eminere videntur : cf. in
§ 127 *quae volunt eminentia videri;*
§ 131 *ut eminerent e tabulis picturae.*

10. legentes meminerint : harks
back to § 50.

§ 93. 12. megabyzi : Strabo xiv,
p. 641 ἱερέας δ' εὐνούχους εἶχον οὓς
ἐκάλουν Μεγαβύζους.

13. pompam : from Herondas iv,
66 ff. we learn that the picture was
at Kos, in the παστός (Sanctuary) of
the Asklepieion, and that it represented
a sacrifice of oxen.   It is amusingly
described by the gossips Kokkale and
Kynno (ed. Crusius).

ΚΟΚ. ὁ βοῦς δὲ χὠ ἄγων αὐτόν, ἥ θ'
            ὁμαρτεῦσα
      χὠ γρυπὸς οὗτος χὠ ἀνάσιμος
            ἄνθρωπος,
      οὐχὶ ζόην βλέπουσιν ἡμέρην
            πάντες ;
      εἰ μὴ ἐδόκευν τι μέζον ἢ γυνὴ
            πρήσσειν,
      ἀνηλάλαξ' ἄν, μή μ' ὁ βοῦς τι
            πημήνῃ,

When the lower portion was damaged no one could be found to restore it, and thus the very injury redounded to the glory of the artist.   In course of time the panel of the picture fell into decay, *Its restora-*
and Nero when Emperor substituted for it another picture by the *tion by*
hand of Dorotheos.   Apelles had begun another Aphrodite at 92 *Dorotheos.*
Kos, intending to surpass even the fame of his earlier achievement, but when only a part was finished envious death interposed, and no one was found to finish the outlines already traced.   He *'Alexander*
also painted in the temple of Artemis at Ephesos a portrait of *holding the*
Alexander holding a thunderbolt for twenty talents [£4,200 *bolt.'*
circ.]: the fingers seem to stand out and the thunderbolt to project from the picture;—the reader should remember that all this was done with four colours.   For this picture he was paid in gold coins, reckoned not by number but by measure.   He painted 93 too the train of a μεγάβυζος, or priest of Artemis of Ephesos, Kleitos on horseback going out to battle, and the picture of a squire handing a helmet to one who asks for it.   It were vain to enumerate the number of times he painted Alexander and Philip.   At Samos we admire his Habron, at Rhodes his Menander, king of Karia, and his Antaios, at Alexandria Gorgo-

οὕτω ἐπιλοξοῖ, Κυννί, τῇ ἐτέρῃ
   κούρῃ
ΚΥΝ. ἀληθιναί, φίλη, γὰρ αἱ Ἐφεσίου
   χεῖρες
ἐς πάντ' Ἀπελλέω γράμματ',
   οὐδ' ἐρεῖς "κεῖνος
ὤνθρωπος ἐν μὲν εἶδεν, ἐν δ'
   ἀπηρνήθη."
ἀλλ' ᾧ ἐπὶ νοῦν γένοιτο, καὶ
   θεῶν ψαύειν
ἠπείγεθ' . . .
The use of the past tense ἠπείγετο shows that Apelles was no longer alive at the time Herondas wrote the Mimiamboi (circ. B. C. 280–273). For similar subjects cf. on § 126 (Pausias) and § 137 (Aristolaos). A curious but arbitrary explanation of the Koan picture, as representing the Egyptian bull Apis, is given by R. Meister in his ed. of Herondas, p. 222.
   Clitum: surnamed ὁ μέλας (Plutarch, *Alex.* 16), the bosom friend of Alexander, whose life he saved at the Granikos, and by whom he was

afterwards slain: Arrian. iv, 8, &c.
   14. **galeam poscenti:** [generally taken as descriptive of the portrait of Kleitos.   But the change from the accusative to the dative would be barbarous, while the asyndetic enumeration shows that we have here a fresh subject.   It was perhaps a grave picture (*expir. imago*); very similar subjects appear on grave reliefs (1) in Syracuse, rider with horn of plenty, standing by his horse, to r. attendant leaning on spear, to l. boy bringing helmet, snake between boy and horse, unpublished; (2) the relief from Thyrea in Athens, Friederichs-Wolters, 1812, cf. Deneken, *ap.* Roscher ii, art. 'Heros,' col. 2563.   Also on vases, Naples, Heydemann 2192, from Canosa.—H. L. U.]
   15. **quotiens pinxerit:** cf. xxxiv, 63, of Alexander's portraits by Lysippos.
   16. **Habronem:** probably the painter mentioned below, § 141.
   Sami: where the Heraion con-

K

drum regem Cariae Rhodi, item Antaeum, Alexandreae
Gorgosthenen tragoedum, Romae Castorem et Pollucem
cum Victoria et Alexandro Magno, item Belli imaginem
restrictis ad terga manibus, Alexandro in curru triumphante,
94 quas utrasque tabulas divus Augustus in fori sui celeberrimis 5
partibus dicaverat simplicitate moderata, divus Claudius
pluris existimavit utrique excisa Alexandri facie divi
Augusti imagines addere. eiusdem arbitrantur manu esse
et in Dianae templo Herculem aversum, ut, quod est difficillimum, faciem eius ostendat verius pictura quam promittat. 10
pinxit et heroa nudum, eaque pictura naturam ipsam provo-
95 cavit. est et equus eius sive fuit pictus in certamine, quo
iudicium ad mutas quadripedes provocavit ab hominibus.
namque ambitu praevalere aemulos sentiens singulorum
picturas inductis equis ostendit, Apellis tantum equo adhin- 15
nivere, idque et postea semper evenit, ut experimentum
96 artis illud ostentaretur. fecit et Neoptolemum ex equo
adversus Persas, Archelaum cum uxore et filia, Antigonum
thoracatum cum equo incedentem. peritiores artis praefe-
runt omnibus eius operibus eundem regem sedentem in equo 20
et Dianam sacrificantium virginum choro mixtam, quibus

tained a collection of pictures (Strabo
xiv, p. 637 τὸ Ἡραῖον ... νεὼς μέγας,
ὃς νῦν πινακοθήκη ἐστί).

Menandrum: one τῶν ἑταίρων,
Arrian, *Anabasis* iii, 6, 8; iv, 13, 7;
vii, 24, 1, Diodoros xviii, 59; he
was satrap of Lydia, and as no king
of Karia of the name of Menander is
known, it may be that we have here
a confusion on Pliny's part, cf. Brunn,
K. G. ii, p. 212.

1. Antaeum: unknown.

Alexandreae: above, § 89.

2. tragoedum: cf. the *temulenta
tibicina* of Lysippos, xxxiv, 63, the
saltator Alcisthenes in § 147, &c.

Castorem...Magno: above, § 27.
The type of Alexander between the
Dioskouroi was at a later date adapted
to triumphal pictures of the Emperors,
cf. *Mon. d. Inst.* iii, 10.

4. restrictis ad terga manibus:

in § 27 the subject of the picture is
described as Triumph and War.
Servius on *Aen.* i, 294 (ed. Thilo i, p.
109) *in foro Augusti introeuntibus ad
sinistram fuit bellum pictum et furor
sedens super arma devinctus eo habitu
quo poeta dixit;* it is of course
possible that Pliny forgot to mention
the *Furor*, but, as Jacobi (*Museogr.*
p. 73) has pointed out, it is more likely
that Servius, in order to give a more
striking explanation of the Virgilian
lines (*Claudentur Belli portae; Furor
impius intus | saeva sedens super
arma et centum vinctus aenis | post
tergum nodis fremet horridus ore
cruento*), split the personification of
War into two. We may assume from
Servius, *loc. cit.*, that the first picture
was on the R. of the spectator entering
the Forum.

§ 94. 8. arbitrantur: i.e. a judge-sthenes the tragic actor, at Rome Kastor and Polydeukes with *Allegorical* Victory and Alexander the Great, and also a figure of War with *pictures of Alexander* his hands bound behind his back, and Alexander riding in triumph *the Great.* in a chariot. These two pictures had been placed in the most 94 crowded parts of his forum with the restraint of good taste by the god Augustus, but the god Claudius thought fit to cut out in both the face of Alexander and substitute that of Augustus. The Herakles with averted face, in the temple of Diana, is also attributed to Apelles; by a triumph of art the picture seems not only to suggest, but actually to give the face. He also painted a nude hero, a picture which challenges comparison with Nature herself. A horse also exists, or did exist, painted for a com- 95 petition, in which he appealed from the judgement of men to that *An unfair verdict.* of dumb beasts. When he saw that his rivals were likely to be *The horses* placed above him through intrigue, he caused some horses to be *approve the picture of* brought in and showed them each picture in turn; they neighed *Apelles.* only at the horse of Apelles, and this was invariably the case ever afterwards, so that the test was applied purposely to afford a display of his skill. He also painted Neoptolemos on horse- 96 back fighting against the Persians, Archelaos in a group with his wife and daughter, and a portrait of Antigonos in armour advancing with his horse. Skilled judges of painting prefer among all his works his equestrian portrait of Antigonos and his Artemis amid a band of maidens offering sacrifice, a painting

ment of connoisseurs not certified by the artist's signature.

9. **Dianae**: in the campus *Flaminius* dedicated by Lepidus B.C. 179; Liv. xl, 52. The reading *Annae* (sc. *Perennae*) is defended by Jordan (*ap.* Preller, *Röm. Mythol.* 2nd ed. i, p. 344, note 1), but against his view see Wissowa *ap.* Pauly, *s. v.* Anna Perenna.

§ 95. 12. **est et equus**: according to Ailian, Ποικ. Ἱστ. ii, 3, the story was told of Alexander and the horse in his equestrian portrait. The *est* ... *sive fuit* show how little importance Pliny himself attaches to such anecdotes.

§ 96. 17. **Neoptolemum**: *not* the son of Achilles, as Welcker and others have supposed, but the ἑταῖρος of

Alexander, son of Arrhabaios, Arrian i, 20, 10; ii, 27, 6, Diodoros xviii, 29.

ex equo: sc. *pugnantem.*

18. **Archelaum**: two Archelaoi are known among the soldiers of Alexander, (1) the son of Androkles, one τῶν ἑταίρων; he was placed in command of the garrison left at Aornos (Arr. iii, 29, 1); (2) the son of Theodoros, who was placed in command at Susa (Arr. iii, 16, 9).

21. **sacrificantium**: since the words are at variance with the Homeric description, endless emendations of the passage have been suggested (see Overbeck, *Schriftquell.* 1870). The best explanation seems that of Dilthey (*Rhein. Mus.* xxv, p. 327), who supposes that in translating

vicisse Homeri versus videtur id ipsum describentis. pinxit
et quae pingi non possunt, tonitrua, fulgetra, fulgura, quae
97 Bronten, Astrapen, Ceraunobolian appellant.   inventa eius
et ceteris profuere in arte, unum imitari nemo potuit, quod
absoluta opera atramento inlinebat ita tenui ut id ipsum 5
repercussu claritatis colorem album excitaret custodiretque
a pulvere et sordibus, ad manum intuenti demum appareret,
sed etiam ratione magna, ne claritas colorum aciem offende-
ret veluti per lapidem specularem intuentibus et e longin-
quo eadem res nimis floridis coloribus austeritatem occulte 10
daret.

98   Aequalis eius fuit Aristides Thebanus. is omnium primus
animum pinxit et sensus hominis expressit, quae vocant
Graeci ethe, item perturbationes, durior paulo in coloribus.
huius opera : oppido capto ad matris morientis ex volnere 15

6. album] *Traube* ; alvum *Bamb.* ; alium *Bamb. e corr., Detlefsen* ; *om.
reliqui.*   8. etiam] *Bamb. e corr.* ; etiam *Bamb.* ; et cum *Voss., Detlefsen.*
15. opera] *Bamb.* ; pictura *reliqui, Detlefsen.*

some Greek epigram beginning for
instance :
θυούσαις δὲ κόραισιν ὁμορρόθος ἰοχέαιρα
ἐξάρχουσα χορόν, σεύεται ἀγροτέρη.
Pliny or his author mistook θυούσαις
from θυέω for the partic. of θύω.
   1. Homeri versus : Od. vi, 102—
οἵη δ᾽ ῎Αρτεμις εἶσι κατ᾽ οὔρεα ἰοχέαιρα
      *   *   *   *   *
τῇ δέ θ᾽ ἅμα Νύμφαι, κοῦραι Διὸς
αἰγιόχοιο,
ἀγρονόμοι παίζουσι.
   3. Bronten . . . Ceraunobolian :
personifications [κεραυνοβολία was
the personification of κεραυνός (Diels,
Doxographi Graeci, p. 367 foll. and
Aetios Mac. ii, 2, 3, p. 368); for Bronte
cf. Philostr. the Elder *Imag.* i, 14
Βροντὴ ἐν εἴδει σκληρῷ καὶ ᾽Αστραπὴ
σέλας ἐκ τῶν ὀφθαλμῶν ἱεῖσα πῦρ . . .
Possibly the three figures were united
in an allegory of a storm and formed
a votive offering to Zeus κεραυνο-
βόλος ; cf. *C. I. G.* 1513 ; *βροντῶν* and
κεραύνιος, *C. I. G.* 2641, 3446, 3810,
and often.—H. L. U.].
   § 97. 5. atramento : the exact

composition of Apelles's *atramentum*
still remains obscure ; we can only
gather that although some black substance formed its basis, this was so
diluted and spread out as to become
transparent and practically colourless.
   6. colorem album excitaret :
this passage offers grave difficulties.
(1) If we follow the remaining codices
in omitting the word *album* we get
pure nonsense, since it is absurd to
talk of a glazing that raised the
picture's colour as a whole, and yet
toned it down.   (2) If we follow
Detlefsen and adopt the *alium* which
a later hand wrote for the *alvum* of
cod. Bamb. we get worse nonsense,
for what is this *color alius?*   (3) I
cannot help suspecting that *albus* (used
of a dead, opaque white) is a mistranslation of the Greek λευκός in its
sense of ' brilliant ' ; the object of the
glazing, then, was to give a brilliant
surface to the whole picture ; this
brought the colours into unison, and
at the same time served the practical
purpose of protecting the painting
from dust.

thought to have excelled the lines of Homer that describe the same scene. He also painted the unpaintable, thunder, for example, lightning and thunderbolts, βροντή, ἀστραπή and κεραυνοβολία as they are called.

All have profited by his innovations, though one of these could **97** never be imitated; he used to give his pictures when finished a black glazing so thin that by sending back the light it could call forth a whitish colour, while at the same time it afforded protection from dust and dirt, only becoming visible itself on the closest inspection. In using this glazing, one main purpose of his was to prevent the brilliance of the colours from offending the eyes,—the effect was as when they are looked at through talc, —and also that when seen at a distance those which were vivid to excess might be imperceptibly toned down.

Aristeides of Thebes was his contemporary: he was the first **98** among all painters to paint the soul, and gave expression to the *Aristeides* affections of man—I mean to what the Greeks call ἤθη—and also *of Thebes.* the emotions. His colouring is rather harsh. His works are:

9. **lapidem specularem**: xxxvi, 160; it was a transparent highly laminated substance, used also for windows (*specularia*), cf. Plin. *Ep.* ii, 17, 4; Juv. iv, 21, &c.

§ 98. 12. **Aristides Thebanus**: below, § 111; he was the second of the name, son of Nikomachos, § 108, and grandson of the first Aristeides, *ib.*, above, § 75.

omnium primus: note on § 16.

13. **sensus . . . perturbationes**: as O. Jahn points out (*Kunsturtheile*, p. 115), Pliny is here giving a closer definition of *animus* by dividing it into ἤθη and πάθη, for the first of which, according to Quinct. vi, 2, 8, no precise Latin equivalent existed: *horum* (sc. *affectuum*) *autem, sicut antiquitus traditum accepimus, duae sunt species: alteram Graeci* πάθος *vocant, quod nos vertentes recte ac proprie affectum dicimus, alteram* ἤθος, *cuius nomine, ut ego equidem sentio, caret sermo Romanus: mores appellantur, atque inde pars quoque illa philosophiae* ἠθική *moralis est dicta* (cf. above, note on *mores* in § 63).

Pliny, therefore, to avoid misunderstanding, gives the Greek word also for ἤθη, while for πάθη he felt himself on safe ground in using *perturbationes*, the translation introduced by Cicero (*Tusc. Disp.* iii, 4, 7). Not a few commentators have considered ἤθος, πάθος to be incompatible qualities in one artist, yet Quinct. (vi, 2, 12) shows that in a sense πάθος is complementary to ἤθος, while Ailian (Ποικ. Ἱστ. iv, 3) especially attributes both qualities to Polygnotos—the ἀγαθὸς ἠθογράφος. (For a thorough and subtle discussion of the question cf. O. Jahn, *op. cit.* pp. 105–117.)

15. **matris morientis**: the motive was employed in sculpture by Epigonos (xxxiv, 88). The picture is described *Anth. Pal.* vii, 623. The Plinian passage doubtless inspired the group of a dead mother with a young child seeking her breast, on the left of the celebrated 'Morbetto' or 'Phrygian Plague' engraved by Marc. Antonio (reproduced Delaborde, *M. Antoine Raimondi*, to face p. 214) according to general supposition from

mammam adrepens infans, intellegiturque sentire mater et
timere ne emortuo lacte sanguinem lambat, quam tabulam
Alexander Magnus transtulerat Pellam in patriam suam.
99 idem pinxit proelium cum Persis, centum homines tabula ea
conplexus pactusque in singulos minas denas a tyranno 5
Elatensium Mnasone.   pinxit et currentes quadrigas et
supplicantem paene cum voce et venatores cum captura et
Leontion Epicuri et anapauomenen propter fratris amorem,
item Liberum et Ariadnen spectatos Romae in aede Cereris,
100 tragoedum et puerum in Apollinis, cuius tabulae gratia 10
interiit pictoris inscitia cui tergendam eam mandaverat M.
Iunius praetor sub die ludorum Apollinarium.   spectata est

a drawing of Raphael. But the drawing in sepia wash and white in the
Uffizi (cornice 265, no. 525) is only,
Mr. B. Berenson informs me, a copy
after an original, now lost, that may
have been by Perino del Vaga.

3. transtulerat Pellam : after the
sack of Thebes in B.C. 335.

§ 99. 4. proelium cum Persis :
since Aristeides is a contemporary of
Apelles and Alexander, the picture must
have represented one of the battles of
this king. It is tempting to identify
the *proelium* with the battle of Issos
and to recognize its copy in the famous
mosaic from Pompei in Naples : the
powerfully characterized Alexander,
the Dareios with his gesture of de-
spairing command are conceptions
worthy of the great master of ἦθος and
πάθος, while motives such as the fallen
Persian in the foreground recall the
mater moriens. It is possible, however, that the Pompeian mosaic should
be rather traced back to Aristeides's
fellow-pupil Philoxenos (§ 109)
(Michaelis, *Jahrb*. vii, 1893, p. 134),
whose battle-piece is more closely defined as *proelium cum Dario*. It is, at
any rate, time to claim the picture for
powerful artists such as Aristeides or
Philoxenos, and to discard the opinion
which attributes it to a lady-painter
Helena, reputed indeed to have
painted a battle of Issos, but only on

the authority of so notorious a liar as
Ptolemaios Chennos. Addenda.

6. Mnasone : a pupil and friend
of Aristotle, circ. B.C. 349 (Timaios
apud Athenaios, vi, p. 264 D, Ailian,
Ποικ. Ἱστ. iii, 19). He was made
tyrant of Elateia after the battle of
Chaironeia in B.C. 338.

currentes quadrigas : votive offerings for victories in the chariot course,
cf. note on xxxiv, 71.

7. supplicantem : making a gesture of entreaty, probably the picture
was that of an *adorans ;* cf. xxxiv, 73,
90, &c. *Cum voce* epigr. cf. Introd.
p. lxxi.

venatores cum captura : note on
xxxiv, 66 ; cf. the hunt of Ptolemaios
Soter by Antiphilos in § 138.

8. Leontion Epicuri : friend and
pupil of Epikouros (B.C. 341–270), and
mistress of his favourite pupil Metrodoros ; she was a rival of Glykera
(Athen. xiii, p. 585 D), who came to
Athens with Harpalos, B.C. 326.
Aristeides probably painted her not
much later than B.C. 320. Although
Epikouros did not reside in Athens
before B.C. 306, it is natural that her
portrait, whenever painted, should be
described as that of the famous '*Leontion Epicuri*,' Kroker, *Gleichnamige
Gr. Künstler*, p. 28 ; Urlichs, *Rhein.
Mus*. xxv, p. 511 f. Another portrait
of her by Theoros below, § 144.

a picture of a mother lying wounded to death in the sack of *Wounded*
a city; she appears conscious that her babe is creeping towards *mother and her child.*
her breast, and afraid lest, now that her milk is dried up, he
should suck blood. This picture Alexander the Great carried off
to his native Pella. He also painted a battle with the Persians; 99
the picture contains a hundred figures, for each of which Mnason
the tyrant of Elateia had agreed to pay him ten minae [£35];
and furthermore a chariot race, and a suppliant whose very accents
we seem to hear, huntsmen with their game, Leontion the pupil
of Epikouros, a girl dying for love of her brother, the Dionysos
and Ariadne now to be seen at Rome in the temple of Ceres, and
a tragic actor and a boy in the temple of Apollo. This picture 100
was ruined through the ignorance of the painter to whom Marcus
Junius as praetor entrusted it to be cleaned before the games of
Apollo. In the temple of Faith on the Capitol was to be seen

---

anapauomenen . . . amorem:
[the subject, which has given rise to
much controversy (see especially Dilthey and L. Urlichs in *Rhein. Mus.*
xxv and xxvi) is sufficiently easy to
explain by reference to *Anth. Pal.* vii,
517—

'Ἠῷοι Μελάνιππον ἐθάπτομεν, ἠελίου δὲ
    δυομένου Βασιλὼ κάτθανε παρθενεκὴ
αὐτοχερί· ζώειν γὰρ ἀδελφεὸν ἐν πυρὶ
        θεῖσα,
οὐκ ἔτλη. δίδυμον δ'οἶκος ἐσεῖδε κακὸν
πατρὸς 'Αριστίπποιο· κατήφησεν δὲ Κυ-
        ρήνη
    πᾶσα, τὸν εὔτεκνον χῆρον ἰδοῦσα
        δόμον.

Evidently the *anapauomene* was a girl
who had died in grief at her brother's
death. The picture was a grave picture, an *expirantis imago* (§ 90), and
the name anapauomene was doubtless
derived from the epigram inscribed
upon it: ἀναπαύεσθαι, here of rest in
death.—H. L. U.] Introd. p. lxxi.

9. spectatos: before the fire which
took place in the reign of Augustus,
Strabo, viii, p. 381; see note above on
§ 24, where the Dionysos alone is
mentioned.

aede Cereris: note on xxxiv, 15.

10. tragoedum et puerum: has

sometimes been explained of a tragic
actor playing his part with a boy (e.g.
Maas, *Ann. d. Inst*, 1881, p. 142,
155, suggests Priam and Troilos), but
it more probably simply represented
an older actor teaching a boy his part;
for the subject cf. Schreiber, *Hell. Rel.*
pl. 47, 48; Helbig, *Wandgemälde*,
1455 (actor with poet), and the cylix by
Douris in Berlin (Furtwängler, *Vasen*,
ii, 2285), also a similar subject below;
an old man with a lyre teaching a
boy.

Apollinis: in the temple on the
Campus Flaminius, near the *porticus Octaviae*, xxxvi, 34; dedicated
B.C. 430, for the removal of a plague
(Liv. iv, 25), it remained down to the
age of Augustus the only temple to
the god in Rome (Asconius on Cic.
In toga candida, p. 91). In B.C. 32,
C. Sosius dedicated in it a cedar-wood
statue of the god which he brought
from Seleukia (xiii, 53); hence the
temple is sometimes called *templum
Apollinis Sosiani.*

§ 100. 11. M. Junius: probably
Silanus, cos. B.C. 25.

12. ludorum Apollinarium: held
on July 13; instituted B.C. 212.

et in aede Fidei in Capitolio senis cum lyra puerum docentis.
pinxit et aegrum sine fine laudatum, tantumque arte valuit
ut Attalus rex unam tabulam eius centum talentis emisse
101 tradatur. simul, ut dictum est, et Protogenes floruit. patria
ei Caunus, gentis Rhodiis subiectae. summa paupertas 5
initio artisque summa intentio et ideo minor fertilitas.
quis eum docuerit non putant constare, quidam et naves
pinxisse usque ad quinquagensimum annum, argumentum
esse, quod cum Athenis celeberrimo loco Minervae delubri
propylon pingeret, ubi fecit nobilem Paralum et Hammoni- 10
ada, quam quidam Nausicaan vocant, adiecerit parvolas
naves longas in iis quae pictores parergia appellant, ut appareret a quibus initiis ad arcem ostentationis opera sua
102 pervenissent. palmam habet tabularum eius Ialysus, qui
est Romae dicatus in templo Pacis. cum pingeret eum, 15

---

1. **aede Fidei**: Livy (i, 21), attributes its foundation to Numa ; restored
B.C. 115 by M. Aemilius Scaurus ; it
was on the Capitol, see Gilbert, *Rom*,
iii, p. 399, note 2.

2. **aegrum**: votive picture for a
recovery ; for the subject Furtwängler
(*Jahrb.* iii, p. 218) compares an excellent bronze statuette of a sick man (in
the Cook coll. at Richmond).

3. **Attalus rex**: vii, 126. = App. I.
§ 101. 4. **ut dictum est**: in § 81.

patria Caunus: so also Paus. i, 3,
5, Plut. *Demetr.* 22, while Souidas
names Xanthos in Lykia as his birthplace.

7. **quis eum docuerit**: cf. Seilanion xxxiv, 51 ; Lysippos, *ibid.* 61 ;
see Introd. p. xlvi ff.

naves pinxisse: i. e. he would
paint the παράσημα and ἐπίσημα of
ships.

9. **Athenis**: he was probably
twice at Athens ; Curtius conjectures
that his picture of the 'Thesmothetai'
(Paus. i, 3, 5), in the *Bouleuterion*,
was connected with the re-organization
of the νομοφύλακες by Demetrios of
Phaleron, but that in the days of
Pausanias, the origin of the picture

being forgotten, it was called after
the old republican θεσμοθέται (*Stadt-
Geschichte von Athen*, p. 229). Add.—
The second visit was under his special
patron Demetrios Poliorketes, on the
occasion alluded to here.

10. **propylon**: cf. xxxvi, 32 *Charites in propylo Atheniensium quas
Socrates fecit;* the unusual form
propylon for the more familiar *propy-
laeum* or *propylaea* justifies us in
attributing both passages to the same
authority ; Wachsmuth, *Stadt Athen*,
i, 36, 2 ; Introd. p. l.

Paralum et Hammoniada: i.e.
the patron-heroes of the two holy
triremes. The Ammonias—ἡ τοῦ
Ἄμμωνος ἱερὰ τριήρης—(see Kenyon's
note on Aristotle, Ἀθην. Πολ. p. 152)
replaced the old Salaminia. The choice
of the name is characteristic of the
Antigonids and their strenuous efforts
to keep alive the memory of the
deified Alexander (Curtius, *op. cit.*
p. 233); for the holy triremes cf.
Boeckh-Fränkel, *Staatsalterthümer*,
p. 305 ff. ; Boeckh, *Seeurkunden*, p.
76 ff.

11. **Nausicaan**: both figures were,
it seems, united in one picture which

a picture of an old man with a lyre teaching a boy. Aristeides also painted a sick man, a picture never sufficiently praised, and so great was his name that king Attalos, we are told, paid a hundred talents [£21,000 circ.] for a single picture by his hand.

Protogenes, as I have already said, was a painter of the same 101 date. He was a native of Kaunos, a city subject to Rhodes. *Protogenes of Kaunos.* The great poverty of his early days and his scrupulous devotion *Obscurity* to his art were the causes that he produced but few pictures. *of his early life.* The name of his master is supposed to be unknown, while some say that he painted ships until his fiftieth year, and adduce in proof thereof that when he was at Athens decorating, in the most celebrated of spots, the gateway to the temple of Athene, for which he painted his famous Paralos and Hammonias,—a figure sometimes called Nausikaa,—he introduced some tiny warships in the part of the picture called the παρέργια, purposing to show the humble origin of the painter whose works had risen to such a height of glory. Among his pictures the Ialysos, dedicated in 102 the Temple of Peace at Rome, bears off the palm. The story *The 'Ialysos.'*

lent itself to interpretation as Odysseus and Nausikaa ; but see C. Torr, *Class. Rev.* iv, 1890, p. 231.

parvolas naves : perhaps along the edge of the picture ; they were merely ornamental, or, at the most, served to indicate that the hero and heroine depicted were connected with ships. C. Torr (*loc. cit.*) suggests that the little warships were represented in the background out at sea, the figures themselves being in the foreground upon the shore. In this case the 'smallness' was due simply to the necessities of perspective. The explanation given by Pliny is evidently aitiological, nor is it necessary to follow Curtius (*loc. cit.*) in bracketing the *et*, and taking these small triremes to indicate ' to what a height of glory — from what small beginnings—ship-building had attained.'

12. **parergia** : diminutive of πάρεργον. No specific part of the picture is intended, but only a subordinate or incidental detail. The word is best explained by reference to Strabo xiv, p. 652, where it is related that Protogenes was vexed because in his picture of the Satyr (below, § 105) the admiration roused by the partridge had caused the work itself—τὸ ἔργον—to become a πάρεργον.

§ 102. 14. **Ialysus** : a Rhodian hero, after whom the city of 'Ιάλυσος was named ; son of Kerkaphos and Kydippe, whose other sons were the eponymous heroes Lindos and Kameiros (Pindar, *Ol.* vii, 74). The dog shows that Ialysos was represented as a huntsman. Possibly the picture was one of a cycle of Rhodian heroes, likewise including the *Kydippe* and *Tlepolemos* (below, § 106). When Strabo wrote (*loc. cit.*), the picture was still at Rhodes ; it was probably brought away by Vespasian and placed at once in his Temple of Peace. Plutarch (*Dem.* 22) says it was already burnt in his day.

15. **templo Pacis** : note on xxxiv, 84.

traditur madidis lupinis vixisse, quo simul et famem susti-
neret et sitim nec sensus nimia dulcedine obstrueret. huic
picturae quater colorem induxit contra obsidia iniuriae et
vetustatis, ut decedente superiore inferior succederet. est
in ea canis mire factus ut quem pariter et casus pinxerit. 5
non iudicabat se in eo exprimere spumam anhelantis, cum
in reliqua parte omni, quod difficillimum erat, sibi ipse
103 satisfecisset. displicebat autem ars ipsa nec minui poterat,
et videbatur nimia ac longius a veritate discedere, spumaque
illa pingi, non ex ore nasci ; anxio animi cruciatu, cum in 10
pictura verum esse, non verisimile vellet, absterserat saepius
mutaveratque penicillum, nullo modo sibi adprobans. postremo iratus arti, quod intellegeretur, spongeam inpegit
inviso loco tabulae, et illa reposuit ablatos colores qualiter
104 cura optaverat, fecitque in pictura fortuna naturam. hoc 15
exemplo eius similis et Nealcen successus spumae equi
similiter spongea inpacta secutus dum celetem pingit ac
poppyzonta retinentem eum. ita Protogenes monstravit et
fortunam. propter hunc Ialysum, ne cremaret tabulam,
Demetrius rex, cum ab ea parte sola posset Rhodum capere, 20
non incendit, parcentemque picturae fugit occasio victoriae.
105 erat tunc Protogenes in suburbano suo hortulo, hoc est
Demetrii castris, neque interpellatus proeliis inchoata opera

1. quo] *Traube*; quoniam, *codd.*, *Detlefsen.* sustineret] *codd.*; sustinerent
Detlefsen. 2. obstrueret] *Bamb.*; obstruerent *reliqui, Detlefsen.* 17. dum
celetem pingit ac] *Traube* ; disceret cum pingitur *Bamb.*; dicitur, cum
pingeret, *Detlefsen.*

3. **obsidia iniuriae ac vetustatis :** hendiadys, to avoid the
awkward co-ordination of genitives;
cf. Petron. 84 *nondum vetustatis iniuria victus.* In spite of the ingenious
remarks of Berger (*Beiträge*, ii, p. 19),
I think the story of the four coats
of colour may still be considered
apocryphal.

§ 103. 15. **fortuna:** the whole anecdote is an amusing illustration of the
saying of Agathon (*ap.* Arist. *Nic.
Ethics*, vi, 4), τέχνη τύχην ἔστερξε
καὶ τύχη τέχνην. Introd. p. xli f.

§ 104. 16. **Nealcen:** below,
§§ 142, 145. The following anecdote

is told also by Plut. περὶ Τύχης, p.
99 B. (= Bernardakis I, p. 240) and
by Val. Max. viii, 11, ext. 7 (without
naming the artist). Dio Chrysostom
and Sextus Empiricus (see *S. Q.* 1889)
tell the story of Apelles.

17. **celetem . . . poppyzonta :**
for the subject in sculpture cf. (*a*)
Winter *Jahrb.* viii, 1893, p. 142 ; (*b*)
Parthenon W. frieze, viii, 15, 22 (*Cat.*
p. 180) &c. ; (*c*) a gem in the Coll.
Tyskiewiez (Furtwängler *Ant. Gemmen*, pl. ix, 14).

20. **ab ea parte sola :** cf. vii, 126.
The picture was in the temple of
Dionysos just outside the city (Strabo,

runs that while he was painting it he lived on lupins steeped in water, that he might thus satisfy at once his hunger and his thirst without blunting his faculties by over-indulgence. He gave this picture four coats of colour to preserve it from the approach of injury and age, so that if the first coat peeled off the one below might take its place. The dog in this picture is the outcome as *The foam* it were of miracle, since chance, and not art alone, went to the *of the dog is painted* painting of it. The artist felt that he had not perfectly rendered *by miracle.* the foam of the panting animal, although he had satisfied himself —a difficult task—in the rest of the painting. It was the very 103 skill which displeased him and which could not be concealed, but obtruded itself too much, thus making the effect unnatural; it was foam painted with the brush, not frothing from the mouth. Chafing with anxiety, for he aimed at absolute truth in his painting and not at a makeshift, he had wiped it out again and again, and changed his brush without finding any satisfaction. At last, enraged with the art which was too evident, he threw his sponge at the hateful spot, and the sponge left on the picture the colours it had wiped off, giving the exact effect he had intended, and chance thus became the mirror of nature. Nealkes likewise 104 *The same* once succeeded in rendering the foam of a horse in the same *happens to* way, by throwing his sponge at the picture he was painting of *a horse in* a groom coaxing a race-horse. Thus Protogenes even taught the *a picture by Nealkes.* uses of fortune. It was to preserve this Ialysos that king Demetrios refrained from setting fire to the city, which was open to attack on that side only, and by sparing the picture he forfeited his chance of victory. At the time of the siege Protogenes was living 105 in his little garden beyond the walls, within the lines of Demetrios. He did not allow the war to interrupt his work, but went on with *Generosity* the pictures he was painting, except when summoned to the *of Deme-trios* presence of the king, and when asked what gave him courage to *towards Protogenes.*

loc. *cit.*); for a fuller account of the episode see in especial Plutarch, *Dem.* 22; the story has little historical credibility, but, as Helbig (*Unters.* p. 181) points out, serves to emphasize the love of art which characterized 'the most genial of the Diadochoi.'

Rhodum: i. e. the new city founded in B. C. 408; for the siege cf. xxxiv, 41.

§ 105. 22. **erat tunc Protogenes**:

the story, which recurs in a variety of forms, is suspicious: thus Archimedes was found quietly drawing geometric figures when the Romans stormed Syracuse (Liv. xxv, 31, 9); in modern times the painter Parmegianino was found calmly painting a Madonna when the Spanish and Dutch troops, under Constable of Bourbon, stormed Rome in 1527, &c.

intermisit omnino nisi accitus a rege, interrogatusque qua
fiducia extra muros ageret respondit scire se cum Rhodiis
illi bellum esse, non cum artibus. disposuit rex in tutelam
eius stationes, gaudens quod posset manus servare quibus
pepercerat, et ne saepius avocaret, ultro ad eum venit hostis 5
relictisque victoriae suae votis inter arma et murorum ictus
spectavit artificem, sequiturque tabulam illius temporis haec
106 fama, quod eam Protogenes sub gladio pinxerit. Satyrus
hic est quem anapauomenon vocant, ne quid desit temporis
eius securitati, tenentem tibias. fecit et Cydippen, Tlepo- 10
lemum, Philiscum tragoediarum scriptorem meditantem et
athletam et Antigonum regem, matrem Aristotelis philosophi, qui ei suadebat ut Alexandri Magni opera pingeret
propter aeternitatem rerum. impetus animi et quaedam
artis libido in haec potius eum tulere. novissime pinxit 15
Alexandrum ac Pana. fecit et signa ex aere, ut diximus.
107 eadem aetate fuit Asclepiodorus, quem in symmetria mirabatur Apelles. huic Mnaso tyrannus pro duodecim diis
dedit in singulos mnas tricenas, idemque Theomnesto in
108 singulos heroas vicenas. his adnumerari debet et Nico- 20
machus Aristidi filius ac discipulus. pinxit raptum
Proserpinae, quae tabula fuit in Capitolio in Minervae
delubro supra aediculam Iuventatis, et in eodem Capitolio,

21. Aristidi] *Urlichs in Chrestom.*; aristiaci *Bamb. Detlefsen*; aristicheimi *Riccard*; ariste //// *Voss.*; aristecheimi *Lips.*

§ 106. 9. ne . . . securitati :
Strabo describes the Satyr as leaning
on a column, apparently somewhat in
the scheme of the celebrated 'Resting
Satyr' by Praxiteles, Helbig, *Class. Ant.*
525. Furtwängler, *Masterpieces*, p. 329.

10. Cydippen, Tlepolemum :
above, note on *Ialysus* in § 102.
Tlepolemos led the Rhodian contin-
gent to Troy (*Il.* ii, 653).

11. Philiscum trag. script. : he
was a native of Kerkyra. According
to Athen. v, 198 c he took part in the
great πομπή of Ptolemy Philadelphos,
B.C. 284, in virtue of his office of
priest of Dionysos. The theory that
the beautiful relief in the Lateran

(Benndorf-Schöne, 245 = Helbig, *Class.
Ant.* 663) is a copy of Protogenes'
picture is quite uncertain.

12. Antigonum regem : painted
by Apelles, above, §§ 90, 96.

matrem Aristotelis : her name
was Phaestis. Cf. Introd. p. lxi.

16. Alexandrum ac Pana : probably Alexander was represented as
Dionysos, to whom, according to the
legend, Pan acted as shieldbearer
during his progress through India,
Lucian, *Dionys.* 2 ; Helbig, *Untersuchungen*, p. 50.

ut diximus : xxxiv, § 91.

§ 107. 17. Asclepiodorus : above,
§ 80 ; he may be identical with the

remain outside the walls, he replied that he knew the king was making war against Rhodes, not against art. Demetrios placed sentinels to guard him, and took a pride in protecting the artist he had spared. Unwilling to call him from his work, Demetrios, enemy though he was, visited him in person, and in the midst of arms and of assaults neglected his hopes of victory to watch the painter. Hence comes the saying about the picture which Protogenes was engaged on at the time, that he had painted it under the sword. This is the Satyr called the ἀναπαυόμενος [resting], 106 and he is holding the pipes, to emphasize the painter's sense of security at the moment. He also painted a Kydippe, and a Tlepolemos, Philiskos the tragedian in meditation, an athlete, a portrait of king Antigonos, and the mother of Aristotle the philosopher, who had tried to persuade him to paint the exploits of Alexander the Great, on the ground that they deserved immortality, but the natural turn of his genius, and his artist's caprice drew the painter rather to these other themes. Alexander and Pan were the last subjects he ever painted; as already noted, he also made bronze statues.

The *Asklepiodoros* whose knowledge of symmetry was praised 107 by Apelles, belonged to the same epoch; the tyrant Mnason *Asklepio-doros.* gave him thirty minae [100 guineas circ.] for each of his twelve gods, and to †*Theomnestos* twenty minae [£70 circ.] for each of his heroes.

We must rank with these artists *Nikomachos*, the son and pupil 108 of Aristeides. He painted the rape of Persephone, which was in *Nikoma-chos, son of* the temple of Minerva on the Capitol, above the little chapel of *Aristeides.*

---

sculptor xxxiv, 86. He must have held a high position, since Plutarch, *Glor. Athen.* 2, mentions him along with Apollodoros (above, § 60), Euphranor (below, § 128); Nikias (§ 132), and Panainos (§ 59), as one of the masters who made Athens glorious through their paintings.

18. **Mnaso** : above, note on § 99.

§ **108.** 20. **Nicomachus** : the mention in Cic. *Brutus*, 18, 70, is alone sufficient to prove his high reputation, yet his works are known from Pliny only; to the list given here must be added the unfinished Tyndaridai, in § 145.

21. **Aristidi** : i. e. the Elder, cf. above, § 75; Urlichs' reading is confirmed by the fact that whereas in § 110 Ariston appears as brother and pupil of Nikomachos, he appears in § 111 as a son and pupil of Aristeides, hence Nikomachos too must have been the son of an Aristeides, Kroker, *Gleichnamige Gr. Künstler*, p. 26.

raptum Proserpinae : for the subject cf. note on xxxiv, 69.

22. **fuit** : before the fire of 69 A.D.; above, note on xxxiv, 38.

23. **aediculam Iuventatis** : in the actual cella of Minerva, near the statue of the goddess; the cult of *Iuventas*,

quam Plancus imperator posuerat, Victoria quadrigam in
sublime rapiens. Ulixi primus addidit pilleum. pinxit et
109 Apollinem ac Dianam, deumque matrem in leone sedentem,
item nobiles Bacchas obreptantibus Satyris, Scyllamque
quae nunc est Romae in templo Pacis. nec fuit alius in ea 5
arte velocior. tradunt namque conduxisse pingendum ab
Aristrato Sicyoniorum tyranno quod is faciebat Telesti
poetae monimentum praefinito die intra quem perageretur,
nec multo ante venisse tyranno in poenam accenso paucisque
110 diebus absolvisse et celeritate et arte mira. discipulos 10
habuit Aristonem fratrem et Aristiden filium et Philo-
xenum Eretrium, cuius tabula nullis postferenda Cassandro
regi picta continuit Alexandri proelium cum Dario. idem
pinxit et lasciviam, in qua tres Sileni comissantur. hic
celeritatem praeceptoris secutus breviores etiamnum quas- 15
111 dam picturae conpendiarias invenit. adnumeratur his et
Nicophanes elegans ac concinnus ita ut venustate ei pauci
conparentur. cothurnus ei et gravitas artis multum a

like that of *Terminus* (in the same
temple) was one of the oldest in
Rome; Liv. i, 55, 4; v, 54, 7 ; for
full literature cf. Wissowa, *ap.* Roscher,
ii, pp. 666, 708, *s. v.* Jupiter; *ib.*
p. 764, *s.v.* Juventas.

1. **Plancus imperator** : sc. L.
Munatius, triumphed B. C. 43 (for his
assumption of the title of *imperator* cf.
Cic. *Phil.* iii, 38, and the letters of
Plancus, *ap.* Cic. *ad Fam.* x, 8; 24).
His brother L. Plautius Plancus
(adopted by L. Plautius) struck in B.C.
45 a coinage with a type of Nike and
horses, which is apparently a copy of
the picture by Nikomachos (see next
note and cf. Helbig, *Untersuchungen*,
p. 154). Furtwängler (*Jahrb.* iv,
1889, p. 62) hence suspects an error on
the part of Pliny in naming the more
famous *Plancus Imp.* as dedicator of
the statue.

**Victoria quadrigam in sub-
lime rapiens:** Furtwängler (*loc. cit.*)
emphasizes the opinion already expressed by Panofka (13th *Winckelmannsprogramm*) and Schuchardt

(*Nikomachos*, p. 20 ff.) that the composition survives on a beautiful gem
signed Ροῦφος (*Jahrb.* iii, 1888, pl. xi,
10), in St. Petersburg, representing
Nike with outspread wings, bearing
away a team of four horses. This
theory is confirmed by the fact that
the composition is repeated on the
coins of the *gens Plautia* (Babelon,
Monnaies de la Rép. Rom. ii, p. 325).
The painting of Nikomachos was of
course a votive offering for a victory
in the chariot race. 'Instead of the
usual traditional type, in which the
winner appears in his chariot crowned
by victory, or else Nike standing in
the chariot guides the horses, Nikomachos ventured on a daring invention ; ignoring the chariot and the
earthly chariot course, he painted the
triumphant horses as they are borne
aloft to victory by Nike herself.'
(F.)

2. **Ulixi primus:** Servius on
Aeneid ii, 44 (Thilo. i, p. 222) *huic
Ulixi primus Nicomachus pictor pilleo
caput texisse fertur*, but the Schol.

Youth, and a Victory snatching up to Heaven a team of horses; this was also to be seen in the Capitol, where Plancus had dedicated it when general. He was the first to give a cap to Ulysses. He also painted an Apollo and Artemis, a Mother of the Gods 109 seated on her lion, a celebrated picture of Mainades with Satyrs stealing upon them, and a Scylla now at Rome in the temple of Peace. No artist surpassed him in rapidity of execution. It *His* is said, for instance, that Aristratos, tyrant of Sikyon, com- *rapidity.* missioned him to paint before a fixed day the monument which he was raising to the poet Telestes; Nikomachos arrived only a little before the appointed time, and the tyrant in his annoyance wished to punish him, but the painter finished the work in a few days with a promptitude as marvellous as his success. His pupils 110 were his brother †*Ariston*, his son *Aristeides* and †*Philoxenos* of Eretria, who painted for king Kassander the battle between Alexander and Dareios, a picture second to none; he also painted a scene of revelry in which three Seilenoi are making merry. He imitated the swiftness of his master, and himself invented some shortened methods of technique. We must include in this list 111 *Nikophanes*, a painter at once graceful and precise, whose delicacy *Niko-* few can equal, though he lacks the grandeur and dignity found in *phanes.*

on *Iliad* x, 265 attributes the innovation to Apollodoros.

3. **Apollinem ac Dianam**: a group.

deumque matrem: i. e. Kybele sitting on her lion, as for instance on the Pergamene frieze, and on the frieze from the temple at Priene (fragment in Br. Mus.).

§ **109.** 4. **nobiles Bacchas obrept. Sat.**: for the subject, cf. *Wandgemälde*, 542–556; Schreiber, *Hell. Reliefs*, xxiv. None of these compositions can, however, be referred with certainty to Nikomachos.

Scyllamque: Schuchardt (*Nikomachos*, p. 40 ff.) proposes to recognize a copy of the picture of Nikomachos in the *Scylla*, *Mon. d. Inst.* iii, pl. liii, 3 = Helbig, *Wandgemälde*, 1063; the same composition recurs on coins struck by S. Pompeius.

7. **Aristrato**: tyrant of Sikyon, Ol. 105 = B.C. 360–357.

Telesti: a dithyrambic poet, native

of Selinos, who had apparently migrated to Sikyon (Athen. xiv, p. 616, 625). In B.C. 401 he won the first prize at Athens.

§ **110.** 11. **Aristidem filium**: i. e. *Aristides Thebanus*, above, § 98, cf. below, § 111.

12. **Cassandro regi**: B.C. 306–296.

13. **proelium cum Dario**: at Issos in B.C. 433, or Gaugamela in B.C. 431. See note above on *proelium cum Persis*, in § 99.

16. **compendiarias**: what this 'shortened method' may have been it is impossible to tell; cf. Petron. 2 *pictura quoque non alium exitum fecit, postquam Aegyptiorum audacia tam magnae artis compendiariam invenit.* See Addenda.

§ **111.** 17. **Nicophanes**: below, § 137; *adnumeratur his*, because he belongs to approximately the same date.

Zeuxide et Apelle abest. Apellis discipulus Perseus, ad
quem de hac arte scripsit, huius fuerat aetatis. Aristidis
Thebani discipuli fuerunt et filii Niceros et Ariston, cuius
est Satyrus cum scypho coronatus, discipuli Antorides et
Euphranor, de quo mox dicemus.   5

112   Namque subtexi par est minoris picturae celebres in
penicillo, e quibus fuit Piraeicus. arte paucis postferendus
proposito nescio an destruxerit se, quoniam humilia quidem
secutus humilitatis tamen summam adeptus est gloriam.
tonstrinas sutrinasque pinxit et asellos et obsonia ac similia, 10
ob haec cognominatus rhyparographos, in iis consummatae
voluptatis, quippe eae pluris veniere quam maximae multo-
113 rum.   e diverso Maeniana, inquit Varro, omnia operiebat
Serapionis tabula sub Veteribus. hic scaenas optime pinxit,
sed hominem pingere non potuit. contra Dionysius nihil 15
aliud quam homines pinxit, ob id anthropographos cogno-
114 minatus.   parva et Callicles fecit, item Calates comicis
tabellis, utraque Antiphilus. namque et Hesionam nobilem
pinxit et Alexandrum ac Philippum cum Minerva, qui sunt
in schola in Octaviae porticibus, et in Philippi Liberum 20

---

2. de . . . arte scripsit: above,
§ 79, Introd. p. xl.

Aristidis Thebani: above, §§ 98–
100, 110; he appears here as master
of Nikeros-Euphranor, by confusion
with his grandfather Aristeides I,
above, note on § 108.

5. Euphranor: he is erroneously
made into a pupil of Aristeides of
Thebes, whereas he was the pupil of
the older Aristeides, above, § 75. *mox
dicemus*, in § 128.

§ **112. 7. Piraeicus** = Πειραϊκός fr.
Πειραιεύς, Helbig, *Untersuch.* 366 ff.
This artist is still known only from
Pliny, the *Pireicus* of Propert. iii, 9,
12, which rested on mere interpolation, having been abandoned for *Parrhasius* by recent editors: *Parrhasius
parva vindicat arte locum.*

10. **tonstrinas sutrinasque**: cf.
the *lanificium* by Antiphilos in § 138,
the workshops by Philiskos and Simos
in § 143.

§ **113. 13. e diverso**: in contradiction to the small pictures by Peiraikos.

Maeniana: *maeniana appellata
sunt a Maenio censore qui primus in
foro ultra columnas tigna proiecit, quo
ampliarentur superiora spectacula*,
Festus, 134. This derivation is probably correct, though the word soon
became a common appellative, cf.
Vitruvius, v, 1, 1. Jordan (*Top. der
Stadt Rom*, vol. i, part 2, p. 383,
note 94) believes that Pliny alludes to
a temporary exhibition of a picture by
Serapion, and not to painted decorations of the *maeniana*. The date of
Serapion is unknown, except that it
must have been previous to Varro,
from whom the information as to his
pictures is derived.

inquit Varro: from whom §§ 112–
114 appear to be almost wholly derived, Münzer, *op. cit.* p. 540 f.

14. **sub Veteribus**: note on § 25.

Zeuxis and Apelles. *Perseus*, the pupil to whom Apelles dedicated his book on art, also belongs to this period. The pupils of Aristeides of Thebes were his sons †*Nikeros* and †*Ariston* (by the *Pupils of Aristeides.* second of whom we have a crowned Satyr holding a cup) and also †*Antorides* and *Euphranor*, of whom I shall speak presently.

It is well to add an account of the artists who won fame with 112 the brush in painting smaller pictures. Amongst them was *Genre painters.* †*Peiraïkos*. In mastery of his art but few take rank above him, *Peiraïkos.* yet by his choice of a path he has perhaps marred his own success, for he followed a humble line, winning however the highest glory that it had to bring. He painted barbers' shops, cobblers' stalls, asses, eatables and similar subjects, earning for himself the name of ῥυπαρογράφος [painter of odds and ends]. In these subjects he could give consummate pleasure, selling them for more than other artists received for their large pictures. As a contrast, Varro 113 mentions a picture by †*Serapion* which covered the whole of the *Serapion.* balconies by the Old Shops. This Serapion was an excellent scene-painter, but could not paint the figure. *Dionysios* on the *Dionysios,* contrary painted figures only, and was called ἀνθρωπογράφος [painter *the 'painter* of men]. *of men.'*

Kallikles also painted small pictures, and so did †*Kalates*, who 114 chose comic subjects; while *Antiphilos* painted in both styles, his *Kallikles. Kalates.* being a famous Hesione, and the picture of Alexander and Philip *Antiphilos.* with Athene now to be seen in the 'schools' of the gallery of Octavia. In the gallery of Philip are his Dionysos, his young

15. **Dionysius**: probably identical with the portrait painter named § 148, but not to be confused with the painter Dionysios of Kolophon, a contemporary of Polygnotos (Arist. *Poet.* 2).

§ **114. 17. parva et Callicles**: known besides only from the following passage of Varro, *neque ille Callicles quaternum digitum tabellis nobilis cum esset factus, tamen in pingendo adscendere potuit ad Euphranoris altitudinem*, Varro, *de Vita P. R.* 1, *ap.* Charisius, p. 126, 25.

comicis: i.e. in subjects borrowed from comedy, cf. § 140.

18. **utraque**: i.e. both small and large pictures; Urlichs, *Chrest.* p. 367.

Antiphilus: appears again in § 138 as a painter in encaustic. He was an Alexandrian and a rival of Apelles (above, note on § 89). Quinctilian (xii, 10, 6) praises him for his facility (*facilitate Antiphilus*); he is probably one of those who introduced that *ars compendiaria* (above, § 110, cf. on Pausias, in § 124), with the invention of which Petronius charged the Egyptians.

Hesionam: probably her deliverance by Herakles. For the subject cf. the large picture, Helbig, *Wandgemälde*, 1129.

19. **Alex. ac Phil. cum Minerva**: probably on a chariot, with Athena acting as charioteer, Furtwängler, *Jahrb.* iv, 1889, p. 86, note 42.

patrem, Alexandrum puerum, Hippolytum tauro emisso
expavescentem, in Pompeia vero Cadmum et Europen.
idem iocosis nomine Gryllum deridiculi habitus pinxit, unde
id genus picturae grylli vocantur. ipse in Aegypto natus
115 didicit a Ctesidemo. decet non sileri et Ardeatis templi 5
pictorem, praesertim civitate donatum ibi et carmine quod
est in ipsa pictura his versibus:

Dignis digna.   Loco picturis condecoravit
reginae Iunonis supremi coniugis templum
Plautius Marcus, cluet Asia lata esse oriundus,   10
quem nunc et post semper ob artem hanc Ardea laudat,

116 eaque sunt scripta antiquis litteris Latinis; non fraudando et
Studio divi Augusti aetate qui primus instituit amoenissi-
mam parietum picturam, villas et portus ac topiaria opera,
lucos, nemora, colles, piscinas, euripos, amnes, litora, qualia 15
quis optaret, varias ibi obambulantium species aut navigan-
tium terraque villas adeuntium asellis aut vehiculis, iam
piscantes aucupantesque aut venantes aut etiam vindemi-
117 antes. sunt in eius exemplaribus nobiles palustri accessu
villae, succollatis sponsione mulieribus labantes trepidis quae 20
feruntur, plurimae praeterea tales argutiae facetissimi salis.

12. Latinis, non *Detlefsen*.

1. **Hippolytum tauro emisso**:
under the influence of the Euripidean
play, Kalkmann, *A. Z.* 1883 (41),
p. 43 ff.

2. **in Pompeia**: note on § 59.
Cf. again Varro, *de Re Rust.* iii, 2, 5,
and Münzer, *loc.cit.*; Introd. p. lxxxiv.

Cadmum et Europen: its great
reputation is apparent from Martial
ii, 14, 3, who uses the name of the
picture as synonymous for the porticus Pompeia (*currit ad Europen*).
The picture, which was doubtless originally in Alexandria, may, as Helbig
(*Untersuch.* p. 224 f.) points out, have
inspired Moschos during his stay in
that city to write the famous description in *Idyll* i, 125 ff. A number of
extant later representations of the
myth—the most celebrated of which
is the mosaic from Palestrina, Roscher,

i, p. 1414, are probably influenced
more or less remotely by the composition of Antiphilos.

3. **Gryllum**: the name, which was
that of the father and of one of the
sons of Xenophon, was common enough.
The *deridiculus habitus* must have
been in allusion to γρύλλος = a dancer
of the γρυλισμός, in which the per-
formers were originally masked as
pigs, though in time the term seems
to have come to include every kind of
wanton dancing (see Phrynichos, ed.
Lobeck, p. 101).   Such performances
were especially in favour at Alexandria, so that it is natural to find
such a subject influencing an Alexandrian artist (cf. Urlichs, *Das hölzerne
Pferd,* p. 20 f.).

§ 115. 5. **Ctesidemo**: below,
§ 140.

Alexander, and Hippolytos terrified at the bull sent up from the
sea, and in the gallery of Pompeius his Kadmos and Europa.
Among his comic pictures is one of a man called Gryllos in a
ridiculous costume, from which all such pictures are called γρύλλοι.
Antiphilos was born in Egypt, and studied under †*Ktesidemos.*   *His master Ktesidemos.*

I ought not to pass over in silence the painter of the temple at 115
Ardea, especially as he was honoured by receiving the citizenship
of the town and the following verses written on the picture : ' To
the deserving be due honour paid.   The temple of queenly Juno,
wife of the almighty, did Lykon adorn with paintings, even Plautius *Plautius*
Marcus, born in wide Asia, whom for this his art Ardea praises   *Marcus Lykon.*
now and for ever more.'   The lines are in old-fashioned Latin
characters.

Nor must I neglect †*Studius,* a painter of the days of Augustus, 116
who introduced a delightful style of decorating walls with repre-   *Studius.*
sentations of villas, harbours, landscape gardens, sacred groves,
woods, hills, fishponds, straits, streams and shores, any scene in
short that took the fancy.   In these he introduced figures of people
on foot, or in boats, and on land of people coming up to the
country-houses either on donkeys or in carriages, besides figures
of fishers and fowlers, or of hunters or even of vintagers.   Among 117
his works we know well the men approaching a villa through
a swamp, and staggering beneath the weight upon their shoulders
of the terrified women whom they have bargained to carry over,
with many other scenes of like vivacity and infinite humour.   He

---

Ardeatis templi : Verg. *Aen.* vii,
411 ff. ; cf. above, § 17.

8. **Loco** = Λύκων ; in addition to
his Greek name he would, on receiving the citizenship of Ardea, assume
the name of Plautius Marcus. M.
Hertz, in *Index Lect. Vratislav.* (1867),
suggests that he may have been both
painter and poet, as was Pacuvius
(above, § 19), and that he is identical
with *Plautius,* a writer whose comedies
passed under the name of Plautus,
Varro, *ap.* A. Gellius, iii, 3, 3. The inscription on his picture being in hexa-
meter, he cannot be dated earlier than
Ennius (B.C. 239–169) ; cf. Mommsen,
Röm. Gesch. ed. 7, i, p. 941 note.

§ 116. 13. **qui primus** : note on
§ 16 : as a fact from Vitruvius vii, 5,
(cf. *Rhein. Mus.* xxv, 1870, p. 394

ff.) it appears that the painting of
topiaria opera was older than the age
of Augustus. Studius gave it a new
impulse or perhaps made it for the
first time really fashionable at Rome.

15. **topiaria opera** : in Livia's
Villa at Prima Porta the walls of one
room were decorated with the plan of
a garden (see *Antike Denkmäler,* i, pl.
11, 24), and afford an excellent example
of the style of Studius (Brunn, *Bull.*
1863, p. 81 ff.) ; cf. also, Helbig,
Untersuchungen, p. 62. Pliny the
younger (*Ep.* v, 6, 22) describes
a bedroom in his villa as follows :
*nec cedit gratiae marmoris ramos in-
cidentesque ramis aves imitata pictura.*

§ 117. 19. **exemplaribus** : sc. *ingenii* ; cf. § 74 *ingenii . . . exempla.*
21. **argutiae** : § 67 ; xxxiv, 65.

idem subdialibus maritimas urbes pingere instituit, blandis-
118 simo aspectu minimoque inpendio.   sed nulla gloria artificum est nisi qui tabulas pinxere, eo venerabilior antiquitatis
prudentia apparet.   non enim parietes excolebant dominis
tantum, nec domos uno in loco mansuras quae ex incendiis 5
rapi non possent.   casa Protogenes contentus erat in hortulo
suo, nulla in Apellis tectoriis pictura erat.   nondum libebat
parietes totos tinguere, omnium eorum ars urbibus excuba-
119 bat pictorque res communis terrarum erat.   fuit et Arellius
Romae celeber paulo ante divum Augustum, ni flagitio 10
insigni corrupisset artem, semper ei lenocinans cuius feminae
amore flagraret, ob id deas pingens, sed dilectarum imagine.
120 itaque in pictura eius scorta numerabantur.   fuit et nuper
gravis ac severus idemque floridus et vividus pictor Famulus.   huius erat Minerva spectantem spectans quacumque 15
aspiceretur.   paucis diei horis pingebat, id quoque cum
gravitate, quod semper togatus, quamquam in machinis.
carcer eius artis domus aurea fuit, et ideo non extant
exempla alia magnopere.   post eum fuere in auctoritate
Cornelius Pinus et Attius Priscus, qui Honoris et Virtutis 20
aedes Imp. Vespasiano Aug. restituenti pinxerunt, Priscus
antiquis similior.

121   Non est omittenda in picturae mentione celebris circa
A.U.C. 711– Lepidum fabula, siquidem in triumviratu quodam loco
718.   deductus a magistratibus in nemorosum hospitium minaciter 25
cum iis postero die expostulavit somnum ademptum sibi
volucrum concentu, at illi draconem in longissima membrana

---

14. floridis (floridus *e corr.*) umidus *Bamb.*, *corr. Traube*; floridissimus
Urlichs in Chrest., Detlefsen.

1. subdialibus : cf. xxxvi, 186.
    § 118. 4. excolebant dominis :
private patrons, cf. in § 30 (colores)
quos dominus pingenti praestat; in
§ 44 *e reliquis coloribus quos a dominis dari diximus* . . .
    6. casa in hortulo : above, § 105.
The 'cottage' doubtless belonged to
the same class of *loci communes* as the
anus (note on § 81).
    § 120. 14. gravis ac severus : i.e.

in his person (cf. below, *cum gravitate,
togatus*), whereas his painting was
floridus and *vividus;* the adjectives
are transferred from the colour to the
painter, cf. § 134 *austerior colore*,
though *austerus* like *floridus* was
a technical qualification of certain
colours, *sunt autem colores austeri
aut floridi*, § 30.
    17. quod semper togatus : so
Vandyck painted in full dress.

also brought in the fashion of painting seaside towns on the walls
of open galleries, producing a delightful effect at a very small cost.
No artists, however, enjoy a real glory unless they have painted 118
easel pictures, and herein the wisdom of past generations claims
our greater respect.   They did not decorate walls to be seen only
by their owners, nor houses that must always remain in one place
and could not be carried away in case of fire.   Protogenes was
content with a cottage in his little garden, and no fresco was to be
seen in the house of Apelles.   It was not yet men's pleasure to
dye whole surfaces of wall ; all the masters laboured for the cities,
and the artist was the possession of the whole world.

Not long before the time of the god Augustus, *Arellius* had 119
earned distinction at Rome, save for the sacrilege by which he *Arellius.*
notoriously degraded his art.   Always desirous of flattering some
woman or other with whom he chanced to be in love, he painted
goddesses in the person of his mistresses, of whom his paintings
are a mere catalogue.   The painter †*Famulus* also lived not 120
long ago ; he was grave and severe in his person, while his *Famulus.*
painting was rich and vivid.   He painted an Athena whose eyes
are turned to the spectator from whatever side he may be looking.
Famulus painted for a few hours only in the day, and treated his
art seriously, always wearing the toga, even when mounted on
scaffolding.   The Golden House was the prison of his art, and
hence not many examples of it are known.   After him †*Cornelius* Cornelius
Pinus and †*Attius Priscus* were painters of repute, who painted *Pinus.*
the twin temples of Honour and Virtue when they were restored *Priscus.*
by the emperor Vespasian Augustus.   Priscus approached more
nearly to the old masters.

While on the subject of painting I must not omit the well- 121
known story of Lepidus.   Once during his triumvirate he had 43–36 B.C.
been escorted by the magistrates of a certain town to a lodging in *'Scare-
crow,'*
the middle of a wood, and on the next morning complained with *painted for Lepidus.*
threats that the singing of the birds prevented him from sleeping.
They painted a snake on an immense strip of parchment and
stretched it all round the grove.   We are told that by this means

---

machinis : here of scaffolding,
Blümner, *Technol.* iv, 430 : for
machina = easel, above, § 81.

18. career eius artis : for Pliny's
hatred of Nero cf. above, § 51 ; xxxiv,
45, 84.

20. Honoris et Virtutis aedes :
built or rather restored by Marcellus,
in B. C. 212, to contain part of the art
treasures brought from Syracuse, Liv.
xxv, 40, cf. xxvii, 25 ; Cic. *Verr.* II, iv,
54, 120 ; Gilbert, *Rom,* iii. p. 97 f.

depictum circumdedere luco eoque terrore aves tunc siluisse
narratur et postea potuisse compesci.

122   Ceris pingere ac picturam inurere quis primus excogita-
verit non constat.   quidam Aristidis inventum putant postea
consummatum a Praxitele, sed aliquanto vetustiores encau- 5
stae picturae exstitere, ut Polygnoti et Nicanoris ac Mnasilai
Pariorum.   Elasippus quoque Aeginae picturae suae in-
scripsit ἐνέκαεν, quod profecto non fecisset nisi encaustica
inventa.

123   Pamphilus quoque Apellis praeceptor non pinxisse solum 10
encausta sed etiam docuisse traditur Pausian Sicyonium
primum in hoc genere nobilem.   Bryetis filius hic fuit eius-
demque primo discipulus.   pinxit et ipse penicillo parietes
Thespis, cum reficerentur quondam a Polygnoto picti,
multumque conparatione superatus existimabatur, quoniam 15
124 non suo genere certasset. idem et lacunaria primus pingere
instituit, nec camaras ante eum taliter adornari mos fuit.
parvas pingebat tabellas maximeque pueros.   hoc aemuli
interpretabantur facere eum, quoniam tarda picturae ratio
esset illa.   quamobrem daturus et celeritatis famam absolvit 20
uno die tabellam quae vocata est hemeresios puero picto.

125 amavit in iuventa Glyceram municipem suam, inventricem
coronarum, certandoque imitatione eius ad numerosissimam
florum varietatem perduxit artem illam.   postremo pinxit

---

§ 122. 3. ceris pingere . . .
inurere: i. e. encaustic; note on
§ 149.

4. quidam . . . inventum: for this
variant tradition, Introd. p. xxxiii.

Aristidis: presumably the first of
the name, above, § 75.

5. consumm. a Praxitele: who
would use encaustic for the *circumlitio*
of his statues (below, § 133).

6. Polygnoti: above, §§ 58–59.

8. ἐνέκαεν: cf. above, § 27.

§ 123. 10. Pamphilus: §§ 75–76.
We now come again upon distinct
traces of Xenokrates.   Stress is laid
upon the pre-eminence of Sikyon, and
the painters are connected with definite stages of progress.   Pamphilos

is awkwardly dragged in a second
time, in order to introduce his pupil
Pausias, who in the original Greek
account, where no arbitrary division
seems to have been drawn between
the painters in encaustic and others,
would certainly be discussed in connexion with his master and his contemporaries of §§ 75–76, Introd.
p. xxxiv.

13. pinxit . . . certasset: this
mention of wall-paintings shows that
encaustic was not treated separately
by the Greek authors.

14. Thespis: the wall paintings
by Polygnotos had probably been
injured at the destruction of Thespiai
by the Thebans in B. C. 374.   The

they terrified the birds into silence and that this has ever since been a recognized device for quieting them.

We do not know with certainty who first invented the art of **122** painting with wax colours and burning in the painting. Some *Encaustic painting.* believe that it was invented by Aristeides and afterwards brought to perfection by Praxiteles, but encaustic paintings of a somewhat earlier date exist, for example, by Polygnotos, and by †Nikanor and †Mnasilaos of Paros. †Elasippos of Aigina also wrote on one of his paintings ἐνέκαεν [burnt it in], which he certainly would not have done before the invention of encaustic painting.

Tradition further says that Pamphilos the master of Apelles **123** not only painted in encaustic but also taught *Pausias* of Sikyon, *Practised by Pamphi-* the first well-known master in this style. Pausias was the son of *los, and by* †*Bryetes*, under whom he first studied. He also painted with the *Pausias* *of Sikyon.* brush certain walls at Thespiai, which had originally been painted by Polygnotos and needed restoration. His work was held to suffer very greatly by the comparison, as he had competed in a style that was not his own. He was the first to paint panelled **124** ceilings, nor was it the practice to decorate vaulted roofs in this way before his day. He habitually painted small pictures, boys being his favourite subject. His rivals declared that this was because his method of encaustic painting was slow, whereupon he determined to acquire a reputation for rapid execution, and painted in a single day a picture of a boy called the ἡμερήσιος [day's work]. As a youth he loved his townswoman Glykera, **125** who first invented flower wreaths. By copying and rivalling her *Glykera,* *the flower-* he enabled encaustic painting to represent a great variety of *girl, beloved* flowers. Finally he painted a portrait of Glykera herself seated *of Pausias.*

restoration of the paintings would take place on the restoration of the city, after the capture of Thebes by Alexander in 335 B.C.

§ 124. 16. **idem et lacunaria primus**: Furtwängler (*Fleck. Jahrb.* xxii, 1876, p. 507) has pointed out that these words correspond to *qui primus lacunaria pinxit* in the table of contents, while the following *nec camaras ante eum* corresponds to *quando primum camarae pictae* (*ib.*). The statements accordingly are quite distinct.

20. **absolvit uno die**: cf. the praise for swiftness bestowed upon Nikomachos, § 109, and his pupil Philoxenos, § 110; upon Iaia, in § 148, and Quinctilian's estimate of Antiphilos (note on § 114).

§ **125.** 22. **Glyceram**: xxi, 4, whence we obtain *post Olympiada C* (= B.C. 380) as a further guide to the artist's date. Append. V.

inventricem: the passage in xxi shows that she was really thought of as the inventor of the art of plaiting garlands; thus the old conjecture *venditricem* (Gesner) becomes impossible.

et ipsam sedentem cum corona, quae e nobilissimis tabula
est appellata stephaneplocos, ab aliis stephanopolis, quoniam
Glycera venditando coronas sustentaverat paupertatem.
huius tabulae exemplar, quod apographon vocant, L. Lucul-
126 lus duobus talentis emit Dionysiis Athenis.   Pausias autem 5
fecit et grandis tabulas, sicut spectatam in Pompei porticu
boum immolationem.   eam primus invenit picturam, quam
postea imitati sunt multi, aequavit nemo.   ante omnia, cum
longitudinem bovis ostendi vellet, adversum eum pinxit, non
127 traversum, et abunde intellegitur amplitudo.   dein, cum 10
omnes quae volunt eminentia videri candicanti faciant colore, quae condunt nigro, hic totum bovem atri coloris fecit
umbraeque corpus ex ipsa dedit magna prorsus arte in aequo
extantia ostendente et in confracto solida omnia.   Sicyone
et hic vitam egit, diuque illa fuit patria picturae.   tabulas 15
A.U.C. 698. inde e publico omnis propter aes alienum civitatis addictas
128 Scauri aedilitas Romam transtulit.   post eum eminuit longe
ante omnis Euphranor Isthmius olympiade CIIII, idem qui
inter fictores dictus est nobis.   fecit et colossos et marmorea
et typos scalpsit, docilis ac laboriosus ante omnis et in quo- 20
cumque genere excellens ac sibi aequalis.   hic primus vide-

---

4. **apographon**: there were at the
time many artists who were solely
occupied in the business of copying;
at Athens Lucian, *Zeux.* 3, sees a
copy of the ‘ Kentaurs ’ of Zeuxis; cf.
also Dionysios περὶ Δινάρχου vii,
p. 644; Quinct. x, 2, 6 ; x, 2, 2 ;
above, § 91 (Helbig, *Untersuchungen*,
p. 63). From the exorbitant price
paid, however, it is possible that the
apographon was a replica by the
artist himself.

5. **Athenis**: Lucullus visited
Athens in B.C. 88–87 as Sulla’s
Quaestor; cf. below, on § 156.

§ 126. 7. **boum immolationem**:
for the subject cf. § 93 (note on *pompam*).

§ 127. 11. **eminentia**: §§ 92 (*digiti eminere videntur*); 131.

13. **umbrae corpus ex ipsa
dedit**: the effect was simply pro-

duced by modelling, without the help
of any extraneous colour, precisely as
the Kentaurs of the white marble
slab at Naples (Helbig, *Wandgem.*
1241) appear in strong relief through
the skilful though slight modelling,
Wickhoff, *Wiener Genesis*, p. 47.

in aequo omnia: in modern
parlance Pausias excelled at giving
the ‘ impression of artistic reality with
only two dimensions ’ (cf. Berenson,
*The Florentine painters of the Renais-
sance*, p. 4), i. e. at representing depth,
the third dimension, on a flat surface.

15. **patria picturae**: cf. xxxvi, 9.

16. **propter aes alienum**: since
Sulla’s Mithridatic war the Sikyonians
had fallen into debt and distress
(see especially Cic. *ad Att.* i, 19, 9;
ib. 20, 4; *Tusc. Disp.* iii, 22,
§ 53) and were consequently forced
to sell their art treasures.

with a wreath, one of the famous pictures of the world, called the στεφανηπλόκος [wreath-binder], or by others the στεφανόπωλις [wreath-seller], because Glykera had supported herself by selling wreaths. A copy of the picture, an ἀπόγραφον as it is called, was bought by Lucius Lucullus for two talents [£420 circ.] at the festival of Dionysos at Athens. Pausias, however, also painted 126 large pictures, as for example the famous sacrifice of oxen in the Gallery of Pompeius. He devised an innovation which has often *He devises* been imitated but never equalled. The most striking instance is *a new application* that wishing to display an ox's length of body, he painted a front *of light* and not a side view of the animal, and yet contrived to show *and shade.* its size. Again, while all others put in the high lights in white 127 and paint the less salient parts in dark colour, he painted the whole ox black, and gave substance to the shadow out of the shadow itself, showing great art in giving all his figures full relief upon the flat surface, and in indicating their form when fore-shortened. He spent his life at Sikyon, for many years the home of painting. Later on, in the aedileship of Scaurus, all the 56 B.C. pictures of Sikyon were sold to liquidate the public debt, and were brought to Rome.

After Pausias in the hundred and fourth Olympiad [364–361 128 B.C.], *Euphranor* of the Isthmos, whom I have already mentioned *Euphra-* among the statuaries, far excelled all rivals. He furthermore *nor.* produced colossal statues, works in marble and reliefs. Receptive and of indefatigable industry, he attained in every branch a high level, below which he never fell. He first, it is believed, gave to

17. **Scauri aedilitas:** viii, 64, and often.

§ 128. **post eum:** of time (Furtwängler, *Plinius*, p. 15); but a date posterior to Pausias is irreconcilable with Ol. 104 below and xxxiv, 50. The mistake arises, as Robert, *Arch. Märchen*, p. 89, points out, from Pliny's confusion between the Elder Aristeides (§ 75) and Aristeides of Thebes. In his original scheme he doubtless intended to keep E. in his right chronology immediately after Euxeinidas and his pupil Aristeides; but as in that case the account of the supposed pupil would have preceded that of the supposed master (§§ 98, 111), Pliny was misled

into the present anachronism.

18. **qui inter fictores:** xxxiv, 77, *et colossos* ib. § 78, Euphranor's marble works are only mentioned here.

20. **typos:** in which he would be able to bring out his double skill as painter and artist; the Greek relief, as we know it from the Sidonian Sarkophagi, being in reality a sort of raised picture (Wickhoff, *Wiener Genesis*, p. 46 ff.; cf. Winter, *Arch. Anzeiger*, 1894, p. 8 ff.); a γραπτὸς τύπος, *Anth. Pal.* vii, 730.

in quocumque genere excellens: Quinct. xii, 10, 12 *Euphranorem circa plurium artium species praestantem.*

21. **hic primus:** introduces his

tur expressisse dignitatis heroum et usurpasse symmetrian,
sed fuit in universitate corporum exilior et capitibus articu-
129 lisque grandior. volumina quoque composuit de symmetria
et coloribus. opera eius sunt equestre proelium, XII dei,
Theseus, in quo dixit eundem apud Parrhasium rosa pastum 5
esse, suum vero carne. nobilis eius tabula Ephesi est, Ulixes
simulata insania bovem cum equo iungens et palliati cogi-
130 tantes, dux gladium condens. eodem tempore fuere Cydias
et . . . , cuius tabulam Argonautas HS. CXXXXIIII Hortensius orator mercatus est eique aedem fecit in Tuscu- 10
lano suo, Euphranoris autem discipulus Antidotus. huius
est clipeo dimicans Athenis et luctator tubicenque inter
pauca laudatus. ipse diligentior quam numerosior et in
coloribus severus maxime inclaruit discipulo Nicia Atheni-
131 ense qui diligentissime mulieres pinxit. lumen et umbras 15
custodiit atque ut eminerent e tabulis picturae maxime

8. cydi et cydias *codd.*; Cydias *Detlefsen.*

special contribution to his art, cf.
Introd. p. xxvii f.

1. **dignitatis heroum**: so Varro,
Vita Pop. Rom., ap. Char. p. 126,
praises E. for his *altitudo* or loftiness.

symmetrian: note on xxxiv, 65.

2. **exilior**: see Addenda.

capitibus articulisque: the
judgement is identical with that passed
on Zeuxis in § 64, where see note.

§ 129. 3. **volumina . . . composuit**: like Apelles, § 79, Pamphilos (note on § 76), Melanthios, &c.
Introd. p. xl f.

4. **equestre proelium**: in the Stoa
of Zeus Eleutherios at Athens, Paus.
i, 3, 4; the picture represented the
cavalry engagement which preceded
the battle of Mantineia (B. C. 362, cf.
Plut. *Glor. Ath.* ii, p. 346); according
to Paus. viii, 9, 8, a copy of it was to
be seen in the gymnasium at Mantineia.

XII dei: in the same Stoa,
Paus. i, 3, 3; for the Zeus in this
picture see Val. Max. viii, ext. 5; for
the Hera, Luc. εἰκόνες 7.

5. **Theseus**: likewise in the Stoa
Eleutherios; the hero was represented

with Demokratia and Demos, Paus.
loc. cit. Both Theseus and Demos
were subjects that had been treated
by Parrhasios (above § 69). Demos
was also painted by Aristolaos, § 137.
For the distribution of Euphranor's
pictures in the Stoa Eleutherios see
Hitzig and Blümner, *Pausanias,* p. 141.

in quo dixit eundem: Plut.
Glor. Athen. ii, p. 346 Εὐφράνωρ
τὸν Θησέα τὸν ἑαυτοῦ τῷ Παρρασίου
παρέβαλε λέγων, τὸν μὲν ἐκείνου ῥόδα
βεβρωκέναι, τὸν δὲ ἑαυτοῦ κρέα βύεια.
Münzer (*op. cit.* p. 527) aptly compares
the Aristophanic verse (Fr. 180) upon
Euripides, recorded by Antigonos of
Karystos, *ap.* Diogenes iv, 3, 18 παρη-
τημένος (sc. Πολέμων) ἅ φησιν Ἀριστο-
φάνης περὶ Εὐριπίδου " ὀξωτὰ καὶ σιλ-
φιωτά," ἅπερ, ὡς ὁ αὐτός φησι, " κατα-
πυγοσύνη ταῦτ' ἐστὶ πρὸς κρέας μέγα."
Introd. p. lxiii f.

7. **simulata insania**: ὅτε συστρα-
τεύει τοῖς Ἀτρείδαις μὴ θέλων, Lucian,
περὶ οἴκου 30, where the whole picture is
described in detail. The same subject
was painted by Parrhasios (Plut. *aud.
poet.* 3), we are not told for what city.

heroes their full dignity, and mastered the theory of symmetry; he made the body, however, too slim and the head and limbs too large. He also wrote on symmetry and colour. His works are : 129 a cavalry engagement, the Twelve Gods and a Theseus, of which *He com-pares his* he said that the Theseus of Parrhasios had fed on roses, but his *'Theseus'* on flesh. At Ephesos is his famous picture of Odysseus feigning *to that of Parrhasios.* madness and yoking an ox with a horse, with cloaked figures in meditation, and their leader sheathing his sword. *Kydias* 130 and . . . lived at the same time; his picture of the Argonauts was purchased for 144,000 sesterces [£1250 circ.] by the orator Hortensius, who built a shrine for it on his estate at Tusculum. †*Antidotos* was a pupil of Euphranor. He painted a warrior *Antidotos.* fighting with a shield, to be seen at Athens, a wrestler and a trumpeter, a picture praised as are but few. He was a laborious rather than a prolific artist, and severe in his scheme of colouring; his chief claim to renown is that he was the master of *Nikias* of *Nikias of Athens.* Athens, who painted women with minute care. Nikias was pains- 131 taking in his treatment of light and shade, and took special care

palliati cogitantes: these must be identical with the πρέσβεις in Lucian's description.

8. gladium condens: Παλαμήδης . . . πρόκωπον ἔχων τὸ ξίφος, i. e. the sword was half out of the sheath, and it was uncertain whether Palamedes was drawing or replacing it. So too in § 59, Pliny says of a picture by Polygnotos that it was uncertain whether the man represented was ' ascending' or ' descending.'

§ 130. fuere Cydias et . . . : the *fuere* combined with the evidence of the MSS. compels one to assume the loss of an artist's name. Whether Cydias should appear in the first place or the second is uncertain. Over-beck's explanation *Schriftquell.* 1969[a] (which I presume is also Detlefsen's), that *fuere* refers to both Cydias and Antidotus, is quite unwarranted.

9. Hortensius orator : xxxiv, 48.

12. luctator tubicenque : votive pictures; for the latter, probably of a winner in a herald's competition, see note on xxxiv, 88.

13. numerosior : see on xxxiv, 58.

in coloribus severus : for similar judgements ; § 98 *durior paulo in coloribus;* § 134 *austerior colore Athenion;* § 137 *e severissimis pic-toribus* (*Aristolaus*) ; ib. *durus in coloribus* (*Nikophanes*).

14. discipulo Nicia : Euphranor and Praxiteles being contemporaries (xxxiv, 50), a chronological difficulty arises from the statement that Nikias, who assisted Praxiteles to paint his statues, was the pupil of a pupil of Euphranor. Pliny himself felt the difficulty ; in § 133 he hints at the solution in the words *non satis discer-nitur . . .* ; there were evidently two artists named Nikias ; to the Elder, the assistant of Praxiteles (fl. ab. B. C. 37c–330), and probably the painter of Alexander (r. B. C. 336–323), belongs the date Ol. CXII, while the Younger, who was the pupil of Antidotos, flourished about the time of Athenion (on whom see note).

§ 131. 15. lumen et umbras: §§ 29, 127. Cf. Introd. p. xxxiv.

16. ut eminerent : §§ 92, 127.

A.U.C. 679. curavit.   opera eius: Nemea advecta ex Asia Romam a
Silano quam in curia diximus positam, item Liber pater in
A.U.C. 724. aede Concordiae, Hyacinthus, quem Caesar Augustus delectatus eo secum deportavit Alexandrea capta—et ob id
Tiberius Caesar in templo eius dicavit hanc tabulam et 5
132 Danaen—, Ephesi vero est megabyzi sacerdotis Ephesiae
Dianae sepulchrum, Athenis necyomantea Homeri.   hanc
vendere Attalo regi noluit talentis LX, potiusque patriae
suae donavit abundans opibus.   fecit et grandes picturas,
in quibus sunt Calypso et Io et Andromeda, Alexander 10
quoque in Pompei porticibus praecellens et Calypso sedens.
133 huic eidem adscribuntur quadripedes, prosperrime canes
expressit.   hic est Nicias de quo dicebat Praxiteles interrogatus quae maxime opera sua probaret in marmoribus:
quibus Nicias manum admovisset, tantum circumlitioni eius 15

5. tabulam et Danaen] *Bamb.*; tabulam—et Danae *Detlefsen.*

2. **Silano**: ii, 100; governor of
Bithynia, B. C. 76–75.   The picture
had possibly belonged to Pergamon.
  diximus: § 27, where see note.
  3. **Hyacinthus**: from Paus. iii,
19, 4, it appears he was represented
in the bloom of youth, in special
allusion to Apollo's love for him.
  4. **Alexandria capta**: on the
works of art brought by Augustus
from Alexandria, and dedicated by
him at Rome, see Wunderer's monograph, *Manibiae Alexandrinae,* Würzburg, 1894.
  5. **in templo eius**: i. e. in the
temple built to the memory of
Augustus by Livia and Tiberius in
14 A. D., Dio Cassius lvi, 46; cf.
Plin. xii, 94.   To it belonged both
a porticus and a library (xxxiv, 43).
  et Danaen: the Danae is awkwardly coordinated with the *Hyacinthus.*   That it did not come from
Egypt, as Urlichs (*Chrest.* p. 372)
supposes, is shown by the fact that
Pliny would in that case have made
the relative sentence refer to both
pictures (Wunderer, *op. cit.* p. 9).

§ 132. 6. **megabyzi**: note on
§ 93.
  7. **sepulchrum**: for another grave
picture, by Nikias, at Triteia in
Achaia, see Paus. vii, 22, 6; cf. the
expirantium imagines of Apelles, in
§ 90; the *anapauomene* of Aristeides,
in § 99.
  necyom. Homeri: *Odyssey* xi.
The picture, described *Anth. Pal.*
ix, 792, was the artist's most celebrated work.   While he was engaged
upon it, according to an entertaining
tale told by Plutarch, *An sen. sit ger.
rep.* v, 4, Nikias used to ask those of
his household whether he had washed
or breakfasted.
  8. **Attalo regi**: familiarity with
the high prices paid by Attalos (vii,
126; xxxv, 24) induced Pliny into
error.   The date of Attalos is irreconcilable with that of Nikias, so
that Plutarch is probably right in
telling the story of Ptolemaios
(Soter, B. C. 306–284), Πτολεμαίου
δὲ τοῦ βασιλέως ἑξήκοντα τάλαντα τῆς
γραφῆς συντελεσθείσης πέμψαντος αὐτῷ
μὴ λαβεῖν μηδ᾽ ἀποδόσθαι τὸ ἔργον.

that his figures should be relieved against the background.   His *His treat-ment of light and shade.*
works are : the picture of Nemea brought to Rome from Asia by
Silanus, and placed, as I have said, in the Council Chamber ;
a Dionysos in the temple of Concord; the Hyakinthos carried 75 B.C.
away on the fall of Alexandria by Caesar Augustus, who took such 30 B.C.
great delight in the picture that as a consequence Tiberius Caesar
dedicated it in the temple of Augustus together with the Danae ;
at Ephesos a painting for the grave of a μεγάβυζος or priest of 132
Artemis of Ephesos, and at Athens the νεκυομαντεία [questioning
of the dead] of Homer.   This picture the artist refused to sell to
King Attalos for sixty talents [£12,600 circ.] but preferred, as he
was a rich man, to present it to his own country.   He also painted
large pictures, amongst them Kalypso, Io, Andromeda, the excellent portrait of Alexander which is in the Gallery of Pompeius, and
a Kalypso seated.   Pictures of animals are also ascribed to him, 133
and he was very successful in painting dogs.   It is of this Nikias *He colours*
that Praxiteles, when asked which of his marble statues pleased *the statues*
him most, said, 'Those which the hand of Nikias has touched,' *of Praxi-teles.*
such was his tribute to this artist's colouring of the accessories.
It is not clear whether this or another Nikias is the one placed

Non posse suav. vivere sec. Ep. xi, 2. The court of Alexandria had been more fortunate in purchasing the Hyakinthos (§ 131).

patriae suae donavit: cf. in § 62 the similar statement concerning Zeuxis.

9. **grandes picturas**: in opposi-tion to the smaller pictures painted in encaustic.

10. **Calypso**: a standing figure from the fact that the second Kalypso is expressly described as *sedens*.

Io: Helbig (*Untersuchungen*, pp. 113, 140), inclines to see in the Io of the House of Livia on the Palatine, a copy of the Io of Nikias, a composi-tion which seems to have inspired Prop. i, 3, 20.

Andromeda: the composition seems preserved in the well-known relief of the Capitol, Helbig, *Class. Ant.*461 = Schreiber,*Hell. Reliefs*, xii; cf. the Pompeian paintings, Helbig, *Wandgemälde*, 1186-1189. Add.

11. **Pompei porticibus**: note on § 59.

§ 133. 12. **prosperrime canes**: κεῖται δὲ ἐνταῦθα ... Νικίας τε ὁ Νικο-μήδους (cf. Köhler, *Ath. Mitth.* 1885, p. 234, 2), ζῷα ἄριστος γράψαι τῶν ἐφ' αὑτοῦ, Paus. i, 29, 15. The descrip-tion appears to be from the inscription on the grave.

15. **circumlitioni**: the process must be kept distinct from the γάνωσις or toning down of the whole statue (Vitr. vii, 9, 4); *circuml.* was admirably explained by Welcker (in Müller, *Handbuch*, p. 431), to consist in a painting of hair and accessories, intended to give *relief* to the statue— to be in a word identical with *circum-litio* as understood in painting,Quinct. viii, 5, 26 *nec pictura, in qua nihil circumlitum est eminet* (cf. *id.* xii, 9, 8). Since then, the discovery of the Sidonian sarkophagoi has revealed precisely such a use of colour for hair, dress, &c., as was divined by Welcker,

tribuebat. non satis discernitur alium eodem nomine an
134 hunc eundem quidam faciant olympiade CXII. Niciae
conparatur et aliquando praefertur Athenion Maronites
Glaucionis Corinthii discipulus, austerior colore et in auste-
ritate iucundior, ut in ipsa pictura eruditio eluceat. pinxit 5
in templo Eleusine Phylarchum et Athenis frequentiam
quam vocavere syngenicon, item Achillem virginis habitu
occultatum Ulixe deprendente, et in una tabula VI signa,
quaque maxime inclaruit agasonem cum equo. quod nisi
135 in iuventa obiisset, nemo compararetur. est nomen et 10
A.U.C. 586. Heraclidi Macedoni. initio naves pinxit, captoque Perseo
rege Athenas commigravit, ubi eodem tempore erat Metrodorus pictor idemque philosophus, in utraque scientia magnae
auctoritatis. itaque cum L. Paulus devicto Perseo petiisset
ab Atheniensibus uti sibi quam probatissimum philosophum 15
mitterent ad erudiendos liberos, item pictorem ad triumphum
excolendum, Athenienses Metrodorum elegerunt professi
eundem in utroque desiderio praestantissimum, quod ita

---

while flesh parts are seen to have been
left in the tone of the marble ; cf. the
Artemis of Vienna, *Jahrb. d. Oesterr.*
Kunstsamml. v, 1887, pl. i, ii, and
R. v. Schneider's remarks, *ib.* p. 22, on
the former colouring of the Hermes
of Praxiteles. See also Wickhoff, in
Wiener Genesis, p. 48.

1. **non satis discernitur**: above,
note on *discipulo Nicia.*

§ **134. 4. austerior**: i.e. *Nicia,*
cui comparabatur ; cf. above, note on
severus in § 130.

5. **eruditio** : cf. § 76 *omnibus*
litteris eruditus of Pamphilos.

pinxit . . . syngenicon : the two
pictures mentioned here belonging
to the class of votive offerings, and the
locality of each being specially noted,
B. Keil (*Hermes*, xxx, 1895, p. 229 ;
cf. Münzer, *ib.* p. 540) considers the
whole sentence to be an addition
to the main account from the work
of Heliodoros περὶ ἀναθημάτων, see
Introd. p. lxxiv f.

6. **Phylarchum** : Pausanias (i,

26, 3) mentions a cavalry captain
Olympiodoros (presumably identical
with the archon of Ol. 121, 3 = B.C.
294) in the time of Kassander (d. Ol.
121 = B.C. 296), who distinguished
himself in an engagement at Eleusis
against the Makedonians, and was
accordingly honoured with a portrait
there. He may quite well, therefore,
be identical with the Olympiodoros
painted by Athenion, a contemporary of the younger Nikias. For
lit. see Hitzig-Blümner, *Pausanias,*
p. 283.

7. **syngenicon** : the Greek word
introduced because P. is not quite
assured of his Latin equivalent ; for
the subject see note on *cognatio,* in
§ 76.

Achillem . . . deprendente: the
subject had been treated by Polygnotos in the Pinakotheke of the
Propylaia (Paus. i, 22, 6) and often.
We know it from a series of Pompeian
wall paintings, Helbig, *Wandgemälde,*
1296-1303 (the most famous, 1297, is

by some authorities in the hundred and twelfth Olympiad
[332-329 B. C.]. †*Athenion* of Maroneia, the pupil of Glaukion of **134**
Corinth, is compared with Nikias, and preferred to him by some. *Athenion,*
He used a severer scheme of colouring than Nikias, and pro- *pupil of*
duced a more pleasing effect withal, thus manifesting in his *Glaukion.*
execution his grasp of the abstract principles of his art. He
painted in the temple of Eleusis a captain of cavalry ; at Athens
an assembly called a συγγενικόν ; also Achilles, in the guise of
a maiden, at the moment of detection by Odysseus ; a picture
containing six figures, and the groom with a horse on which his
fame chiefly rests. Had he not died young, no artist would be
comparable to him.

†*Herakleides* of Makedon, who began life as a ship painter, also **135**
enjoys a great reputation. After King Perseus was taken prisoner, *Hera-*
he repaired to Athens, where was then living *Metrodoros,* who was *kleides.*
at once painter and philosopher, and had won high distinction **168 B.C.**
in either capacity. Accordingly, when Lucius Paulus after his *Metro-*
victories over Perseus asked the Athenians to send him their best *doros.*
philosopher to teach his children, and a painter to commemorate
his triumph, they chose Metrodoros, declaring that he could best
fulfil both requirements, as indeed Paulus found to be the case.

given in Roscher, i, p. 27), none of which however can be traced back with any certainty to Athenion ; cf. Helbig, *Untersuch.* p. 158. Addenda.

§ **135. 11. Heraclidi**: below, § 146.

captoque Perseo rege : Ol. 153, 1, Robert, *Arch. Märch.* p. 135, note, points out that the last date for a painter having been Ol. 121 (§ 134), there was precisely the same gap in the chronology of the painters as in that of the bronze sculptors (xxxiv, 52 *cessavit deinde ars* (Ol. 121) *ac rursus Ol.* 116 *revixit*). It is evident that the Greek sources ended for painting as for sculpture with approximately the same period, and that the additions concerning Herakleides and Metrodoros, both of whom are connected with Roman exploits, like the additions made in xxxiv, 52 to the Greek lists of the sculptors, are extraneous to the original history of art

forming the basis of the Plinian account, Introd. p. lxxx f.

12. **Metrodorus** : he is most likely identical with the Metrodoros in the Index to this book. Further he is possibly the same as the Metrodoros of Stratonikaia, mentioned by Diogenes Laertios x, 9, and Cic. *De Orat.* i, 11, 45, as being a pupil of Karneades (cf. Brunn, *K. G.* ii, p. 293; Urlichs, *Malerei,* p. 16 ; Helbig, *Untersuch.* p. 5).

16. **ad erudiendos liberos**: the two younger sons who died at the time of the triumph ; cf. the charming passage in Plutarch, *Aem. Paul.* vi Οὐ γὰρ μόνον γραμματικοὶ καὶ σοφισταὶ καὶ ῥήτορες, ἀλλὰ καὶ πλάσται καὶ ζωγράφοι καὶ πώλων καὶ σκυλάκων ἐπιστάται καὶ διδάσκαλοι θήρας Ἕλληνες ἦσαν περὶ τοὺς νεανίσκους (i. e. the elder sons, the younger Scipio and Fabius Maximus, after their father's triumph over the Ligurians, B.C. 181).

136 Paulus quoque iudicavit. Timomachus Byzantius Caesaris
dictatoris aetate Aiacem et Mediam pinxit ab eo in Veneris
Genetricis aede positas, LXXX talentis venundatas. talentum Atticum ✕ VI taxat M. Varro. Timomachi aeque
laudantur Orestes, Iphigenia in Tauris et Lecythion agili- 5
tatis exercitator, cognatio nobilium, palliati quos dicturos
pinxit, alterum stantem, alterum sedentem. praecipue
137 tamen ars ei favisse in Gorgone visa est. Pausiae filius et
discipulus Aristolaus e severissimis pictoribus fuit, cuius
sunt Epaminondas, Pericles, Media, Virtus, Theseus, imago 10
Atticae plebis, boum immolatio. sunt quibus et Nicophanes eiusdem Pausiae discipulus placeat diligentia quam

§ 136. 1. Timomachus Byz.
Caesaris ... aetate : from what we
know of the famous Aias and Medeia
(see following note), Pliny seems guilty
of an anachronism in placing Timomachos in this period (so Brunn,
Dilthey, Helbig, Urlichs and Furtwängler ; see Brandstätter, *Der Maler
Timomachos*, where all the evidence
concerning the artist's date is collected) ; he presumably found no date
in his author, and tried to obtain
one out of the purchase by Caesar
(Furtwängler, *Plinius*, p. 14), [*Caesaris dictatoris aetate* in imitation of
Magni Pompei aetate xx, 144 ; xxii,
128 ; xxvi, 12 ; xxxiii, 130, 156.—
H. L. U.]

2. Veneris G. aede : above, § 26
where see note.

Aiacem et Mediam : apparently
identical with the Aias and Medeia
mentioned by Cicero, *Verr.* II,
iv, 60, 135, where he enumerates
thirteen works of art, each of which
was the pride of the city that owned
it : *quid arbitramini merere velle
Cycicenos, ut Aiacem aut Mediam
amittant?* Now the Verrine orations
date from B. C. 70, and since the
pictures had then attained a world-
wide celebrity, similar to that enjoyed
by the Eros of Praxiteles, the heifer
of Myron, &c., we must suppose they

had been some time in existence ;
thus the latest date which could well
be assigned to the pictures would be
about 100-90 B. C., but this cannot be
called the ‚ ‘ age of Caesar.’ Indeed
since all the artists (i. e. Pythagoras,
Myron, the two Praxiteles, Protogenes
and Apelles) mentioned by Cicero are
of the fifth and fourth centuries, it
seems reasonable to suppose that
Timomachos also lived not later than
the fourth century. From the subjects
of his pictures he was probably a contemporary of Apelles (Brandstätter,
op. cit.). The two pictures were composed as pendants, at least so we
gather from the juxtaposition of the
subjects in Ovid, *Trist.* ii, 525 :
*Utque sedet vultu fassus Telamonius
iram
Inque oculis facinus barbara mater
habet.*
The composition has survived on a
number of gems (Berlin, Cat. 673,
674, 1357, 4319, 4327, 6491 ; Br.
Mus. Cat. 1426, 1427). Copies of
the Medeia have survived in two wall-
paintings (1) from Pompei, Helbig,
Wandgemälde, 1262, (2) from Herculaneum, Helbig, 1264 (single figure
of Medeia, but taken apparently
from a large composition similar
to the former) : Medeia meditating
the murder, while the children

Timomachos of Byzantion in the time of the dictator Caesar 136
painted the Aias and the Medeia, placed by Caesar in the temple *Timoma-*
of Venus the Mother, which cost eighty talents [£16,800 circ.]. *chos.*
(Marcus Varro values the Attic talent at 6000 denarii.) Other
pictures by Timomachos meet with a like praise ; his Orestes and
Iphigeneia among the Tauroi ; his portrait of Lekythion, a master
of gymnastics ; an assembly of notable persons, and two men in
cloaks just ready to speak, one standing, the other sitting. Art,
however, is thought to have granted to him his greatest success in
the Gorgon which he painted.

†*Aristolaos*, the son and pupil of Pausias, was an artist of the 137
severest school ; he painted pictures of Epameinondas, Perikles, *Aristolaos,*
Medeia, Valour, Theseus, a personification of the populace of *son and pupil of*
Athens, and a sacrifice of oxen. *Pausias.*

†*Nikophanes*, another pupil of Pausias, is admired by a small *Niko-*
phanes.

quietly play in charge of the paidagogos—a scheme which corresponds to Lucian's description περὶ οἴκου, 31. The picture was very probably inspired by the Medeia of Euripides. From § 145 we learn that it was left unfinished. The Medeia gave occasion for a number of epigrams (see Overbeck's *Schriftquellen* 2126–2139). *Anth. Plan.* iv, 137, shows that it was painted in encaustic—ἐν κηρῷ. (Against the view advanced here that Timomachos is a painter of the fourth century, see Robert, in *Arch. Märchen*, p. 132, who defends Pliny's *Caesaris aetate*, and lately Wickhoff, in *Wiener Genesis*, p. 72). Addenda.

5. Orestes, Iphigenia in Tauris: one picture, the two parts of which are given asyndetically, see J. Müller, *Stil*, p. 39 f. For the subject cf. the Pompeian wall-painting, *A. Z.* 1875, pl. xiii : on the right, above, Iphigenia with her maidens emerging from the temple, on the left, below, Orestes and Pylades brought prisoners to the temple ; as Robert points out (*ib.* p. 133 f.), there are no grounds for identifying the Pompeian picture as a copy of the original by Timomachos. See also the composition on the

sarkophagos, Robert, *Sarkoph. Reliefs* pl. lvii. Addenda.

agilitatis exercitator : he would be a less exalted personage than an ἐπιστάτης ἀθλητῶν (xxxiv, 82), but more on a level with the *praestigiator* Theodoros, and the *saltator* Alkisthenes in § 147. The picture was presumably a votive portrait.

6. cognatio nobilium : above, note on § 76.

palliati : i. e. wrapped in the *pallium* = ἱμάτιον, whence they were presumably portraits ; cf. on the *duo palliata* in xxxiv, 54.

quos dicturos : [cf. the Elder Philostratos εἰκόνες ii, 31 ὅρα καὶ τὸν Θεμιστοκλέα τὴν μὲν τοῦ προσώπου στάσιν παραπλήσιον τοῖς λέγουσιν. —H. L. U.] ; also Sittl, *Gebärde*, p. 7, note 5.

8. in Gorgone : i.e. a Gorgoneion or mask of Medusa ; we may compare in sculpture the 'Medusa Rondanini' (Munich, Glypt. 128).

§ 137. Pausiae : above, § 123. The account of Aristolaus has been torn asunder from its original context.

9. e severissimis : note on § 130.

11. boum immolatio : note on § 93 ; cf. § 127.

Nicophanes : above, § 111.

intellegant soli artifices, alias durus in coloribus et sile
multus ; nam Socrates iure omnibus placet ; tales sunt
eius cum Aesculapio filiae Hygia, Aegle, Panacea, Iaso et
piger qui appellatur Ocnos, spartum torquens quod asellus
138 adrodit. hactenus indicatis proceribus in utroque genere 5
non silebuntur et primis proximi : Aristoclides qui pinxit
aedem Apollinis Delphis. Antiphilus puero ignem conflante
laudatur ac pulchra alias domo splendescente ipsiusque pueri
ore, item lanificio in quo properant omnium mulierum
pensa, Ptolemaeo venante, sed nobilissimo Satyro cum pelle 10
pantherina, quem aposcopeuonta appellant. Aristophon
Ancaeo vulnerato ab apro cum socia doloris Astypale
numerosaque tabula in qua sunt Priamus, Helena, Credulitas,
139 Ulixes, Deiphobus, Dolus. Androbius pinxit Scyllum
ancoras praecidentem Persicae classis, Artemon Danaen 15

---

12. Ancaium (Angaium *e corr.*) vineratumo *Bamb.* ; Ancaeum vulneratum
Detlefsen.   Astypalaea *coni. Brunn K. G.* ii, p. 53, *Detlefsen.*

---

1. **soli artifices** : Münzer, *op. cit.*
p. 519, points out that this reference
to the opinion of artists recalls the
passage on Telephanes, xxxiv, 68.

durus in coloribus : § 130 *in
coloribus severus*, where see note.

2. **nam** : [elliptical, i. e. the case
of the painter Sokrates is different,
for *he* pleases everybody (*omnibus*),
whereas Nikophanes is only for the
few (*sunt quibus*) ; cf. the use of
nam in xxxiv, 7 ; x, 210 ; xvii, 58,
151.—H. L. U.]

Sokrates : he appears in such
close connexion with Aristolaos and
Nikophanes, that he is presumably also
a pupil of Pausias. In xxxvi, 32, Pliny
mentions a sculptor Sokrates, whom
he distinguishes from the painter,
though according to some authorities
they were identical.   Introd. p. l. f.

3. **Aesculapio** : i. e. a votive
picture for a recovery ; for the subject
cf. the reliefs, Friederichs-Wolters,
1148, 1150.

4. **Ocnos** : for the subject, which
had already been represented by
Polygnotos in the Delphian Lesche

(Paus. x, 29, 2), cf. the *puteal* in the
Vatican (Helbig, 373).

§ **138. 5. utroque genere** : i. e.
both large and small pictures.

7. **aedem Ap. Delphis** : nothing
further is known of these paintings.

Antiphilus : above, §§ 89, 114.

puero ign. confl. : for the same subject in statuary cf. the splanchnoptes
of Styppax, xxxiv, 81.

8. **domo splendescente** : for effects
of reflected light cf. above, note on
§ 78, and Wickhoff, *Wiener Genesis*,
p. 79.

9. **lanificio** : cf. the subjects of
Peiraïkos in § 112, of Philiskos in
§ 143.

10. **Ptolemaeo** : above, § 89.

11. **aposcopeuonta** : i. e. raising
his hand to shade his eyes in the
satyric dance called σκώπευμα (Athen.
xiv, p. 629 f.).   Variations of the
motive have been recovered in a number of statues and statuettes, which
can all be traced back to one original
type of which the finest instance is a
bronze at Berlin ; Furtwängler, *Satyr
aus Pergamon*, p. 14 ff.

circle for an industry which painters alone can really appreciate ; apart from this merit he was too harsh in colouring, and too lavish in his use of yellow ochre. The merit of †*Sokrates* on the other *Sokrates.* hand is, as it should be, patent to everybody, thanks to his pictures of Asklepios with his daughters Hygieia, Aigle, Panakeia and Iaso, and of a sluggard, called Ὄκνος [sloth], twisting a rope which an ass is gnawing.

So far I have spoken only of the leading artists in both styles, **138** but I do not purpose to omit those of the second rank.

Painters of second rank arranged alphabetically

†*Aristokleides* painted the temple of Apollo at Delphoi. *Anti-* *philos* is praised for his picture of a boy blowing a fire, and for the reflection cast by the fire on the room, which is in itself beautiful, and on the boy's face ; for his picture of wool-weaving, where all the women busily ply their tasks ; for his Ptolemaios hunting, and, most famous of all, for his Satyr with a panther's skin, called the ἀποσκοπεύων, or Gazer.

Aristo- *kleides.* *Antiphilos.*

Aristophon is celebrated for his Ankaios wounded by the boar, *Aristo-* grouped with Astypale, the partner of his woe, and a crowded *phon.* picture containing Priam, Helen, Credulity, Odysseus, Deiphobos and Guile. †*Androbios* painted Skyllos cutting the cables of the **139** Persian fleet ; †*Artemon* a Danae and the pirates marvelling at her ;

Aristophon : brother of Polygnotos, above, note on § 60.

12. Ancaeo : not the Arkadian Ankaios, but the Argonaut with his mother Astypale. Benndorf, *Gjölbaschi*, p. 114 f., inclines to believe the wounded hero was supported by his mother, a Polygnotan scheme, echoes of which seem to have survived on both the Phigaleian and Gjölbaschi friezes. The hero being a Samian, the picture was probably at Samos.

Astypale : [shortened for *Asty-* *palaia,* so Zeuxis commonly for Zeux-ippos ; cf. A. Fick, *Die Griechischen Personennamen,* 2nd. ed., p. 35. In Hyginus, *Fab.* 167 (ed. Bunte, 122, 1, 6), *Astyphile* is unnecessarily restored by Bunte to Astyphalaea.— H. L. U.] The reading *Astypale* is also kept by Benndorf (*op. cit.*).

13 numerosa : Brunn, *K. G.* ii, p. 53, explains this adjective applied to a picture which contained only six figures, from Quinct. v, 10, 10 *vulgoque* (*inter opifices*) *paullo numerosius opus dicitur argumentosum.*

Priamus . . . Dolus : from the presence of Helen and of Deiphobos it appears that the picture represented a scene from the siege of Troy subsequent to the death of Paris ; on the whole composition cf. Jahn, *A. Z.* 1847, p. 127. For the personifications of *Dolus* and *Credulitas* cf. the διαβολή in Apelles' picture (above, note on § 89).

§ 139. 14. Scyllum : he dived and cut the cables of the Persian fleet, Paus. x, 19, 1 ; cf. Herod. viii, 8.

15. D. mirantibus eam praedonibus : according to the legend, it was Dictys. a fisherman, who rescued Danae. There may have been a variant tradition or the *praedones* may come from misinterpretation of the picture. Helbig, *Untersuchungen,* p. 145, brings *Wandgemälde* 119 into connexion with the 'Danae.'

mirantibus eam praedonibus, reginam Stratonicen, Herculem
et Deianiram, nobilissimas autem, quae sunt in Octaviae
operibus, Herculem ab Oeta monte Doridos exusta mortali-
tate consensu deorum in caelum euntem, Laomedontis circa
Herculem et Neptunum historiam. Alcimachus Dioxip- 5
pum, qui pancratio Olympiae citra pulveris iactum, quod
140 vocant ἀκονιτί, vicit, Coenus stemmata. Ctesilochus Apellis
discipulus petulanti pictura innotuit, Iove Liberum parturi-
ente depicto mitrato et muliebriter ingemescente inter
opstetricia dearum, Cleon Cadmo, Ctesidemus Oechaliae 10
expugnatione, Laodamia, Ctesicles reginae Stratonices
iniuria. nullo enim honore exceptus ab ea pinxit volutan-
tem cum piscatore quem reginam amare sermo erat, eamque
tabulam in portu Ephesi proposuit ipse velis raptus. regina
tolli vetuit utriusque similitudine mire expressa. Cratinus 15
141 comoedos Athenis in Pompeio pinxit, Eutychides bigam,
regit Victoria. Eudorus scaena spectatur—idem et ex

---

1. **reginam Stratonicen**: there
were several queens of this name;
the most celebrated, who may be the
one intended here, was daughter of
Demetrios Poliorketes (Plut. *Dem.*
liii), married first to Seleukos Nikator,
then to his son Antiochos (Val. Max.
v, 7, *Ext.* 1); Introd. p. lx.

Herculem et Deianiram: this
and the following picture seem part
of a cycle representing the Labours of
Herakles. Addenda.

3. **Herculem . . . in caelum
euntem**: for the Apotheosis of
Herakles in later art see Furtwängler,
ap. Roscher, i, 2250.

5. **historiam**: probably in a series
of pictures. One scene, the freeing of
Hesione by Herakles, was also the
subject of a picture by Antiphilos
(above, § 114).

Dioxippum: he was in the army
of Alexander the Great, and in B.C.
326, during the Median campaign,
he overcame in an athletic contest
the Makedonian Koragos who had
challenged him. By this feat, however, he drew upon himself the dis-

pleasure of Alexander, and being
slandered to the king he finally took
his own life. Diod. xvii, 100–101;
Ailian, Ποικ. Ἱστ. x, 22 (see G. H.
Förster, *Sieger in den Olympischen
Spielen*, i, p. 27, 381), Ol. 113, 3 =
326 B.C.

6. **Olympiae**: instead of the usual
construction, *Olympia vincere*, imitated from the Greek.

7. ἀκονιτί = χωρὶς κόνεως: usually
because the appointed antagonist
failed to appear; according to Paus.
vi, 11, 4, Dromeus of Mantineia was
the first to gain a victory ἀκονιτί; cf.
id. vi, 7, 4; *I. G. B.* 29. See for
all possible conditions of such a
victory K. E. Heinrichs, *Ueber das
Pentathlon der Griechen* (Würzburg,
1892), p. 74. For the expression
sine pulvere, which was proverbial,
Otto, *Sprichwörter*, p. 290.

stemmata: portraits fitted into
some kind of genealogical tree (xxxv,
§ 6); cf. note on *cognatio*, in § 76.

§ 140. **Ctesilochus**: if identical, as is generally supposed with
the Κτησιόχος of Souidas (*s. v.*

a portrait of queen Stratonike ; a Herakles and Deianeira, and the celebrated pictures in the galleries of Octavia : the one represents Herakles on Mount Oite in Doris, putting off his mortality in the flames, and going up to heaven by consent of all the gods ; the other shows the story of Laomedon, Herakles and Poseidon. †*Alkimachos* painted a picture of Dioxippos, who won in the pankration at Olympia a victory without dust, ἀκονιτί, as it is called. †*Koinos* painted family trees. *Ktesilochos*, a pupil of Apelles, became famous by a burlesque painting of Zeus giving birth to Dionysos ; the god wears a head-dress and, moaning like a woman, is receiving the good offices of the goddesses. †*Kleon* owes his reputation to a picture of Kadmos, †*Ktesidemos* to a siege of Oichalia and a Laodameia, while †*Ktesikles* is best known by the affront he offered to queen Stratonike, who had received him without any mark of honour. He in consequence painted her lying in the arms of a fisherman, her reputed lover, and had the picture exhibited in the port of Ephesos, after he himself had sped away with all sails set. The queen, however, would not allow the picture to be removed, as both portraits were excellent likenesses. †*Kratinos* painted comic actors in the Pompeion at Athens, *Eutychides*, a two-horsed chariot driven by Nike. †*Eudoros*, who

Apelles), he was the brother of Apelles.

8. petulanti pictura : the picture was probably intended as a parody. Heydemann, *Hall. Winckelmannspr.* x (1885), p. 5 ff.

Iove . . . mitrato : an absurdity because, among Greeks at any rate, the μίτρα was only a feminine adornment ; above, § 58 *capita earum* (sc. *mulierum*) *mitris versicoloribus operuit ;* but vi, 162 *Arabes mitrati.*

9. inter opstet. dearum : i. e. the *Eileithyiai.*

10. Ctesidemus : the master of Antiphilos, above, § 114.

Oechaliae expugn. : by Herakles, Strabo, ix, p. 438.

11. Laodamia : the subject is of frequent occurrence (gem Br. Mus. Cat. p. 67, no. 327 ; numerous sarkophagi, cp. especially Baumeister, *Denkm.,* p. 1422, fig. 1574), but there is no ascertained copy of Ktesidemos's picture.

Stratonices iniuria : cf. on § 139.

15. Cratinus comoedus : I see no need for doubting his identity with the writer of comedies (fl. middle of fifth cent.). This first mention of Kratinos was detached from its context with Eirene, daughter of Kratinos (§ 147), in order to be introduced into the alphabetical list (see Münzer, *op. cit.* p. 535 ; Introd. p. lxv.).

16. in Pompeio : at the entrance to the Kerameikos, Paus. 1, 2, 4.

§ 141. Eutychides : in xxxiv, 78, he is mentioned as a sculptor in bronze.

bigam, regit Victoria : for the subject cf. Helbig, *Wandgemälde,* 938, 939.

17. scaena : i. e. a scenic decoration intended to be fastened to the *scaenae frons ;* cf. § 23.

et ex aere signa fecit : he is however not mentioned in xxxiv.

aere signa fecit—Hippys Neptuno et Victoria. Habron amicam et Concordiam pinxit et deorum simulacra, Leontiscus Aratum victorem cum tropaeo, psaltriam, Leon Sappho, Nearchus Venerem inter Gratias et Cupidines,
142 Herculem tristem insaniae poenitentia, Nealces Venerem— 5 ingeniosus et sollers iste, siquidem, cum proelium navale Persarum et Aegyptiorum pinxisset, quod in Nilo, cuius est aqua maris similis, factum volebat intellegi, argumento declaravit quod arte non poterat ; asellum enim bibentem
143 in litore pinxit et crocodilum insidiantem ei—Oenias 10 syngenicon, Philiscus officinam pictoris ignem conflante puero, Phalerion Scyllam, Simonides Agatharchum et Mnemosynen, Simus iuvenem requiescentem, officinam fullonis quinquatrus celebrantem, idemque Nemesim egreg-
144 iam, Theorus se inunguentem, idem ab Oreste matrem 15

15. se inunguentem] *Sillig*; emungentem *Bamb.*; et inungentem *Ricc.*; erumpentem *Detlefsen* (*coni. Benndorf*).

1. **Hippys**: the name has been conjecturally restored from Polemon, *ap.* Athen. xi, p. 474 d ; cf. above, note on *anus* in § 78.

2. **amicam**: simply the portrait of a *hetaira* (cf. Furtwängler, *Dornauszieher*, p. 94, n. 53). Some commentators, however, assume a misunderstanding on Pliny's part of the Greek φιλία, and suggest the reading *Amicitiam*, by analogy with *Concordia* = ὁμόνοια.

3 **Aratum ... tropaeo**: according to Hardouin (*ad loc.*), to commemorate the victory over Aristippos, Plut. *Aratus*, xxix ; the identification with the Sikyonian Aratos (frees Sikyon B.C. 251), however, seems doubtful, since none of the known painters in the list belong to so late a period ; below, note on *Nealces ;* cf. Brunn, *K. G.* ii, p. 292.

psaltriam : cf. xxxiv, 63 and note.

§ **142. 5. Herculem tristem** : i.e. after the murder of his children ; cf. in sculpture the kindred subject of Athamas, xxxiv, 140. A gem, which Stephani (*Ausruh. Her.* p. 145)

thought he could trace back to the picture of Nearchos, has been shown by Furtwängler (*ap.* Roscher, i, 2175) to be merely an adaptation by an artist of the Renascence of a type created for Aias (above, note on § 136).

Nealces: Münzer, *op. cit.* p. 532, note 2, rightly disputes his identity with the painter Nealkes, the friend of Aratos (Plut. *loc. cit.* xiii), since in that case Pasias, the pupil of Nealkes's own pupil Erigonos (§ 145), would belong to the late second century, outside the lower limit of the lists ; to this consideration may be added that the story recounted of Erigonos (*loc. cit.*) is closely connected with a number of other stories, which cannot have arisen later than the commencement of the third century. Münzer's discovery, however, with regard to the picture by Nealkes (note on *proelium*) at once settles the question in favour of an earlier painter of the name.

6. **ingeniosus**: cf. the praise bestowed upon Timanthes in § 73.

proelium ... asellum. Münzer

also made statues in bronze, is known by a scene painted for a theatre, *Hippys* by a Poseidon and a Nike, †*Habron* by a portrait of his mistress, a picture of Concord and figures of the Gods. †*Leontiskos* painted Aratos as victor with a trophy, and a woman playing on the cithara, †*Leon* a Sappho, †*Nearchos* an Aphrodite attended by the Graces and Loves, and a Herakles in grief repenting of his madness, †*Nealkes*, an Aphrodite. This Nealkes was a man of ingenious devices; he had painted a naval battle between the Egyptians and Persians, and wishing to show that it was fought on the Nile (the waters of which are like those of the sea) he indicated by a symbol that which art alone could not express, painting an ass drinking on the river's brim and a crocodile lying in wait for it. †*Oinias* painted a family gather-ing; †*Philiskos* an artist's studio with a boy blowing the fire; †*Phalerion* a Skylla; †*Simonides* an Agatharchos and Mnemo-syne; *Simos* a youth resting, the workshop of a fuller who is keeping the festival of Minerva, and a Nemesis of great beauty. †*Theoros* painted an athlete anointing himself, an Orestes slaying

142
Nealkes.

143

144
Theoros :
his picture

(*loc. cit.*) has had the signal merit of fixing the occasion for the picture and thereby the date of the artist. It must have referred to one of the battles by which Artaxerxes III Ochos, (B. C. 358–337), successively reduced Egypt in B. C. 350. 'Popular conceptions of the wicked enemy, of the ass-shaped Seth Typhon, had won for the hated king the nickname of the "Ass" among the Egyptians, while among the Greeks who fought in thousands on either side, the pun ὦχος—ὄνος had quickly spread (cf. Deinon, *ap.* Plut. *de Iside*, 31 διὸ καὶ τῶν Περσικῶν βασιλέων ἐχθραίνοντες μάλιστα τὸν Ὦχον ὡς ἐναγῆ καὶ μιαρόν, ὄνον ἐπωνόμασαν : Ailian, Ποικ. Ἰστ. iv, 8). The allusion which Neal-kes introduced into his picture was clear to his contemporaries and to the point; later its meaning was forgotten, and people had recourse to the silly explanation recorded by Pliny.'

§ 143. 11. **syngenicon**: above, § 136; cf. note on § 76.

ignem conflante puero. The studio must have been that of a

painter in encaustic; cf. the picture by Antiphilos, in § 138. Introd. p. lxxi.

12. **Scyllam**: uncertain whether the sea monster or the daughter of Nisos; cf. Brunn, *K. G.* 300; a Scylla by Nikomachos in § 109.

13. **Mnemosynen**: cf. the relief of Archelaos of Priene in Br. Mus.

Simus: possibly identical with the sculptor Simos of Salamis (in Kypros), known from two inscriptions (*I. G. B.* 163, 164), which from the character of the epigraphy may be dated about the third century B. C., Brunn, *K. G.* i, p. 467; H. v. Gaer-tringen, *Jahrb.* ix, 1894, p. 39.

iuvenem requiescentem : [per-haps a grave picture, in which the dead youth was represented lying down, i. e. an ἀναπαυόμενος (§ 99 and note), an *expirantis imago* (§ 90).—H. L. U.]

14. **quinquatrus** : the feast, which was of two kinds, the Greater and the Lesser, was kept by all those whose trades were under the special protec-tion of Minerva. Addenda.

§ 144. 15. **Theorus** : the name belongs to the class of those given,

et Aegisthum interfici, bellumque Iliacum pluribus tabulis,
quod est Romae in Philippi porticibus, et Cassandram, quae
est in Concordiae delubro, Leontium Epicuri cogitantem,
Demetrium regem, Theon Orestis insaniam, Thamyram
citharoedum, Tauriscus discobolum, Clytaemestram, Pani- 5
145 scon, Polynicen regnum repetentem et Capanea. non omit-
tetur inter hos insigne exemplum. namque Erigonus tritor
colorum Nealcae pictoris in tantum ipse profecit ut celebrem
etiam discipulum reliquerit Pasian, fratrem Aeginetae
pictoris. illud vero perquam rarum ac memoria dignum 10
est suprema opera artificum inperfectasque tabulas, sicut
Irim Aristidis, Tyndaridas Nicomachi, Mediam Timomachi
et quam diximus Venerem Apellis, in maiore admiratione
esse quam perfecta, quippe in is liniamenta reliqua ipsaeque
cogitationes artificum spectantur, atque in lenocinio com- 15
mendationis dolor est manus, cum id ageret, exstinctae.
146 sunt etiamnum non ignobiles quidem, in transcursu tamen

according to Fick (*Gr.Personennamen*,
p. 360), in allusion to the bearer's
profession (see, however, H.L.Urlichs'
note on *Euchira*, in § 152). That
there is not the slightest evidence for
following Brunn (*K. G.* ii, p. 255), in
charging Pliny with the fabrication of
Theorus out of a misunderstanding
of *Theon*, has been shown by Urlichs
in *Hölz. Pferd*, p. 18, n. 17.

se inungentem : votive portrait
of an athlete, represented in the
act of anointing himself, a subject
familiar in statuary, Furtwängler,
Masterpieces, p. 257 ff. ; against the
Benndorf-Detlefsen reading *erumpentem* see H. L. Urlichs, in *Woch. f.
Klass. Phil.* 1895, p. 548.

ab Oreste matrem et Aegis-
thum interfici : cf. the construction
in xxxiv, 59 (*fecit*) *Apollinem serpentemque eius sagittis configi.* For
the subject cf. the Pompeian picture,
A. Z. xli, 1883, pl. ix, 1 (Robert, *ib.*
p. 259), and the Sarkophagos in St.
Petersburg, Robert, *Sark. Rel.* pl. liv,
p. 166 f. Wickhoff, *Wiener Genesis,*
p. 85.

1. bellumque Iliacum pluribus
tabulis : probably one of the oldest
instances of a serial representation of
scenes from the Trojan war, such as
became so fashionable in imperial
days (cf. the *Troiae halosis*, Petron.
87, also the pictures of the Fall of
Troy, seen by Aineias in the Palace
of Dido, Virg. *Aen.* i, 456-493). From
Pompeii we have a series of pictures,
which, even if not close imitations of
the pictures by Theoros (see Helbig,
Untersuch. p. 142), serve to illustrate
how these cycles were conceived ; see
Brüning, *Jahrb.* ix, 1894, p. 164
(*Ueber die lildlichen Vorlagen der
Ilischen Tafeln*).

2. Philippi porticibus : note on
§ 66.

Cassandram : it may have been
part of the Trojan series (above), and
have become separated from it ; more
probably it was a picture by itself.

3. Leontium : note on § 99.

4. Demetrium : i.e. Poliorketes ;
cf. note on xxxiv, 42.

Theon : of Samos ; mentioned by
Quinct. xii, 10, 6, among the seven

his mother and Aigisthos, a cycle of pictures of the Trojan war, *of ' Orestes slaying his Mother.'*
now in Rome in the Gallery of Philip, a Kassandra, now in the
temple of Concord, Leontion, the pupil of Epikouros, in medita-
tion, and king Demetrios.   *Theon* painted the madness of Orestes, *Theon: his picture of the 'Madness of Orestes.'*
and a portrait of Thamyras, a player on the cithara; *Tauriskos*
painted the portrait of a quoit - thrower, a Klytaimnestra, a
Πανίσκος or young Pan, a Polyneikes claiming the throne, and
a Kapaneus.

Nor must I forget to mention here the noteworthy case of **145**
†*Erigonos*, who ground the colours of Nealkes, and eventually *Erigonos: his rise from obscurity to fame.*
became so good a painter that he could even train a great artist in
his pupil †*Pasias*, the brother of the painter †*Aiginetas*.   Another
most curious fact and worthy of record is, that the latest works of *Singular value and charm of unfinished works.*
artists and the pictures left unfinished at their death are valued
more than any of their finished paintings, for example the Iris by
Aristeides, the children of Tyndaros by Nikomachos, the Medeia
by Timomachos and the Aphrodite by Apelles, mentioned above.
The reason is that in these we see traces of the design and the
original conception of the artists, while sorrow for the hand that
perished at its work beguiles us into the bestowal of praise.

There still remain certain painters whom, though artists of **146**
repute, I can do no more than name in passing, †*Aristokydes*, *Second alphabetical list.*

---

most important painters of the age of
Alexander, as *praestantissimus . . .
concipiendis visionibus quas φαντασίας
vocant ;* cf. also Ailian, Ποικ. Ἱστ. ii.
44, where the warrior charging out of
a panel is described.

Orestis insaniam: τὴν Ὀρέστου
μητροκτονίαν, Plut. *de aud. Poet.* 3.

Thamyram citharoedum: cf. the
Gorgosthenes tragoedus, by Apelles,
in § 93, the *tibicina* of Lysippos, xxxiv,
63, the *psaltria* by Leontiskos, in
§ 141, &c.

5. Tauriscus: his identity with
one of the sculptors of the ' Farnese
Bull ' can neither be proved nor disproved.   He is perhaps the same as
the silver-chaser of xxxiii, 156, whom
in xxxvi, 33, Pliny is careful to distinguish from the sculptor.

discobolum: votive picture for
an athletic contest.

§ 145. 7. tritor colorum: cf.
above, § 85 *qui colores tererent ;* for
the story of Erigonos's rise from
poverty to fame, cf. Lysippos, xxxiv,
61, Protogenes, above, § 101, Introd.
p. xlix.

8. Nealcae: above, §§ 104, 142.

ut discipulum rel. : so likewise
Seilanion, xxxiv, 51, though himself
a self-taught artist, leaves a celebrated
pupil in Zeuxiades, Introd. *loc. cit.*

9. Aeginetae: for the ethnic as
proper name cf. Fick, *Gr. Personennamen,* p. 333.

12. Aristidis: above, §§ 75, 98,
108; for Nikomachos, § 108.

Mediam Timomachi: §§ 26, 136.

13. quam diximus: above, §§ 87,
91.

14. quippe . . . extinctae: rhetorical; for *liniamenta reliqua* cf. note
on § 68.

dicendi Aristocydes, Anaxander, Aristobulus Surus,
Arcesilas Tisicratis filius, Coroebus Nicomachi discipulus,
Charmantides Euphranoris, Dionysodorus Colophonius,
Dicaeogenes qui cum Demetrio rege vixit, Euthymides,
Heraclides Macedo, Milon Soleus Pyromachi statuari 5
discipuli, Mnasitheus Sicyonius, Mnasitimus Aristonidae
filius et discipulus, Nessus Habronis filius, Polemon
Alexandrinus, Theodorus Samius et Stadios Nicosthenis
147 discipuli, Xenon Neoclis discipulus Sicyonius. pinxere
et mulieres : Timarete Miconis filia Dianam quae in tabula 10
Ephesi est antiquissimae picturae, Irene Cratini pictoris filia
et discipula puellam quae est Eleusine, Calypso senem et
praestigiatorem Theodorum, Alcisthenen saltatorem, Aristarete Nearchi filia et discipula Aesculapium. Iaia Cyzicena
perpetua virgo M. Varronis iuventa Romae et penicillo 15
pinxit et cestro in ebore imagines mulierum maxime et
Neapoli anum in grandi tabula, suam quoque imaginem ad
148 speculum. nec ullius velocior in pictura manus fuit, artis
vero tantum ut multum manipretiis antecederet celeberrimos
eadem aetate imaginum pictores Sopolim et Dionysium, 20
quorum tabulae pinacothecas inplent. pinxit et quaedam
Olympias, de qua hoc solum memoratur, discipulum eius
fuisse Autobulum.

§ 146. 2. **Arcesilae** : from his
date he may be identical with the
Arkesilaos, Paus. i, 1, 3, whose picture
of Leosthenes and his sons (a συγγενικόν) was in the sanctuary of Athena
and Zeus in the Peiraieus. The exploits of Leosthenes, mentioned by
Pausanias, took place B.C. 323.

Tisicratis : pupil of Euthykrates
of Sikyon, xxxiv, 83.

Nicomachi : §§ 108, 145.

3. **Euphranoris** : § 128.

5. **Heraclides** : above, § 135.

Pyromachi : note on xxxiv, § 84.

6. **Mnasitheus** : the identification
with the Mnasitheos of Plut. *Arat.*
vii, suggested by Brunn, *K. G.* ii,
p. 292, is more than doubtful.

Mnasitimos : son of Aristonidas,
I. G. B. 197, above xxxiv, 140.

7. **Habronis** : above, §§ 93, 141.

8. **Theodorus Samius** : on the
different painters of this name see
Brunn, *K. G.* ii, p. 285 ; if the identity
of his fellow-pupil *Stadios* with the
sculptor Stadieus of Paus. vi, 4, 5,
the master of Polykles (note on xxxvi,
35), were certain, his date would be
towards Ol. 150 = B.C. 180.

§ 147. 10. **Timarete** : the account
of the women painters bears strong
traces of Duris ; cf. Münzer, *op. cit.*
p. 525 ; Introd. p. lxv. The names
are given in inverted alphabetical
order. In connexion with the lady
painters it is interesting to note the
charming Pompeian wall paintings,
Helbig, *Wandgemälde*, 1443, 1444 =
Blümner, *Techn.* iii, p. 226, iv, p. 460,
the first of a woman painting a statue,

171

†*Anaxander*, †*Aristoboulos* of Syria, *Arkesilas* the son of Teisikrates, †*Koroibos* the pupil of Nikomachos, †*Charmantides* the
pupil of Euphranor, †*Dionysodorus* of Kolophon, †*Dikaiogenes*
who lived at the court of king Demetrios, †*Euthymides*, †*Herakleides* of Makedon and †*Milon* of Soloi, both pupils of Pyromachos the statuary, †*Mnasitheus* of Sikyon, *Mnasitimos* the son
and pupil of Aristonidas, †*Nessos* the son of Habron, †*Polemon*
of Alexandria, *Theodoros* of Samos and *Stadios*, pupils of †Niko-
sthenes, and †*Xenon* of Sikyon, the pupil of Nealkes.

Women too have been painters: †*Timarete* the daughter of 147
Mikon, painted an Artemis at Ephesos in a picture of very archaic
style. *Eirene*, the daughter and pupil of the painter Kratinos,
painted a maiden at Eleusis, †*Kalypso* painted portraits of an old
man, of the juggler Theodoros, and of the dancer Alkisthenes;
†*Aristarete*, the daughter and pupil of Nearchos, painted an Asklepios. †*Iaia* of Kyzikos, who remained single all her life, worked
at Rome in the youth of Marcus Varro, both with the brush and
with the cestrum on ivory. She painted chiefly portraits of women,
and also a large picture of an old woman at Naples, and a portrait
of herself, executed with the help of a mirror. No artist worked 148
more rapidly than she did, and her pictures had such merit that
they sold for higher prices than those of †Sopolis and Dionysios,
well-known contemporary painters, whose works fill our galleries.
†*Olympias* also was a painter; of her we only know that †*Auto-
boulos* was her pupil.

Women painters. Timarete. Eirene. Kalypso. Aristarete. Iaia of Kyzikos. Olympias.

the second of a woman seated at her easel.

Miconis filia: § 59; Eirene and Aristarete likewise figure both as daughters and pupils; cf. Münzer, *loc. cit.*

11. **antiquiss. picturae:** the exact meaning is difficult to comprehend; Brunn suggests that she affected an archaicising style.

Irene: Εἰρήνην τὴν Κρατίνου θυγατέρα, Clemens Alex. (quoting from Didymos) *Strom.* iv, 124, p. 620, Pott; cf. § 140.

12. **puellam:** translation of the Greek κόρα, so first Raoul Rochette, *Peint. Inédites*, p. 222; cf. Brunn, *K. G.* ii, p. 299.

13. **praestigiatorem ... saltatorem:** chiastic order.

14. **Nearchi:** above, § 141.

Iaia Cyzicena: the alphabetical order is broken to insert a passage taken from Varro, Introd. p. lxxxiii.

16. **cestro in ebore:** i.e. in encaustic on ivory (below, § 149), as opposed to *penicillo* in the ordinary method of tempera.

17. **in grandi tabula:** on a wood panel of course, and presumably with the brush; cf. Blümner, *Technol.* iv, p. 445, note 1.

§ 148. 20. **Sopolim:** the name is still known only from Pliny, for in Cic. *ad. Att.* iv, 18, 4, it seems certain that *solidis pectoribus* is the reading, and not *e Sopolidis pictoribus* (see Baiter & Kayzer's critical apparatus).

Dionysium: § 113.

21. **inplent:** rhetorical, cf. xxxiv, 36, *replevit urbem.*

149   encausto pingendi duo fuere antiquitus genera, cera et in ebore cestro, id est vericulo, donec classes pingi coepere. hoc tertium accessit resolutis igni ceris penicillo utendi, quae pictura navibus nec sole nec sale ventisque corrumpitur.

5

§ 149. 1. **Encausto pingendi:** § 122. Owing to Pliny's obscure wording of the following passage the whole subject of ancient encaustic is beset with the gravest difficulties. For the literature up to 1887 see Blümner, *Technol.* iv, pp. 442 ff.; a good *résumé*, with new suggestions, by Cecil Smith, art. *Pictura,* in Smith's *Dict. of Ant.* ii, pp. 392 ff.; cf. also A. S. Murray, *Handbook,* pp. 394 ff.; a highly important contribution has lately been made by the painter Berger, *Beiträge zur Entwickelungsgeschichte der Malertechnik,* i, ii (1893 and 1895), who has succeeded in proving painting in encaustic to be a totally different process from the καῦσις of walls painted with an admixture of olive-oil and Punic wax (Plin. xxi, 83), described by Vitruvius (vii, 9). This discovery has freed the subject from some of its worst difficulties.

duo genera: (1) *cera et cestro* on the usual materials, i.e. wood. (2) *cera et cestro,* on ivory, a less common material, so that Pliny mentions it specially. Of the first method, the portraits from the Fayoum now afford numerous examples (see Berger, ii, pp. 50 ff.; Cecil Smith, *loc. cit.,* &c.). The second method remains obscure, but cf. the painted ivory fragments mentioned by Berger, i, p. 41 (in *Pal. Conserv.* at Rome) and the ivory panel in the British Museum with figure of a nymph, Murray, *Handbook,* p. 396, fig. 117. It is noteworthy that the lady painter Iaia (§ 147) is the only artist known to have employed this technique.

From the earliest times two methods of painting in encaustic 149 existed—one with wax, the other further on ivory—by means of *Painting in wax.* a cestrum or sharp point. When it became the fashion to paint ships of war, a third method was introduced, of melting the wax by fire and using a brush. Paint applied to ships in this way cannot be destroyed either by the action of the sun or of the brine or wind.

2. **cestro ... vericulo**: it is Berger's merit (*Beiträge*, i, p. 35 ff.) to have identified the *cestrum* among the instruments found in the grave of St. Médard (*ib.* figs. 2, 3; Blümner, *Technol.* iv, figs. 66, 67), and among the Naples bronzes (*Beitr.* i, p. 43 ff.). The one end is shaped like a spoon: with it the colours are held to melt over the *cauterium* or fire-pan (the misnamed *boîte à couleurs* of the St. Médard grave), and then poured over the panel; the long handle thickens at the upper end, which is used to level the colours.

donec classes pingi coepere: Berger, i, p. 38, explains the introduction of the brush for ship painting to have been necessitated by the impossibility of pouring fluid colour from the *cestrum* on to the *vertical* sides of a ship. This explanation seems correct, in so far at least as the meaning of the writer of the Plinian passage is concerned. It would be in the manner of certain ancient art-writers to imagine a conventional development of technique from cestrum to brush, and then to prove the point by appeal to practice.

3. **resolutis ceris**: i.e. in a separate, preliminary process, whereas in the first two methods the colours were both heated and applied by means of the cestrum.

II. PLASTICE.

151 DE pictura satis superque. contexuisse his et plasticen conveniat. eiusdem opere terrae fingere ex argilla simili-tudines Butades Sicyonius figulus primus invenit Corinthi filiae opera quae capta amore iuvenis, abeunte illo peregre, umbram ex facie eius ad lucernam in pariete lineis circum- 5 scripsit, quibus pater eius inpressa argilla typum fecit et cum ceteris fictilibus induratum igni proposuit, eumque

A.U.C. 608. servatum in Nymphaeo, donec Mummius Corinthum ever-
152 terit, tradunt. sunt qui in Samo primos omnium plasticen invenisse Rhoecum et Theodorum tradant multo ante 10

A.U.C. 97. Bacchiadas Corintho pulsos, Damaratum vero ex eadem urbe profugum, qui in Etruria Tarquinium regem populi Romani genuit, comitatos fictores Euchira, Diopum, Eugram-mum, ab iis Italiae traditam plasticen. Butadis inventum

§ **151. 2. eiusdem opere terrae:** with these words Pliny harks back to his main theme in § 1 (*Restant terrae ipsius genera lapidumque*) of which the History of the Painters has been but an episode ; so again in § 166 he begins *Verum et ipsius terrae;* see Fröhner, in *Rhein. Mus.* 47, 1892, p. 294.

2. similitudines primus inve-nit: Boutades ' invents' (1) faces in relief, (2) faces applied as tile-ends, (3) how to take the cast of the model for a statue, whereas Lysistratos (4) shows, finally, how to take the cast from a living model. The whole de-velopment has a strong Xenokratic tinge ; see Introd. p. xxxiv. f.

3. Butades Sicyonius: the fol-lowing anecdote is told with slight variations by Athenagoras, Πρεσβεία,

17 ed. Schwartz, p. 18 (see App. xi).

Corinthi: cf. § 16 ; Corinth and Sikyon now appear as the cradles of the art of modelling. As Cecil Smith points out (*Pictura*, p. 401), the legend that the Sikyonian Bou-tades worked at Corinth, suggests an attempt to compromise the rival claims of both cities to artistic priority.

4. abeunte illo peregre: accord-ing to Athenagoras, the youth was not going away, but asleep.

8. donec Mummius Corinthum: the sack of Corinth in B.C. 146 had evidently become a conventional date with which to connect the disappear-ance or destruction of works of art in Greece.

9. sunt qui: introduces paren-thetically a variant version of the origin of πλαστική ; from the mention

II. MODELLING.

Of painting I have said enough and more than enough, but it may be well to add some account of clay modelling. It was by the service of the selfsame earth that †*Boutades*, a potter of Sikyon, discovered, with the help of his daughter, how to model portraits in clay. She was in love with a youth, and when he was leaving the country she traced the outline of the shadow which his face cast on the wall by lamplight. Her father filled in the outline with clay and made a model ; this he dried and baked with the rest of his pottery, and we hear that it was preserved in the temple of the Nymphs, until Mummius overthrew Corinth. According to some authorities clay modelling was first introduced in Samos by *Rhoikos* and *Theodoros*, long before the expulsion of the Bacchiadai from Corinth, and when Damaratos fled from that city to Etruria, where his son Tarquinius, afterwards king of Rome, was born, he was accompanied by three potters, *Eucheir*, †*Diopos*, and †*Eugrammos*, who introduced the art of modelling into Italy. Boutades first added red ochre or modelled in red clay, and

151
Boutades of Sikyon discovers modelling in clay.

146 B.C.

152
Rhoikos and Theodoros of Samos.
657 B.C.
(Grote)
Greek potters follow Damaratos to Etruria.

of the followers of Damaratos this alternative account seems taken from Cornelius Nepos (above, § 17, Introd. p. lxxxv). The subject of Boutades is resumed below at *Boutadis inventum*, and again at *idem et de signis*.

10. **Rhoecum et Theodorum** : xxxiv, 83.

11. **Damaratum** ; above. § 16.

13. **fictores** : πλάσται, *fingere* like πλάσσω being used of the artist who works in soft substances such as earth or wax, also who fashions by the hand (cf. the *fingitque premendo* of Vergil, *Aen.* vi, 80) ; see on xxxiv, 7, and below, on § 153.

Euchira . . . Eugrammum : respectively the skilled handicraftsman

(εὔχειρ), and the skilled draughtsman (εὔγραμμος), while Diopus = δίοπος is connected with διόπτης or διόπτρα, an instrument for taking levels,' the invention of which (vii, 198) is attributed by Pliny to Theodoros, Urlichs, *Chrestom.* p. 373. [A. Fick, *Die Griechischen Personennamen*, 2nd ed. p. 254, believes these names to be given with regard to the bearer's trade or occupation, and in many cases to have supplanted the real name (cf. note on *Theorus*, in § 144). They seem to me more likely to have been favourite names in artist families, and to have been given at birth.— H. L. U.] For Eucheiros see Comm. on p. 220.

est rubricam addere aut ex rubra creta fingere, primusque
personas tegularum extremis imbricibus inposuit, quae inter
initia prostypa vocavit, postea idem ectypa fecit.   hinc et
fastigia templorum orta.   propter hunc plastae appellati.

153   Hominis autem imaginem gypso e facie ipsa primus 5
omnium expressit ceraque in eam formam gypsi infusa
emendare instituit Lysistratus Sicyonius, frater Lysippi de
quo diximus.   hic et similitudines reddere instituit, ante
eum quam pulcherrimas facere studebatur.   idem et de
signis effigies exprimere invenit, crevitque res in tantum ut 10
nulla signa statuaeve sine argilla fierent.   quo apparet antiquiorem hanc fuisse scientiam quam fundendi aeris.

154   Plastae laudatissimi fuere Damophilus et Gorgasus, idem
pictores, qui Cereris aedem Romae ad circum maximum

2. personas tegularum: numbers
of these tile-faces from Etruria are to
be seen in almost every Museum ; cf.
also the terra-cotta fragments from
the treasuries at Olympia (*Olympia* ii,
Baudenkmäler, taf. cxx).

4. fastigia : in Pliny used as a rule
of the figures of the akroteria, and
not of the actual pedimental figures,
cf. xxxvi, 13 ; xxviii, 16 ; xxxvii, 14 ;
xxxvi, 6, &c., below § 157 ; this meaning is borne out (1) by Vitruv. iii, 3,
5 *ornantque signis fictilibus aut
aereis inauratis earum fastigia Tusca-
nico more, uti est ad Circum maximum
Cereris, et Herculis Pompeiani, item
Capitolii*, (2) by Cicero, *de Divin.* i,
10, 16 *cum Summanus in fastigio
Iovis opt. max.*, *qui tum erat fictilis,
e caelo ictus esset, etc.*, (3) by Festus,
s.v. *Ratumena*.   Further, in Plut.
Caesar lxiii, ἀκρωτήριον corresponds to
the *fastigium* of Suet. *Jul.* 81 ; see
Furtwängler, *A. Z.* 1882, p. 346;
Fowler in *Amer. Journ. of Archaeol.*
viii, 1893, p. 385.

orta : because the figured akroteria
arose out of the earlier tile-faces.

§ 153. 5. Hominis . . . studebatur : the proper place for the 'invention' of Lysistratos is after the third
invention of Boutades, below (B. dis-

covered how to make models of
statues; Lysistratos, however (*autem*),
found out how to take casts of living
people, see note on § 151).   The displacement arose, doubtless, from confusion of notes ; it may be due to Pliny
himself, or to his nephew when he prepared the last books of the *Hist. Nat.*
for publication ; cf. Brunn, *K. G.* i,
p. 403, Furtwängler, *Plinius*, p. 59 f.,
Münzer, *op. cit.* p. 510.

e facie ipsa : i.e. from the living
model ; the invention attributed to
Lysistratos has nothing whatever to
do with the custom of taking masks
from the face of the dead.

8. ante eum q. pulcherrimas :
the observation is correct ; by the time
of Lysippos realistic portraiture had,
if not superseded ideal or typical representation, yet asserted its right to
co-existence. It was, in a word, the age
when an athlete could be idealized as
the '*Apoxyomenos*,' or portrayed with
the brutal realism of the bronze boxer
from Olympia (*Olympia* iv, *Bronzen*,
taf. ii), cf. the note on xxxiv, 16.

9. idem et : refers back to Boutades.

11. sine argilla : Pliny means that
to make a bronze statue without a clay
model is impossible, though he—or

placed masks as tile-fronts on the eaves of buildings, originally called πρόστυπα, or low reliefs; later on he made ἔκτυπα, or high reliefs, and these led to the ornamentation of the gables of temples. Since the time of Boutades artists who worked in clay have been called modellers. (*Lysistratos* of Sikyon, brother of the Lysippos whom I have mentioned in an earlier book, was however the first who obtained portraits by making a plaster mould on the actual features, and introduced the practice of taking from the plaster a wax cast on which he made the final corrections. He also first rendered likenesses with exactitude, for previous artists had only tried to make them as beautiful as possible.) The said Boutades discovered how to take casts from statues, a practice which was extended to such a degree that no figure or statue was made without a clay model. Hence it is clear that the art of clay modelling is older than that of bronze casting.

Most highly praised among modellers were †*Damophilos* and †*Gorgasos;* they were also painters, and united both arts in the decorations of the temple of Ceres at Rome near the Great

153
Lysistratos of Sikyon takes casts from the living face.

Boutades makes clay models for statues.

154
Damophilos and Gorgasos decorate the Temple of Ceres.

---

his author—have used an ambiguous expression, which might imply that there had been previous bronze statues, but made without a clay model, cf. Furtwängler, *Plinius*, p. 60. The use of clay models for marble statues seems to have been of altogether later date, cf. § 155.

antiquiorem: so in xxxiv, 35, *prior* (sc. *plastice*) *quam statuaria fuit.*

§ 154. 13. Damophilus: [although Damophilos is the Doric form of Demophilos, and both represent the same name, it is yet impossible to deduce from this fact the identity of the Damophilus mentioned here with the *Demophilus Himeraeus* who appears in § 61, the master of Zeuxis. Himera was an Ionic city, and it is out of the question that one of its citizens should ever have called himself by a Doric form of his name. Yet we cannot on the other hand doubt the form *Damophilus* given here by Pliny; for he evidently had it from an authority who was familiar with the actual in-

scription (*versibus inscriptis Graece*) Thus if we get rid of the false assumption that this Damophilus could be identical with the master of Zeuxis, we get rid of all the far-fetched combinations necessary to reconcile the date of D. of Himera (whose pupil Zeuxis fl. about B.C. 404) with the date of the temple of Ceres, B.C. 493. —H. L. U.]. The difficulty of reconciling *Demophilus* and *Damophilus* has been perceived by Freeman, *Hist. of Sicily*, ii, p. 411 : 'It is a little startling to hear that the master of Zeuxis, with his colleague Gorgasos, painted the Roman temple which was vowed by Aulus Postumius, victor at Regillus.' Freeman, however, inclines to a conciliation: 'Chronology may be appeased by the easy conjecture that the painting of the temple, and the Greek letters which recorded the names of the artists, came a generation or two later than the temple itself.'

14. Cereris aedem: note on xxxiv, 15, and the passage from Vitruvius quoted above under *fastigia*.

utroque genere artis suae excoluerant versibus inscriptis
Graece quibus significarent ab dextra opera Damophili esse,
ab laeva Gorgasi.   ante hanc aedem Tuscanica omnia in
aedibus fuisse auctor est Varro, et ex hac, cum reficeretur,
crustas parietum excisas tabulis marginatis inclusas esse, 5
155 item signa ex fastigiis dispersa.   fecit et Chalcosthenes
cruda opera Athenis, qui locus ab officina eius Ceramicos
appellatur.   M. Varro tradit sibi cognitum Romae Possim
nomine, a quo facta poma et uvas alitem nescisse aspectu
discernere a veris.   idem magnificat Arcesilaum, L. Luculli 10
familiarem, cuius proplasmata pluris venire solita artificibus
156 ipsis quam aliorum opera; ab hoc factam Venerem Genetricem in foro Caesaris et prius quam absolveretur festina-
tione dedicandi positam, eidem a Lucullo HS. |X̄| signum
Felicitatis locatum, cui mors utriusque inviderit; Octavio 15

9. alitem nescisse] *Traube*; item piscis (pisces, *Bamb.*) *codd.*; item pisces
non possis *Jan, Detlefsen.*

1. **utroque genere artis** : i.e. the
decorations consisted of painted terra-
cottas; fine examples (from T. of
Jupiter Capitolinus?) exist at Rome
in Pal. Conserv., Helbig, i, p. 447 f.

2. **ab dextra . . . ab laeva** : cf. the
similar inscription, *Anth. Pal.* ix, 758 :
Κίμων ἔγραψε τὴν θύραν τὴν δεξιάν,
τὴν δ' ἐξιόντων δεξιὰν Διονύσιος.

4. **cum reficeretur** : after the fire
of B.C. 31; restored by Augustus, B.C.
27, re-dedicated B.C. 17 (Tac. *Ann.*
ii, 49).

5. **crustas** : for reliefs cf. xxxiii,
157, *crustarius.*

excisas : cf. Vitruv. ii, 8, 9, a
typical instance of the care taken in
the first century B.C. to preserve
archaic works.

tabulis marginatis : below, §
173.

6. **ex fastigiis** : above, note on
§ 152.

§ **155. Chalcosthenes** : more
correctly *Kaïkosthenes ;* see on xxxiv,
87. From a basis (Δελτίον, 1891,
p. 25 f. and p. 84) found in the actual
Kerameikos, we learn that K. was

of the deme Thria. Lolling (*loc.
cit.*) dates the inscr. towards the close
of the third century B.C.

7. **cruda opera** : these have been
identified by Milchhöfer (*Arch. Studien,
H. Brunn dargebr.* 1893, p. 50 ff.)
with the ἀγάλματα ἐκ πηλοῦ, representing Dionysos feasting in the house of
Amphiktyon, which adorned a chapel
—οἴκημα—of the god's τέμενος, in the
Kerameikos (Paus. i, 2, 5); the monument was presumably the votive offering of a guild of Dionysiac artists.
The Italian work of the Della Robbias
may help us to a notion of what the
group or relief looked like.

8. **appellatur** : the etymological
attempt suggests Varronian authorship; cf. note on xxxiv, 11, on xxxvi,
14 (*lychniten*).

9. **poma et uvas** : cf. the excellent
carvings of fruit, leaves and flowers on
a relief of the Museo d. Terme, Wickhoff,
Wiener Genesis, p. 22, figs. 7, 8, 9,
10, and the beautiful garlands of fruit
and flowers that adorned the *Ara
Pacis* of Augustus.

alitem nescisse : cf., in con-

Circus, placing on it a metrical inscription in Greek to say that on the right hand were the works of Damophilos, on the left the works of Gorgasos. Varro tells us that in all earlier temples decorations in the Etruscan style only were to be found, and that when this temple was restored the ornamentation of the walls was cut out and framed, and the statues that crowned the roof were dispersed.

Chalkosthenes also modelled in unbaked clay in the Potter's 155 Quarter at Athens, so called after his workshop. Marcus Varro *Chalko-sthenes.* says that at Rome a man named +*Possis* was known to him who *Possis.* made clay apples and grapes which the very birds could not distinguish from nature. He also praises +*Arkesilaos*, the friend *Arkesilaos.* of Lucius Lucullus, for whose clay models artists would pay more *Value of his clay* than was given for the finished works of others ; he made the *models.* statue of Venus the Mother in the forum of Caesar, which was 156 set up before it was really finished, so eager were his patrons to dedicate it. He also accepted a commission from Lucullus to make a statue of Good Fortune for 1,000,000 sesterces [£8750 circ.]. Death, however, cut them both off before the statue was completed. Arkesilaos also made a plaster model for a talent [£210 circ.] for a Roman knight named Octavius, who proposed

firmation of Traube's reading, above, §§ 23, 65, 66.

10. idem magnificat: cf. in xxxvi, 41 *Arcesilaum quoque magnificat Varro*, hence the identity of authorship for both passages.

Arcesilaum : for his marble works see xxxvi, 33, 41 ; his *Venus Genitrix* and his *Felicitas* are mentioned here because they apparently remained at the stage of clay models.

L. Luculli familiarem : Urlichs (*Arkesilaos*, p. 4) suggests that Lucullus brought back Arkesilaos with him from Athens when he visited that city in B.C. 88–7, cf. above, § 125.

11. proplasmata: see the excellent remarks of Wickhoff, *Wiener Genesis*, p. 25 f. and p. 41, on the extensive use of the clay model in the first century B.C., and its influence on the technique of marble ; cf. above, on § 153.

§ 156. 12. Venerem Genetricem: from the Roman coins which most probably reproduce the statue, it appears that the *Genetrix* of Arkesilaos was adapted from a Greek statuary type which recent criticism has traced back to the 'Aphrodite in the gardens' of Alkamenes (note on xxxvi, 16) ; cf. Furtwängler, *ap.* Roscher i, p. 413.

14. signum Felicitatis : the temple of *Felicitas* had been built by C. Licinius Lucullus, xxxiv, 69; xxxvi, 39.

15. mors utriusque : Marcus Lucullus died B.C. 58, and his brother only survived him a short time (Plut. *Luc.* xliii); hence since Arkesilaos was still at work for Caesar in B.C. 46 (below), we must either imagine that he left an order of his patron unattended to for fifteen years, or follow Urlichs (*op. cit.* p. 5), in supposing that it is the young Lucullus (*clarissimus adulescens*, Cic. *Phil.* x, 48), whose death (at Philippi in B.C. 42) is alluded to here. From

equiti Romano cratera facere volenti exemplar e gypso
factum talento. laudat et Pasitelen qui plasticen matrem
caelaturae et statuariae scalpturaeque dixit et, cum esset in
omnibus his summus, nihil umquam fecit antequam finxit.
157 praeterea elaboratam hanc artem Italiae et maxime Etru- 5
riae, Vulcam Veis accitum cui locaret Tarquinius Priscus
Iovis effigiem Capitolio dicandam, fictilem eum fuisse et
ideo miniari solitum, fictiles in fastigio templi eius quadrigas,
de quibus saepe diximus, ab hoc eodem factum Herculem
qui hodieque materiae nomen in urbe retinet. hae enim 10
tum effigies deorum erant lautissimae, nec poenitet nos
illorum qui tales deos coluere, aurum enim et argentum ne
158 diis quidem conficiebant. durant etiamnum plerisque in
locis talia simulacra. fastigia quidem templorum etiam
in urbe crebra et municipiis, mira caelatura et arte suique 15
firmitate, sanctiora auro, certe innocentiora.

xxxiv, 93 (where see note) we learn
that he rededicated a statue of
Herakles originally set up by his
father; it is therefore not surprising
to find him commissioning Arkesilaos,
an old friend of his family, with
a statue for the temple built by his
grandfather.

Octavio equiti : according to Urlichs, *Arkesilaos*, p. 17, perhaps identical with the upstart (*terrae filius*) who
pestered Cicero with invitations to
dinner, Cic. *Fam.* vii, 9, 16.

2. Pasitelen : xxxiii, 156; xxxvi,
40.

3. scalpturae : here = *sculptura*
[so also Plin. the Y. *Ep.* i, 10, has
scalptor for *sculptor*.—H. L. U.]; the
term is generally used of the graver's
art, as an equivalent of the Greek
γλυπτική.

§ 157. 5. maxime Etruriae : the
remark is fully confirmed by the
splendid remains of large terra-cotta
figures, discovered in Italy; cf.
especially the pedimental figures from

the temple at Luni, Milani, *Mus. d.
Ant. Classica*, i, 1884, pp. 89-112;
where see further literature.

7. Iovis effigiem . . . fictilem :
cf. Juv. xi, 115 *fictilis et nullo vio-
latus Iupiter auro*. From Servius'
(on *Eclog.* x, 27) description of the
Roman *triumphatores*, who were
adorned *Iovis optimi maximi ornatu*
we learn that the god was represented
standing with the thunderbolt in his
right (cf. Ovid *Fast.* i, 202 *inque
Iovis dextra fictile fulmen erat*) and
the sceptre in his left. This ancient
image was destroyed B.C. 83, in the
fire which laid the temple in ashes.
It was replaced by a gold-ivory
Jupiter—the work of an Apollonios
—after the model of the Olympian
Zeus of Pheidias (cf. Chalcidius on
Plato's *Timaios*, 338 C, p. 361, ed.
Wrobel, and Loewy on *I. G. B.* 343,
p. 242).

Capitolio : note on xxxiv, 38.

8. miniari solitum : *enumerat
auctores Verrius quibus credere ne-*

to have a goblet cast from it. Varro further praises *Pasiteles, Pasiteles.* who said that modelling was the mother of chasing, statuary and *He pronounces* sculpture, and who, though he excelled in all these arts, never *upon the* executed any work without first making a clay model. The art *157 value of* of modelling, again, according to Varro, was developed in Italy, *the clay* and more especially in Etruria, and Tarquin the Ancient summoned *model.* an artist called †Vulca from Veii to make a statue of Jupiter for the Capitol. This statue was of clay and was therefore painted red ; the four-horse chariots on the gables of the temple, which I have mentioned so often, were also of clay. Vulca further made the Hercules still known at Rome as ' the clay Hercules.' These were the most magnificent statues known in those days, and we have no reason to be ashamed of the men who worshipped deities of clay, and would not, even for their gods, change gold and silver into images. Effigies of clay still exist in different *158* places, while gable ornaments in clay are still to be seen even at Rome as well as in provincial towns. The admirable execution *Beauty and* of these figures, their artistic merits and their durability make *simplicity of the* them more worthy of honour than gold, and they are at any rate *ancient clay* more innocent. *images.*

---

cesse sit Iovis ipsius simulacri faciem diebus festis minio inlini solitam . . . Plin. xxxiii, 111 ; see also Servius on *Ecl.* vi, 62 ; x, 27 ; cf. in Greece the painting with white, at her festival, of the image of Athena Skirrophoria.

fictiles . . . quadrigas : also the work of Veientine artists, Plut. *Poplic.* xiii ἅρμα κατὰ κορυφὴν (sc. νεὼ τοῦ Καπ. Δι.) ἐπιστῆσαι κεραμεοῦν ἐξέδωκε (sc. ὁ Ταρκονίνιος) Τυρρηνοῖς τισιν ἐξ Οὐηίων δημιουργοῖς. These are the chariots whose miraculous swelling in the potter's furnace was interpreted as an omen of the future greatness of Rome (Plin. xxviii, 16 *cum in fastigium eiusdem delubri* (Jup. Cap.) *praeparatae quadrigae fictiles in fornace crevissent*). These chariots were replaced in B.C. 296 by a *Iovem in culmine cum quadrigis,* apparently of bronze (Liv. x, 23, 12). The roof of the temple of the Tarquins

was richly adorned with painted decorations ; cf. Cic. *de Div.* i, 10, 16 ; Liv. *per.* 14 ; and see note on § 154 for possible remains of these decorations.

9. **saepe diximus :** viii, 161 ; xxviii, 16.

Herculem : often identified (but on the very slightest grounds) with the *Hercules fictilis* of Martial xiv, 178.

10. **hae enim tum effigies :** this rhetorical tribute to the simplicity of the ancient Roman images was as old as —Cato, or as Cato reported by Livy (xxxiv, 4, 4) *infesta, mihi credite, signa ab Syracusis illata sunt huic urbi. iam nimis multos audio Corinthi et Athenarum ornamenta laudantis mirantisque et antefixa fictilia deorum Romanorum ridentis. ego hos malo propitios deos et ita spero futuros, si in suis manere sedibus patiemur.*

C. PLINII SECUNDI

NATURALIS HISTORIAE

LIBER XXXVI, §§ 9-44

(*SCULPTURA*)

SCULPTURA.

9   MARMORE scalpendo primi omnium inclaruerunt Dipoenus et Scyllis geniti in Creta insula etiamnum Medis imperantibus priusque quam Cyrus in Persis regnare inciperet, hoc est olympiade circiter quinquagensima. hi Sicyonem se contulere, quae diu fuit officinarum omnium talium patria. 5 deorum simulacra publice locaverant iis Sicyoni, quae prius quam absolverentur artifices iniuriam questi abiere in 10 Aetolos. protinus Sicyonem fames invasit ac sterilitas maerorque dirus. remedium petentibus Apollo Pythius respondit: si Dipoenus et Scyllis deorum simulacra per- 10 fecissent, quod magnis mercedibus obsequiisque impetratum

5. talium] metallum *omnes praeter Bamb.*

§ 9.1. **Marmore scalpendo**: with the exception of the ἄγαλμα of the Lindian Athena ἐκ λίθου σμαράγδου, mentioned on the doubtful authority of George Kedrenos (Overbeck, *Schriftqu.* 327; cf. Brunn, *K. G.* i, p. 44), Dip. and Skyllis seem only to have made wooden images, Paus. ii, 15, 1; 22, 5; Clement of Alex. προτρεπτ. λόγ. iv, p. 42; the gilt bronze images mentioned by Moses of Chorene (*Schriftqu.* 326) were more probably of gilt wood. It is evident that in the original Greek authority (Xenokrates from the character of the passage and the stress laid on Sikyon; see Introd. p. xxv) these artists had been discussed in connexion with the beginnings of bronze statuary; Münzer, *Hermes*, xxx, 1895, p. 523; cf. Robert, *Arch. Märch.* p. 22.

2. **geniti in Creta**: contains a trace of the legend preserved in Paus. ii, 15, 1, that they were the sons of the Athenian Daidalos and a woman of Gortyn. By representing artists born in Crete as active in Sikyon, a similar compromise between the rival claims of ancient art centres is effected to that noted in the case of Boutades, xxxv, 151; cf. Münzer, *loc. cit.*

Medis imperantibus; the Armenian historian Moses of Chorene recounts that Ardashir (= Kyros) took away from Kroisos three statues of Artemis, Herakles and Apollo by Dipoinos and Skyllis. The date assigned to the artists seems calculated with reference to this event as follows: Kyros could take away works by D. and S. at the time of his

SCULPTURE IN MARBLE.

As sculptors in marble, the first to win fame were *Dipoinos* and *Skyllis*, born before the fall of the Median empire, and before Cyrus began to reign in Persia, that is about the fiftieth Olympiad [580-577 B.C.], in the island of Crete. They migrated to Sikyon, which was long the home of all such crafts. The state of Sikyon gave them a commission for certain images of the gods, but before these were completed the artists, aggrieved at the treatment they met with, departed into Aitolia. Sikyon soon 10 afterwards was visited by famine, failure of the crops and dire affliction. The inhabitants sought relief from the Pythian Apollo, and received the answer that the evil would cease when Dipoinos and Skyllis should complete their statues of the gods, a concession which was hardly won from them by money and by personal defer-

conquest of Kroisos (B. C. 546), therefore the artists must have been of repute even before the accession of Kyros (B.C. 556), Robert, *op. cit.* p. 18 f.

4. **circiter**: cf. xxxiv, 49 : *circiter CCC urbis nostrae annum.*

Sicyonem ... patria: cf. xxxv, 127 *diuque* (Sikyon) *illa fuit patria picturae.*

6. **prius quam absolv.** : the following anecdote, whose artificial character is obvious, has been shown by Petersen, *de Cerere Phigalensi,* p. 13 ff., to be a mere adaptation of the local myth recorded Paus. ii, 7, 7.

7. **iniuriam questi**: γενομένου δέ σφισι (Apollo and Artemis) δείματος ... οἱ μὲν ἐς Κρήτην ... ἀπετράποντο, Paus. *loc. cit.*

in **Aetolos**: named by the legend as the artists' place of refuge because there existed in that region works by D. and S., i. e. at Ambrakia (§ 14), which, though not in Aitolia, was towards the close of the third century the most prominent city of the Aitolian league. A Greek writer of that date (Antigonos? cf. Introd. p. xxxvii) might say indifferently εἰς Ἀμβρακίαν or εἰς Αἰτωλούς; Münzer, *op. cit.* p. 524.

§ 10. 8. **protinus ... dirus**: τοὺς δὲ ἀνθρώπους ... νόσος ἐπέλαβεν, Paus. *loc. cit.*

9. **remedium ... impetratum est**: καὶ σφᾶς ἐκέλευον οἱ μάντεις Ἀπόλλωνα ἱλάσασθαι καὶ Ἄρτεμιν ... ὑπὸ τούτων δὲ πεισθέντας τοὺς θεούς φασιν ἐς τὴν ἀκρόπολιν ἐλθεῖν.

est. fuere autem simulacra ea Apollinis, Dianae, Herculis, Minervae quod e caelo postea tactum est.

11   Cum hi essent, iam fuerat in Chio insula Melas scalptor, dein filius eius Micciades, ac deinde nepos Archermus, cuius filii Bupalus et Athenis vel clarissimi in ea scientia fuere 5 Hipponactis poetae aetate, quem certum est LX olympiade fuisse. quodsi quis horum familiam ad proavom usque retro agat, inveniat artis eius originem cum olympiadum

12   initio coepisse. Hipponacti notabilis foeditas voltus erat, quamobrem imaginem eius lascivia iocorum hi proposuere 10 ridentium circulis, quod Hipponax indignatus destrinxit amaritudinem carminum in tantum ut credatur aliquis ad laqueum eos conpulisse. quod falsum est, conplura enim in finitimis insulis simulacra postea fecere, sicut in Delo, quibus subiecerunt carmen non vitibus tantum censeri 15 Chion sed et operibus Archermi filiorum. ostendunt et

13   Iasii Dianam manibus eorum factam. in ipsa Chio narrata est operis eorum Dianae facies in sublimi posita, cuius voltum intrantes tristem, abeuntes exhilaratum putant. Romae eorum signa sunt in Palatina aede Apollinis in 20

17. Iasii] *Riccard.*; Lasii *Bamb., Detlefsen*; lasi *Voss.*

1. **Apollinis ... Minervae** : the list is alphabetical ; the statues therefore were no part of a group but single works, H. L. Urlichs in *Görlitz. Verhandl.* p. 330, note 2.

Dianae : possibly identical with the ξόανον of Artemis Munychia mentioned by Clement, προτρεπτ. λόγος, iv, p. 42 : cf. Urlichs *loc. cit.*; Robert, *Arch. März.* p. 22.

§ **11. 3. Cum hi essent** : to the account of D. and S. is now opposed (from another source) that of the Chian school. Introd. p. xxvi.

Melas ... Micciades ... Archermus : the three names appear on the famous inscription from Delos (*I. G. B.* 1 ; best restored by Lolling, Ἐφ. ἀρχ. 1888, p. 71 ff. ; cf. E. A. Gardner in *Class. Rev.* 1893, p. 140), where Ἀρχερμος (2nd line) appears as son of Μικκιάδης (1st line). The

Melas (Μέ[λ]α[ν]ος πατρώϊον ἀσ[τυ νέμοντες]) of the third line is presumably not the father of Mikkiades, but, as Schöll and Robert pointed out (*Arch. März.* p. 116 f.), a local hero of Chios, son of Oinopion ; Ion *ap.* Paus. vii, 4, 8. The account in Pliny rests upon this or a similar inscription ; the blunder with regard to Melas may have been committed early by a Greek writer ; cf. note on Demarate in xxxiv, 88.

scalptor = *sculptor ;* cf. note on xxxv, 156.

4. **Archermus** : besides the Delos inscription, the name occurs on a later inscr., in the Ionic alphabet, from the Athenian Akropolis, C. I. A. iv, 373, 95.

5. **Bupalus et Ath.** : the fact that they were sons of Archermos was doubtless also taken from an inscription ; Münzer, *op. cit.* p. 524.

ence. The statues in question were of Apollo, Artemis, Herakles, and Athene: this last was afterwards struck by lightning.

Before their day, however, the sculptor *Melas* had already lived 11 in the island of Chios, succeeded by his son *Mikkiades* and his *The school of Chios.* grandson *Archermos*, whose sons, *Boupalos* and *Athenis*, were masters of great renown in their craft in the time of the poet Hipponax, who certainly lived in the sixtieth Olympiad [540–537 B.C.]. Thus counting four generations backwards to their great grandfather, the birth of sculpture is found to coincide with the first Olympiad [776–773 B.C.]. Hipponax was conspicuous for 12 his ill-favoured countenance, which incited the sculptors in wanton jest to display his portrait to the ridicule of their assembled friends. Incensed at this Hipponax lampooned them so bitterly that, as some believe, they were driven to hang themselves. This, however, cannot be true, for they afterwards made in the neighbouring islands, as for example, in Delos, a number of images of the gods, under which they carved verses saying that Chios was not honoured for her vines alone but for the works of the sons of Archermos. Iasos too can show an Artemis made by their hands, 13 while in Chios itself we hear of a mask of Artemis by them, which is placed at a height in the temple, and presents a gloomy countenance to those who enter the temple, a cheerful one to those who are leaving. At Rome statues by them are to be seen on the summit of the temple of Apollo on the Palatine, and

6. **LX olympiade :** the Parian Chronicle gives his date as Ol. 59, 3 = B. C. 542.

8. **olymp. initio :** the calculation is based on the false assumption that a generation = the average full life of sixty years; cf. Furtwängler, *Plinius*, p. 17.

§ 12. 9. **notabilis foeditas :** cf. Metrodoros of Skepsis, *ap.* Athen. xii, 552 c. The only ascertained factor in the whole anecdote is the poet's attacks (*acer hostis Bupalo*) upon the two artists (Bergk, *Lyr. Gr.* ed. 4, fr. 10–14; Collignon, *Hist. Sculpt.* i, p. 141); it is probable that when the real cause for these attacks had been forgotten, a new one was elaborated out of the statues of Boupalos and Athenis, the archaic character of which struck later generations as simply grotesque; cf. Robert, *Arch.*

März. p. 115 f.

12. **ad laqueum :** this portion of the story is the *doublette* of the story of Lycambes and Archilochos. The *credatur aliquis* introduces it as apocryphal, while in the following sentence it is proved an invention.

14. **in Delo :** like their father Archermos.

17. **Iasii :** in the neighbourhood of Chios. The words *ostendunt . . . putant* betray mere periegetic curiosity (Furtwängler, *Plinius*, p. 61); they are from a different source to the earlier part of the account, which is based upon a study of inscriptions. Since Mucianus visited Iasos (ix, 33) it is reasonable to attribute this information to him; Introd. p. lxxxix.

§ 13. 20. **in Palatina aede :** xxxiv, 14.

fastigio et omnibus fere quae fecit divus Augustus. patris
quoque eorum et Deli fuere opera et in Lesbo insula.
14 Dipoeni quidem Ambracia, Argos, Cleonae operibus refertae fuere. omnes autem candido tantum marmore usi
sunt e Paro insula, quem lapidem coepere lychniten appel- 5
lare, quoniam ad lucernas in cuniculis caederetur, ut auctor
est Varro, multis postea candidioribus repertis, nuper vero
etiam in Lunensium lapidicinis. sed in Pariorum mirabile
proditur glaeba lapidis unius cuneis dividentium soluta
15 imaginem Sileni intus extitisse. non omittendum hanc 10
artem tanto vetustiorem fuisse quam picturam aut statuariam, quarum utraque cum Phidia coepit octogensima tertia
olympiade, post annos circiter CCCXXXII. et ipsum Phidian tradunt scalpsisse marmora, Veneremque eius esse
16 Romae in Octaviae operibus eximiae pulchritudinis. Al- 15
camenen Atheniensem, quod certum est, docuit in primis
nobilem, cuius sunt opera Athenis complura in aedibus
sacris praeclarumque Veneris extra muros quae appellatur
Aphrodite ἐν κήποις. huic summam manum ipse Phidias

in fastigio: i.e. the *signa* were
akroterial figures (see note on xxxv,
152), the pedimental and other decorations also consisting of archaic sculpture; cf. the archaic Amazon published
by Petersen, *Röm. Mitth.* iv, 1889,
p. 36 f.

1. et omnibus fere: rhetorical
exaggeration: cf. the *ex omnibus
clarissima quaeque* in xxxiv, 84, H. L.
Urlichs, *Rhein. Mus.* 1889, p. 487.

§ 14. 3. Dipoeni: harks back
to § 10.

Ambracia: see note on *Aetolos*
in § 9; the foundation of Ambrakia by Gorgos son of Kypselos
(Strab. x, 452) affords us an upper
limit for the activity of D. and S. in
that city. The Ambrakiot works
of art were taken away to Rome by
Fulvius Nobilior, B.C. 189.

Argos: for which D. and S.
made of ebony wood a group of the
Dioskouroi and their families; Paus.
ii, 22, 5.

Cleonae: for which they made
the image of Athena; Paus. ii,
15, 1.

refertae: rhetorical: cf. in xxxv,
148 *quorum tabulae pinacothecas
implent.*

4. omnes autem: i.e. the Chian
sculptors as well.

5. lychniten: the etymology is
thoroughly Varronian, cf. notes on
xxxiv, 11; xxxv, 155; according to
Lepsius, *Griechische Marmorstudien*,
p. 45, it rests on fact: the marble
came from the underground quarries
about five miles N.E. of the ancient
city of Paros; Lepsius noticed here
a number of holes cut obliquely into
the walls of the rock, the purpose of
which he believes was to suspend the
workmen's lamps by their hooked
handles.

10. imaginem Sileni: cf. the similar story, Cic. *Div.* i, 13, 23: *fingebat
Carneades in Chiorum lapicidinis
saxo diffiso caput exstitisse Panisci.*

indeed in almost all the temples built by the god Augustus.
Works by their father Archermos existed at Delos and in the
island of Lesbos. Ambrakia, Argos, and Kleonai were filled full 14
of the works of Dipoinos. All these artists used none but white
Parian marble, called lychnites [λυχνίτης], as Varro says, because *Marble of*
it was quarried by lamplight in underground passages. Since *Paros.*
then many marbles of a purer white have been discovered, and
again quite recently in the quarries of Luna. A marvellous story
tells how in the quarries of Paros a block which was being split
with wedges, opened and disclosed a figure of Seilenos.

Nor must I forget to say that the art of sculpture is much 15
older than that of painting or of bronze statuary, both of which *Sculpture*
began with Pheidias in the eighty-third olympiad [448-445 B. C.], *painting*
some 332 years later. It is said that *Pheidias* also worked in *statuary.*
marble, and that an Aphrodite by him of surpassing beauty is
at Rome in the gallery of Octavia. It is certain at all events
that he taught *Alkamenes* of Athens, a sculptor of the first rank, 16.
many of whose works are in the temples of Athens, while out- *Alka-*
side the city is his famous statue, known as 'Aphrodite ἐν κήποις,' *menes.*
or 'in the gardens.' Pheidias himself, according to tradition,

§ 15. hanc artem : sc. *sculp-*
turam by implication, although the
kind of art has not been previously
mentioned; cf. notes on xxxiv, 56
(*hanc scientiam*); xxxv, 153 (*hanc*
scientiam).

12. quarum utraque : xxxiv, 49;
xxxv, 54; as regards painting Pliny
forgets that he had himself argued
that its beginnings were still earlier
than Pheidias. Introd. p. xxx.

14. tradunt : [tradition as opposed
to real fact, i. e. whether he was a
sculptor in marble or not, it is certain
(*quod certum est*) that he taught
Alkamenes. So in xxxv, 54, *tradatur*
is opposed to *in confesso sit;* in xvii,
49, *sunt qui . . . adspergant. quod*
certum est . . . sol confert, H. L. U.]

scalpsisse marmora : Pliny's
Greek authors had laid chief stress on
the bronze works of Pheidias, xxxiv,
54; that he must have been equally
celebrated for his works in marble
is evident from the sculptures of the

Parthenon and the whole tendencies
of his school, and from the express
testimony of Aristotle, *Eth. Nicom.*
vi, 7 : τὴν δὲ σοφίαν ἔν τε ταῖς τέχναις
τοῖς ἀκριβεστάτοις τὰς τέχνας ἀποδίδο-
μεν, οἷον Φειδίαν λιθουργὸν σοφὸν καὶ
Πολύκλειτον ἀνδριαντοποιόν, ἐνταῦθα
μὲν οὖν οὐδὲν ἄλλο σημαίνοντες τὴν
σοφίαν, ἢ ὅτι ἀρετὴ τέχνης ἐστίν.

15. Octaviae operibus: cf. § 35,
where another Aphrodite (*aliam*
Venerem) by Philiskos is mentioned
as being in the same gallery.

§ 16. Alcamenen: xxxiv, 49 and
72. The only dateable work by Alka-
menes is his group of Athena and Hera-
kles, dedicated in the Herakleion at
Thebes after the downfall of the Thirty
Tyrants in 403 B. C. (Paus. ix, 11, 6).
Pliny's account of Alkamenes and
Agorakritos seems borrowed from
Antigonos, Introd. p. xlii.

17. Athenis: see note on xxxiv,
49, *Olymp.* lxxxiii.

19. ἐν κήποις: on the Ilissos, Paus.

17 inposuisse dicitur. eiusdem discipulus fuit Agoracritus
Parius et aetate gratus, itaque e suis operibus pleraque
nomini eius donasse fertur. certavere autem inter se ambo
discipuli Venere facienda, vicitque Alcamenes non opere
sed civitatis suffragiis contra peregrinum suo faventis. 5
quare Agoracritus ea lege signum suum vendidisse traditur,
ne Athenis esset, et appellasse Nemesin. id positum est
Rhamnunte pago Atticae, quod M. Varro omnibus signis
praetulit. est et in Matris magnae delubro eadem civitate
18 Agoracriti opus. Phidian clarissimum esse per omnes gentes 10
quae Iovis Olympii famam intellegunt nemo dubitat, sed ut
laudari merito sciant etiam qui opera eius non videre, pro-
feremus argumenta parva et ingeni tantum. neque ad hoc
Iovis Olympii pulchritudine utemur, non Minervae Athenis
factae amplitudine, cum sit ea cubitorum XXVI,—ebore haec 15
et auro constat—sed in scuto eius Amazonum proelium
caelavit intumescente ambitu, in parmae eiusdem concava
parte deorum et Gigantum dimicationes, in soleis vero
Lapitharum et Centaurorum, adeo momenta omnia capacia

i. 19, 2. According to a generally
accepted theory of Furtwängler, the
Alkamenian statue is reproduced in the
statues of the 'Venus Genitrix' type
(Louvre, Giraudon, 1175; Florence
Alinari, 1331).

huic summam manum: the
words almost imply that the same
reproach attached to Alkamenes as
to Agorakritos, namely, that Pheidias
allowed his own work to pass off as
his pupil's, cf. Pallat in *Jahrb*. ix,
1894, p. 14.

§ 17. 1. Agoracritus: Overbeck,
Schriftquellen, 829–843.

3. nomini . . . donasse: the
scandal recorded here without special
allusion to any one work was used
by Polemon (*ap*. Zenobios v, 82)
as an argument wherewith to vin-
dicate for Pheidias the authorship of
the Agorakritan Nemesis. Introd.
p. xxxix.

certavere : cf. the story of the
competition between Pheidias and

Alkamenes recorded by John Tzetzes,
χιλιάδες, 931.

7. Nemesin : Wilamowitz (*Antigonos v. Karystos*, p. 11) points out
that the story of the Nemesis having
been intended for an Aphrodite
originated in the fact that the
Rhamnusian Nemesis differed from
the type usual at a later date. Cf.
Paus. i, 33, 7: Πτερὰ δ' ἔχον οὔτε
τοῦτο τὸ ἄγαλμα Νεμέσεως οὔτε ἄλλο
πεποίηται τῶν ἀρχαίων ... οἱ δὲ ὕστερον,
ἐπιφαίνεσθαι γὰρ τὴν θεὸν μάλιστα ἐπὶ
τῷ ἐρᾶν ἐθέλουσιν, ἐπὶ τούτῳ Νεμέσει
πτερὰ ὥσπερ Ἔρωτι ποιοῦσι; cf. Am-
mianus Marcellinus, xiv, 11, 25–26
(ed. Gardthausen, p. 42), and Kalkmann, *Pausanias der Perieget*, p. 206.

8. Rhamnunte : a fragment of
the colossal head of the Nemesis was
discovered here, and is now in the
Brit. Mus. (*Cat. Sculpt*. i, 460).
Numerous fragments of the basis (Leda
bringing Helen to Nemesis, Paus. *loc.
cit.*) were recovered in 1890, and are

put the last touches to this work. He also taught *Agorakritos* of **17**
Paros, whom he so loved for his youthful grace, that he allowed *Agora-kritos.*
several of his own works to pass under his name. The two
pupils made statues of Aphrodite for a competition, and Alkamenes received the prize, not from the merit of his work, but
because the Athenians voted for their fellow-citizen against
a foreigner. The story runs that Agorakritos thereupon sold his
statue, imposing the condition that it should not be set up at
Athens, and called it Nemesis. It now stands in Rhamnous,
a deme of Attica, and Marcus Varro esteems it above all other
statues. There is another statue by Agorakritos in the same city,
in the shrine of the Great Mother.

The renown of Pheidias among all peoples who realize the **18**
glory of his Olympian Zeus cannot be brought in doubt ; yet so *Pheidias. His in-*
that even those who have not seen his works may know that his *ventive*
praises are well deserved, I shall cite those minute details in which *genius in details.*
it was only left to him to display the resources of his inventive
faculty. For this purpose I shall not appeal to the beauty of his
Olympian Zeus, nor to the size of his Athena at Athens, though
she is 26 cubits [37 ft. 10 in.] in height, made all of gold and
ivory ; but I shall instance her shield, on the convex face of which
he represented the battle of the Amazons, and on the concave
surface the conflict between the gods and giants, while on the side
of her sandals were the Lapithai and the Kentaurs. So true was
it that in his eyes every tiny space afforded a field for art. The

published, *Jahrb.* ix, 1894, pl. 1–7,
pp. 1–22 (Pallat). Pausanias, who is
never curious in the matter of ascrip-
tions, simply attributes the work to
Pheidias, as he likewise did the
' Mother of the Gods ' by Agorakritos,
and the Athena by Kolotes (see
note on xxxv, 54).

9. **Matris magnae del.** : Μητρὸς
θεῶν ἱερόν, Paus. i, 3, 5, where
the statue is erroneously ascribed to
Pheidias himself. For the type of the
goddess see the fine relief of undoubted
Pheidian style, *A. Z.* 38, 1880, pl. i ;
Roscher, ii, p. 1663, fig. 5. Addenda.

§ 18. 11. **Iovis Olympii** : xxxiv,
49 ; 54 ; full description of the statue in
Paus. v, 10, 2 : beneath the feet of
Zeus was the artist's inscription, Φειδίας
Χαρμίδου υἱὸς ᾿Αθηναῖος μ᾿ ἐποίησε : the

numerous references in other authors
coll. by Overb. *Schriftquell.* 692–754.

14. **Minervae** : xxxiv, 54 ; Paus.
i, 24, 5 ; Overbeck, 645–696 ; a rough
Roman copy in the statuette from the
Varvakeion (Athens, Central Mus. ;
cast in Br. Mus., *Cat. Sculpt.* i, 300 ;
cf. 301).

16. **scuto** : a small late copy is
preserved in the ' Strangford ' shield,
Brit. Mus. *Cat. Sculpt.* i, 302 ; for the
latest discussion of the style of the
reliefs and of the supposed portraits
of Pheidias and Perikles, see Furtwängler, *Masterpieces*, p. 48.

18. **soleis** : cf. in the Mus. Conserv.
at Rome the colossal foot wearing
a sandal adorned along the edge with
a train of Tritons (Helbig, *Class. Ant.*
596).

19 artis illi fuere. in basi autem quod caelatum est Pandoras genesin appellant: dii adsunt nascenti XX numero. Victoria praecipue mirabili periti mirantur et serpentem ac sub ipsa cuspide aeream sphingem. haec sint obiter dicta de artifice numquam satis laudato, simul ut noscatur illam magnifi- 5
20 centiam aequalem fuisse et in parvis. Praxitelis aetatem inter statuarios diximus, qui marmoris gloria superavit etiam semet. opera eius sunt Athenis in Ceramico, sed ante omnia est non solum Praxitelis verum in toto orbe terrarum Venus quam ut viderent multi navigaverunt 10 Cnidum. duas fecerat simulque vendebat, alteram velata specie, quam ob id praetulerunt quorum condicio erat Coi, cum eodem pretio detulisset, severum id ac pudicum arbitrantes. reiectam Cnidi emerunt inmensa differentia famae.
21 voluit eam a Cnidiis postea mercari rex Nicomedes, totum 15 aes alienum quod erat ingens civitatis dissoluturum se promittens. omnia perpeti maluere, nec inmerito, illo enim signo Praxiteles nobilitavit Cnidum. aedicula eius tota aperitur ut conspici possit undique effigies dea favente ipsa,

1. caelatum est — Pandoras genesin appellant — dii *Gerhard, Detlefsen.*
2. adsunt nascenti] *Urlichs in Chrest.*; sunt nascentis *Riccard.*; sunt nascentes *reliqui*; sunt adstantes *Detlefsen.*   3. ac] *post verbum* aeream *pos. Panofka, Detlefsen.*   4. aeream] *Bamb., reliqui*; aureum *Urlichs, Detlefsen.*

§ 19. 1. **Pandoras genesin**: Paus. i, 24, 7 : from the hesitating manner in which the statement is introduced by *appellant*, it appears that either Pliny or his Latin author had not thoroughly grasped the meaning of the Greek; cf. Jahn, *Kunsturtheile*, p. 127.

2. **dii adsunt**: the composition is preserved on the basis of the Pergamene copy of the Athena Parthenos, *Jahrb.* v, 1890, p. 114, fig. 9.

Victoria: καὶ Νίκην ὅσον τε τεσσάρων πηχῶν . . . ἔχει. Paus. *loc. cit.*

3. **ac sub ipsa . . : sphingem**: the reading adopted by Detlefsen brings Pliny into agreement with Pausanias (καὶ πλησίον τοῦ δόρατος δράκων ἐστίν), but does intolerable violence to the MSS. (cf. Gurlitt,

Pausanias, p. 98). We have therefore retained the MSS. reading, which can be construed though the sense is not absolutely clear. The confusion, however, is more likely due to Pliny's hurrying over details, than to the copyists. *Sub ipsa* I take to mean 'about on a level with'; *aeream* is evidently correct, for had the sphinx— according to Pliny—been of gold, like the rest of the statue, there would have been no need to mention its material.

§ 20. 7. **diximus**: xxxiv, 69–70.

8. **in Ceramico**: refers to grave statues by Praxiteles in the Athenian cemetery. Pausanias (i, 2, 3) mentions a grave ἐπίθημα ἔχων στρατιώτην ἵππῳ παρεστηκότα· ὅντινα μὲν οὐκ οἶδα, Πραξιτέλης δὲ καὶ τὸν ἵππον καὶ τὸν στρατιώτην ἐποίησεν (notes on xxxiv,

relief on the base is known as the γένεσις of Pandora ; the **19**
gods present at the birth are twenty in number. The Victory is
most wondrous, but connoisseurs admire also the serpent and
further the bronze sphinx beneath the spear of the goddess. Let
these passing remarks on a sculptor whose praises can never end,
serve at the same time to show that even in the smallest details
the opulence of his genius never fell short.

Praxiteles, whose date I gave among the bronze workers, outdid **20**
even himself by the fame of his works in marble. Statues by his *Praxiteles.*
hand exist at Athens in the Kerameikos, while famous not only
among the works of Praxiteles, but throughout the whole world,
is the Aphrodite which multitudes have sailed to Knidos to look *Aphrodite*
upon. He had offered two statues of Aphrodite for sale at the *of Knidos.*
same time, the second being a draped figure, which for that
reason was preferred by the people of Kos with whom lay the
first choice ; the price of the two figures was the same, but they
flattered themselves they were giving proof of a severe modesty.
The rejected statue, which was bought by the people of Knidos,
enjoys an immeasurably greater reputation. King Nikomedes **21**
subsequently wished to buy it from them, offering to discharge
the whole of their public debt, which was enormous. They, however, preferred to suffer the worst that could befall, and they
showed their wisdom, for by this statue Praxiteles made Knidos
illustrious. It stands in a small shrine, open all round so that

70, 71, and on the *expir. imagines* of
Apelles in xxxv, 90). For the Plinian
phrase, cf. Cicero, *de Leg.* ii, 26, 64 :
*amplitudines sepulcrorum, quas in
Ceramico videmus;* Wolters, *Athen.
Mitth.* xviii, 1893, p. 5 f. and note 1.

10. **Venus . . . Cnidum** : the
statue is represented on coins of
Knidos, Gardner, *Types*, xv, 21 ; for
a revised list of the marble copies, see
Furtwängler, *Masterpieces*, p. 322,
note 3 ; the best known is in the
Vatican, Helbig 316 (good cast without drapery in South Kensington
Museum). The notices in ancient
writers coll. by Overbeck, *Schriftquell.*
1227–1248. The information as to
the Knidian Aphrodite is from Mucianus. Introd. p. lxxxvii.

11. **velata specie** : this second
Aphrodite is still to seek ; for a possible echo of the work, see Furtwängler, *op. cit.* p. 322 f.

§ 21. 15. **voluit . . . mercari** : at
the close of the first Mithridatic war,
B.C. 84, when Nikomedes III (King of
Bithynia B.C. 90–74), who had been
expelled from his kingdom by Mithridates, was reinstated by the Romans.

16. **aes alienum** : for the heavy
contributions exacted by Sulla from
the Greek states of Asia Minor, cf.
Appian, Μιθριδ. 63.

18. **aedicula** : for a detailed description of the statue and its shrine,
cf. Lucian, Ἔρωτες, 13.

19. **dea favente ipsa** : in allusion
to the legend that the goddess herself

ut creditur, facta. nec minor ex quacumque parte admiratio est. ferunt amore captum quendam, cum delituisset
noctu, simulacro cohaesisse, eiusque cupiditatis esse indicem
22 maculam. sunt in Cnido et alia signa marmorea inlustrium
artificum, Liber pater Bryaxidis et alter Scopae et Minerva, 5
nec maius aliud Veneris Praxiteliae specimen quam quod
inter haec sola memoratur. eiusdem est et Cupido obiectus
a Cicerone Verri, ille propter quem Thespiae visebantur,
nunc in Octaviae scholis positus, eiusdem et alter nudus in
Pario colonia Propontidis, par Veneri Cnidiae nobilitate et 10
iniuria, adamavit enim Alcetas Rhodius atque in eo quoque
23 simile amoris vestigium reliquit. Romae Praxitelis opera
sunt Flora, Triptolemus, Ceres in hortis Servilianis, Boni
Eventus et Bonae Fortunae simulacra in Capitolio, item
Maenades et quas Thyiadas vocant et Caryatidas, et Sileni 15
in Pollionis Asini monumentis, et Apollo et Neptunus.
24 Praxitelis filius Cephisodotus et artis heres fuit. cuius
laudatum est Pergami symplegma nobile digitis corpori

served the artist as model. Clement of
Alexandria, προτρεπτ. λόγος 53, names
the courtesan Kratina as model.

2. amore captum: cf. below,
§ 22, § 39. Similar stories were told
also of a Hebe by Ktesikles, Adaios,
ap. Athen. xiii, p. 606 a, of an Ἀγαθὴ
τύχη near th Prytaneion in Athens,
Ailian, ποικ. ἰστ. ix, 39.

§ 22. 5. Bryaxidis: below, § 30;
xxxiv, 42, 73.

Scopae: below, §§ 25, 28, 30, 31 ;
xxxiv, 49.

7. Cupido: given as a present to
Phryne, Paus. i, 20, 1 ; cf. Athen. xiii,
p. 591 b. The Eros was brought from
Thespiai to Rome by Gaius Caligula,
restored to Thespiai by Claudius, and
finally brought back to Rome by
Nero ; it was destroyed in a fire, in
the reign of Titus (Paus. ix, 27, 3).
Furtwängler (Masterp. p. 314 ff.)
follows Visconti in recognizing copies
of the statue in the 'Eros of Cento-
celle' (Helbig, 185) and its numerous
replicas.

obiectus : Verres had robbed Heius
of Messana of another Eros by
Praxiteles ; Cicero's allusion to the
Thespian statue was to impress upon
the judges mirum quendam dolorem
accipere eos, ex quorum urbibus haec
auferantur.

8. propter . . . visebantur: Cic.
Verr. II, iv, 2, 4: Cupidinem fecit
(Praxiteles) illum qui est Thespiis,
propter quem Thespiae visuntur; nam
alia visendi causa nulla est; cf. ib.
60, 135.

9. Octaviae scholis : part of the
complex of buildings known as the
Opera Octaviae ; these were probably
rooms opening on to the gallery or
porticus itself.

alter nudus: the type was first
identified by Furtwängler on coins
of Parion (ap. Roscher, i, 1358);
later Benndorf (Bull. della Comm.
Arch. 1886, p. 74) recognized a marble copy in the 'Genius Borghese'
of the Louvre (phot. Giraudon,
1201).

the statue, which was made, as is believed, under the direct inspiration of the goddess, can be seen from every side, nor is there any point of view from which it is less admirable than from another.

There are in Knidos other marble statues by great sculptors, **22** a Dionysos by *Bryaxis*, another Dionysos, and also an Athena by *Skopas*, and there is no more forcible panegyric of the Aphrodite of Praxiteles than the fact that among all these it alone is remembered. Praxiteles also made the Eros with which Cicero *Eros of* taunted Verres, that Eros for whose sake men travelled to *Thespiai.* Thespiai. It is now in the 'schools' of Octavia. He made a second nude Eros in the colony of Parion, on the Propontis, a figure as celebrated as the Aphrodite of Knidos.

At Rome the works of Praxiteles are: Flora, Triptolemos and **23** Demeter in the gardens of Servilius, the images of Good Luck and Good Fortune in the Capitol, further the Mainads, the figures known as Thyiades and Karyatides, the Seilenoi in the gallery of Asinius Pollio, and an Apollo and Poseidon.

Kephisodotos, the son of Praxiteles, was also the heir to his **24** genius. Greatly admired is his celebrated group at Pergamon of *Kephiso-dotos.*

in Pario colonia: v, 141; xxxiv, 78; it was the seat of a very ancient cult of Eros, Paus. ix, 27, 1 (Furt-wängler, *ap.* Roscher, i, 1342).

§ 23. 12. **Romae**: at this point begins a description of works of art in Rome, which is continued with only a few interruptions to the close of the history of the marble sculptors in § 43.

13. **Flora, Tript., Ceres**: pre-sumably in a group; *Flora* must be the Greek Κόρα, and owes her Latin name to the wreath she was holding as on the relief. Overbeck, *Kunst. Myth.* pl. xiv, 3, 4; Ἐφημ. ἀρχ. 1893, p. 35.

hortis Servilianis: from Suet. *Nero*, 47, this must have been on the *Via Ostiensis;* cf. Tacitus, *Ann.* xv, 55; *Hist.* iii, 38; *C. I. L.* vi, 8673, 8674.

Boni Ev. et Bonae Fort. = Ἀγαθὸς δαίμων and Ἀγαθὴ τύχη; for the received Attic type of these divi-nities see the votive relief in the Brit. Mus. (*Mus. Marbles*, xi, pl. 47).

15. **Maenades**: for Attic fourth-century types of the maenads see Rapp *ap.* Roscher, ii. 2270.

Thyiadas: γυναῖκες μέν εἰσιν Ἀττικαί, φοιτῶσαι δὲ ἐς τὸν Παρνασὸν παρὰ ἔτος . . . ἄγουσιν ὄργια Διονύσῳ, Paus. x, 4, 3. Καρυατίδες, maidens of Karyai, who danced at the festival of Artemis, Paus. iv, 16, 9.

16. **Pollionis Asini mon.** : in the Museum connected with the famous library, Plin. vii, 115; both apparently adjoined the *Atrium Libertatis*, which was restored by Asinius Pollio, cf. Suet. *Aug.* 29; Ovid, *Tristia*, iii, 1, 72; Gilbert, *Rom*, iii, p. 338, note 2.

§ 24. 17. **Cephisodotus**: xxxiv, 51, 87.

18. **Pergami**: the information is from Mucianus, Introd. p. lxxxix. [From Tac. *Ann.* xvi, 23, it appears that a number of works of art were still at Pergamon in the reign of Nero.—H.L.U.]

symplegma: [probably here of

verius quam marmori inpressis. Romae eius opera sunt
Latona in Palati delubro, Venus in Pollionis Asini monumentis et intra Octaviae porticus in Iunonis aede Aescula-
25 pius ac Diana. Scopae laus cum his certat. is fecit
Venerem et Pothon, qui Samothrace sanctissimis caerimonis 5
coluntur, item Apollinem Palatinum, Vestam sedentem
laudatam in Servilianis hortis duosque campteras circa eam,
quorum pares in Asini monimentis sunt, ubi et canephoros
26 eiusdem. sed in maxima dignatione delubro Cn. Domitii
in circo Flaminio Neptunus ipse et Thetis atque Achilles, 10
Nereides supra delphinos et cete aut hippocampos sedentes,
item Tritones chorusque Phorci et pistrices ac multa alia
marina, omnia eiusdem manu, praeclarum opus, etiam si
totius vitae fuisset. nunc vero praeter supra dicta quaeque
nescimus Mars etiamnum est sedens colossiaeus eiusdem 15
manu in templo Bruti Callaeci apud circum eundem, prae-

7. campteras] *Bamb.*; camiteras *reliqui*; lampteras *Jan, Detlefsen*.

an erotic couple, cf. Martial, xii,
43; Arnobius, vii, 33 (ed. Reifferscheid, p. 267), and for this use of
σύμπλεγμα, Soph. Fr. 556, Plato,
Symp. 191, Aeta.—H. L. U.] That
this *symplegma* had an erotic significance is proved by the comparison
with the group of Pan and Olympos
(§ 35) *quod est alterum in terris symplegma nobile.*
digitis . . . inpressis : cf. Herondas,
iv, 59 f. (ed. Crusius) :
τὸν παῖδα δὴ ⟨τὸν⟩ γυμνὸν ἦν κνίσω
τοῦτον
οὐχ ἕλκος ἕξει, Κύννα;
2. Latona: Crusius (German transl.
of *Herondas*, p. xiv, note) suggests
possible identity with the Leto which
had stood in Kos, Herondas, ii, 98.
Palati delubro: below, § 32.
3. Iunonis aede: below, § 35;
§ 42.
Aesculapius: according to Crusius (*loc. cit.*), possibly identical
with the Asklepios by 'the sons of
Praxiteles' (οἱ Πρηξιτέλεω παῖδες) in
the temple of Kos; Herond. iv, 20 ff.

§ 25. 4. Scopae laus : § 22 ; § 30.
5. Venerem et Pothon : the Samo-
thrakian cult seems to have developed
out of that of Demeter and Hermes
Kadmos ; cf. Crusius, *Fleckeisen's
Jahrb.* 128, p. 298; *Beiträge z.
Griech. Myth.* p. 15. For the temple
of Aphrodite at Megara. Skopas had
made statues of Eros, Himeros, and
Pothos : Paus. i, 43, 6.
Samothrace : Mucianus, who had
visited Samothrake, is again Pliny's
authority here, Introd. p. xc.
6. Apoll. Palatinum : for the
temple, cf. xxxiv, 14; above, § 24;
below, § 32. Propertius, ii, 31, 15,
describes the statue as follows :—
deinde inter matrem deus ipse in-
terque sororem
Pythius in longa carmina ueste
sonat.
(The Apollo referred to in l. 5 f. of
the same elegy has been shown by
Hülsen, *Röm. Mitth.* ix, 1894, p.
240 f., to refer to a quite distinct statue
which stood in the courtyard of the
temple.) The Skopasian Apollo, the

figures interlaced [σύμπλεγμα], in which the fingers seem to press on flesh rather than on marble. At Rome his works are: the Leto in the temple on the Palatine, an Aphrodite in the gallery of Asinius Pollio, and the Asklepios and Artemis in the temple of Juno within the portico of Octavia. The praise of *Skopas* vies with theirs. He made the Aphrodite 25 and Πόθος, or Desire, which are worshipped in Samothrake with *Skopas.* the holiest ritual, also the Apollo on the Palatine and, in the gardens of Servilius, a seated Hestia which is praised, and beside her two pillars whose pendants are in the galleries of Asinius, where also is his κανηφόρος [basket-bearer]. But most highly 26 esteemed of all his works is the group in the temple built by Gnaeus Domitius in the Circus of Flaminius: it comprises Poseidon himself with Thetis and Achilles, Nereids riding on dolphins and sea monsters or on sea horses, and Tritons and the train of Phorkos, with sea beasts and a tumult of creatures of the deep, the whole by the same hand, a wondrous work, even were it that of a life-time. Yet in addition to the works I have named and those which are unknown to us, we have by the same artist an Ares, a colossal seated figure, now in the temple built by Brutus Callaecus close to the Circus of Flaminius, besides a nude

---

Kitharoidos, is represented on coins of Nero (Overb. *Apoll. Münztaf.* v, 47, 48, 50, 51).

7. **campteras**: i. e. goals or columns marking in the *stadium* the turning-point for runners or chariots (κάμπτειν); cf. the *metae* on the sarkophagos, Helbig, *Class. Ant.* 339; these columns might be profusely adorned with sculpture.

§ **26**. 9. delubro: i. e. of Neptune. It is uncertain which of the Domitii built it; Urlichs (*Griechische Statuen im Rep. Rom*, p. 19) inclines to attribute the original building to the consul of B. C. 121, who celebrated with great splendour his triumph over the Arverni, and its restoration to his greatgrandson, the consul of B. C. 32; this later Domitius now placed in the temple the great Skopasian group, presumbly brought from Bithynia, of which he was governor B. C. 40-35, and where was a famous temple of

Poseidon at Astakos-Olbia (Urlichs, *Skopas*, p. 130).

10. **circo Flaminio**: cf. Gilbert, *Rom*, iii, p. 89.

ipse: i.e. the temple-statue; Becker, *Top.* p. 619, note 13; cf. *simulacrum ipsum* in xxxiv, 66.

Thetis . . . marina: the group represented the passing of Achilles to the Isles of the Blest; Urlichs, *Skopas*, p. 133 ff.; cf. Fleischer *ap.* Roscher, i, p. 53. Pliny's description is tinged by reminiscences of Virgil, *Aen.* v, 240.

15. **Mars . . . sedens**: the Ares Ludovisi (Helbig, 883)—a statue distinctly Skopasian in style—is probably a reduced copy of this work; see Furtwängler, *Masterpieces*, p. 304.

16. **Bruti Callaeci**: (D. Junius) cos. B. C. 138; celebrated his triumph over the *Callaici* B. C. 132; the architect of the temple was Hermodoros of Salamis, Nepos *ap.* Priscian, *Fragm.*

terea Venus in eodem loco nuda Praxiteliam illam ante-
27 cedens et quemcumque alium locum nobilitatura. Romae
quidem multitudo operum, etiam obliteratio ac magis offi-
ciorum negotiorumque acervi omnis a contemplatione tamen
abducunt, quoniam otiosorum et in magno loci silentio talis 5
admiratio est. qua de causa ignoratur artifex eius quoque
Veneris quam Vespasianus imperator in operibus Pacis suae
28 dicavit antiquorum dignam fama. par haesitatio est in
templo Apollinis Sosiani, Niobae liberos morientes Scopas
an Praxiteles fecerit, item Ianus pater in suo templo dicatus 10
ab Augusto ex Aegypto advectus utrius manu sit, iam
quidem et auro occultatus. similiter in curia Octaviae
quaeritur de Cupidine fulmen tenente. id demum adfirma-
29 tur, Alcibiaden esse principem forma in ea aetate. multa
in eadem schola sine auctoribus placent: Satyri quattuor, 15
ex quibus unus Liberum patrem palla velatum umeris
praefert, alter Liberam similiter, tertius ploratum infantis

Hist. Rom. 13, p. 227; cf. Gilbert,
Rom, iii, p. 88.

§ 27. 2. **Romae quidem**: for the
sentiment of the whole passage, cf.
Hor. *Ep.* i, 10. [It became a commonplace of silver Latinity to contrast the
noise of the city with the quiet of the
villas, see also Pliny's Introd. to Bk.
xiv; Pliny,*Ep.*iii,18,4 *nunquam porro
aut valde vacat Romae, aut com-
modum est audire recitantem; Ep.*
iii, 5, 13 *haec inter medios labores
urbisque fremitum;* and *Ep.* i, 9;
cf. C. F. Herrmann *über d. Kunstsinn
der Römer*, p. 46.—H. L. U.]

7. **operibus Pacis**: connected
with the Temple and Forum of Peace,
xxxiv, 84.

§ 28. 9. **Apollinis Sosiani**: xiii,53,
the surname from C. Sosius (the legate
of Antony), who brought the sacred
cedar-wood image of the god from
Seleukia, and restored the temple;
note on xxxv, 99.

Niobae: if the group was identical
with the original of the Florence
statues, the style—especially of the
heads—can leave no doubt that it

was by Skopas (cf. Amelung, *Basis
des Praxiteles*, p. 67). The ancient
critics evidently confused Skopas
and Praxiteles, precisely as do the
moderns.

10. **Ianus pater**: a bearded double
terminal bust, rechristened at Rome as
Janus. [What divinity it originally
represented is impossible to tell, for
the Romans were absolutely without scruple in renaming statues; cf.
Pseud. Dio Chrys. xxxvii, 42 Κορινθ.
for a Poseidon rededicated as Jupiter.
—H. L. U.] According to Wernicke,
Jahrb. v, 1890, p. 148, this 'Janus'
may be identical with the Skopasian
herm (*not* Hermes), *Anth. Plan.* 192.

in suo templo: the shrine in the
Forum (xxxiv, 33) can scarcely have
been spacious enough to hold a second
statue: it is still doubtful which
temple is meant; Roscher, (*Lex.* ii,
26 f.) suggests a temple of Janus
belonging to the Forum Augustum,
while Jordan (*Hermes*, iv, p. 239)
thought of the temple in the Forum
Holitorium; cf. Peter, Ovid's *Fasti*,
ii, p. 11.

Aphrodite now in the same place, which surpasses even the Praxitelean goddess, and would suffice to make famous any other spot. At Rome indeed the works of art are legion ; besides, one 27 effaces another from the memory, and above all, beautiful as they *Multitude of works in* are, people are distracted by the overpowering claims of duty and *Rome ob-* business, for to admire art we need leisure and profound stillness. *scures their fame.* For this same reason we are ignorant of the sculptor of the Aphrodite dedicated by the emperor Vespasian in the galleries of his temple of Peace, a work worthy of the old masters. It is likewise 28 uncertain whether Skopas or Praxiteles made the dying children of Niobe in the temple of the Apollo of Sosius, and again which of them made the Father Janus brought by Augustus from Egypt and dedicated in his own temple; the Janus, moreover, is now disguised by gilding. The same difficulty arises in the case of the Eros holding a thunderbolt, in the Council Chamber of Octavia ; this only is certain, that it is the portrait of Alkibiades, the handsomest man of his day. Many groups by unknown 29 artists attract us in this gallery ; such as the four Satyrs, one of whom is carrying on his shoulders a cloaked Dionysos, the second carries Ariadne in the same way, the third is soothing a crying

---

11. **ex Aegypto** : cf. xxxv, 131, 28, and notes.

iam quidem : in exculpation.

12. **auro occultatus** : the gilding is specially mentioned, as unusual in the case of a marble statue; cf. Wunderer, *Manibiae*, p. 10 ; note on xxxiv, 63.

similiter . . . quaeritur : from works as to which it was doubtful whether they were by Skopas or Praxiteles Pliny passes on to general doubts, and thence to statues by unknown masters (*sine auctoribus*) ; Wernicke, *op. cit.* p. 150.

in curia : certain rooms of the *opera Octaviae* served occasionally for meetings of the Senate ; Dio Cassius, lv, 8 ; Josephus, *Bell. Jud.* vii, 5, 4 ; Gilbert, *Rom,* iii, p. 249, note 1.

13. **fulmen tenente** : Ἔρως κεραυνοφόρος.

id . . . adfirmatur : Wernicke (*loc. cit.*) explains Pliny's meaning to be as follows : the individuality of the features leads people to suppose this is a

portrait—and a portrait of Alkibiades ; I take no responsibility in the matter, but thus far is certain, that Alkibiades was the most beautiful man in the period to which the statue belongs.

14. **Alcibiaden** : the statue had most probably nothing to do with Alkibiades, but the connexion in the popular mind arose from the well-known ἐπίσημον on his shield (Plut. *Alkib.* 16).

§ 29. 15. **eadem schola** : Gilbert, *loc. cit.*

16. **Liberum . . . palla velatum** : the description of the fully draped figure suggests the Dionysos supported (not carried) by a Satyr in the 'Ikarios' relief (Schreiber, *Hell. Reliefs,* xxxvii). *palla = πέπλος,* usually understood of the cloak worn by women, though practically identical with the ἱμάτιον.

17. **Liberam similiter** : a Maenad carried by a Satyr, misunderstood as an Ariadne ; cf. Furtwängler, *Plinius,* p. 10.

cohibet, quartus cratere alterius sitim sedat, duaeque Aurae
velificantes sua veste.   nec minor quaestio est in saeptis
Olympum et Pana, Chironem cum Achille qui fecerint,
praesertim cum capitali satisdatione fama iudicet dignos.
30 Scopas habuit aemulos eadem aetate Bryaxim et Timo- 5
theum et Leocharen, de quibus simul dicendum est, quoniam
pariter caelavere Mausoleum.   sepulchrum hoc est ab uxore
Artemisia factum Mausolo Cariae regulo, qui obiit olympiadis CVII anno secundo.   opus id ut esset inter septem
miracula hi maxime fecere artifices.   patet ab austro et 10
septentrione centenos sexagenos ternos pedes, brevius a

11. centenos] *Urlichs in Chrest., Detlefsen* ; *om. Bamb., reliqui.*

ploratum infantis cohibet: recalls the well-known group in the
Louvre (phot. Giraudon, 1182) and
its numerous replicas (Rome, Helbig,
11; phot. Alinari, 6673) of Seilenos
nursing the babe Dionysos.

1. duaeque Aurae: cf. the so-
called ' Nereids ' of the Xanthian tomb
(Brit. Mus.), which have been shown by
Six, *J. H. S.* xiii, p. 131, to represent
the Αὖραι : Pindar, *Ol.* ii, 70, μακάρων
νᾶσος ὠκεανίδες περιπνέοισιν ; see also
Max. Mayer *ap.* Roscher, ii, 2147 ff.

2. nec minor quaestio: above,
note in § 28 on *similiter . . . quaeritur.*

in saeptis: i. e. in the galleries
which surrounded the voting-place
of the Comitia, after the luxurious
alterations planned by Caesar (Cic.
Att. iv, 16, 14) and completed by
Augustus ; cf. Dio Cassius, liii, 23.

3. Olympum et Pana : the group
in Naples of the bearded Pan teaching
a young boy the syrinx (Friederichs,
Bausteine, 654; Helbig, *Untersuch.*
p. 156) is commonly thought to
reproduce this work.

Chironem cum Achille: the
subject is preserved in wall-paintings
(Helbig, *Wandgem.* 1291-1295), of
which the best preserved and most
famous is Helbig 1291. A head
from a marble copy is in the Pal.
Conservat. ; Helbig, *Class. Ant.* 572.

4. capitali satisdatione : xxxiv,
38.

§ 30. 5. Scopas : the dates for
his activity are comprised between
his work for the temple of Athena
Alea at Tegea (after the fire B. C.
394, Paus. viii, 45, 4) and his work
for the Mausoleion (about B. C. 353)
and for the Artemision of Ephesos
(after the fire of B. C. 356, below § 95).

aemulos : cf. xxxiv, 49, *aemuli ;*
xxxv, 64.

Bryaxim : xxxiv, 73 ; for his signature Βρύαξις ἐπόησεν on the basis
adorned with reliefs of horsemen see
Δελτίον, 1891, p. 35; *Bull. Corr. Hell.,*
xv, 1891, p. 369, plate vii ; 'Εφημ. ἀρχ.
1893, plates 6, 7. The inscription is
of about the date of the Mausoleion
(cf. plates 4, 5, for a torso of Nike
found not far from the basis, and
which Kavvadias, *ib.* p. 46, supposes
to have crowned the monument).

Timotheum : xxxiv, 91 ; he
may have been already advanced in
years when he worked upon the
Mausoleion ; the inscription (Kavvadias, *Fouilles d'Epidaure*, no. 241,
l. 36 f.) recording his contract for fur-
nishing models and sculptures for the
Temple of Asklepios at Epidauros,
Paus. ii, 32, 4, is dated by Kavvadias
(p. 85) at the commencement of the
fourth century, while Foucart, *Bull.*

child, and the fourth quenches the thirst of another child out of a goblet ; further, the two wind goddesses spreading their robes as sails.   It is equally uncertain who made the groups in the voting enclosures of Olympos and Pan, and of Achilles and Cheiron, and yet such is their renown that the custodians are obliged to pledge their lives for their safety.

Bryaxis, Timotheos, and *Leochares* were rivals and contemporaries of Skopas, and must be mentioned with him, as they worked together on the Mausoleion.   This is the tomb erected by Artemisia in honour of her husband Mausolos, prince of Karia, who died in the second year of the hundred and seventh Olympiad [351 B.C.], and its place among the seven wonders of the world is largely due to these great sculptors.   The length of the south and north sides is 163 feet ; the two façades are

30
*The Mauso-
leion.*

Corr. Hell. xiv, 1890, p. 589 ff., places it at about B. C 375.

6. **Leocharen :** for his date see on xxxiv, 50.

7. **Mausoleum:** a history of its discovery, a discussion of the restorations proposed, and the chief literature up to 1891 are given by Newton in Smith's *Dict. Ant.* ii, p. 155 ff. Students will read with interest the latest restoration, attempted by E. Oldfield, *Archaeologia,* 1895, pp. 273-362. But it is as useless and unsatisfactory as others so far as the Plinian text is concerned.   Mr. Oldfield starts by rejecting *in toto* the variant readings of *cod. Bamb.,* and does this without adequate knowledge of the character of this MS.   Especially unsatisfactory is his rejection of *circumitum,* for the besetting sin of the *Bamb.* is not the introduction of words or syllables, but their omission (cf. H. L. Urlichs' note on xxxiv, 69 *Liberum patrem*).   Further, the facts that Mr. Oldfield writes in ignorance of anything more recent than Sillig's second edition, that he is unacquainted either with Detlefsen's edition, or with his article on the Plinian MSS. in the *Philologus* (t. xxviii), or with the *Chrestom.* of Urlichs, and that he confuses *Otto Jahn* (p. 284 and p. 290) with *Ludwig von Jan,* show how

little trust can be placed in his criticism of the text.—On architectural grounds alone, Mr. Oldfield's reconstruction may have merits of which the present writer feels incompetent to judge.   We have translated faithfully from *cod. Bamb.,* and in the notes I attempt no harmonizing of the Plinian description with monumental evidence, nor can I point out discrepancies, for the simple reason that any impartial student must admit that the real shape of the Mausoleion and distribution of its parts remain as much a riddle now as before.—The whole description of the Mausoleion is taken from Mucianus, Introd. p. lxxxviii.

8. **Mausolo . . . regulo:** he was, as a fact, only a satrap under the king of Persia ; Diodoros, xvi, 36, gives B. C. 353 as the date of his death.

9. **inter septem miracula :** it figures in the oldest canonical lists. The various lists of the 'Seven Wonders' are conveniently printed together by Orelli in the Appendix to his edition of Philo Byzantius, pp. 141-150.   *Ib.* pp. 192-194 will be found all the ancient descriptions of the Mausoleion.

11. **centenos:** this addition is unavoidable if we are to accept the total 440 feet as correct.

frontibus, toto circumitu pedes CCCCXXXX, attollitur in
altitudinem XXV cubitis, cingitur columnis XXXVI. pteron
31 vocavere circumitum.   ab oriente caelavit Scopas, a septentrione Bryaxis, a meridie Timotheus, ab occasu Leochares,
priusque quam peragerent regina obit.   non tamen recesse- 5
runt nisi absoluto iam, id gloriae ipsorum artisque monimentum iudicantes, hodieque certant manus.   accessit et
quintus artifex.   namque supra·pteron pyramis altitudine
inferiorem aequat, viginti quattuor gradibus in metae
cacumen se contrahens.   in summo est quadriga marmorea 10
quam fecit Pythis.   haec adiecta CXXXX pedum altitudine
32 totum opus includit.   Timothei manu Diana Romae est in
Palatio Apollinis delubro, cui signo caput reposuit Avianius
Evander.   in magna admiratione est Hercules Menestrati
et Hecate Ephesi in templo Dianae post aedem in cuius 15

1. CCCCXXXX] *Bamb.*; quadringentos undecim *reliqui.*   2. XXXV
Detlefsen.   11. altitudine] *Bamb., Riccard., Lips.*; altitudinem, *Detlefsen.*

2. pteron vocavere : cf. in § 19,
Πανδώρας γένεσιν *appellant.*
§ 31. 3. ab oriente . . . Scopas
. . . Leochares : the endeavours to
identify the styles of each sculptor
in the extant slabs have up to now
been unsatisfactory.   The dominant
thought and design seem Skopasian.
Vitruvius (vii, *praef.* 12), in his account
of the Mausoleion, names Praxiteles
as one of the sculptors (on this point
see Amelung, *Die Basis des Praxiteles
aus Mantinea,* p. 55 f.).
9. inferiorem : Newton, *loc. cit.,*
rightly points out that, according to
ordinary rules, the word to be supplied
would be *pyramidem,* which, however,
he considered inadmissible, as he
found no evidence for a pyramidal
substructure.   On the other hand,
Detlefsen's *altitudine[m]* does unwarranted violence to the text.
10. quadriga marmorea: a restoration of the extant fragments may now
be seen in the Mausoleion room of
the Brit. Mus.   That the so-called
'Artemisia' and 'Mausolos' can,
however, never have been placed in

the chariot has been made clear by
P. Gardner, *J. H. S.* xiii, p. 188 ff.
11. Pythis: Vitruvius, *loc. cit.,* gives
the name Phyteus (MSS.), but the
identity is not certain.
§ 32. 12. Timothei manu: the style
of this artist can now be satisfactorily
studied in the sculptured decorations
of the Asklepieion at Epidauros ; from
the inscription (above, note on § 30, 5)
we learn that he contracted (ἔλετο) to
construct (ἐργάσασθαι) and provide
(παρέχεν) models (τύπος)—presumably
for the pedimental sculptures—and for
the akroteria or angle figures of one of
the gables (ἄτερον αἰετόν).   From the
relation of the akroterial figures of
the west front (Centr. Mus. Catal.
155-157) to one another and to the
figures of the Amazon battle from the
corresponding west pediment, there
is every ground for regarding them as
the work of one artist, i. e. of
Timotheos ; Amelung, *Basis des Praxiteles,* p. 69 f., where the kinship of
the group of Leda and the Swan (best-
known replica in the Capitol ; Helbig,
459) to the Epidaurian sculptures is

shorter, and the whole perimeter is 440 feet; its height is 25 cubits [37½ feet], and it has thirty-six columns. This colonnade is called a πτερόν. The sculptures of the eastern front are 31 carved by Skopas, those on the north by Bryaxis, on the south by Timotheos, and on the west by Leochares. The queen died before the work was finished, but the artists carried it through to the end, deeming that it would be an abiding monument of their own glory and of the glory of art, and to this day they compete for the prize. A fifth sculptor also worked on the monument. Above the colonnade is a pyramid, of the same height as the lower structure, consisting of twenty-four retreating steps rising into a cone. On the apex stands a chariot and four horses in marble made by *Pythis*. Including this the height is 140 feet.

In the temple of Apollo on the Palatine at Rome stands an 32 Artemis by Timotheos, the head of which has been restored by Avianius Evander. Greatly admired is a Herakles by †*Menestratos*, and a Hekate at Ephesos in the temple of Artemis, behind the

pointed out (the likeness noted simultaneously by Winter, *Ath. Mitth.* xix, 1894, p. 157 ff.). Add.

13. **Avianius Evander**: cf. Hor. *Sat.* i, 3, 90 :—

  Comminxit lectum potus mensave catillum

Evandri manibus tritum deiecit; where the scholiast Porphyrio remarks that Evander was both chaser and sculptor (*plastes statuarum*), that Alexander brought him from Athens to Alexandria, whence he was taken to Rome *inter captivos*, doubtless on the capture of the city by Augustus in 25 B.C.; cf. further Cic. *Fam.* xiii, 2 ; 21 ; 27, and vii, 23, where Avianius figures rather as art-dealer than as artist ; cf. Brunn, *K. G.* i, p. 547.

14. **in magna admiratione**: these words introduce the fifth parenthetical mention of works elsewhere than in Rome. [The construction of the passage down to *incluta* is curious ; we get (i) admirable works (in *magna adm.*) ; (ii) works equally admirable (*non postferuntur*) ; (iii) a work of which nothing need be said,

for all the world understands the greatness of the drunken old woman by Myron—this last work being abruptly introduced by a *nam*, which implies an ellipse of the preceding sentence, according to a usage noted in xxxiv, 7, xxxv, 137. H. L. U.]

Menestrati: possibly identical with the sculptor of a statue of the unknown poetess Learchis ; Tatian, πρὸς Ἑλλ. p. 34, ed. Schwartz.

15. **Hecate Ephesi**: the information, like that on the Mausoleion, appears derived from Mucianus (*Introd.* p. lxxxviii).

post aedem : interpreted by Sillig (*Dict. of Artists*, s. v. Menestratos) as 'the back part of the temple,' i.e. the ὀπισθόδομος. But it is doubtful whether *post* can be susceptible of such a meaning. It therefore seems more reasonable to suppose that the Hekate of M. was contained in a separate shrine, within the precinct (*in templo*), but behind the great temple (*post aedem*). That the Hekate was in a closed locality, and not merely outside the temple in the open air, as

contemplatione admonent aeditui parcere oculis, tanta
marmoris radiatio est. non postferuntur et Charites in
propylo Atheniensium quas Socrates fecit alius ille quam
pictor, idem ut aliqui putant. nam Myronis illius qui in
aere laudatur anus ebria est Zmyrnae in primis incluta. 5
33 Pollio Asinius, ut fuit acris vehementiae, sic quoque spectari
monumenta sua voluit. in his sunt Centauri Nymphas
gerentes Arcesilae, Thespiades Cleomenis, Oceanus et Iuppiter Heniochi, Appiades Stephani, Hermerotes Taurisci,
34 non caelatoris illius sed Tralliani, Iuppiter hospitalis Papyli 10
Praxitelis discipuli, Zethus et Amphion ac Dirce et taurus

9. Heniochi] *Jan*; eniochi *Bamb.*; enthochi *Riccard.*, *Voss.*; Antiochi
Urlichs in Chrest, Detlefsen.

some authorities suppose, is evident
from the story of the *marmoris
radiatio;* the mysterious gleam of the
marble can only be understood if the
statue was seen in the half-light of a
shrine, and becomes nonsense if the
Hekate was out of doors.

1. **aeditui**: the fact that the
statue was shown by temple attendants
is another argument in favour of its
being in a closed locality.

2. **marmoris radiatio**: the face
of the statue, like the hands and feet,
would be left in the original colour
of the marble, or just toned by wax
(see in xxxv, 133 note on *circumlitioni*); the white face would be seen
gleaming through the dusk of the
shrine—the imagination being doubtless stimulated by a sense of the
mysterious personality of Hekate.—
M. S. Reinach kindly points out to
me that we seem to detect in the
legend traces of the old belief that
mortals might not look in the face of
the gods without being struck blind;
cf. Teiresias and the mysterious
Epizelos of Herodotos.

Charites: the type is known from
two reliefs in Rome (most famous
in the Vatican, Helbig, 83) and three
in Athens, two of which were found on
the Akropolis (*Ath. Mitth.* iii, 1878,

p. 181 ff., Furtwängler). They are all
after an original of the period ab. B. C.
470; cf. Furtwängler, *Masterpieces*,
p. 23, note 1, Introd. p. 1, note 2.

in propylo Athen.: Paus. i, 22,
8: κατὰ δὲ τὴν ἔσοδον αὐτὴν ἤδη
τὴν ἐς ἀκρόπολιν Ἑρμῆν, ὃν Προπύλαιον
ὀνομάζουσι καὶ Χάριτας Σωκράτην
ποιῆσαι τὸν Σωφρονίσκου λέγουσι; cf.
note on xxxv, 101 for the unusual form
propylon, and Introd. p. 1.

3. **Socrates fecit**: it is curious
to note that Pliny knows nothing of the
popular identification of the sculptor
Sokrates with the philosopher,
accepted by Pausanias, *loc. cit.*, and
a number of other authorities (Overb.
S. Q. 907-914), Introd. *loc. cit.*

alius . . . idem: contains the
trace of a similar controversy to that
noted in the case of Pythagoras,
xxxiv, 60; Introd. p. 1.

4. **Myronis illius**: xxxiv, 49;
57-59.

5. **anus ebria**: the identification
of the work with the well-known
statue of an old woman nursing an ivy-
crowned wine-jar (Helbig, *Class. Ant.*
431, p. 318, where see list of replicas
and literature) is nothing less than
certain. Nor do the grounds for
attributing the work, on account of
the subject, to a later Myron seem

shrine, in looking at which the temple guardians advise visitors to be cautious, so dazzling is the lustre of the marble. Not inferior are the Charites in the gateway at Athens; the *Sokrates* who made them is to be distinguished from the painter, though some believe in their identity. As to *Myron*, the celebrated *Myron.* bronze caster, his statue at Smyrna of an intoxicated old woman ranks among the most famous works.

Asinius Pollio with his characteristic enterprise was eager that his 33 galleries should attract attention. They contain Kentaurs with *Gallery of Asinius Pollio.* nymphs on their backs by †*Arkesilas*, Thespiades by *Kleomenes*, figures of Okeanos and Zeus by †*Heniochos*, nymphs of the Appia by *Stephanos*, terminal busts of Eros by *Tauriskos* (not the famous chaser, but Tauriskos of Tralles), a Zeus of strangers by †*Papylos* 34 the pupil of Praxiteles, and Zethos and Amphion, with Dirke, the

reasonable. The figures from the angle of the west pediment of the temple at Olympia show that the presentation of aged women was not alien to the art of the early fifth century. The epithet *ebria*, like the *temulenta* applied to the flute-player of Lysippos in xxxiv, 63, rests perhaps on some slight misapprehension of the motive, or mistranslation from the Greek.

§ 33. 7. monumenta: above, note on § 23.

Centauri Nymph. gerentes: for the subject cf. the wall-painting, Helbig, *Wandgem.* 499; cf. also the Kentaurs (bearing Erotes) of Aristeas and Papias (Capitol, Helbig, 512, 513).

8. Arcesilae: xxxv, 155; below, § 41.

Thespiades: same subject by Teisikra'es, xxxiv, 66; by Praxiteles, below, § 39.

Cleomenis: his identity with— or relationship to—the sculptor of the so-called 'Germanicus' in the Louvre (*I. G. B.* 344), or of the altar with sacrifice of Iphigeneia in Florence (*I. G. B.* 380), is quite uncertain. (*I. G. B.* 513, from Medicean Venus, is a modern forgery.)

9. Heniochi: [von Jan's reading may be considered certain, the names *Arcesilae . . . Taurisci* being in alphabetical order.—H. L. U.].

Appiades: so called doubtless from their resemblance to the statues of the nymphs of the Appian aqueduct which adorned a fountain of the Forum Julium; cf. Ovid, *Ars Amat.* i, 79; iii, 451; cf. *Rem. Amor.* 660; Gilbert, *Rom*, iii, p. 226, note 1.

Stephani: probably identical with the pupil of Pasiteles, whose inscription is read on the statue of an athlete in the Villa Albani, *I. G. B.* 574; cf. *ib.* 375, where he is named as the master of Menelaos, the artist of the famous group in the Museo Boncompagni (Helbig, 887).

Hermerotes: terminal busts of Eros; for extant instances in statuary see Furtwängler, *Masterpieces*, p. 69 (Eros), p. 60 (Athena), p. 234 ff. (Herakles). The old interpretation that the several divinities were combined with Hermes in a double terminal bust is without support from the monuments, though it is favoured by Cicero, *Att.* i, iv. 3: *quod ad me de Hermathena scribis, per mihi gratum est: est ornamentum Academiae proprium meae, quod et Hermes commune omnium et Minerva singulare est eius gymnasii.* Add.

10. caelatoris: xxxiii, 156.

§ 34. hospitalis = ξένιος.

11. Zethus . . . taurus: a group

vinculumque ex eodem lapide, a Rhodo advecta opera
Apolloni et Taurisci. parentum hi certamen de se fecere,
Menecraten videri professi, sed esse naturalem Artemidorum.
eodem loco Liber pater Eutychidis laudatur, ad Octaviae
vero porticum Apollo Philisci Rhodi in delubro suo, item 5
Latona et Diana et Musae novem et alter Apollo nudus.
35 eum qui citharam in eodem templo tenet Timarchides fecit,
intra Octaviae vero porticus aedem Iunonis ipsam deam
Dionysius et Polycles, aliam Venerem eodem loco Philiscus,
cetera signa Pasiteles. idem Polycles et Dionysius Timar- 10

9. Polycles aliam, Venerem *Detlefsen.*

('Toro Farnese,' Naples, Friederichs-
Wolters, 1402), which is generally
accepted as the identical one mentioned by Pliny, was discovered in
1546 in the Thermae of Caracalla.
    1. ex eodem lapide : cf. below,
§ 36 ; § 37 ; § 41 ; the 'Bull' and
the 'Laokoon' are however constructed
of several pieces, and the same was
most likely the case with the 'Lioness'
of Arkesilaos, and the chariot-group of
Lysias. With regard to the 'Laokoon'
and the 'Lioness' Robert, *Arch.
März.* p. 143, note, had suggested
that *ex uno lapide* meant a group
disposed on one basis, in opposition
to groups composed of statues set
each upon a separate basis. But the
grammatical propriety of this interpretation is doubtful, cf. Urlichs,
Arkesilaos, p. 16, note 2. Förster
(*Görlitz. Verhandl.* p. 298) believes
that Pliny in saying that the Bull and
the Laokoon were *ex uno lapide* had
been deceived by the appearance of
the groups. As a fact, the expression
seems, in all four cases, to imply little
beyond the desire to heighten the
impression of technical difficulty, by
adding one of those details which
readily appeal to popular imagination; cf. *Anth.* ix, 759 (εἰς ἅρμα
λίθινον) :—
Εἶς λίθος, ἅρμ', ἐλατήρ, ἵπποι, ζυγόν,
    ἡνία, μάστιξ.

Ib. 760 :—
Εἶς δίφρος, ἅρμ', ἐλατήρ, ἵπποι, ζυγός,
    ἡνία, νίκη.
Rhodo: much light has recently
been thrown on the dates of the
Rhodian school by two papers of
Maurice Holleaux (*Rev. de Phil.*
xvii, 1893, pp. 171-185), and H. von
Gaertringen (*Jahrb.* ix, 1894, pp. 23-
43). According to the latter, the
inscriptions fall into two periods : (i)
from close of third century to B. C.
163 (Pydna) ; (ii) from B. C. 88, at
the close of the Mithridatic war, to
the total reduction of the Rhodian
state by Cassius Longinus and Cassius
of Parma in B. C. 43 (Appian, Ἐμφ.
iv, 60-74 ; v, 2). It was then that
many a Rhodian work of art was taken
to Rome.
    2. **Apolloni et Taurisci** :   a
basis found in the theatre of Magnesia
on the Maiander bears the inscription
Ἀπολλώνιος Ταυρίσκου [Τραλλιανὸς]
ἐποίει : it is published by H. v. Gaertringen (*Athen. Mitth.* xix, 1894,
p. 37 ff.), who dates it from early
Imperial times, so that the Ταυρίσκος
of the inscription (though of course not
the Ἀπολλώνιος) may be one of the
sculptors of the Bull, which would be
executed previous to B. C. 43 (see previous note). The names were probably
recurrent in a family of artists.
    parentum hi certamen :   the

bull and the cord, all carved out of one block. It is the joint work of *Apollonios* and *Tauriskos*, and was brought from Rhodes. These two sculptors occasioned a controversy as to their parentage, by declaring that Menekrates was their nominal, Artemidoros their real father. In the same collection is a fine Dionysos by Eutychides. Near the gallery of Octavia in the *Other Roman galleries* temple of Apollo stands a statue of the god by *Philiskos* of Rhodes, together with Leto, Artemis, and the nine Muses and another nude Apollo. *Timarchides* made the Apollo with the cithara in the same temple, and *Dionysios* and *Polykles* the statue 35 of Juno within her temple in the portico of Octavia. A second Aphrodite in the same place is by *Philiskos*, and the other statues by *Pasiteles*. The same Polykles and Dionysios, the sons of

words are rhetorical, or rest on a Roman misunderstanding of the Greek inscription. According to a custom of which the Rhodian inscriptions afford numerous instances (cf. *inter alia, I. G. B.* 174, 181), the artists had added to their signature not only the name of their real father, but that of their father by adoption. H. v. G. suggests the following restoration : Ἀπολλώνιος καὶ Ταυρίσκος Ἀρτεμιδώρου, καθ᾽ ὑοθεσίαν δὲ Μενεκράτεος, Τραλλιανοὶ ἐποίησαν.

4. **Eutychidis** : probably not the pupil of Lysippos (xxxiv, 78), who was a bronze statuary ; the name was common ; see Loewy in *I. G. B.* 143.

5. **in delubro suo** : i. e. the temple of Apollo Sosianus ; notes on xxxv, 99, above, § 28.

6. **Musae novem** : Amelung (*Basis des Praxiteles*, p. 44 f. and Append.) shows that this is probably the group which inspired the artists of the Muses on the basis from Halikarnassos (Trendelenburg, *Der Musen Chor*, Winckelmannspr. xxxvi, 1876) and of the Muses on the relief of the Apotheosis of Homer (Brunn-Bruckmann, plate 50), both in the Brit. Mus. It is significant that both works are from Southern Asia-Minor, i. e. from the neighbourhood of Rhodes.

§ 35. 7. **Timarchides** : son of Polykles of Athens, xxxiv, 52, and brother of Timokles, *ib.* ; his two sons, Polykles II and Dionysios, are mentioned below ; together with his brother (οἱ Πολυκλέους παῖδες) he made for Olympia the statue of the pugilist Agesarchos of Triteia, and for Elateia statues of Asklepios and of Athena (Paus. vi. 12, 9 ; x, 34, 6 ; 8).

8. **aedem Iunonis** : erected together with the adjacent temple (*proxima aedes*) of Jupiter by Q. Caecilius Metellus after his triumph of B. C. 149 ; Vell. Paterc. I, 11.

ipsam deam : the temple statue ; cf. *Neptunus ipse*, above, § 26 ; *simulacrum ipsum Trophonii*, xxxiv, 66.

9. **Dionysius et Polycles** : identical with the *Polycles et Dionysius Timarchidis filii*, below.

aliam Venerem : Urlichs (*Quellenreg.* p. 8) has shown that these words refer back to § 15, where an Aphrodite by Pheidias, in the *porticus Oct.*, had already been mentioned.

10. **Pasiteles** : note on § 39.

Dionysius : together with his nephew Timarchides II, he made the statue of C. Ofellius, found in Delos ; it bears the inscription Διονύσιος Τιμαρχίδου καὶ Τιμαρχίδης Πολυκλέους Ἀθηναῖοι, *I. G. B.* 242.

chidis fili Iovem qui est in proxima aede fecerunt, Pana et
Olympum luctantes eodem loco Heliodorus, quod est
alterum in terris symplegma nobile, Venerem lavantem se
36 *sedaedalsas* stantem Polycharmus. ex honore apparet
in magna auctoritate habitum Lysiae opus, quod in Palatio 5
super arcum divus Augustus honori Octavi patris sui dicavit
in aedicula columnis adornata, id est quadriga currusque et
Apollo ac Diana ex uno lapide. in hortis Servilianis reperio
laudatos Calamidis Apollinem illius caelatoris, Dercylidis
pyctas, Amphistrati Callisthenen historiarum scriptorem. 10
37 nec deinde multo plurium fama est, quorundam claritati in
operibus eximiis obstante numero artificum, quoniam nec
unus occupat gloriam nec plures pariter nuncupari possunt,
sicut in Laocoonte, qui est in Titi imperatoris domo, opus
omnibus et picturae et statuariae artis praeferendum. ex 15
uno lapide eum ac liberos draconumque mirabiles nexus de
consili sententia fecere summi artifices Hagesander et Poly-

4. Sesedaedalsas stantem *Bamb.* ; sesededalsa stantem *Ricc., Voss.* ; se sed et
aliam stantem *Sillig*; sese Daedalus, aliam stantem *Detlefsen.*

1. **Iovem** : above, note on *aedem
Iunonis.*

Pana et Olympum : the names
are significant as showing that these
συμπλέγματα were mostly erotic
groups, composed perhaps in the
scheme familiar from the groups in
Dresden.

Heliodorus : xxxiv, 91 ; the signature of his son (Πλούταρχος
Ἡλιοδώρου Ῥόδιος ἐποίησε) closes the
great inscription, discovered in Rhodes
by Hiller v. Gaertringen, which since
it contains the names of L. Murena
and L. Lucullus has been dated by
Mommsen at B.C. 82-74 (*Jahrb.* ix,
1894, p. 25 ff.; cf. also Maurice
Holleaux, *Rev. de Philol.* xvii, 1893,
p. 173; and *I. G. B.* 194-196).

3. **alterum**: harks back to the similar group by Kephisodotos in § 24.

Venerem lavantem se: the
'Vénus Accroupie' in the Louvre
(Friederichs-Wolters 1467) is looked
upon as a copy of this work, but
see Add.

§ **36. 6. super arcum**: the arch was
part of the *Propylaea* which formed
the entrance to the *area* of Apollo,
Gardthausen *Augustus I*, p. 962 ; *ib.
II*, p. 575.

Octavii patris: Suet. *Aug.* 3.

8. **ex uno lapide** : note on § 34.

hortis Servilianis : above, § 23.

9. **illius caelatoris**: xxxiii, 155 ;
xxxiv, 47 ; he is presumably identical
with the bronze statuary, xxxiv, 71.

10. **Amphistrati** : known also
from Tatian (πρὸς Ἕλλην. p. 34, ed.
Schwartz) as sculptor of the portrait
of an unknown poetess Kleito.

Callisthenem : of Olynthos, pupil
and nephew of Aristotle ; according
to Diodoros, xiv, 117, his 'Hellenika'
were a history of the years B.C.
387-357 (Peace of Antalkidas to the
Phokaian war).

§ **37. 14. in Laocoonte**: the original group was found on Jan. 14, 1506,
near the Baths of Titus, whither it may
have been moved from his Palace at
a date posterior to Pliny (on the cir-

A. THE FAMILY OF POLYKLES.

[Stadieus of Athens]
Paus. vi, 4, 5.

|

POLYKLES I OF ATHENS { *Plin.* xxxiv, 52.
fl. about 156 B.C. { *Paus.* vi, 4, 5.
{ *I. G. Insul.* i, 855 ?

TIMOKLES { *Plin.* xxxiv, 52.
fl. ab. { *Paus.* vi, 12, 9.
156 B.C. { „ x, 34, 6; 8.

TIMARCHIDES I *Plin.* xxxiv, 91 ?
fl. after 140 B.C. { „ xxxvi, 35.
{ *Paus.* vi, 12, 9.
{ „ x, 34, 6; 8.
{ *I. G. B.* 328? cf.
{ *Ath. Mitth.* xx,
1895, p. 219.

POLYKLES II (*Plin.* xxxvi, 35)
after 140 B.C.

DIONYSIOS OF ATHENS
140–90 B.C. (*Plin.*
xxxv, 35, and *I. G. B.*
242).

TIMARCHIDES II (νεώτερος)
OF ATHENS (Θορίκιος):
I. G. B. 242 and the inscr.
Athen. Mitth. xx, 1895,
p. 216.

B. THE FAMILY OF ATHANODOROS.

ATHANODOROS I (Paton inscr.)

HAGESANDROS I (Paton inscr. Lindian decree, &c.)

HAGESANDROS II*   POLYDOROS*   ATHANODOROS II*
(adopted by Dionysios,
Lindian inscr.)

* The sculptors of the Laokoon.

Timarchides, made the Zeus in the adjoining temple, where are also the Pan and Olympos interlaced by *Heliodoros*, second in renown among such groups in all the world, an Aphrodite bathing . . . . standing by †*Polycharmos*. The 36 distinction conferred on the work of *Lysias* shows how highly it was esteemed, inasmuch as the god Augustus dedicated it in honour of his father Octavius; it was placed within a small building adorned with columns upon the arch on the Palatine. It consisted of a team of four horses, a chariot, Apollo and Artemis, all carved out of one block of marble. I find that in the gardens of Servilius are an Apollo by *Kalamis*, the well-known silver chaser, boxers by †*Derkylidas*, and a portrait of Kallisthenes the historian by *Amphistratos*, all of which are mentioned with praise.

Not many celebrated artists remain to be named; in the case 37 of certain masterpieces the very number of the collaborators is an *Collaboration of different sculptors.* obstacle to their individual fame, since neither can one man take to himself the whole glory, nor have a number so great a claim to honour. This is the case with the Laokoon in the palace of the Emperor Titus, a work superior to all the pictures and bronzes of the world. Out of one block of marble did the illustrious artists *Hagesander*, *Polydoros*, and *Athanodoros* of Rhodes, after taking counsel together, carve Laokoon, his children, and the

---

cumstances of the find see Michaelis, *Jahrb.* v, 1890, p. 16); it is now in the Vatican (Helbig, 153). The full literature from 1755 to 1879 is given by Blümner, Comm. to Lessing's *Laokoon*, 2nd ed. p. 722; cf. also Friederichs-Wolters, 1422, and the three papers by Förster, (1) in *Görlitz. Verhandlungen*, pp. 75–94, and 293 to 307; (2) *Jahrb.* vi, 1891, p. 177 ff.; (3) *Jahrb.* ix, 1894, p. 43 ff.

in Titi imp. domo; xxxiv, 55.

15. statuariae : note on xxxiv, 54 (*toreuticen*).

ex uno lapide : note above on § 34: Michelangelo Buonarotti and Giovanni Cristofano, 'che sono i primi scultori di Roma, negano ch'ella sia d'un sol marmo, e mostrano circa a quattro commettiture'; Trivulzio, quoted by Michaelis, *loc. cit.* note 49.

16. de consili sententia : that these words mean neither 'by decree of the Emperor's Privy Council' (Lachmann, *A. Z.* 1848, p. 236 = *Kleine Schriften*, p. 273), nor 'by decree of the Council of Rhodes,' nor yet 'after consultation of the artists with their friends' (Mommsen, *Hermes*, xx, 1885, p. 268), but are to be understood in the simple sense given to them above, has been brilliantly proved by Förster in *Görlitz. Verhandl.* pp. 75 ff.; for the usage, cf. Cicero *Verres*, II, iii, 18; v, 12, 53, 54, 114; *pro Balbo*, 11, 19, 38, and often: Caesar, *B. G.* iii, 16; Livy, xlv, 26 and 29; Plin. *Ep.* v, 1, 6; 3, 8; vi. 31, 12.

17. Hag. et Pol. et Ath. Rhodi : the name of Athanodoros occurs in seven inscriptions published in facsimile by Förster, *Jahrb.* vi, 1891, pp.

P

38 dorus et Athenodorus Rhodi. similiter Palatinas domos
Caesarum replevere probatissimis signis Craterus cum Py-
thodoro, Polydeuces cum Hermolao, Pythodorus alius cum
Artemone, et singularis Aphrodisius Trallianus. Agrippae
Pantheum decoravit Diogenes Atheniensis, in columnis 5
templi eius Caryatides probantur inter pauca operum, sicut
in fastigio posita signa sed propter altitudinem loci minus
39 celebrata. inhonorus est nec in templo ullo Hercules ad
quem Poeni omnibus annis humana sacrificaverant victima,
humi stans ante aditum porticus ad nationes. sitae fuere 10
et Thespiades ad aedem Felicitatis, quarum unam amavit
eques Romanus Iunius Pisciculus, ut tradit Varro ; admirator

12. admirator] *Bamb.* ; admiratur *reliqui, Detlefsen.*

191–195. Of these, the Lindian decree
in honour of Athanodoros, son of
Hagesander, has been lately fully
published by H. v. Gaertringen
(*Jahrb.* ix, 1894, p. 34), and shown to
be not earlier, but possibly somewhat
later, than the Ploutarchos-Helio-
doros inscription (B.C. 82–74) mentioned above. With the help of lines
16, 17 of the inscription published
by Paton, *B. C. H.* xiv, p. 278,
['Aγήσ]ανδρος ῾Aγησάνδρου [τοῦ]
'Aθανοδ[ώ]ρο[υ], H. von Gaertringen
(*op. cit.*) reconstructs the annexed
table. The Hagesander who worked
on the Laokoon would more probably
be the elder brother than the father of
the other two sculptors. The present
writer can see nothing in the technique
or style of the Laokoon to prevent our
accepting for it the date suggested by
the inscriptions. Helbig however
has again quite lately (*Class. Ant., loc.
cit.*) maintained that the Laokoon
belongs to the period previous to the
Pergamene altar, and that the Athanodoros inscriptions belonged to copies
of his works.

§ 38. 2. replevere : rhetorical, cf.
refertae in § 14 ; *implent*, xxxv, 148,
&c.

Craterus ... Aphrodisius : Pliny's

contention is quaintly confirmed,
since not a single one of these artists
is known outside his text (see however
I. G. B. 427).

4. Agrippae Pantheum : xxxiv,
13.

5. Diogenes : identity with the
Diogenes of the inscription found at
Nineveh (Brit. Mus., *I. G. B.* 561 ;
A. S. Murray in *J. H. S.* iii, p. 240 ff.)
is possible, but doubtful.

in columnis ... Caryatides : the
late discoveries in connexion with
the Pantheon have, unfortunately,
thrown no light on the architectural
function performed by these Caryatides. Stark, *Arch. Zeit.* xviii, 1866,
p. 249 f., supposes *in col.* to mean
down among the columns as opposed
to the statues *in fastigio ;* in this case
the Kar. would be not architectonic,
but dancing figures like the Karyatides
of Praxiteles ; above, § 23. Addenda.

§ 39. 8. inhonorus est : rhetorical indignation ; cf. in xxxiv, 89,
the passage on the Bull of Phalaris.

Hercules : a Phoenician or Tyrian
Melkart, presumably brought from
Carthage by the younger Scipio B. C.
146 (cf. Peter, *ap.* Roscher, i, 246 ;
Urlichs, *Griech. Statuen im Rep.
Rom*, p. 13).

wondrous coils of the snakes. So, too, on the Palatine, †*Krateros* 38
and his colleague †*Pythodoros*, †*Polydeukes* and †*Hermolaos*, a
second †*Pythodoros* and †*Artemon*, and †*Aphrodisios* of Tralles,
who worked alone, have filled the mansions of the Caesars with
excellent statues. The sculptures of the Pantheum of Agrippa are *Pantheon.*
by †*Diogenes* of Athens; the Karyatides of the temple columns
are in the very first rank, and so are the statues of the pediment,
though less well known because of the great height at which they
stand. Dishonoured and without a shrine is the Hercules to 39
whom the Carthaginians offered annual human sacrifice; it
stands on the ground in front of the entrance to the Gallery
of the Nations. By the temple of Felicity stood also the
Thespiades, of one of which, according to Varro, a Roman knight,
Junius Pisciculus, was enamoured. Varro likewise admires

10. **humi stans**: i. e. the statue
was without pedestal or basis.

port. ad nationes: Serv. on
Aen. 8, 721: *porticum Augustus
fecerat in qua simulacra omnium
gentium collocaverat, quae porticus
adpellabatur ad nationes;* it must not
be confused with Pompeius' *porticus*
of the fourteen nations, below, § 41.

11. **Thespiades**: Cic. *Verr.* II, iv,
4: *atque ille L. Mummius, cum Thespiadas, quae ad aedem Felicitatis sunt,
ceteraque profana ex illo oppido [Thes-
piis] signa tolleret, hunc...Cupidinem*
(above, § 22) . . . *non attigit.* The
statues must have been among those
which L. Lucullus borrowed from
Mummius, to adorn the temple up to
the day of his election, and cleverly
managed not to return (Strabo, viii,
p. 381; cf. Dio Cassius, fr. 75). From
Varro (*Ling. Lat.* vi, 2) we learn that
the *Thespiades = Musae.* It is usually
assumed that the *Thespiades* are identical with the *signa quae ante aedem
Fel. fuere,* by Praxiteles, cf. xxxiv, 69,
where see note; but the fact that the
latter were of bronze sufficiently disposes of the identification. The pro-
venance, however, of the *Thespiades,*
their celebrity, the subject and the
story of Pisciculus, show them to have
been Praxitelean works. The famous

group of the Muses found at Tivoli,
now in the Vatican (Helbig, 268–274),
may be looked upon as copies; their
Praxitelean character has been search-
ingly analysed by Amelung, *Basis
des Prax. aus Mantinea,* 1895, pp.
25–49.

aedem Felicitatis: xxxiv, 69;
built by L. Lucullus to commemorate
his Spanish campaigns of B.C. 150–
151 (Urlichs, *Arkesilaos,* p. 7), ded.
142 B. C., Dio Cass. fr. 75. On the
temple-statue, see xxxv, 156.

12. **ut tradit Varro**: V. is evidently the authority for the whole
passage from *sitae fuere . . . auctor est*
in § 41. His name is brought in at
this point because Pliny looks upon
the story of Pisciculus as of doubtful
authenticity, and therefore lays all
responsibility upon his author.

admirator et Pasitelis: the
reading is proved by the context
Arcesilaum quoque magn. Varro in
§ 41, where the *quoque* has no sense
unless Varro's admiration of some
other artist had been previously recorded; Furtwängler, *Plinius,* p. 41;
cf. the citations from Varro in xxxv,
155–157 : *Varro tradit sibi cognitum
Possim . . . idem magn. Arcesil . . .
laudat et Pasitelen.* On Pasiteles, see
Introd. p. lxxvii.

et Pasitelis, qui et quinque volumina scripsit nobilium
40 operum in toto orbe.   natus hic in Graeca Italiae ora et
civitate Romana donatus cum his oppidis Iovem fecit ebo-
reum in Metelli aede qua campus petitur.   accidit ei, cum
in navalibus ubi ferae Africanae erant per caveam intuens 5
leonem caelaret, ut ex alia cavea panthera erumperet non
levi periculo diligentissimi artificis.   fecisse opera complura
41 dicitur, quae fecerit nominatim non refertur.   Arcesilaum
quoque magnificat Varro, cuius se marmoream habuisse
leaenam aligerosque ludentis cum ea Cupidines, quorum 10
alii religatam tenerent, alii cornu cogerent bibere, alii calci-
arent soccis, omnes ex uno lapide.   idem et a Coponio
quattuordecim nationes quae sunt circa Pompeium factas
auctor est.   invenio et Canachum laudatum inter statuarios
42 fecisse marmorea.   nec Sauram atque Batrachum obliterari 15
convenit qui fecere templa Octaviae porticibus inclusa natione ipsi Lacones.   quidam et opibus praepotentes fuisse
eos putant ac sua inpensa construxisse inscriptionem sperantes, qua negata hoc tamen alio modo usurpasse.   sunt

1. fraxiteles *Bamb.*; passitelis *reliqui*; Pasiteles *Detlefsen.*

1. **nobilium operum**: the Greek
title would be περὶ ἐνδόξων ἔργων.
§ **40. 3. civitate . . . oppidis**:
during the social war of B.C. 90–89,
when by the *Leges Iulia* and *Plautia
Papiria* the right of citizenship was
extended to all the cities of Italy.
4. **in Metelli aede**: i.e. the temple of Jupiter mentioned above, § 35.
qua campus: sc. *Martius*, therefore the temple was on the north side
of the *porticus Octaviae.*
5. **navalibus**: the naval docks
of the Campus Martius, on the Tiber,
over against the *prata Quinctia;* cf.
Liv. iii, 26, 8, and xlv, 42, *sub fin.*;
Gilbert, *Rom*, pp. 146–150. The event
referred to may have happened in B.C.
55, when wild beasts were brought
from Africa for the games of Pompeius; Plin. viii, 53, 64.
8. **non refertur**: i.e. by Varro.
§ **41. Arcesilaum**: xxxv, 155,
where see notes.

9. **se . . . habuisse**: xxxiii, 154,
where Varro is likewise cited as owner
and authority.   His works of art were
scattered in the proscriptions of B.C.
43.   Introd. p. lxxxiv.
marmoream . . . leaenam: the
subject recalls the beautiful relief in
Vienna of a lioness (Schreiber, *Hell.
Rel.*, pl. i), which, with its companion (sheep suckling a lamb), can
help us to recover the style of sculptures of animals executed by Arkesilaos
and Pasiteles, Wickhoff, *Wiener
Genesis*, p. 26.
13. **quattuordecim nationes**: to
correspond to the number of nations
subjugated by Pompeius (Plut. *Pomp.*
xlv; cf. Vell. ii, 40; Plin. vii, 98
mentions only thirteen nations; the
fourteenth statue was apparently added
to commemorate the triumph over the
pirates, a mention of which closes
the Act. Triumph. for the year 693;
Gilbert, *Rom*, p. 326, note 2). These

Pasiteles, the author of five books on the celebrated works of art *Pasiteles.* in all the world. This artist was born on the Greek coast of **40** Italy, and received the Roman citizenship when it was given to the cities of that district. He made the ivory statue of Jupiter in the temple of Metellus on the way to the Field of Mars. It happened that once at the docks where were the wild beasts from Africa, as he was looking into a den to make a study of a lion on a relief, a panther broke out of another cage, to the great peril of the conscientious artist. His works are said to be numerous, but they are nowhere mentioned by name. †*Arkesilaos* also is highly **41** esteemed by Varro, who possessed a marble group by his hand *Arkesilaos.* of a lioness with winged Loves sporting about her ; some are holding her by a cord, others are forcing her to drink out of a horn, and others are putting shoes upon her ; the whole is carved out of one block. Varro is again my authority for saying that †*Coponius* made the fourteen statues of the nations which stand round the theatre of Pompeius. I find too that *Kanachos*, famous for his bronzes, worked also in marble, nor must I overlook †*Sauras* and †*Batrachos*, Lakonians by birth, who built the temples **42** enclosed by the galleries of Octavia. Some say that they were *Sauras and* rich men who built the temples at their own cost, hoping that *Batrachos.* their names would be inscribed upon them. Foiled in this, they yet achieved their object in another way, so it is said, and it is

statues are the earliest instances of those personifications of conquered peoples so conspicuous in Roman art. It is noteworthy that the artist was a Roman (Brunn, *K. G.* i, p. 602). These may be the statues concerning the placing of which Atticus advised Pompeius, Cic. *Att.* iv, 9.

circa Pompeium : Suet. *Nero*, 46.

14. Canachum : xxxiv, 50, 75.

§ 42. 15. Sauram atque Batrachum : names of animals were familiar in Greece as proper names (cf. Ταῦρος, Σκύμνος, Τέττιξ, Μῦς, and the long lists in Fick, *Gr. Personennamen*, p. 314 ff.). Moreover, it was a usual Roman custom to introduce—on grave-reliefs—some allusive emblem to the name of the deceased : a boar for Titus Statilius Aper (*C. I. L.* vi, 1975 ; Helbig, *Class. Ant.* 423); a calf

for C. Tullius Vitulus (Fabretti, *Inscr.* p. 187). By an extension of this custom, the architects S. and B. might carve a frog and a lizard in lieu of signature among the ornaments of a column. The serious objection to the story is that Vitruvius (iii, 2, 5) names Hermodoros of Salamis as the architect of the temples. We must therefore conclude either that the story is aitiological—the ornaments of the columns giving rise to a story to which the custom of allusive emblems noted above lent plausibility— or that S. and B. were architects-adjoint, or perhaps merely donors of the said columns, whom at a later date legend turned into architects of the temples.

18. inscriptionem sperantes : this portion of the anecdote is, in any case, apocryphal.

certe etiamnum in columnarum spiris inscalptae nominum
43 eorum argumento lacerta atque rana.   in Iovis aede ex iis
pictura cultusque reliquus omnis femineis argumentis constat, erat enim facta Iunoni, sed, cum inferrentur signa,
permutasse geruli traduntur, et id religione custoditum 5
velut ipsis diis sedem ita partitis.   ergo et in Iunonis aede
cultus est qui Iovis esse debuit.   sunt et in parvolis marmoreis famam consecuti Myrmecides, cuius quadrigam cum
agitatore operuit alis musca, et Callicrates, cuius formicarum
pedes atque alia membra pervidere non est.   10
44   Haec sint dicta de marmoris scalptoribus summaque
claritate artificum.

2. lacerta atque rana: cf. the
lizard and frog carved on the capital
of one of the columns of San Lorenzo
fuori le mura, transferred from some
ancient building.

§ 43. in Iovis aede: above, §§
35, 40; according to Vell. Paterc.
i, 11, who states that the temple of
Jupiter was the first in Rome to be
built of marble; the temples being
sine inscriptione, legend naturally
soon became active on the subject.

7. parvolis marmoreis: a confusion of Pliny's, who in vii, 85,
mentions Myrm. and Kall. as workers
in ivory.

8. Myrmecides: of Athens, according to Choiroboskos (quoted by
Schol. to Dionysios Thrax = Overb.

Schriftquell. 2194), or of Miletos
(Ailian, ποικ. ἱστ. i, 17). He is generally represented as making the chariot
conjointly with K. Another marvel
of their μικροτεχνία was a grain of
sesame engraved with an elegiac
distich (according to Plutarch, *adv.
Stoicos*, xiv, 5, two lines of Homer).
There is no clue to the date of either
artist.

quadrigam: in vii, 85 it is
mentioned as of ivory, while Choiroboskos (above) says iron; and the
grammarian Theodosios (*S. Q.* 2201),
bronze; it looks suspiciously as if the
quadriga were apocryphal. Yet the
execution of a microscopic chariot was
quite within the power of the ancient
goldsmith, cf. the tiny chariot led by

undeniably true that a lizard and a frog, typifying their names, are still to be seen carved on the bases of the columns. Of these **43** two temples the one dedicated to Jupiter contains only paintings and decorations relating to women, for as a matter of fact it was built for Juno; but the porters made a mistake, it is said, when they brought in the statues, and superstition consecrated the error, as though this division of their shrines were due to the gods themselves. In the same way the temple of Juno has the ornaments appropriate to Jupiter.

Miniature works in marble likewise secured renown for *Myrme-* *Miniature* *kides*, whose four-horse chariot and charioteer could be covered *works.* by the wings of a fly, and for *Kallikrates*, whose ants have feet and limbs too small to be distinguished by the human eye.

This closes what I have to say of workers in marble and of the **44** most famous sculptors.

---

a Nike, with Erotes at each side, belonging to the ear-pendant, *Ant. du Bosphore Cimmérien*, ed. Reinach, pl. xii, 5, 5ª. Reinach (p. 4) justly sees in it a confirmation of the praises bestowed by the ancients on the μικρο-τεχνία of Theodoros, Myrmekides, and Kallikrates. Perhaps, therefore, we should look upon all these artists as practising the art of goldsmiths by the side of the greater art of statuary in bronze or marble (see note on xxxiv, 83).

9. **Callicrates :** of Lakedaimon (Ailian and Choiroboskos).

formicarum : the fashioning of ants and bees is attributed by Cicero (*Acad. prior.* ii, 38, 120) to Myrmekides—rightly, to judge from the man's name, which is doubtless a nickname won for him by his skill.

10. **pervidere non est:** cf. Varro (*Ling. Lat.* vii, i), who says of the works of Myrmekides that they could only be properly seen when placed on black silk.

APPENDIX.

I.

125   IDEM hic imperator edixit ne quis ipsum alius quam
Apelles pingeret, quam Pyrgoteles scalperet, quam Lysippus ex aere duceret, quae artes pluribus inclaruere exemplis.
126 Aristidis Thebani pictoris unam tabulam centum talentis
rex Attalus licitus est, octoginta emit duas Caesar dictator, 5
Mediam et Aiacem Timomachi, in templo Veneris Genetricis dicaturus.   Candaules rex Bularchi picturam Magnetum exiti, haud mediocris spati, pari rependit auro.   Rhodum
non incendit rex Demetrius expugnator cognominatus, ne
tabulam Protogenis cremaret a parte ea muri locatam. 10
127 Praxiteles marmore nobilitatus est Gnidiaque Venere praecipue vesano amore cuiusdam iuvenis insigni, sed et Nico-
medis aestimatione regis grandi Gnidiorum aere alieno
permutare eam conati.   Phidiae Iuppiter Olympius cotidie
testimonium perhibet, Mentori Capitolinus et Diana Ephesia, 15
quibus fuere consecrata artis eius vasa.

II.

198   Normam autem et libellam et tornum et clavem Theodorus Samius (*sc.* invenit).

VII, 125. 2. **Apelles** : xxxv, 8₅ ;
cf. Hor. *Ep.* II, 1, 239 ; *Edicto vetuit,
ne quis se praeter Apellen | Pingeret,
aut alius Lysippo duceret aera | Fortis
Alexandri vultum simulantia* . . .

    Pyrgoteles : xxxvii, 8.

    Lysippus : see note on xxxiv,
63.

    § **126. 4. Aristidis Thebani** :
xxxv, 98.

    centum talentis : after the sack

of Corinth this sum was offered by
Attalos, or rather by Philopoimen
on his behalf, for the 'Dionysos and
Ariadne' of Aristeides ; upon which
Mummius, staggered at the value set
upon the picture, retained it (xxxv, 24
and note).

    6. **Mediam et Aiacem Timom.** :
xxxv, 26 ; 136.

    7. **Bularchi picturam** : xxxv, 55
and note.

I.

THE emperor Alexander also issued an edict that none but 125
Apelles might paint his portrait, none but Pyrgoteles engrave it,
and none but Lysippos cast his statue in bronze. Several famous
likenesses of him exist of these three kinds.

King Attalos bought a single picture by Aristeides of Thebes 126
for a hundred talents [£21,000 circ.], and the dictator Caesar
gave eighty [£16,800 circ.] for two by Timomachos, a Medeia
and an Aias, which he intended to dedicate in the temple of
Venus the Mother. King Kandaules paid its weight in gold for
a picture of no small dimensions by Boularchos, representing the
destruction of the Magnetes. King Demetrios, surnamed the
Destroyer of Cities, refrained from setting fire to Rhodes, for fear
he should burn a painting by Protogenes which was near the
part of the city wall threatened. Praxiteles owes his fame to his 127
marble sculptures and to his Aphrodite at Knidos, which is best
known by the story of the youth who fell madly in love with it,
and also by the value King Nikomedes set on it when he offered
to take it in acquittal of the heavy state debt of the Knidians. Zeus
of Olympia daily bears testimony in honour of Pheidias, as for
Mentor do Jupiter of the Capitol and Artemis of Ephesos, to
whom the cups made by his hand have been consecrated.

I.

The rule and line, the lathe and lever, were invented by 198
Theodoros of Samos.

8. **Rhodum non incendit:** xxxv, 104.

§ 127. 11. **marmore nobilitatus:** xxxvi, 20; cf. xxxiv, 69 *Prax. quoque marmore felicior.*

14. **Iuppiter Olympius:** xxxiv, 49, 54; xxxvi, 18.

15. **Capitolinus . . . Ephesia:** xxxiii, 154 and note.

§ 198. 17. **Theodorus Samius:** xxxiv, 83 and note.

BOOK VII.

III.

205 Picturam Aegypti et in Graecia Euchir Daedali cognatus
ut Aristoteli placet, ut Theophrasto Polygnotus Atheniensis
(*sc.* condere instituerunt).

IV.

Lib. XVI.

213 Maxime aeternam putant hebenum et cupressum cedrum-
que, claro de omnibus materiis iudicio in templo Ephesiae 5
Dianae, utpote cum tota Asia exstruente CXX annis per-
actum sit. convenit tectum eius esse e cedrinis trabibus.
de simulacro ipso deae ambigitur. ceteri ex hebeno esse
tradunt, Mucianus ter cos. ex his qui proxime viso scripsere vitigineum et numquam mutatum septies restituto 10
214 templo, hanc materiam elegisse Endoeon, etiam nomen
artificis nuncupans, quod equidem miror, cum antiquiorem
Minerva quoque, non modo Libero patre, vetustatem ei
tribuat.

V.

Lib. XXI.

4. Arborum enim ramis coronari in sacris certaminibus 15
mos erat primum. postea variare coeptum mixtura versi-
colori florum, quae invicem odores coloresque accenderet,
Sicyone ingenio Pausiae pictoris atque Glycerae coronariae
dilectae admodum illi, cum opera eius pictura imitaretur,
illa provocans variaret, essetque certamen artis ac naturae, 20
quales etiam nunc exstant artificis illius tabellae atque in
primis appellata stephaneplocos qua pinxit ipsam.

11. Endoeon] *Sillig*; eandem con *codices.*

§ 205. 1. **Aegypti**: xxxv, 15.

Euchir: in xxxv, 152 he figures as
one of the Corinthian modellers who
accompanied Damaratos to Italy; in
Paus. vi, 4, 4 as the master of Klearchos
of Rhegion, the master of Pythagoras.
At least it seems probable that it is
one and the same personage to whom
different parts are assigned in various
apocryphal traditions concerning the
beginnings of the several arts, cf.
Robert *Arch. Märch.* p. 131, note 2.
For an artist of the name in late
historic times see xxxiv, 91.

2. **Theophrasto**: on the misunderstanding involved here see
Introd. p. xxx.

XVI, 213. 5. **templo Ephesiae**:
below, xxxvi, 95.

9. **Mucianus**: Introd. p. lxxxv ff.

11. **Endoeon**: the name was restored by Sillig from Athenag. Πρεσβ.
17 (below, App. xi) for the corrupt
eandem con of the MSS. Besides
Ephesos, Endoios also worked in
Asia Minor at Eruthrai (Paus. vii,
5, 9); further, in one of his two inscriptions (*I. G. B.* 8, stele of

III.

Painting was first invented by the Egyptians, and introduced 205 into Greece, according to Aristotle, by *Eucheir*, a kinsman of Daidalos, but according to Theophrastos by *Polygnotos* of Athens.

IV.

BOOK XVI.

Ebony, cypress, and cedar wood are thought to be the most 213 durable, every wood having been signally tested in the temple of Artemis at Ephesos, which all Asia joined to build, and which was completed in a hundred and twenty years. While all agree that the roof is made of cedar beams, we have varying accounts of the image of the goddess. All other writers say that it is of ebony, but among those who have written after close inspection, Mucianus, who was thrice consul, declares that it is of vine-wood, and has remained unchanged though the temple has been restored seven times. The material, he says, was the choice of *Endoios*, the 214 maker, whose name he gives somewhat to my surprise, since he holds the image to be not only earlier than the Dionysos, but also than the Athene.

V.

BOOK XXI.

Branches of trees were originally used for crowns in the sacred 4 games. Later on the fashion of intertwining flowers of different hues, to strengthen each other's scent and colour, was invented and introduced at Sikyon by the painter Pausias and Glykera, a wreath-seller whom he loved. He imitated her wares in painting, and she varied them to challenge him, thus making art and nature vie together. Pictures by Pausias in this style are still extant, the most noteworthy being the στεφανηπλόκος, or wreath-binder, a portrait of Glykera herself.

Lampito) he uses the Ionic dialect, while in the other ('Αρχ. Δελτ., 1888, p. 208) he uses the Ionic alphabet. It is probable, therefore, that he was an Ionian, whom the later art-historians turned into an Athenian, as they did Alkamenes and others (see *Add. to Introd.* p. 232). From their epigraphy the inscriptions must be dated between B.C. 532 and 508; for the latest discussion of Endoios and his date see Lechat in *Rev. des Études Grecques*, v, 1892, p. 385 ff. The most famous work of Endoios was the seated Athena (below, App. xi ; Paus. i, 26, 4) dedicated on the Athenian Akropolis by one Kallias.

XXI, 4. 18. Pausiae . . . Glycerae : xxxv, 125 and note.

VI.

90   Lemnius (*sc.* labyrinthus) similis illi columnis tantum
CL memorabilior fuit, quarum in officina turbines ita librati
pependerunt ut puero circumagente tornarentur. architecti
fecere Zmilis et Rhoecus et Theodorus indigenae.

VII.

95   Graecae magnificentiae vera admiratio exstat templum 5
Ephesiae Dianae CXX annis factum a tota Asia. in solo
id palustri fecere, ne terrae motus sentiret aut hiatus timeret,
rursus ne in lubrico atque instabili fundamenta tantae molis
locarentur, calcatis ea substravere carbonibus, dein velleribus
lanae. universo templo longitudo est CCCCXXV pedum, 10
latitudo CCXXV, columnae CXXVII a singulis regibus
factae LX pedum altitudine, ex is XXXVI caelatae, una
a Scopa. operi praefuit Chersiphron architectus.

VIII.

177   Elide aedis est Minervae in qua frater Phidiae Panaenus
tectorium induxit lacte et croco subactum, ut ferunt, ideo, 15
si teratur hodie in eo saliva pollice, odorem croci sapo-
remque reddit.

IX.

184   Pavimenta originem apud Graecos habent elaborata ante
picturae ratione donec lithostrota expulere eam. celeberri-

12. una a] *Bamb.* ; una *Ricc., Voss.*

XXXVI, 90. 1. **Lemnius (lab.)**:
by error for the Samian labyrinth,
see note on xxxiv, 83.

§ 95. 5. **templum Ephesiae Dianae**: the description seems borrowed
from Mucianus, Introd. p. lxxxviii;
cf. xvi, 213, but the account is very
confused, referring partly to the first
temple (begun close of seventh century
B.C. and burnt 356 B. C. by Herostratos,
Strabo, xiv, p. 640) and partially to
the second, upon which Skopas would
be employed. The reconstruction of
the Ephesian Artemision is beset with

almost as grave difficulties as that of
the Mausoleion, but see the interesting
attempt lately made by A. S. Murray,
*Journal of the R. Inst. of Brit.
Archit.*, 1895, p. 41 ff. The ancient
literature is fully given and discussed
by Brunn, *K. G.* ii, p. 345 ff.

8. **ne in lubrico . . . lanae**: this
was done by the advice of Theodoros,
Diogenes Laertios, ii, 8, 103.

10. **universo templo**: i.e. measuring the length along the lowermost
step of the platform, see A. S. Murray,
op. cit. p. 44.

VI.

The labyrinth of Lemnos is like that of Krete, but is distinguished by its columns, a hundred and fifty in number. Their drums were raised from the ground in the stone-yard and balanced on a pivot, so that a boy could set them spinning round and smooth their surface. The architects who built it were *Smilis*, *Rhoikos*, and *Theodoros*, natives of the island.

VII.

Our genuine admiration for the magnificence of the Greek genius 95 is roused by the temple of Artemis at Ephesos, which was built in a hundred and twenty years by the exertions of all Asia. The temple was placed on a marshy site, that it might not suffer from earthquakes, or be in danger from the cracking of the ground, while on the other hand, to prevent any insecurity or shifting in the foundation on which the massive weight of the temple was to rest, a substratum was laid of pounded charcoal covered with fleeces. The full length of the temple is 425 feet, and its breadth 225; there are 127 columns 60 feet high, each made by a different king. Of these 36 are carved, one of them by *Skopas*. The chief architect was *Chersiphron*.

VIII.

There is at Elis a temple of Athena in which we are told that 177 Panainos, the brother of Pheidias, mixed the plaster on the walls with saffron and milk; hence to this very day if the finger is wetted in the mouth and rubbed on the wall, it smells and tastes of saffron.

IX.

The Greeks were the first to introduce paved floors, which they 184 decorated with painting until mosaic took its place. The most

12. **una a Scopa**: this is the reading of Cod. Bamb.; it was kindly verified for this edition by Mr. Fischer. Chronologically it is quite possible that Skopas worked for the second Ephesian temple, see note on xxxvi, 30.

13. **Chersiphron**: the first architect of the first temple, vii, 125.

§ 177. 14. **Elide**: xxxv, 54, both Panainos and Kolotes had been employed on the statue of Athena, and it is evident from the present passage that Panainos must have decorated the temple with wall-paintings.

§ 184. 19. **lithostrota**: the earliest instance of a mosaic floor in Greece

mus fuit in hoc genere Sosus qui Pergami stravit quem
vocant asaroton oecon, quoniam purgamenta cenae in pavi-
mentis quaeque everri solent velut relicta fecerat parvis
e tessellis tinctisque in varios colores. mirabilis ibi columba
bibens et aquam umbra capitis infuscans. apricantur aliae 5
scabentes sese in canthari labro.

LIB.   X.
XXXVII.
8   Polycratis gemma quae demonstratur intacta inlibataque
est. Ismeniae aetate multos post annos apparet scalpi
etiam smaragdos solitos. confirmat hanc eandem opinionem
edictum Alexandri magni quo vetuit in hac gemma ab alio 10
se scalpi quam ab Pyrgotele non dubie clarissimo artis eius.
Post eum Apollonides et Cronius in gloria fuere quique
divi Augusti imaginem simillime expressit, qua postea
principes signant, Dioscurides.

                               XI.

Athena-   Αἱ δ' εἰκόνες μέχρι μήπω πλαστικὴ καὶ γραφικὴ καὶ ἀνδριαν- 15
goras,   τοποιητικὴ ἦσαν, οὐδὲ ἐνομίζοντο· Σαυρίου δὲ τοῦ Σαμίου καὶ
Πρεσβεία

is that of the *Pronaos* of the temple of
Zeus at Olympia, *Olympia, Baudenkm.*
ii, pl. cv (cf. *ib.* i, pl. ix). Mosaic came
into general use in the time of the Diadochoi ; cf. Athen. xii, 542 d, *ib.* v,
206 d.

2. asaroton oecon: cf. the mosaic
in the Lateran (Helbig,*Class. Ant.*694)
strewn with fragments of food, and
the mosaic (Brit. Mus.) representing
strewn leaves.—Statius *Silv.* i, 3, 56.

4. columba bibens: a similar
subject in the famous mosaic of the
Capitol, found in the villa of Hadrian ;
Helbig, *Class. Ant.* 450 ; cf. the
mosaics in Naples, *Mo.* 9992 and
114281. From the words *mirabilis
ibi* it appears that the dove drinking
was part of the larger composition
representing the unswept floor.
Doves on the edge of a vase are a
subject of frequent occurrence on

coins, cf. Drexler, *Zeitschrift f.
Numismatik*, vol. xix.

XXXVII, 8. 7. Polycratis gem-
ma : according to Pliny in § 4 of this
book it was a sardonyx, and was
preserved at Rome, in the Temple of
Concord, set in a horn, the offering of
Augusta (sc. Livia).

intacta inlibataque : on the other
hand, Strabo, xiv, p. 638, speaks
of its being splendidly graved, and
Herodotos (iii, 41) of its being a seal
of emerald (i. e. emerald-prase, see
Brunn, *K. G.* ii, p. 468; Furtwängler,
Jahrb. iii, 1888, p. 194) mounted in
a gold ring σφρηγὶς χρυσόδετος ; it
was reputed the work of Theodoros,
cf. Paus. viii, 14, 1, and see note
above on xxxiv, 83.

8. Ismeniae : Plut. *Per.* 1 ;
Apuleius, *de Deo Socr.* 21 ; Boethius,
Inst. Mus. I, 1 (ed. Friedlein, p. 185,

celebrated worker in mosaic is †*Sosos*, who laid the floors of a house at Pergamon, known as the ἀσάρωτος οἶκος, or Unswept House, because he represented in small bits of many-coloured mosaic the scraps from the table and everything that is usually swept away, as if they had been left lying on the floor. Among these mosaics is a marvellous dove drinking and casting the shadow of its head on the water. Other doves are pluming their feathers in the sun on the lip of a goblet.

X.

The gem shown as that of Polykrates is uncut and untouched. 8 We find that at a much later date, in the days of Ismenias, even emeralds were engraved. An edict of Alexander the Great confirms this : he forbade any one but *Pyrgoteles*, who was beyond doubt the greatest master of the art, to engrave his likeness on these gems. After Pyrgoteles, †*Apollonides* and †*Kronios* won fame, and *Dioskourides* who engraved that perfect likeness of the god Augustus which later emperors have used as their seal. 9

XI.

Images of the gods were not had in honour at all before the arts of modelling, of painting and of statuary were introduced,

20). Dionysodoros is known only from Pliny.

9. **smaragdos** : emerald, however, does not appear to have come into use till Hellenistic times, and then only unimportant gems were cut in this stone.

11. **ab Pyrgotele** : vii, 125 (App. I) ; cf. Apuleius, *Florida*, i, p. 7 (ed. Krueger, 1865) ; he is unknown outside literature.

13. **Augusti imaginem** : a full list (needing revision however) of portraits of Augustus on gems is given by Bernoulli, *Röm. Iconographie*, ii, p. 46. None can be traced back to Dioskourides.

14. **Dioscurides** : of the numerous extant gems bearing the signature of D. six only are recognized as genuine

by Furtwängler, *Jahrb.* iii, 1888, pp. 218-224; *ib.* pl. iii, 1 ; pl. viii, 22, 23, 24, 25, 26. To these signed instances should be added, according to R. von Schneider (*Album der Wiener Sammlungen*, p. 16, text to plate 41), the great Vienna cameo representing the family of Augustus. —Three sons of Dioskourides,— Hierophilos, Hyllos, and Eutyches, —are known from their signatures on gems to have been gem-engravers; see Furtwängler, *op. cit.* p. 304 ff.

15. **Αἱ δ’ εἰκόνες** . . . : the rhetoric of Athenagoras seems evolved out of the same curious notion appearing in Plin. xxxiv, 9, 16, that art progressed from lesser objects to statues of the gods.

16. **Σαυρίου . . . Σαμίου**: we again

περὶ Χρισ-
τιανῶν, 17
(ed.
Schwartz,
p. 18).

Κράτωνος τοῦ Σικυωνίου καὶ Κλεάνθους τοῦ Κορινθίου καὶ κόρης
Κορινθίας γενομένων καὶ σκιαγραφίας μὲν εὑρεθείσης ὑπὸ Σαυρίου
ἵππον ἐν ἡλίῳ περιγράψαντος, γραφικῆς δὲ ὑπὸ Κράτωνος ἐν πίνακι
λελευκωμένῳ σκιὰς ἀνδρὸς καὶ γυναικὸς ἐναλείψαντος, ἀπὸ δὲ τῆς
κόρης κοροπλαθικῆς [εὑρέθη] (ἐρωτικῶς γάρ τινος ἔχουσα περι- 5
έγραψεν αὐτοῦ κοιμωμένου ἐν τοίχῳ τὴν σκιάν, εἶθ᾽ ὁ πατὴρ ἡσθεὶς
ἀπαραλλάκτῳ οὔσῃ τῇ ὁμοιότητι (κέραμον δὲ εἰργάζετο) ἀνεγλύψας
τὴν περιγραφὴν πηλῷ προσανεπλήρωσεν· ὁ τύπος ἔτι καὶ νῦν ἐν
Κορίνθῳ σῴζεται), τούτοις δὲ ἐπιγενόμενοι Δαίδαλος Θεόδωρος
Σμῖλις ἀνδριαντοποιητικὴν καὶ πλαστικὴν προσεξεῦρον. ὁ μὲν δὴ 10
χρόνος ὀλίγος τοσοῦτος ταῖς εἴκοσι καὶ τῇ περὶ τὰ εἴδωλα πραγ-
ματείᾳ, ὡς ἔχειν εἰπεῖν τὸν ἑκάστου τεχνίτην θεοῦ. τὸ μὲν γὰρ
ἐν Ἐφέσῳ τῆς Ἀρτέμιδος καὶ τὸ τῆς Ἀθηνᾶς (μᾶλλον δὲ Ἀθηλᾶς·
ἀθήλη γὰρ ὡς οἱ μυστικώτερον οὕτω γὰρ) τὸ ἀπὸ τῆς ἐλαίας τὸ
παλαιὸν καὶ τὴν Καθημένην Ἔνδοιος εἰργάσατο μαθητὴς Δαιδάλου, 15
ὁ δὲ Πύθιος ἔργον Θεοδώρου καὶ Τηλεκλέους καὶ ὁ Δήλιος καὶ
ἡ Ἄρτεμις Τεκταίου καὶ Ἀγγελίωνος τέχνη, ἡ δὲ ἐν Σάμῳ Ἥρα
καὶ ἐν Ἄργει Σμίλιδος χεῖρες καὶ Φειδίου τὰ λοιπὰ εἴδωλα ἡ
Ἀφροδίτη ⟨ἡ⟩ ἐν Κνίδῳ ἑτέρα Πραξιτέλους τέχνη, ὁ ἐν Ἐπιδαύρῳ
Ἀσκληπιὸς ἔργον Φειδίου. συνελόντα φάναι, οὐδὲν αὐτῶν δια- 20
πέφευγεν τὸ μὴ ὑπ᾽ ἀνθρώπου γεγονέναι. εἰ τοίνυν θεοί, τί οὐκ
ἦσαν ἐξ ἀρχῆς; τί δέ εἰσιν νεώτεροι τῶν πεποιηκότων; τί δὲ
ἔδει αὐτοῖς πρὸς τὸ γενέσθαι ἀνθρώπων καὶ τέχνης; γῆ ταῦτα καὶ
λίθοι καὶ ὕλη καὶ περίεργος τέχνη.

catch here the echo of some art-
writer who had contrasted the claims
of island and mainland schools; cf.
Introd. pp. xxiii, xxvi.

1. **Κλεάνθους**: Plin. xxxv, 15.
κόρης Κορινθίας: Plin. xxxv, 151.
6. **αὐτοῦ κοιμωμένου**: while in
Pliny the lover is represented as going
away.
8. **ἔτι καὶ νῦν ἐν Κορίνθῳ**: *donec
Mummius Corinthum everterit*, Plin.
xxxv, 151; hence it appears that

Athenagoras is quoting—though not
necessarily at first hand—from an
author older than B.C. 146.

14. **τὸ ἀπὸ τῆς ἐλαίας**: Paus. i, 26,
6. Athenagoras is the only writer
who attributes the statue to Endoios.

15. **Ἔνδοιος**: above note on xvi,
214 = App. IV.
μαθητὴς Δαιδάλου: Paus. i, 26, 4.
16. **ὁ δὲ Πύθιος**: Diodoros, i, 98.
ὁ Δήλιος: Paus. ii, 32, 5; cf.
Plut. *de Mus.* 14 (= Bernardakis, vi,

but are later than the days of †*Saurias* of Samos, †*Kraton* of Sikyon, *Kleanthes* of Corinth, and a maiden, also of Corinth. Linear drawing was discovered by Saurias, who traced the outline of the shadow cast by a horse in the sun, and painting by Kraton, who painted on a whitened tablet the shadows of a man and woman. The maiden invented the art of modelling figures in relief. She was in love with a youth, and while he lay asleep she sketched the outline of his shadow on the wall. Delighted with the perfection of the likeness, her father, who was a potter, cut out the shape and filled in the outline with clay ; the figure is still preserved at Corinth. After these came *Daidalos*, *Theodoros*, and *Smilis*, who introduced the arts of statuary and modelling. In fact so short a time has passed since statues and the making of images were introduced, that we can name the maker of each several god. *Endoios*, the pupil of Daidalos, made the statue of Artemis at Ephesos, the old olive-wood image of Athena (or rather of Athela [the unsuckled], for so those better acquainted with her mysteries call her), and the seated image ; the Pythian Apollo is the work of *Theodoros* and *Telekles ;* the Apollo and Artemis at Delos are by *Tektaios* and *Angelion ;* the statues of Hera in Samos and in Argos are by the hand of Smilis, and the other statues are by *Pheidias ; Praxiteles* made the second Aphrodite at Knidos, and Pheidias the Asklepios at Epidauros. In a word, there is not one of them but is the work of man's hands. If, then, these are gods, why were they not from the beginning, and why are they younger than those who made them ? What need had they of men and human art to bring them into being ? They are but earth and stones and wood and cunning art.

p. 500) ; for the type see P. Gardner and Imhoof-Blumer, *Num. Comm.* CC xi–xiv.

17. ἡ ᾿Αρτεμις : known only from Athenagoras.

ἡ δὲ ἐν Σ. ῞Ηρα : Paus. vii, 4, 4 ; for the type cf. P. Gardner, *Samos and Samian Coins*, pp. 19, 75 ff, pl. v, 1–9. Smilis was himself a Samian,

above notes on App. VI. and on xxxiv, 83.

18. ἐν ᾿Αργει : this Argive Hera by Smilis is known only from Athenagoras ; but see Brunn, *K. G.* i, p. 27.

19. ᾿Αφροδ. ἐν Κνίδῳ : Plin. xxxvi, 20.

20. ᾿Ασκληπιός : see Introd. p. liv, note 1.

ADDENDA

I. INTRODUCTION

Page xliii, note 2. F. Münzer provides me with a final proof of the indebtedness of Antigonos to Duris for the story of the Nemesis; he points out (in a private letter) the striking similarity between the story told in Pliny, of the vengeance taken by Agorakritos, and the following fragment from Duris in Plutarch (*Lysander* 18 = Fr. 65, Müller) : Ἀντιμάχου δὲ τοῦ Κολοφωνίου καὶ Νικηράτου τινὸς Ἡρακλεώτου ποιήμασι Λυσάνδρεια διαγωνισαμένων ἐπ' αὐτοῦ (sc. Lysander) τὸν Νικήρατον ἐστεφάνωσεν, ὁ δὲ Ἀντίμαχος ἀχθεσθεὶς ἠφάνισε τὸ ποίημα. Πλάτων δὲ νέος ὢν τότε καὶ θαυμάζων τὸν Ἀντίμαχον ἐπὶ τῇ ποιητικῇ, βαρέως φέροντα τὴν ἧτταν ἀνελάμβανε καὶ παρεμυθεῖτο, τοῖς ἀγνοοῦσι. . . . ' There were two other poets, Antimachus Colophonian, and Niceratus born at Heraclea, which did both wryte verses to honour him (Lysander), striving whether of them should do best. Lysander *judged the crown and victory unto Niceratus: wherewith Antimachus was so angry that he rased out all that he had written of him.* But Plato, who at that time was young, and loved Antimachus because he was an excellent poet, did comforte him, and tolde him that ignoraunce . . .' (North, ed. Wyndham, vol. iii, p. 247).

P. li. Still another story of a self-taught artist, preserved this time not in Pliny but in Pausanias, has been pointed out to me by F. Münzer, whose communication on the subject I translate verbally : ' The account of Pausanias (v, 20, 2) concerning Kolotes may be classed with the stories from Duris noted *Hermes*, xxx, p. 532 f.: εἶναι δέ φασιν ἐξ Ἡρακλείας τὸν Κολώτην. οἱ δὲ πολυπραγμονήσαντες σπουδῇ τὰ ἐς τοὺς πλάστας Πάριον ἀποφαίνουσιν ὄντα αὐτόν, μαθητὴν Πασιτέλους, Πασιτέλην δὲ αὐτοδιδαχθῆναι (Buttmann's reading for the αὐτὸν διδαχθῆναι of the MSS., which it is impossible to retain except by assuming a lacuna). Thus the same is recounted here of Pasiteles as of the several men noted *loc. cit.* Like the Seilanion, Protogenes, Erigonos, and Lysippos of Duris, Pasiteles is represented as having had no teacher; like Seilanion, Erigonos and Pythagoras of Rhegion, he had one pupil. Pasiteles is as completely unknown as these three pupils, and as the master of the philosopher Demokritos invented by Duris (fr. 56). I accordingly believe that the view combated by Pausanias must be traced back to Duris. It is uncertain whether Antigonos had already combated it, or whether he combined it with the current tradition, inasmuch as he transferred Kolotes from the Parian to the Athenian school. To alter the birthplace of Kolotes from Herakleia to Paros, whereby he was made into the countryman of his fellow-pupil Agorakritos, was a slight matter in the eyes of Duris, for he had turned Kleoboulos of Lindos into a Karian, and proclaimed the foreign origin of other of the seven sages (Müller, *F. H. G.* ii, p. 482, fr. 53–55) ; probably also he had transferred the scene of an anecdote from Kroton to Agrigentum (Plin. xxxiv, 64, cf. *Hermes*, xxx, p. 537, n. 1).' In the light of the preceding note of Münzer's, it has become plain to me that Duris must be held responsible for the tradition that represented Alkamenes as a native of Lemnos (Λήμνιος, Souidas, s. v. ᾿Αλκαμένης ; νησιώτης, Tzetzes, *Chil.* viii, 340), whereas Antigonos turned him into an Athenian (Plin. xxxvi, 16). It is natural to find Duris—a Samian—repeatedly championing the claims of the Greeks of Asia Minor and the islands to artistic pre-eminence. Nor must we forget that, careless of accuracy though he was, he doubtless had at his command detailed information which was no longer within reach of the later art-historians, who were content to group artists about the chief art-centres. Thus Endoios, who was probably really an Ionian (note on Appendix XI), is represented in Pausanias simply as ᾿Αθηναῖος. One great error of modern archaeologists is to attempt to harmonize the variant traditions instead of tracing them to their different sources, which will generally be discovered in periods wide apart.

P. li, note 6 : *The masters of Pheidias.* I am pleased to find what I wrote six months back concerning the masters of Pheidias confirmed by the comments of Michaelis (*Deutsche Litteraturzeitung*, 1896, no. 25, p. 788 ; rev. of E. Gardner's *Handbook of Greek Sculpture*) on the untrustworthiness of the Hagelaïdas tradition : the same scholion on Aristoph. *Frogs*, 504, which names Hagelaïdas as the master of Pheidias, also contains a mistake concerning the Herakles Alexikakos of Hagelaïdas; this same untrustworthy scholion is the source for the information of Tzetzes and Souidas (above, p. li, note 3). Michaelis accordingly disputes the strange contention of E. Gardner (*Handbook*, p. 194; cf. pp. 248, 265) that ' the relation of Pheidias to Ageladas is the best established by literary evidence,' '*vielmehr ist Phidias' Schülerverhältniss zu dem Attiker Hegias einmal, aber gut, das zu Hagelades viermal, aber schlecht bezeugt.*' To the unsatisfactory character of E. Gardner's proposed emendation of Dio Chrys. Or. lv. 1 (*Class. Rev.* viii, 1894, p. 70) I have drawn attention elsewhere (*ib.* p. 171, note 1).

P. lxi. The story of the angry artist and the sponge is told by Dio Chrysostom (Or. lxiii, 4 = *Schriftqu.* 1889) of Apelles and his picture of a war horse. I find that Mr. A. S. Murray (*Handbook*, p. 384) has already pointed out, in connexion with Apelles, that the story seemed the anecdotic illustration of the line of Agathon.

P. lxii. From a remark in note 1 on p. 537 of his article in the *Hermes*, it would seem that Münzer also inclines to attribute the story of Zeuxis and the five maidens to Duris. But Münzer makes Duris responsible for the transference of the scene of the story from Kroton to Agrigentum (cf. above, Add. to p. li). Possibly, therefore, we may some day be able to drive the story home to a source whence Duris himself quoted—or misquoted.

P. lxxxv. *Fabius Vestalis* : it is worth noting that, since in each of the three notices his name appears last on the Plinian lists, he was probably only a supplementary author (comm. by Dr. Münzer).

BOOK XXXIII

P. 6, 2. *crustarius* : there are superb examples of ἐμβλήματα among the cups of both the treasures of Hildesheim (Berlin) and of Bosco Reale (Louvre); cf. Winter, *Arch. Anz.* 1896, p. 93. For the most part the *emblema* appears in the shape of a bust in full relief, soldered to a silver plate.

BOOK XXXIV

P. 6, 18. *proscriptum ab Antonio*: cf. Gardthausen, *Augustus*, i, p. 136.

P. 8, 19. *tricliniorum pedibus fulcrisque* : that the *fulcrum* was 'the framework on which the pillows of a couch or the cushions of a chair were placed' has been maintained and fully proved by W. C. F. Anderson, *Class. Rev.* iii, 1889, p. 322 ff.

P. 14, 7. *ubi omnium . . . iconicas vocant* : the latest discussion of this passage is by Dittenberger and Purgold, *Olympische Inschriften*, col. 236, 295 f, where it is pointed out that in the inscr. recording the Olympic victory of Xenombrotos of Kos (*ib.* no. 170 ; Paus. vi, 14, 12) the τοῖος ὁποῖον ὁρᾷς of the fifth line proves that the statue was iconic; yet the epigram and the silence of Pausanias both show that X. was no τρισολυμπιονίκης.

P. 16, 13. *elephanti* : on triumphal chariots drawn by elephants see, however, Gardthausen, *Augustus*, ii, p. 257.

P. 23, 13. *Statues of Demetrios of Phaleron* : the lines from Varro run—

> *Hic Demetrius aeneas tot aptust*
> *Quot luces habet annus absolutus*

(for the first line, as emended by Scaliger, Bormann, *Arch. Ep. Mitth.* xvii, 1894, p. 233 f., proposes *hic Demetrius est [tot aera nac]tus*). Wachsmuth (*loc. cit.*) is probably right in tracing back the legend of the number of statues put up to Demetrios to an epigram—'as many statues as there are days in the year'—a playful turn which was afterwards accepted as serious fact, giving rise not only to the statements in Varro and Pliny, but to the improved version in Diogenes that all these statues were erected to Demetrios in a period less than a year: εἰκόνων ἠξιώθη χαλκῶν ἑξήκοντα πρὸς ταῖς τριακοσίαις, ὧν αἱ πλείους ἐφ' ἵππων ἦσαν καὶ ἁρμάτων καὶ συνωρίδων, συντελεσθεῖσαι ἐν οὐδὲ τριακοσίαις ἡμέραις.—Cornelius Nepos, *Miltiades*, vi, and Plutarch, *Praec. reip. gerend.* 27 E (Bernardakis, v, p. 116), mention 300 as the number of the statues, a round sum, more or less representing the truth. The 1,500 statues mentioned by Dio Chrysostom (xxxvii, 41) are mere foolish rhetoric. The distich from Varro was presumably inscribed, in his *Imagines* (cf. Plin. xxxv, 11 ; A. Gellius, *Noct. Att.* iii, 10, 1 ; 11, 7), beneath a portrait of Demetrios; see Bormann, *loc. cit.*

P. 28, 18. *Rhodi etiamnum* : the passage from Jerome is referred by Mommsen (*Ueber den Chronographen, &c.*, p. 692) to a Roman history ' of the period of Caesar and Augustus,' by Reifferscheid (p. 360, n. 224) to Suetonius; cf· Gardthausen, *Augustus*, i, p. 67.

P. 32, 25. *Arvernis* : the temple is presumably the one described by Gregory of Tours (i, 30), of which the foundations were discovered in 1874, see Mowat, *Rev. Arch.* 1875, p. 31 ff., where the five inscriptions *Mercurio Arverno* are discussed. As to the type of Zenodoros' Mercury, Mowat, *Bull. Monum.* 1875, p. 557 ff., conjectures that we possess an echo of it in the seated Mercury on an altar from Horn in Holland (inscr. Brambach, *C. I. R.* 2029, p. xxvii); cf. S. Reinach, *Bronzes Figurés*, p. 80, no. 68.

P. 34, 5. *in officina* : perhaps it is scarcely correct to refer this to the workshop or studio of Zenodoros. From the size of the colossus it is probable that a special workshop was erected for the artist.

P. 34, 21. *sphingem* : Münzer points out to me that Quinct. vi, 3, 98, accords with Pliny in giving bronze as the material of the sphinx. Now ' in this chapter of Quinctilian several *bons mots* of the personages of the Ciceronian age and of Cicero himself have been shown by Wissowa (*Hermes*, xvi, p. 499 ff.) to be borrowed from the book of Domitius Marsus, *de urbanitate*, which Quinctilian frequently quotes in this chapter.' Therefore we may assume the same D. Marsus, who appears in the Index to Bk. xxxiv, to have been Pliny's authority for the story of Hortensius and the sphinx. (This observation of Münzer's will shortly be published in his *Beiträge zur Quellenkritik der Naturgeschichte des Plinius.*)

P. 36, 11. *Hagelades*: E. Gardner, *Handbook of Greek Sculpture*, p. 192, proposes to read the Ἀγελαΐδα of *I. G. B.* 30 (bathron of Praxiteles) as ὁ Ἀγελαΐδα, and, accordingly, takes the name of the Argive master to have been Agelaïdas. The form Hagelaidas (Greek Hagelaΐdas), which we print in the translation, is also retained by Dittenberger and Purgold, *Inschr. von Olympia* 631, where see literature.

P. 38, 1. *Argium*: owing to its position a proper name, and not, as often surmised, the ethnic of Asopodoros, in which case it would have been placed after the name it qualified, cf. *Gorgias Lacon* (§ 49), *Demean Clitorium;* Dittenberger and Purgold in *Inschriften von Olympia*, col. 647, where see literature.

P. 38, 1. *Asopodorum*: for the inscription on the bathron of Praxiteles, see now *Inschr. von Olympia*, 630, 631, where Dittenberger and Purgold rightly reject Röhl's proposed identification of the Plinian *Asopodorus* and *Athenodorus* with the artists of the bathron.

P. 38, 2. *Clitorium*: Paus. x, 9, 7, οὗτοι (sc. Ἀθην. καὶ Δαμέας) δὲ Ἀρκάδες εἰσὶν ἐκ Κλείτορος.

P. 38, 5. *Leochares*: I refer the passage concerning the statue of Isokrates by Leochares in *Vit. X Orat.* 27 to Heliodoros on the authority of Keil, *Hermes*, xxx, 1895, p. 202.

P 40, 1. *Date of Seilanion*: Furtwängler, *Statuenkopien im Alterthum*, p. 562, shows, however, that the connexion attempted by Delamare between *C. I. G. S.* 414, and *C. I. G. S.* 4253, 4254, is unfounded: D.'s conjecture that the latter refers to the revival of the games in 329-8 B.C. is unproven; 4253 refers not to the games but generally to the *Hieron* of Amphiaraos and the *Penteteris,* while 4254 is a decree in honour of the officials in charge of the games. There is nothing in either inscription implying a revival. Thus the only evidence we are left with for the date of 414 is derived from the epigraphy; according to Dittenberger the upper limit is 366 B.C. Now if we accept the extant portraits of Plato as copies after an original by Seilanion (Helbig, *Class. Ant.* 265, p. 183 f.), and adopt Furtwängler's identification of the Theseus at Ince-Blundell Hall (*Statuenkopien*, pl. ii, iii, *ib.* p. 559 ff.) as a copy of the Theseus of Seilanion (Plut. *Thes.* iv), there would be artistic grounds for placing the artist as far back in the fourth century as the epigraphy of *C. I. G. S.* 414 allows.—No great weight can be attached to the date assigned to Seilanion in Pliny's chronology, the mention of Seilanion having been loosely tacked on by a later hand to the old Xenokratic chronology, Introd. p. xlix, note 2.

P. 40, 2. *Zeuxiaden*: the identity of the portraitist of Hypereides with the pupil of Seilanion is, however, doubtful, cf. Introd. p. liii.

P. 42, 4. *forma cognomen* = lit. 'the surname of beauty'; for *forma* = beauty, cf. below § 78, *cliduchon eximia forma;* xxxv, 86, *ob admirat. formae;* O. Jahn, *Arch. Zeit.* 1847, p. 63 (cf. Brunn, *K. G.* p. 182), believe the Greek epithet of the goddess to have been Μορφώ, which occurs as an epithet of Aphrodite at Sparta (Paus. iii, 15, 8). Other conjectures are καλλίμορφος and καλλίστη.

P. 42, 5. *cliduchum* : it is Pliny's rule to mention the names of gods, while he almost invariably omits to name mortals; their statues are referred to by their motive, e.g. *diadumenus, discobolus, apoxyomenus, mala ferens nudus, &c.* Hence it is that the *cliduchus* cannot be regarded as the Athena Promachos (so Urlichs in *Chrestom.*), nor the *astragalizontes* of Polykleitos as the Dioscuri (so Furtwängler in *Masterpieces*, p. 292, note 1), nor the *mala ferens nudus* as a statue of Herakles.

P. 42, 10. *diadumenum* : another fairly complete copy of this statue, recently found in Delos (*B. C. H.* 1895, pl. viii), is—to judge from the publication—of poor workmanship, inferior to the Madrid copy; cf. Furtwängler, *Statuenkopien im Alterthum*, p. 548.

P. 44, 1. *telo incessentem* : I ought to have stated more fully that Furtwängler (*loc. cit.*) shows the impossibility—on grammatical and other grounds—of the reading *talo*, which is supported by Benndorf. The latter supposes the statue referred to, to have stood on an astragal basis—a forerunner to the Kairos of Lysippos (*Schriftqu.* 1463-1467), further, to have been described by some Greek writer as γυμνὸς ἀστραγάλῳ ἐπικείμενος where Pliny then translated the ἐπικείμενος in its alternative sense of ' advancing' or ' pursuing.' But in that case *talo incessens* could only mean *advancing towards* or *pursuing a knuckle-bone*, which is nonsense. *Talo* can only be the instrument, the weapon *with which* the man is attacking, so that everything combines to commend Benndorf's own earlier conjecture *telo*.

P. 44, 3. *in Titi imperatoris atrio* : the reading of *Cod. Bamb.* seems to be: in titi imperīs atrio duo (see our facsimile) ; incliti in patrio duo *Bamb. e corr.*

P. 44, 6. *Portrait of Artemon* : in *Class. Rev.* 1894, p. 219, I pointed out that the erection of the portrait should probably be connected with the Samian expedition of 439 B.C., at which date Furtwängler (*Masterpieces*, p. 119) conjectures the Perikles by Kresilas to have been put up. Meanwhile grave doubts have arisen in my mind as to the authenticity of the Polykleitan Artemon. The confusion already noted by Plutarch with the Artemon of Anakreon is suspicious. The notice in Pliny is clearly derived from an anecdotic source other than that from which his main narrative is borrowed. Possibly, as Münzer hints, *Hermes*, xxx, p. 537, we have here further traces of Duris.

P. 46, 1. *pristas*: the MSS. are unanimous ; hence, since H. L. Urlichs (*loc. cit.*) has satisfactorily shown that a group of sawyers—put up doubtless by some successful master-builder—is absolutely in harmony with fifth-century traditions, I had not thought it necessary to refer to Loeschcke's proposed emendation of *pristas* to *pyctas*—an emendation, however, which threatens to come into favour again.

P. 46, 14. *puerum . . . tabellam*: for the motive Reisch (*l. c.*) compares the vase in Munich (Cat. 51), Benndorf, *Griechische u. Sicilische Vasenbilder*, i, pl. ix.

P. 48, 16. *The Apoxyomenos of Lysippos* : the copy in the Braccio Nuovo of the Vatican (Helbig, 31) seemed to me too well known to need mention. For the writer from whom Pliny got the story of Tiberius's passion for the statue, see Introd. p. xcii, n. 4.

P. 50, 6 : for portraits of Alexander, see also Helbig, *Sopra un Busto Colossale d'Alessandro Magno* in Mon. Antichi (R. Acad. Lincei), vol. vi, 1895.

P. 60, 1. *Portrait of Perikles*: Blümner and Hitzig (*Pausanias*, p. 307) remark that the word ἀνδριάς, used by Pausanias (i, 25, 1), does not apply to a terminal bust. Cf. further Bernoulli in *Jahrb.* xi, 1896, p. 107 f.

P. 60, 3. *Minervam mirabilem . . . et aram*: while still proposing to see a copy of this Athena in the 'Pallas de Velletri' whose original he refers to Kresilas (see Introd. p. lxxv, n. 2), Furtwängler recognizes a copy of the Zeus in a fine statue at Ince-Blundell Hall, *Statuenkopien im Alterthum*, plates i and iii, 1, *ib.* p. 551 ff., the original of which he attributes on stylistic grounds neither to Kresilas nor to the unknown Kephisodoros, but to the elder Kephisodotos. The reasons adduced, however, are scarcely strong enough to warrant the alteration in the Plinian text of the MS. reading *Cephisodorus* to *Cephisodotus*.

P. 60, 10. *celetizontas* : for the motive cf. further a statue in the Palazzo Orlandi at Florence, Arndt-Bruckmann, *Einzelverk.* 242.

P. 66, 7. *Hermaphrodite of Polykles* : the Berlin statue (193) is now published by Furtwängler, *Statuenkopien*, pl. xii, who sees in it a copy of the work of Polykles (*ib.* p. 582 ff.).

P. 68, 3. *nec hominem ex aere fecit, sed iracundiam* : while admitting—what is indeed incontrovertible—that this phraseology is common to Silver Latinity, I now believe that an epigram is after all concealed behind it (Introd. p. lxx), all the Plinian criticism and analysis of Greek works of art being Greek in their origin ; cf. note on xxxv, 61.

P. 68, 8. *Theodorus* : cf. also vii, 198 ; xxxv, 152. Identity with the artist of *C. I. A.* 373, 90 (from Akropolis, middle of sixth century) is probable but not certain.

P. 70, 4. *infans . . . anserem strangulat* : in his translation of Herondas (1893), p. xiv, Crusius alludes to the group in Herondas as being wholly marble. The attempt to establish identity with the Plinian group seems futile, seeing how common the subject was in antiquity; cf. E. Gardner in *J. H. S.* vi, 1885, pp. 7 ff.

P. 72, 2. *Apellas* : cf. also *I. G. B.* 100 (= *Inschriften von Olympia*, 634), from the basis supporting the horses of Kyniska in the Pronaos of the Temple of Zeus, Paus. v, 12, 5 (*I. G. B.* 99 = *Inschr. von Ol.* 160).

P. 72, 8. *Hermes nursing the infant Dionysos by Kephisodotos* : the identity of this group with the famous group at Olympia seems to me probable. The latter is attributed to Praxiteles on the authority of Pausanias (v, 17, 1) only. I believe that in this case, as often in that of works attributed to Pheidias (xxxv, 54, Athena by Kolotes ; xxxvi, 17, Nemesis and Mother of the Gods by Agorakritos), all of which are put down to Pheidias by Paus. (Introd. p. xl, cf. p. liii, note 1), Pliny represents the more detailed—and perchance the more trustworthy—tradition, while Pausanias gives only the popular attributions. If the Hermes of Olympia was really by Praxiteles, but could pass in the eyes of certain critics as the work of his father or elder brother, it follows that the statue belonged, as Brunn has maintained, to the artist's earlier period and not to his later as recently argued by Furtwängler (*Masterpieces*, p. 307 f). It may be questioned whether we are not too completely under the spell of Pausanias, whose untrustworthiness in the matter of attributions is notorious, and who, writing some 600 years after the artists of the great period, was as liable to blunder concerning their works as the compiler of a modern guide-book concerning the artists of the Renascence and their works. However, I am at present neither prepared nor equipped to challenge the Praxitelean authorship of the Hermes on morphological or aesthetic grounds. A long and complete reinvestigation of all the extant material would first be necessary, but I think it worth while to point out distinctly that there were probably two ancient traditions concerning the authorship of the statue, and that the comparative trustworthiness of each should be investigated. I may add that the resemblance of the Kephisodotian Eirene holding the child Ploutos to the Hermes nursing the child Dionysos is so strong as only to be satisfactorily accounted for by referring them to the same artist: both figures are posed in the same manner, while the children are, as has often been noted, practically identical (cf. Furtwängler, *op. cit.* p. 296).

P. 72, 12. *Cenchramis*: cf. for Kenchramos, Purgold on *Inschriften von Ol.* 638.

P. 74, 2. *tubicine*: cf. Urlichs, *Pergamenische Inschriften*, p. 24. The commentary is not quite clear at this point; the explanation of Winckelmann (*Geschichte*, ed. 1776, p. 660 ff.=tr. Lodge, vol. ii, p. 204 ff.) applies to the ' dying Gaul' of the Capitol, and not to the Plinian *tubicen*.

P. 74, 2. *matri interfectae*: that this was a Gaulish woman seems to have been *first* suggested by Urlichs, *loc. cit.* ; on the whole subject of these works by Epigonos see G. Habich, *Die Amazonengruppe des Attalischen Weihgeschenks* (Eine Studie zur Pergamenischen Kunstgeschichte), Berlin, 1896, p. 14 ff.

P. 76, 8. *Scopas uterque*: G. Habich, *Die Amazonengruppe*, p. 66, note 2, is of opinion that *scopas* refers to the works of art made by each of two artists (*uterque*), and explains these works to have been dancing satyrs. Habich supports his theory by appeal to the Munich vase. I must abide, however, by the opinion which I arrived at about a year ago after careful study of the vase in question, and which I have expressed in the Commentary.

P. 78, 1. *Callimachus*: for his date consult Winckelmann, *Geschichte* (ed. 1776), p. 460 (=tr. Lodge, vol. ii, p. 123), Furtwängler, *Masterpieces*, p. 437.

BOOK XXXV.

P. 92, 13. *M. Agrippa*: for Agrippa's interest in art, see now Gardthausen, *Augustus*, i. p. 749 ff.

P. 102, § 57. § 59. For the pictures in the *Poikile Stoa*, see now Hitzig and Blümner, *Pausanias*, p. 201 f.

P. 106, 2. *Zeuxis of Herakleia* : I have not sufficiently emphasized the difficulties at the commencement of Pliny's account of Zeuxis. It seems to me probable that the two conflicting dates of his birth given by Pliny represent the conflicting opinions of Greek art-historians (Antigonos and Duris? cf. Introd. p. xxxiii, on the beginnings of encaustic; Introd. p. xxvi, on the origin of sculpture). The epigram against Zeuxis attributed to Apollodoros should have been alluded to among the epigrams discussed, Introd. p. lvii.

P. 108, 7. *Herakles strangling the snakes in presence of Alkmena and Amphitryon.* The vase-painting in the Brit. Mus. (F. 479) is now published, *Cat. of Vases in Brit. Mus.* vol. iv, pl. xiii. The clumsiness of the figures, the coarseness of the picture as a whole, and the absence of Amphitryo must make us wary of accepting it as more than a distant echo of the picture by Zeuxis.

P. 134. *The Pompeian Mosaic*: now at last well photographed by Alinari, Naples 12050.

P. 136. *The ' Thesmothetai' of Protogenes*: the view of Curtius seems to me probable. For dissentient opinions and the full literature of the subject, see Hitzig-Blümner, *Pausanias*, p. 145.

P. 140. *The Resting Satyr*: the subject occurs likewise in painting ; a well preserved instance in the *Casa Nuova* at Pompei, phot. Brogi, Naples 11216. But, at present, no safe connexion can be established between these paintings and the work of Protogenes.

P. 142, 17. *shortened methods of technique*: recent study in the Museum of Naples has convinced me that the clue to these words is afforded by a singular group of ' Campanian ' pictures—the most striking of which is Helbig 1111 (= phot. Alinari, Naples 12035), known since the days of Böttiger as ' Evening prayer in front of the Temple of Isis.' The picture is not a work of the first rank, but it proves that the ancients possessed to as great a degree as any moderns all the secrets of impressionism : the broad flight of steps is indicated by a few bold dashes of white ; the heads of the crowd on either side are roughly modelled within two bands of dark shadow ; white is applied with extraordinary intelligence and variety, now for an effect of light, now for the white garments that contrast with the dark skin of the Egyptian priests. Closely connected with this picture is the similar subject, Helbig 1112, and the two pictures of the ' Trojan horse ' ((1) phot. Sommer, Pompei 9218, (2) Helbig 1326). Egyptian origin is attested from their subjects for the Isis pictures, while for those of the Trojan horse it has been proved both from the treatment and motives by L. von Urlichs (*das Hölzerne Pferd*). There seems little doubt that these pictures are an example of that *compendiaria*, that shortened method hated by Petronius, as in modern times by Ruskin, which was successfully cultivated and perhaps first brought into fashion by Antiphilos, and imitated in Greece by Nikomachos.

P. 154, 2. *exilior*: Robert, *Hall. Winckelmannsprogramm*, xix, 1895, p. 25, maintains that the adjective in its usual sense of *slender, slim* or *thin*, cannot be properly applied to the figures of an artist who expressed the *dignitates* of heroes, or who boasted that ' his Theseus had been fed on meat.' Robert, accordingly, proposed to see in *exilior* the (mis)translation of some such word as βραχύτερος = *short, thick-set* or *stumpy*. Robert's arguments have been vigorously controverted by Furtwängler (*Statuenkopien im Alterthum*, p. 568 f.), who defends the received interpretation of the passage. It seems to me that the contradictions in the criticisms passed upon Parrhasios, which vex Robert, and which Furtwängler attempts to reconcile, are the effect of the present juxtaposition in Pliny of two or more appreciations of Euphranor, derived from totally different sources : the sentence *videtur expressisse dignitatis heroum . . . articulisque grandior* is plainly Xenokratic in its origin (Introd. p. xxvii) ; here there can be no real contradiction between the *dignitates* which Euphranor expressed and the fact that he was *in universitate corporum exilior*, for the first refers to the artist's ethical conception of his heroes, the latter to their physical presentment. As regards the saying attributed to Euphranor concerning his Theseus, I have pointed out both in the note on the passage and in the Introduction (p. lxiii f.) that its source is anecdotic, and can be traced back—perhaps through Antigonos—to Duris of Samos.

P. 155. *Andromeda*: for the finest and best preserved of the Pompeian pictures see phot. Alinari, Naples 12034.

P. 156. *Achilles detected by Ulysses*: phot. Alinari, Naples 12001, *id.*
12000 ; a different scheme seems preserved in the recently discovered picture
in the *Casa Nuova* at Pompei, phot. Brogi 11226.

P. 159. *Medeia of Timomachos*: the picture Helbig 1262 (= phot. Alinari,
Naples 12024) seems to me on close inspection to be really a copy after
a good original, presumably, then, after the Medeia by Timomachos. The
single figure of Medeia, on the other hand, appears to me extremely inferior
in conception and execution ; pose and accessories are different, and I can see
not the slightest reason for referring it to the same original as the former picture.

P. 159. *Orestes and Iphigeneia*: phot. Alinari, Naples 12020.

P. 162. *Herakles and Deianeira*: for the subject, treated with considerable
mastery, and evidently after a good original, see the Pompeian picture, phot.
Alinari, Naples 12026 (cf. Helbig, *Wandgemälde*, 1146).

P. 166, 14. *quinquatrus celebrantem*: Simos' picture apparently lent itself
to a Roman interpretation, which by Pliny's time had superseded the true
Greek explanation of the subject.

BOOK XXXVI.

P. 190, 9. *Statue of Mother of Gods by Agorakritos*: Furtwängler, *Statuenkopien*, p. 577 ff., claims to have discovered a copy of this work in a statue of
the Villa Pamfili in Rome.

P. 202, 12. *Timotheos*: I have lately examined the 'Leda and the Swan'
in the Capitol ; the connexion established between it and the Epidaurian
sculptures by both Amelung and Winter seems to me to stand the test of minute
criticism ; it is, however, disputed by Arndt (Arndt-Bruckmann, *Phot. Einzelverk.* ii, p. 30).

P. 205, 9. *Hermerotes*: the point made by Cicero (*loc. cit.*) was probably
suggested by the word *Hermathena*, rather than by the actual monument. Cf.
also *Att.* i, 1, 5 ; *ib.* 10, 3 (*Hermeracles*). A terminal figure at Newby Hall
(Michaelis, *Anc. Marbles in Great Britain*, p. 531) affords a doubtful instance
of an *Hermeros*. Michaelis brings it into connexion with the work of Tauriskos.

P. 208, l. 4. *Venerem lavantem se . . . Polycharmus*: concerning this
difficult passage I can only arrive at negative results. (1) The reading *sese
Daedalus* must, I think, be rejected, the best codices offering no evidence for it
whatsoever ; the corrupt *sedaedalsas* of *Cod. Bamb.* conceals either further
descriptive words or the name of the locality where the statue was. (2) The
current attribution of the *Venus lavans se* to one Daidalos of Bithynia, known
only on the authority of Eustathios (*Schriftqu.* 2045), which seemed to receive support from the recurrence of a crouching or bathing Aphrodite on Bithynian coins
(see Bernoulli, *Aphrodite*, p. 317), must also be renounced ; the type on the
coins occurs elsewhere, and belongs to a series whose origin can be traced back
to high antiquity (cf. Friederichs-Wolters, p. 571). (3) The notion that two
statues are mentioned in the passage, and that the first was *crouching*, in opposition to the *Venus stans* of Polycharmos, is entirely without support ; *stantem*
may be used here, not necessarily of an upright *versus* a stooping figure, but in
the sense of 'placed,' 'situated.' Brunn, *K. G.* ii, p. 528, Müller, *Handbuch*,
377, note 5, take the whole sentence to be descriptive of *one* statue by Polycharmos.

P. 210. *Caryatids of the Pantheon*: see also Helbig, *Class. Ant.* i, and Gardthausen, *Augustus*, ii, p. 429 f.

P. 212. *Lioness by Arkesilaos*: Mr. Cecil Smith kindly reminds me, in this connexion, of a 'fine mosaic in the Brit. Mus., from Pompei (an early one), representing a lion and three Cupids : one has bound the lion with a cord, one seems to hold a drinking-vessel, and the third holds an object which seems to be a large dart. It is a good illustration of the Arkesilaos subject, and is evidently a copy from a Hellenistic relief.'

N.B.—The student will find all references concerning Roman topography admirably put together by Hülsen in the *Nomenclator Topographicus* to Kiepert and Hülsen's *Formae Urbis Romae Antiquae*, Berlin, 1896.

INDEXES

INDEX I

NAMES OF ARTISTS

INDEX II

MUSEOGRAPHIC

Rome (*continued*).

Trigemina Gate, outside the, column of L. Minucius, xxxiv, 21.

Golden House of Nero, bronzes collected by Nero, xxxiv, 84; paintings by Famulus in, xxxv, 120.

Palatine, House of the Caesars, panel with lines by Apelles and Protogenes, xxxv, 83; filled with statues by Krateros and Pythodoros, Polydeukes and Hermolaos, Pythodoros and Artemon, and Aphrodisios of Tralles, xxxvi, 38.

Palatine, Chapel above Arch, chariot and horses. Apollo, Artemis, marble group by Lysias, xxxvi, 36.

Pantheum, bronze capitals of columns, xxxiv, 13; decorated with sculptures by Diogenes, xxxvi, 38.

Saepta, Olympos and Pan, Cheiron and Achilles, groups by unknown sculptors, xxxvi, 29.

Tarquin, House of, Valeria, statue of, xxxiv, 29.

Temples :

Apollo in Circus of Flaminius, tragic actor and boy, picture of, by Aristeides, xxxv, 99; children of Niobe, statues of, by Skopas or Praxiteles, xxxvi, 28; Apollo by Philiskos; Leto, Artemis, nine Muses and Apollo; Apollo by Timarchides with cithara, statues of, xxxvi, 34.

Apollo of the Palatine, Apollo, statue of, by Skopas, xxxvi, 25; Artemis, statue of, by Timotheos, xxxvi, 32; Leto, statue of, by Kephisodotos, xxxvi. 24; bronze lamp, xxxiv, 14; statues by Boupalos and Athenis, *in fastigio,* xxxvi, 13.

Augustus, pictures dedicated there by Tiberius, xxxv, 28; pictures of Hyakinthos, by Nikias, from Alexandria, and of Danae, xxxv, 131; *Library of,* Tuscan Apollo, colossal statue of, xxxiv, 43.

Castor and Pollux, in front of, Q. Marcius Tremulus, statue of, xxxiv, 23.

Ceres, decorated with painted terracottas by Damophilos and Gorgasos, xxxv, 154; Dionysos and Ariadne, picture of, by Aristeides, xxxv, 24, 99.

Concord, statues of Asklepios and Hygieia, by Nikeratos, xxxiv, 80; Apollo and Hera, by Baton,

Rome (*continued*).

xxxiv, 73; Ares and Hermes, by Piston, xxxiv, 89; Demeter, Zeus, Athena, by Sthennis, xxxiv, 90; Leto with infant Apollo and Artemis, by Euphranor, xxxiv, 77. Pictures of Dionysos, by Nikias, xxxv, 131; Kassandra, by Theoros, xxxv, 144; Marsyas bound, by Zeuxis, xxxv, 66.

Diana, in Circus of Flaminius, Herakles painted by Apelles, xxxv, 94.

Earth, in vicinity of, Spurius Cassius, statue of, xxxiv, 30.

Faith, on Capitol, old man and boy, picture of, by Aristeides, xxxv, 100.

Felicitas, Thespiades, statues of, xxxvi, 39; Aphrodite, statue of, by Praxiteles, xxxiv, 69; in front of, bronze statues by Praxiteles, xxxiv, 69.

Fortune of the Day, statues in, Athena, two draped figures, nude Colossus, all by Pheidias, xxxiv, 54; seven nude and one of old man, by Pythagoras of Samos, xxxiv, 60.

Hercules, in Cattle Market, paintings by Pacuvius, xxxv, 19.

Hercules Musarum, muses, statues of, xxxv, 66.

Hercules Pompei, Hercules, statue of, by Myron, xxxiv, 57.

Honour and Virtue (twin temples), paintings by Cornelius Pinus and Attius Priscus, xxxv, 120.

Janus, statue of Janus by Skopas or Praxiteles, brought from Egypt, xxxvi, 28.

Janus, Janus, statue of, dedicated by Numa, xxxiv, 33.

Julius Caesar, Aphrodite Anadyomene, picture by Apelles, xxxv, 27, 91; Aphrodite, picture of, by Dorotheos, xxxv, 91.

Juno on Capitol, bronze dog, xxxiv, 38.

Juno within gallery of Octavia, Asklepios and Artemis, statues of, by Kephisodotos, xxxvi, 24; statues of Juno by Dionysios and Polykles, and Aphrodite by Philiskos; statues by Pasiteles, xxxvi, 35; decorations appropriate to Jupiter, xxxvi, 43.

Jupiter of the Capitol, statue of Jupiter in clay by Vulca, xxxv, 157; four horse chariots in clay on roof of, xxxv, 157; cups by

THE END

THE ARGONAUT LIBRARY OF ANTIQUITIES

Standard Reference Works on Greek Art and Numismatics

● **MASTERPIECES OF GREEK SCULPTURE. Adolf Furtwängler.** xvi + 439, illus. + 24 plates. LC 64-910. $20.00

A reissue of the first systematic work (1895) on the works and styles of the great Greek masters, considered to be the fundamental reference for any modern study. The originals and ancient copies in the great museums and art galleries of the world identified as the works of Pheidias, Praxiteles, Polykleitos, Skopas, etc. are carefully analyzed stylistically and the most famous appear in the 300 text illustrations and the 24 plates of the new edition. New select bibliography, notes and indices. (D—)

● **ANCIENT COINS ILLUSTRATING LOST MASTERPIECES OF GREEK ART— NUMISMATIC COMMENTARY ON PAUSANIAS. F. Imhoof-Blumer and Percy Gardner.** lxxx + 176 + 32 plates. LC 64-23435. $10.00

A new enlarged edition of a long out of print work (1885-7) important for the study of numismatic sources related to the history of Greek sculpture and Greek art in general. On the basis of the detailed descriptions of famous works of art by Pausanias, the authors identified the representations of the works on Greek coins. In this way a unique gallery of destroyed, lost or yet undiscovered great works of art has been formed, showing us what once adorned the cities and shrines of ancient Greece. (D—)

● **THE ELDER PLINY'S CHAPTERS ON THE HISTORY OF ART. K. Jex-Blake and Eugenie Sellers Strong.** c + 252. LC 66-19183. $10.00

A reissue of another basic reference work for the history of Greek sculpture much in demand since 1896. Updated with a new introduction and select bibliography by R. V. Schoder, S.J. of Loyola University. Pliny's original texts are accompanied by long commentaries on what ancient sculptures have been identified on the basis of his writings. (D 2)

● **ANCIENT WRITERS ON GREEK SCULPTURE. H. Stuart Jones.** 320 pp. LC 65-26123. $10.00

A reprint of this long out of print reference work (1895) enlarged with a new preface, bibliographically updated and carefully indexed for the first time. Includes all the basic passages and references from the classical authors which are necessary for the study of Greek sculpture. The original texts are given with English translations and commentaries. (D—)

● **ANCIENT GREEK AND ROMAN BRONZES. Winifred Lamb.** 360 pp., illus., plates. LC 67-17575. $10.00

The most widely acclaimed reference work on ancient bronze works of art, long out of print and unavailable. Illustrated with a fine selection of bronzes from museums and galleries around the world and accompanied by an instructive and well documented text, this work is rightfully considered the basic source in all courses and seminars on ancient art. Enlarged with an introduction and select bibliography by Dr. Lenore Keene Congdon. (D 3)

● **ALEXANDER THE GREAT IN GREEK AND ROMAN ART. Margaret Bieber.** 108 + 64 plates. LC 64-23430. $7.50

A new work of important reference value examining all the known portraits of the great conqueror made during his lifetime and later during the Hellenistic and Roman periods. The plates illustrate 122 examples of sculpture, bronzes, gems and coins. The lengthy fully documented text, together with many plates, make this monograph the best introduction to Hellenistic and Roman art written by one of the foremost authorities in the field. (D—)

● **ANCIENT GREEK DRESS. Ethel Abrahams and Lady Evans.** xx + 228, illus. + 48 plates. LC 64-23436. $7.50

A new volume combining for the first time the two basic reference works for the study of ancient Greek dress in the English language with a new introduction, select bibliography, notes and many new illustrations of works of Greek art from all over the world. Considered to be an indispensable reference work by the reviewers of *Library Journal, The Classical Journal* and many leading classical scholars. (D—)

- **SELECT NUMISMATIC BIBLIOGRAPHY. Elvira Clain-Stefanelli.** xiv + 406 pp. $12.50

  The first extensive bibliography of its kind, compiled by the AssociateCurator of Numismatics in the Smithsonian Institution. Critical listings of all the most important works on numismatics in all languages,covering ancient, mediaeval and modern coinage, paper money, medals and early and primitive forms of money. Indispensable for reference rooms in all public and university libraries. (D—)

- **A BIBLIOGRAPHY OF APPLIED NUMISMATICS IN THE FIELDS OF GREEK AND ROMAN ARCHAEOLOGY AND THE FINE ARTS. Cornelius C. Vermeule.** viii + 172. $4.00

  A most useful list of over 1300 works demonstrative of the usefulness of numismatic evidence in classical archaeology and the fine arts. The material is especially helpful to anyone wishing to locate references in fields in which numismatics are fundamental for the understanding of non-numismatic problems. (A—)

- **THE PADUANS: MEDALS BY GIOVANNI CAVINO. Richard Hoe Lawrence.** 31 pp., illus.* $1.50

  A book enabling the neophyte or advanced collector to identify the well-executed imitations of Roman medals made by the skilled Renaissance artist Giovanni Cavino. (C—)

- **BECKER THE COUNTERFEITER. George F. Hill.** 111 + 19 plates. $12.00

  A reprint of the brief biography of this nineteenth century counterfeiter of ancient coins, followed by a detailed list of illustrations of 361 of Becker's counterfeits for immediate identification. Becker was one of the most expert counterfeiters of ancient coins ever known and even some of the experts have been deceived by his work. (A—)

- **A GEOGRAPHIC LEXICON OF GREEK COIN INSCRIPTIONS. A. Florance.** 112 pp. LC 66-19173. $5.00

  The first American publication of this handy lexicon identifying both the abbreviated and complete ethnics (inscriptions) of the Greek city-states inscribed on their coins, most of which are not found in the usual Greek lexicons. Each has an indication of the general area in which the city was located, and in the case of the Greek Imperial issues, the province of the Roman Empire. With maps of ancient Greece and Rome plus lists of cities which issued non-inscribed coins and coins with bilingual inscriptions. A basic tool for any student of Greek archaeology and philology and the numismatist. (D—)

- **A DICTIONARY OF GREEK COIN INSCRIPTIONS. Severin Icard.** Limited edition of 450 numbered copies. xlviii + 564 + 2 plates. $30.00

  A limited edition of the famous lexicographic work *Identification des Monnaies par la Nouvelle méthode des lettres-jalons et des Légendes Fragmentées* in which are included all known Greek coin inscriptions. The introduction appears in an English translation. In the corpus all inscriptions, complete and fragmentary, of kings, emperors, mint officials, generals, states, cities, etc. are listed alphabetically with descriptive epithets in many cases. A major reference work and an invaluable help in identifying coins. Each word of the inscription is also listed separately for easy identification in the case of worn or partially destroyed inscriptions. (D 2)

- **ANCIENT, MEDIEVAL, MODERN COINS AND HOW TO KNOW THEM. Gertrude B. Rawlings.** xix + 360 + 30 plates. LC 66-19186. $10.00

  A reprint of a much in demand manual which is an introduction to the history and development of coins and coinage from the earliest period to the first decade of the 20th century. A valuable book for those specializing in one period of coinage who wish to extend their knowledge to another. (D—)

- **COINS AND MEDALS: THEIR PLACE IN HISTORY AND ART. Stanley Lane Poole.** 200 pp., approx., illus. LC 66-19182. $10.00

  A reissue, with new typesetting, of the 1885 edition containing essays on the ancient coins of Europe and Asia by the editors of the famed British Museum catalogues of coins. Excellent introduction in one handy volume to the following coins: ancient Greek, Roman, Indian, Japanese, Chinese, Mohammedan, Phoenician, Parthian, Judaean, Sassanian, Nabathean, early English and the coinage of Christian Europe, plus a chapter on medals. (D 2)

- **COIN TYPES. THEIR ORIGIN AND DEVELOPMENT 700 B.C. — 1604 A.D. Sir George Macdonald.** 286 pp., illus. + 16 plates. LC 67-17581. $10.00

  A reprint of the famous and much in demand text of the author's lectures on the history of coins (1905). A book designed for the average reader, but due to the importance, validity and originality of its contents, it has been raised to a prominent position among numismatic reference books. Important for the study of the history, problems and general background of numismatics beginning with the most primitive coinage of the ancient world through Byzantium, the medieval period, the Renaissance and the dawn of modern world coinage. (D 2)

● **HISTORIA NUMORUM: A MANUAL OF GREEK NUMISMATICS. Barclay V. Head.** lxxxviii + 978, illus. $30.00

Reprinted from the 1911 edition, this manual remains a masterpiece of numismatic scholarship. The author produced a handbook in one volume containing in condensed form a complete and detailed sketch of the numismatic history of nearly every city, king or dynast known to have struck coins in the ancient Greek world. Considered by Shaw (*List of Books for College Libraries*, p. 32) to be the basic reference volume on Greek numismatics. With 7 indices and an extensive reference bibliography. (D 2)

● **THE ILLUSTRATIONS OF THE HISTORIA NUMORUM. Barclay V. Head and N. Svoronos.** Royal octavo. 64 pp. + 40 plates $7.50

Users of the famous *Historia Numorum* in all its English editions have long agreed that if it lacks anything it is illustrations of the most famous coins described in it. Very few know that Barclay Head actually prepared a set of 35 plates illustrating about 420 coins in obverse and reverse which, with their descriptions, formed the third volume of the modern Greek translation of *Historia Numorum* published in Athens in 1898 by the also famous numismatist Nicholas Svoronos.

This small volume is now reprinted with the addition of 5 plates and is a necessary addition to each copy of *Historia Numorum* already in any library or personal collection. (D 4)

● **ANCIENT GREEK AND ROMAN COINS: A HANDBOOK. George F. Hill.** xvi + 296, illus. + 16 plates. LC 64-23439. $10.00

The fundamental introductory work (1899) to the coinages of the ancient world, now re-issued with a new bibliography and other addenda. Ideal for the student of archaeology and the collector of ancient coins. The most important coins are catalogued and illustrated. (D—)

● **ANCIENT ARCHITECTURE ON GREEK AND ROMAN COINS AND MEDALS; ARCHITECTURA NUMISMATICA. T. L. Donaldson.** 382 + 54 plates. LC 65-15464. $10.00

A reprint of a very valuable and unique collection (1856) of the representations of ancient temples, shrines, theatres, public buildings, city walls, gates, bridges, etc. illustrated on ancient coins and medals issued in Greece and Rome. These architectural monuments are seen on the coins in the state of preservation in which they existed when the coins were struck, thus giving us an excellent record of ancient architecture, much of which is now lost, destroyed or unexcavated. With a new select annotated bibliography, introduction, biographical note of the author and a detailed index. (D—)

● **HISTORICAL GREEK COINS. George F. Hill.** xxvi + 182 + 16 plates. LC 66-19179. $10.00

An excellent and methodical numismatic commentary to the highlights of the history of ancient Greece from the rise of archaic Greece to the Persian Wars, from the brilliance of the Athenian Empire until its downfall in the Peloponnesian War and the decline of the city-states. Coins illuminate history most vividly here and illustrate the growth of Alexander's empire and the history of the Hellenistic states and kingdoms until the final conquest by Rome. (D—)

● **HISTORICAL ROMAN COINS. George F. Hill.** xvi + 196 + 16 plates. LC 66-19180. $10.00

The companion volume to *Historical Greek Coins*, in which coins tell the story of Rome from the earliest period to the highlights of the Republic and its final submission to the Empire established during the rule of Augustus Octavianus. (D—)

● **THE COINS OF THE GREEK AND SCYTHIC KINGS OF BACTRIA AND INDIA. Percy Gardner.** 272 pp. + 32 plates. LC 66-25813. $15.00

Originally issued in 1886 in an edition of just 300 copies, this amazing corpus of the historical coins minted by the Greek and Scythic kings of Bactria and India, appears again for the first time. This is the basic sourcebook for the chronicles of almost 200 years of the eastern-most Hellenistic empire, unknown from any other source. Planned and issued as the first volume of the Catalogue of Indian Coins in the British Museum, this rare reference work was expanded by the author to include coins from other museums and private collections. This edition has been enlarged by a preface, a select bibliography, and a new dynastic chart of the Greco-Bactrian kings according to the most recent authorities. (D—)

● **GREEK IMPERIAL COINS AND THEIR MINTS. Tom B. Jones.** 112 pp., illus. LC 66-19174. $5.00

A new book tracing through coins for the first time the eastward expansion of the Roman Empire. A unique reference for the study of Greek inscribed Imperial coins issued in the Greek-speaking provinces. Also for the first time a complete list and map appear showing all the city mints known to date. Very little has been written on this coinage, making this book of especial importance to the historian and numismatist. (D 2)

● **BYZANTIUM AND NUMISMATICS. Aloisius Barozzi.** 96 pp., plates. LC 66-19181. $3.00